BRIEF PRINCIPLES OF

MACROECONOMICS

FOURTH EDITION

N. GREGORY MANKIW

HARVARD UNIVERSITY

THOMSON

SOUTH-WESTERN

Australia · Brazil · Canada · Mexico · Singapore · Spain · United Kingdom · United States

THOMSON
SOUTH-WESTERN

Brief Principles of Macroeconomics, Fourth Edition
N. Gregory Mankiw

VP/Editorial Director:
Jack W. Calhoun

Editor-in-Chief:
Alex von Rosenberg

Publisher:
Steve Momper

Sr. Acquisitions Editor:
Mike Worls

Developmental Editor:
Jane Tufts

Contributing Editors:
Sarah K. Dorger
Jennifer E. Baker

Sr. Marketing Manager:
Brian Joyner

Assoc. Marketing Communications Manager:
Sarah Greber

Sr. Production Project Manager:
Emily S. Gross

Manager of Technology, Editorial:
Vicky True

Technology Project Editor:
Dana Cowden

Web Coordinator:
Karen Schaffer

Sr. Manufacturing Coordinator:
Sandee Milewski

Production House:
Lachina Publishing Services

Printer:
R.R. Donnelley
Willard, OH

Art Director:
Michelle Kunkler

Internal and Cover Designer:
Stratton Design

Cover Illustration:
Tate Gallery, London/Art Resource, NY

Internal Illustrator:
William Low/Cobalt Illustration Services

Photography Manager:
John Hill

Photo Researcher:
Susan Van Etten

Library of Congress Control Number: 2005938053

For more information about our products, contact us at:

Thomson Learning Academic Resource Center

1-800-423-0563

Thomson Higher Education
5191 Natorp Boulevard
Mason, OH 45040
USA

To Catherine, Nicholas, and Peter,
my other contributions to the next generation

N. Gregory Mankiw is professor of economics at Harvard University. As a student, he studied economics at Princeton University and MIT. As a teacher, he has taught macroeconomics, microeconomics, statistics, and principles of economics. He even spent one summer long ago as a sailing instructor on Long Beach Island.

Professor Mankiw is a prolific writer and a regular participant in academic and policy debates. His work has been published in scholarly journals, such as the *American Economic Review, Journal of Political Economy*, and *Quarterly Journal of Economics*, and in more popular forums, such as *The New York Times, The Financial Times, The Wall Street Journal*, and *Fortune*. He is also author of the best-selling intermediate-level textbook *Macroeconomics* (Worth Publishers). In addition to his teaching, research, and writing, Professor Mankiw has been a research associate of the National Bureau of Economic Research, an adviser to the Federal Reserve Bank of Boston and the Congressional Budget Office, and a member of the ETS test development committee for the advanced placement exam in economics. From 2003 to 2005, he served as chairman of the President's Council of Economic Advisers.

Professor Mankiw lives in Wellesley, Massachusetts, with his wife, Deborah, three children, Catherine, Nicholas, and Peter, and their border terrier, Tobin.

During my 20-year career as a student, the course that excited me most was the two-semester sequence on the principles of economics that I took during my freshman year in college. It is no exaggeration to say that it changed my life.

I had grown up in a family that often discussed politics over the dinner table. The pros and cons of various solutions to society's problems generated fervent debate. But in school, I had been drawn to the sciences. Whereas politics seemed vague, rambling, and subjective, science was analytic, systematic, and objective. While political debate continued without end, science made progress.

My freshman course on the principles of economics opened my eyes to a new way of thinking. Economics combines the virtues of politics and science. It is, truly, a social science. Its subject matter is society—how people choose to lead their lives and how they interact with one another. But it approaches the subject with the dispassion of a science. By bringing the methods of science to the questions of politics, economics tries to make progress on the challenges that all societies face.

I was drawn to write this book in the hope that I could convey some of the excitement about economics that I felt as a student in my first economics course. Economics is a subject in which a little knowledge goes a long way. (The same cannot be said, for instance, of the study of physics or the Japanese language.) Economists have a unique way of viewing the world, much of which can be taught in one or two semesters. My goal in this book is to transmit this way of thinking to the widest possible audience and to convince readers that it illuminates much about the world around them.

I believe that everyone should study the fundamental ideas that economics has to offer. One purpose of general education is to inform people about the world and thereby make them better citizens. The study of economics, as much as any discipline, serves this goal. Writing an economics textbook is, therefore, a great honor and a great responsibility. It is one way that economists can help promote better government and a more prosperous future. As the great economist Paul Samuelson put it, "I don't care who writes a nation's laws, or crafts its advanced treaties, if I can write its economics textbooks."

What's New in the Fourth Edition?

More of this book is devoted to applications—and less to formal economic theory—than is the case with many other books written for the principles course. Most chapters include case studies illustrating how the principles of economics are applied. In addition, "In The News" boxes offer excerpts from newspaper articles showing how economic ideas shed light on current issues facing society. After students finish their first course in economics, they should think about news stories from a new perspective and with greater insight.

Although the principles of economics are timeless, the application of those principles changes over time as events unfold and as policymakers consider new initiatives. To keep the study of economics fresh and relevant for each new cohort of students, teachers of economics must constantly update their courses. This new edition contributes to that effort by including dozens of new case studies and boxes.

The new features in this edition are too numerous to list in their entirety, but here is a sample:

- A new box describes how football coach Bill Belichick has used economic research to improve his team's 4th-down strategy.
- A new box summarizes recent research by Nobel Prize winner Ed Prescott on how taxes influence work effort in Europe.
- A new box discusses the winners and losers from the increased textile trade with China.
- A new box considers the economics of offshore outsourcing.
- A new case study describes the fiscal challenge ahead that arises from an aging population.
- A new box describes how London has reduced congestion with road pricing.
- A new box discusses how rapid growth in Asia is making the global distribution of income more equal.
- A new box summarizes recent research into the causes of child labor in poor nations.
- A new case study examines the moral hazard problem as applied to corporate managers.
- A new box discusses what behavioral economics says about the determinants of saving.
- A new box considers how economic statistics can miss the underground economy.
- A new box uses three striking photos to illustrate the differences in living standards in Great Britain, Mexico, and Mali.
- A new box includes an article by the presidents of Mali and Burkina Faso on how freer world trade would benefit their nations' poor farmers.
- A new box examines some of the peculiar features of U.S. health insurance.
- A new box discusses the problem of high unemployment in Germany.
- A new case study considers whether the U.S. economy could ever experience a bout of capital flight.
- Two new boxes analyze the economics of Hurricane Katrina—one focusing on the short-run macroeconomic impact and the second on the reconstruction effort.
- And finally, a new case study in Chapter 2 discusses my own recent experience as an economic adviser to President Bush.

Only the complete 36-chapter version of this book includes all of these new applications. See below for outlines of each of the five available versions.

In addition to updating the book, I have refined its coverage and pedagogy with input from many users of the previous edition. There are many changes, both large and small, aimed at making the book clearer and more student-friendly.

All the changes that I made, and the many others that I considered, were evaluated in light of the benefits of brevity. Like most things that we study in economics, a student's time is a scarce resource. I always keep in mind a dictum from the great novelist Robertson Davies: "One of the most important things about writing is to boil it down and not bore the hell out of everybody."

How Is This Book Organized?

To write a brief and student-friendly book, I had to consider new ways to organize familiar material. What follows is a whirlwind tour of this text. The tour will, I hope, give instructors some sense of how the pieces fit together.

Introductory Material

Chapter 1, "Ten Principles of Economics," introduces students to the economist's view of the world. It previews some of the big ideas that recur throughout economics, such as opportunity cost, marginal decision making, the role of incentives, the gains from trade, and the efficiency of market allocations. Throughout the book, I refer regularly to the *Ten Principles of Economics* introduced in Chapter 1 to remind students that these principles are the foundation for most economic analysis. An icon in the margin calls attention to these references.

Chapter 2, "Thinking Like an Economist," examines how economists approach their field of study. It discusses the role of assumptions in developing a theory and introduces the concept of an economic model. It also discusses the role of economists in making policy. The appendix to this chapter offers a brief refresher course on how graphs are used and how they can be abused.

Chapter 3, "Interdependence and the Gains from Trade," presents the theory of comparative advantage. This theory explains why individuals trade with their neighbors, as well as why nations trade with other nations. Much of economics is about how market forces coordinate many individual production and consumption decisions. As a starting point for this analysis, students see in this chapter why specialization, interdependence, and trade can benefit everyone.

I next introduce the basic tools of supply and demand. Chapter 4, "The Market Forces of Supply and Demand," develops the supply curve, the demand curve, and the notion of market equilibrium. This microeconomic model is the starting point for much of macroeconomic theory.

Macroeconomics

My overall approach to teaching macroeconomics is to examine the economy in the long run (when prices are flexible) before examining the economy in the short run (when prices are sticky). I believe that this organization simplifies learning macroeconomics for several reasons. First, the classical assumption of price flexibility is more closely linked to the basic lessons of supply and demand, which students have already mastered. Second, the classical dichotomy allows the study of the long run to be broken up into several easily digested pieces. Third, because the business cycle represents a transitory deviation from the economy's long-run growth path, studying the transitory deviations is more natural after the long-run equilibrium is understood. Fourth, the macroeconomic theory of the short run is more controversial among economists than the macroeconomic theory of the long run. For these reasons, most upper-level courses in macroeconomics now follow this long-run-before-short-run approach; my goal is to offer introductory students the same advantage.

I start the coverage of macroeconomics with issues of measurement. Chapter 5, "Measuring a Nation's Income," discusses the meaning of gross domestic product and related statistics from the national income accounts. Chapter 6, "Measuring the Cost of Living," discusses the measurement and use of the consumer price index.

The next four chapters describe the behavior of the real economy in the long run. Chapter 7, "Production and Growth," examines the determinants of the large variation in living standards over time and across countries. Chapter 8, "Saving, Investment, and the Financial System," discusses the types of financial institutions in our economy and examines their role in allocating resources. Chapter 9, "The Basic Tools of Finance," introduces present value, risk management, and asset pricing. Chapter 10, "Unemployment," considers the long-run determinants of the unemployment rate, including job search, minimum-wage laws, the market power of unions, and efficiency wages.

Having described the long-run behavior of the real economy, the book then turns to the long-run behavior of money and prices. Chapter 11, "The Monetary System," introduces the economist's concept of money and the role of the central bank in controlling the quantity of money. Chapter 12, "Money Growth and Inflation," develops the classical theory of inflation and discusses the costs that inflation imposes on a society.

The next two chapters present the macroeconomics of open economies, maintaining the long-run assumptions of price flexibility and full employment. Chapter 13, "Open-Economy Macroeconomics: Basic Concepts," explains the relationship among saving, investment, and the trade balance, the distinction between the nominal and real exchange rate, and the theory of purchasing-power parity. Chapter 14, "A Macroeconomic Theory of the Open Economy," presents a classical model of the international flow of goods and capital. The model sheds light on various issues, including the link between budget deficits and trade deficits and the macroeconomic effects of trade policies. Because instructors differ in their emphasis on this material, these chapters are written so they can be used in different ways. Some may choose to cover Chapter 13 but not Chapter 14; others may skip both chapters; and still others may choose to defer the analysis of open-economy macroeconomics until the end of their courses.

After developing the long-run theory of the economy in Chapters 7 through 14, the book turns to explaining short-run fluctuations around the long-run trend. This organization simplifies teaching the theory of short-run fluctuations because, at this point in the course, students have a good grounding in many basic macroeconomic concepts. Chapter 15, "Aggregate Demand and Aggregate Supply," begins with some facts about the business cycle and then introduces the model of aggregate demand and aggregate supply. Chapter 16, "The Influence of Monetary and Fiscal Policy on Aggregate Demand," explains how policymakers can use the tools at their disposal to shift the aggregate-demand curve. Chapter 17, "The Short-Run Trade-off between Inflation and Unemployment," explains why policymakers who control aggregate demand face a trade-off between inflation and unemployment. It examines why this trade-off exists in the short run, why it shifts over time, and why it does not exist in the long run.

The book concludes with Chapter 18, "Five Debates over Macroeconomic Policy." This capstone chapter considers five controversial issues facing policymakers: the proper degree of policy activism in response to the business cycle, the choice between rules and discretion in the conduct of monetary policy, the desirability of reaching zero inflation, the importance of balancing the government's budget, and the need for tax reform to encourage saving. For each issue, the chapter presents both sides of the debate and encourages students to make their own judgments.

Learning Tools

The purpose of this book is to help students learn the fundamental lessons of economics and to show how they can apply these lessons to their lives and to the world in which they live. Toward that end, I have used various learning tools that recur throughout the book.

Case Studies Economic theory is useful and interesting only if it can be applied to understanding actual events and policies. This book, therefore, contains numerous case studies that apply the theory that has just been developed.

In the News Boxes One benefit that students gain from studying economics is a new perspective and greater understanding about news from around the world. To highlight this benefit, I have included excerpts from many newspaper articles, some of which are opinion columns written by prominent economists. These articles, together with my brief introductions, show how basic economic theory can be applied. Most of these boxes are new to this edition.

FYI Boxes These boxes provide additional material "for your information." Some of them offer a glimpse into the history of economic thought. Others clarify technical issues. Still others discuss supplementary topics that instructors might choose either to discuss or skip in their lectures.

Definitions of Key Concepts When key concepts are introduced in the chapter, they are presented in **bold** typeface. In addition, their definitions are placed in the margins. This treatment should aid students in learning and reviewing the material.

Quick Quizzes After each major section, students are offered a Quick Quiz to check their comprehension of what they have just learned. If students cannot readily answer these quizzes, they should stop and reread material before continuing. The answers to all Quick Quizzes are in an appendix at the back of the book.

Chapter Summaries Each chapter ends with a brief summary that reminds students of the most important lessons that they have just learned. Later in their study, it offers an efficient way to review for exams.

List of Key Concepts A list of key concepts at the end of each chapter offers students a way to test their understanding of the new terms that have been introduced. Page references are included so that students can review the terms they do not understand.

Questions for Review At the end of each chapter are questions for review that cover the chapter's primary lessons. Students can use these questions to check their comprehension and to prepare for exams.

Problems and Applications Each chapter also contains a variety of problems and applications that ask students to apply the material that they have learned. Some professors may use these questions for homework assignments. Others may use them as a starting point for classroom discussions.

Alternative Versions of the Books

The book you are holding in your hand is one of five versions of this book that are available for introducing students to economics. Thomson South-Western Publishing and I offer this menu of books because instructors differ in how much time they have and what topics they choose to cover. Here is a brief description of each:

- *Principles of Economics.* This complete version of the book contains all 36 chapters. It is designed for two-semester introductory courses that cover both microeconomics and macroeconomics.
- *Principles of Microeconomics.* This version contains 22 chapters and is designed for one-semester courses in introductory microeconomics.
- *Principles of Macroeconomics.* This version contains 23 chapters and is designed for one-semester courses in introductory macroeconomics. It contains a full development of the theory of supply and demand.
- *Brief Principles of Macroeconomics.* This shortened macro version of 18 chapters contains only one chapter on the basics of supply and demand. It is designed for instructors who want to jump to the core topics of macroeconomics more quickly.
- *Essentials of Economics.* This version of the book contains 24 chapters. It is designed for one-semester survey courses that cover the basics of both microeconomics and macroeconomics.

The accompanying table shows precisely which chapters are included in each book. Instructors who wish more information about these alternative versions should contact their local South-Western representative.

Supplements

Thomson South-Western offers various supplements for instructors and students who use this book. These resources make teaching the principles of economics easy for the professor and learning them easy for the student. David R. Hakes of the University of Northern Iowa, a dedicated teacher and economist, supervised the development of the supplements for this edition. A complete list of available supplements follows this Preface.

Translations and Adaptations

I am delighted that versions of this book are (or will soon be) available in many of the world's languages. Currently scheduled translations include Azeri, Chinese (in both standard and simplified characters), Croatian, Czech, Dutch, French, Georgian, German, Greek, Indonesian, Italian, Japanese, Korean, Macedonian, Montenegrin, Portuguese, Romanian, Russian, Serbian, and Spanish. In addition, adaptations of the book for Australian, Canadian, and European students are also available. Instructors who would like more information about these books should contact Thomson South-Western.

The Five Versions of This Book

AVAILABLE VERSIONS

Chapter	Principles of Economics	Principles of Microeconomics	Principles of Macroeconomics	Brief Principles of Macroeconomics	Essentials of Economics
1. Ten Principles of Economics	X	X	X	X	X
2. Thinking Like an Economist	X	X	X	X	X
3. Interdependence and the Gains from Trade	X	X	X	X	X
4. The Market Forces of Supply and Demand	X	X	X	X	X
5. Elasticity and Its Application	X	X	X		X
6. Supply, Demand, and Government Policies	X	X	X		X
7. Consumers, Producers, and the Efficiency of Markets	X	X	X		X
8. Application: The Costs of Taxation	X	X	X		X
9. Application: International Trade	X	X	X		X
10. Externalities	X	X			X
11. Public Goods and Common Resources	X	X			X
12. The Design of the Tax System	X	X			
13. The Costs of Production	X	X			X
14. Firms in Competitive Markets	X	X			X
15. Monopoly	X	X			X
16. Oligopoly	X	X			
17. Monopolistic Competition	X	X			
18. The Markets for the Factors of Production	X	X			
19. Earnings and Discrimination	X	X			
20. Income Inequality and Poverty	X	X			
21. The Theory of Consumer Choice	X	X			
22. Frontiers of Microeconomics	X	X			
23. Measuring a Nation's Income	X		X	X	X
24. Measuring the Cost of Living	X		X	X	X
25. Production and Growth	X		X	X	X
26. Saving, Investment, and the Financial System	X		X	X	X
27. The Basic Tools of Finance	X		X	X	X
28. Unemployment	X		X	X	X
29. The Monetary System	X		X	X	X
30. Money Growth and Inflation	X		X	X	X
31. Open-Economy Macroeconomics: Basic Concepts	X		X	X	
32. A Macroeconomic Theory of the Open Economy	X		X	X	
33. Aggregate Demand and Aggregate Supply	X		X	X	X
34. The Influence of Monetary and Fiscal Policy on Aggregate Demand	X		X	X	X
35. The Short-Run Trade-off between Inflation and Unemployment	X		X	X	
36. Five Debates over Macroeconomic Policy	X		X	X	

Note: Chapter numbers refer to the complete book, *Principles of Economics.*

Acknowledgments

In writing this book, I benefited from the input of many talented people. Indeed, the list of people who have contributed to this project is so long that it seems an injustice that only a single name appears on the cover.

Let me begin with my colleagues in the economics profession. The four editions of this text and its supplemental materials have benefited enormously from their input. In reviews and surveys, they have offered suggestions, identified challenges, and shared ideas from their own classroom experience. I am indebted to them for the perspectives they have brought to the text. Unfortunately, the list has become too long to thank those who contributed to previous editions, even though students reading the current edition are still benefiting from their insights.

Most important in this process have been Ron Cronovich (University of Nevada at Las Vegas) and David Hakes (University of Northern Iowa). Ron and David are dedicated teachers who have been a reliable sounding board for ideas and hard-working partners with me in putting together the superb package of supplements.

For this new edition, the following diary reviewers recorded their day-to-day experience over the course of a semester, offering detailed suggestions about how to improve the text. These reviewers included instructors and students.

Instructors

Anne Bunton, *Cottey College*
Margaret Chapman, *Illinois Wesleyan University*
Sean Corcoran, *California State University–Sacramento*
Susanne Currier, *University of Central Oklahoma*
Susan Dadres, *Southern Methodist University*
David Eaton, *Murray State University*

Pat Euzent, *University of Central Florida*
Fred Foldvary, *Santa Clara University*
Daniel Marburger, *Arkansas State University*
Jeffrey Michael, *Towson University*
Michael Nieswiadomy, *University of North Texas*
Gyan Pradhan, *Westminster College*
Thomas Rhoads, *Towson University*

Students

Adam Aft, Anthony Barbato, Jared Podnos, and Andy Shiffman, *Indiana University*
Bryanna Barrett, *Murray State University*
Laura Cohen and Juris Pupcenoks, *Westminster College*
Cidrick Espejel and Carah Ronan, *Southern Methodist University*
Lauren Jeffries, Jennifer Seidel, and Bryan Shrode, *University of Central Florida*

Cameron Alexis Moore, *Illinois Wesleyan University*
Xuan Thuong Nguyen and Anne Scudder, *Santa Clara University*
Eric Rader, Stormy Shippy, and Kevin Smith, *University of North Texas*
Sarah Ritterhoff and Jyoti Singh, *Towson University*

The following reviewers of the third edition provided suggestions for refining the content, organization, and approach in the fourth.

Rashid Al Hmoud, *Texas Tech University*

Mark Ashe, *Westminster College*

Greg Brock, *Georgia Southern University*

Bruce Brown, *California Polytechnic–Pomona*

Tom Casey, *DeVry University*

Brad Causey, *Sycamore High School*

Sandy Chau, *The Hong Kong Polytechnic University*

Barbara Craig, *Oberlin College*

Anna DellaValle, *Columbia University*

Elizabeth Dickhaus, *University of Missouri, Saint Louis*

Mike Driver, *Farragut High School*

Ali Faegh, *Houston Community College*

Kent Ford, *Onondaga Community College, Syracuse*

Roger Frantz, *San Diego State University*

Steve Freeman, *Capital High School*

Shailendra Gajanan, *University of Pittsburgh, Bradford*

Tommy Georgiades, *DeVry University*

Larry Hagan, *DeVry University*

Phil Holleran, *Radford University*

Hans Isakson, *University of Northern Iowa*

Leo Kahane, *California State University, Hayward*

Christopher Klein, *Middle Tennessee State University*

Jim Lee, *Texas A&M University, Corpus Christi*

John Lovett, *Texas Christian University*

Fiona C. Maclachlan, *Manhattan College*

Peter Martinez, *Danbury High School*

Kate Matraves, *Albion College*

Pete Mavrokordatos, *Tarrant County College*

Tom Means, *San Jose State University*

Kim Merritt, *Cameron University*

Debrasi Mukherjee, *Western Michigan University*

Chris Nguyen, *Plaza Business Institute*

Matt Nowakowski, *Minnesota School of Business*

Una Osili, *Indiana University–Purdue University, Indianapolis*

Kathy Parkison, *Indiana University, Kokomo*

Thomas Pogue, *University of Iowa*

Diane Primont, *Southeast Missouri State University*

Lou Quiros, *College of Westchester*

James Ragan, *Kansas State University*

Raymond Robertson, *Macalester College*

James Roumasset, *University of Hawaii, Manoa*

Udayan Roy, *Long Island University*

William Sander, *DePaul University*

Sue Lynn Sasser, *University of Central Oklahoma*

Martin Schreiber, *DeVry University*

Robert Schwab, *University of Maryland*

Juha Seppälä, *University of Illinois*

William Seyfried, *Winthrop University*

Tim Sloan, *Jenks High School*

Kenneth Smith, *Millersville University*

Abdulhamid Sukar, *Cameron University*

Phillip Szmedra, *Georgia Southwestern State University*

Serena Tong, *Long Island Business Institute*

Jogindar S. Uppal, *State University of New York, Albany*

Walter Wessels, *North Carolina State University*

Kathryn Wilson, *Kent State University*

Sheng-Ping Yang, *Wayland Baptist University*

Bassam Yousif, *California State University, Fullerton*

I received detailed feedback on specific elements in the text, including all end-of-chapter problems and applications, from the following instructors.

Josiah Baker, *University of Central Florida*

J. Ulysses Balderas, *University of Colorado–Boulder*

King Banaian, *Saint Cloud State University*

Bruce Brown, *California State Polytechnic, Pomona*

Byron Chapman, *Ohio State University*

Margaret Chapman, *Illinois Wesleyan University*

Basanta Chaudhuri, *Rutgers University*

Sean Corcoran, *California State University, Sacramento*

Christopher Cornell, *Fordham University*

Barbara Craig, *Oberlin College*

Eleanor Craig, *University of Delaware*

Susanne Currier, *University of Central Oklahoma*

Susan Dadres, *Southern Methodist University*

Alan Deardorff, *University of Michigan*

Stratford Douglas, *West Virginia University*

David Eaton, *Murray State University*

Can Erbil, *Brandeis University*

Patricia Euzent, *University of Central Florida*

Fred Foldvary, *Santa Clara University*

Lynn Gillette, *University of Kentucky*

Phillip Holleran, *Radford University*

James Hvidding, *Kutztown University*

Hans Isakson, *University of Northern Iowa*

Leo Kahane, *California State University, Hayward*

Brian Kench, *University of Tampa*

Christopher Klein, *Middle Tennessee State University*

Todd Knoop, *Cornell College*

Charles Krusekopf, *Austin College*

John Lovett, *Texas Christian University*

Fiona C. Maclachlan, *Manhattan College*

Thomas Makemson, *Webster University*

Daniel Marburger, *Arkansas State University*

Catherine Matraves, *Michigan State University*

Tom Means, *San Jose State University*

Jeffrey Michael, *Towson University*

Debasri Mukherjee, *Western Michigan University*

Peter Olson, *Indiana University*

Drew Parkes, *University of Northern Iowa*

Jodi Pelkowski, *Wichita State University*

Michael Pisani, *Central Michigan University*

Marlene Reed, *Samford University*

Thomas Rhoads, *Towson University*

Raymond Robertson, *Macalester College*

June Roux, *Salem Community College*

Udayan Roy, *Long Island University*

William Sander, *DePaul University*

Juha Seppälä, *University of Illinois*

William Seyfried, *Winthrop University*

Charles Sicotte, *Rock Valley College*

Kenneth Smith, *Millersville University*

Jogindar S. Uppal, *State University of New York, Albany*

John Volpe, *Trinity College*

David Wihry, *University of Maine*

Virginia Wilcox-Gok, *Northern Illinois University*

William Wood, *James Madison University*

Sheng P. Yang, *Black Hills State University*

The accuracy of a textbook is critically important. Although I am responsible for any remaining errors, I am grateful to the following professors for reading through the final manuscript and page proofs with me:

Josiah Baker, *University of Central Florida*
Ronald Elkins, *Central Washington University*
Marlene Reed, *Baylor University*
Thomas Rhoads, *Towson University*

The team of editors who worked on this book improved it tremendously. Jane Tufts, my developmental editor, provided truly spectacular editing—as she always does. Mike Worls, senior acquisitions editor, did a splendid job of overseeing the many people involved in such a large project. Sarah Dorger, developmental editor, was crucial in assembling an extensive and thoughtful group of reviewers to give me feedback on the previous edition, while putting together an excellent team to revise the supplements. Emily Gross, production project manager, and Mandy Hetrick, project manager at Lachina Publishing Services, had the patience and dedication necessary to turn my manuscript into this book. Michelle Kunkler, art director, and Mike Stratton, designer, gave this book its clean, friendly look. William Low, the illustrator, helped make the book more visually appealing and economics less abstract. Frank Hubert, copyeditor, refined my prose, and Terry Casey, indexer, prepared a careful and thorough index. Brian Joyner, marketing manager, worked long hours getting the word out to potential users of this book. The rest of the Thomson South-Western team was also consistently professional, enthusiastic, and dedicated: Jennifer Baker, Erin Berger, Dana Cowden, Erin Donohoe, Jennifer Garamy, Sarah Greber, Sandee Milewski, and Michael Guendelsberger.

I must also thank my "in-house" editor—Deborah Mankiw. As the first reader of almost everything I write, she continued to offer just the right mix of criticism and encouragement.

Finally, I am grateful to my children, Catherine, Nicholas, and Peter. Their unpredictable visits to my study offered welcome relief from long spans of writing and rewriting. Although now they are only thirteen, eleven, and seven years old, someday they will grow up and study the principles of economics. I hope this book provides its readers some of the education and enlightenment that I wish for my own children.

N. Gregory Mankiw
September 2005

Thomson South-Western will provide copies of these supplements free of charge to those instructors qualified under its adoption policy. Please contact your sales representative to learn how you may qualify, or call the Academic Resource Center at 1-800-423-0563.

Instructor Resources

Instructor's Manual with Solutions Manual

For lecture preparation, the Instructor's Manual, written by Linda Ghent (Eastern Illinois University), offers a detailed outline for each chapter of the text, provides learning objectives, identifies stumbling blocks that students may face, offers helpful teaching tips, and provides suggested in-classroom activities for a more cooperative learning experience. The Instructor's Manual also includes solutions to all end-of-chapter exercises, Quick Quizzes, Questions for Review, and Problems and Applications found in the text.

Instructor's Resource CD

Included on this CD are the key supplements designed to aid instructors. The Instructor's Resource CD contains the Class Planning Guide, Instructor's Manual with Solutions Manual, Traditional PowerPoint Presentation Slides, Transparency Masters, and the Test Bank in both ExamView® Computerized Testing Software and Microsoft Word.

A separate resource CD-Rom features the groundbreaking Premium PowerPoint presentation by Ron Cronovich (University of Nevada, Las Vegas), which engages students through interactive examples and applications, as well as carefully built animated graphs.

Class Planning Guide

The Class Planning Guide simplifies the planning of the principles course and helps the instructor incorporate valuable tools and new activities into the course. Organized according to teaching workflow (plan, manage, teach, reinforce, test, grade, and report), this guide cuts down the time to create the course syllabus.

Printed Test Bank

Daniel K. Biederman (University of North Dakota), Ken Brown (University of Northern Iowa), Lisa Jepsen (University of Northern Iowa), Bryce Kanago (University of Northern Iowa), and Ken McCormick (University of Northern Iowa) have updated and revised the Test Bank. It consists of approximately 230 questions per chapter. Every question has been painstakingly checked to ensure the accuracy and clarity of the answers and revised to address the main text updates. Included are multiple-choice, true/false, and short answer questions that assess students' critical thinking skills. Questions are organized by text section and identified both by level of difficulty (easy, medium, hard) and question type (applicative, analytical, interpretive, and definitional). These features help instructors pick and choose their questions with ease.

ExamView®

ExamView® Computerized Testing Software contains all of the questions in the printed test bank. This program is an easy-to-use test creation software compatible with Microsoft Windows. Instructors can add or edit questions, instructions, and answers and select questions by previewing them on the screen, select them randomly, or select them by number. Instructors can also create and administer quizzes online, whether over the Internet, a local area network (LAN), or a wide area network (WAN). Contact your South-Western/Thomson sales representative for ordering information.

Video for Mankiw's *Principles of Economics*

Ken Witty, a talented documentary filmmaker, has produced a video series to illustrate the *Ten Principles of Economics* introduced in Chapter 1. Instructors can show these videos as an interesting and visually appealing introduction to topics discussed throughout the textbook. The video is also available in streaming video on the text website.

Premium PowerPoint Lecture Slides

New to the 4th edition, Ron Cronovich (University of Nevada, Las Vegas) has designed slides with many innovative features inspired by the principles of effective teaching. Lecture material is "chunked" and peppered with brief active-learning exercises for immediate reinforcement, application, and informal assessment. Handouts provided for students (in PDF format) will encourage attendance and attentiveness. Many slides are annotated with helpful notes for instructors. Graphs are animated as an instructor might draw them on the blackboard. Dr. Cronovich will be updating these slides annually to incorporate user feedback, and update data.

Traditional PowerPoint Lecture Slides

The PowerPoint Lecture Slides have been updated for the 4th edition and provide chapter-by-chapter slides for use during classroom preparation and lecture.

PowerPoint Exhibit Slides

These slides contain the figures, charts, and tables from the text. Instructors can easily incorporate them into their own PowerPoint presentations.

Transparency Acetates

Created to help instructors build text images into their lectures, full color transparency acetates are available with the 4th edition for use on an overhead projector. They are available to adopters upon request.

WebTutor Advantage

More than just an interactive study aid, WebTutor Advantage delivers innovative learning aids that actively engage students. Benefits include automatic and immediate feedback from quizzes; interactive, multimedia-rich explanation of concepts, such as flash-animated graphing tutorials and graphing exercises that utilize an online graph-drawing tool; streaming video applications; online exercises; flashcards; and greater interaction and involvement through online discussion forums. Powerful instructor tools are also provided to assist communication and collaboration between students and faculty.

A Guide to the Mankiw Approach

In this essay, N. Gregory Mankiw explains his well-respected approach to teaching economics—an approach that fosters in students a better understanding of economic principles and encourages the application of the economic way of thinking.

Instructor Resources on the Product Support Website

This password-protected website (*http://mankiw.swlearning.com*) provides a wealth of information about the book and supplements along with student exercises and instructor resources and supplements.

TextChoice

TextChoice is the home of Thomson Learning's online digital content. It provides the fastest, easiest way for you to create your own learning materials. You may select content from hundreds of our best-selling titles, choose material from one of our databases, and add your own material. Contact your South-Western/Thomson Learning sales representative for more information.

Favorite Ways to Learn Economics: Instructor's Edition

Authors David Anderson of Centre College and Jim Chasey of Homewood Flossmoor High School use experiments to bring economic education to life. In its second edition, this lab manual for the classroom and for individual study contains experiments and problem sets that reinforce key economic concepts.

Student Resources

Study Guide

David R. Hakes (University of Northern Iowa) has prepared a study guide that will enhance student success. Each chapter of the study guide includes learning objectives, a description of the chapter's context and purpose, a chapter review, key terms and definitions, advanced critical thinking questions, and helpful hints for understanding difficult concepts. Students can develop their understanding by doing the practice problems and short answer questions and then assess their mastery of the key concepts with the self-test, which includes true/false and multiple choice questions. Solutions to all study guide questions are included in the study guide.

ThomsonNOW to Accompany Mankiw *Principles of Economics*

ThomsonNOW ties together five fundamental learning activities for use with Mankiw's 4th edition: diagnostics, tutorials, homework, quizzing, and testing. The richness of the ThomsonNOW learning environment allows students to work at their own pace, check their comprehension along the way by taking quizzes and receiving feedback and rejoinders, and then set up their own personalized learning plans. The assigned material and unlimited practice improve both retention and remediation. In addition, self-paced tutorials support students with explanations, examples, step-by-step problem solving, and unlimited practice. Students also have access to the Mankiw 4th edition Graphing Workshops, Ask the Instructor video lessons as well as access to EconNews, EconDebate, EconLinks and EconData.

For Mankiw 4th edition instructors, ThomsonNOW provides a powerful gradebook and course management tools, compatible with both WebCT and Blackboard. Instructors can quickly create their own assignments and tests, drawing from the wealth of exercises provided or authoring their own questions. The variety of problem types allows instructors to assess the way they teach. Customized assignments can be copied easily for use in additional sections or future terms, making class management progressively easier.

Website

Valuable resources for students can be found on the Internet at the Mankiw 4th edition textbook support site: *http://mankiw.swlearning .com*. Students will find links to economics-related Internet sites and a sample chapter from the study guide. Also, career listings for students, leading economic indicator information, and an economic URL database can be found at *http:// economics.swlearning.com*.

"Economics is a study of mankind in the ordinary business of life." So wrote Alfred Marshall, the great 19th-century economist, in his textbook, *Principles of Economics.* Although we have learned much about the economy since Marshall's time, this definition of economics is as true today as it was in 1890, when the first edition of his text was published.

Why should you, as a student at the beginning of the 21st century, embark on the study of economics? There are three reasons.

The first reason to study economics is that it will help you understand the world in which you live. There are many questions about the economy that might spark your curiosity. Why are apartments so hard to find in New York City? Why do airlines charge less for a round-trip ticket if the traveler stays over a Saturday night? Why is Robin Williams paid so much to star in movies? Why are living standards so meager in many African countries? Why do some countries have high rates of inflation while others have stable prices? Why are jobs easy to find in some years and hard to find in others? These are just a few of the questions that a course in economics will help you answer.

The second reason to study economics is that it will make you a more astute participant in the economy. As you go about your life, you make many economic decisions. While you are a student, you decide how many years to stay in school. Once you take a job, you decide how much of your income to spend, how much to save, and how to invest your savings. Someday you may find yourself running a small business or a large corporation, and you will decide what prices to charge for your products. The insights developed in the coming chapters will give you a new perspective on how best to make these decisions. Studying economics will not by itself make you rich, but it will give you some tools that may help in that endeavor.

The third reason to study economics is that it will give you a better understanding of the potential and limits of economic policy. As a voter, you help choose the policies that guide the allocation of society's resources. When deciding which policies to support, you may find yourself asking various questions about economics. What are the burdens associated with alternative forms of taxation? What are the effects of free trade with other countries? What is the best way to protect the environment? How does a government budget deficit affect the economy? These and similar questions are always on the minds of policy-makers in mayors' offices, governors' mansions, and the White House.

Thus, the principles of economics can be applied in many of life's situations. Whether the future finds you reading the newspaper, running a business, or sitting in the Oval Office, you will be glad that you studied economics.

N. Gregory Mankiw
September 2005

BRIEF CONTENTS

TABLE OF CONTENTS

PART 1
INTRODUCTION   1

CHAPTER 1
TEN PRINCIPLES OF ECONOMICS   3

CHAPTER 2
THINKING LIKE AN ECONOMIST   19

PART 3
THE DATA OF MACROECONOMICS   89

PART 5
MONEY AND PRICES IN THE LONG RUN 223

PART 6
THE MACROECONOMICS OF OPEN ECONOMIES   273

CHAPTER 13
OPEN-ECONOMY MACROECONOMICS: BASIC CONCEPTS   275

PART 7
SHORT-RUN ECONOMIC FLUCTUATIONS   *321*

PART 8
FINAL THOUGHTS   415

CHAPTER 18
FIVE DEBATES OVER MACROECONOMIC POLICY   417

1

Introduction

Ten Principles of Economics

The word *economy* comes from the Greek word *oikonomos*, which means "one who manages a household." At first, this origin might seem peculiar. But in fact, households and economies have much in common.

A household faces many decisions. It must decide which members of the household do which tasks and what each member gets in return: Who cooks dinner? Who does the laundry? Who gets the extra dessert at dinner? Who gets to choose what TV show to watch? In short, the household must allocate its scarce resources among its various members, taking into account each member's abilities, efforts, and desires.

Like a household, a society faces many decisions. A society must decide what jobs will be done and who will do them. It needs some people to grow food, other people to make clothing, and still others to design computer software. Once society has allocated people (as well as land, buildings, and machines) to various jobs, it must also allocate the output of goods and services that they produce. It must decide who will eat caviar and who will eat potatoes. It must decide who will drive a Ferrari and who will take the bus.

The management of society's resources is important because resources are scarce. **Scarcity** means that society has limited resources and therefore cannot produce all the goods and services people wish to have. Just as a household cannot give every member everything he or she wants, a society cannot give every individual the highest standard of living to which he or she might aspire.

scarcity
the limited nature of society's resources

3

economics
the study of how society
manages its scarce
resources

Economics is the study of how society manages its scarce resources. In most societies, resources are allocated not by an all-powerful dictator but through the combined actions of millions of households and firms. Economists therefore study how people make decisions: how much they work, what they buy, how much they save, and how they invest their savings. Economists also study how people interact with one another. For instance, they examine how the multitude of buyers and sellers of a good together determine the price at which the good is sold and the quantity that is sold. Finally, economists analyze forces and trends that affect the economy as a whole, including the growth in average income, the fraction of the population that cannot find work, and the rate at which prices are rising.

Although the study of economics has many facets, the field is unified by several central ideas. In this chapter, we look at *Ten Principles of Economics*. Don't worry if you don't understand them all at first or if you don't find them completely convincing. In later chapters, we will explore these ideas more fully. The ten principles are introduced here to give you an overview of what economics is all about. You can think of this chapter as a "preview of coming attractions."

HOW PEOPLE MAKE DECISIONS

There is no mystery to what an economy is. Whether we are talking about the economy of Los Angeles, of the United States, or of the whole world, an economy is just a group of people interacting with one another as they go about their lives. Because the behavior of an economy reflects the behavior of the individuals who make up the economy, we start our study of economics with four principles of individual decision making.

Principle 1: People Face Trade-offs

The first lesson about making decisions is summarized in the adage "There is no such thing as a free lunch." To get one thing that we like, we usually have to give up another thing that we like. Making decisions requires trading off one goal against another.

Consider a student who must decide how to allocate her most valuable resource—her time. She can spend all of her time studying economics; she can spend all of her time studying psychology; or she can divide her time between the two fields. For every hour she studies one subject, she gives up an hour she could have used studying the other. And for every hour she spends studying, she gives up an hour that she could have spent napping, bike riding, watching TV, or working at her part-time job for some extra spending money.

Or consider parents deciding how to spend their family income. They can buy food, clothing, or a family vacation. Or they can save some of the family income for retirement or the children's college education. When they choose to spend an extra dollar on one of these goods, they have one less dollar to spend on some other good.

When people are grouped into societies, they face different kinds of trade-offs. The classic trade-off is between "guns and butter." The more we spend on national defense (guns) to protect our shores from foreign aggressors, the less we can spend on consumer goods (butter) to raise our standard of living at home. Also important in modern society is the trade-off between a clean environment and a high level of income. Laws that require firms to reduce pollution raise the cost of producing goods and services. Because of the higher costs, these firms end up earning smaller profits, paying lower wages, charging higher prices, or some combination of these three. Thus, while pollution regulations give us the benefit of a cleaner environment and the improved health that comes with it, they have the cost of reducing the incomes of the firms' owners, workers, and customers.

Another trade-off society faces is between efficiency and equity. **Efficiency** means that society is getting the maximum benefits from its scarce resources. **Equity** means that those benefits are distributed fairly among society's members. In other words, efficiency refers to the size of the economic pie, and equity refers to how the pie is divided. Often, when government policies are designed, these two goals conflict.

Consider, for instance, policies aimed at achieving a more equal distribution of economic well-being. Some of these policies, such as the welfare system or unemployment insurance, try to help the members of society who are most in need. Others, such as the individual income tax, ask the financially successful to contribute more than others to support the government. Although these policies have the benefit of achieving greater equity, they have a cost in terms of reduced efficiency. When the government redistributes income from the rich to the poor, it reduces the reward for working hard; as a result, people work less and produce fewer goods and services. In other words, when the government tries to cut the economic pie into more equal slices, the pie gets smaller.

Recognizing that people face trade-offs does not by itself tell us what decisions they will or should make. A student should not abandon the study of psychology just because doing so would increase the time available for the study of economics. Society should not stop protecting the environment just because environmental regulations reduce our material standard of living. The poor should not be ignored just because helping them distorts work incentives. Nonetheless, acknowledging life's trade-offs is important because people are likely to make good decisions only if they understand the options that they have available.

efficiency
the property of society getting the most it can from its scarce resources

equity
the property of distributing economic prosperity fairly among the members of society

Principle 2: The Cost of Something Is What You Give Up to Get It

Because people face trade-offs, making decisions requires comparing the costs and benefits of alternative courses of action. In many cases, however, the cost of some action is not as obvious as it might first appear.

Consider, for example, the decision to go to college. The benefit is intellectual enrichment and a lifetime of better job opportunities. But what is the cost? To answer this question, you might be tempted to add up the money you spend on tuition, books, room, and board. Yet this total does not truly represent what you give up to spend a year in college.

The first problem with this answer is that it includes some things that are not really costs of going to college. Even if you quit school, you need a place to sleep and food to eat. Room and board are costs of going to college only to the extent that they are more expensive at college than elsewhere. Indeed, the cost of room and board at your school might be less than the rent and food expenses that you would pay living on your own. In this case, the savings on room and board are a benefit of going to college.

The second problem with this calculation of costs is that it ignores the largest cost of going to college—your time. When you spend a year listening to lectures, reading textbooks, and writing papers, you cannot spend that time working at a job. For most students, the wages given up to attend school are the largest single cost of their education.

opportunity cost
whatever must be given up to obtain some item

The **opportunity cost** of an item is what you give up to get that item. When making any decision, such as whether to attend college, decision makers should be aware of the opportunity costs that accompany each possible action. In fact, they usually are. College athletes who can earn millions if they drop out of school and play professional sports are well aware that their opportunity cost of college is very high. It is not surprising that they often decide that the benefit is not worth the cost.

Principle 3: Rational People Think at the Margin

rational people
people who systematically and purposefully do the best they can to achieve their objectives

Economists normally assume that people are rational. **Rational people** systematically and purposefully do the best they can to achieve their objectives, given the opportunities they have. As you study economics, you will encounter firms that decide how many workers to hire and how much of their product to manufacture and sell to maximize profits. You will encounter consumers who buy a bundle of goods and services to achieve the highest possible level of satisfaction, subject to their incomes and the prices of those goods and services.

marginal changes
small incremental adjustments to a plan of action

Rational people know that decisions in life are rarely black and white but usually involve shades of gray. At dinnertime, the decision you face is not between fasting or eating like a pig but whether to take that extra spoonful of mashed potatoes. When exams roll around, your decision is not between blowing them off or studying 24 hours a day but whether to spend an extra hour reviewing your notes instead of watching TV. Economists use the term **marginal changes** to describe small incremental adjustments to an existing plan of action. Keep in mind that *margin* means "edge," so marginal changes are adjustments around the edges of what you are doing. Rational people often make decisions by comparing *marginal benefits* and *marginal costs*.

For example, consider an airline deciding how much to charge passengers who fly standby. Suppose that flying a 200-seat plane across the United States costs the airline $100,000. In this case, the average cost of each seat is $100,000/200, which is $500. One might be tempted to conclude that the airline should never sell a ticket for less than $500. In fact, however, the airline can raise its profits by thinking at the margin. Imagine that a plane is about to take off with ten empty seats, and a standby passenger waiting at the gate will pay $300 for a seat. Should the airline sell the ticket? Of course it should. If the plane has empty seats, the cost of adding one more passenger is minuscule. Although the *average* cost of flying a passenger is $500, the *marginal* cost is merely the cost of the bag of peanuts and can of soda that the extra passenger will consume. As long as the standby passenger pays more than the marginal cost, selling the ticket is profitable.

Marginal decision making can help explain some otherwise puzzling economic phenomena. Here is a classic question: Why is water so cheap, while diamonds are so expensive? Humans need water to survive, while diamonds are unnecessary; but for some reason, people are willing to pay much more for a diamond than for a cup of water. The reason is that a person's willingness to pay for any good is based on the marginal benefit that an extra unit of the good would yield. The marginal benefit, in turn, depends on how many units a person already has. Although water is essential, the marginal benefit of an extra cup is small because water is plentiful. By contrast, no one needs diamonds to survive, but because diamonds are so rare, people consider the marginal benefit of an extra diamond to be large.

A rational decision maker takes an action if and only if the marginal benefit of the action exceeds the marginal cost. This principle can explain why airlines are willing to sell a ticket below average cost and why people are willing to pay more for diamonds than for water. It can take some time to get used to the logic of marginal thinking, but the study of economics will give you ample opportunity to practice.

Principle 4: People Respond to Incentives

An **incentive** is something (such as the prospect of a punishment or a reward) that induces a person to act. Because rational people make decisions by comparing costs and benefits, they respond to incentives. You will see that incentives play a central role in the study of economics. One economist went so far as to suggest that the entire field could be simply summarized: "People respond to incentives. The rest is commentary."

incentive
something that induces
a person to act

Incentives are crucial to analyzing how markets work. For example, when the price of an apple rises, people decide to eat more pears and fewer apples because the cost of buying an apple is higher. At the same time, apple orchards decide to hire more workers and harvest more apples because the benefit of selling an apple is also higher. As we will see, the effect of a good's price on the behavior of buyers and sellers in a market—in this case, the market for apples— is crucial for understanding how the economy allocates scarce resources.

Public policymakers should never forget about incentives because many policies change the costs or benefits that people face and, therefore, alter their behavior. A tax on gasoline, for instance, encourages people to drive smaller, more fuel-efficient cars. That is one reason people drive smaller cars in Europe, where gasoline taxes are high, than in the United States, where gasoline taxes are low. A gasoline tax also encourages people to take public transportation rather than drive and to live closer to where they work. If the tax were larger, more people would be driving hybrid cars, and if it were large enough, they would switch to electric cars.

When policymakers fail to consider how their policies affect incentives, they often end up with results they did not intend. For example, consider public policy regarding auto safety. Today, all cars have seat belts, but this was not true 50 years ago. In the 1960s, Ralph Nader's book *Unsafe at Any Speed* generated much public concern over auto safety. Congress responded with laws requiring seat belts as standard equipment on new cars.

How does a seat belt law affect auto safety? The direct effect is obvious: When a person wears a seat belt, the probability of surviving a major auto accident rises. But that's not the end of the story because the law also affects behavior by altering incentives. The relevant behavior here is the speed and care with which drivers operate their cars. Driving slowly and carefully is costly because it uses the driver's time and energy. When deciding how safely to drive, rational people compare the marginal benefit from safer driving to the marginal cost. They drive more slowly and carefully when the benefit of increased safety is high. It is no surprise, for instance, that people drive more slowly and carefully when roads are icy than when roads are clear.

Consider how a seat belt law alters a driver's cost–benefit calculation. Seat belts make accidents less costly because they reduce the likelihood of injury or

BASKETBALL STAR LEBRON JAMES
UNDERSTANDS OPPORTUNITY COST
AND INCENTIVES. HE DECIDED TO
SKIP COLLEGE AND GO STRAIGHT TO
THE PROS, WHERE HE HAS EARNED
MILLIONS OF DOLLARS AS ONE OF
THE NBA'S TOP PLAYERS.

death. In other words, seat belts reduce the benefits of slow and careful driving. People respond to seat belts as they would to an improvement in road conditions—by driving faster and less carefully. The end result of a seat belt law, therefore, is a larger number of accidents. The decline in safe driving has a clear, adverse impact on pedestrians, who are more likely to find themselves in an accident but (unlike the drivers) don't have the benefit of added protection.

At first, this discussion of incentives and seat belts might seem like idle speculation. Yet in a classic 1975 study, economist Sam Peltzman showed that auto-safety laws have had many of these effects. According to Peltzman's evidence, these laws produce both fewer deaths per accident and more accidents. He concluded that the net result is little change in the number of driver deaths and an increase in the number of pedestrian deaths.

Peltzman's analysis of auto safety is an offbeat example of the general principle that people respond to incentives. When analyzing any policy, we must consider not only the direct effects but also the indirect and sometimes less obvious effects that work through incentives. If the policy changes incentives, it will cause people to alter their behavior.

Quick Quiz   List and briefly explain the four principles of individual decision making.

HOW PEOPLE INTERACT

The first four principles discussed how individuals make decisions. As we go about our lives, many of our decisions affect not only ourselves but other people as well. The next three principles concern how people interact with one another.

Principle 5: Trade Can Make Everyone Better Off

You have probably heard on the news that the Japanese are our competitors in the world economy. In some ways, this is true because American and Japanese firms produce many of the same goods. Ford and Toyota compete for the same customers in the market for automobiles. Apple and Sony compete for the same customers in the market for digital music players.

Yet it is easy to be misled when thinking about competition among countries. Trade between the United States and Japan is not like a sports contest in which one side wins and the other side loses. In fact, the opposite is true: Trade between two countries can make each country better off.

To see why, consider how trade affects your family. When a member of your family looks for a job, he or she competes against members of other families who are looking for jobs. Families also compete against one another when they go shopping because each family wants to buy the best goods at the lowest prices. So in a sense, each family in the economy is competing with all other families.

Despite this competition, your family would not be better off isolating itself from all other families. If it did, your family would need to grow its own food, make its own clothes, and build its own home. Clearly, your family gains much from its ability to trade with others. Trade allows each person to specialize in the

THE WALL STREET JOURNAL

ENGLEMAN

"FOR $5 A WEEK YOU CAN WATCH BASEBALL WITHOUT BEING NAGGED TO CUT THE GRASS!"

activities he or she does best, whether it is farming, sewing, or home building. By trading with others, people can buy a greater variety of goods and services at lower cost.

Countries as well as families benefit from the ability to trade with one another. Trade allows countries to specialize in what they do best and to enjoy a greater variety of goods and services. The Japanese, as well as the French and the Egyptians and the Brazilians, are as much our partners in the world economy as they are our competitors.

Principle 6: Markets Are Usually a Good Way to Organize Economic Activity

The collapse of communism in the Soviet Union and Eastern Europe in the 1980s may be the most important change in the world during the past half century. Communist countries worked on the premise that government officials were in the best position to determine the allocation of scarce resources in the economy. These central planners decided what goods and services were produced, how much was produced, and who produced and consumed these goods and services. The theory behind central planning was that only the government could organize economic activity in a way that promoted economic well-being for the country as a whole.

Today, most countries that once had centrally planned economies have abandoned this system and are trying to develop market economies. In a **market economy,** the decisions of a central planner are replaced by the decisions of millions of firms and households. Firms decide whom to hire and what to make. Households decide which firms to work for and what to buy with their incomes. These firms and households interact in the marketplace, where prices and self-interest guide their decisions.

market economy
an economy that allocates resources through the decentralized decisions of many firms and households as they interact in markets for goods and services

At first glance, the success of market economies is puzzling. After all, in a market economy, no one is looking out for the economic well-being of society as a whole. Free markets contain many buyers and sellers of numerous goods and services, and all of them are interested primarily in their own well-being. Yet despite decentralized decision making and self-interested decision makers, market economies have proven remarkably successful in organizing economic activity in a way that promotes overall economic well-being.

In his 1776 book *An Inquiry into the Nature and Causes of the Wealth of Nations*, economist Adam Smith made the most famous observation in all of economics: Households and firms interacting in markets act as if they are guided by an "invisible hand" that leads them to desirable market outcomes. One of our goals in this book is to understand how this invisible hand works its magic.

As you study economics, you will learn that prices are the instrument with which the invisible hand directs economic activity. In any market, buyers look at the price when determining how much to demand, and sellers look at the price when deciding how much to supply. As a result of the decisions that buyers and sellers make, market prices reflect both the value of a good to society and the cost to society of making the good. Smith's great insight was that prices adjust to guide these individual buyers and sellers to reach outcomes that, in many cases, maximize the welfare of society as a whole.

There is an important corollary to the skill of the invisible hand in guiding economic activity: When the government prevents prices from adjusting naturally to supply and demand, it impedes the invisible hand's ability to coordinate the millions of households and firms that make up the economy. This corollary explains why taxes adversely affect the allocation of resources: Taxes distort prices and thus the decisions of households and firms. It also explains the even greater harm caused by policies that directly control prices, such as rent control. And it explains the failure of communism. In communist countries, prices were not determined in the marketplace but were dictated by central planners. These planners lacked the information that gets reflected in prices that are free to respond to market forces. Central planners failed because they tried to run the economy with one hand tied behind their backs—the invisible hand of the marketplace.

Principle 7: Governments Can Sometimes Improve Market Outcomes

If the invisible hand of the market is so great, why do we need government? One purpose of studying economics is to refine your view about the proper role and scope of government policy.

One reason we need government is that the invisible hand can work its magic only if the government enforces the rules and maintains the institutions that are

FYI

Adam Smith and the Invisible Hand

It may be only a coincidence that Adam Smith's great book *The Wealth of Nations* was published in 1776, the exact year American revolutionaries signed the Declaration of Independence. But the two documents share a point of view that was prevalent at the time: Individuals are usually best left to their own devices, without the heavy hand of government guiding their actions. This political philosophy provides the intellectual basis for the market economy and for free society more generally.

Why do decentralized market economies work so well? Is it because people can be counted on to treat one another with love and kindness? Not at all. Here is Adam Smith's description of how people interact in a market economy:

Man has almost constant occasion for the help of his brethren, and it is vain for him to expect it from their benevolence only. He will be more likely to prevail if he can interest their self-love in his favor, and show them that it is for their own advantage to do for him what he

Adam Smith

requires of them.... It is not from the benevolence of the butcher, the brewer, or the baker that we expect our dinner, but from their regard to their own interest....

Every individual ... neither intends to promote the public interest, nor knows how much he is promoting it.... He intends only his own gain, and he is in this, as in many other cases, led by an invisible hand to promote an end which was no part of his intention. Nor is it always the worse for the society that it was no part of it. By pursuing his own interest he frequently promotes that of the society more effectually than when he really intends to promote it.

Smith is saying that participants in the economy are motivated by self-interest and that the "invisible hand" of the marketplace guides this self-interest into promoting general economic well-being.

Many of Smith's insights remain at the center of modern economics. Our analysis in the coming chapters will allow us to express Smith's conclusions more precisely and to analyze fully the strengths and weaknesses of the market's invisible hand.

key to a market economy. Most important, markets work only if **property rights** are enforced. A farmer won't grow food if he expects his crop to be stolen; a restaurant won't serve meals unless it is assured that customers will pay before they leave; and a music company won't produce CDs if too many potential customers avoid paying by making illegal copies. We all rely on government-provided police and courts to enforce our rights over the things we produce—and the invisible hand counts on our ability to enforce our rights.

Yet there is another, more profound reason we need government: The invisible hand is powerful, but it is not omnipotent. Although markets are often a good way to organize economic activity, this rule has some important exceptions. There are two broad reasons for a government to intervene in the economy and change the allocation of resources that people would choose on their own: to promote efficiency and to promote equity. That is, most policies aim either to enlarge the economic pie or to change how the pie is divided.

Consider first the goal of efficiency. Although the invisible hand usually leads markets to allocate resources efficiently, this is not always the case. Economists use the term **market failure** to refer to a situation in which the market on its own fails to produce an efficient allocation of resources. One possible cause of market failure is an **externality,** which is the impact of one person's actions on the well-being of a bystander. The classic example of an externality is pollution. Another possible cause of market failure is **market power,** which refers to the ability of a single person (or small group) to unduly influence market prices. For example, if everyone in town needs water but there is only one well, the owner of the well is not subject to the rigorous competition with which the invisible hand normally keeps self-interest in check. In the presence of externalities or market power, well-designed public policy can enhance economic efficiency.

The invisible hand may also fail to ensure that economic prosperity is distributed equitably. A market economy rewards people according to their ability to produce things that other people are willing to pay for. The world's best basketball player earns more than the world's best chess player simply because people are willing to pay more to watch basketball than chess. The invisible hand does not ensure that everyone has sufficient food, decent clothing, and adequate healthcare. Many public policies, such as the income tax and the welfare system, aim to achieve a more equitable distribution of economic well-being.

To say that the government *can* improve on market outcomes at times does not mean that it always *will*. Public policy is made not by angels but by a political process that is far from perfect. Sometimes policies are designed simply to reward the politically powerful. Sometimes they are made by well-intentioned leaders who are not fully informed. As you study economics, you will become a better judge of when a government policy is justifiable because it promotes efficiency or equity and when it is not.

property rights
the ability of an individual to own and exercise control over scarce resources

market failure
a situation in which a market left on its own fails to allocate resources efficiently

externality
the impact of one person's actions on the well-being of a bystander

market power
the ability of a single economic actor (or small group of actors) to have a substantial influence on market prices

Quick Quiz   List and briefly explain the three principles concerning people's economic interactions.

HOW THE ECONOMY AS A WHOLE WORKS

We started by discussing how individuals make decisions and then looked at how people interact with one another. All these decisions and interactions together make up "the economy." The last three principles concern the workings of the economy as a whole.

Principle 8: A Country's Standard of Living Depends on Its Ability to Produce Goods and Services

The differences in living standards around the world are staggering. In 2003, the average American had an income of about $37,500. In the same year, the average Mexican earned $8,950, and the average Nigerian earned $900. Not surprisingly, this large variation in average income is reflected in various measures of the quality of life. Citizens of high-income countries have more TV sets, more cars, better nutrition, better healthcare, and a longer life expectancy than citizens of low-income countries.

Changes in living standards over time are also large. In the United States, incomes have historically grown about 2 percent per year (after adjusting for changes in the cost of living). At this rate, average income doubles every 35 years. Over the past century, average income has risen about eightfold.

productivity
the quantity of goods and services produced from each hour of a worker's time

What explains these large differences in living standards among countries and over time? The answer is surprisingly simple. Almost all variation in living standards is attributable to differences in countries' **productivity**—that is, the amount of goods and services produced from each hour of a worker's time. In nations where workers can produce a large quantity of goods and services per unit of time, most people enjoy a high standard of living; in nations where workers are less productive, most people endure a more meager existence. Similarly, the growth rate of a nation's productivity determines the growth rate of its average income.

The fundamental relationship between productivity and living standards is simple, but its implications are far-reaching. If productivity is the primary determinant of living standards, other explanations must be of secondary importance. For example, it might be tempting to credit labor unions or minimum-wage laws for the rise in living standards of American workers over the past century. Yet the real hero of American workers is their rising productivity. As another example, some commentators have claimed that increased competition from Japan and other countries explained the slow growth in U.S. incomes during the 1970s and 1980s. Yet the real villain was not competition from abroad but flagging productivity growth in the United States.

The relationship between productivity and living standards also has profound implications for public policy. When thinking about how any policy will affect living standards, the key question is how it will affect our ability to produce goods and services. To boost living standards, policymakers need to raise productivity by ensuring that workers are well educated, have the tools needed to produce goods and services, and have access to the best available technology.

Principle 9: Prices Rise When the Government Prints Too Much Money

inflation
an increase in the overall level of prices in the economy

In Germany in January 1921, a daily newspaper cost 0.30 marks. Less than 2 years later, in November 1922, the same newspaper cost 70,000,000 marks. All other prices in the economy rose by similar amounts. This episode is one of history's most spectacular examples of **inflation,** an increase in the overall level of prices in the economy.

Although the United States has never experienced inflation even close to that in Germany in the 1920s, inflation has at times been an economic problem. During the 1970s, for instance, the overall level of prices more than doubled, and President Gerald Ford called inflation "public enemy number one." By contrast, inflation in the 1990s was about 3 percent per year; at this rate, it would take more than 20 years for prices to double. Because high inflation imposes various costs on society, keeping inflation at a low level is a goal of economic policymakers around the world.

What causes inflation? In almost all cases of large or persistent inflation, the culprit is growth in the quantity of money. When a government creates large quantities of the nation's money, the value of the money falls. In Germany in the early 1920s, when prices were on average tripling every month, the quantity of money was also tripling every month. Although less dramatic, the economic history of the United States points to a similar conclusion: The high inflation of the 1970s was associated with rapid growth in the quantity of money, and the low inflation of the 1990s was associated with slow growth in the quantity of money.

"WELL IT MAY HAVE BEEN 68 CENTS WHEN YOU GOT IN LINE, BUT IT'S 74 CENTS NOW!"

Principle 10: Society Faces a Short-Run Trade-off between Inflation and Unemployment

Although a higher level of prices is, in the long run, the primary effect of increasing the quantity of money, the short-run story is more complex and more controversial. Most economists describe the short-run effects of monetary injections as follows:

- Increasing the amount of money in the economy stimulates the overall level of spending and thus the demand for goods and services.
- Higher demand may over time cause firms to raise their prices, but in the meantime, it also encourages them to increase the quantity of goods and services they produce and to hire more workers to produce those goods and services.
- More hiring means lower unemployment.

This line of reasoning leads to one final economywide trade-off: a short-run trade-off between inflation and unemployment.

Although some economists still question these ideas, most accept that society faces a short-run trade-off between inflation and unemployment. This simply means that, over a period of a year or two, many economic policies push inflation and unemployment in opposite directions. Policymakers face this trade-off regardless of whether inflation and unemployment both start out at high levels (as they were in the early 1980s), at low levels (as they were in the late 1990s), or someplace in between. This short-run trade-off plays a key role in the analysis of the **business cycle**—the irregular and largely unpredictable fluctuations in economic activity, as measured by the production of goods and services or the number of people employed.

Policymakers can exploit the short-run trade-off between inflation and unemployment using various policy instruments. By changing the amount that the government spends, the amount it taxes, and the amount of money it prints, policymakers can influence the combination of inflation and unemployment that the economy experiences. Because these instruments of economic policy are potentially so powerful, how policymakers should use these instruments to control the economy, if at all, is a subject of continuing debate.

business cycle
fluctuations in economic activity, such as employment and production

FYI

How to Read This Book

Economics is fun, but it can also be hard to learn. My aim in writing this text is to make it as fun and easy as possible. But you, the student, also have a role to play. Experience shows that if you are actively involved as you study this book, you will enjoy a better outcome both on your exams and in the years that follow. Here are a few tips about how best to read this book.

1. *Summarize, don't highlight.* Running a yellow marker over the text is too passive an activity to keep your mind engaged. Instead, when you come to the end of a section, take a minute and summarize what you just learned in your own words, writing your summary in the wide margins we've provided. When you've finished the chapter, compare your summaries with the one at the end of the chapter. Did you pick up the main points?

2. *Test yourself.* Throughout the book, Quick Quizzes offer instant feedback to find out if you've learned what you are supposed to. Take the opportunity to write down your answer and then check it against the answers provided in the back of the book. The quizzes are meant to test your basic comprehension. If your answer is incorrect, you probably need to review the section.

3. *Practice, practice, practice.* At the end of each chapter, Questions for Review test your understanding, and Problems and Applications ask you to apply and extend the material. Perhaps your instructor will assign some of these exercises as homework. If so, do them. If not, do them anyway. The more you use your new knowledge, the more solid it becomes.

4. *Go online.* The publisher of this book maintains an extensive website to help you in your study of economics. It includes additional examples, applications, and problems, as well as quizzes so you can test yourself. Check it out. The website is http://mankiw.swlearning.com.

5. *Study in groups.* After you've read the book and worked problems on your own, get together with classmates to discuss the material. You will learn from each other—an example of the gains from trade.

6. *Don't forget the real world.* In the midst of all the numbers, graphs, and strange new words, it is easy to lose sight of what economics is all about. The Case Studies and In the News boxes sprinkled throughout this book should help remind you. Don't skip them. They show how the theory is tied to events happening in all of our lives. If your study is successful, you won't be able to read a newspaper again without thinking about supply, demand, and the wonderful world of economics.

Quick Quiz List and briefly explain the three principles that describe how the economy as a whole works.

CONCLUSION

You now have a taste of what economics is all about. In the coming chapters, we will develop many specific insights about people, markets, and economies. Mastering these insights will take some effort, but it is not an overwhelming task. The field of economics is based on a few basic ideas that can be applied in many different situations.

Throughout this book, we will refer back to the *Ten Principles of Economics* highlighted in this chapter and summarized in Table 1. Whenever we do so, an icon will be displayed in the margin, as it is now. But even when that icon is absent, you should keep these building blocks in mind. Even the most sophisticated economic analysis is built using the ten principles introduced here.

How People Make Decisions
1: People Face Trade-offs
2: The Cost of Something Is What You Give Up to Get It
3: Rational People Think at the Margin
4: People Respond to Incentives

How People Interact
5: Trade Can Make Everyone Better Off
6: Markets Are Usually a Good Way to Organize Economic Activity
7: Governments Can Sometimes Improve Market Outcomes

How the Economy as a Whole Works
8: A Country's Standard of Living Depends on Its Ability to Produce Goods and Services
9: Prices Rise When the Government Prints Too Much Money
10: Society Faces a Short-Run Trade-off between Inflation and Unemployment

T A B L E 1

Ten Principles of Economics

SUMMARY

- The fundamental lessons about individual decision making are that people face trade-offs among alternative goals, that the cost of any action is measured in terms of forgone opportunities, that rational people make decisions by comparing marginal costs and marginal benefits, and that people change their behavior in response to the incentives they face.

- The fundamental lessons about interactions among people are that trade can be mutually beneficial, that markets are usually a good way of coordinating trade among people, and that the government can potentially improve market outcomes if there is some market failure or if the market outcome is inequitable.

- The fundamental lessons about the economy as a whole are that productivity is the ultimate source of living standards, that money growth is the ultimate source of inflation, and that society faces a short-run trade-off between inflation and unemployment.

KEY CONCEPTS

scarcity, p. 3
economics, p. 4
efficiency, p. 5
equity, p. 5
opportunity cost, p. 6
rational people, p. 6

marginal changes, p. 6
incentive, p. 7
market economy, p. 9
property rights, p. 11
market failure, p. 11
externality, p. 11

market power, p. 11
productivity, p. 12
inflation, p. 12
business cycle, p. 13

QUESTIONS FOR REVIEW

1. Give three examples of important trade-offs that you face in your life.

2. What is the opportunity cost of seeing a movie?

3. Water is necessary for life. Is the marginal benefit of a glass of water large or small?

4. Why should policymakers think about incentives?

5. Why isn't trade among countries like a game with some winners and some losers?

6. What does the "invisible hand" of the marketplace do?

7. Explain the two main causes of market failure and give an example of each.

8. Why is productivity important?

9. What is inflation and what causes it?

10. How are inflation and unemployment related in the short run?

PROBLEMS AND APPLICATIONS

1. Describe some of the trade-offs faced by each of the following:
   a. a family deciding whether to buy a new car
   b. a member of Congress deciding how much to spend on national parks
   c. a company president deciding whether to open a new factory
   d. a professor deciding how much to prepare for class

2. You are trying to decide whether to take a vacation. Most of the costs of the vacation (airfare, hotel, and forgone wages) are measured in dollars, but the benefits of the vacation are psychological. How can you compare the benefits to the costs?

3. You were planning to spend Saturday working at your part-time job, but a friend asks you to go skiing. What is the true cost of going skiing? Now suppose you had been planning to spend the day studying at the library. What is the cost of going skiing in this case? Explain.

4. You win $100 in a basketball pool. You have a choice between spending the money now or putting it away for a year in a bank account that pays 5 percent interest. What is the opportunity cost of spending the $100 now?

5. The company that you manage has invested $5 million in developing a new product, but the development is not quite finished. At a recent meeting, your salespeople report that the introduction of competing products has reduced the expected sales of your new product to $3 million. If it would cost $1 million to finish development and make the product, should you go ahead and do so? What is the most that you should pay to complete development?

6. Three managers of the Magic Potion Company are discussing a possible increase in production. Each suggests a way to make this decision.

   HARRY: We should examine whether our company's productivity—gallons of potion per worker—would rise or fall.

   RON: We should examine whether our average cost—cost per worker—would rise or fall.

   HERMIONE: We should examine whether the extra revenue from selling the additional potion would be greater or smaller than the extra costs.

   Who do you think is right? Why?

7. The Social Security system provides income for people over age 65. If a recipient of Social Security decides to work and earn some income, the amount he or she receives in Social Security benefits is typically reduced.
   a. How does the provision of Social Security affect people's incentive to save while working?
   b. How does the reduction in benefits associated with higher earnings affect people's incentive to work past age 65?

8. A recent bill reforming the government's anti-poverty programs limited many welfare recipients to only 2 years of benefits.
   a. How does this change affect the incentives for working?
   b. How might this change represent a trade-off between equity and efficiency?

9. Your roommate is a better cook than you are, but you can clean more quickly than your roommate can. If your roommate did all of the cooking and you did all of the cleaning, would your chores take you more or less time than if you divided each task evenly? Give a similar example of how specialization and trade can make two countries both better off.

10. Suppose the United States adopted central planning for its economy, and you became the chief planner. Among the millions of decisions that you need to make for next year are how many compact discs to produce, what artists to record, and who should receive the discs.
    a. To make these decisions intelligently, what information would you need about the compact disc industry? What information would you need about each of the people in the United States?
    b. How would your decisions about CDs affect some of your other decisions, such as how many CD players to make or cassette tapes to produce? How might some of your other decisions about the economy change your views about CDs?

11. Nations with corrupt police and court systems typically have lower standards of living than nations with less corruption. Why might that be the case?

12. Explain whether each of the following government activities is motivated by a concern about equity or a concern about efficiency. In the case of efficiency, discuss the type of market failure involved.
    a. regulating cable TV prices

    b. providing some poor people with vouchers that can be used to buy food
    c. prohibiting smoking in public places
    d. breaking up Standard Oil (which once owned 90 percent of all oil refineries) into several smaller companies
    e. imposing higher personal income tax rates on people with higher incomes
    f. instituting laws against driving while intoxicated

13. Discuss each of the following statements from the standpoints of equity and efficiency.
    a. "Everyone in society should be guaranteed the best healthcare possible."
    b. "When workers are laid off, they should be able to collect unemployment benefits until they find a new job."

14. In what ways is your standard of living different from that of your parents or grandparents when they were your age? Why have these changes occurred?

15. Suppose Americans decide to save more of their incomes. If banks lend this extra saving to businesses, which use the funds to build new factories, how might this lead to faster growth in productivity? Who do you suppose benefits from the higher productivity? Is society getting a free lunch?

16. Imagine that you are a policymaker trying to decide whether to reduce the rate of inflation. To make an intelligent decision, what would you need to know about inflation, unemployment, and the trade-off between them?

17. Look at a newspaper or at the website http://www.economist.com to find three stories about the economy that have been in the news lately. For each story, identify one (or more) of the *Ten Principles of Economics* discussed in this chapter that is relevant and explain how it is relevant. Also, for each story, look through this book's Contents and try to find a chapter that might shed light on the news event.

 For further information on topics in this chapter, additional problems, applications, examples, online quizzes, and more, please visit our website at http://mankiw.swlearning.com.

Thinking Like an Economist

Every field of study has its own language and its own way of thinking. Mathematicians talk about axioms, integrals, and vector spaces. Psychologists talk about ego, id, and cognitive dissonance. Lawyers talk about venue, torts, and promissory estoppel.

Economics is no different. Supply, demand, elasticity, comparative advantage, consumer surplus, deadweight loss—these terms are part of the economist's language. In the coming chapters, you will encounter many new terms and some familiar words that economists use in specialized ways. At first, this new language may seem needlessly arcane. But as you will see, its value lies in its ability to provide you with a new and useful way of thinking about the world in which you live.

The single most important purpose of this book is to help you learn the economist's way of thinking. Of course, just as you cannot become a mathematician, psychologist, or lawyer overnight, learning to think like an economist will take some time. Yet with a combination of theory, case studies, and examples of economics in the news, this book will give you ample opportunity to develop and practice this skill.

Before delving into the substance and details of economics, it is helpful to have an overview of how economists approach the world. This chapter discusses the field's methodology. What is distinctive about how economists confront a question? What does it mean to think like an economist?

THE ECONOMIST AS SCIENTIST

"I'M A SOCIAL SCIENTIST, MICHAEL. THAT MEANS I CAN'T EXPLAIN ELECTRICITY OR ANYTHING LIKE THAT, BUT IF YOU EVER WANT TO KNOW ABOUT PEOPLE, I'M YOUR MAN."

Economists try to address their subject with a scientist's objectivity. They approach the study of the economy in much the same way as a physicist approaches the study of matter and a biologist approaches the study of life: They devise theories, collect data, and then analyze these data in an attempt to verify or refute their theories.

To beginners, it can seem odd to claim that economics is a science. After all, economists do not work with test tubes or telescopes. The essence of science, however, is the *scientific method*—the dispassionate development and testing of theories about how the world works. This method of inquiry is as applicable to studying a nation's economy as it is to studying the earth's gravity or a species' evolution. As Albert Einstein once put it, "The whole of science is nothing more than the refinement of everyday thinking."

Although Einstein's comment is as true for social sciences such as economics as it is for natural sciences such as physics, most people are not accustomed to looking at society through the eyes of a scientist. Let's discuss some of the ways in which economists apply the logic of science to examine how an economy works.

The Scientific Method: Observation, Theory, and More Observation

Isaac Newton, the famous 17th-century scientist and mathematician, allegedly became intrigued one day when he saw an apple fall from a tree. This observation motivated Newton to develop a theory of gravity that applies not only to an apple falling to the earth but to any two objects in the universe. Subsequent testing of Newton's theory has shown that it works well in many circumstances (although, as Einstein would later emphasize, not in all circumstances). Because Newton's theory has been so successful at explaining observation, it is still taught today in undergraduate physics courses around the world.

This interplay between theory and observation also occurs in the field of economics. An economist might live in a country experiencing rapid increases in prices and be moved by this observation to develop a theory of inflation. The theory might assert that high inflation arises when the government prints too much money. (As you may recall, this was one of the *Ten Principles of Economics* in Chapter 1.) To test this theory, the economist could collect and analyze data on prices and money from many different countries. If growth in the quantity of money were not at all related to the rate at which prices are rising, the economist would start to doubt the validity of this theory of inflation. If money growth and inflation were strongly correlated in international data, as in fact they are, the economist would become more confident in the theory.

Although economists use theory and observation like other scientists, they do face an obstacle that makes their task especially challenging: Experiments are often difficult in economics. Physicists studying gravity can drop many objects in their laboratories to generate data to test their theories. By contrast, economists studying inflation are not allowed to manipulate a nation's monetary policy simply to generate useful data. Economists, like astronomers and evolutionary biologists, usually have to make do with whatever data the world happens to give them.

To find a substitute for laboratory experiments, economists pay close attention to the natural experiments offered by history. When a war in the Middle East interrupts the flow of crude oil, for instance, oil prices skyrocket around the world. For consumers of oil and oil products, such an event depresses living standards. For economic policymakers, it poses a difficult choice about how best to respond. But for economic scientists, the event provides an opportunity to study the effects of a key natural resource on the world's economies, and this opportunity persists long after the wartime increase in oil prices is over. Throughout this book, therefore, we consider many historical episodes. These episodes are valuable to study because they give us insight into the economy of the past and, more important, because they allow us to illustrate and evaluate economic theories of the present.

The Role of Assumptions

If you ask a physicist how long it would take for a marble to fall from the top of a ten-story building, she will answer the question by assuming that the marble falls in a vacuum. Of course, this assumption is false. In fact, the building is surrounded by air, which exerts friction on the falling marble and slows it down. Yet the physicist will correctly point out that friction on the marble is so small that its effect is negligible. Assuming the marble falls in a vacuum greatly simplifies the problem without substantially affecting the answer.

Economists make assumptions for the same reason: Assumptions can simplify the complex world and make it easier to understand. To study the effects of international trade, for example, we may assume that the world consists of only two countries and that each country produces only two goods. Of course, the real world consists of dozens of countries, each of which produces thousands of different types of goods. But by assuming two countries and two goods, we can focus our thinking on the essence of the problem. Once we understand international trade in an imaginary world with two countries and two goods, we are in a better position to understand international trade in the more complex world in which we live.

The art in scientific thinking—whether in physics, biology, or economics—is deciding which assumptions to make. Suppose, for instance, that we were dropping a beachball rather than a marble from the top of the building. Our physicist would realize that the assumption of no friction is far less accurate in this case: Friction exerts a greater force on a beachball than on a marble because a beachball is much larger. The assumption that gravity works in a vacuum is reasonable for studying a falling marble but not for studying a falling beachball.

Similarly, economists use different assumptions to answer different questions. Suppose that we want to study what happens to the economy when the government changes the number of dollars in circulation. An important piece of this analysis, it turns out, is how prices respond. Many prices in the economy change infrequently; the newsstand prices of magazines, for instance, change only every few years. Knowing this fact may lead us to make different assumptions when studying the effects of the policy change over different time horizons. For studying the short-run effects of the policy, we may assume that prices do not change much. We may even make the extreme and artificial assumption that all prices are completely fixed. For studying the long-run effects of the policy, however, we may assume that all prices are completely flexible. Just as a physicist uses different assumptions when studying falling marbles and falling beachballs, economists use different assumptions when studying the short-run and long-run effects of a change in the quantity of money.

Economic Models

High school biology teachers teach basic anatomy with plastic replicas of the human body. These models have all the major organs: the heart, the liver, the kidneys, and so on. The models allow teachers to show their students in a simple way how the important parts of the body fit together. Of course, no one would mistake these plastic models for a real person. These models are stylized, and they omit many details. Yet despite this lack of realism—indeed, because of this lack of realism—studying these models is useful for learning how the human body works.

Economists also use models to learn about the world, but instead of being made of plastic, they are most often composed of diagrams and equations. Like a biology teacher's plastic model, economic models omit many details to allow us to see what is truly important. Just as the biology teacher's model does not include all of the body's muscles and capillaries, an economist's model does not include every feature of the economy.

As we use models to examine various economic issues throughout this book, you will see that all the models are built with assumptions. Just as a physicist begins the analysis of a falling marble by assuming away the existence of friction, economists assume away many of the details of the economy that are irrelevant for studying the question at hand. All models—in physics, biology, and economics—simplify reality to improve our understanding of it.

Our First Model: The Circular-Flow Diagram

The economy consists of millions of people engaged in many activities—buying, selling, working, hiring, manufacturing, and so on. To understand how the economy works, we must find some way to simplify our thinking about all these activities. In other words, we need a model that explains, in general terms, how the economy is organized and how participants in the economy interact with one another.

circular-flow diagram
a visual model of the economy that shows how dollars flow through markets among households and firms

Figure 1 presents a visual model of the economy called a **circular-flow diagram.** In this model, the economy is simplified to include only two types of decision makers—firms and households. Firms produce goods and services using inputs, such as labor, land, and capital (buildings and machines). These inputs are called the *factors of production.* Households own the factors of production and consume all the goods and services that the firms produce.

Households and firms interact in two types of markets. In the *markets for goods and services,* households are buyers, and firms are sellers. In particular, households buy the output of goods and services that firms produce. In the *markets for the factors of production,* households are sellers, and firms are buyers. In these markets, households provide the inputs that firms use to produce goods and services. The circular-flow diagram offers a simple way of organizing all the economic transactions that occur between households and firms in the economy.

The inner loop of the circular-flow diagram represents the flows of inputs and outputs. The households sell the use of their labor, land, and capital to the firms in the markets for the factors of production. The firms then use these factors to produce goods and services, which in turn are sold to households in the markets for goods and services. Hence, the factors of production flow from households to firms, and goods and services flow from firms to households.

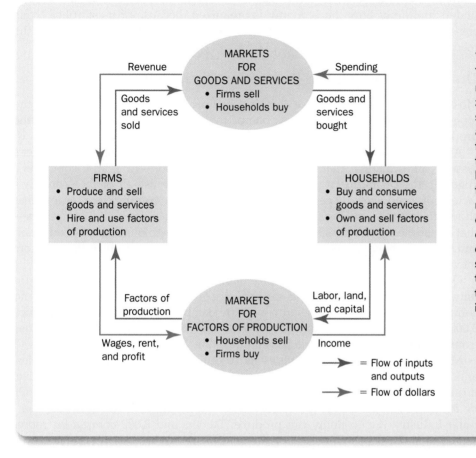

The Circular Flow
This diagram is a schematic representation of the organization of the economy. Decisions are made by households and firms. Households and firms interact in the markets for goods and services (where households are buyers and firms are sellers) and in the markets for the factors of production (where firms are buyers and households are sellers). The outer set of arrows shows the flow of dollars, and the inner set of arrows shows the corresponding flow of inputs and outputs.

The outer loop of the circular-flow diagram represents the corresponding flow of dollars. The households spend money to buy goods and services from the firms. The firms use some of the revenue from these sales to pay for the factors of production, such as the wages of their workers. What's left is the profit of the firm owners, who themselves are members of households. Hence, spending on goods and services flows from households to firms, and income in the form of wages, rent, and profit flows from firms to households.

Let's take a tour of the circular flow by following a dollar bill as it makes its way from person to person through the economy. Imagine that the dollar begins at a household, say, in your wallet. If you want to buy a cup of coffee, you take the dollar to one of the economy's markets for goods and services, such as your local Starbucks coffee shop. There you spend it on your favorite drink. When the dollar moves into the Starbucks cash register, it becomes revenue for the firm. The dollar doesn't stay at Starbucks for long, however, because the firm uses it to buy inputs in the markets for the factors of production. For instance, Starbucks might use the dollar to pay rent to its landlord for the space it occupies or to pay the wages of its workers. In either case, the dollar enters the income of some household and, once again, is back in someone's wallet. At that point, the story of the economy's circular flow starts once again.

The circular-flow diagram in Figure 1 is one simple model of the economy. It dispenses with details that, for some purposes, are significant. A more complex and realistic circular-flow model would include, for instance, the roles of government and international trade. Yet these details are not crucial for a basic understanding of how the economy is organized. Because of its simplicity, this circular-flow diagram is useful to keep in mind when thinking about how the pieces of the economy fit together.

Our Second Model: The Production Possibilities Frontier

Most economic models, unlike the circular-flow diagram, are built using the tools of mathematics. Here we use one of the simplest such models, called the production possibilities frontier, to illustrate some basic economic ideas.

Although real economies produce thousands of goods and services, let's assume an economy that produces only two goods—cars and computers. Together, the car industry and the computer industry use all of the economy's factors of production. The **production possibilities frontier** is a graph that shows the various combinations of output—in this case, cars and computers—that the economy can possibly produce given the available factors of production and the available production technology that firms can use to turn these factors into output.

Figure 2 shows this economy's production possibilities frontier. If the economy uses all its resources in the car industry, it can produce 1,000 cars and no computers. If it uses all its resources in the computer industry, it can produce 3,000 computers and no cars. The two endpoints of the production possibilities frontier represent these extreme possibilities.

More likely, the economy divides its resources between the two industries, and this yields other points on the production possibilities frontier. For example, it can produce 600 cars and 2,200 computers, shown in the figure by point A. Or by moving some of the factors of production to the car industry from the computer industry, the economy can produce 700 cars and 2,000 computers, represented by point B.

production possibilities frontier

a graph that shows the combinations of output that the economy can possibly produce given the available factors of production and the available production technology

2 FIGURE

The Production Possibilities Frontier
The production possibilities frontier shows the combinations of output—in this case, cars and computers—that the economy can possibly produce. The economy can produce any combination on or inside the frontier. Points outside the frontier are not feasible given the economy's resources.

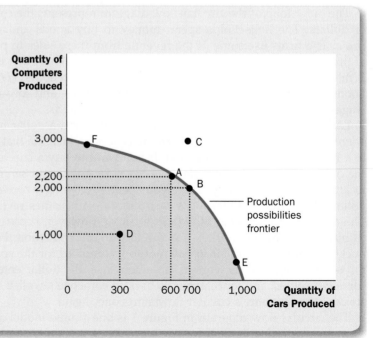

Because resources are scarce, not every conceivable outcome is feasible. For example, no matter how resources are allocated between the two industries, the economy cannot produce the amount of cars and computers represented by point C. Given the technology available for manufacturing cars and computers, the economy simply does not have enough of the factors of production to support that level of output. With the resources it has, the economy can produce at any point on or inside the production possibilities frontier, but it cannot produce at points outside the frontier.

An outcome is said to be *efficient* if the economy is getting all it can from the scarce resources it has available. Points on (rather than inside) the production possibilities frontier represent efficient levels of production. When the economy is producing at such a point, say point A, there is no way to produce more of one good without producing less of the other. Point D represents an *inefficient* outcome. For some reason, perhaps widespread unemployment, the economy is producing less than it could from the resources it has available: It is producing only 300 cars and 1,000 computers. If the source of the inefficiency is eliminated, the economy can increase its production of both goods. For example, if the economy moves from point D to point A, its production of cars increases from 300 to 600, and its production of computers increases from 1,000 to 2,200.

One of the *Ten Principles of Economics* discussed in Chapter 1 is that people face trade-offs. The production possibilities frontier shows one trade-off that society faces. Once we have reached the efficient points on the frontier, the only way of getting more of one good is to get less of the other. When the economy moves from point A to point B, for instance, society produces 100 more cars but at the expense of producing 200 fewer computers.

This trade-off helps us understand another of the *Ten Principles of Economics:* The cost of something is what you give up to get it. This is called the *opportunity cost.* The production possibilities frontier shows the opportunity cost of one good as measured in terms of the other good. When society moves from point A to point B, it gives up 200 computers to get 100 additional cars. That is, at point A, the opportunity cost of 100 cars is 200 computers. Put another way, the opportunity cost of each car is two computers. Notice that the opportunity cost of a car equals the slope of the production possibilities frontier. (If you don't recall what slope is, you can refresh your memory with the graphing appendix to this chapter.)

The opportunity cost of a car in terms of the number of computers is not a constant in this economy but depends on how many cars and computers the economy is producing. This is reflected in the shape of the production possibilities frontier. Because the production possibilities frontier in Figure 2 is bowed outward, the opportunity cost of a car is highest when the economy is producing many cars and fewer computers, such as at point E, where the frontier is steep. When the economy is producing few cars and many computers, such as at point F, the frontier is flatter, and the opportunity cost of a car is lower.

Economists believe that production possibilities frontiers often have this bowed shape. When the economy is using most of its resources to make computers, such as at point F, the resources best suited to car production, such as skilled autoworkers, are being used in the computer industry. Because these workers probably aren't very good at making computers, the economy won't have to lose much computer production to increase car production by one unit. The opportunity cost of a car in terms of computers is small, and the frontier is relatively flat. By contrast, when the economy is using most of its resources to make cars, such as at point E, the resources best suited to making cars are already in the car industry. Producing an additional car means moving some of the best computer technicians out of the computer industry and making them autoworkers. As a result, producing an additional car will mean a substantial loss of computer output. The opportunity cost of a car is high, and the frontier is quite steep.

The production possibilities frontier shows the trade-off between the outputs of different goods at a given time, but the trade-off can change over time. For example, suppose a technological advance in the computer industry raises the number of computers that a worker can produce per week. This advance expands society's set of opportunities. For any given number of cars, the economy can make more computers. If the economy does not produce any computers, it can still produce 1,000 cars, so one endpoint of the frontier stays the same. But the rest of the production possibilities frontier shifts outward, as in Figure 3.

This figure illustrates economic growth. Society can move production from a point on the old frontier to a point on the new frontier. Which point it chooses depends on its preferences for the two goods. In this example, society moves from point A to point G, enjoying more computers (2,300 instead of 2,200) and more cars (650 instead of 600).

The production possibilities frontier simplifies a complex economy to highlight some basic but powerful ideas: scarcity, efficiency, trade-offs, opportunity cost, and economic growth. As you study economics, these ideas will recur in various forms. The production possibilities frontier offers one simple way of thinking about them.

Microeconomics and Macroeconomics

Many subjects are studied on various levels. Consider biology, for example. Molecular biologists study the chemical compounds that make up living things. Cellular biologists study cells, which are made up of many chemical compounds

3 FIGURE

A Shift in the Production Possibilities Frontier
A technological advance in the computer industry enables the economy to produce more computers for any given number of cars. As a result, the production possibilities frontier shifts outward. If the economy moves from point A to point G, then the production of both cars and computers increases.

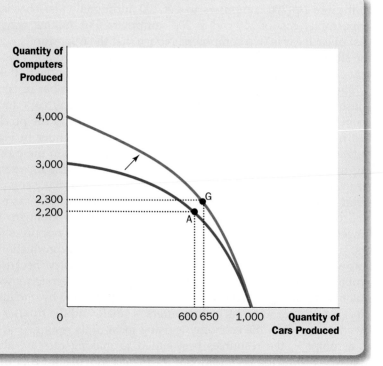

and, at the same time, are themselves the building blocks of living organisms. Evolutionary biologists study the many varieties of animals and plants and how species change gradually over the centuries.

Economics is also studied on various levels. We can study the decisions of individual households and firms. Or we can study the interaction of households and firms in markets for specific goods and services. Or we can study the operation of the economy as a whole, which is the sum of the activities of all these decision makers in all these markets.

The field of economics is traditionally divided into two broad subfields. **Microeconomics** is the study of how households and firms make decisions and how they interact in specific markets. **Macroeconomics** is the study of economy-wide phenomena. A microeconomist might study the effects of rent control on housing in New York City, the impact of foreign competition on the U.S. auto industry, or the effects of compulsory school attendance on workers' earnings. A macroeconomist might study the effects of borrowing by the federal government,

microeconomics
the study of how households and firms make decisions and how they interact in markets

macroeconomics
the study of economy-wide phenomena, including inflation, unemployment, and economic growth

FYI

Who Studies Economics?

As a college student, you might be asking yourself: How many economics classes should I take? How useful will this stuff be to me later in life? Economics can seem abstract at first, but the field is fundamentally very practical, and the study of economics is useful in many different career paths. Here is a small sampling of some well-known people who majored in economics when they were in college.

Meg Witman	Chief Executive Officer, Ebay
Ronald Reagan	Former President of the United States
William F. Buckley	Journalist
Danny Glover	Actor
Barbara Boxer	U.S. Senator
John Elway	NFL Quarterback
Ted Turner	Founder of CNN and Owner of Atlanta Braves
Kofi Annan	Secretary General, United Nations
Lionel Richie	Singer
Michael Kinsley	Journalist
Ben Stein	Political Speechwriter, Actor, and Game Show Host
Cate Blanchett	Actor
Anthony Zinni	General, U.S. Marine Corps

Tiger Woods	Golfer
Steve Ballmer	Chief Executive Officer, Microsoft
Arnold Schwarzenegger	Governor of California
Sandra Day-O'Connor	Former Supreme Court Justice
Mick Jagger	Singer for The Rolling Stones

Having studied at the London School of Economics may not help Mick Jagger hit the high notes, but it has probably given him some insight about how to invest the substantial sums he has earned during his rock-'n'-roll career.

When asked in 2005 why The Rolling Stones were going on tour again, former economics major Mick Jagger replied, "Supply and demand." Keith Richards added, "If the demand's there, we'll supply."

the changes over time in the economy's rate of unemployment, or alternative policies to raise growth in national living standards.

Microeconomics and macroeconomics are closely intertwined. Because changes in the overall economy arise from the decisions of millions of individuals, it is impossible to understand macroeconomic developments without considering the associated microeconomic decisions. For example, a macroeconomist might study the effect of a cut in the federal income tax on the overall production of goods and services. To analyze this issue, he or she must consider how the tax cut affects the decisions of households about how much to spend on goods and services.

Despite the inherent link between microeconomics and macroeconomics, the two fields are distinct. Because they address different questions, each field has its own set of models, which are often taught in separate courses.

Quick Quiz In what sense is economics like a science? • Draw a production possibilities frontier for a society that produces food and clothing. Show an efficient point, an inefficient point, and an infeasible point. Show the effects of a drought. • Define microeconomics and macroeconomics.

THE ECONOMIST AS POLICY ADVISER

Often, economists are asked to explain the causes of economic events. Why, for example, is unemployment higher for teenagers than for older workers? Sometimes economists are asked to recommend policies to improve economic outcomes. What, for instance, should the government do to improve the economic well-being of teenagers? When economists are trying to explain the world, they are scientists. When they are trying to help improve it, they are policy advisers.

Positive versus Normative Analysis

To help clarify the two roles that economists play, we begin by examining the use of language. Because scientists and policy advisers have different goals, they use language in different ways.

For example, suppose that two people are discussing minimum-wage laws. Here are two statements you might hear:

> POLLY: Minimum-wage laws cause unemployment.
>
> NORMA: The government should raise the minimum wage.

Ignoring for now whether you agree with these statements, notice that Polly and Norma differ in what they are trying to do. Polly is speaking like a scientist: She is making a claim about how the world works. Norma is speaking like a policy adviser: She is making a claim about how she would like to change the world.

In general, statements about the world are of two types. One type, such as Polly's, is positive. **Positive statements** are descriptive. They make a claim about how the world *is*. A second type of statement, such as Norma's, is normative. **Normative statements** are prescriptive. They make a claim about how the world *ought to be*.

A key difference between positive and normative statements is how we judge their validity. We can, in principle, confirm or refute positive statements by examining evidence. An economist might evaluate Polly's statement by analyzing data on changes in minimum wages and changes in unemployment over

positive statements
claims that attempt to describe the world as it is

normative statements
claims that attempt to prescribe how the world should be

time. By contrast, evaluating normative statements involves values as well as facts. Norma's statement cannot be judged using data alone. Deciding what is good or bad policy is not merely a matter of science. It also involves our views on ethics, religion, and political philosophy.

Positive and normative statements are fundamentally different, but they are often closely intertwined in a person's set of beliefs. In particular, positive views about how the world works affect normative views about what policies are desirable. Polly's claim that the minimum wage causes unemployment, if true, might lead her to reject Norma's conclusion that the government should raise the minimum wage. Yet normative conclusions cannot come from positive analysis alone; they involve value judgments as well.

As you study economics, keep in mind the distinction between positive and normative statements because it will help you stay focused on the task at hand. Much of economics is positive: It just tries to explain how the economy works. Yet those who use economics often have goals that are normative: They want to learn how to improve the economy. When you hear economists making normative statements, you know they are speaking not as scientists but as policy advisers.

Economists in Washington

President Harry Truman once said that he wanted to find a one-armed economist. When he asked his economists for advice, they always answered, "On the one hand, . . . On the other hand, . . ."

Truman was right in realizing that economists' advice is not always straightforward. This tendency is rooted in one of the *Ten Principles of Economics:* People face trade-offs. Economists are aware that trade-offs are involved in most policy decisions. A policy might increase efficiency at the cost of equity. It might help future generations but hurt current generations. An economist who says that all policy decisions are easy is an economist not to be trusted.

Truman was also not alone among presidents in relying on the advice of economists. Since 1946, the president of the United States has received guidance from the Council of Economic Advisers, which consists of three members and a staff of several dozen economists. The council, whose offices are just a few steps from the White House, has no duty other than to advise the president and to write the annual *Economic Report of the President,* which discusses recent developments in the economy and presents the council's analysis of current policy issues.

The president also receives input from economists in many administrative departments. Economists at the Department of the Treasury help design tax policy. Economists at the Department of Labor analyze data on workers and those looking for work to help formulate labor-market policies. Economists at the Department of Justice help enforce the nation's antitrust laws.

Economists are also found outside the administrative branch of government. To obtain independent evaluations of policy proposals, Congress relies on the advice of the Congressional Budget Office, which is staffed by economists. The Federal Reserve, the institution that sets the nation's monetary policy, employs hundreds of economists to analyze economic developments in the United States and throughout the world. Table 1 lists the websites of some of these agencies.

The influence of economists on policy goes beyond their role as advisers: Their research and writings often affect policy indirectly. Economist John Maynard Keynes offered this observation:

The ideas of economists and political philosophers, both when they are right and when they are wrong, are more powerful than is commonly understood.

"LET'S SWITCH. I'LL MAKE THE POLICY, YOU IMPLEMENT IT, AND HE'LL EXPLAIN IT."

In The News

Super Bowl Economics

Economists often offer advice to policymakers. Sometimes those policymakers are football coaches.

Incremental Analysis, with Two Yards to Go
By David Leonhardt

The academic paper that David Romer began writing two years ago did not look like something that could determine the outcome of a Super Bowl. Sure, it was an analysis of whether professional football teams punt more often than is rational, but it seemed intended mainly for the amusement of sports fans who happen to be professors.

Professor Romer, an economist at the University of California at Berkeley, used the phrases "Bellman equation" and "dynamic-programming analysis"—in the paper's title, no less. His footnotes cited work published in *Econometrica, Cognitive Science,* and other publications that are not exactly must-reads in N.F.L. locker rooms.

But when his conclusion—teams punt too much—began getting attention last summer, a reporter asked Bill Belichick, the coach of the New England

Patriots, about the paper. "I read it," he said, according to *The Boston Herald.* "I don't know much of the math involved, but I think I understand the conclusions and he has some valid points."

Upon hearing that, Professor Romer's jaw dropped, he said. His paper was available only on his Berkeley Internet site, emlab.berkeley.edu/users/dromer, and the site of a group called the National Bureau of Economic Research.

But the most interesting development was yet to come. Two weeks ago, facing a fourth down in the Patriots' own territory on the very first drive of the game—a sure punting situation in the N.F.L.—Belichick decided to go for a first down and made it. The Patriots soon scored a touchdown and were on their way to today's Super Bowl, against the Carolina Panthers.

Football analysts immediately called the decision an instance of a coach's instinct triumphing over cold analysis. In fact, Professor Romer said last week, Belichick seemed to be "throwing gut

instinct out the window and going on analysis." The information is right there in Figure 5 of the economist's paper: on fourth and 1 on your own 44-yard line, the potential benefit of keeping the drive going outweighs the cost of giving the opponents good field position.

The coach may not have been thinking about Professor Romer's paper at that moment, but he has clearly adopted the methods of a social scientist in a way that few other sports coaches have. Belichick, who majored in economics at Wesleyan University, approaches his job much the way a financial analyst pores over a balance sheet. He seems to view every decision as a chance to perform better cost–benefit analysis than his peers do. Richard Miller, a Wesleyan economist with whom the coach remains in touch, calls the approach "incremental analysis." In plain English, it involves looking for subtle differences in one small area that can affect an entire system, whether that system is a company, a stock market, or a football game.

Source: *The New York Times,* Week in Review, February 1, 2004, page 12.

Indeed, the world is ruled by little else. Practical men, who believe themselves to be quite exempt from intellectual influences, are usually the slaves of some defunct economist. Madmen in authority, who hear voices in the air, are distilling their frenzy from some academic scribbler of a few years back.

Although these words were written in 1935, they remain true today. Indeed, the "academic scribbler" now influencing public policy is often Keynes himself.

Here are the websites for a few of the government agencies that are responsible for collecting economic data and making economic policy.

T A B L E 1

Websites

Department of Commerce	http://www.commerce.gov
Bureau of Labor Statistics	http://www.bls.gov
Congressional Budget Office	http://www.cbo.gov
Federal Reserve Board	http://www.federalreserve.gov

CASE STUDY | MR. MANKIW GOES TO WASHINGTON

The author of the textbook you are now reading is, I will readily admit, a typical, nerdy college professor, more comfortable in the world of dusty books than in the world of glad-handing politicians. But from 2003 to 2005, I had the opportunity to leave the ivory tower and become the chairman of Council of Economic Advisers. For two years, I was President Bush's chief economist.

As chair of the CEA, I met with the President about twice a week. Some of these meetings were briefings on the state of the economy; most were discussions of current issues in economic policy. I worked closely with other members of the White House staff to analyze policy options and brief the President on a wide range of topics, such as tax policy, the federal budget, Social Security, and international trade. I also met regularly with economic officials outside the White House, such as Secretary of the Treasury John Snow and Federal Reserve Chairman Alan Greenspan, and with leaders of the business community.

For anyone used to the measured pace and quiet reflection of university life, taking such a job is exhilarating. Sitting in the Oval Office, flying on *Air Force One,* and spending the weekend with the President at Camp David are unforgettable experiences. Testifying as the President's representative before congressional committees, which include members who are usually partisan and sometimes hostile, is also an experience a person does not easily forget—no matter how hard one might try.

During my two years in Washington, I learned a lot about the process by which economic policy is made. It differs in many ways from the idealized policy process assumed in economics textbooks.

Throughout this text, whenever we discuss economic policy, we often focus on one question: What is the best policy for the government to pursue? We act as if policy were set by a benevolent king. Once the king figures out the right policy, he has no trouble putting his ideas into action.

In the real world, figuring out the right policy is only part of a leader's job, sometimes the easiest part. After the President hears from his economic advisers about what policy is best from their perspective, he turns to other advisers for related input. His communications advisers will tell him how best to explain the proposed policy to the public, and they will try to anticipate any misunderstandings that might arise to make the challenge more difficult. His press advisers will tell him how the news media will report on his proposal and what opinions will likely be expressed on the nation's editorial pages. His legislative affairs advisers will tell him how Congress will view the proposal, what amendments members of Congress will suggest, and the likelihood that Congress will pass some version of the President's proposal into law. His political advisers will tell him which groups will organize to support or oppose the proposed policy, how this proposal will affect his standing among different groups in the electorate, and whether it will affect support for any of the President's other policy initiatives. After hearing and weighing all this advice, the President then decides how to proceed.

My two years in Washington were a vivid reminder of an important lesson: Making economic policy in a representative democracy is a messy affair—and there are often good reasons presidents (and other politicians) do not advance the policies that economists advocate. Economists offer crucial input into the policy process, but their advice is only one ingredient of a complex recipe. •

Quick Quiz Give an example of a positive statement and an example of a normative statement. • Name three parts of government that regularly rely on advice from economists.

WHY ECONOMISTS DISAGREE

"If all economists were laid end to end, they would not reach a conclusion." This quip from George Bernard Shaw is revealing. Economists as a group are often criticized for giving conflicting advice to policymakers. President Ronald Reagan once joked that if the game Trivial Pursuit were designed for economists, it would have 100 questions and 3,000 answers.

Why do economists so often appear to give conflicting advice to policymakers? There are two basic reasons:

- Economists may disagree about the validity of alternative positive theories about how the world works.
- Economists may have different values and therefore different normative views about what policy should try to accomplish.

Let's discuss each of these reasons.

Differences in Scientific Judgments

Several centuries ago, astronomers debated whether the earth or the sun was at the center of the solar system. More recently, meteorologists have debated whether the earth is experiencing global warming and, if so, why. Science is a search for understanding about the world around us. It is not surprising that as the search continues, scientists can disagree about the direction in which truth lies.

Economists often disagree for the same reason. Economics is a young science, and there is still much to be learned. Economists sometimes disagree because they have different hunches about the validity of alternative theories or about the size of important parameters that measure how economic variables are related.

For example, economists disagree about whether the government should tax a household's income or its consumption (spending). Advocates of a switch from the current income tax to a consumption tax believe that the change would encourage households to save more because income that is saved would not be taxed. Higher saving, in turn, would lead to more rapid growth in productivity and living standards. Advocates of the current income tax system believe that household saving would not respond much to a change in the tax laws. These two groups of economists hold different normative views about the tax system because they have different positive views about the responsiveness of saving to tax incentives.

Differences in Values

Suppose that Peter and Paula both take the same amount of water from the town well. To pay for maintaining the well, the town taxes its residents. Peter has income of $50,000 and is taxed $5,000, or 10 percent of his income. Paula has income of $10,000 and is taxed $2,000, or 20 percent of her income.

Is this policy fair? If not, who pays too much and who pays too little? Does it matter whether Paula's low income is due to a medical disability or to her decision to pursue a career in acting? Does it matter whether Peter's high income is due to a large inheritance or to his willingness to work long hours at a dreary job?

These are difficult questions on which people are likely to disagree. If the town hired two experts to study how the town should tax its residents to pay for the well, we would not be surprised if they offered conflicting advice.

This simple example shows why economists sometimes disagree about public policy. As we learned earlier in our discussion of normative and positive analysis, policies cannot be judged on scientific grounds alone. Economists give conflicting advice sometimes because they have different values. Perfecting the science of economics will not tell us whether Peter or Paula pays too much.

Perception versus Reality

Because of differences in scientific judgments and differences in values, some disagreement among economists is inevitable. Yet one should not overstate the amount of disagreement. There are many cases in which economists agree.

Table 2 contains ten propositions about economic policy. In a survey of economists in business, government, and academia, these propositions were endorsed by an overwhelming majority of respondents. Most of these propositions would fail to command a similar consensus among the general public.

The first proposition in the table is about rent control, a policy that sets a legal maximum on the amount landlords can charge for their apartments. Almost all economists believe that rent control adversely affects the availability and quality of housing and is a very costly way of helping the neediest members of society. Nonetheless, many city governments choose to ignore the advice of economists and place ceilings on the rents that landlords may charge their tenants.

The second proposition in the table concerns tariffs and import quotas, two policies that restrict trade among nations. For reasons we will discuss more fully later in this text, almost all economists oppose such barriers to free trade. Nonetheless, over the years, presidents and Congress have chosen to restrict the import of certain goods. In 2002, for example, the Bush administration imposed temporary tariffs on steel to protect domestic steel producers from foreign competition. In this case, economists did offer united advice, but policymakers chose to ignore it.

Why do policies such as rent control and trade barriers persist if the experts are united in their opposition? The reason may be that economists have not yet convinced the general public that these policies are undesirable. One purpose of this book is to help you understand the economist's view of these and other subjects and, perhaps, to persuade you that it is the right one.

2 TABLE

Ten Propositions about Which Most Economists Agree

Proposition (and percentage of economists who agree)
1. A ceiling on rents reduces the quantity and quality of housing available. (93%)
2. Tariffs and import quotas usually reduce general economic welfare. (93%)
3. Flexible and floating exchange rates offer an effective international monetary arrangement. (90%)
4. Fiscal policy (e.g., tax cut and/or government expenditure increase) has a significant stimulative impact on a less than fully employed economy. (90%)
5. If the federal budget is to be balanced, it should be done over the business cycle rather than yearly. (85%)
6. Cash payments increase the welfare of recipients to a greater degree than do transfers-in-kind of equal cash value. (84%)
7. A large federal budget deficit has an adverse effect on the economy. (83%)
8. A minimum wage increases unemployment among young and unskilled workers. (79%)
9. The government should restructure the welfare system along the lines of a "negative income tax." (79%)
10. Effluent taxes and marketable pollution permits represent a better approach to pollution control than imposition of pollution ceilings. (78%)

Source: Richard M. Alston, J. R. Kearl, and Michael B. Vaughn, "Is There Consensus among Economists in the 1990s?" *American Economic Review* (May 1992): 203–209. Reprinted by permission.

Quick Quiz Why might economic advisers to the president disagree about a question of policy?

LET'S GET GOING

The first two chapters of this book have introduced you to the ideas and methods of economics. We are now ready to get to work. In the next chapter, we start learning in more detail the principles of economic behavior and economic policy.

As you proceed through this book, you will be asked to draw on many of your intellectual skills. You might find it helpful to keep in mind some advice from the great economist John Maynard Keynes:

> The study of economics does not seem to require any specialized gifts of an unusually high order. Is it not ... a very easy subject compared with the higher branches of philosophy or pure science? An easy subject, at which very few excel! The paradox finds its explanation, perhaps, in that the master-economist must possess a rare *combination* of gifts. He must be mathematician, historian, statesman, philosopher—in some degree. He must understand symbols and speak in words. He must contemplate the particular in terms of the general, and touch abstract and concrete in the same flight of thought. He must study the present in the light of the past for the purposes of the future. No part of man's nature or his institutions must lie entirely outside his regard. He must be purposeful and disinterested in a simultaneous mood; as aloof and incorruptible as an artist, yet sometimes as near the earth as a politician.

It is a tall order. But with practice, you will become more and more accustomed to thinking like an economist.

In The News

Why You Should Study Economics

In this excerpt from a commencement address, the former president of the Federal Reserve Bank of Dallas makes the case for studying economics.

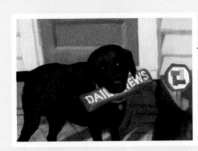

The Dismal Science? Hardly!

By Robert D. McTeer, Jr.

Weeks ago, I had lunch with the smartest woman in the world: Marilyn vos Savant, the "Ask Marilyn" columnist in *Parade* magazine.

According to the folks at the *Guinness Book,* Marilyn has the world's highest recorded I.Q. She is interested in economics education, of all things, and we met at a board meeting of the National Council on Economic Education. I told her I think economics is a good major for smart students, but if they are really, really smart, I'd rather they become doctors so they could do somebody some good. She said, "Yes, but doctors help people one at a time, while an Alan Greenspan can help millions of people at a time." She has a point. Mr. Greenspan is an excellent example of someone making a big difference by applying good economics.

My take on training in economics is that it becomes increasingly valuable as you move up the career ladder. I can't imagine a better major for corporate CEOs, congressmen, or American presidents. . . . Economics training will help you understand fallacies and unintended consequences. In fact, I am inclined to define economics as the study of how to anticipate unintended consequences. . . .

Little in the literature seems more relevant to contemporary economic debates than what usually is called the broken window fallacy. Whenever a government program is justified not on its merits but by the jobs it will create, remember the broken window: Some teenagers, being the little beasts that they are, toss a brick through a bakery window. A crowd gathers and laments, "What a shame." But before you know it, someone suggests a silver lining to the situation: Now the baker will have to spend money to have the window repaired. This will add to the income of the repairman, who will spend his additional income, which will add to another seller's income, and so on. You know the drill. The chain of spending will multiply and generate higher income and employment. If the broken window is large enough, it might produce an economic boom! . . .

Most voters fall for the broken window fallacy, but not economics majors. They will say, "Hey, wait a minute!" If the baker hadn't spent his money on window repair, he would have spent it on the new suit he was saving to buy. Then the tailor would have the new income to spend, and so on. The broken window didn't create net new spending; it just diverted spending from somewhere else. The broken window does not create new activity, just different activity. People see the activity that takes place. They don't see the activity that *would* have taken place.

The broken window fallacy is perpetuated in many forms. Whenever job creation or retention is the primary objective I call it the job-counting fallacy. Economics majors understand the nonintuitive reality that real progress comes from job destruction. It once took 90 percent of our population to grow our food. Now it takes 3 percent. Pardon me, Willie, but are we worse off because of the job losses in agriculture? The would-have-been farmers are now college professors and computer gurus. . . .

So instead of counting jobs, we should make every job count. We will occasionally hit a soft spot when we have a mismatch of supply and demand in the labor market. But that is temporary. Don't become a Luddite and destroy the machinery, or become a protectionist and try to grow bananas in New York City.

Source: *The Wall Street Journal,* June 4, 2003, p. A18. Copyright © 2003 by Robert D. McTeer, Jr.

SUMMARY

- Economists try to address their subject with a scientist's objectivity. Like all scientists, they make appropriate assumptions and build simplified models to understand the world around them. Two simple economic models are the circular-flow diagram and the production possibilities frontier.

- The field of economics is divided into two subfields: microeconomics and macroeconomics. Microeconomists study decision making by households and firms and the interaction among households and firms in the marketplace. Macroeconomists study the forces and trends that affect the economy as a whole.

- A positive statement is an assertion about how the world *is*. A normative statement is an assertion about how the world *ought to be*. When economists make normative statements, they are acting more as policy advisers than scientists.

- Economists who advise policymakers offer conflicting advice either because of differences in scientific judgments or because of differences in values. At other times, economists are united in the advice they offer, but policymakers may choose to ignore it.

KEY CONCEPTS

circular-flow diagram, p. 22
production possibilities frontier, p. 24

microeconomics, p. 27
macroeconomics, p. 27

positive statements, p. 28
normative statements, p. 28

QUESTIONS FOR REVIEW

1. How is economics like a science?
2. Why do economists make assumptions?
3. Should an economic model describe reality exactly?
4. Draw and explain a production possibilities frontier for an economy that produces milk and cookies. What happens to this frontier if disease kills half of the economy's cow population?
5. Use a production possibilities frontier to describe the idea of "efficiency."

6. What are the two subfields into which economics is divided? Explain what each subfield studies.
7. What is the difference between a positive and a normative statement? Give an example of each.
8. What is the Council of Economic Advisers?
9. Why do economists sometimes offer conflicting advice to policymakers?

PROBLEMS AND APPLICATIONS

1. Draw a circular-flow diagram. Identify the parts of the model that correspond to the flow of goods and services and the flow of dollars for each of the following activities.
   a. Selena pays a storekeeper $1 for a quart of milk.
   b. Stuart earns $4.50 per hour working at a fast-food restaurant.
   c. Shanna spends $7 to see a movie.
   d. Sally earns $10,000 from his 10 percent ownership of Acme Industrial.

2. Imagine a society that produces military goods and consumer goods, which we'll call "guns" and "butter."

   a. Draw a production possibilities frontier for guns and butter. Using the concept of opportunity cost, explain why it most likely has a bowed-out shape.

   b. Show a point that is impossible for the economy to achieve. Show a point that is feasible but inefficient.

   c. Imagine that the society has two political parties, called the Hawks (who want a strong military) and the Doves (who want a smaller military). Show a point on your production possibilities frontier that the Hawks might choose and a point the Doves might choose.

   d. Imagine that an aggressive neighboring country reduces the size of its military. As a result, both the Hawks and the Doves reduce their desired production of guns by the same amount. Which party would get the bigger "peace dividend," measured by the increase in butter production? Explain.

3. The first principle of economics discussed in Chapter 1 is that people face trade-offs. Use a production possibilities frontier to illustrate society's trade-off between two "goods"—a clean environment and the quantity of industrial output. What do you suppose determines the shape and position of the frontier? Show what happens to the frontier if engineers develop a new way of producing electricity that emits fewer pollutants.

4. An economy consists of three workers: Larry, Moe, and Curly. Each works 10 hours a day and can produce two services: mowing lawns and washing cars. In an hour, Larry can either mow one lawn or wash one car; Moe can either mow one lawn or wash two cars; and Curly can either mow two lawns or wash one car.

   a. Calculate how much of each service is produced under the following circumstances, which we label A, B, C, and D:

      • all three spend all their time mowing lawns (A)

      • all three spend all their time washing cars (B)

      • all three spend half their time on each activity (C)

      • Larry spends half his time on each activity, while Moe only washes cars and Curly only mows lawns (D)

   b. Graph the production possibilities frontier for this economy. Using your answers to part (a), identify points A, B, C, and D on your graph.

   c. Explain why the production possibilities frontier has the shape it does.

   d. Are any of the allocations calculated in part (a) inefficient? Explain.

5. Classify the following topics as relating to microeconomics or macroeconomics.

   a. a family's decision about how much income to save

   b. the effect of government regulations on auto emissions

   c. the impact of higher national saving on economic growth

   d. a firm's decision about how many workers to hire

   e. the relationship between the inflation rate and changes in the quantity of money

6. Classify each of the following statements as positive or normative. Explain.

   a. Society faces a short-run trade-off between inflation and unemployment.

   b. A reduction in the rate of growth of money will reduce the rate of inflation.

   c. The Federal Reserve should reduce the rate of growth of money.

   d. Society ought to require welfare recipients to look for jobs.

   e. Lower tax rates encourage more work and more saving.

7. Classify each of the statements in Table 2 as positive, normative, or ambiguous. Explain.

8. If you were president, would you be more interested in your economic advisers' positive views or their normative views? Why?

9. Find a recent copy of the *Economic Report of the President* at your library or on the Internet. Read a chapter about an issue that interests you. Summarize the economic problem at hand and describe the council's recommended policy.

10. Look up one of the websites listed in Table 1. What recent economic trends or issues are addressed there?

For further information on topics in this chapter, additional problems, examples, applications, online quizzes, and more, please visit our website at http://mankiw.swlearning.com.

APPENDIX

GRAPHING: A BRIEF REVIEW

Many of the concepts that economists study can be expressed with numbers—the price of bananas, the quantity of bananas sold, the cost of growing bananas, and so on. Often, these economic variables are related to one another. When the price of bananas rises, people buy fewer bananas. One way of expressing the relationships among variables is with graphs.

Graphs serve two purposes. First, when developing economic theories, graphs offer a way to visually express ideas that might be less clear if described with equations or words. Second, when analyzing economic data, graphs provide a way of finding how variables are in fact related in the world. Whether we are working with theory or with data, graphs provide a lens through which a recognizable forest emerges from a multitude of trees.

Numerical information can be expressed graphically in many ways, just as a thought can be expressed in words in many ways. A good writer chooses words that will make an argument clear, a description pleasing, or a scene dramatic. An effective economist chooses the type of graph that best suits the purpose at hand.

In this appendix, we discuss how economists use graphs to study the mathematical relationships among variables. We also discuss some of the pitfalls that can arise in the use of graphical methods.

Graphs of a Single Variable

Three common graphs are shown in Figure A-1. The *pie chart* in panel (a) shows how total income in the United States is divided among the sources of income, including compensation of employees, corporate profits, and so on. A slice of the pie represents each source's share of the total. The *bar graph* in panel (b) compares

A-1 FIGURE

Types of Graphs

The pie chart in panel (a) shows how U.S. national income is derived from various sources. The bar graph in panel (b) compares the average income in four countries. The time-series graph in panel (c) shows the productivity of labor in U.S. businesses from 1950 to 2000.

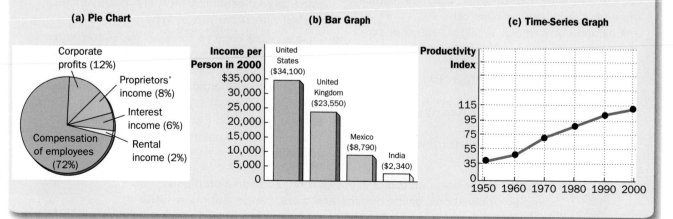

(a) Pie Chart

Corporate profits (12%)
Proprietors' income (8%)
Interest income (6%)
Rental income (2%)
Compensation of employees (72%)

(b) Bar Graph

Income per Person in 2000
$35,000
30,000
25,000
20,000
15,000
10,000
5,000
0
United States ($34,100)
United Kingdom ($23,550)
Mexico ($8,790)
India ($2,340)

(c) Time-Series Graph

Productivity Index
115
95
75
55
35
0
1950 1960 1970 1980 1990 2000

income for four countries. The height of each bar represents the average income in each country. The *time-series graph* in panel (c) traces the rising productivity in the U.S. business sector over time. The height of the line shows output per hour in each year. You have probably seen similar graphs in newspapers and magazines.

Graphs of Two Variables: The Coordinate System

Although the three graphs in Figure A-1 are useful in showing how a variable changes over time or across individuals, such graphs are limited in how much they can tell us. These graphs display information only on a single variable. Economists are often concerned with the relationships between variables. Thus, they need to display two variables on a single graph. The *coordinate system* makes this possible.

Suppose you want to examine the relationship between study time and grade point average. For each student in your class, you could record a pair of numbers: hours per week spent studying and grade point average. These numbers could then be placed in parentheses as an *ordered pair* and appear as a single point on the graph. Albert E., for instance, is represented by the ordered pair (25 hours/week, 3.5 GPA), while his "what-me-worry?" classmate Alfred E. is represented by the ordered pair (5 hours/week, 2.0 GPA).

We can graph these ordered pairs on a two-dimensional grid. The first number in each ordered pair, called the *x-coordinate*, tells us the horizontal location of the point. The second number, called the *y-coordinate*, tells us the vertical location of the point. The point with both an *x*-coordinate and a *y*-coordinate of zero is known as the *origin*. The two coordinates in the ordered pair tell us where the point is located in relation to the origin: *x* units to the right of the origin and *y* units above it.

Figure A-2 graphs grade point average against study time for Albert E., Alfred E., and their classmates. This type of graph is called a *scatterplot* because it plots scattered points. Looking at this graph, we immediately notice that

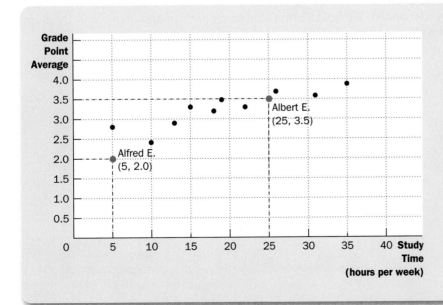

FIGURE A-2

Using the Coordinate System
Grade point average is measured on the vertical axis and study time on the horizontal axis. Albert E., Alfred E., and their classmates are represented by various points. We can see from the graph that students who study more tend to get higher grades.

points farther to the right (indicating more study time) also tend to be higher (indicating a better grade point average). Because study time and grade point average typically move in the same direction, we say that these two variables have a *positive correlation*. By contrast, if we were to graph party time and grades, we would likely find that higher party time is associated with lower grades; because these variables typically move in opposite directions, we call this a *negative correlation*. In either case, the coordinate system makes the correlation between the two variables easy to see.

Curves in the Coordinate System

Students who study more do tend to get higher grades, but other factors also influence a student's grade. Previous preparation is an important factor, for instance, as are talent, attention from teachers, even eating a good breakfast. A scatterplot like Figure A-2 does not attempt to isolate the effect that study has on grades from the effects of other variables. Often, however, economists prefer looking at how one variable affects another, holding everything else constant.

To see how this is done, let's consider one of the most important graphs in economics: the *demand curve*. The demand curve traces out the effect of a good's price on the quantity of the good consumers want to buy. Before showing a demand curve, however, consider Table A-1, which shows how the number of novels that Emma buys depends on her income and on the price of novels. When novels are cheap, Emma buys them in large quantities. As they become more expensive, she borrows books from the library instead of buying them or chooses to go to the movies instead of reading. Similarly, at any given price, Emma buys more novels when she has a higher income. That is, when her income increases, she spends part of the additional income on novels and part on other goods.

We now have three variables—the price of novels, income, and the number of novels purchased—which are more than we can represent in two dimensions. To put the information from Table A-1 in graphical form, we need to hold one of the three variables constant and trace out the relationship between the other two. Because the demand curve represents the relationship between price and quantity demanded, we hold Emma's income constant and show how the number of novels she buys varies with the price of novels.

TABLE

Novels Purchased by Emma
This table shows the number of novels Emma buys at various incomes and prices. For any given level of income, the data on price and quantity demanded can be graphed to produce Emma's demand curve for novels, as shown in Figures A-3 and A-4.

		Income	
Price	$20,000	$30,000	$40,000
$10	2 novels	5 novels	8 novels
9	6	9	12
8	10	13	16
7	14	17	20
6	18	21	24
5	22	25	28
	Demand curve, D_3	Demand curve, D_1	Demand curve, D_2

Suppose that Emma's income is $30,000 per year. If we place the number of novels Emma purchases on the *x*-axis and the price of novels on the *y*-axis, we can graphically represent the middle column of Table A-1. When the points that represent these entries from the table—(5 novels, $10), (9 novels, $9), and so on—are connected, they form a line. This line, pictured in Figure A-3, is known as Emma's demand curve for novels; it tells us how many novels Emma purchases at any given price. The demand curve is downward sloping, indicating that a higher price reduces the quantity of novels demanded. Because the quantity of novels demanded and the price move in opposite directions, we say that the two variables are *negatively related*. (Conversely, when two variables move in the same direction, the curve relating them is upward sloping, and we say the variables are *positively related*.)

Now suppose that Emma's income rises to $40,000 per year. At any given price, Emma will purchase more novels than she did at her previous level of income. Just as earlier we drew Emma's demand curve for novels using the entries from the middle column of Table A-1, we now draw a new demand curve using the entries from the right column of the table. This new demand curve (curve D_2) is pictured alongside the old one (curve D_1) in Figure A-4; the new curve is a similar line drawn farther to the right. We therefore say that Emma's demand curve for novels *shifts* to the right when her income increases. Likewise, if Emma's income were to fall to $20,000 per year, she would buy fewer novels at any given price and her demand curve would shift to the left (to curve D_3).

In economics, it is important to distinguish between *movements along a curve* and *shifts of a curve*. As we can see from Figure A-3, if Emma earns $30,000 per year and novels cost $8 apiece, she will purchase 13 novels per year. If the price

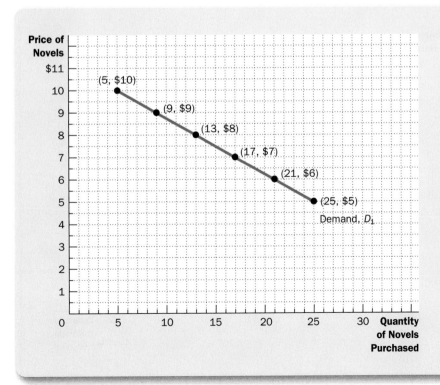

FIGURE A-3

Demand Curve
The line D_1 shows how Emma's purchases of novels depend on the price of novels when her income is held constant. Because the price and the quantity demanded are negatively related, the demand curve slopes downward.

of novels falls to $7, Emma will increase her purchases of novels to 17 per year. The demand curve, however, stays fixed in the same place. Emma still buys the same number of novels *at each price,* but as the price falls, she moves along her demand curve from left to right. By contrast, if the price of novels remains fixed at $8 but her income rises to $40,000, Emma increases her purchases of novels from 13 to 16 per year. Because Emma buys more novels *at each price,* her demand curve shifts out, as shown in Figure A-4.

There is a simple way to tell when it is necessary to shift a curve. When a variable that is not named on either axis changes, the curve shifts. Income is on neither the *x*-axis nor the *y*-axis of the graph, so when Emma's income changes, her demand curve must shift. Any change that affects Emma's purchasing habits besides a change in the price of novels will result in a shift in her demand curve. If, for instance, the public library closes and Emma must buy all the books she wants to read, she will demand more novels at each price, and her demand curve will shift to the right. Or if the price of movies falls and Emma spends more time at the movies and less time reading, she will demand fewer novels at each price, and her demand curve will shift to the left. By contrast, when a variable on an axis of the graph changes, the curve does not shift. We read the change as a movement along the curve.

Slope

One question we might want to ask about Emma is how much her purchasing habits respond to price. Look at the demand curve pictured in Figure A-5. If this curve is very steep, Emma purchases nearly the same number of novels regard-

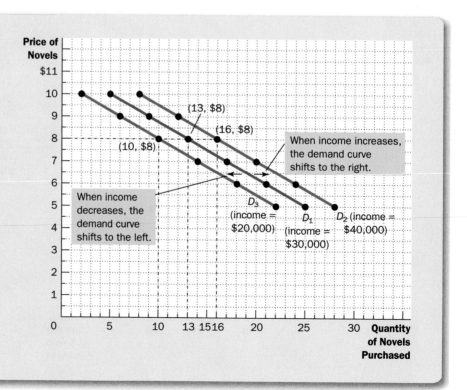

A-4 FIGURE

Shifting Demand Curves
The location of Emma's demand curve for novels depends on how much income she earns. The more she earns, the more novels she will purchase at any given price, and the farther to the right her demand curve will lie. Curve D_1 represents Emma's original demand curve when her income is $30,000 per year. If her income rises to $40,000 per year, her demand curve shifts to D_2. If her income falls to $20,000 per year, her demand curve shifts to D_3.

less of whether they are cheap or expensive. If this curve is much flatter, Emma purchases many fewer novels when the price rises. To answer questions about how much one variable responds to changes in another variable, we can use the concept of *slope*.

The slope of a line is the ratio of the vertical distance covered to the horizontal distance covered as we move along the line. This definition is usually written out in mathematical symbols as follows:

$$\text{slope} = \frac{\Delta y}{\Delta x},$$

where the Greek letter Δ (delta) stands for the change in a variable. In other words, the slope of a line is equal to the "rise" (change in y) divided by the "run" (change in x). The slope will be a small positive number for a fairly flat upward-sloping line, a large positive number for a steep upward-sloping line, and a negative number for a downward-sloping line. A horizontal line has a slope of zero because in this case the y-variable never changes; a vertical line is said to have an infinite slope because the y-variable can take any value without the x-variable changing at all.

What is the slope of Emma's demand curve for novels? First of all, because the curve slopes down, we know the slope will be negative. To calculate a numerical value for the slope, we must choose two points on the line. With Emma's income at $30,000, she will purchase 21 novels at a price of $6 or 13 novels at a price of $8. When we apply the slope formula, we are concerned with the change between these two points; in other words, we are concerned with the difference between

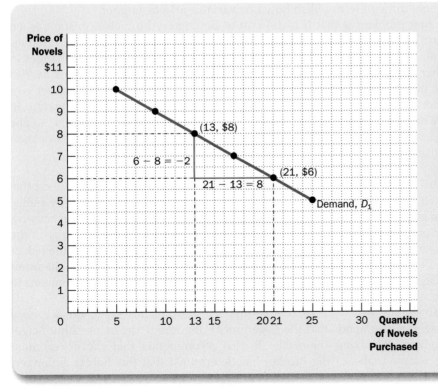

FIGURE A-5

Calculating the Slope of a Line
To calculate the slope of the demand curve, we can look at the changes in the x- and y-coordinates as we move from the point (21 novels, $6) to the point (13 novels, $8). The slope of the line is the ratio of the change in the y-coordinate (−2) to the change in the x-coordinate (+8), which equals −1/4.

them, which lets us know that we will have to subtract one set of values from the other, as follows:

$$\text{slope} = \frac{\Delta y}{\Delta x} = \frac{\text{first } y\text{-coordinate} - \text{second } y\text{-coordinate}}{\text{first } x\text{-coordinate} - \text{second } x\text{-coordinate}} = \frac{6 - 8}{21 - 13} = \frac{-2}{8} = \frac{-1}{4}$$

Figure A-5 shows graphically how this calculation works. Try computing the slope of Emma's demand curve using two different points. You should get exactly the same result, $-1/4$. One of the properties of a straight line is that it has the same slope everywhere. This is not true of other types of curves, which are steeper in some places than in others.

The slope of Emma's demand curve tells us something about how responsive her purchases are to changes in the price. A small slope (a number close to zero) means that Emma's demand curve is relatively flat; in this case, she adjusts the number of novels she buys substantially in response to a price change. A larger slope (a number farther from zero) means that Emma's demand curve is relatively steep; in this case, she adjusts the number of novels she buys only slightly in response to a price change.

Cause and Effect

Economists often use graphs to advance an argument about how the economy works. In other words, they use graphs to argue about how one set of events *causes* another set of events. With a graph like the demand curve, there is no doubt about cause and effect. Because we are varying price and holding all other variables constant, we know that changes in the price of novels cause changes in the quantity Emma demands. Remember, however, that our demand curve came from a hypothetical example. When graphing data from the real world, it is often more difficult to establish how one variable affects another.

The first problem is that it is difficult to hold everything else constant when measuring how one variable affects another. If we are not able to hold variables constant, we might decide that one variable on our graph is causing changes in the other variable when actually those changes are caused by a third *omitted variable* not pictured on the graph. Even if we have identified the correct two variables to look at, we might run into a second problem—*reverse causality*. In other words, we might decide that A causes B when in fact B causes A. The omitted-variable and reverse-causality traps require us to proceed with caution when using graphs to draw conclusions about causes and effects.

Omitted Variables   To see how omitting a variable can lead to a deceptive graph, let's consider an example. Imagine that the government, spurred by public concern about the large number of deaths from cancer, commissions an exhaustive study from Big Brother Statistical Services, Inc. Big Brother examines many of the items found in people's homes to see which of them are associated with the risk of cancer. Big Brother reports a strong relationship between two variables: the number of cigarette lighters that a household owns and the probability that someone in the household will develop cancer. Figure A-6 shows this relationship.

What should we make of this result? Big Brother advises a quick policy response. It recommends that the government discourage the ownership of cigarette lighters by taxing their sale. It also recommends that the government require warning labels: "Big Brother has determined that this lighter is dangerous to your health."

Graph with an Omitted Variable
The upward-sloping curve shows that members of households with more cigarette lighters are more likely to develop cancer. Yet we should not conclude that ownership of lighters causes cancer because the graph does not take into account the number of cigarettes smoked.

In judging the validity of Big Brother's analysis, one question is paramount: Has Big Brother held constant every relevant variable except the one under consideration? If the answer is no, the results are suspect. An easy explanation for Figure A-6 is that people who own more cigarette lighters are more likely to smoke cigarettes and that cigarettes, not lighters, cause cancer. If Figure A-6 does not hold constant the amount of smoking, it does not tell us the true effect of owning a cigarette lighter.

This story illustrates an important principle: When you see a graph used to support an argument about cause and effect, it is important to ask whether the movements of an omitted variable could explain the results you see.

Reverse Causality   Economists can also make mistakes about causality by misreading its direction. To see how this is possible, suppose the Association of American Anarchists commissions a study of crime in America and arrives at Figure A-7, which plots the number of violent crimes per thousand people in major cities against the number of police officers per thousand people. The anarchists note the curve's upward slope and argue that because police increase

Graph Suggesting Reverse Causality
The upward-sloping curve shows that cities with a higher concentration of police are more dangerous. Yet the graph does not tell us whether police cause crime or crime-plagued cities hire more police.

rather than decrease the amount of urban violence, law enforcement should be abolished.

If we could run a controlled experiment, we would avoid the danger of reverse causality. To run an experiment, we would set the number of police officers in different cities randomly and then examine the correlation between police and crime. Figure A-7, however, is not based on such an experiment. We simply observe that more dangerous cities have more police officers. The explanation for this may be that more dangerous cities hire more police. In other words, rather than police causing crime, crime may cause police. Nothing in the graph itself allows us to establish the direction of causality.

It might seem that an easy way to determine the direction of causality is to examine which variable moves first. If we see crime increase and then the police force expand, we reach one conclusion. If we see the police force expand and then crime increase, we reach the other. Yet there is also a flaw with this approach: Often, people change their behavior not in response to a change in their present conditions but in response to a change in their *expectations* of future conditions. A city that expects a major crime wave in the future, for instance, might hire more police now. This problem is even easier to see in the case of babies and minivans. Couples often buy a minivan in anticipation of the birth of a child. The minivan comes before the baby, but we wouldn't want to conclude that the sale of minivans causes the population to grow!

There is no complete set of rules that says when it is appropriate to draw causal conclusions from graphs. Yet just keeping in mind that cigarette lighters don't cause cancer (omitted variable) and minivans don't cause larger families (reverse causality) will keep you from falling for many faulty economic arguments.

3

Interdependence and the Gains from Trade

Consider your typical day. You wake up in the morning, and you pour yourself juice from oranges grown in Florida and coffee from beans grown in Brazil. Over breakfast, you watch a news program broadcast from New York on your television made in Japan. You get dressed in clothes made of cotton grown in Georgia and sewn in factories in Thailand. You drive to class in a car made of parts manufactured in more than a dozen countries around the world. Then you open up your economics textbook written by an author living in Massachusetts, published by a company located in Ohio, and printed on paper made from trees grown in Oregon.

Every day, you rely on many people from around the world, most of whom you do not know, to provide you with the goods and services that you enjoy. Such interdependence is possible because people trade with one another. Those people who provide you with goods and services are not acting out of generosity or concern for your welfare. Nor is some government agency directing them to make what you want and give it to you. Instead, people provide you and other consumers with the goods and services they produce because they get something in return.

In subsequent chapters, we will examine how our economy coordinates the activities of millions of people with varying tastes and abilities. As a starting point for this analysis, here we consider the reasons for economic interdependence. One of the *Ten Principles of Economics* highlighted in Chapter 1 is that trade can make everyone better off. This principle explains why people trade with their neighbors and why nations trade with other nations. In this chapter, we examine this principle more closely. What exactly do people gain when they trade with one another? Why do people choose to become interdependent?

A PARABLE FOR THE MODERN ECONOMY

To understand why people choose to depend on others for goods and services and how this choice improves their lives, let's look at a simple economy. Imagine that there are two goods in the world: meat and potatoes. And there are two people in the world—a cattle rancher and a potato farmer—each of whom would like to eat both meat and potatoes.

The gains from trade are most obvious if the rancher can produce only meat and the farmer can produce only potatoes. In one scenario, the rancher and the farmer could choose to have nothing to do with each other. But after several months of eating beef roasted, boiled, broiled, and grilled, the rancher might decide that self-sufficiency is not all it's cracked up to be. The farmer, who has been eating potatoes mashed, fried, baked, and scalloped, would likely agree. It is easy to see that trade would allow them to enjoy greater variety: Each could then have a steak with a baked potato or a burger with fries.

Although this scene illustrates most simply how everyone can benefit from trade, the gains would be similar if the rancher and the farmer were each capable of producing the other good, but only at great cost. Suppose, for example, that the potato farmer is able to raise cattle and produce meat, but that he is not very good at it. Similarly, suppose that the cattle rancher is able to grow potatoes but that her land is not very well suited for it. In this case, it is easy to see that the farmer and the rancher can each benefit by specializing in what he or she does best and then trading with the other.

The gains from trade are less obvious, however, when one person is better at producing *every* good. For example, suppose that the rancher is better at raising cattle *and* better at growing potatoes than the farmer. In this case, should the rancher or farmer choose to remain self-sufficient? Or is there still reason for them to trade with each other? To answer this question, we need to look more closely at the factors that affect such a decision.

Production Possibilities

Suppose that the farmer and the rancher each work 8 hours per day and can devote this time to growing potatoes, raising cattle, or a combination of the two. Table 1 shows the amount of time each person requires to produce 1 ounce of each good. The farmer can produce an ounce of potatoes in 15 minutes and an ounce of meat in 60 minutes. The rancher, who is more productive in both activities, can produce an ounce of potatoes in 10 minutes and an ounce of meat in 20 minutes. The last two columns in the table show the amounts of meat or potatoes the farmer and rancher can produce if they work an 8-hour day producing only that good.

Panel (a) of Figure 1 illustrates the amounts of meat and potatoes that the farmer can produce. If the farmer devotes all 8 hours of his time to potatoes, he produces 32 ounces of potatoes (measured on the horizontal axis) and no meat. If he devotes all his time to meat, he produces 8 ounces of meat (measured on

	Minutes Needed to Make 1 Ounce of:		Amount Produced in 8 Hours		TABLE 1
	Meat	Potatoes	Meat	Potatoes	**The Production Opportunities of the Farmer and the Rancher**
Farmer	60 min/oz	15 min/oz	8 oz	32 oz	
Rancher	20 min/oz	10 min/oz	24 oz	48 oz	

FIGURE 1

Panel (a) shows the combinations of meat and potatoes that the farmer can produce. Panel (b) shows the combinations of meat and potatoes that the rancher can produce. Both production possibilities frontiers are derived from Table 1 and the assumption that the farmer and rancher each work 8 hours per day.

The Production Possibilities Frontier

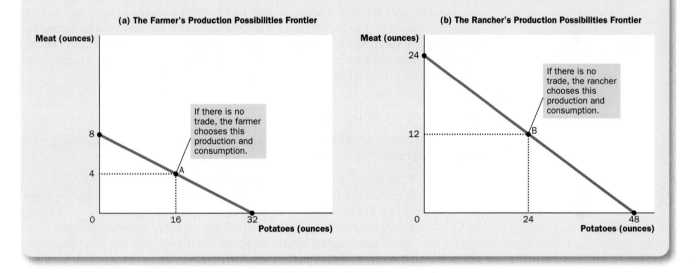

the vertical axis) and no potatoes. If the farmer divides his time equally between the two activities, spending 4 hours on each, he produces 16 ounces of potatoes and 4 ounces of meat. The figure shows these three possible outcomes and all others in between.

This graph is the farmer's production possibilities frontier. As we discussed in Chapter 2, a production possibilities frontier shows the various mixes of output that an economy can produce. It illustrates one of the *Ten Principles of Economics* in Chapter 1: People face trade-offs. Here the farmer faces a trade-off between producing meat and producing potatoes.

You may recall that the production possibilities frontier in Chapter 2 was drawn bowed out. In that case, the rate at which society could trade one good for the other depended on the amounts that were being produced. Here, however, the farmer's technology for producing meat and potatoes (as summarized in Table 1) allows him to switch between the two goods at a constant rate. Whenever the farmer spends 1 hour less producing meat and 1 hour more producing potatoes, he reduces his output of meat by 1 ounce and raises his output of potatoes by 4 ounces—and this is true regardless of how much he is already producing. As a result, the production possibilities frontier is a straight line.

Panel (b) of Figure 1 shows the production possibilities frontier for the rancher. If the rancher devotes all 8 hours of her time to potatoes, she produces 48 ounces of potatoes and no meat. If she devotes all her time to meat, she produces 24 ounces of meat and no potatoes. If the rancher divides her time equally, spending 4 hours on each activity, she produces 24 ounces of potatoes and 12 ounces of meat. Once again, the production possibilities frontier shows all the possible outcomes.

If the farmer and rancher choose to be self-sufficient, rather than trade with each other, then each consumes exactly what he or she produces. In this case, the production possibilities frontier is also the consumption possibilities frontier. That is, without trade, Figure 1 shows the possible combinations of meat and potatoes that the farmer and rancher can each consume.

Although these production possibilities frontiers are useful in showing the trade-offs that the farmer and rancher face, they do not tell us what the farmer and rancher will actually choose to do. To determine their choices, we need to know the tastes of the farmer and the rancher. Let's suppose they choose the combinations identified by points A and B in Figure 1: The farmer produces and consumes 16 ounces of potatoes and 4 ounces of meat, while the rancher produces and consumes 24 ounces of potatoes and 12 ounces of meat.

Specialization and Trade

After several years of eating combination B, the rancher gets an idea and goes to talk to the farmer:

RANCHER: Farmer, my friend, have I got a deal for you! I know how to improve life for both of us. I think you should stop producing meat altogether and devote all your time to growing potatoes. According to my calculations, if you work 8 hours a day growing potatoes, you'll produce 32 ounces of potatoes. If you give me 15 of those 32 ounces, I'll give you 5 ounces of meat in return. In the end, you'll get to eat 17 ounces of potatoes and 5 ounces of meat every day, instead of the 16 ounces of potatoes and 4 ounces of meat you now get. If you go along with my plan, you'll have more of *both* foods. [To illustrate her point, the rancher shows the farmer panel (a) of Figure 2.]

FARMER: (sounding skeptical) That seems like a good deal for me. But I don't understand why you are offering it. If the deal is so good for me, it can't be good for you too.

RANCHER: Oh, but it is! Suppose I spend 6 hours a day raising cattle and 2 hours growing potatoes. Then I can produce 18 ounces of meat and 12 ounces of potatoes. After I give you 5 ounces of my meat in exchange for 15 ounces of your potatoes, I'll end up with 13 ounces of meat and 27 ounces of potatoes, instead of the 12 ounces of meat

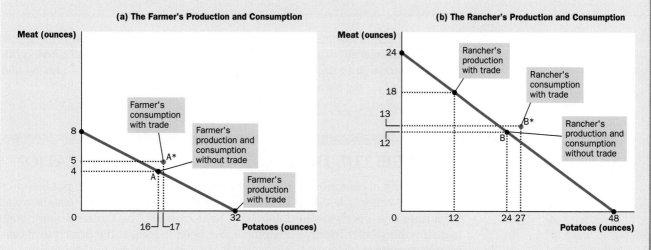

FIGURE 2

The proposed trade between the farmer and the rancher offers each of them a combination of meat and potatoes that would be impossible in the absence of trade. In panel (a), the farmer gets to consume at point A* rather than point A. In panel (b), the rancher gets to consume at point B* rather than point B. Trade allows each to consume more meat and more potatoes.

How Trade Expands the Set of Consumption Opportunities

(a) The Farmer's Production and Consumption

Meat (ounces)

Farmer's consumption with trade

Farmer's production and consumption without trade

Farmer's production with trade

Potatoes (ounces)

(b) The Rancher's Production and Consumption

Meat (ounces)

Rancher's production with trade

Rancher's consumption with trade

Rancher's production and consumption without trade

Potatoes (ounces)

(c) The Gains from Trade: A Summary

	Farmer		Rancher	
	Meat	**Potatoes**	**Meat**	**Potatoes**
Without Trade:				
Production and Consumption	4 oz	16 oz	12 oz	24 oz
With Trade:				
Production	0 oz	32 oz	18 oz	12 oz
Trade	Gets 5 oz	Gives 15 oz	Gives 5 oz	Gets 15 oz
Consumption	5 oz	17 oz	13 oz	27 oz
GAINS FROM TRADE:				
Increase in Consumption	+1 oz	+1 oz	+1 oz	+3 oz

and 24 ounces of potatoes that I now get. So I will also consume more of both foods than I do now. [She points out panel (b) of Figure 2.]

FARMER: I don't know. . . . This sounds too good to be true.

RANCHER: It's really not as complicated as it seems at first. Here—I've summarized my proposal for you in a simple table. [The rancher shows the farmer a copy of the table at the bottom of Figure 2.]

FARMER: (after pausing to study the table) These calculations seem correct, but I am puzzled. How can this deal make us both better off?

RANCHER: We can both benefit because trade allows each of us to specialize in doing what we do best. You will spend more time growing potatoes and less time raising cattle. I will spend more time raising cattle and less time growing potatoes. As a result of specialization and trade, each of us can consume more meat and more potatoes without working any more hours.

Quick Quiz   Draw an example of a production possibilities frontier for Robinson Crusoe, a shipwrecked sailor who spends his time gathering coconuts and catching fish. Does this frontier limit Crusoe's consumption of coconuts and fish if he lives by himself? Does he face the same limits if he can trade with natives on the island?

COMPARATIVE ADVANTAGE: THE DRIVING FORCE OF SPECIALIZATION

The rancher's explanation of the gains from trade, though correct, poses a puzzle: If the rancher is better at both raising cattle and growing potatoes, how can the farmer ever specialize in doing what he does best? The farmer doesn't seem to do anything best. To solve this puzzle, we need to look at the principle of *comparative advantage*.

As a first step in developing this principle, consider the following question: In our example, who can produce potatoes at lower cost—the farmer or the rancher? There are two possible answers, and in these two answers lie the solution to our puzzle and the key to understanding the gains from trade.

Absolute Advantage

One way to answer the question about the cost of producing potatoes is to compare the inputs required by the two producers. Economists use the term **absolute advantage** when comparing the productivity of one person, firm, or nation to that of another. The producer that requires a smaller quantity of inputs to produce a good is said to have an absolute advantage in producing that good.

In our example, time is the only input, so we can determine absolute advantage by looking at how much time each type of production takes. The rancher has an absolute advantage both in producing meat and in producing potatoes because she requires less time than the farmer to produce a unit of either good. The rancher needs to input only 20 minutes to produce an ounce of meat, whereas the farmer needs 60 minutes. Similarly, the rancher needs only 10 minutes to produce an ounce of potatoes, whereas the farmer needs 15 minutes. Based on this information, we can conclude that the rancher has the lower cost of producing potatoes, if we measure cost by the quantity of inputs.

absolute advantage
the ability to produce a good using fewer inputs than another producer

Opportunity Cost and Comparative Advantage

There is another way to look at the cost of producing potatoes. Rather than comparing inputs required, we can compare the opportunity costs. Recall from Chapter 1 that the **opportunity cost** of some item is what we give up to get that item. In our example, we assumed that the farmer and the rancher each spend 8 hours a day working. Time spent producing potatoes, therefore, takes away from time available for producing meat. As the rancher and farmer reallocate time between producing the two goods, they move along their production possibility frontiers; they give up units of one good to produce units of the other. The opportunity cost measures the trade-off between the two goods that each producer faces.

Let's first consider the rancher's opportunity cost. According to Table 1, producing 1 ounce of potatoes takes 10 minutes of work. When the rancher spends those 10 minutes producing potatoes, she spends 10 minutes less producing meat. Because the rancher needs 20 minutes to produce 1 ounce of meat, 10 minutes of work would yield $1/2$ ounce of meat. Hence, the rancher's opportunity cost of producing 1 ounce of potatoes is $1/2$ ounce of meat.

Now consider the farmer's opportunity cost. Producing 1 ounce of potatoes takes him 15 minutes. Because he needs 60 minutes to produce 1 ounce of meat, 15 minutes of work would yield $1/4$ ounce of meat. Hence, the farmer's opportunity cost of 1 ounce of potatoes is $1/4$ ounce of meat.

Table 2 shows the opportunity costs of meat and potatoes for the two producers. Notice that the opportunity cost of meat is the inverse of the opportunity cost of potatoes. Because 1 ounce of potatoes costs the rancher $1/2$ ounce of meat, 1 ounce of meat costs the rancher 2 ounces of potatoes. Similarly, because 1 ounce of potatoes costs the farmer $1/4$ ounce of meat, 1 ounce of meat costs the farmer 4 ounces of potatoes.

Economists use the term **comparative advantage** when describing the opportunity cost of two producers. The producer who gives up less of other goods to produce Good X has the smaller opportunity cost of producing Good X and is said to have a comparative advantage in producing it. In our example, the farmer has a lower opportunity cost of producing potatoes than does the rancher: An ounce of potatoes costs the farmer only $1/4$ ounce of meat, but it costs the rancher $1/2$ ounce of meat. Conversely, the rancher has a lower opportunity cost of producing meat than does the farmer: An ounce of meat costs the rancher 2 ounces of potatoes, but it costs the farmer 4 ounces of potatoes. Thus, the farmer has a comparative advantage in growing potatoes, and the rancher has a comparative advantage in producing meat.

Although it is possible for one person to have an absolute advantage in both goods (as the rancher does in our example), it is impossible for one person to have a comparative advantage in both goods. Because the opportunity cost of one good is the inverse of the opportunity cost of the other, if a person's opportunity cost of one good is relatively high, the opportunity cost of the other good must be relatively low. Comparative advantage reflects the relative opportunity cost. Unless two people have exactly the same opportunity cost, one person will

opportunity cost
whatever must be given up to obtain some item

comparative advantage
the ability to produce a good at a lower opportunity cost than another producer

	Opportunity Cost of:		TABLE 2
	1 Ounce of Meat	1 Ounce of Potatoes	The Opportunity Cost of Meat and Potatoes
Farmer	4 oz potatoes	¼ oz meat	
Rancher	2 oz potatoes	½ oz meat	

have a comparative advantage in one good, and the other person will have a comparative advantage in the other good.

Comparative Advantage and Trade

The gains from specialization and trade are based not on absolute advantage but on comparative advantage. When each person specializes in producing the good for which he or she has a comparative advantage, total production in the economy rises. This increase in the size of the economic pie can be used to make everyone better off.

In our example, the farmer spends more time growing potatoes, and the rancher spends more time producing meat. As a result, the total production of potatoes rises from 40 to 44 ounces, and the total production of meat rises from 16 to 18 ounces. The farmer and rancher share the benefits of this increased production.

There is another way to look at the gains from trade—in terms of the price that each party pays the other. Because the farmer and rancher have different opportunity costs, they can each think they are getting a bargain. That is, each benefits from trade by obtaining a good at a price that is lower than his or her opportunity cost of that good.

Consider the proposed deal from the viewpoint of the farmer. The farmer gets 5 ounces of meat in exchange for 15 ounces of potatoes. In other words, the farmer buys each ounce of meat for a price of 3 ounces of potatoes. This price of meat is lower than his opportunity cost for 1 ounce of meat, which is 4 ounces of potatoes. Thus, the farmer benefits from the deal because he gets to buy meat at a good price.

Now consider the deal from the rancher's viewpoint. The rancher buys 15 ounces of potatoes for a price of 5 ounces of meat. That is, the price of potatoes is $1/3$ ounce of meat. This price of potatoes is lower than her opportunity cost of 1 ounce of potatoes, which is $1/2$ ounce of meat. The rancher benefits because she gets to buy potatoes at a good price.

The principle of comparative advantage establishes that there are gains from specialization and trade, but it leaves open a couple of related questions: What determines the price at which trade takes place? How are the gains from trade shared between the trading parties? The precise answer to these questions is beyond the scope of this chapter, but we can state one general rule: For both parties to gain from trade, the price at which they trade must lie between the two opportunity costs. In our example, the farmer and rancher agreed to trade at a rate of 3 ounces of potatoes for each ounce of meat. This price is between the farmer's opportunity cost (4 ounces of potatoes per ounce of meat) and the rancher's opportunity cost (2 ounces of potatoes per ounce of meat). As long as the trading price lies somewhere in this range, each party will benefit by buying a good at a price that is lower than his or her opportunity cost.

The moral of the story of the farmer and the rancher should now be clear: *Trade can benefit everyone in society because it allows people to specialize in activities in which they have a comparative advantage.*

Quick Quiz   Robinson Crusoe can gather 10 coconuts or catch 1 fish per hour. His friend Friday can gather 30 coconuts or catch 2 fish per hour. What is Crusoe's opportunity cost of catching one fish? What is Friday's? Who has an absolute advantage in catching fish? Who has a comparative advantage in catching fish?

FYI

The Legacy of Adam Smith and David Ricardo

Economists have long understood the principle of comparative advantage. Here is how the great economist Adam Smith put the argument:

It is a maxim of every prudent master of a family, never to attempt to make at home what it will cost him more to make than to buy. The tailor does not attempt to make his own shoes, but buys them of the shoemaker. The shoemaker does not attempt to make his own clothes but employs a tailor. The farmer attempts to make neither the one nor the other, but employs those different artificers. All of them find it for their interest to employ their whole industry in a way in which they have some advantage over their neighbors, and to purchase with a part of its produce, or what is the same thing, with the price of part of it, whatever else they have occasion for.

This quotation is from Smith's 1776 book *An Inquiry into the Nature and Causes of the Wealth of Nations,* which was a landmark in the analysis of trade and economic interdependence.

David Ricardo

Smith's book inspired David Ricardo, a millionaire stockbroker, to become an economist. In his 1817 book *Principles of Political Economy and Taxation,* Ricardo developed the principle of comparative advantage as we know it today. His defense of free trade was not a mere academic exercise. Ricardo put his economic beliefs to work as a member of the British Parliament, where he opposed the Corn Laws, which restricted the import of grain.

The conclusions of Adam Smith and David Ricardo on the gains from trade have held up well over time. Although economists often disagree on questions of policy, they are united in their support of free trade. Moreover, the central argument for free trade has not changed much in the past two centuries. Even though the field of economics has broadened its scope and refined its theories since the time of Smith and Ricardo, economists' opposition to trade restrictions is still based largely on the principle of comparative advantage.

APPLICATIONS OF COMPARATIVE ADVANTAGE

The principle of comparative advantage explains interdependence and the gains from trade. Because interdependence is so prevalent in the modern world, the principle of comparative advantage has many applications. Here are two examples, one fanciful and one of great practical importance.

Should Tiger Woods Mow His Own Lawn?

Tiger Woods spends a lot of time walking around on grass. One of the most talented golfers of all time, he can hit a drive and sink a putt in a way that most casual golfers only dream of doing. Most likely, he is talented at other activities too. For example, let's imagine that Woods can mow his lawn faster than anyone else. But just because he *can* mow his lawn fast, does this mean he *should*?

In The News

Evolution and Economics

The theory of comparative advantage may lie at the heart of humanity's evolutionary success.

Homo Economicus?

Since the days of Adam Smith and David Ricardo, advocates of free trade and the division of labor, including this newspaper, have lauded the advantages of those economic principles. Until now, though, no one has suggested that they might be responsible for the very existence of humanity. But that is the thesis propounded by Jason Shogren, of the University of Wyoming, and his colleagues. For Dr Shogren is suggesting that trade and specialization are the reasons *Homo sapiens* displaced previous members of the genus, such as

Homo neanderthalensis (Neanderthal man), and emerged triumphant as the only species of humanity.

Neanderthal man has had a bad cultural rap over the years since the discovery of the first specimen in the Neander valley in Germany, in the mid-19th century. The "caveman" image of a stupid, grunting, hairy, thick-skulled parody of graceful modern humanity has stuck in the public consciousness. But current scholarship suggests Neanderthals were probably about as smart as modern humans, and also capable of speech. If they were hairy, strong and tough—

which they were—that was an appropriate adaptation to the ice-age conditions in which they lived. So why did they become extinct?

Neanderthals existed perfectly successfully for 200,000 years before *Homo sapiens* arrived in their European homeland about 40,000 years ago, after a circuitous journey from Africa via central Asia. But 10,000 years later they were gone, so it seems likely that the arrival of modern man was the cause. The two species certainly occupied more or less the same ecological niche (hunting a wide range of animals, and gathering a

---

To answer this question, we can use the concepts of opportunity cost and comparative advantage. Let's say that Woods can mow his lawn in 2 hours. In that same 2 hours, he could film a television commercial for Nike and earn $10,000. By contrast, Forrest Gump, the boy next door, can mow Woods's lawn in 4 hours. In that same 4 hours, he could work at McDonald's and earn $20.

In this example, Woods's opportunity cost of mowing the lawn is $10,000 and Forrest's opportunity cost is $20. Woods has an absolute advantage in mowing lawns because he can do the work with a lower input of time. Yet Forrest has a comparative advantage in mowing lawns because he has the lower opportunity cost.

The gains from trade in this example are tremendous. Rather than mowing his own lawn, Woods should make the commercial and hire Forrest to mow the lawn. As long as Woods pays Forrest more than $20 and less than $10,000, both of them are better off.

Should the United States Trade with Other Countries?

Just as individuals can benefit from specialization and trade with one another, as the farmer and rancher did, so can populations of people in different countries.

similarly eclectic range of plant food), and would thus have been competitors.

One theory is that *Homo sapiens* had more sophisticated tools, which gave him an advantage in hunting or warfare. Another is that the modern human capacity for symbolic thinking (manifest at that time in the form of cave paintings and carved animal figurines) provided an edge. Symbolic thinking might have led to more sophisticated language and better co-operation. But according to Dr Shogren's paper in a forthcoming edition of the *Journal of Economic Behavior and Organization*, it was neither cave paintings nor better spear points that led to *Homo sapiens's* dominance. It was a better economic system.

One thing *Homo sapiens* does that *Homo neanderthalensis* shows no sign of having done is trade. The evidence suggests that such trade was going on even 40,000 years ago. Stone tools made of non-local materials, and sea-shell jewelry found far from the coast, are witnesses to long-distance exchanges. That *Homo sapiens* also practiced division of labor and specialization is suggested not only by the skilled nature of his craft work, but also by the fact that his dwellings had spaces apparently set aside for different uses.

To see if trade might be enough to account for the dominance of *Homo sapiens*, Dr Shogren and his colleagues created a computer model of population growth that attempts to capture the relevant variables for each species. These include fertility, mortality rates, hunting efficiency and the number of skilled and unskilled hunters in each group, as well as levels of skill in making objects such as weapons, and the ability to specialise and trade.

Initially, the researchers assumed that on average Neanderthals and modern humans had the same abilities for most of these attributes. They therefore set the values of those variables equal for both species. Only in the case of the trading and specialization variables did they allow *Homo sapiens* an advantage: specifically, they assumed that the most efficient human hunters specialized in hunting, while bad hunters hung up their spears and made things such as clothes and tools instead. Hunters and craftsmen then traded with one another.

According to the model, this arrangement resulted in everyone getting more meat, which drove up fertility and thus increased the population. Since the supply of meat was finite, that left less for Neanderthals, and their population declined. . . .

Of course, none of this proves absolutely that economics led to modern humanity inheriting the Earth. But it does raise the intriguing possibility that the dismal science is responsible for even more than Smith and Ricardo gave it credit.

Many of the goods that Americans enjoy are produced abroad, and many of the goods produced in the United States are sold abroad. Goods produced abroad and sold domestically are called **imports.** Goods produced domestically and sold abroad are called **exports.**

> **imports**
> goods produced abroad and sold domestically
>
> **exports**
> goods produced domestically and sold abroad

To see how countries can benefit from trade, suppose there are two countries, the United States and Japan, and two goods, food and cars. Imagine that the two countries produce cars equally well: An American worker and a Japanese worker can each produce 1 car per month. By contrast, because the United States has more and better land, it is better at producing food: A U.S. worker can produce 2 tons of food per month, whereas a Japanese worker can produce only 1 ton of food per month.

The principle of comparative advantage states that each good should be produced by the country that has the smaller opportunity cost of producing that good. Because the opportunity cost of a car is 2 tons of food in the United States but only 1 ton of food in Japan, Japan has a comparative advantage in producing cars. Japan should produce more cars than it wants for its own use and export some of them to the United States. Similarly, because the opportunity cost of a ton of food is 1 car in Japan but only 1/2 car in the United States, the United States has a comparative advantage in producing food. The United States should produce more food than it wants to consume and export some to Japan. Through specialization and trade, both countries can have more food and more cars.

In reality, of course, the issues involved in trade among nations are more complex than this example suggests. Most important among these issues is that each country has many citizens with different interests. International trade can at times make some individuals worse off, even as it makes the country as a whole better off. When the United States exports food and imports cars, the impact on an American farmer is not the same as the impact on an American autoworker. Yet, contrary to the opinions sometimes voiced by politicians and political commentators, international trade is not like war, in which some countries win and others lose. Trade allows all countries to achieve greater prosperity.

Quick Quiz Suppose that the world's fastest typist happens to be trained in brain surgery. Should he do his own typing or hire a secretary? Explain.

CONCLUSION

The principle of comparative advantage shows that trade can make everyone better off. You should now understand more fully the benefits of living in an interdependent economy. But having seen why interdependence is desirable, you might naturally ask how it is possible. How do free societies coordinate the diverse activities of all the people involved in their economies? What ensures that goods and services will get from those who should be producing them to those who should be consuming them?

In a world with only two people, such as the rancher and the farmer, the answer is simple: These two people can directly bargain and allocate resources between themselves. In the real world with billions of people, the answer is less obvious. We take up this issue in the next chapter, where we see that free societies allocate resources through the market forces of supply and demand.

SUMMARY

- Each person consumes goods and services produced by many other people both in the United States and around the world. Interdependence and trade are desirable because they allow everyone to enjoy a greater quantity and variety of goods and services.

- There are two ways to compare the ability of two people in producing a good. The person who can produce the good with the smaller quantity of inputs is said to have an *absolute advantage* in producing the good. The person who has the smaller

opportunity cost of producing the good is said to have a *comparative advantage*. The gains from trade are based on comparative advantage, not absolute advantage.

- Trade makes everyone better off because it allows people to specialize in those activities in which they have a comparative advantage.

- The principle of comparative advantage applies to countries as well as to people. Economists use the principle of comparative advantage to advocate free trade among countries.

KEY CONCEPTS

absolute advantage, p. 52
opportunity cost, p. 53

comparative advantage, p. 53
imports, p. 57

exports, p. 57

QUESTIONS FOR REVIEW

1. Explain how absolute advantage and comparative advantage differ.

2. Give an example in which one person has an absolute advantage in doing something but another person has a comparative advantage.

3. Is absolute advantage or comparative advantage more important for trade? Explain your reason-

ing using the example in your answer to Question 2.

4. Will a nation tend to export or import goods for which it has a comparative advantage? Explain.

5. Why do economists oppose policies that restrict trade among nations?

PROBLEMS AND APPLICATIONS

1. Maria can read 20 pages of economics in an hour. She can also read 50 pages of sociology in an hour. She spends 5 hours per day studying.
   a. Draw Maria's production possibilities frontier for reading economics and sociology.
   b. What is Maria's opportunity cost of reading 100 pages of sociology?

2. American and Japanese workers can each produce 4 cars a year. An American worker can produce 10 tons of grain a year, whereas a Japanese worker can produce 5 tons of grain a year. To keep things simple, assume that each country has 100 million workers.
   a. For this situation, construct a table analogous to Table 1.
   b. Graph the production possibilities frontier of the American and Japanese economies.
   c. For the United States, what is the opportunity cost of a car? Of grain? For Japan, what is the opportunity cost of a car? Of grain? Put this information in a table analogous to Table 2.
   d. Which country has an absolute advantage in producing cars? In producing grain?
   e. Which country has a comparative advantage in producing cars? In producing grain?
   f. Without trade, half of each country's workers produce cars and half produce grain. What

quantities of cars and grain does each country produce?
   g. Starting from a position without trade, give an example in which trade makes each country better off.

3. Pat and Kris are roommates. They spend most of their time studying (of course), but they leave some time for their favorite activities: making pizza and brewing root beer. Pat takes 4 hours to brew a gallon of root beer and 2 hours to make a pizza. Kris takes 6 hours to brew a gallon of root beer and 4 hours to make a pizza.
   a. What is each roommate's opportunity cost of making a pizza? Who has the absolute advantage in making pizza? Who has the comparative advantage in making pizza?
   b. If Pat and Kris trade foods with each other, who will trade away pizza in exchange for root beer?
   c. The price of pizza can be expressed in terms of gallons of root beer. What is the highest price at which pizza can be traded that would make both roommates better off? What is the lowest price? Explain.

4. Suppose that there are 10 million workers in Canada and that each of these workers can produce either 2 cars or 30 bushels of wheat in a year.

a. What is the opportunity cost of producing a car in Canada? What is the opportunity cost of producing a bushel of wheat in Canada? Explain the relationship between the opportunity costs of the two goods.

b. Draw Canada's production possibilities frontier. If Canada chooses to consume 10 million cars, how much wheat can it consume without trade? Label this point on the production possibilities frontier.

c. Now suppose that the United States offers to buy 10 million cars from Canada in exchange for 20 bushels of wheat per car. If Canada continues to consume 10 million cars, how much wheat does this deal allow Canada to consume? Label this point on your diagram. Should Canada accept the deal?

5. England and Scotland both produce scones and sweaters. Suppose that an English worker can produce 50 scones per hour or 1 sweater per hour. Suppose that a Scottish worker can produce 40 scones per hour or 2 sweaters per hour.

a. Which country has the absolute advantage in the production of each good? Which country has the comparative advantage?

b. If England and Scotland decide to trade, which commodity will Scotland trade to England? Explain.

c. If a Scottish worker could produce only 1 sweater per hour, would Scotland still gain from trade? Would England still gain from trade? Explain.

6. The following table describes the production possibilities of two cities in the country of Baseballia:

	Pairs of Red Socks per Worker per Hour	Pairs of White Socks per Worker per Hour
Boston	3	3
Chicago	2	1

a. Without trade, what is the price of white socks (in terms of red socks) in Boston? What is the price in Chicago?

b. Which city has an absolute advantage in the production of each color sock? Which city has a comparative advantage in the production of each color sock?

c. If the cities trade with each other, which color sock will each export?

d. What is the range of prices at which trade can occur?

7. Suppose that in a year an American worker can produce 100 shirts or 20 computers, while a Chinese worker can produce 100 shirts or 10 computers.

a. Graph the production possibilities curve for the two countries. Suppose that without trade the workers in each country spend half their time producing each good. Identify this point in your graph.

b. If these countries were open to trade, which country would export shirts? Give a specific numerical example and show it on your graph. Which country would benefit from trade? Explain.

c. Explain what price of computers (in terms of shirts) the two countries might trade.

d. Suppose that China catches up with American productivity so that a Chinese worker can produce 100 shirts or 20 computers. What pattern of trade would you predict now? How does this advance in Chinese productivity affect the economic well-being of the citizens of the two countries?

8. Are the following statements true or false? Explain in each case.

a. "Two countries can achieve gains from trade even if one of the countries has an absolute advantage in the production of all goods."

b. "Certain very talented people have a comparative advantage in everything they do."

c. "If a certain trade is good for one person, it can't be good for the other one."

d. "If trade is good for a country, it must be good for everyone in the country."

9. The United States exports corn and aircraft to the rest of the world, and it imports oil and clothing from the rest of the world. Do you think this pattern of trade is consistent with the principle of comparative advantage? Why or why not?

For further information on topics in this chapter, additional problems, examples, applications, online quizzes, and more, please visit our website at http://mankiw.swlearning.com.

2

How Markets Work

The Market Forces of Supply and Demand

When a cold snap hits Florida, the price of orange juice rises in supermarkets throughout the country. When the weather turns warm in New England every summer, the price of hotel rooms in the Caribbean plummets. When a war breaks out in the Middle East, the price of gasoline in the United States rises, and the price of a used Cadillac falls. What do these events have in common? They all show the workings of supply and demand.

Supply and *demand* are the two words economists use most often—and for good reason. Supply and demand are the forces that make market economies work. They determine the quantity of each good produced and the price at which it is sold. If you want to know how any event or policy will affect the economy, you must think first about how it will affect supply and demand.

This chapter introduces the theory of supply and demand. It considers how buyers and sellers behave and how they interact with one another. It shows how supply and demand determine prices in a market economy and how prices, in turn, allocate the economy's scarce resources.

MARKETS AND COMPETITION

The terms *supply* and *demand* refer to the behavior of people as they interact with one another in competitive markets. Before discussing how buyers and sellers behave, let's first consider more fully what we mean by the terms *market* and *competition*.

What Is a Market?

market
a group of buyers and sellers of a particular good or service

A **market** is a group of buyers and sellers of a particular good or service. The buyers as a group determine the demand for the product, and the sellers as a group determine the supply of the product.

Markets take many forms. Sometimes markets are highly organized, such as the markets for many agricultural commodities. In these markets, buyers and sellers meet at a specific time and place, where an auctioneer helps set prices and arrange sales.

More often, markets are less organized. For example, consider the market for ice cream in a particular town. Buyers of ice cream do not meet together at any one time. The sellers of ice cream are in different locations and offer somewhat different products. There is no auctioneer calling out the price of ice cream. Each seller posts a price for an ice-cream cone, and each buyer decides how much ice cream to buy at each store. Nonetheless, these consumers and producers of ice cream are closely connected. The ice-cream buyers are choosing from the various ice-cream sellers to satisfy their hunger, and the ice-cream sellers are all trying to appeal to the same ice-cream buyers to make their businesses successful. Even though it is not organized, the group of ice-cream buyers and ice-cream sellers forms a market.

What Is Competition?

The market for ice cream, like most markets in the economy, is highly competitive. Each buyer knows that there are several sellers from which to choose, and each seller is aware that his product is similar to that offered by other sellers. As a result, the price of ice cream and the quantity of ice cream sold are not determined by any single buyer or seller. Rather, price and quantity are determined by all buyers and sellers as they interact in the marketplace.

competitive market
a market in which there are many buyers and many sellers so that each has a negligible impact on the market price

Economists use the term **competitive market** to describe a market in which there are so many buyers and so many sellers that each has a negligible impact on the market price. Each seller of ice cream has limited control over the price because other sellers are offering similar products. A seller has little reason to charge less than the going price, and if he charges more, buyers will make their purchases elsewhere. Similarly, no single buyer of ice cream can influence the price of ice cream because each buyer purchases only a small amount.

In this chapter, we assume that markets are *perfectly competitive*. To reach this highest form of competition, a market must have two characteristics: (1) the goods offered for sale are all exactly the same, and (2) the buyers and sellers are so numerous that no single buyer or seller has any influence over the market price. Because buyers and sellers in perfectly competitive markets must accept the price the market determines, they are said to be *price takers*. At the market price, buyers can buy all they want, and sellers can sell all they want.

There are some markets in which the assumption of perfect competition applies perfectly. In the wheat market, for example, there are thousands of farmers who sell wheat and millions of consumers who use wheat and wheat products. Because no single buyer or seller can influence the price of wheat, each takes the price as given.

Not all goods and services, however, are sold in perfectly competitive markets. Some markets have only one seller, and this seller sets the price. Such a seller is called a *monopoly*. Your local cable television company, for instance, may be a monopoly. Residents of your town probably have only one cable company from which to buy this service. Some markets (covered in the study of microeconomics) fall between the extremes of perfect competition and monopoly.

Despite the diversity of market types we find in the world, assuming perfect competition is a useful simplification and, therefore, a natural place to start. Perfectly competitive markets are the easiest to analyze because everyone participating in the market takes the price as given by market conditions. Moreover, because some degree of competition is present in most markets, many of the lessons that we learn by studying supply and demand under perfect competition apply in more complicated markets as well.

Quick Quiz   What is a market?   •   What are the characteristics of a competitive market?

DEMAND

We begin our study of markets by examining the behavior of buyers. To focus our thinking, let's keep in mind a particular good—ice cream.

The Demand Curve: The Relationship between Price and Quantity Demanded

The **quantity demanded** of any good is the amount of the good that buyers are willing and able to purchase. As we will see, many things determine the quantity demanded of any good, but when analyzing how markets work, one determinant plays a central role—the price of the good. If the price of ice cream rose to $20 per scoop, you would buy less ice cream. You might buy frozen yogurt instead. If the price of ice cream fell to $0.20 per scoop, you would buy more. Because the quantity demanded falls as the price rises and rises as the price falls, we say that the quantity demanded is *negatively related* to the price. This relationship between price and quantity demanded is true for most goods in the economy and, in fact, is so pervasive that economists call it the **law of demand:** Other things equal, when the price of a good rises, the quantity demanded of the good falls, and when the price falls, the quantity demanded rises.

The table in Figure 1 shows how many ice-cream cones Catherine buys each month at different prices of ice cream. If ice cream is free, Catherine eats 12 cones per month. At $0.50 per cone, Catherine buys 10 cones each month. As the price rises further, she buys fewer and fewer cones. When the price reaches $3.00, Catherine doesn't buy any ice cream at all. This table is a **demand schedule,** a table that shows the relationship between the price of a good and the quantity demanded, holding constant everything else that influences how much consumers of the good want to buy.

The graph in Figure 1 uses the numbers from the table to illustrate the law of demand. By convention, the price of ice cream is on the vertical axis, and the

quantity demanded
the amount of a good that buyers are willing and able to purchase

law of demand
the claim that, other things equal, the quantity demanded of a good falls when the price of the good rises

demand schedule
a table that shows the relationship between the price of a good and the quantity demanded

1 **FIGURE**

Catherine's Demand
Schedule and Demand Curve

The demand schedule shows the quantity demanded at each price. The demand curve, which graphs the demand schedule, shows how the quantity demanded of the good changes as its price varies. Because a lower price increases the quantity demanded, the demand curve slopes downward.

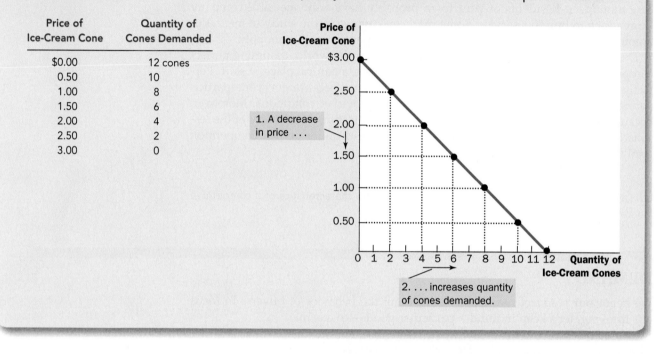

Price of Ice-Cream Cone	Quantity of Cones Demanded
$0.00	12 cones
0.50	10
1.00	8
1.50	6
2.00	4
2.50	2
3.00	0

1. A decrease in price . . .

2. . . . increases quantity of cones demanded.

demand curve
a graph of the relationship between the price of a good and the quantity demanded

quantity of ice cream demanded is on the horizontal axis. The downward-sloping line relating price and quantity demanded is called the **demand curve.**

Market Demand versus Individual Demand

The demand curve in Figure 1 shows an individual's demand for a product. To analyze how markets work, we need to determine the *market demand*, the sum of all the individual demands for a particular good or service.

The table in Figure 2 shows the demand schedules for ice cream of two individuals—Catherine and Nicholas. At any price, Catherine's demand schedule tells us how much ice cream she buys, and Nicholas's demand schedule tells us how much ice cream he buys. The market demand at each price is the sum of the two individual demands.

The graph in Figure 2 shows the demand curves that correspond to these demand schedules. Notice that we sum the individual demand curves horizontally to obtain the market demand curve. That is, to find the total quantity demanded at any price, we add the individual quantities found on the horizontal axis of the individual demand curves. Because we are interested in analyzing how markets work, we will work most often with the market demand curve. The market demand curve shows how the total quantity demanded of a good varies as the price of the good varies, while all the other factors that affect how much consumers want to buy are held constant.

The quantity demanded in a market is the sum of the quantities demanded by all the buyers at each price. Thus, the market demand curve is found by adding horizontally the individual demand curves. At a price of $2.00, Catherine demands 4 ice-cream cones, and Nicholas demands 3 ice-cream cones. The quantity demanded in the market at this price is 7 cones.

Price of Ice-Cream Cone	Catherine		Nicholas		Market
$0.00	12	+	7	=	19 cones
0.50	10		6		16
1.00	8		5		13
1.50	6		4		10
2.00	4		3		7
2.50	2		2		4
3.00	0		1		1

Shifts in the Demand Curve

The demand curve for ice cream shows how much ice cream people buy at any given price, holding constant the many other factors beyond price that influence consumers' buying decisions. As a result, this demand curve need not be stable over time. If something happens to alter the quantity demanded at any given price, the demand curve shifts. For example, suppose the American Medical Association discovered that people who regularly eat ice cream live longer, healthier lives. The discovery would raise the demand for ice cream. At any given price, buyers would now want to purchase a larger quantity of ice cream, and the demand curve for ice cream would shift.

Figure 3 illustrates shifts in demand. Any change that increases the quantity demanded at every price, such as our imaginary discovery by the American Medical Association, shifts the demand curve to the right and is called an *increase in demand.* Any change that reduces the quantity demanded at every price shifts the demand curve to the left and is called a *decrease in demand.*

There are many variables that can shift the demand curve. Here are the most important.

3 F I G U R E

Shifts in the Demand Curve
Any change that raises the quantity that buyers wish to purchase at a given price shifts the demand curve to the right. Any change that lowers the quantity that buyers wish to purchase at a given price shifts the demand curve to the left.

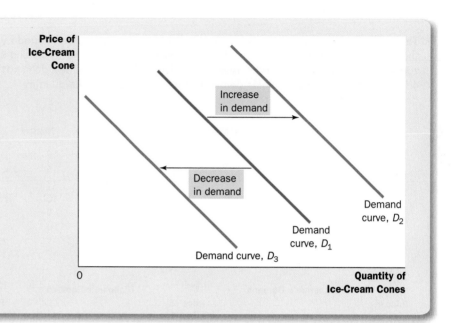

Income   What would happen to your demand for ice cream if you lost your job one summer? Most likely, it would fall. A lower income means that you have less to spend in total, so you would have to spend less on some—and probably most—goods. If the demand for a good falls when income falls, the good is called a **normal good.**

Not all goods are normal goods. If the demand for a good rises when income falls, the good is called an **inferior good.** An example of an inferior good might be bus rides. As your income falls, you are less likely to buy a car or take a cab and more likely to ride a bus.

Prices of Related Goods   Suppose that the price of frozen yogurt falls. The law of demand says that you will buy more frozen yogurt. At the same time, you will probably buy less ice cream. Because ice cream and frozen yogurt are both cold, sweet, creamy desserts, they satisfy similar desires. When a fall in the price of one good reduces the demand for another good, the two goods are called **substitutes.** Substitutes are often pairs of goods that are used in place of each other, such as hot dogs and hamburgers, sweaters and sweatshirts, and movie tickets and video rentals.

Now suppose that the price of hot fudge falls. According to the law of demand, you will buy more hot fudge. Yet in this case, you will buy more ice cream as well because ice cream and hot fudge are often used together. When a fall in the price of one good raises the demand for another good, the two goods are called **complements.** Complements are often pairs of goods that are used together, such as gasoline and automobiles, computers and software, and peanut butter and jelly.

Tastes   The most obvious determinant of your demand is your tastes. If you like ice cream, you buy more of it. Economists normally do not try to explain people's tastes because tastes are based on historical and psychological forces that are beyond the realm of economics. Economists do, however, examine what happens when tastes change.

normal good
a good for which, other things equal, an increase in income leads to an increase in demand

inferior good
a good for which, other things equal, an increase in income leads to a decrease in demand

substitutes
two goods for which an increase in the price of one leads to an increase in the demand for the other

complements
two goods for which an increase in the price of one leads to a decrease in the demand for the other

Variable	A Change in This Variable. . .
Price	Represents a movement along the demand curve
Income	Shifts the demand curve
Prices of related goods	Shifts the demand curve
Tastes	Shifts the demand curve
Expectations	Shifts the demand curve
Number of buyers	Shifts the demand curve

T A B L E   1

Variables That Influence Buyers
This table lists the variables that affect how much consumers choose to buy of any good. Notice the special role that the price of the good plays: A change in the good's price represents a movement along the demand curve, whereas a change in one of the other variables shifts the demand curve.

Expectations   Your expectations about the future may affect your demand for a good or service today. For example, if you expect to earn a higher income next month, you may choose to save less now and spend more of your current income buying ice cream. As another example, if you expect the price of ice cream to fall tomorrow, you may be less willing to buy an ice-cream cone at today's price.

Number of Buyers   Because market demand is derived from individual demands, it depends on all those factors that determine the demand of individual buyers, including buyers' incomes, tastes, expectations, and the prices of related goods. In addition, it depends on the number of buyers. If Peter, another consumer of ice cream, were to join Catherine and Nicholas, the quantity demanded in the market would be higher at every price, and the demand curve would shift to the right.

Summary   The demand curve shows what happens to the quantity demanded of a good when its price varies, holding constant all the other variables that influence buyers. When one of these other variables changes, the demand curve shifts. Table 1 lists the variables that influence how much consumers choose to buy of a good.

If you have trouble remembering whether you need to shift or move along the demand curve, it helps to recall a lesson from the appendix to Chapter 2. A curve shifts when there is a change in a relevant variable that is not measured on either axis. Because the price is on the vertical axis, a change in price represents a movement along the demand curve. By contrast, income, the prices of related goods, tastes, expectations, and the number of buyers are not measured on either axis, so a change in one of these variables shifts the demand curve.

CASE STUDY | TWO WAYS TO REDUCE THE QUANTITY OF SMOKING DEMANDED

© ROYALTY-FREE/CORBIS

WHAT IS THE BEST WAY TO STOP THIS?

Public policymakers often want to reduce the amount that people smoke. There are two ways that policy can attempt to achieve this goal.

One way to reduce smoking is to shift the demand curve for cigarettes and other tobacco products. Public service announcements, mandatory health warnings on cigarette packages, and the prohibition of cigarette advertising on television are all policies aimed at reducing the quantity of cigarettes demanded at

4 FIGURE

Shifts in the Demand Curve versus Movements along the Demand Curve

If warnings on cigarette packages convince smokers to smoke less, the demand curve for cigarettes shifts to the left. In panel (a), the demand curve shifts from D_1 to D_2. At a price of $2.00 per pack, the quantity demanded falls from 20 to 10 cigarettes per day, as reflected by the shift from point A to point B. By contrast, if a tax raises the price of cigarettes, the demand curve does not shift. Instead, we observe a movement to a different point on the demand curve. In panel (b), when the price rises from $2.00 to $4.00, the quantity demanded falls from 20 to 12 cigarettes per day, as reflected by the movement from point A to point C.

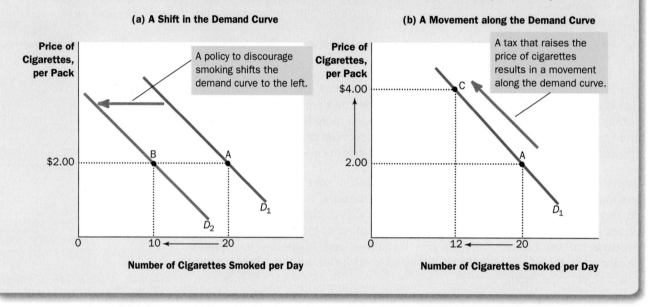

(a) A Shift in the Demand Curve

Price of Cigarettes, per Pack

A policy to discourage smoking shifts the demand curve to the left.

$2.00

B   A

D_2 D_1

0   10 ← 20

Number of Cigarettes Smoked per Day

(b) A Movement along the Demand Curve

Price of Cigarettes, per Pack

A tax that raises the price of cigarettes results in a movement along the demand curve.

$4.00   C

2.00   A

D_1

0   12 ← 20

Number of Cigarettes Smoked per Day

any given price. If successful, these policies shift the demand curve for cigarettes to the left, as in panel (a) of Figure 4.

Alternatively, policymakers can try to raise the price of cigarettes. If the government taxes the manufacture of cigarettes, for example, cigarette companies pass much of this tax on to consumers in the form of higher prices. A higher price encourages smokers to reduce the numbers of cigarettes they smoke. In this case, the reduced amount of smoking does not represent a shift in the demand curve. Instead, it represents a movement along the same demand curve to a point with a higher price and lower quantity, as in panel (b) of Figure 4.

How much does the amount of smoking respond to changes in the price of cigarettes? Economists have attempted to answer this question by studying what happens when the tax on cigarettes changes. They have found that a 10 percent increase in the price causes a 4 percent reduction in the quantity demanded. Teenagers are found to be especially sensitive to the price of cigarettes: A 10 percent increase in the price causes a 12 percent drop in teenage smoking.

A related question is how the price of cigarettes affects the demand for illicit drugs, such as marijuana. Opponents of cigarette taxes often argue that tobacco and marijuana are substitutes so that high cigarette prices encourage marijuana use. By contrast, many experts on substance abuse view tobacco as a "gateway drug" leading the young to experiment with other harmful substances. Most studies of the data are consistent with this view: They find that lower cigarette prices are associated with greater use of marijuana. In other words, tobacco and marijuana appear to be complements rather than substitutes.

Quick Quiz Make up an example of a demand schedule for pizza and graph the implied demand curve. • Give an example of something that would shift this demand curve. • Would a change in the price of pizza shift this demand curve?

SUPPLY

We now turn to the other side of the market and examine the behavior of sellers. Once again, to focus our thinking, let's consider the market for ice cream.

The Supply Curve: The Relationship between Price and Quantity Supplied

The **quantity supplied** of any good or service is the amount that sellers are willing and able to sell. There are many determinants of quantity supplied, but once again, price plays a special role in our analysis. When the price of ice cream is high, selling ice cream is profitable, and so the quantity supplied is large. Sellers of ice cream work long hours, buy many ice-cream machines, and hire many workers. By contrast, when the price of ice cream is low, the business is less profitable, and so sellers produce less ice cream. At a low price, some sellers may even choose to shut down, and their quantity supplied falls to zero. Because the quantity supplied rises as the price rises and falls as the price falls, we say that the quantity supplied is *positively related* to the price of the good. This relationship between price and quantity supplied is called the **law of supply:** Other things equal, when the price of a good rises, the quantity supplied of the good also rises, and when the price falls, the quantity supplied falls as well.

The table in Figure 5 shows the quantity of ice-cream cones supplied each month by Ben, an ice-cream seller, at various prices of ice cream. At a price below $1.00, Ben does not supply any ice cream at all. As the price rises, he supplies a greater and greater quantity. This is the **supply schedule,** a table that shows the relationship between the price of a good and the quantity supplied, holding constant everything else that influences how much producers of the good want to sell.

The graph in Figure 5 uses the numbers from the table to illustrate the law of supply. The curve relating price and quantity supplied is called the **supply curve.** The supply curve slopes upward because, other things equal, a higher price means a greater quantity supplied.

Market Supply versus Individual Supply

Just as market demand is the sum of the demands of all buyers, market supply is the sum of the supplies of all sellers. The table in Figure 6 shows the supply schedules for two ice-cream producers—Ben and Jerry. At any price, Ben's supply schedule tells us the quantity of ice cream Ben supplies, and Jerry's supply schedule tells us the quantity of ice cream Jerry supplies. The market supply is the sum of the two individual supplies.

quantity supplied
the amount of a good that sellers are willing and able to sell

law of supply
the claim that, other things equal, the quantity supplied of a good rises when the price of the good rises

supply schedule
a table that shows the relationship between the price of a good and the quantity supplied

supply curve
a graph of the relationship between the price of a good and the quantity supplied

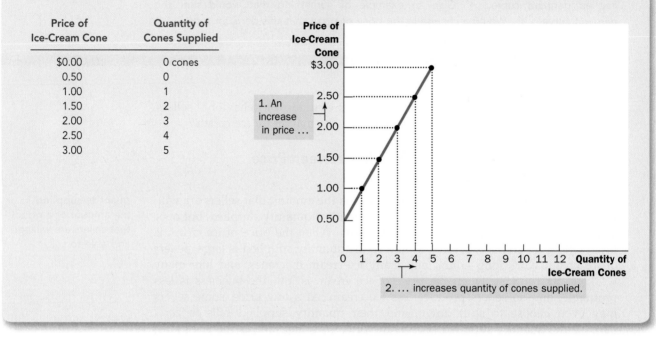

5 FIGURE

Ben's Supply Schedule and Supply Curve

The supply schedule shows the quantity supplied at each price. This supply curve, which graphs the supply schedule, shows how the quantity supplied of the good changes as its price varies. Because a higher price increases the quantity supplied, the supply curve slopes upward.

Price of Ice-Cream Cone	Quantity of Cones Supplied
$0.00	0 cones
0.50	0
1.00	1
1.50	2
2.00	3
2.50	4
3.00	5

The graph in Figure 6 shows the supply curves that correspond to the supply schedules. As with demand curves, we sum the individual supply curves *horizontally* to obtain the market supply curve. That is, to find the total quantity supplied at any price, we add the individual quantities found on the horizontal axis of the individual supply curves. The market supply curve shows how the total quantity supplied varies as the price of the good varies.

Shifts in the Supply Curve

The supply curve for ice cream shows how much ice cream producers offer for sale at any given price, holding constant all the other factors beyond price that influence producers' decisions about how much to sell. This relationship can change over time, which is represented by a shift in the supply curve. For example, suppose the price of sugar falls. Because sugar is an input into producing ice cream, the fall in the price of sugar makes selling ice cream more profitable. This raises the supply of ice cream: At any given price, sellers are now willing to produce a larger quantity. Thus, the supply curve for ice cream shifts to the right.

Figure 7 illustrates shifts in supply. Any change that raises quantity supplied at every price, such as a fall in the price of sugar, shifts the supply curve to the right and is called an *increase in supply*. Similarly, any change that reduces the quantity supplied at every price shifts the supply curve to the left and is called a *decrease in supply*.

FIGURE 6

Price of Ice-Cream Cone	Ben		Jerry		Market
$0.00	0	+	0	=	0 cones
0.50	0		0		0
1.00	1		0		1
1.50	2		2		4
2.00	3		4		7
2.50	4		6		10
3.00	5		8		13

Market Supply as the Sum of Individual Supplies
The quantity supplied in a market is the sum of the quantities supplied by all the sellers at each price. Thus, the market supply curve is found by adding horizontally the individual supply curves. At a price of $2.00, Ben supplies 3 ice-cream cones, and Jerry supplies 4 ice-cream cones. The quantity supplied in the market at this price is 7 cones.

FIGURE 7

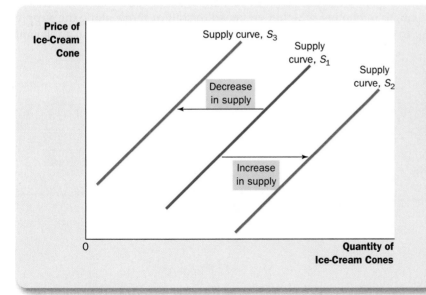

Shifts in the Supply Curve
Any change that raises the quantity that sellers wish to produce at a given price shifts the supply curve to the right. Any change that lowers the quantity that sellers wish to produce at a given price shifts the supply curve to the left.

There are many variables that can shift the supply curve. Here are some of the most important.

Input Prices   To produce its output of ice cream, sellers use various inputs: cream, sugar, flavoring, ice-cream machines, the buildings in which the ice cream is made, and the labor of workers to mix the ingredients and operate the machines. When the price of one or more of these inputs rises, producing ice cream is less profitable, and firms supply less ice cream. If input prices rise substantially, a firm might shut down and supply no ice cream at all. Thus, the supply of a good is negatively related to the price of the inputs used to make the good.

Technology   The technology for turning inputs into ice cream is another determinant of supply. The invention of the mechanized ice-cream machine, for example, reduced the amount of labor necessary to make ice cream. By reducing firms' costs, the advance in technology raised the supply of ice cream.

Expectations   The amount of ice cream a firm supplies today may depend on its expectations of the future. For example, if a firm expects the price of ice cream to rise in the future, it will put some of its current production into storage and supply less to the market today.

Number of Sellers   Market supply depends on all those factors that influence the supply of individual sellers, such as the prices of inputs used to produce the good, the available technology, and expectations. In addition, the supply in a market depends on the number of sellers. If Ben or Jerry were to retire from the ice-cream business, the supply in the market would fall.

Summary   The supply curve shows what happens to the quantity supplied of a good when its price varies, holding constant all the other variables that influence sellers. When one of these other variables changes, the supply curve shifts. Table 2 lists the variables that influence how much producers choose to sell of a good.

Once again, to remember whether you need to shift or move along the supply curve, keep in mind that a curve shifts only when there is a change in a relevant

2 TABLE

Variables That Influence Sellers
This table lists the variables that affect how much producers choose to sell of any good. Notice the special role that the price of the good plays: A change in the good's price represents a movement along the supply curve, whereas a change in one of the other variables shifts the supply curve.

Variable	A Change in This Variable...
Price	Represents a movement along the supply curve
Input prices	Shifts the supply curve
Technology	Shifts the supply curve
Expectations	Shifts the supply curve
Number of sellers	Shifts the supply curve

variable that is not named on either axis. The price is on the vertical axis, so a change in price represents a movement along the supply curve. By contrast, because input prices, technology, expectations, and the number of sellers are not measured on either axis, a change in one of these variables shifts the supply curve.

Quick Quiz Make up an example of a supply schedule for pizza and graph the implied supply curve. • Give an example of something that would shift this supply curve. • Would a change in the price of pizza shift this supply curve?

SUPPLY AND DEMAND TOGETHER

Having analyzed supply and demand separately, we now combine them to see how they determine the quantity of a good sold in a market and its price.

Equilibrium

Figure 8 shows the market supply curve and market demand curve together. Notice that there is one point at which the supply and demand curves intersect. This point is called the market's **equilibrium.** The price at this intersection is called the **equilibrium price,** and the quantity is called the **equilibrium quantity.** Here the equilibrium price is $2.00 per cone, and the equilibrium quantity is 7 ice-cream cones.

The dictionary defines the word *equilibrium* as a situation in which various forces are in balance—and this also describes a market's equilibrium. *At the equilibrium price, the quantity of the good that buyers are willing and able to buy exactly balances the quantity that sellers are willing and able to sell.* The equilibrium price is sometimes called the *market-clearing price* because, at this price, everyone in the

equilibrium
a situation in which the market price has reached the level at which quantity supplied equals quantity demanded

equilibrium price
the price that balances quantity supplied and quantity demanded

equilibrium quantity
the quantity supplied and the quantity demanded at the equilibrium price

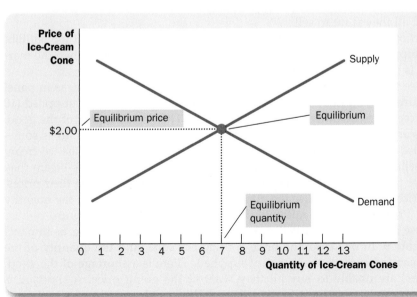

FIGURE 8

The Equilibrium of Supply and Demand
The equilibrium is found where the supply and demand curves intersect. At the equilibrium price, the quantity supplied equals the quantity demanded. Here the equilibrium price is $2.00: At this price, 7 ice-cream cones are supplied, and 7 ice-cream cones are demanded.

FIGURE

Markets Not in Equilibrium

In panel (a), there is a surplus. Because the market price of $2.50 is above the equilibrium price, the quantity supplied (10 cones) exceeds the quantity demanded (4 cones). Suppliers try to increase sales by cutting the price of a cone, and this moves the price toward its equilibrium level. In panel (b), there is a shortage. Because the market price of $1.50 is below the equilibrium price, the quantity demanded (10 cones) exceeds the quantity supplied (4 cones). With too many buyers chasing too few goods, suppliers can take advantage of the shortage by raising the price. Hence, in both cases, the price adjustment moves the market toward the equilibrium of supply and demand.

market has been satisfied: Buyers have bought all they want to buy, and sellers have sold all they want to sell.

The actions of buyers and sellers naturally move markets toward the equilibrium of supply and demand. To see why, consider what happens when the market price is not equal to the equilibrium price.

Suppose first that the market price is above the equilibrium price, as in panel (a) of Figure 9. At a price of $2.50 per cone, the quantity of the good supplied (10 cones) exceeds the quantity demanded (4 cones). There is a **surplus** of the good: Suppliers are unable to sell all they want at the going price. A surplus is sometimes called a situation of *excess supply*. When there is a surplus in the ice-cream market, sellers of ice cream find their freezers increasingly full of ice cream they would like to sell but cannot. They respond to the surplus by cutting their prices. Falling prices, in turn, increase the quantity demanded and decrease the quantity supplied. Prices continue to fall until the market reaches the equilibrium.

Suppose now that the market price is below the equilibrium price, as in panel (b) of Figure 9. In this case, the price is $1.50 per cone, and the quantity of the good demanded exceeds the quantity supplied. There is a **shortage** of the good: Demanders are unable to buy all they want at the going price. A shortage is sometimes called a situation of *excess demand*. When a shortage occurs in the ice-

surplus
a situation in which quantity supplied is greater than quantity demanded

shortage
a situation in which quantity demanded is greater than quantity supplied

cream market, buyers have to wait in long lines for a chance to buy one of the few cones available. With too many buyers chasing too few goods, sellers can respond to the shortage by raising their prices without losing sales. As the price rises, the quantity demanded falls, the quantity supplied rises, and the market once again moves toward the equilibrium.

Thus, the activities of the many buyers and sellers automatically push the market price toward the equilibrium price. Once the market reaches its equilibrium, all buyers and sellers are satisfied, and there is no upward or downward pressure on the price. How quickly equilibrium is reached varies from market to market depending on how quickly prices adjust. In most free markets, surpluses and shortages are only temporary because prices eventually move toward their equilibrium levels. Indeed, this phenomenon is so pervasive that it is called the **law of supply and demand:** The price of any good adjusts to bring the quantity supplied and quantity demanded for that good into balance.

law of supply and demand
the claim that the price of any good adjusts to bring the quantity supplied and the quantity demanded for that good into balance

Three Steps to Analyzing Changes in Equilibrium

So far, we have seen how supply and demand together determine a market's equilibrium, which in turn determines the price of the good and the amount of the good that buyers purchase and sellers produce. Of course, the equilibrium price and quantity depend on the position of the supply and demand curves. When some event shifts one of these curves, the equilibrium in the market changes, resulting in a new price and a new quantity exchanged between buyers and sellers.

When analyzing how some event affects the equilibrium in a market, we proceed in three steps. First, we decide whether the event shifts the supply curve, the demand curve, or in some cases, both curves. Second, we decide whether the curve shifts to the right or to the left. Third, we use the supply-and-demand diagram to compare the initial and the new equilibrium, which shows how the shift affects the equilibrium price and quantity. Table 3 summarizes these three steps. To see how this recipe is used, let's consider various events that might affect the market for ice cream.

Example: A Change in Demand   Suppose that one summer the weather is very hot. How does this event affect the market for ice cream? To answer this question, let's follow our three steps.

<table>

3 T A B L E	1. Decide whether the event shifts the supply or demand curve (or perhaps both).
Three Steps for Analyzing Changes in Equilibrium	2. Decide in which direction the curve shifts.
	3. Use the supply-and-demand diagram to see how the shift changes the equilibrium price and quantity.

</table>

1. The hot weather affects the demand curve by changing people's taste for ice cream. That is, the weather changes the amount of ice cream that people want to buy at any given price. The supply curve is unchanged because the weather does not directly affect the firms that sell ice cream.

2. Because hot weather makes people want to eat more ice cream, the demand curve shifts to the right. Figure 10 shows this increase in demand as the shift in the demand curve from D_1 to D_2. This shift indicates that the quantity of ice cream demanded is higher at every price.

3. As Figure 10 shows, the increase in demand raises the equilibrium price from $2.00 to $2.50 and the equilibrium quantity from 7 to 10 cones. In other

10 F I G U R E

How an Increase in Demand Affects the Equilibrium

An event that raises quantity demanded at any given price shifts the demand curve to the right. The equilibrium price and the equilibrium quantity both rise. Here an abnormally hot summer causes buyers to demand more ice cream. The demand curve shifts from D_1 to D_2, which causes the equilibrium price to rise from $2.00 to $2.50 and the equilibrium quantity to rise from 7 to 10 cones.

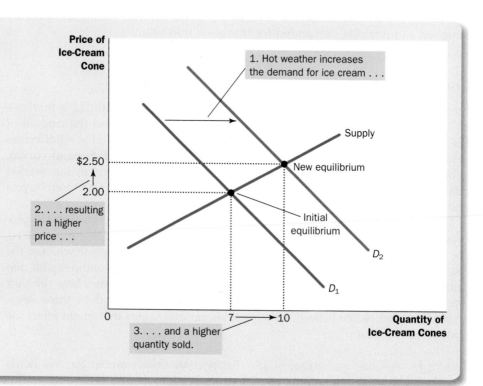

words, the hot weather increases the price of ice cream and the quantity of ice cream sold.

Shifts in Curves versus Movements along Curves   Notice that when hot weather drives up the price of ice cream, the quantity of ice cream that firms supply rises, even though the supply curve remains the same. In this case, economists say there has been an increase in "quantity supplied" but no change in "supply."

Supply refers to the position of the supply curve, whereas the *quantity supplied* refers to the amount suppliers wish to sell. In this example, supply does not change because the weather does not alter firms' desire to sell at any given price. Instead, the hot weather alters consumers' desire to buy at any given price and thereby shifts the demand curve. The increase in demand causes the equilibrium price to rise. When the price rises, the quantity supplied rises. This increase in quantity supplied is represented by the movement along the supply curve.

To summarize, a shift *in* the supply curve is called a "change in supply," and a shift *in* the demand curve is called a "change in demand." A movement *along* a fixed supply curve is called a "change in the quantity supplied," and a movement *along* a fixed demand curve is called a "change in the quantity demanded."

Example: A Change in Supply   Suppose that during another summer, a hurricane destroys part of the sugarcane crop and drives up the price of sugar. How does this event affect the market for ice cream? Once again, to answer this question, we follow our three steps.

1. The change in the price of sugar, an input into making ice cream, affects the supply curve. By raising the costs of production, it reduces the amount of ice cream that firms produce and sell at any given price. The demand curve does not change because the higher cost of inputs does not directly affect the amount of ice cream households wish to buy.
2. The supply curve shifts to the left because, at every price, the total amount that firms are willing and able to sell is reduced. Figure 11 illustrates this decrease in supply as a shift in the supply curve from S_1 to S_2.
3. As Figure 11 shows, the shift in the supply curve raises the equilibrium price from $2.00 to $2.50 and lowers the equilibrium quantity from 7 to 4 cones. As a result of the sugar price increase, the price of ice cream rises, and the quantity of ice cream sold falls.

Example: A Change in Both Supply and Demand   Now suppose that a heat wave and a hurricane occur during the same summer. To analyze this combination of events, we again follow our three steps.

1. We determine that both curves must shift. The hot weather affects the demand curve because it alters the amount of ice cream that households want to buy at any given price. At the same time, when the hurricane drives up sugar prices, it alters the supply curve for ice cream because it changes the amount of ice cream that firms want to sell at any given price.
2. The curves shift in the same directions as they did in our previous analysis: The demand curve shifts to the right, and the supply curve shifts to the left. Figure 12 illustrates these shifts.

11 FIGURE

How a Decrease in Supply Affects the Equilibrium

An event that reduces quantity supplied at any given price shifts the supply curve to the left. The equilibrium price rises, and the equilibrium quantity falls. Here an increase in the price of sugar (an input) causes sellers to supply less ice cream. The supply curve shifts from S_1 to S_2, which causes the equilibrium price of ice cream to rise from $2.00 to $2.50 and the equilibrium quantity to fall from 7 to 4 cones.

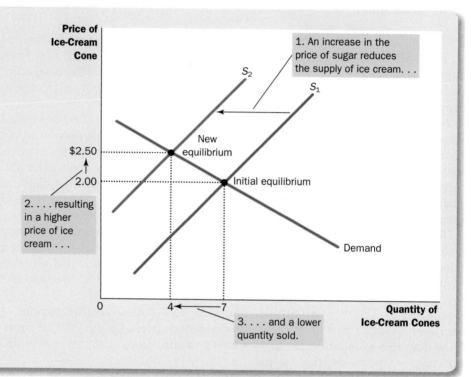

12 FIGURE

A Shift in Both Supply and Demand

Here we observe a simultaneous increase in demand and decrease in supply. Two outcomes are possible. In panel (a), the equilibrium price rises from P_1 to P_2, and the equilibrium quantity rises from Q_1 to Q_2. In panel (b), the equilibrium price again rises from P_1 to P_2, but the equilibrium quantity falls from Q_1 to Q_2.

In The News

Political Unrest Shifts the Supply Curve

According to our analysis, a natural disaster that reduces supply reduces the quantity sold and raises the price. Sometimes the same is true with disasters caused by humans.

Chocolate Lovers Fret over Ivory Cocoa Woes

By Jennifer Heldt Powell

Political unrest overseas threatens to disrupt the supply of America's sweetest temptations.

Fighting on the Ivory Coast, which supplies 45 percent of the world's cocoa, has sent cocoa prices soaring just as the harvest season begins. And unless peacekeepers can bring order, chocolate prices could soar as well.

"There is hope that international pressure will quell the fighting," said Ann Prendergast, an analyst with Refco, a commodities trading company in New York. "If it doesn't, it's going to be just horrible and there won't be much cocoa coming out of the Ivory Coast."

The most recent troubles began last week when Ivory Coast government forces attacked the rebel-held towns in the northern part of the country. That was followed by air strikes on a French camp that killed nine soldiers and an American civilian.

Cocoa prices rose 9.7 percent, the steepest increase in five years. . . .

The surge could affect high end chocolate makers who rely on the prime cocoa butter produced by the Ivory Coast, said Prendergast. How much of an effect depends on peace efforts and the farmers.

"As the price goes up, farmers have motivation to do anything they can to get their product to the market," said Prendergast.

Source: *The Boston Herald*, November 9, 2004, p. 3. Reprinted with permission by *The Boston Herald*.

3. As Figure 12 shows, two possible outcomes might result depending on the relative size of the demand and supply shifts. In both cases, the equilibrium price rises. In panel (a), where demand increases substantially while supply falls just a little, the equilibrium quantity also rises. By contrast, in panel (b), where supply falls substantially while demand rises just a little, the equilibrium quantity falls. Thus, these events certainly raise the price of ice cream, but their impact on the amount of ice cream sold is ambiguous (that is, it could go either way).

Summary We have just seen three examples of how to use supply and demand curves to analyze a change in equilibrium. Whenever an event shifts the supply curve, the demand curve, or perhaps both curves, you can use these tools to predict how the event will alter the amount sold in equilibrium and the price

4 TABLE

What Happens to Price and Quantity When Supply or Demand Shifts?
As a quick quiz, make sure you can explain each of the entries in this table using a supply-and-demand diagram.

	No Change in Supply	An Increase in Supply	A Decrease in Supply
No Change in Demand	P same Q same	P down Q up	P up Q down
An Increase in Demand	P up Q up	P ambiguous Q up	P up Q ambiguous
A Decrease in Demand	P down Q down	P down Q ambiguous	P ambiguous Q down

at which the good is sold. Table 4 shows the predicted outcome for any combination of shifts in the two curves. To make sure you understand how to use the tools of supply and demand, pick a few entries in this table and make sure you can explain to yourself why the table contains the prediction it does.

Quick Quiz Analyze what happens to the market for pizza if the price of tomatoes rises. • Analyze what happens to the market for pizza if the price of hamburgers falls.

CONCLUSION: HOW PRICES ALLOCATE RESOURCES

This chapter has analyzed supply and demand in a single market. Although our discussion has centered around the market for ice cream, the lessons learned here apply in most other markets as well. Whenever you go to a store to buy something, you are contributing to the demand for that item. Whenever you look for a job, you are contributing to the supply of labor services. Because supply and demand are such pervasive economic phenomena, the model of supply and demand is a powerful tool for analysis. We will be using this model repeatedly in the following chapters.

 One of the *Ten Principles of Economics* discussed in Chapter 1 is that markets are usually a good way to organize economic activity. Although it is still too early to judge whether market outcomes are good or bad, in this chapter we have begun to see how markets work. In any economic system, scarce resources have to be allocated among competing uses. Market economies harness the forces of supply and demand to serve that end. Supply and demand together determine the prices of the economy's many different goods and services; prices in turn are the signals that guide the allocation of resources.

For example, consider the allocation of beachfront land. Because the amount of this land is limited, not everyone can enjoy the luxury of living by the beach. Who gets this resource? The answer is whoever is willing and able to pay the price. The price of beachfront land adjusts until the quantity of land demanded exactly balances the quantity supplied. Thus, in market economies, prices are the mechanism for rationing scarce resources.

Similarly, prices determine who produces each good and how much is produced. For instance, consider farming. Because we need food to survive, it is crucial that some people work on farms. What determines who is a farmer and who is not? In a free society, there is no government planning agency making this decision and ensuring an adequate supply of food. Instead, the allocation of workers to farms is based on the job decisions of millions of workers. This decentralized system works well because these decisions depend on prices. The prices of food and the wages of farmworkers (the price of their labor) adjust to ensure that enough people choose to be farmers.

If a person had never seen a market economy in action, the whole idea might seem preposterous. Economies are large groups of people engaged in many interdependent activities. What prevents decentralized decision making from degenerating into chaos? What coordinates the actions of the millions of people with their varying abilities and desires? What ensures that what needs to get done does in fact get done? The answer, in a word, is *prices*. If market economies are guided by an invisible hand, as Adam Smith famously suggested, then the price system is the baton that the invisible hand uses to conduct the economic orchestra.

"Two dollars"   "—and seventy-five cents."

SUMMARY

- Economists use the model of supply and demand to analyze competitive markets. In a competitive market, there are many buyers and sellers, each of whom has little or no influence on the market price.

- The demand curve shows how the quantity of a good demanded depends on the price. According to the law of demand, as the price of a good falls, the quantity demanded rises. Therefore, the demand curve slopes downward.

- In addition to price, other determinants of how much consumers want to buy include income, the prices of substitutes and complements, tastes, expectations, and the number of buyers. If one of these factors changes, the demand curve shifts.

- The supply curve shows how the quantity of a good supplied depends on the price. According to the law of supply, as the price of a good rises, the quantity supplied rises. Therefore, the supply curve slopes upward.

- In addition to price, other determinants of how much producers want to sell include input prices, technology, expectations, and the number of sellers. If one of these factors changes, the supply curve shifts.

- The intersection of the supply and demand curves determines the market equilibrium. At the equilibrium price, the quantity demanded equals the quantity supplied.

- The behavior of buyers and sellers naturally drives markets toward their equilibrium. When the market price is above the equilibrium price, there is a surplus of the good, which causes the market price to fall. When the market price is below the equilibrium price, there is a shortage, which causes the market price to rise.

- To analyze how any event influences a market, we use the supply-and-demand diagram to examine how the event affects the equilibrium price and quantity. To do this, we follow three steps. First, we decide whether the event shifts the supply curve or the demand curve (or both). Second, we decide which direction the curve shifts. Third, we compare the new equilibrium with the initial equilibrium.

- In market economies, prices are the signals that guide economic decisions and thereby allocate scarce resources. For every good in the economy, the price ensures that supply and demand are in balance. The equilibrium price then determines how much of the good buyers choose to purchase and how much sellers choose to produce.

KEY CONCEPTS

market, p. 64
competitive market, p. 64
quantity demanded, p. 65
law of demand, p. 65
demand schedule, p. 65
demand curve, p. 66
normal good, p. 68

inferior good, p. 68
substitutes, p. 68
complements, p. 68
quantity supplied, p. 71
law of supply, p. 71
supply schedule, p. 71
supply curve, p. 71

equilibrium, p. 75
equilibrium price, p. 75
equilibrium quantity, p. 75
surplus, p. 76
shortage, p. 76
law of supply and demand, p. 77

QUESTIONS FOR REVIEW

1. What is a competitive market? Briefly describe a type of market that is not perfectly competitive.

2. What determines the quantity of a good that buyers demand?

3. What are the demand schedule and the demand curve and how are they related? Why does the demand curve slope downward?

4. Does a change in consumers' tastes lead to a movement along the demand curve or a shift in the demand curve? Does a change in price lead to a movement along the demand curve or a shift in the demand curve?

5. Popeye's income declines, and as a result, he buys more spinach. Is spinach an inferior or a normal good? What happens to Popeye's demand curve for spinach?

6. What determines the quantity of a good that sellers supply?

7. What are the supply schedule and the supply curve and how are they related? Why does the supply curve slope upward?

8. Does a change in producers' technology lead to a movement along the supply curve or a shift in the supply curve? Does a change in price lead to a movement along the supply curve or a shift in the supply curve?

9. Define the equilibrium of a market. Describe the forces that move a market toward its equilibrium.

10. Beer and pizza are complements because they are often enjoyed together. When the price of beer rises, what happens to the supply, demand, quantity supplied, quantity demanded, and price in the market for pizza?

11. Describe the role of prices in market economies.

PROBLEMS AND APPLICATIONS

1. Explain each of the following statements using supply-and-demand diagrams.
   a. "When a cold snap hits Florida, the price of orange juice rises in supermarkets throughout the country."
   b. "When the weather turns warm in New England every summer, the price of hotel rooms in Caribbean resorts plummets."
   c. "When a war breaks out in the Middle East, the price of gasoline rises, and the price of a used Cadillac falls."

2. "An increase in the demand for notebooks raises the quantity of notebooks demanded but not the quantity supplied." Is this statement true or false? Explain.

3. Consider the market for minivans. For each of the events listed here, identify which of the determinants of demand or supply are affected. Also indicate whether demand or supply increases or decreases. Then draw a diagram to show the effect on the price and quantity of minivans.
   a. People decide to have more children.
   b. A strike by steelworkers raises steel prices.
   c. Engineers develop new automated machinery for the production of minivans.
   d. The price of sports utility vehicles rises.
   e. A stock-market crash lowers people's wealth.

4. Consider the markets for DVD movies, TV screens, and tickets at movie theaters.
   a. For each pair, identify whether they are complements or substitutes:
      • DVDs and TV screens
      • DVDs and movie tickets
      • TV screens and movie tickets
   b. Suppose a technological advance reduces the cost of manufacturing TV screens. Draw a diagram to show what happens in the market for TV screens.
   c. Draw two more diagrams to show how the change in the market for TV screens affects the markets for DVDs and movie tickets.

5. Over the past 20 years, technological advances have reduced the cost of computer chips. How do you think this affected the market for computers? For computer software? For typewriters?

6. Consider these two statements from the In The News box:
   a. "Political unrest overseas threatens to disrupt the supply of America's sweetest temptations."
   b. "As the price goes up, farmers have motivation to do anything they can to get their product to the market."

   Which of these statements refers to a movement along the supply curve? Which refers to a shift in the supply curve? Explain.

7. Using supply-and-demand diagrams, show the effect of the following events on the market for sweatshirts.
   a. A hurricane in South Carolina damages the cotton crop.
   b. The price of leather jackets falls.
   c. All colleges require morning exercise in appropriate attire.
   d. New knitting machines are invented.

8. Suppose that in the year 2010 the number of births is temporarily high. How does this baby boom affect the price of baby-sitting services in 2015 and 2025? (Hint: 5-year-olds need baby-sitters, whereas 15-year-olds can be baby-sitters.)

9. Ketchup is a complement (as well as a condiment) for hot dogs. If the price of hot dogs rises, what happens to the market for ketchup? For tomatoes? For tomato juice? For orange juice?

10. The market for pizza has the following demand and supply schedules:

Price	Quantity Demanded	Quantity Supplied
$4	135 pizzas	26 pizzas
5	104	53
6	81	81
7	68	98
8	53	110
9	39	121

Graph the demand and supply curves. What is the equilibrium price and quantity in this market? If the actual price in this market were *above* the equilibrium price, what would drive the market toward the equilibrium? If the actual price in this market were *below* the equilibrium price, what would drive the market toward the equilibrium?

11. Because bagels and cream cheese are often eaten together, they are complements.
    a. We observe that both the equilibrium price of cream cheese and the equilibrium quantity of bagels have risen. What could be responsible for this pattern—a fall in the price of flour or a fall in the price of milk? Illustrate and explain your answer.
    b. Suppose instead that the equilibrium price of cream cheese has risen but the equilibrium quantity of bagels has fallen. What could be responsible for this pattern—a rise in the price of flour or a rise in the price of milk? Illustrate and explain your answer.

12. Suppose that the price of basketball tickets at your college is determined by market forces. Currently, the demand and supply schedules are as follows:

Price	Quantity Demanded	Quantity Supplied
$4	10,000 tickets	8,000 tickets
8	8,000	8,000
12	6,000	8,000
16	4,000	8,000
20	2,000	8,000

a. Draw the demand and supply curves. What is unusual about this supply curve? Why might this be true?

b. What are the equilibrium price and quantity of tickets?

c. Your college plans to increase total enrollment next year by 5,000 students. The additional students will have the following demand schedule:

Price	Quantity Demanded
$4	4,000 tickets
8	3,000
12	2,000
16	1,000
20	0

Now add the old demand schedule and the demand schedule for the new students to calculate the new demand schedule for the entire college. What will be the new equilibrium price and quantity?

13. Market research has revealed the following information about the market for chocolate bars: The demand schedule can be represented by the equation $Q^D = 1{,}600 - 300P$, where Q^D is the quantity demanded and P is the price. The supply schedule can be represented by the equation $Q^S = 1{,}400 + 700P$, where Q^S is the quantity supplied. Calculate the equilibrium price and quantity in the market for chocolate bars.

For further information on topics in this chapter, additional problems, examples, applications, online quizzes, and more, please visit our website at http://mankiw.swlearning.com.

3

The Data of Macroeconomics

Measuring a Nation's Income

When you finish school and start looking for a full-time job, your experience will, to a large extent, be shaped by prevailing economic conditions. In some years, firms throughout the economy are expanding their production of goods and services, employment is rising, and jobs are easy to find. In other years, firms are cutting back production, employment is declining, and finding a good job takes a long time. Not surprisingly, any college graduate would rather enter the labor force in a year of economic expansion than in a year of economic contraction.

Because the condition of the overall economy profoundly affects all of us, changes in economic conditions are widely reported by the media. Indeed, it is hard to pick up a newspaper without seeing some newly reported statistic about the economy. The statistic might measure the total income of everyone in the economy (GDP), the rate at which average prices are rising (inflation), the percentage of the labor force that is out of work (unemployment), total spending at stores (retail sales), or the imbalance of trade between the United States and the rest of the world (the trade deficit). All these statistics are *macroeconomic*. Rather than telling us about a particular household or firm, they tell us something about the entire economy.

As you may recall from Chapter 2, economics is divided into two branches: microeconomics and macroeconomics. **Microeconomics** is the study of how

microeconomics
the study of how households and firms make decisions and how they interact in markets

macroeconomics
the study of economy-wide phenomena, including inflation, unemployment, and economic growth

individual households and firms make decisions and how they interact with one another in markets. **Macroeconomics** is the study of the economy as a whole. The goal of macroeconomics is to explain the economic changes that affect many households, firms, and markets simultaneously. Macroeconomists address diverse questions: Why is average income high in some countries while it is low in others? Why do prices rise rapidly in some periods of time while they are more stable in other periods? Why do production and employment expand in some years and contract in others? What, if anything, can the government do to promote rapid growth in incomes, low inflation, and stable employment? These questions are all macroeconomic in nature because they concern the workings of the entire economy.

Because the economy as a whole is just a collection of many households and many firms interacting in many markets, microeconomics and macroeconomics are closely linked. The basic tools of supply and demand, for instance, are as central to macroeconomic analysis as they are to microeconomic analysis. Yet studying the economy in its entirety raises some new and intriguing challenges.

In this and the next chapter, we discuss some of the data that economists and policymakers use to monitor the performance of the overall economy. These data reflect the economic changes that macroeconomists try to explain. This chapter considers *gross domestic product,* or simply GDP, which measures the total income of a nation. GDP is the most closely watched economic statistic because it is thought to be the best single measure of a society's economic well-being.

THE ECONOMY'S INCOME AND EXPENDITURE

If you were to judge how a person is doing economically, you might first look at his or her income. A person with a high income can more easily afford life's necessities and luxuries. It is no surprise that people with higher incomes enjoy higher standards of living—better housing, better healthcare, fancier cars, more opulent vacations, and so on.

The same logic applies to a nation's overall economy. When judging whether the economy is doing well or poorly, it is natural to look at the total income that everyone in the economy is earning. That is the task of gross domestic product (GDP).

GDP measures two things at once: the total income of everyone in the economy and the total expenditure on the economy's output of goods and services. The reason that GDP can perform the trick of measuring both total income and total expenditure is that these two things are really the same. *For an economy as a whole, income must equal expenditure.*

Why is this true? An economy's income is the same as its expenditure because every transaction has two parties: a buyer and a seller. Every dollar of spending by some buyer is a dollar of income for some seller. Suppose, for instance, that Karen pays Doug $100 to mow her lawn. In this case, Doug is a seller of a service, and Karen is a buyer. Doug earns $100, and Karen spends $100. Thus, the transaction contributes equally to the economy's income and to its expenditure. GDP, whether measured as total income or total expenditure, rises by $100.

Another way to see the equality of income and expenditure is with the circular-flow diagram in Figure 1. As you may recall from Chapter 2, this diagram describes all the transactions between households and firms in a simple economy. It simplifies matters by assuming that all goods and services are bought by house-

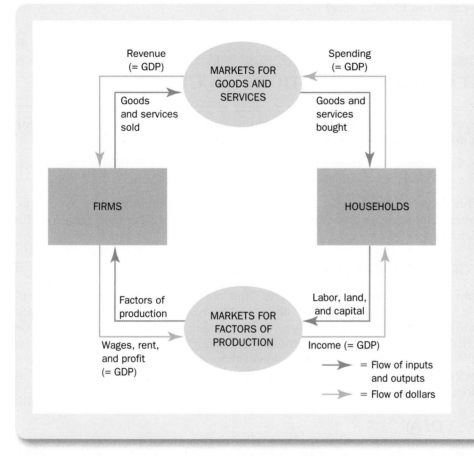

FIGURE 1

The Circular-Flow Diagram
Households buy goods and services from firms, and firms use their revenue from sales to pay wages to workers, rent to landowners, and profit to firm owners. GDP equals the total amount spent by households in the market for goods and services. It also equals the total wages, rent, and profit paid by firms in the markets for the factors of production.

holds and that households spend all of their income. In this economy, when households buy goods and services from firms, these expenditures flow through the markets for goods and services. When the firms in turn use the money they receive from sales to pay workers' wages, landowners' rent, and firm owners' profit, this income flows through the markets for the factors of production. Money continuously flows from households to firms and then back to households.

GDP measures this flow of money. We can compute it for this economy in one of two ways: by adding up the total expenditure by households or by adding up the total income (wages, rent, and profit) paid by firms. Because all expenditure in the economy ends up as someone's income, GDP is the same regardless of how we compute it.

The actual economy is, of course, more complicated than the one illustrated in Figure 1. Households do not spend all of their income; they pay some of it to the government in taxes, and they save some for use in the future. In addition, households do not buy all goods and services produced in the economy; some goods and services are bought by governments, and some are bought by firms that plan to use them in the future to produce their own output. Yet regardless of whether a household, government, or firm buys a good or service, the transaction has a buyer and seller. Thus, for the economy as a whole, expenditure and income are always the same.

Quick Quiz   What two things does gross domestic product measure? How can it measure two things at once?

THE MEASUREMENT OF GROSS DOMESTIC PRODUCT

Now that we have discussed the meaning of gross domestic product in general terms, let's be more precise about how this statistic is measured. Here is a definition of GDP that focuses on GDP as a measure of total expenditure:

gross domestic product (GDP)
the market value of all final goods and services produced within a country in a given period of time

- **Gross domestic product (GDP)** is the market value of all final goods and services produced within a country in a given period of time.

This definition might seem simple enough. But in fact, many subtle issues arise when computing an economy's GDP. Let's therefore consider each phrase in this definition with some care.

"GDP Is the Market Value . . ."

You have probably heard the adage, "You can't compare apples and oranges." Yet GDP does exactly that. GDP adds together many different kinds of products into a single measure of the value of economic activity. To do this, it uses market prices. Because market prices measure the amount people are willing to pay for different goods, they reflect the value of those goods. If the price of an apple is twice the price of an orange, then an apple contributes twice as much to GDP as does an orange.

" . . . Of All . . ."

GDP tries to be comprehensive. It includes all items produced in the economy and sold legally in markets. GDP measures the market value of not just apples and oranges but also pears and grapefruit, books and movies, haircuts and healthcare, and on and on.

GDP also includes the market value of the housing services provided by the economy's stock of housing. For rental housing, this value is easy to calculate—the rent equals both the tenant's expenditure and the landlord's income. Yet many people own the place where they live and, therefore, do not pay rent. The government includes this owner-occupied housing in GDP by estimating its rental value. In effect, GDP is based on the assumption that the owner is renting the house to himself. The imputed rent is included both in the homeowner's expenditure and in his income, so it adds to GDP.

There are some products, however, that GDP excludes because measuring them is so difficult. GDP excludes most items produced and sold illicitly, such as illegal drugs. It also excludes most items that are produced and consumed at home and, therefore, never enter the marketplace. Vegetables you buy at the grocery store are part of GDP; vegetables you grow in your garden are not.

These exclusions from GDP can at times lead to paradoxical results. For example, when Karen pays Doug to mow her lawn, that transaction is part of GDP. If Karen were to marry Doug, the situation would change. Even though Doug may continue to mow Karen's lawn, the value of the mowing is now left out of GDP because Doug's service is no longer sold in a market. Thus, when Karen and Doug marry, GDP falls.

". . . Final . . ."

When International Paper makes paper, which Hallmark then uses to make a greeting card, the paper is called an *intermediate good,* and the card is called a *final good.* GDP includes only the value of final goods. The reason is that the value of intermediate goods is already included in the prices of the final goods. Adding the market value of the paper to the market value of the card would be double counting. That is, it would (incorrectly) count the paper twice.

An important exception to this principle arises when an intermediate good is produced and, rather than being used, is added to a firm's inventory of goods for use or sale at a later date. In this case, the intermediate good is taken to be "final" for the moment, and its value as inventory investment is added to GDP. When the inventory of the intermediate good is later used or sold, the firm's inventory investment is negative, and GDP for the later period is reduced accordingly.

". . . Goods and Services . . ."

GDP includes both tangible goods (food, clothing, cars) and intangible services (haircuts, housecleaning, doctor visits). When you buy a CD by your favorite band, you are buying a good, and the purchase price is part of GDP. When you pay to hear a concert by the same band, you are buying a service, and the ticket price is also part of GDP.

". . . Produced . . ."

GDP includes goods and services currently produced. It does not include transactions involving items produced in the past. When General Motors produces and sells a new car, the value of the car is included in GDP. When one person sells a used car to another person, the value of the used car is not included in GDP.

". . . Within a Country . . ."

GDP measures the value of production within the geographic confines of a country. When a Canadian citizen works temporarily in the United States, his production is part of U.S. GDP. When an American citizen owns a factory in Haiti, the production at his factory is not part of U.S. GDP. (It is part of Haiti's GDP.) Thus, items are included in a nation's GDP if they are produced domestically, regardless of the nationality of the producer.

". . . In a Given Period of Time."

GDP measures the value of production that takes place within a specific interval of time. Usually, that interval is a year or a quarter (three months). GDP measures the economy's flow of income and expenditure during that interval.

When the government reports the GDP for a quarter, it usually presents GDP "at an annual rate." This means that the figure reported for quarterly GDP is the amount of income and expenditure during the quarter multiplied by 4. The government uses this convention so that quarterly and annual figures on GDP can be compared more easily.

In addition, when the government reports quarterly GDP, it presents the data after they have been modified by a statistical procedure called *seasonal adjustment.* The unadjusted data show clearly that the economy produces more goods and services during some times of year than during others. (As you might guess,

December's holiday shopping season is a high point.) When monitoring the condition of the economy, economists and policymakers often want to look beyond these regular seasonal changes. Therefore, government statisticians adjust the quarterly data to take out the seasonal cycle. The GDP data reported in the news are always seasonally adjusted.

Now let's repeat the definition of GDP:

- Gross domestic product (GDP) is the market value of all final goods and services produced within a country in a given period of time.

This definition focuses on GDP as total expenditure in the economy. But don't forget that every dollar spent by a buyer of a good or service becomes a dollar of income to the seller of that good or service. Therefore, in addition to applying this definition, the government also adds up total income in the economy. The two ways of calculating GDP give almost exactly the same answer. (Why "almost"? Although the two measures should be precisely the same, data sources are not perfect. The difference between the two calculations of GDP is called the *statistical discrepancy*.)

It should be apparent that GDP is a sophisticated measure of the value of economic activity. In advanced courses in macroeconomics, you will learn more about the subtleties that arise in its calculation. But even now you can see that each phrase in this definition is packed with meaning.

Quick Quiz   Which contributes more to GDP—the production of a pound of hamburger or the production of a pound of caviar? Why?

THE COMPONENTS OF GDP

Spending in the economy takes many forms. At any moment, the Smith family may be having lunch at Burger King; General Motors may be building a car factory; the Navy may be procuring a submarine; and British Airways may be buying an airplane from Boeing. GDP includes all of these various forms of spending on domestically produced goods and services.

To understand how the economy is using its scarce resources, economists are often interested in studying the composition of GDP among various types of spending. To do this, GDP (which we denote as Y) is divided into four components: consumption (C), investment (I), government purchases (G), and net exports (NX):

$$Y = C + I + G + NX.$$

This equation is an *identity*—an equation that must be true because of how the variables in the equation are defined. In this case, because each dollar of expenditure included in GDP is placed into one of the four components of GDP, the total of the four components must be equal to GDP. Let's look at each of these four components more closely.

consumption
spending by households on goods and services, with the exception of purchases of new housing

Consumption

Consumption is spending by households on goods and services. Goods include household spending on durable goods, such as automobiles and appliances, and

FYI

Other Measures of Income

When the U.S. Department of Commerce computes the nation's GDP every three months, it also computes various other measures of income to get a more complete picture of what's happening in the economy. These other measures differ from GDP by excluding or including certain categories of income. What follows is a brief description of five of these income measures, ordered from largest to smallest.

- *Gross national product* (GNP) is the total income earned by a nation's permanent residents (called *nationals*). It differs from GDP by including income that our citizens earn abroad and excluding income that foreigners earn here. For example, when a Canadian citizen works temporarily in the United States, his production is part of U.S. GDP, but it is not part of U.S. GNP. (It is part of Canada's GNP.) For most countries, including the United States, domestic residents are responsible for most domestic production, so GDP and GNP are quite close.

- *Net national product* (NNP) is the total income of a nation's residents (GNP) minus losses from depreciation. *Depreciation* is the wear and tear on the economy's stock of equipment and structures, such as trucks rusting and computers becoming obsolete. In the national income accounts prepared by the Department of Commerce, depreciation is called the "consumption of fixed capital."

- *National income* is the total income earned by a nation's residents in the production of goods and services. It differs from net national product by excluding indirect business taxes (such as sales taxes) and including business subsidies. NNP and national income also differ because of the *statistical discrepancy* that arises from problems in data collection.

- *Personal income* is the income that households and noncorporate businesses receive. Unlike national income, it excludes *retained earnings,* which is income that corporations have earned but have not paid out to their owners. It also subtracts corporate income taxes and contributions for social insurance (mostly Social Security taxes). In addition, personal income includes the interest income that households receive from their holdings of government debt and the income that households receive from government transfer programs, such as welfare and Social Security.

- *Disposable personal income* is the income that households and noncorporate businesses have left after satisfying all their obligations to the government. It equals personal income minus personal taxes and certain nontax payments (such as traffic tickets).

Although the various measures of income differ in detail, they almost always tell the same story about economic conditions. When GDP is growing rapidly, these other measures of income are usually growing rapidly. And when GDP is falling, these other measures are usually falling as well. For monitoring fluctuations in the overall economy, it does not matter much which measure of income we use.

---

nondurable goods, such as food and clothing. Services include such intangible items as haircuts and medical care. Household spending on education is also included in consumption of services (although one might argue that it would fit better in the next component).

Investment

Investment is the purchase of goods that will be used in the future to produce more goods and services. It is the sum of purchases of capital equipment, inventories, and structures. Investment in structures includes expenditure on new housing. By convention, the purchase of a new house is the one form of household spending categorized as investment rather than consumption.

investment
spending on capital equipment, inventories, and structures, including household purchases of new housing

As mentioned earlier in this chapter, the treatment of inventory accumulation is noteworthy. When IBM produces a computer and, instead of selling it, adds it to its inventory, IBM is assumed to have "purchased" the computer for itself. That is, the national income accountants treat the computer as part of IBM's investment spending. (If IBM later sells the computer out of inventory, IBM's inventory investment will then be negative, offsetting the positive expenditure of the buyer.) Inventories are treated this way because one aim of GDP is to measure the value of the economy's production, and goods added to inventory are part of that period's production.

Notice that GDP accounting uses the word *investment* differently from how you might hear the term in everyday conversation. When you hear the word *investment*, you might think of financial investments, such as stocks, bonds, and mutual funds—topics that we study later in this book. By contrast, because GDP measures expenditure on goods and services, here the word *investment* means purchases of investment goods, including capital equipment, inventories, and structures.

Government Purchases

government purchases
spending on goods and services by local, state, and federal governments

Government purchases include spending on goods and services by local, state, and federal governments. It includes the salaries of government workers and spending on public works. Recently, the U.S. national income accounts have switched to the longer label *government consumption expenditure and gross investment*, but in this book, we will use the traditional and shorter term *government purchases*.

The meaning of government purchases requires a bit of clarification. When the government pays the salary of an Army general, that salary is part of government purchases. But what happens when the government pays a Social Security benefit to one of the elderly? Such government spending is called a *transfer payment* because it is not made in exchange for a currently produced good or service. Transfer payments alter household income, but they do not reflect the economy's production. (From a macroeconomic standpoint, transfer payments are like negative taxes.) Because GDP is intended to measure income from, and expenditure on, the production of goods and services, transfer payments are not counted as part of government purchases.

Net Exports

net exports
spending on domestically produced goods by foreigners (exports) minus spending on foreign goods by domestic residents (imports)

Net exports equal the purchases of domestically produced goods by foreigners (exports) minus the domestic purchases of foreign goods (imports). A domestic firm's sale to a buyer in another country, such as the Boeing sale to British Airways, increases net exports.

The *net* in *net exports* refers to the fact that imports are subtracted from exports. This subtraction is made because imports of goods and services are included in other components of GDP. For example, suppose that a household buys a $30,000 car from Volvo, the Swedish carmaker. That transaction increases consumption by $30,000 because car purchases are part of consumer spending. It also reduces net exports by $30,000 because the car is an import. In other words, net exports include goods and services produced abroad (with a minus sign) because these goods and services are included in consumption, investment, and government purchases (with a plus sign). Thus, when a domestic household, firm, or government buys a good or service from abroad, the purchase reduces net exports—but because it also raises consumption, investment, or government purchases, it does not affect GDP.

	Total (in billions of dollars)	Per Person (in dollars)	Percent of Total	
Gross domestic product, Y	$11,728	$39,904	100%	
Consumption, C	8,232	28,009	70	
Investment, I	1,922	6,539	16	
Government purchases, G	2,184	7,431	19	
Net exports, NX	−609	−2,072	−5	

Source: U.S. Department of Commerce.

T A B L E **1**

GDP and Its Components
This table shows total GDP for the U.S. economy in 2004 and the breakdown of GDP among its four components. When reading this table, recall the identity $Y = C + I + G + NX$.

CASE STUDY   THE COMPONENTS OF U.S. GDP

Table 1 shows the composition of U.S. GDP in 2004. In this year, the GDP of the United States was almost $12 trillion. Dividing this number by the 2004 U.S. population of 294 million yields GDP per person (sometimes called GDP per capita). We find that in 2004 the income and expenditure of the average American was $39,904.

Consumption made up 70 percent of GDP, or $28,009 per person. Investment was $6,539 per person. Government purchases were $7,431 per person. Net exports were –$2,072 per person. This number is negative because Americans earned less from selling to foreigners than they spent on foreign goods.

These data come from the Bureau of Economic Analysis, which is the part of the U.S. Department of Commerce that produces the national income accounts. You can find more recent data on GDP at its website http://www.bea.doc.gov.   •

Quick Quiz   List the four components of expenditure. Which is the largest?

REAL VERSUS NOMINAL GDP

As we have seen, GDP measures the total spending on goods and services in all markets in the economy. If total spending rises from one year to the next, one of two things must be true: (1) the economy is producing a larger output of goods and services, or (2) goods and services are being sold at higher prices. When studying changes in the economy over time, economists want to separate these two effects. In particular, they want a measure of the total quantity of goods and services the economy is producing that is not affected by changes in the prices of those goods and services.

To do this, economists use a measure called *real GDP*. Real GDP answers a hypothetical question: What would be the value of the goods and services produced this year if we valued these goods and services at the prices that prevailed in some specific year in the past? By evaluating current production using prices that are fixed at past levels, real GDP shows how the economy's overall production of goods and services changes over time.

To see more precisely how real GDP is constructed, let's consider an example.

A Numerical Example

Table 2 shows some data for an economy that produces only two goods: hot dogs and hamburgers. The table shows the quantities of the two goods produced and their prices in the years 2005, 2006, and 2007.

To compute total spending in this economy, we would multiply the quantities of hot dogs and hamburgers by their prices. In the year 2005, 100 hot dogs are sold at a price of $1 per hot dog, so expenditure on hot dogs equals $100. In the same year, 50 hamburgers are sold for $2 per hamburger, so expenditure on hamburgers also equals $100. Total expenditure in the economy—the sum of expenditure on hot dogs and expenditure on hamburgers—is $200. This amount, the production of goods and services valued at current prices, is called **nominal GDP.**

The table shows the calculation of nominal GDP for these three years. Total spending rises from $200 in 2005 to $600 in 2006 and then to $1,200 in 2007. Part of this rise is attributable to the increase in the quantities of hot dogs and hamburgers, and part is attributable to the increase in the prices of hot dogs and hamburgers.

To obtain a measure of the amount produced that is not affected by changes in prices, we use **real GDP,** which is the production of goods and services valued at constant prices. We calculate real GDP by first choosing one year as a *base year.* We then use the prices of hot dogs and hamburgers in the base year to compute the value of goods and services in all of the years. In other words, the prices in the base year provide the basis for comparing quantities in different years.

nominal GDP
the production of goods and services valued at current prices

real GDP
the production of goods and services valued at constant prices

2 TABLE

Real and Nominal GDP
This table shows how to calculate real GDP, nominal GDP, and the GDP deflator for a hypothetical economy that produces only hot dogs and hamburgers.

Prices and Quantities

Year	Price of Hot dogs	Quantity of Hot dogs	Price of Hamburgers	Quantity of Hamburgers
2005	$1	100	$2	50
2006	$2	150	$3	100
2007	$3	200	$4	150

Calculating Nominal GDP

Year	
2005	($1 per hot dog × 100 hot dogs) + ($2 per hamburger × 50 hamburgers) = $200
2006	($2 per hot dog × 150 hot dogs) + ($3 per hamburger × 100 hamburgers) = $600
2007	($3 per hot dog × 200 hot dogs) + ($4 per hamburger × 150 hamburgers) = $1,200

Calculating Real GDP (base year 2005)

Year	
2005	($1 per hot dog × 100 hot dogs) + ($2 per hamburger × 50 hamburgers) = $200
2006	($1 per hot dog × 150 hot dogs) + ($2 per hamburger × 100 hamburgers) = $350
2007	($1 per hot dog × 200 hot dogs) + ($2 per hamburger × 150 hamburgers) = $500

Calculating the GDP Deflator

Year	
2005	($200/$200) × 100 = 100
2006	($600/$350) ×100 = 171
2007	($1,200/$500) × 100 = 240

Suppose that we choose 2005 to be the base year in our example. We can then use the prices of hot dogs and hamburgers in 2005 to compute the value of goods and services produced in 2005, 2006, and 2007. Table 2 shows these calculations. To compute real GDP for 2005, we use the prices of hot dogs and hamburgers in 2005 (the base year) and the quantities of hot dogs and hamburgers produced in 2005. (Thus, for the base year, real GDP always equals nominal GDP.) To compute real GDP for 2006, we use the prices of hot dogs and hamburgers in 2005 (the base year) and the quantities of hot dogs and hamburgers produced in 2006. Similarly, to compute real GDP for 2007, we use the prices in 2005 and the quantities in 2007. When we find that real GDP has risen from $200 in 2005 to $350 in 2006 and then to $500 in 2007, we know that the increase is attributable to an increase in the quantities produced because the prices are being held fixed at base-year levels.

To sum up: *Nominal GDP uses current prices to place a value on the economy's production of goods and services. Real GDP uses constant base-year prices to place a value on the economy's production of goods and services.* Because real GDP is not affected by changes in prices, changes in real GDP reflect only changes in the amounts being produced. Thus, real GDP is a measure of the economy's production of goods and services.

Our goal in computing GDP is to gauge how well the overall economy is performing. Because real GDP measures the economy's production of goods and services, it reflects the economy's ability to satisfy people's needs and desires. Thus, real GDP is a better gauge of economic well-being than is nominal GDP. When economists talk about the economy's GDP, they usually mean real GDP rather than nominal GDP. And when they talk about growth in the economy, they measure that growth as the percentage change in real GDP from one period to another.

The GDP Deflator

As we have just seen, nominal GDP reflects both the prices of goods and services and the quantities of goods and services the economy is producing. By contrast, by holding prices constant at base-year levels, real GDP reflects only the quantities produced. From these two statistics, we can compute a third, called the GDP deflator, which reflects the prices of goods and services but not the quantities produced.

The **GDP deflator** is calculated as follows:

$$\text{GDP deflator} = \frac{\text{Nominal GDP}}{\text{Real GDP}} \times 100.$$

GDP deflator
a measure of the price level calculated as the ratio of nominal GDP to real GDP times 100

Because nominal GDP and real GDP must be the same in the base year, the GDP deflator for the base year always equals 100. The GDP deflator for subsequent years measures the change in nominal GDP from the base year that cannot be attributable to a change in real GDP.

The GDP deflator measures the current level of prices relative to the level of prices in the base year. To see why this is true, consider a couple of simple examples. First, imagine that the quantities produced in the economy rise over time but prices remain the same. In this case, both nominal and real GDP rise together, so the GDP deflator is constant. Now suppose, instead, that prices rise over time but the quantities produced stay the same. In this second case, nominal GDP rises but real GDP remains the same, so the GDP deflator rises as well. Notice that, in both cases, the GDP deflator reflects what's happening to prices, not quantities.

Let's now return to our numerical example in Table 2. The GDP deflator is computed at the bottom of the table. For year 2005, nominal GDP is $200, and real GDP is $200, so the GDP deflator is 100. For the year 2006, nominal GDP is $600, and real GDP is $350, so the GDP deflator is 171. Because the GDP deflator rose in year 2006 from 100 to 171, we can say that the price level increased by 71 percent. The percentage increase in the price level is the rate of inflation.

The GDP deflator is one measure that economists use to monitor the average level of prices in the economy and thus the rate of inflation. The GDP deflator gets its name because it can be used to take inflation out of nominal GDP—that is, to "deflate" nominal GDP for the rise that is due to increases in prices. We examine another measure of the economy's price level, called the consumer price index, in the next chapter, where we also describe the differences between the two measures.

CASE STUDY | REAL GDP OVER RECENT HISTORY

Now that we know how real GDP is defined and measured, let's look at what this macroeconomic variable tells us about the recent history of the United States. Figure 2 shows quarterly data on real GDP for the U.S. economy since 1965.

The most obvious feature of these data is that real GDP grows over time. The real GDP of the U.S. economy in 2004 was almost four times its 1965 level. Put differently, the output of goods and services produced in the United States has grown on average 3.2 percent per year. This continued growth in real GDP enables the typical American to enjoy greater economic prosperity than his or her parents and grandparents did.

A second feature of the GDP data is that growth is not steady. The upward climb of real GDP is occasionally interrupted by periods during which GDP declines, called *recessions*. Figure 2 marks recessions with shaded vertical bars. (There is no ironclad rule for when the official business cycle dating committee will declare that a recession has occurred, but an old rule of thumb is two consecutive quarters of falling real GDP.) Recessions are associated not only with

2 FIGURE

Real GDP in the United States
This figure shows quarterly data on real GDP for the U.S. economy since 1965. Recessions—periods of falling real GDP—are marked with the shaded vertical bars.

Source: U.S. Department of Commerce.

In The News

GDP Lightens Up

GDP measures the value of the economy's output of goods and services. What do you think we would learn if, instead, we measured the weight of the economy's output?

From Greenspan, a (Truly) Weighty Idea

By David Wessel

Having weighed the evidence carefully, Federal Reserve Chairman Alan Greenspan wants you to know that the U.S. economy is getting lighter.

Literally.

When he refers to "downsizing" in this instance, Mr. Greenspan means that a dollar's worth of the goods and services produced in the mighty U.S. economy weighs a lot less than it used to, even after adjusting for inflation.

A modern 10-story office building, he says, weighs less than a 10-story building erected in the late 19th century. With synthetic fibers, clothes weigh less. And the electronics revolution has produced televisions so light they can be worn on the wrist.

By conventional measures, the [real] gross domestic product—the value of all goods and services produced in the nation—is five times as great as it was 50 years ago. Yet "the physical weight of our gross domestic product is evidently only modestly higher than it was 50 or 100 years ago," Mr. Greenspan told an audience in Dallas recently.

When you think about it, it's not so surprising that the economy is getting lighter. An ever-growing proportion of the U.S. GDP consists of things that don't weigh anything at all—lawyers' services, psychotherapy, e-mail, online information.

But Mr. Greenspan has a way of making the obvious sound profound. Only "a small fraction" of the nation's economic growth in the past several decades "represents growth in the tonnage of physical materials—oil, coal, ores, wood, raw chemicals," he has observed. "The remainder represents new insights into how to rearrange those physical materials to better serve human needs." . . .

The incredible shrinking GDP helps explain why American workers can produce more for each hour of work than ever before. . . . [It] also helps explain why there is so much international trade these days. "The . . . downsizing of output," Mr. Greenspan said recently, "meant that products were easier and hence less costly to move, and most especially across national borders." . . .

"The world of 1948 was vastly different," Mr. Greenspan observed a few years back. "The quintessential model of industry might in those days was the array of vast, smoke-encased integrated steel mills . . . on the shores of Lake Michigan. Output was things, big physical things."

Today, one exemplar of U.S. economic might is Microsoft Corp., with its almost weightless output. "Virtually unimaginable a half-century ago was the extent to which concepts and ideas would substitute for physical resources and human brawn in the production of goods and services," he has said.

Of course, one thing made in the U.S. is heavier than it used to be: people. The National Institutes of Health says 22.3% of Americans are obese, up from 12.8% in the early 1960s. But Mr. Greenspan doesn't talk about that.

Source: *The Wall Street Journal*, May 20, 1999, p. B1. Copyright 1999 by DOW JONES & CO INC. Reproduced with permission of DOW JONES & CO INC.

lower incomes but also with other forms of economic distress: rising unemployment, falling profits, increased bankruptcies, and so on.

Much of macroeconomics is aimed at explaining the long-run growth and short-run fluctuations in real GDP. As we will see in the coming chapters, we need different models for these two purposes. Because the short-run fluctuations represent deviations from the long-run trend, we first examine the behavior of key macroeconomic variables, including real GDP, in the long run. Then in later chapters, we build on this analysis to explain short-run fluctuations.   •

In The News

The Underground Economy

The gross domestic product misses many transactions that take place in the underground economy.

Searching for the Hidden Economy

By Doug Campbell

Here is the brief, unremarkable story of how I recently came to participate in the underground economy:

Midafternoon on the iciest day this past winter, a man knocked at my front door. "Shovel your walk?" he asked. "Only $5."

Outside, it was a bone-chilling 15 degrees. "Sold," I said. A half-hour later I handed over a five-dollar bill and thanked him for saving me the trouble.

Officially, this was an unofficial transaction—off the books, with no taxes paid or safety regulations followed. (At least, I assume this hired hand didn't bother to report that income or register with the proper authorities.) As such, it was technically illegal. And,

of course, it's the sort of thing that happens all the time.

International Differences in the Underground Economy

Country	Underground Economy as a Percent of GDP
Bolivia	68 percent
Zimbabwe	63
Peru	61
Thailand	54
Mexico	33
Argentina	29
Sweden	18
Australia	13
United Kingdom	12
Japan	11
Switzerland	9
United States	8

Source: Friedrich Schneider. Figures are for 2002.

The size of the official U.S. economy, as measured by Gross Domestic Product (GDP), was almost $12 trillion in 2004. Measurements of the unofficial economy—not including illegal activities like drug dealing and prostitution—differ substantially. But it's generally agreed to be significant, somewhere between 6 percent and 20 percent of GDP. At the midpoint, this would be about $1.5 trillion a year.

Broadly defined, the underground, gray, informal, or shadow economy involves otherwise legal transactions that go unreported or unrecorded. That's a wide net, capturing everything from babysitting fees, to bartering home repairs with a neighbor, to failing to report pay from moonlighting gigs. The "underground" label tends to make it sound much more sinister than it really is.

Quick Quiz Define *real GDP* and *nominal GDP*. Which is a better measure of economic well-being? Why?

IS GDP A GOOD MEASURE OF ECONOMIC WELL-BEING?

Earlier in this chapter, GDP was called the best single measure of the economic well-being of a society. Now that we know what GDP is, we can evaluate this claim.

As we have seen, GDP measures both the economy's total income and the economy's total expenditure on goods and services. Thus, GDP per person tells us the income and expenditure of the average person in the economy. Because most people

Criminal activities make up a large portion of what could be termed the total underground economy. Many studies have been done on the economics of drug dealing, prostitution, and gambling. But because money from crime is almost never recovered, many policymakers are more interested in portions of the underground economy that otherwise would be legal if not hidden from authorities. Things like shoveling walks.

Despite its intrigue, the informal economy's importance and consequences remain in debate. The reason: "You're trying to measure a phenomenon whose entire purpose is to hide itself from observation," says Ed Feige, an economist at the University of Wisconsin.

This uncertainty poses problems for policymakers. Without knowing the precise size, scope, and causes of the underground economy, how can they decide what—if anything—to do about it?

Was the man who shoveled my walk engaging in a socially positive or negative activity? Was I? Suffice it to say, some economists have dedicated their entire careers to answering questions about the underground economy—and still there is nothing close to a consensus about its size or description. . . .

Economists generally agree that the shadow economy is worse in developing nations, whose webs of bureaucratic red tape and corruption are notorious. For instance, [economist Friedrich] Schneider in 2003 published "shadow economy" estimates (defined broadly as all market-based, legal production of goods and services deliberately concealed from the authorities) for countries including: Zimbabwe, estimated at a whopping 63.2 percent of GDP, Thailand's at 54.1 percent, and Bolivia's at 68.3 percent. Among former Soviet bloc nations, Georgia led the way with a 68 percent of GDP shadow economy, and together those nations had an average 40.1 percent of GDP underground. This contrasts with an average of 16.7 percent among Western nations. . . .

In his 2003 book, *Reefer Madness: Sex, Drugs and Cheap Labor in the American Black Market,* investigative writer Eric Schlosser invokes Adam Smith's "invisible hand" theory that men pursuing their own self-interest will generate benefits for society as a whole. This invisible hand has produced a fairly sizable underground economy, and we cannot understand our entire economic

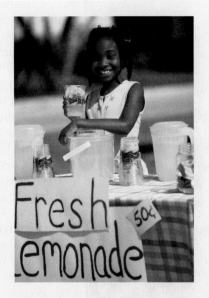

A SHADOWY ENTERPRISE?

system without understanding how the hidden underbelly functions, too. "The underground is a good measure of the progress and the health of nations," Schlosser writes. "When much is wrong, much needs to be hidden." Schlosser's implication was that much is wrong in the United States. If he had taken a more global view, he might have decided relatively little is hidden here.

Source: "Region Focus," Federal Reserve Bank of Richmond, Spring 2005.

would prefer to receive higher income and enjoy higher expenditure, GDP per person seems a natural measure of the economic well-being of the average individual.

Yet some people dispute the validity of GDP as a measure of well-being. When Senator Robert Kennedy was running for president in 1968, he gave a moving critique of such economic measures:

> [Gross domestic product] does not allow for the health of our children, the quality of their education, or the joy of their play. It does not include the beauty of our poetry or the strength of our marriages, the intelligence of our public debate or the integrity of our public officials. It measures neither our courage, nor our wisdom, nor our devotion to our country. It measures everything, in short, except that which makes life worthwhile, and it can tell us everything about America except why we are proud that we are Americans.

Much of what Robert Kennedy said is correct. Why, then, do we care about GDP?

© PHOTODISC/GETTY IMAGES

GDP REFLECTS THE
FACTORY'S PRODUCTION,
BUT NOT THE HARM THAT
IT INFLICTS ON THE
ENVIRONMENT.

The answer is that a large GDP does in fact help us to lead a good life. GDP does not measure the health of our children, but nations with larger GDP can afford better healthcare for their children. GDP does not measure the quality of their education, but nations with larger GDP can afford better educational systems. GDP does not measure the beauty of our poetry, but nations with larger GDP can afford to teach more of their citizens to read and enjoy poetry. GDP does not take account of our intelligence, integrity, courage, wisdom, or devotion to country, but all of these laudable attributes are easier to foster when people are less concerned about being able to afford the material necessities of life. In short, GDP does not directly measure those things that make life worthwhile, but it does measure our ability to obtain the inputs into a worthwhile life.

GDP is not, however, a perfect measure of well-being. Some things that contribute to a good life are left out of GDP. One is leisure. Suppose, for instance, that everyone in the economy suddenly started working every day of the week, rather than enjoying leisure on weekends. More goods and services would be produced, and GDP would rise. Yet despite the increase in GDP, we should not conclude that everyone would be better off. The loss from reduced leisure would offset the gain from producing and consuming a greater quantity of goods and services.

Because GDP uses market prices to value goods and services, it excludes the value of almost all activity that takes place outside markets. In particular, GDP omits the value of goods and services produced at home. When a chef prepares a delicious meal and sells it at his restaurant, the value of that meal is part of GDP. But if the chef prepares the same meal for his family, the value he has added to the raw ingredients is left out of GDP. Similarly, childcare provided in day-care centers is part of GDP, whereas childcare by parents at home is not. Volunteer work also contributes to the well-being of those in society, but GDP does not reflect these contributions.

Another thing that GDP excludes is the quality of the environment. Imagine that the government eliminated all environmental regulations. Firms could then produce goods and services without considering the pollution they create, and GDP might rise. Yet well-being would most likely fall. The deterioration in the quality of air and water would more than offset the gains from greater production.

GDP also says nothing about the distribution of income. A society in which 100 people have annual incomes of $50,000 has GDP of $5 million and, not surprisingly, GDP per person of $50,000. So does a society in which 10 people earn $500,000 and 90 suffer with nothing at all. Few people would look at those two situations and call them equivalent. GDP per person tells us what happens to the average person, but behind the average lies a large variety of personal experiences.

In the end, we can conclude that GDP is a good measure of economic well-being for most—but not all—purposes. It is important to keep in mind what GDP includes and what it leaves out.

C A S E STUDY | INTERNATIONAL DIFFERENCES IN GDP AND THE QUALITY OF LIFE

One way to gauge the usefulness of GDP as a measure of economic well-being is to examine international data. Rich and poor countries have vastly different lev-

Country	Real GDP per Person (2002)	Life Expectancy	Adult Literacy (% of Population)	Internet Usage (% of Population)
United States	$35,750	77 years	99%	55%
Germany	27,100	78	99	41
Japan	26,940	81	99	45
Mexico	8,970	73	91	10
Russia	8,230	67	99	4
Brazil	7,770	68	86	8
China	4,580	71	91	5
Indonesia	3,230	67	88	4
India	2,670	64	61	2
Pakistan	1,940	61	42	1
Bangladesh	1,700	61	41	<0.5
Nigeria	860	52	67	<0.5

TABLE 3

GDP and the Quality of Life
The table shows GDP per person and three other measures of the quality of life for twelve major countries.

Source: *Human Development Report 2004*, United Nations.

els of GDP per person. If a large GDP leads to a higher standard of living, then we should observe GDP to be strongly correlated with various measures of the quality of life. And, in fact, we do.

Table 3 shows twelve of the world's most populous countries ranked in order of GDP per person. The table also shows life expectancy (the expected life span at birth), literacy (the percentage of the adult population who can read), and Internet usage (the percentage of the population that regularly uses the Internet). These data show a clear pattern. In rich countries, such as the United States, Germany, and Japan, people can expect to live into their late seventies, almost all of the population can read, and about half the population uses the Internet. In poor countries, such as Nigeria, Bangladesh, and Pakistan, people typically live only until their fifties or early sixties, only about half of the population is literate, and Internet usage is very rare.

Data on other aspects of the quality of life tell a similar story. Countries with low GDP per person tend to have more infants with low birth weight, higher rates of infant mortality, higher rates of maternal mortality, higher rates of child malnutrition, and less common access to safe drinking water. In countries with low GDP per person, fewer school-age children are actually in school, and those who are in school must learn with fewer teachers per student. These countries also tend to have fewer televisions, fewer telephones, fewer paved roads, and fewer households with electricity. International data leave no doubt that a nation's GDP is closely associated with its citizens' standard of living.   •

CASE STUDY | WHO WINS AT THE OLYMPICS?

Every four years, the nations of the world compete in the Olympic Games. When the games end, commentators use the number of medals a nation takes home as a measure of success. This measure seems very different from the GDP that economists use to measure success. It turns out, however, that this is not so.

Economists Andrew Bernard and Meghan Busse examined the determinants of Olympic success in a study published in the *Review of Economics and Statistics* in 2004. The most obvious explanation is population: Countries with more people will, other things equal, have more star athletes. But this is not the full story. China, India, Indonesia, and Bangladesh together have more than 40 percent of the world's population, but they typically win only 6 percent of the medals. The reason is that these countries are poor: Despite their large populations, they account for only 5 percent of the world's GDP. Their poverty prevents many gifted athletes from reaching their potential.

Bernard and Busse find that the best gauge of a nation's ability to produce world-class athletes is total GDP. A large total GDP means more medals, regardless of whether the total comes from high GDP per person or a large number of people. In other words, if two nations have the same total GDP, they can be expected to win the same number of medals, even if one nation (India) has many people and low GDP per person and the other nation (Netherlands) has few people and high GDP per person.

In addition to GDP, two other factors influence the number of medals won. The host country usually earns extra medals, reflecting the benefit that athletes get from competing on their home turf. In addition, the former communist countries of Eastern Europe (the Soviet Union, Romania, East Germany, and so on) earned more medals than other countries with similar GDP. These centrally planned economies devoted more of the nation's resources to training Olympic athletes than did free-market economies, where people have more control over their own lives.   •

Quick Quiz   Why should policymakers care about GDP?

CONCLUSION

This chapter has discussed how economists measure the total income of a nation. Measurement is, of course, only a starting point. Much of macroeconomics is aimed at revealing the long-run and short-run determinants of a nation's gross domestic product. Why, for example, is GDP higher in the United States and Japan than in India and Nigeria? What can the governments of the poorest countries do to promote more rapid growth in GDP? Why does GDP in the United States rise rapidly in some years and fall in others? What can U.S. policymakers do to reduce the severity of these fluctuations in GDP? These are the questions we will take up shortly.

At this point, it is important to acknowledge the significance of just measuring GDP. We all get some sense of how the economy is doing as we go about our lives. But the economists who study changes in the economy and the policymakers who formulate economic policies need more than this vague sense—they need concrete data on which to base their judgments. Quantifying the behavior of the economy with statistics such as GDP is, therefore, the first step to developing a science of macroeconomics.

SUMMARY

- Because every transaction has a buyer and a seller, the total expenditure in the economy must equal the total income in the economy.

- Gross domestic product (GDP) measures an economy's total expenditure on newly produced goods and services and the total income earned from the production of these goods and services. More precisely, GDP is the market value of all final goods and services produced within a country in a given period of time.

- GDP is divided among four components of expenditure: consumption, investment, government purchases, and net exports. Consumption includes spending on goods and services by households, with the exception of purchases of new housing. Investment includes spending on new equipment and structures, including households' purchases of new housing. Government

purchases include spending on goods and services by local, state, and federal governments. Net exports equal the value of goods and services produced domestically and sold abroad (exports) minus the value of goods and services produced abroad and sold domestically (imports).

- Nominal GDP uses current prices to value the economy's production of goods and services. Real GDP uses constant base-year prices to value the economy's production of goods and services. The GDP deflator—calculated from the ratio of nominal to real GDP—measures the level of prices in the economy.

- GDP is a good measure of economic well-being because people prefer higher to lower incomes. But it is not a perfect measure of well-being. For example, GDP excludes the value of leisure and the value of a clean environment.

KEY CONCEPTS

microeconomics, p. 91
macroeconomics, p. 92
gross domestic product (GDP), p. 94

consumption, p. 96
investment, p. 97
government purchases, p. 98
net exports, p. 98

nominal GDP, p. 100
real GDP, p. 100
GDP deflator, p. 101

QUESTIONS FOR REVIEW

1. Explain why an economy's income must equal its expenditure.

2. Which contributes more to GDP—the production of an economy car or the production of a luxury car? Why?

3. A farmer sells wheat to a baker for $2. The baker uses the wheat to make bread, which is sold for $3. What is the total contribution of these transactions to GDP?

4. Many years ago, Peggy paid $500 to put together a record collection. Today, she sold her albums at a garage sale for $100. How does this sale affect current GDP?

5. List the four components of GDP. Give an example of each.

6. Why do economists use real GDP rather than nominal GDP to gauge economic well-being?

7. In the year 2005, the economy produces 100 loaves of bread that sell for $2 each. In the year 2006, the economy produces 200 loaves of bread that sell for $3 each. Calculate nominal GDP, real GDP, and the GDP deflator for each year. (Use 2005 as the base year.) By what percentage does each of these three statistics rise from one year to the next?

8. Why is it desirable for a country to have a large GDP? Give an example of something that would raise GDP and yet be undesirable.

PROBLEMS AND APPLICATIONS

1. What components of GDP (if any) would each of the following transactions affect? Explain.
   a. A family buys a new refrigerator.
   b. Aunt Jane buys a new house.
   c. Ford sells a Mustang from its inventory.
   d. You buy a pizza.
   e. California repaves Highway 101.
   f. Your parents buy a bottle of French wine.
   g. Honda expands its factory in Marysville, Ohio.

2. The government purchases component of GDP does not include spending on transfer payments such as Social Security. Thinking about the definition of GDP, explain why transfer payments are excluded.

3. As the chapter states, GDP does not include the value of used goods that are resold. Why would including such transactions make GDP a less informative measure of economic well-being?

4. Below are some data from the land of milk and honey.

Year	Price of Milk	Quantity of Milk (quarts)	Price of Honey	Quantity of Honey (quarts)
2005	$1	100	$2	50
2006	$1	200	$2	100
2007	$2	200	$4	100

   a. Compute nominal GDP, real GDP, and the GDP deflator for each year, using 2005 as the base year.
   b. Compute the percentage change in nominal GDP, real GDP, and the GDP deflator in 2006 and 2007 from the preceding year. For each year, identify the variable that does not change. Explain in words why your answer makes sense.
   c. Did economic well-being rise more in 2006 or 2007? Explain.

5. Consider the following data on U.S. GDP:

Year	Nominal GDP (in billions $)	GDP Deflator (base year 1996)
2000	9,873	118
1999	9,269	113

   a. What was the growth rate of nominal GDP between 1999 and 2000? (Note: The growth rate is the percentage change from one period to the next.)
   b. What was the growth rate of the GDP deflator between 1999 and 2000?
   c. What was real GDP in 1999 measured in 1996 prices?
   d. What was real GDP in 2000 measured in 1996 prices?
   e. What was the growth rate of real GDP between 1999 and 2000?
   f. Was the growth rate of nominal GDP higher or lower than the growth rate of real GDP? Explain.

6. If prices rise, people's income from selling goods increases. The growth of real GDP ignores this gain, however. Why, then, do economists prefer real GDP as a measure of economic well-being?

7. Revised estimates of U.S. GDP are usually released by the government near the end of each month. Find a newspaper article that reports on the most recent release, or read the news release yourself at http://www.bea.doc.gov, the website of the U.S. Bureau of Economic Analysis. Discuss the recent changes in real and nominal GDP and in the components of GDP.

8. One day, Barry the Barber, Inc., collects $400 for haircuts. Over this day, his equipment depreciates in value by $50. Of the remaining $350, Barry sends $30 to the government in sales taxes, takes home $220 in wages, and retains $100 in his business to add new equipment in the future. From the $220 that Barry takes home, he pays $70 in income taxes. Based on this information, compute Barry's contribution to the following measures of income.
   a. gross domestic product
   b. net national product
   c. national income
   d. personal income
   e. disposable personal income

9. A farmer grows wheat, which he sells to a miller for $100. The miller turns the wheat into flour, which he sells to a baker for $150. The baker turns the wheat into bread, which he sells to consumers for $180. Consumers eat the bread.

a. What is GDP in this economy? Explain.

b. *Value added* is defined as the value of a producer's output minus the value of the intermediate goods that the producer buys. Assuming there are no intermediate goods beyond those described above, calculate the value added of each of the three producers.

c. What is total value added of the three producers in this economy? How does it compare to the economy's GDP? Does this example suggest another way of calculating GDP?

10. Goods and services that are not sold in markets, such as food produced and consumed at home, are generally not included in GDP. Can you think of how this might cause the numbers in the second column of Table 3 to be misleading in a comparison of the economic well-being of the United States and India? Explain.

11. Until the early 1990s, the U.S. government emphasized GNP rather than GDP as a measure of economic well-being. Which measure should the government prefer if it cares about the total income of Americans? Which measure should it prefer if it cares about the total amount of economic activity occurring in the United States?

12. The participation of women in the U.S. labor force has risen dramatically since 1970.

a. How do you think this rise affected GDP?

b. Now imagine a measure of well-being that includes time spent working in the home and taking leisure. How would the change in this measure of well-being compare to the change in GDP?

c. Can you think of other aspects of well-being that are associated with the rise in women's labor-force participation? Would it be practical to construct a measure of well-being that includes these aspects?

 For further information on topics in this chapter, additional problems, examples, applications, online quizzes, and more, please visit our website at http://mankiw.swlearning.com.

Measuring the Cost of Living

In 1931, as the U.S. economy was suffering through the Great Depression, the New York Yankees paid famed baseball player Babe Ruth a salary of $80,000. At the time, this pay was extraordinary, even among the stars of baseball. According to one story, a reporter asked Ruth whether he thought it was right that he made more than President Herbert Hoover, who had a salary of only $75,000. Ruth replied, "I had a better year."

In 2005, the median player on the New York Yankees was paid $5.8 million, and shortstop Alex Rodriquez was paid $26 million. At first, this fact might lead you to think that baseball has become vastly more lucrative over the past seven decades. But as everyone knows, the prices of goods and services have also risen. In 1931, a nickel would buy an ice-cream cone, and a quarter would buy a ticket at the local movie theater. Because prices were so much lower in Babe Ruth's day than they are today, it is not clear whether Ruth enjoyed a higher or lower standard of living than today's players.

In the preceding chapter, we looked at how economists use gross domestic product (GDP) to measure the quantity of goods and services that the economy is producing. This chapter examines how economists measure the overall cost of living. To compare Babe Ruth's salary of $80,000 with salaries from today, we need to find some way of turning dollar figures into meaningful measures of purchasing power. That is exactly the job of a statistic called the *consumer price index.* After seeing how the consumer price index is constructed, we discuss how we can use such a price index to compare dollar figures from different points in time.

The consumer price index is used to monitor changes in the cost of living over time. When the consumer price index rises, the typical family has to spend more dollars to maintain the same standard of living. Economists use the term *inflation* to describe a situation in which the economy's overall price level is rising. The *inflation rate* is the percentage change in the price level from the previous period. As we will see in the coming chapters, inflation is a closely watched aspect of macroeconomic performance and is a key variable guiding macroeconomic policy. This chapter provides the background for that analysis by showing how economists measure the inflation rate using the consumer price index.

THE CONSUMER PRICE INDEX

consumer price index (CPI)

a measure of the overall cost of the goods and services bought by a typical consumer

The **consumer price index (CPI)** is a measure of the overall cost of the goods and services bought by a typical consumer. Each month, the Bureau of Labor Statistics (BLS), which is part of the Department of Labor, computes and reports the consumer price index. In this section, we discuss how the consumer price index is calculated and what problems arise in its measurement. We also consider how this index compares to the GDP deflator, another measure of the overall level of prices, which we examined in the preceding chapter.

How the Consumer Price Index Is Calculated

When the Bureau of Labor Statistics calculates the consumer price index and the inflation rate, it uses data on the prices of thousands of goods and services. To see exactly how these statistics are constructed, let's consider a simple economy in which consumers buy only two goods: hot dogs and hamburgers. Table 1 shows the five steps that the BLS follows.

1. *Fix the basket.* Determine which prices are most important to the typical consumer. If the typical consumer buys more hot dogs than hamburgers, then the price of hot dogs is more important than the price of hamburgers and, therefore, should be given greater weight in measuring the cost of living. The Bureau of Labor Statistics sets these weights by surveying consumers and finding the basket of goods and services that the typical consumer buys. In the example in the table, the typical consumer buys a basket of 4 hot dogs and 2 hamburgers.
2. *Find the prices.* Find the prices of each of the goods and services in the basket for each point in time. The table shows the prices of hot dogs and hamburgers for 3 different years.
3. *Compute the basket's cost.* Use the data on prices to calculate the cost of the basket of goods and services at different times. The table shows this calculation for each of the 3 years. Notice that only the prices in this calculation change. By keeping the basket of goods the same (4 hot dogs and 2 hamburgers), we are isolating the effects of price changes from the effect of any quantity changes that might be occurring at the same time.

TABLE **1**

Calculating the Consumer Price Index and the Inflation Rate: An Example

This table shows how to calculate the consumer price index and the inflation rate for a hypothetical economy in which consumers buy only hot dogs and hamburgers.

Step 1: Survey Consumers to Determine a Fixed Basket of Goods

Basket = 4 hot dogs, 2 hamburgers

Step 2: Find the Price of Each Good in Each Year

Year	Price of Hot Dogs	Price of Hamburgers
2005	$1	$2
2006	2	3
2007	3	4

Step 3: Compute the Cost of the Basket of Goods in Each Year

2005	($1 per hot dog × 4 hot dogs) + ($2 per hamburger × 2 hamburgers) = $8 per basket
2006	($2 per hot dog × 4 hot dogs) + ($3 per hamburger × 2 hamburgers) = $14 per basket
2007	($3 per hot dog × 4 hot dogs) + ($4 per hamburger × 2 hamburgers) = $20 per basket

Step 4: Choose One Year as a Base Year (2005) and Compute the Consumer Price Index in Each Year

2005	($8/$8) × 100 = 100
2006	($14/$8) × 100 = 175
2007	($20/$8) × 100 = 250

Step 5: Use the Consumer Price Index to Compute the Inflation Rate from Previous Year

2006	(175 − 100)/100 × 100 = 75%
2007	(250 − 175)/175 × 100 = 43%

4. *Choose a base year and compute the index.* Designate one year as the base year, which is the benchmark against which other years are compared. (The choice of base year is arbitrary, as the index is used to measure *changes* in the cost of living.) Once the base year is chosen, the index is calculated as follows:

$$\text{Consumer price index} = \frac{\text{Price of basket of goods and services}}{\text{Price of basket in base year}} \times 100.$$

That is, the price of the basket of goods and services in each year is divided by the price of the basket in the base year, and this ratio is then multiplied by 100. The resulting number is the consumer price index.

In the example in the table, 2005 is the base year. In this year, the basket of hot dogs and hamburgers costs $8. Therefore, the price of the basket in all years is divided by $8 and multiplied by 100. The consumer price index is 100 in 2005. (The index is always 100 in the base year.) The consumer price index is 175 in 2006. This means that the price of the basket in 2006 is 175 percent of its price in the base year. Put differently, a basket of goods that costs $100 in the base year costs $175 in 2006. Similarly, the consumer price index is 250 in 2007, indicating that the price level in 2007 is 250 percent of the price level in the base year.

inflation rate
the percentage change in the price index from the preceding period

5. *Compute the inflation rate.* Use the consumer price index to calculate the **inflation rate,** which is the percentage change in the price index from the preceding period. That is, the inflation rate between two consecutive years is computed as follows:

$$\text{Inflation rate in year 2} = \frac{\text{CPI in year 2} - \text{CPI in year 1}}{\text{CPI in year 1}} \times 100.$$

In our example, the inflation rate is 75 percent in 2006 and 43 percent in 2007.

Although this example simplifies the real world by including only two goods, it shows how the Bureau of Labor Statistics computes the consumer price index and the inflation rate. The BLS collects and processes data on the prices of thousands of goods and services every month and, by following the five foregoing steps, determines how quickly the cost of living for the typical consumer is rising. When the BLS makes its monthly announcement of the consumer price index, you can usually hear the number on the evening television news or see it in the next day's newspaper.

producer price index
a measure of the cost of a basket of goods and services bought by firms

In addition to the consumer price index for the overall economy, the BLS calculates several other price indexes. It reports the index for specific metropolitan areas within the country (such as Boston, New York, and Los Angeles) and for some narrow categories of goods and services (such as food, clothing, and energy). It also calculates the **producer price index** (PPI), which measures the cost of a basket of goods and services bought by firms rather than consumers. Because firms eventually pass on their costs to consumers in the form of higher consumer prices, changes in the producer price index are often thought to be useful in predicting changes in the consumer price index.

Problems in Measuring the Cost of Living

The goal of the consumer price index is to measure changes in the cost of living. In other words, the consumer price index tries to gauge how much incomes must rise to maintain a constant standard of living. The consumer price index, however, is not a perfect measure of the cost of living. Three problems with the index are widely acknowledged but difficult to solve.

The first problem is called *substitution bias.* When prices change from one year to the next, they do not all change proportionately: Some prices rise more than others. Consumers respond to these differing price changes by buying less of the goods whose prices have risen by large amounts and by buying more of the goods whose prices have risen less or perhaps even have fallen. That is, consumers substitute toward goods that have become relatively less expensive. If a price index is computed assuming a fixed basket of goods, it ignores the possibility of consumer substitution and, therefore, overstates the increase in the cost of living from one year to the next.

FYI

What Is in the CPI's Basket?

When construct-
ing the consumer
price index, the
Bureau of Labor Statistics tries to include all the goods and services that the typical consumer buys. Moreover, it tries to weight
these goods and services according to how much consumers
buy of each item.

Figure 1 shows the breakdown of consumer spending into
the major categories of goods and services. By far the largest
category is housing, which makes up 42 percent of the typical
consumer's budget. This category includes the cost of shelter (33
percent), fuel and other utilities (5 percent), and household fur-
nishings and operation (4 percent). The next largest category, at
17 percent, is transportation, which includes spending on cars,
gasoline, buses, subways, and so on. The next category, at 15
percent, is food and beverages; this includes food at home (8
percent), food away from home (6 percent), and alcoholic beverages (1 percent). Next are medical care, recreation, and education and communication, each at about 6 percent. This last category includes, for example, college tuition and personal
computers. Apparel, which includes clothing, footwear, and jewelry, makes up 4 percent of the typical consumer's budget.

Also included in the figure, at 4 percent of spending, is a category for other goods and services. This is a catchall for things
consumers buy that do not naturally fit into the other categories, such as cigarettes, haircuts, and funeral expenses.

FIGURE 1

The Typical Basket of Goods and Services
This figure shows how the typical consumer divides
spending among various categories of goods and
services. The Bureau of Labor Statistics calls each
percentage the "relative importance" of the
category.

Source: Bureau of Labor Statistics.

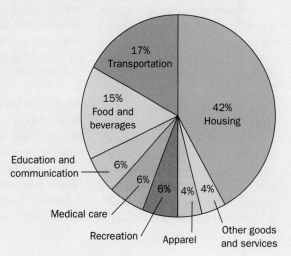

Let's consider a simple example. Imagine that in the base year, apples are
cheaper than pears, and so consumers buy more apples than pears. When the
Bureau of Labor Statistics constructs the basket of goods, it will include more
apples than pears. Suppose that next year pears are cheaper than apples. Consumers will naturally respond to the price changes by buying more pears and
fewer apples. Yet when computing the consumer price index, the BLS uses a
fixed basket, which in essence assumes that consumers continue buying the now
expensive apples in the same quantities as before. For this reason, the index will
measure a much larger increase in the cost of living than consumers actually
experience.

The second problem with the consumer price index is the *introduction of new
goods.* When a new good is introduced, consumers have more variety from which

In The News

Accounting for Quality Change

Behind every macroeconomic statistic are thousands of individual pieces of data, as well as a few key judgment calls.

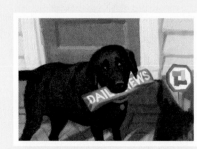

An Inflation Debate Brews over Intangibles at the Mall

By Timothy Aeppel

To most people, when the price of a 27-inch television set remains $329.99 from one month to the next, the price hasn't changed.

But not to Tim LaFleur. He's a commodity specialist for televisions at the Bureau of Labor Statistics, the government agency that assembles the Consumer Price Index. In this case, which landed on his desk last December, he decided the newer set had important improvements, including a better screen. After running the changes through a complex government computer model, he determined that the improvement in the screen was valued at more than $135. Factoring that in, he concluded the price of the TV had actually fallen 29%.

Mr. LaFleur was applying the principles of hedonics, an arcane statistical technique that's become a flashpoint in a debate over how the U.S. government measures inflation. Hedonics is essentially a way of accounting for the changing quality of products when calculating price movements. That's vital in the dynamic U.S. economy, marked by rapid technological advances. Without hedonics, the effect of consumers getting more for their money wouldn't get fully reflected in inflation numbers.

But even as the Federal Reserve raises interest rates amid a recent uptick in inflation, many critics complain the hedonic method is distorting the picture of what's going on in the economy. They say hedonics is too subjective and fear it helps keep inflation figures artificially low—meaning the Fed may already be lagging in its inflation-fighting mission.

It's critically important for consumers, business, the government and the economy as a whole that the CPI is as accurate as possible. The CPI is used to benchmark how much is paid to Social Security recipients, who last year received outlays of $487 billion. It also plays a role in adjusting lease payments, wages in union contracts, food-stamp benefits, alimony and tax brackets. . . .

Bill Gross, head of the world's largest bond fund, Pimco, caused a stir last fall by proclaiming that the way the CPI is calculated amounts to a "con job" by the government aimed at con-

to choose, and this in turn reduces the cost of maintaining the same level of economic well-being. To see why, consider a hypothetical situation: Suppose you could choose between a $100 gift certificate at a large store that offered a wide array of goods and a $100 gift certificate at a small store with the same prices but a more limited selection. Which would you prefer? Most people would pick the store with greater variety. In essence, the increased set of possible choices makes each dollar more valuable. The same is true with the evolution of economy over time: As new goods are introduced, consumers have more choices, and each dollar is worth more. Yet because the consumer price index is based on a fixed basket of goods and services, it does not reflect the increase in the value of the dollar that arises from the introduction of new goods.

Again, let's consider an example. When VCRs were introduced, consumers were able to watch their favorite movies at home. Although not a perfect substicealing the true rate of inflation. A key culprit, he said, was the CPI's growing reliance on hedonics. . . .

Inflation watchers at the statistics bureau say critics exaggerate the significance of hedonics, noting that it's used in only seven out of 211 product categories in the CPI. In most of those, officials say, hedonics actually magnifies price increases rather than suppressing them.

Take housing, which makes up about 30% of the CPI. . . . The bureau says hedonics actually helps boost the housing component of CPI. In order to take into account the aging of housing, and presumably falling quality that goes with it, the CPI applies a form of hedonics that links the age of a housing unit to rents. If someone is paying the equivalent of $500 a month in rent for several years, the rent has actually gone up as the unit ages and becomes less desirable, according to the government. . . .

The hub of this effort is a warren of beige-walled cubicles at the Bureau of Labor Statistics a few blocks from the Capitol. Here 40 commodity specialists hunch over reports with 85,000 price quotes that flow in from around the country every month. The numbers are gathered by 400 part-time data collectors. They visit stores and note prices on the items that make up the basket of goods in the CPI, ranging from ladies' shoes to skim milk to microwave ovens.

One of the biggest challenges in this process is finding substitutes for products that disappear from store shelves or change so much that they are hard to recognize from one month to the next. With TVs, for instance, data collectors find the models they priced the previous month missing about 19% of the time over the course of a year.

When that happens, the data gatherer goes through a four-page checklist of features such as screen size and the type of remote control to find the nearest comparable model. Once this process identifies a product that appears to be the closest match, the data gatherer notes its price. The commodity specialists back in Washington check over these choices and decide whether to accept them. . . .

Many price adjustments in the CPI are straightforward: When candy bars get smaller, but are sold for the same price, the CPI reflects that as a price increase.

Todd Reese, the commodity specialist for autos, says he doesn't need hedonics to extrapolate the value of quality changes, because auto makers present him with a list of changes to the car and the corresponding prices. Still, Mr. Reese must make some tough calls as he does his job. For instance, he recently considered a 2005 model in which the sticker price went from $17,890 to $18,490. The manufacturer cited an extra cost of $230 to make antilock brakes standard, while it said it saved $5 by dropping the cassette portion of the CD player.

The bureau accepted both those items, so the ostensible price increase shrank by $225. But the car maker also told Mr. Reese it wanted to subtract $30 from the price increase for the cost of putting audio controls on the steering wheel, allowing drivers to change channels without reaching for the radio dial. "We didn't allow that claim," says Mr. Reese. "We didn't judge that to be a functional change."

Source: *The Wall Street Journal*, May 9, 2005, p. A1. Copyright 2005 by DOW JONES & CO INC. Reproduced with permission of DOW JONES & CO INC.

tute for a first-run movie on a large screen, an old movie in the comfort of your family room was a new option that increased consumers' set of opportunities. For any given number of dollars, the introduction of the VCR made people better off; conversely, to achieve the same level of economic well-being required a smaller number of dollars. A perfect cost-of-living index would have reflected the introduction of the VCR with a decrease in the cost of living. The consumer price index, however, did not decrease in response to the introduction of the VCR. Eventually, the Bureau of Labor Statistics did revise the basket of goods to include VCRs, and subsequently, the index reflected changes in VCR prices. But the reduction in the cost of living associated with the initial introduction of the VCR never showed up in the index.

The third problem with the consumer price index is *unmeasured quality change*. If the quality of a good deteriorates from one year to the next, the value of a dollar falls, even if the price of the good stays the same, because you are getting a lesser good for the same amount of money. Similarly, if the quality rises from one year to the next, the value of a dollar rises. The Bureau of Labor Statistics does its best to account for quality change. When the quality of a good in the basket changes—for example, when a car model has more horsepower or gets better gas mileage from one year to the next—the Bureau adjusts the price of the good to account for the quality change. It is, in essence, trying to compute the price of a basket of goods of constant quality. Despite these efforts, changes in quality remain a problem because quality is so hard to measure.

There is still much debate among economists about how severe these measurement problems are and what should be done about them. Several studies written during the 1990s concluded that the consumer price index overstated inflation by about 1 percentage point per year. In response to this criticism, the Bureau of Labor Statistics adopted several technical changes to improve the CPI, and many economists believe the bias is now only about half as large as it once was. The issue is important because many government programs use the consumer price index to adjust for changes in the overall level of prices. Recipients of Social Security, for instance, get annual increases in benefits that are tied to the consumer price index. Some economists have suggested modifying these programs to correct for the measurement problems by, for instance, reducing the magnitude of the automatic benefit increases.

The GDP Deflator versus the Consumer Price Index

In the preceding chapter, we examined another measure of the overall level of prices in the economy—the GDP deflator. The GDP deflator is the ratio of nominal GDP to real GDP. Because nominal GDP is current output valued at current prices and real GDP is current output valued at base-year prices, the GDP deflator reflects the current level of prices relative to the level of prices in the base year.

Economists and policymakers monitor both the GDP deflator and the consumer price index to gauge how quickly prices are rising. Usually, these two statistics tell a similar story. Yet there are two important differences that can cause them to diverge.

The first difference is that the GDP deflator reflects the prices of all goods and services *produced domestically,* whereas the consumer price index reflects the prices of all goods and services *bought by consumers.* For example, suppose that the price of an airplane produced by Boeing and sold to the Air Force rises. Even though the plane is part of GDP, it is not part of the basket of goods and services bought by a typical consumer. Thus, the price increase shows up in the GDP deflator but not in the consumer price index.

As another example, suppose that Volvo raises the price of its cars. Because Volvos are made in Sweden, the car is not part of U.S. GDP. But U.S. consumers buy Volvos, and so the car is part of the typical consumer's basket of goods. Hence, a price increase in an imported consumption good, such as a Volvo, shows up in the consumer price index but not in the GDP deflator.

This first difference between the consumer price index and the GDP deflator is particularly important when the price of oil changes. Although the United States does produce some oil, much of the oil we use is imported from the Mid-

"THE PRICE MAY SEEM A LITTLE HIGH, BUT YOU HAVE TO REMEMBER THAT'S IN TODAY'S DOLLARS."

dle East. As a result, oil and oil products such as gasoline and heating oil are a much larger share of consumer spending than of GDP. When the price of oil rises, the consumer price index rises by much more than does the GDP deflator.

The second and subtler difference between the GDP deflator and the consumer price index concerns how various prices are weighted to yield a single number for the overall level of prices. The consumer price index compares the price of a *fixed* basket of goods and services to the price of the basket in the base year. Only occasionally does the Bureau of Labor Statistics change the basket of goods. By contrast, the GDP deflator compares the price of *currently produced* goods and services to the price of the same goods and services in the base year. Thus, the group of goods and services used to compute the GDP deflator changes automatically over time. This difference is not important when all prices are changing proportionately. But if the prices of different goods and services are changing by varying amounts, the way we weight the various prices matters for the overall inflation rate.

Figure 2 shows the inflation rate as measured by both the GDP deflator and the consumer price index for each year since 1965. You can see that sometimes the two measures diverge. When they do diverge, it is possible to go behind these numbers and explain the divergence with the two differences we have discussed. (For example, in 1979 and 1980, CPI inflation spiked up more than the GDP deflator largely because oil prices more than doubled during these two years.) The figure shows, however, that divergence between these two measures is the exception rather than the rule. In the 1970s, both the GDP deflator and the consumer price index show high rates of inflation. In the late 1980s, 1990s, and early 2000s, both measures show low rates of inflation.

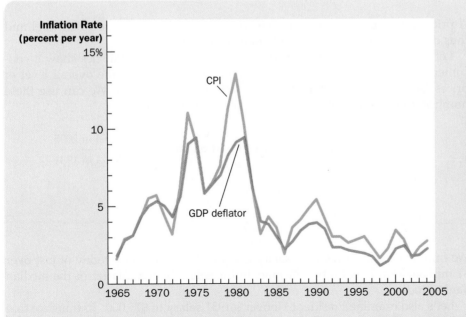

FIGURE 2

Two Measures of Inflation
This figure shows the inflation rate—the percentage change in the level of prices—as measured by the GDP deflator and the consumer price index using annual data since 1965. Notice that the two measures of inflation generally move together.

Source: U.S. Department of Labor; U.S. Department of Commerce.

Quick Quiz   Explain briefly what the consumer price index is trying to measure and how it is constructed.

CORRECTING ECONOMIC VARIABLES FOR THE EFFECTS OF INFLATION

The purpose of measuring the overall level of prices in the economy is to permit comparison between dollar figures from different points in time. Now that we know how price indexes are calculated, let's see how we might use such an index to compare a dollar figure from the past to a dollar figure in the present.

Dollar Figures from Different Times

We first return to the issue of Babe Ruth's salary. Was his salary of $80,000 in 1931 high or low compared to the salaries of today's players?

To answer this question, we need to know the level of prices in 1931 and the level of prices today. Part of the increase in baseball salaries merely compensates players for the higher level of prices today. To compare Ruth's salary to those of today's players, we need to inflate Ruth's salary to turn 1931 dollars into today's dollars.

The formula for turning dollar figures from year T into today's dollars is the following:

$$\text{Amount in today's dollars} = \text{Amount in year } T \text{ dollars} \times \frac{\text{Price level today}}{\text{Price level in year } T}.$$

A price index such as the consumer price index measures the price level and thus determines the size of the inflation correction.

Let's apply this formula to Ruth's salary. Government statistics show a consumer price index of 15.2 for 1931 and 195 for 2005. Thus, the overall level of prices has risen by a factor of 12.8 (which equals 195/15.2). We can use these numbers to measure Ruth's salary in 2005 dollars, as follows:

$$\text{Salary in 2005 dollars} = \text{Salary in 1931 dollars} \times \frac{\text{Price level in 2005}}{\text{Price level in 1931}}$$

$$= \$80,000 \times \frac{195}{15.2}$$

$$= \$1,026,316.$$

We find that Babe Ruth's 1931 salary is equivalent to a salary today of just over $1 million. That is not a bad income, but it is less than a quarter of the median Yankee today.

Let's also examine President Hoover's 1931 salary of $75,000. To translate that figure into 2005 dollars, we again multiply the ratio of the price levels in the two years. We find that Hoover's salary is equivalent to $75,000 × (195/15.2), or $962,171, in 2005 dollars. This is well above President George W. Bush's salary of $400,000. It seems that President Hoover did have a pretty good year after all.

CASE STUDY | MR. INDEX GOES TO HOLLYWOOD

What was the most popular movie of all time? The answer might surprise you.

Movie popularity is usually gauged by box office receipts. By that measure, *Titanic* is the number 1 movie of all time, followed by *Star Wars, Shrek II,* and *E.T.* But this ranking ignores an obvious but important fact: Prices, including those of movie tickets, have been rising over time. When we correct box office receipts for the effects of inflation, the story is very different.

Table 2 shows the top ten movies of all time ranked by inflation-adjusted box office receipts. The number 1 movie is *Gone with the Wind,* which was released in 1939 and is well ahead of *Titanic.* In the 1930s, before everyone had televisions in their homes, about 90 million Americans went to the cinema each week, compared to about 25 million today. But the movies from that era rarely show up in popularity rankings because ticket prices were only a quarter. Scarlett and Rhett fare a lot better once we correct for the effects of inflation.   •

© BETTMANN/CORBIS

"Frankly, my dear, I don't care much for the effects of inflation."

Indexation

As we have just seen, price indexes are used to correct for the effects of inflation when comparing dollar figures from different times. This type of correction shows up in many places in the economy. When some dollar amount is automatically corrected for inflation by law or contract, the amount is said to be *indexed* for inflation.

Film	Year of Release	Total Domestic Gross (in millions of 2004 dollars)
1. *Gone with the Wind*	1939	$1,254
2. *Star Wars*	1977	1,084
3. *The Sound of Music*	1965	870
4. *E.T.: The Extra-Terrestrial*	1982	861
5. *The Ten Commandments*	1956	801
6. *Titanic*	1997	789
7. *Jaws*	1975	783
8. *Doctor Zhivago*	1965	740
9. *The Jungle Book*	1967	662
10. *Snow White and the Seven Dwarfs*	1937	650

T A B L E 2

The Most Popular Movies of All Time, Inflation Adjusted

Source: http://www.the-movie-times.com.

indexation
the automatic correction of a dollar amount for the effects of inflation by law or contract

For example, many long-term contracts between firms and unions include partial or complete **indexation** of the wage to the consumer price index. Such a provision is called a *cost-of-living allowance,* or COLA. A COLA automatically raises the wage when the consumer price index rises.

Indexation is also a feature of many laws. Social Security benefits, for example, are adjusted every year to compensate the elderly for increases in prices. The brackets of the federal income tax—the income levels at which the tax rates change—are also indexed for inflation. There are, however, many ways in which the tax system is not indexed for inflation, even when perhaps it should be. We discuss these issues more fully when we discuss the costs of inflation later in this book.

Real and Nominal Interest Rates

Correcting economic variables for the effects of inflation is particularly important, and somewhat tricky, when we look at data on interest rates. The very concept of an interest rate necessarily involves comparing amounts of money at different points in time. When you deposit your savings in a bank account, you give the bank some money now, and the bank returns your deposit with interest in the future. Similarly, when you borrow from a bank, you get some money now, but you will have to repay the loan with interest in the future. In both cases, to fully understand the deal between you and the bank, it is crucial to acknowledge that future dollars may have different value from current dollars. That is, you have to correct for the effects of inflation.

Let's consider an example. Suppose that Sally Saver deposits $1,000 in a bank account that pays an annual interest rate of 10 percent. A year later, after Sally has accumulated $100 in interest, she withdraws her $1,100. Is Sally $100 richer than she was when she made the deposit a year earlier?

The answer depends on what we mean by "richer." Sally does have $100 more than she had before. In other words, the number of dollars in her possession has risen by 10 percent. But Sally does not care about the amount of money itself: She cares about what she can buy with it. If prices have risen while her money was in the bank, each dollar now buys less than it did a year ago. In this case, her purchasing power—the amount of goods and services she can buy—has not risen by 10 percent.

To keep things simple, let's suppose that Sally is a music fan and buys only music CDs. When Sally made her deposit, a CD at her local music store cost $10. Her deposit of $1,000 was equivalent to 100 CDs. A year later, after getting her 10 percent interest, she has $1,100. How many CDs can she buy now? It depends on what has happened to the price of a CD. Here are some examples:

- Zero inflation: If the price of a CD remains at $10, the amount she can buy has risen from 100 to 110 CDs. The 10 percent increase in the number of dollars means a 10 percent increase in her purchasing power.
- Six percent inflation: If the price of a CD rises from $10 to $10.60, then the number of CDs she can buy has risen from 100 to approximately 104. Her purchasing power has increased by about 4 percent.
- Ten percent inflation: If the price of a CD rises from $10 to $11, then even though Sally's dollar wealth has risen from $1,000 to $1,100, she can still buy only 100 CDs. Her purchasing power is the same as it was a year earlier.

- Twelve percent inflation: If the price of a CD increases from $10 to $11.20, then even with her greater number of dollars, the number of CDs she can buy has fallen from 100 to approximately 98. Her purchasing power has decreased by about 2 percent.

And if Sally were living in an economy with deflation—falling prices—another possibility could arise:

- Two percent deflation: If the price of a CD falls from $10 to $9.80, then the number of CDs she can buy rises from 100 to approximately 112. Her purchasing power increases by about 12 percent.

These examples show that the higher the rate of inflation, the smaller the increase in Sally's purchasing power. If the rate of inflation exceeds the rate of interest, her purchasing power actually falls. And if there is deflation (that is, a negative rate of inflation), her purchasing power rises by more than the rate of interest.

To understand how much a person earns in a savings account, we need to consider both the interest rate and the change in the prices. The interest rate that measures the change in dollar amounts is called the **nominal interest rate,** and the interest rate corrected for inflation is called the **real interest rate.** The nominal interest rate, the real interest rate, and inflation are related approximately as follows:

$$\text{Real interest rate} = \text{Nominal interest rate} - \text{Inflation rate.}$$

The real interest rate is the difference between the nominal interest rate and the rate of inflation. The nominal interest rate tells you how fast the number of dollars in your bank account rises over time. The real interest rate tells you how fast the purchasing power of your bank account rises over time.

nominal interest rate
the interest rate as usually reported without a correction for the effects of inflation

real interest rate
the interest rate corrected for the effects of inflation

CASE STUDY   INTEREST RATES IN THE U.S. ECONOMY

Figure 3 shows real and nominal interest rates in the U.S. economy since 1965. The nominal interest rate in this figure is the rate on 3-month Treasury bills (although data on other interest rates would be similar). The real interest rate is computed by subtracting the rate of inflation from this nominal interest rate. Here the inflation rate is measured as the percentage change in the consumer price index.

One feature of this figure is that the nominal interest rate always exceeds the real interest rate. This reflects the fact that the U.S. economy has experienced rising consumer prices in every year during this period. By contrast, if you looked at the U.S. economy during the late 19th century or at the Japanese economy in some recent years, you will find periods of deflation. During deflation, the real interest rate exceeds the nominal interest rate.

The figure also shows that real and nominal interest rates do not always move together. For example, in the late 1970s, nominal interest rates were high. But because inflation was very high, real interest rates were low. Indeed, during much of the 1970s, real interest rates were negative, for inflation eroded people's

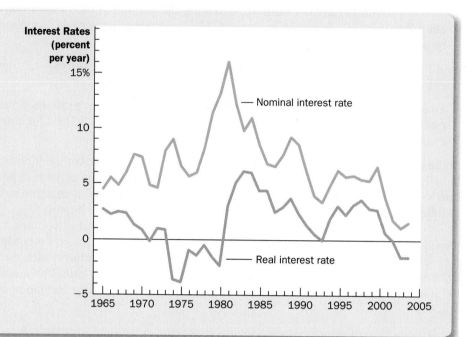

3 FIGURE

Real and Nominal Interest Rates

This figure shows nominal and real interest rates using annual data since 1965. The nominal interest rate is the rate on a 3-month Treasury bill. The real interest rate is the nominal interest rate minus the inflation rate as measured by the consumer price index. Notice that nominal and real interest rates often do not move together.

Source: U.S. Department of Labor; U.S. Department of Treasury.

savings more quickly than nominal interest payments increased them. By contrast, in the late 1990s, nominal interest rates were lower than they had been two decades earlier. But because inflation was much lower, real interest rates were higher. The early 2000s were a period when both real and nominal interest rates were low. In the coming chapters, we will examine the economic forces that determine both real and nominal interest rates. •

Quick Quiz   Henry Ford paid his workers $5 a day in 1914. If the consumer price index was 10 in 1914 and 195 in 2005, how much is the Ford paycheck worth in 2005 dollars?

CONCLUSION

"A nickel ain't worth a dime anymore," baseball player Yogi Berra once observed. Indeed, throughout recent history, the real values behind the nickel, the dime, and the dollar have not been stable. Persistent increases in the overall level of prices have been the norm. Such inflation reduces the purchasing power of each unit of money over time. When comparing dollar figures from different times, it is important to keep in mind that a dollar today is not the same as a dollar 20 years ago or, most likely, 20 years from now.

This chapter has discussed how economists measure the overall level of prices in the economy and how they use price indexes to correct economic variables for the effects of inflation. Price indexes allow us to compare dollar figures from different points in time and, therefore, get a better sense of how the economy is changing.

The discussion of price indexes in this chapter, together with the last chapter's discussion of GDP, is only a first step in the study of macroeconomics. We have not yet examined what determines a nation's GDP or the causes and effects of inflation. To do that, we need to go beyond issues of measurement. Indeed, that is our next task. Having explained how economists measure macroeconomic quantities and prices in the past two chapters, we are now ready to develop the models that explain movements in these variables.

Here is our strategy in the upcoming chapters. First, we look at the long-run determinants of real GDP and related variables, such as saving, investment, real interest rates, and unemployment. Second, we look at the long-run determinants of the price level and related variables, such as the money supply, inflation, and nominal interest rates. Last of all, having seen how these variables are determined in the long run, we examine the more complex question of what causes short-run fluctuations in real GDP and the price level. In all of these chapters, the measurement issues we have just discussed will provide the foundation for the analysis.

SUMMARY

- The consumer price index shows the cost of a basket of goods and services relative to the cost of the same basket in the base year. The index is used to measure the overall level of prices in the economy. The percentage change in the consumer price index measures the inflation rate.

- The consumer price index is an imperfect measure of the cost of living for three reasons. First, it does not take into account consumers' ability to substitute toward goods that become relatively cheaper over time. Second, it does not take into account increases in the purchasing power of the dollar due to the introduction of new goods. Third, it is distorted by unmeasured changes in the quality of goods and services. Because of these measurement problems, the CPI overstates true inflation.

- Like the consumer price index, the GDP deflator measures the overall level of prices in the economy. Although the two price indexes usually move together, there are important differences. The GDP deflator differs from the CPI because it includes goods and services produced rather than goods and services consumed. As a result, imported goods affect the consumer price index

but not the GDP deflator. In addition, while the consumer price index uses a fixed basket of goods, the GDP deflator automatically changes the group of goods and services over time as the composition of GDP changes.

- Dollar figures from different points in time do not represent a valid comparison of purchasing power. To compare a dollar figure from the past to a dollar figure today, the older figure should be inflated using a price index.

- Various laws and private contracts use price indexes to correct for the effects of inflation. The tax laws, however, are only partially indexed for inflation.

- A correction for inflation is especially important when looking at data on interest rates. The nominal interest rate is the interest rate usually reported; it is the rate at which the number of dollars in a savings account increases over time. By contrast, the real interest rate takes into account changes in the value of the dollar over time. The real interest rate equals the nominal interest rate minus the rate of inflation.

KEY CONCEPTS

consumer price index (CPI), p. 114

inflation rate, p. 116

producer price index, p. 116

indexation, p. 124

nominal interest rate, p. 125

real interest rate, p. 125

QUESTIONS FOR REVIEW

1. Which do you think has a greater effect on the consumer price index: a 10 percent increase in the price of chicken or a 10 percent increase in the price of caviar? Why?

2. Describe the three problems that make the consumer price index an imperfect measure of the cost of living.

3. If the price of a Navy submarine rises, is the consumer price index or the GDP deflator affected more? Why?

4. Over a long period of time, the price of a candy bar rose from $0.10 to $0.60. Over the same period, the consumer price index rose from 150 to 300. Adjusted for overall inflation, how much did the price of the candy bar change?

5. Explain the meaning of *nominal interest rate* and *real interest rate*. How are they related?

PROBLEMS AND APPLICATIONS

1. Suppose that the residents of Vegopia spend all of their income on cauliflower, broccoli, and carrots. In 2006, they buy 100 heads of cauliflower for $200, 50 bunches of broccoli for $75, and 500 carrots for $50. In 2007, they buy 75 heads of cauliflower for $225, 80 bunches of broccoli for $120, and 500 carrots for $100.

   a. Calculate the price of each vegetable in each year.

   b. Using 2006 as the base year, calculate the CPI for each year.

   c. What is the inflation rate in 2007?

2. Go to the website of the Bureau of Labor Statistics (http://www.bls.gov) and find data on the consumer price index. By how much has the index including all items risen over the past year? For which categories of spending have prices risen the most? The least? Have any categories experienced price declines? Can you explain any of these facts?

3. Suppose that people consume only three goods, as shown in this table:

	Tennis Balls	Golf Balls	Bottle of Gatorade
2006 price	$2	$4	$1
2006 quantity	100	100	200
2007 price	$2	$6	$2
2007 quantity	100	100	200

   a. What is the percentage change in the price of each of the three goods?

   b. Using a method similar to the consumer price index, compute the percentage change in the overall price level.

   c. If you were to learn that a bottle of Gatorade increased in size from 2006 and 2007, should that information affect your calculation of the inflation rate? If so, how?

   d. If you were to learn that Gatorade introduced new flavors in 2007, should that information affect your calculation of the inflation rate? If so, how?

4. Beginning in 1994, environmental regulations have required that gasoline contain a new additive to reduce air pollution. This requirement raised the cost of gasoline. The Bureau of Labor Statistics decided that this increase in cost represented an improvement in quality.
   a. Given this decision, did the increased cost of gasoline raise the CPI?
   b. What is the argument in favor of the BLS's decision? What is the argument for a different decision?

5. Which of the problems in the construction of the CPI might be illustrated by each of the following situations? Explain.
   a. the invention of the Sony Walkman
   b. the introduction of air bags in cars
   c. increased personal computer purchases in response to a decline in their price
   d. more scoops of raisins in each package of Raisin Bran
   e. greater use of fuel-efficient cars after gasoline prices increase

6. *The New York Times* cost $0.15 in 1970 and $0.75 in 2000. The average wage in manufacturing was $3.23 per hour in 1970 and $14.32 in 2000.
   a. By what percentage did the price of a newspaper rise?
   b. By what percentage did the wage rise?
   c. In each year, how many minutes does a worker have to work to earn enough to buy a newspaper?
   d. Did workers' purchasing power in terms of newspapers rise or fall?

7. The chapter explains that Social Security benefits are increased each year in proportion to the increase in the CPI, even though most economists believe that the CPI overstates actual inflation.
   a. If the elderly consume the same market basket as other people, does Social Security provide the elderly with an improvement in their standard of living each year? Explain.
   b. In fact, the elderly consume more healthcare than younger people, and healthcare costs have risen faster than overall inflation. What would you do to determine whether the elderly are actually better off from year to year?

8. Income tax brackets were not indexed until 1985. When inflation pushed up people's nominal incomes during the 1970s, what do you think happened to real tax revenue? (Hint: This phenomenon was known as "bracket creep.")

9. When deciding how much of their income to save for retirement, should workers consider the real or the nominal interest rate that their savings will earn? Explain.

10. Suppose that a borrower and a lender agree on the nominal interest rate to be paid on a loan. Then inflation turns out to be higher than they both expected.
    a. Is the real interest rate on this loan higher or lower than expected?
    b. Does the lender gain or lose from this unexpectedly high inflation? Does the borrower gain or lose?
    c. Inflation during the 1970s was much higher than most people had expected when the decade began. How did this affect homeowners who obtained fixed-rate mortgages during the 1960s? How did it affect the banks that lent the money?

 For further information on topics in this chapter, additional problems, examples, applications, online quizzes, and more, please visit our website at http://mankiw.swlearning.com.

The Real Economy in the Long Run

Production and Growth

W hen you travel around the world, you see tremendous variation in the standard of living. The average income in a rich country, such as the United States, Japan, or Germany, is more than ten times the average income in a poor country, such as India, Indonesia, or Nigeria. These large differences in income are reflected in large differences in the quality of life. People in richer countries have more automobiles, more telephones, more televisions, better nutrition, safer housing, better healthcare, and longer life expectancy.

Even within a country, there are large changes in the standard of living over time. In the United States over the past century, average income as measured by real GDP per person has grown by about 2 percent per year. Although 2 percent might seem small, this rate of growth implies that average income doubles every 35 years. Because of this growth, average income today is about eight times as high as average income a century ago. As a result, the typical American enjoys much greater economic prosperity than did his or her parents, grandparents, and great-grandparents.

Growth rates vary substantially from country to country. In some East Asian countries, such as Singapore, South Korea, and Taiwan, average income has risen about 7 percent per year in recent decades. At this rate, average income doubles every 10 years. These countries have, in the length of one generation, gone from being among the poorest in the world to being among the richest. By contrast, in some African countries, such as Chad, Ethiopia, and Nigeria, average income has been stagnant for many years.

What explains these diverse experiences? How can the rich countries be sure to maintain their high standard of living? What policies should the poor countries pursue to promote more rapid growth and join the developed world? These are among the most important questions in macroeconomics. As economist Robert Lucas put it, "The consequences for human welfare in questions like these are simply staggering: Once one starts to think about them, it is hard to think about anything else."

In the previous two chapters, we discussed how economists measure macroeconomic quantities and prices. In this chapter, we start studying the forces that determine these variables. As we have seen, an economy's gross domestic product (GDP) measures both the total income earned in the economy and the total expenditure on the economy's output of goods and services. The level of real GDP is a good gauge of economic prosperity, and the growth of real GDP is a good gauge of economic progress. Here we focus on the long-run determinants of the level and growth of real GDP. Later in this book, we study the short-run fluctuations of real GDP around its long-run trend.

We proceed here in three steps. First, we examine international data on real GDP per person. These data will give you some sense of how much the level and growth of living standards vary around the world. Second, we examine the role of *productivity*—the amount of goods and services produced for each hour of a worker's time. In particular, we see that a nation's standard of living is determined by the productivity of its workers, and we consider the factors that determine a nation's productivity. Third, we consider the link between productivity and the economic policies that a nation pursues.

ECONOMIC GROWTH AROUND THE WORLD

As a starting point for our study of long-run growth, let's look at the experiences of some of the world's economies. Table 1 shows data on real GDP per person for thirteen countries. For each country, the data cover more than a century of history. The first and second columns of the table present the countries and time periods. (The time periods differ somewhat from country to country because of differences in data availability.) The third and fourth columns show estimates of real GDP per person about a century ago and for a recent year.

The data on real GDP per person show that living standards vary widely from country to country. Income per person in the United States, for instance, is about 7 times that in China and about 13 times that in India. The poorest countries have average levels of income that have not been seen in the developed world for many decades. The typical citizen of India in 2003 had less real income as the typical resident of England in 1870. The typical person in Bangladesh in 2003 had about one-half the real income of a typical American a century ago.

The last column of the table shows each country's growth rate. The growth rate measures how rapidly real GDP per person grew in the typical year. In the United States, for example, real GDP per person was $3,412 in 1870 and $37,500 in 2003. The growth rate was 1.82 percent per year. This means that if real GDP per person, beginning at $3,412, were to increase by 1.82 percent for each of 133 years, it would end up at $37,500. Of course, real GDP per person did not actually rise exactly 1.82 percent every year: Some years it rose by more and other years by less. The growth rate of 1.82 percent per year ignores short-run fluctua-

Country	Period	Real GDP per Person at Beginning of Period[a]	Real GDP per Person at End of Period[a]	Growth Rate (per year)
Japan	1890–2003	$1,280	$28,620	2.79%
Brazil	1900–2003	663	7,480	2.38
Mexico	1900–2003	987	8,950	2.16
China	1900–2003	610	4,990	2.06
Germany	1870–2003	1,859	27,460	2.05
Canada	1870–2003	2,022	29,740	2.04
United States	1870–2003	3,412	37,500	1.82
Argentina	1900–2003	1,952	10,920	1.69
India	1900–2003	575	2,880	1.58
United Kingdom	1870–2003	4,094	27,650	1.45
Indonesia	1900–2003	759	3,210	1.41
Pakistan	1900–2003	628	2,060	1.16
Bangladesh	1900–2003	531	1,870	1.16

[a]Real GDP is measured in 2003 dollars.

TABLE 1

The Variety of Growth Experiences

Source: Robert J. Barro and Xavier Sala-i-Martin, *Economic Growth* (New York: McGraw-Hill, 1995), tables 10.2 and 10.3; *World Development Report 2005*, Table 1; and author's calculations.

tions around the long-run trend and represents an average rate of growth for real GDP per person over many years.

The countries in Table 1 are ordered by their growth rate from the most to the least rapid. Japan tops the list, with a growth rate of 2.79 percent per year. A hundred years ago, Japan was not a rich country. Japan's average income was only somewhat higher than Mexico's, and it was well behind Argentina's. The standard of living in Japan in 1890 was lower than in India today. But because of its spectacular growth, Japan is now an economic superpower, with average income more than twice that of Mexico and Argentina and similar to Germany, Canada, and the United Kingdom. At the bottom of the list of countries are Bangladesh and Pakistan, which have experienced growth of only 1.16 percent per year over the past century. As a result, the typical resident of these countries continues to live in abject poverty.

Because of differences in growth rates, the ranking of countries by income changes substantially over time. As we have seen, Japan is a country that has risen relative to others. One country that has fallen behind is the United Kingdom. In 1870, the United Kingdom was the richest country in the world, with average income about 20 percent higher than that of the United States and about twice that of Canada. Today, average income in the United Kingdom is below the average income in its two former colonies.

These data show that the world's richest countries have no guarantee they will stay the richest and that the world's poorest countries are not doomed forever to remain in poverty. But what explains these changes over time? Why do some countries zoom ahead while others lag behind? These are precisely the questions that we take up next.

Quick Quiz   What is the approximate growth rate of real GDP per person in the United States? Name a country that has had faster growth and a country that has had slower growth.

FYI

A Picture Is Worth a Thousand Statistics

George Bernard Shaw once said, "The sign of a truly educated man is to be deeply moved by statistics." Most of us, however, have trouble being deeply moved by data on GDP—until we see what these statistics represent.

The three photos on these pages show a typical family from each of three countries—the United Kingdom, Mexico, and Mali. Each family was photographed outside their home, together with all of their material possessions.

These nations have very different standards of living, as judged by these photos, GDP, or other statistics.

• The United Kingdom is an advanced economy. In 2003, its GDP per person was $27,650. A negligible share of the population lives in extreme poverty, defined here as less than $2 a day. Educational attainment is high: Among children of high-school age, 95 percent are in school. Residents of the United Kingdom can expect to enjoy a long life: The probability of a person surviving to age 65 is 83 percent for men and 89 percent for women.

• Mexico is a middle-income country. In 2003, its GDP per person was $8,950. About a quarter of the population lives on less than $2 a day. Among children of high-school age, 60 percent are in school. The probability of a person surviving to age 65 is 71 percent for men and 82 percent for women.

• Mali is a poor country. In 2003, its GDP per person was only $960. Extreme poverty is the norm: More than half of the population lives on less than $2 per day. Educational attainment in Mali is low: Among children of high-school age, less than 10 percent are in school. And life is often cut short: The probability of a person surviving to age 65 is only 37 percent for men and 41 percent for women.

Economists who study economic growth try to understand what causes such large differences in the standard of living.

A Typical Family in the United Kingdom

© DAVID REED

A Typical Family in Mexico

A Typical Family in Mali

FYI

Are You Richer Than the Richest American?

The magazine *American Heritage* once published a list of the richest Americans of all time. The number 1 spot went to John D. Rockefeller, the oil entrepreneur who lived from 1839 to 1937. According to the magazine's calculations, his wealth would today be the equivalent of $200 billion, more than twice that of Bill Gates, the software entrepreneur who is today's richest American.

Despite his great wealth, Rockefeller did not enjoy many of the conveniences that we now take for granted. He couldn't watch television, play video games, surf the Internet, or send an e-mail. During the heat of summer, he couldn't cool his home with air conditioning. For much of his life, he couldn't travel by car or plane, and he couldn't use a telephone to call friends or family. If he became ill, he couldn't take advantage of many medicines, such as antibiotics, that doctors today routinely use to prolong and enhance life.

John D. Rockefeller

Now consider: How much money would someone have to pay you to give up for the rest of your life all the modern conveniences that Rockefeller lived without? Would you do it for $200 billion? Perhaps not. And if you wouldn't, is it fair to say that you are better off than John D. Rockefeller, allegedly the richest American ever?

The preceding chapter discussed how standard price indexes, which are used to compare sums of money from different points in time, fail to fully reflect the introduction of new goods in the economy. As a result, the rate of inflation is overestimated. The flip side of this observation is that the rate of real economic growth is underestimated. Pondering Rockefeller's life shows how significant this problem might be. Because of tremendous technological advances, the average American today is arguably "richer" than the richest American a century ago, even if that fact is lost in standard economic statistics.

PRODUCTIVITY: ITS ROLE AND DETERMINANTS

Explaining the large variation in living standards around the world is, in one sense, very easy. As we will see, the explanation can be summarized in a single word—*productivity*. But in another sense, the international variation is deeply puzzling. To explain why incomes are so much higher in some countries than in others, we must look at the many factors that determine a nation's productivity.

Why Productivity Is So Important

Let's begin our study of productivity and economic growth by developing a simple model based loosely on Daniel Defoe's famous novel *Robinson Crusoe*. Robinson Crusoe, as you may recall, is a sailor stranded on a desert island. Because Crusoe lives alone, he catches his own fish, grows his own vegetables, and makes his own clothes. We can think of Crusoe's activities—his production and consumption of fish, vegetables, and clothing—as a simple economy. By examining Crusoe's economy, we can learn some lessons that also apply to more complex and realistic economies.

What determines Crusoe's standard of living? In a word, **productivity,** the quantity of goods and services produced from each unit of labor input. If Crusoe

productivity
the quantity of goods and services produced from each unit of labor input

is good at catching fish, growing vegetables, and making clothes, he lives well. If he is bad at doing these things, he lives poorly. Because Crusoe gets to consume only what he produces, his living standard is tied to his productivity.

In the case of Crusoe's economy, it is easy to see that productivity is the key determinant of living standards and that growth in productivity is the key determinant of growth in living standards. The more fish Crusoe can catch per hour, the more he eats at dinner. If Crusoe finds a better place to catch fish, his productivity rises. This increase in productivity makes Crusoe better off: He can eat the extra fish, or he can spend less time fishing and devote more time to making other goods he enjoys.

Productivity's key role in determining living standards is as true for nations as it is for stranded sailors. Recall that an economy's gross domestic product (GDP) measures two things at once: the total income earned by everyone in the economy and the total expenditure on the economy's output of goods and services. The reason GDP can measure these two things simultaneously is that, for the economy as a whole, they must be equal. Put simply, an economy's income is the economy's output.

Like Crusoe, a nation can enjoy a high standard of living only if it can produce a large quantity of goods and services. Americans live better than Nigerians because American workers are more productive than Nigerian workers. The Japanese have enjoyed more rapid growth in living standards than Argentineans because Japanese workers have experienced more rapidly growing productivity. Indeed, one of the *Ten Principles of Economics* in Chapter 1 is that a country's standard of living depends on its ability to produce goods and services.

Hence, to understand the large differences in living standards we observe across countries or over time, we must focus on the production of goods and services. But seeing the link between living standards and productivity is only the first step. It leads naturally to the next question: Why are some economies so much better at producing goods and services than others?

How Productivity Is Determined

Although productivity is uniquely important in determining Robinson Crusoe's standard of living, many factors determine Crusoe's productivity. Crusoe will be better at catching fish, for instance, if he has more fishing poles, if he has been trained in the best fishing techniques, if his island has a plentiful fish supply, and if he invents a better fishing lure. Each of these determinants of Crusoe's productivity—which we can call *physical capital, human capital, natural resources,* and *technological knowledge*—has a counterpart in more complex and realistic economies. Let's consider each of these factors in turn.

Physical Capital per Worker   Workers are more productive if they have tools with which to work. The stock of equipment and structures that are used to produce goods and services is called **physical capital,** or just *capital.* For example, when woodworkers make furniture, they use saws, lathes, and drill presses. More tools allow the woodworkers to produce their output more quickly and more accurately: A worker with only basic hand tools can make less furniture each week than a worker with sophisticated and specialized woodworking equipment.

physical capital
the stock of equipment and structures that are used to produce goods and services

As you may recall, the inputs used to produce goods and services—labor, capital, and so on—are called the *factors of production.* An important feature of capital is that it is a *produced* factor of production. That is, capital is an input into the production process that in the past was an output from the production process. The woodworker uses a lathe to make the leg of a table. Earlier, the lathe itself was the output of a firm that manufactures lathes. The lathe manufacturer in turn used other equipment to make its product. Thus, capital is a factor of production used to produce all kinds of goods and services, including more capital.

Human Capital per Worker   A second determinant of productivity is human capital. **Human capital** is the economist's term for the knowledge and skills that workers acquire through education, training, and experience. Human capital includes the skills accumulated in early childhood programs, grade school, high school, college, and on-the-job training for adults in the labor force.

Although education, training, and experience are less tangible than lathes, bulldozers, and buildings, human capital is like physical capital in many ways. Like physical capital, human capital raises a nation's ability to produce goods and services. Also like physical capital, human capital is a produced factor of production. Producing human capital requires inputs in the form of teachers, libraries, and student time. Indeed, students can be viewed as "workers" who have the important job of producing the human capital that will be used in future production.

Natural Resources per Worker   A third determinant of productivity is **natural resources.** Natural resources are inputs into production that are provided by nature, such as land, rivers, and mineral deposits. Natural resources take two forms: renewable and nonrenewable. A forest is an example of a renewable resource. When one tree is cut down, a seedling can be planted in its place to be harvested in the future. Oil is an example of a nonrenewable resource. Because oil is produced by nature over many thousands of years, there is only a limited supply. Once the supply of oil is depleted, it is impossible to create more.

Differences in natural resources are responsible for some of the differences in standards of living around the world. The historical success of the United States was driven in part by the large supply of land well suited for agriculture. Today, some countries in the Middle East, such as Kuwait and Saudi Arabia, are rich simply because they happen to be on top of some of the largest pools of oil in the world.

Although natural resources can be important, they are not necessary for an economy to be highly productive in producing goods and services. Japan, for instance, is one of the richest countries in the world, despite having few natural resources. International trade makes Japan's success possible. Japan imports many of the natural resources it needs, such as oil, and exports its manufactured goods to economies rich in natural resources.

Technological Knowledge   A fourth determinant of productivity is **technological knowledge**—the understanding of the best ways to produce goods and services. A hundred years ago, most Americans worked on farms because farm technology required a high input of labor to feed the entire population. Today, thanks to advances in the technology of farming, a small fraction of the population can produce enough food to feed the entire country. This technological change made labor available to produce other goods and services.

Technological knowledge takes many forms. Some technology is common knowledge—after one person uses it, everyone becomes aware of it. For example, once Henry Ford successfully introduced production in assembly lines, other carmakers quickly followed suit. Other technology is proprietary—it is known only by the company that discovers it. Only the Coca-Cola Company, for

human capital
the knowledge and skills that workers acquire through education, training, and experience

natural resources
the inputs into the production of goods and services that are provided by nature, such as land, rivers, and mineral deposits

technological knowledge
society's understanding of the best ways to produce goods and services

FYI

The Production Function

Economists often use a *production function* to describe the relationship between the quantity of inputs used in production and the quantity of output from production. For example, suppose Y denotes the quantity of output, L the quantity of labor, K the quantity of physical capital, H the quantity of human capital, and N the quantity of natural resources. Then we might write

$$Y = A\, F(L, K, H, N),$$

where $F(\ )$ is a function that shows how the inputs are combined to produce output. A is a variable that reflects the available production technology. As technology improves, A rises, so the economy produces more output from any given combination of inputs.

Many production functions have a property called *constant returns to scale*. If a production function has constant returns to scale, then doubling all inputs causes the amount of output to double as well. Mathematically, we write that a production function has constant returns to scale if, for any positive number x,

$$xY = A\, F(xL, xK, xH, xN).$$

A doubling of all inputs would be represented in this equation by $x = 2$. The right side shows the inputs doubling, and the left side shows output doubling.

Production functions with constant returns to scale have an interesting implication. To see what it is, it will prove instructive to set $x = 1/L$. Then the preceding equation becomes

$$Y/L = A\, F(1, K/L, H/L, N/L).$$

Notice that Y/L is output per worker, which is a measure of productivity. This equation says that labor productivity depends on physical capital per worker (K/L), human capital per worker (H/L), and natural resources per worker (N/L). Productivity also depends on the state of technology, as reflected by the variable A. Thus, this equation provides a mathematical summary of the four determinants of productivity we have just discussed.

instance, knows the secret recipe for making its famous soft drink. Still other technology is proprietary for a short time. When a pharmaceutical company discovers a new drug, the patent system gives that company a temporary right to be its exclusive manufacturer. When the patent expires, however, other companies are allowed to make the drug. All these forms of technological knowledge are important for the economy's production of goods and services.

It is worthwhile to distinguish between technological knowledge and human capital. Although they are closely related, there is an important difference. Technological knowledge refers to society's understanding about how the world works. Human capital refers to the resources expended transmitting this understanding to the labor force. To use a relevant metaphor, knowledge is the quality of society's textbooks, whereas human capital is the amount of time that the population has devoted to reading them. Workers' productivity depends on both.

CASE STUDY | ARE NATURAL RESOURCES A LIMIT TO GROWTH?

Today, the world's population is over 6 billion, about four times what it was a century ago. At the same time, many people are enjoying a much higher standard of living than did their great-grandparents. A perennial debate concerns whether this growth in population and living standards can continue in the future.

Many commentators have argued that natural resources will eventually limit how much the world's economies can grow. At first, this argument might seem hard to ignore. If the world has only a fixed supply of nonrenewable natural resources, how can population, production, and living standards continue to grow over time? Eventually, won't supplies of oil and minerals start to run out? When these shortages start to occur, won't they stop economic growth and, perhaps, even force living standards to fall?

Despite the apparent appeal of such arguments, most economists are less concerned about such limits to growth than one might guess. They argue that technological progress often yields ways to avoid these limits. If we compare the economy today to the economy of the past, we see various ways in which the use of natural resources has improved. Modern cars have better gas mileage. New houses have better insulation and require less energy to heat and cool them. More efficient oil rigs waste less oil in the process of extraction. Recycling allows some nonrenewable resources to be reused. The development of alternative fuels, such as ethanol instead of gasoline, allows us to substitute renewable for nonrenewable resources.

Fifty years ago, some conservationists were concerned about the excessive use of tin and copper. At the time, these were crucial commodities: Tin was used to make many food containers, and copper was used to make telephone wire. Some people advocated mandatory recycling and rationing of tin and copper so that supplies would be available for future generations. Today, however, plastic has replaced tin as a material for making many food containers, and phone calls often travel over fiberoptic cables, which are made from sand. Technological progress has made once crucial natural resources less necessary.

But are all these efforts enough to permit continued economic growth? One way to answer this question is to look at the prices of natural resources. In a market economy, scarcity is reflected in market prices. If the world were running out of natural resources, then the prices of those resources would be rising over time. But in fact, the opposite is more nearly true. The prices of most natural resources (adjusted for overall inflation) are stable or falling. It appears that our ability to conserve these resources is growing more rapidly than their supplies are dwindling. Market prices give no reason to believe that natural resources are a limit to economic growth.   •

Quick Quiz   List and describe four determinants of a country's productivity.

ECONOMIC GROWTH AND PUBLIC POLICY

So far, we have determined that a society's standard of living depends on its ability to produce goods and services and that its productivity depends on physical capital per worker, human capital per worker, natural resources per worker, and technological knowledge. Let's now turn to the question faced by policymakers around the world: What can government policy do to raise productivity and living standards?

Saving and Investment

Because capital is a produced factor of production, a society can change the amount of capital it has. If today the economy produces a large quantity of new capital goods, then tomorrow it will have a larger stock of capital and be able to produce more of all types of goods and services. Thus, one way to raise future productivity is to invest more current resources in the production of capital.

One of the *Ten Principles of Economics* presented in Chapter 1 is that people face trade-offs. This principle is especially important when considering the accumulation of capital. Because resources are scarce, devoting more resources to producing capital requires devoting fewer resources to producing goods and services for current consumption. That is, for society to invest more in capital, it must consume less and save more of its current income. The growth that arises from capital accumulation is not a free lunch: It requires that society sacrifice consumption of goods and services in the present to enjoy higher consumption in the future.

The next chapter examines in more detail how the economy's financial markets coordinate saving and investment. It also examines how government policies influence the amount of saving and investment that takes place. At this point, it is important to note that encouraging saving and investment is one way that a government can encourage growth and, in the long run, raise the economy's standard of living.

Diminishing Returns and the Catch-Up Effect

Suppose that a government pursues policies that raise the nation's saving rate—the percentage of GDP devoted to saving rather than consumption. What happens? With the nation saving more, fewer resources are needed to make consumption goods, and more resources are available to make capital goods. As a result, the capital stock increases, leading to rising productivity and more rapid growth in GDP. But how long does this higher rate of growth last? Assuming that the saving rate remains at its new higher level, does the growth rate of GDP stay high indefinitely or only for a period of time?

The traditional view of the production process is that capital is subject to **diminishing returns:** As the stock of capital rises, the extra output produced from an additional unit of capital falls. In other words, when workers already have a large quantity of capital to use in producing goods and services, giving them an additional unit of capital increases their productivity only slightly. This is illustrated in Figure 1, which shows how the amount of capital per worker determines the amount of output per worker, holding constant all the other determinants of output.

diminishing returns
the property whereby the benefit from an extra unit of an input declines as the quantity of the input increases

Because of diminishing returns, an increase in the saving rate leads to higher growth only for a while. As the higher saving rate allows more capital to be accumulated, the benefits from additional capital become smaller over time, and so growth slows down. *In the long run, the higher saving rate leads to a higher level of productivity and income but not to higher growth in these variables.* Reaching this long run, however, can take quite a while. According to studies of international data on economic growth, increasing the saving rate can lead to substantially higher growth for a period of several decades.

The diminishing returns to capital has another important implication: Other things equal, it is easier for a country to grow fast if it starts out relatively poor.

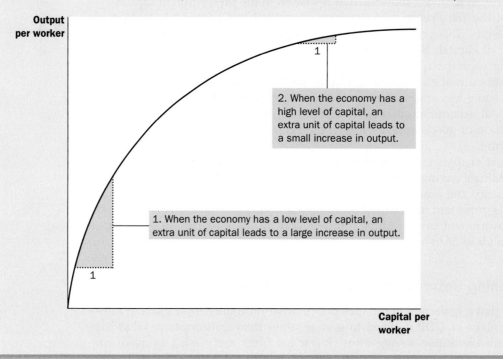

1 FIGURE

Illustrating the
Production Function

This figure shows how the amount of capital per worker influences the amount of output per worker. Other determinants of output, including human capital, natural resources, and technology, are held constant. The curve becomes flatter as the amount of capital increases because of diminishing returns to capital.

Output per worker

2. When the economy has a high level of capital, an extra unit of capital leads to a small increase in output.

1. When the economy has a low level of capital, an extra unit of capital leads to a large increase in output.

Capital per worker

catch-up effect
the property whereby countries that start off poor tend to grow more rapidly than countries that start off rich

This effect of initial conditions on subsequent growth is sometimes called the **catch-up effect.** In poor countries, workers lack even the most rudimentary tools and, as a result, have low productivity. Small amounts of capital investment would substantially raise these workers' productivity. By contrast, workers in rich countries have large amounts of capital with which to work, and this partly explains their high productivity. Yet with the amount of capital per worker already so high, additional capital investment has a relatively small effect on productivity. Studies of international data on economic growth confirm this catch-up effect: Controlling for other variables, such as the percentage of GDP devoted to investment, poor countries do tend to grow at a faster rate than rich countries.

This catch-up effect can help explain some of otherwise puzzling facts. Here's an example: From 1960 to 1990, the United States and South Korea devoted a similar share of GDP to investment. Yet over this time, the United States experienced only mediocre growth of about 2 percent, while Korea experienced spectacular growth of more than 6 percent. The explanation is the catch-up effect. In 1960, Korea had GDP per person less than one-tenth the U.S. level, in part because previous investment had been so low. With a small initial capital stock, the benefits to capital accumulation were much greater in Korea, and this gave Korea a higher subsequent growth rate.

This catch-up effect shows up in other aspects of life. When a school gives an end-of-year award to the "Most Improved" student, that student is usually one who began the year with relatively poor performance. Students who began the year not studying find improvement easier than students who always worked hard. Note that it is good to be "Most Improved," given the starting point, but it is even better to be "Best Student." Similarly, economic growth over the last several decades has been much more rapid in South Korea than in the United States, but GDP per person is still higher in the United States.

Investment from Abroad

So far, we have discussed how policies aimed at increasing a country's saving rate can increase investment and, thereby, long-term economic growth. Yet saving by domestic residents is not the only way for a country to invest in new capital. The other way is investment by foreigners.

Investment from abroad takes several forms. Ford Motor Company might build a car factory in Mexico. A capital investment that is owned and operated by a foreign entity is called *foreign direct investment*. Alternatively, an American might buy stock in a Mexican corporation (that is, buy a share in the ownership of the corporation); the Mexican corporation can use the proceeds from the stock sale to build a new factory. An investment that is financed with foreign money but operated by domestic residents is called *foreign portfolio investment*. In both cases, Americans provide the resources necessary to increase the stock of capital in Mexico. That is, American saving is being used to finance Mexican investment.

When foreigners invest in a country, they do so because they expect to earn a return on their investment. Ford's car factory increases the Mexican capital stock and, therefore, increases Mexican productivity and Mexican GDP. Yet Ford takes some of this additional income back to the United States in the form of profit. Similarly, when an American investor buys Mexican stock, the investor has a right to a portion of the profit that the Mexican corporation earns.

Investment from abroad, therefore, does not have the same effect on all measures of economic prosperity. Recall that gross domestic product (GDP) is the income earned within a country by both residents and nonresidents, whereas gross national product (GNP) is the income earned by residents of a country both at home and abroad. When Ford opens its car factory in Mexico, some of the income the factory generates accrues to people who do not live in Mexico. As a result, foreign investment in Mexico raises the income of Mexicans (measured by GNP) by less than it raises the production in Mexico (measured by GDP).

Nonetheless, investment from abroad is one way for a country to grow. Even though some of the benefits from this investment flow back to the foreign owners, this investment does increase the economy's stock of capital, leading to higher productivity and higher wages. Moreover, investment from abroad is one way for poor countries to learn the state-of-the-art technologies developed and used in richer countries. For these reasons, many economists who advise governments in less developed economies advocate policies that encourage investment from abroad. Often, this means removing restrictions that governments have imposed on foreign ownership of domestic capital.

An organization that tries to encourage the flow of capital to poor countries is the World Bank. This international organization obtains funds from the world's advanced countries, such as the United States, and uses these resources to make loans to less developed countries so that they can invest in roads, sewer systems, schools, and other types of capital. It also offers the countries advice about how the funds might best be used. The World Bank, together with its sister organization, the International Monetary Fund, was set up after World War II. One lesson from the war was that economic distress often leads to political turmoil, international tensions, and military conflict. Thus, every country has an interest in promoting economic prosperity around the world. The World Bank and the International Monetary Fund were established to achieve that common goal.

Education

Education—investment in human capital—is at least as important as investment in physical capital for a country's long-run economic success. In the United States, each year of schooling has historically raised a person's wage on average by about 10 percent. In less developed countries, where human capital is especially scarce, the gap between the wages of educated and uneducated workers is even larger. Thus, one way government policy can enhance the standard of living is to provide good schools and to encourage the population to take advantage of them.

Investment in human capital, like investment in physical capital, has an opportunity cost. When students are in school, they forgo the wages they could have earned. In less developed countries, children often drop out of school at an early age, even though the benefit of additional schooling is very high, simply because their labor is needed to help support the family.

Some economists have argued that human capital is particularly important for economic growth because human capital conveys positive externalities. An *externality* is the effect of one person's actions on the well-being of a bystander. An educated person, for instance, might generate new ideas about how best to produce goods and services. If these ideas enter society's pool of knowledge so everyone can use them, then the ideas are an external benefit of education. In this case, the return to schooling for society is even greater than the return for the individual. This argument would justify the large subsidies to human-capital investment that we observe in the form of public education.

One problem facing some poor countries is the *brain drain*—the emigration of many of the most highly educated workers to rich countries, where these workers can enjoy a higher standard of living. If human capital does have positive externalities, then this brain drain makes those people left behind poorer than they otherwise would be. This problem offers policymakers a dilemma. On the one hand, the United States and other rich countries have the best systems of higher education, and it would seem natural for poor countries to send their best students abroad to earn higher degrees. On the other hand, those students who have spent time abroad may choose not to return home, and this brain drain will reduce the poor nation's stock of human capital even further.

Health and Nutrition

Although the term *human capital* usually refers to education, it can also be used to describe another type of investment in people: expenditures that lead to a healthier population. Other things equal, healthier workers are more productive. Making the right investments in the health of the population is one way for a nation to increase productivity and raise living standards.

Economic historian Robert Fogel has suggested that a significant factor in long-run economic growth is improved health from better nutrition. He estimates that in Great Britain in 1780, about one in five people were so malnour-

In The News

Promoting Human Capital

Human capital is a key to economic growth. With this in mind, some developing countries now give parents an immediate financial incentive to keep their children in school.

Brazil Pays Parents to Help Poor Be Pupils, Not Wage Earners

By Celia W. Dugger

ORTALEZA, Brazil—Vandelson Andrade, 13, often used to skip school to work 12-hour days on the small, graceful fishing boats that sail from the picturesque harbor here. His meager earnings helped pay for rice and beans for his desperately poor family.

But this year he qualified for a small monthly cash payment from the government that his mother receives on the condition that he shows up in the classroom.

"I can't skip school anymore," said Vandelson, whose hand-me-down pants were so big that the crotch ended at his knees and the legs bunched up around his ankles. "If I miss one more day, my mother won't get the money."

This year, Vandelson will finally pass the fourth grade on his third try—a small victory in a new breed of social program that is spreading swiftly across Latin America. It is a developing-country version of American welfare reform: to break the cycle of poverty, the government gives the poor small cash payments in exchange for keeping their children in school and taking them for regular medical checkups.

"I think these programs are as close as you can come to a magic bullet in development," said Nancy Birdsall, president of the Center for Global Development, a nonprofit research group in Washington. "They're creating an incentive for families to invest in their own children's futures. Every decade or so, we see something that can really make a difference, and this is one of those things." . . .

Antônio Souza, 48, and Maria Torres, 37, are raising seven children in a mud hut a couple of hills away from Ms. Andrade. Every member of the family is sinewy and lean. The parents cannot remember the last time the family ate meat or vegetables. But their grant of $27 a month makes it possible to buy rice, sugar, pasta and oil.

Mr. Souza and Ms. Torres, illiterate believers in the power of education,

VANDELSON ANDRADE, STUDENT

have always sent their children to school. "If they don't study, they'll turn into dummies like me," said their father, whose weathered, deeply creased face broke into a wide smile as he surveyed his bright-eyed daughters, Ana Paula, 11, and Daniele, 8, among them. "All I can do is work in the fields."

His wife said proudly: "There are fathers who don't want their children to go to school. But this man here has done everything he could to send his children to school."

Source: *The New York Times*, January 3, 2004.

PHOTO: © JOHN MAIER, JR. / THE IMAGE WORKS

ished that they were incapable of manual labor. Among those who could work, insufficient caloric intake substantially reduced the work effort they could put forth. As nutrition improved, so did workers' productivity.

Fogel studies these historical trends in part by looking at the height of the population. Short height can be an indicator of malnutrition, especially during pregnancy and the early years of life. Fogel finds that as nations develop economically, people eat more, and the population gets taller. From 1775 to 1975, the average caloric intake in Great Britain rose by 26 percent, and the height of the average man rose by 3.6 inches. Similarly, during the spectacular economic growth in South Korea from 1962 to 1995, caloric consumption rose by 44 percent, and average male height rose by 2 inches. Of course, a person's height is determined by a combination of genetic predisposition and environment. But because the genetic makeup of a population is slow to change, such increases in average height are most likely due to changes in the environment—nutrition being the obvious explanation.

Moreover, studies have found that height is an indicator of productivity. Looking at data on a large number of workers at a point in time, researchers have found that taller workers tend to earn more. Because wages reflect a worker's productivity, this finding suggests that taller workers tend to be more productive. The effect of height on wages is especially pronounced in poorer countries, where malnutrition is a bigger risk.

Fogel won the Nobel prize in economics in 1993 for his work in economic history, which includes not only his studies of nutrition but also his studies of American slavery and the role of railroads in the development of the American economy. In the lecture he gave when he was awarded the prize, he surveyed the evidence on health and economic growth. He concluded that "improved gross nutrition accounts for roughly 30 percent of the growth of per capita income in Britain between 1790 and 1980."

Today, malnutrition is fortunately rare in developed nations such as Great Britain and the United States. (Obesity is a more widespread problem.) But for people in developing nations, poor health and inadequate nutrition remain obstacles to higher productivity and improved living standards. The United Nations has recently estimated that almost a third of the population in sub-Saharan Africa is undernourished.

The causal link between health and wealth runs in both directions. Poor countries are poor in part because their populations are not healthy, and their populations are not healthy in part because they are poor and cannot afford adequate healthcare and nutrition. It is a vicious circle. But this fact opens the possibility of a virtuous circle: Policies that lead to more rapid economic growth would naturally improve health outcomes, which in turn would further promote economic growth.

Property Rights and Political Stability

Another way policymakers can foster economic growth is by protecting property rights and promoting political stability. This issue goes to the very heart of how market economies work.

Production in market economies arises from the interactions of millions of individuals and firms. When you buy a car, for instance, you are buying the output of a car dealer, a car manufacturer, a steel company, an iron ore mining company, and so on. This division of production among many firms allows the economy's factors of production to be used as effectively as possible. To achieve this outcome, the economy has to coordinate transactions among these firms, as well as between firms and consumers. Market economies achieve this coordination through market prices. That is, market prices are the instrument with which the invisible hand of the marketplace brings supply and demand into balance in each of the many thousands of markets that make up the economy.

An important prerequisite for the price system to work is an economy-wide respect for *property rights*. Property rights refer to the ability of people to exercise authority over the resources they own. A mining company will not make the effort to mine iron ore if it expects the ore to be stolen. The company mines the ore only if it is confident that it will benefit from the ore's subsequent sale. For this reason, courts serve an important role in a market economy: They enforce property rights. Through the criminal justice system, the courts discourage direct theft. In addition, through the civil justice system, the courts ensure that buyers and sellers live up to their contracts.

Although those of us in developed countries tend to take property rights for granted, those living in less developed countries understand that lack of property rights can be a major problem. In many countries, the system of justice does not work well. Contracts are hard to enforce, and fraud often goes unpunished. In more extreme cases, the government not only fails to enforce property rights but actually infringes upon them. To do business in some countries, firms are expected to bribe powerful government officials. Such corruption impedes the coordinating power of markets. It also discourages domestic saving and investment from abroad.

One threat to property rights is political instability. When revolutions and coups are common, there is doubt about whether property rights will be respected in the future. If a revolutionary government might confiscate the capital of some businesses, as was often true after communist revolutions, domestic residents have less incentive to save, invest, and start new businesses. At the same time, foreigners have less incentive to invest in the country. Even the threat of revolution can act to depress a nation's standard of living.

Thus, economic prosperity depends in part on political prosperity. A country with an efficient court system, honest government officials, and a stable constitution will enjoy a higher economic standard of living than a country with a poor court system, corrupt officials, and frequent revolutions and coups.

Free Trade

Some of the world's poorest countries have tried to achieve more rapid economic growth by pursuing *inward-oriented policies*. These policies attempt to increase productivity and living standards within the country by avoiding interaction with the rest of the world. Domestic firms, claiming they need protection from foreign competition to thrive and grow, often support this infant-industry argument. Together with a general distrust of foreigners, it has at times led policymakers in less developed countries to impose tariffs and other trade restrictions.

Most economists today believe that poor countries are better off pursuing *outward-oriented policies* that integrate these countries into the world economy. When we studied international trade earlier in this book, we showed how trade can improve the economic well-being of a country's citizens. Trade is, in some ways, a type of technology. When a country exports wheat and imports steel, the country benefits as if it had invented a technology for turning wheat into steel. A country that eliminates trade restrictions will, therefore, experience the same kind of economic growth that would occur after a major technological advance.

The adverse impact of inward orientation becomes clear when one considers the small size of many less developed economies. The total GDP of Argentina, for instance, is about that of Philadelphia. Imagine what would happen if the Philadelphia city council were to prohibit city residents from trading with people living outside the city limits. Without being able to take advantage of the gains from trade, Philadelphia would need to produce all the goods it consumes. It would also have to produce all its own capital goods, rather than importing state-of-the-art equipment from other cities. Living standards in Philadelphia would fall immediately, and the problem would likely only get worse over time. This is precisely what happened when Argentina pursued inward-oriented policies throughout much of the 20th century. By contrast, countries that pursued outward-oriented policies, such as South Korea, Singapore, and Taiwan, enjoyed high rates of economic growth.

The amount that a nation trades with others is determined not only by government policy but also by geography. Countries with good natural seaports find trade easier than countries without this resource. It is not a coincidence that many of the world's major cities, such as New York, San Francisco, and Hong Kong, are located next to oceans. Similarly, because landlocked countries find international trade more difficult, they tend to have lower levels of income than countries with easy access to the world's waterways. Many African countries, for example, are landlocked, and some economists point to this fact as one reason the continent is so poor.

Research and Development

The primary reason that living standards are higher today than they were a century ago is that technological knowledge has advanced. The telephone, the transistor, the computer, and the internal combustion engine are among the thousands of innovations that have improved the ability to produce goods and services.

Although most technological advance comes from private research by firms and individual inventors, there is also a public interest in promoting these efforts. To a large extent, knowledge is a *public good:* Once one person discovers an idea, the idea enters society's pool of knowledge, and other people can freely use it. Just as government has a role in providing a public good such as national defense, it also has a role in encouraging the research and development of new technologies.

The U.S. government has long played a role in the creation and dissemination of technological knowledge. A century ago, the government sponsored research about farming methods and advised farmers how best to use their land. More recently, the U.S. government has, through the Air Force and NASA, supported aerospace research; as a result, the United States is a leading maker of rockets and planes. The government continues to encourage advances in knowledge with research grants from the National Science Foundation and the National Institutes of Health and with tax breaks for firms engaging in research and development.

Yet another way in which government policy encourages research is through the patent system. When a person or firm invents a new product, such as a new drug, the inventor can apply for a patent. If the product is deemed truly original, the government awards the patent, which gives the inventor the exclusive right to make the product for a specified number of years. In essence, the patent gives the inventor a property right over his invention, turning his new idea from a public good into a private good. By allowing inventors to profit from their inventions—even if only temporarily—the patent system enhances the incentive for individuals and firms to engage in research.

Population Growth

Economists and other social scientists have long debated how population growth affects a society. The most direct effect is on the size of the labor force: A large population means more workers to produce goods and services. At the

In The News

Rich Farmers versus the World's Poor

According to the presidents of Mali and Burkina Faso, if the United States and other developed countries more consistently followed the tenets of free trade, the world's poor would benefit.

Your Farm Subsidies Are Strangling Us

By Amadou Toumani Toure and Blaise Compaore

After too many years of Africa's being pushed to the global background, it's heartening to see the world's attention being focused on our continent. International support—both financial and otherwise—is certainly needed to help combat the severe poverty and disease gripping our nations. But first and foremost, Africa needs to be allowed to take its destiny into its own hands. Only self-reliance and economic growth and development will allow Africa to become a full member of the world community.

With the creation of the New Economic Partnership for African Development in 2001, African leaders have committed themselves to following the principles of good governance and a market economy. Nothing is more central to this goal than participating in world trade. As the presidents of two of Africa's least developed nations—Mali and Burkina Faso—we are eager to participate in the multilateral trading system and to take on its rights and obligations.

Cotton is our ticket into the world market. Its production is crucial to economic development in West and Central Africa, as well as to the livelihood of millions of people there. Cotton accounts for up to 40 percent of export revenues and 10 percent of gross domestic product in our two countries, as well as in Benin and Chad. . . .

This vital economic sector in our countries is seriously threatened by agricultural subsidies granted by rich countries to their cotton producers. According to the International Cotton Advisory Committee, cotton subsidies amount to about $5.8 billion in the production year of 2001 to 2002, nearly equal the amount of cotton trade for the same period. Such subsidies lead to worldwide overproduction and distort cotton prices, depriving poor African countries of their only comparative advantage in world trade. . . .

America's 25,000 cotton farmers received more in subsidies—some $3 billion—than the entire economic output of Burkina Faso, where two million people depend on cotton. Further, United States subsidies are concentrated on just 10 percent of its cotton farmers. Thus, the payments to about 2,500 relatively well-off farmers have the unintended but nevertheless very real effect of impoverishing some 10 million rural poor people in West and Central Africa. . . .

Our demand is simple: apply free trade rules not only to those products that are of interest to the rich and powerful, but also to those products where poor countries have a proven comparative advantage. We know that the world will not ignore our plea for a fair playing field. The World Trade Organization has said it is committed to addressing the problems of developing countries. The United States has convinced us that a free market economy provides the best opportunities for all members of the world community. Let us translate these principles into deeds.

Source: *The New York Times*, July 11, 2003.

same time, it means more people to consume those goods and services. Beyond these obvious effects, population growth interacts with the other factors of production in ways that are less obvious and more open to debate.

Stretching Natural Resources Thomas Robert Malthus (1766–1834), an English minister and early economic thinker, is famous for his book called *An Essay on the Principle of Population as It Affects the Future Improvement of Society*. In

In The News

Foreign Aid

Improving the lives of the world's poor is not an easy task.

World Bank Challenged: Are the Poor Really Helped?

By Celia Dugger

Wealthy nations and international organizations, including the World Bank, spend more than $55 billion annually to better the lot of the world's 2.7 billion poor people. Yet they have scant evidence that the myriad projects they finance have made any real difference, many economists say.

That important fact has left some critics of the World Bank, the largest financier of antipoverty programs in de-

veloping countries, dissatisfied, and they have begun throwing down an essential challenge. It is not enough, they say, just to measure how many miles of roads are built, schools constructed or micro-credit loans provided. You must also measure whether those investments actually help poor people live longer, more prosperous lives.

It is a common-sense approach that is harder than it sounds, just like the question it seeks to answer: Does aid really work?

A small band of development economists, who a year ago founded the Poverty Action Lab at the Massachusetts

Institute of Technology, have become influential advocates for randomized evaluations as the best way to answer that question. Such trials, generally regarded as the gold standard in social policy research, involve randomly assigning people eligible for an antipoverty program to get the help or not, then comparing outcomes to see whether those who got the help fared better than those who did not.

It is the same approach that has helped drug companies figure out what medicines are effective and Americans decide how best to reform welfare. Advocates for rigorous evaluations hope to

---

THOMAS ROBERT MALTHUS

it, he offered what may be history's most chilling forecast. Malthus argued that an ever-increasing population would continually strain society's ability to provide for itself. As a result, mankind was doomed to forever live in poverty.

Malthus's logic was simple. He began by noting that "food is necessary to the existence of man" and that "the passion between the sexes is necessary and will remain nearly in its present state." He concluded that "the power of population is infinitely greater than the power in the earth to produce subsistence for man." According to Malthus, the only check on population growth was "misery and vice." Attempts by charities or governments to alleviate poverty were counterproductive, he argued, because they merely allowed the poor to have more children, placing even greater strains on society's productive capabilities.

Fortunately, Malthus's dire forecast was far off the mark. Although the world population has increased about sixfold over the past two centuries, living standards around the world are on average much higher. As a result of economic growth, chronic hunger and malnutrition are less common now than they were in Malthus's day. Famines occur from time to time, but they are more often the result of an unequal income distribution or political instability than inadequate food production.

Where did Malthus go wrong? As we discussed in a case study earlier in this chapter, growth in human ingenuity has offset the effects of a larger population.

make aid more effective, not by directing money to particular countries, but by spending it on programs proven to work.

The Poverty Action Lab scholars have made startling discoveries in their own randomized evaluations.

Adding an extra teacher to classrooms in rural India did not improve children's test scores. But hiring high-school graduates who were paid only $10 to $15 a month to give remedial tutoring to groups of lagging students in a Bombay slum markedly improved reading and math skills.

A series of education experiments in Kenya found that providing poor students with free uniforms or a simple porridge breakfast substantially increased attendance. But giving them drugs to treat the intestinal worms that infect more than a quarter of the world's population was more cost effective, with a price tag of only $3.50 for each extra year of schooling achieved.

Healthier children are more likely to go to school. "You can't answer the general question: Does aid work?" said Esther Duflo, an economist and co-founder of the Poverty Action Lab. "You have to go project by project and accumulate the evidence."

The World Bank, a lumbering giant that employs more than 1,200 Ph.D.'s, is beginning to listen to critics like her. This summer, it is organizing large-scale impact evaluations, including randomized trials, of programs to upgrade slums, improve the performance of schools and keep children healthy and in class. The programs will be tested in dozens of countries.

François Bourguignon, the bank's chief economist, said he hoped this new effort would help the bank, other donors and developing countries "learn what does and does not work."

Rigorous impact evaluations should become part of the bank's culture, he said.

That will require deep change. A recent in-house review of bank projects during the past four to five years found that only 2 percent had been properly evaluated for whether they made a difference, according to Mr. Bourguignon. . . .

"The World Bank spent more than a billion dollars without knowing why they were doing what they were doing—that's the tragedy," said Abhijit Banerjee, an M.I.T. economics professor and co-founder of the Poverty Action Lab. . . .

Mr. Pritchett, a veteran bank economist, tried to explain why rigorous evaluations were such a rarity in the culture of the bank. Its highly trained, well-meaning professionals too often think they know the solutions. "They have too little doubt," he said.

Source: *The New York Times*, July 28, 2004.

Pesticides, fertilizers, mechanized farm equipment, new crop varieties, and other technological advances that Malthus never imagined have allowed each farmer to feed ever greater numbers of people. Even with more mouths to feed, few farmers are necessary because each farmer is so productive.

Diluting the Capital Stock Whereas Malthus worried about the effects of population on the use of natural resources, some modern theories of economic growth emphasize its effects on capital accumulation. According to these theories, high population growth reduces GDP per worker because rapid growth in the number of workers forces the capital stock to be spread more thinly. In other words, when population growth is rapid, each worker is equipped with less capital. A smaller quantity of capital per worker leads to lower productivity and lower GDP per worker.

This problem is most apparent in the case of human capital. Countries with high population growth have large numbers of school-age children. This places a larger burden on the educational system. It is not surprising, therefore, that educational attainment tends to be low in countries with high population growth.

The differences in population growth around the world are large. In developed countries, such as the United States and those in Western Europe, the population has risen only about 1 percent per year in recent decades and is expected to rise even more slowly in the future. By contrast, in many poor African countries, population grows at about 3 percent per year. At this rate, the population doubles every 23 years. This rapid population growth makes it harder to provide workers with the tools and skills they need to achieve high levels of productivity.

Although rapid population growth is not the main reason that less developed countries are poor, some analysts believe that reducing the rate of population growth would help these countries raise their standards of living. In some countries, this goal is accomplished directly with laws that regulate the number of children families may have. China, for instance, allows only one child per family; couples who violate this rule are subject to substantial fines. In countries with greater freedom, the goal of reduced population growth is accomplished less directly by increasing awareness of birth control techniques.

Another way in which a country can influence population growth is to apply one of the *Ten Principles of Economics:* People respond to incentives. Bearing a child, like any decision, has an opportunity cost. When the opportunity cost rises, people will choose to have smaller families. In particular, women with the opportunity to receive good education and desirable employment tend to want fewer children than those with fewer opportunities outside the home. Hence, policies that foster equal treatment of women are one way for less developed economies to reduce the rate of population growth and, perhaps, raise their standards of living.

Promoting Technological Progress   Although rapid population growth may depress economic prosperity by reducing the amount of capital each worker has, it may also have some benefits. Some economists have suggested that world population growth has been an engine of technological progress and economic prosperity. The mechanism is simple: If there are more people, then there are more scientists, inventors, and engineers to contribute to technological advance, which benefits everyone.

Economist Michael Kremer has provided some support for this hypothesis in an article titled "Population Growth and Technological Change: One Million B.C. to 1990," which was published in the *Quarterly Journal of Economics* in 1993. Kremer begins by noting that over the broad span of human history, world growth rates have increased as world population has. For example, world growth was more rapid when the world population was 1 billion (which occurred around the year 1800) than when the population was only 100 million (around 500 B.C.). This fact is consistent with the hypothesis that having more people induces more technological progress.

Kremer's second piece of evidence comes from comparing regions of the world. The melting of the polar icecaps at the end of the Ice Age around 10,000 B.C. flooded the land bridges and separated the world into several distinct regions that could not communicate with one another for thousands of years. If technological progress is more rapid when there are more people to discover things, then larger regions should have experienced more rapid growth.

According to Kremer, that is exactly what happened. The most successful region of the world in 1500 (when Columbus reestablished technological contact) comprised the "Old World" civilizations of the large Eurasia-Africa region. Next in technological development were the Aztec and Mayan civilizations in the Americas, followed by the hunter-gatherers of Australia, and then the primitive people of Tasmania, who lacked even fire-making and most stone and bone tools.

The smallest isolated region was Flinders Island, a tiny island between Tasmania and Australia. With the smallest population, Flinders Island had the fewest opportunities for technological advance and, indeed, seemed to regress.

Around 3000 B.C., human society on Flinders Island died out completely. A large population, Kremer concludes, is a prerequisite for technological advance.

Quick Quiz   Describe three ways a government policymaker can try to raise the growth in living standards in a society. Are there any drawbacks to these policies?

CONCLUSION: THE IMPORTANCE OF LONG-RUN GROWTH

In this chapter, we have discussed what determines the standard of living in a nation and how policymakers can endeavor to raise the standard of living through policies that promote economic growth. Most of this chapter is summarized in one of the *Ten Principles of Economics:* A country's standard of living depends on its ability to produce goods and services. Policymakers who want to encourage growth in standards of living must aim to increase their nation's productive ability by encouraging rapid accumulation of the factors of production and ensuring that these factors are employed as effectively as possible.

Economists differ in their views of the role of government in promoting economic growth. At the very least, government can lend support to the invisible hand by maintaining property rights and political stability. More controversial is whether government should target and subsidize specific industries that might be especially important for technological progress. There is no doubt that these issues are among the most important in economics. The success of one generation's policymakers in learning and heeding the fundamental lessons about economic growth determines what kind of world the next generation will inherit.

SUMMARY

- Economic prosperity, as measured by GDP per person, varies substantially around the world. The average income in the world's richest countries is more than ten times that in the world's poorest countries. Because growth rates of real GDP also vary substantially, the relative positions of countries can change dramatically over time.

- The standard of living in an economy depends on the economy's ability to produce goods and services. Productivity, in turn, depends on the amounts of physical capital, human capital, natural resources, and technological knowledge available to workers.

- Government policies can try to influence the economy's growth rate in many ways: by encouraging saving and investment, encouraging invest-

ment from abroad, fostering education, promoting good health, maintaining property rights and political stability, allowing free trade, promoting the research and development of new technologies, and controlling population growth.

- The accumulation of capital is subject to diminishing returns: The more capital an economy has, the less additional output the economy gets from an extra unit of capital. Because of diminishing returns, higher saving leads to higher growth for a period of time, but growth eventually slows down as the economy approaches a higher level of capital, productivity, and income. Also because of diminishing returns, the return to capital is especially high in poor countries. Other things equal, these countries can grow faster because of the catch-up effect.

- Population growth has a variety of effects on economic growth. On the one hand, more rapid population growth may lower productivity by stretching the supply of natural resources and by reducing the amount of capital available for each worker. On the other hand, a larger population may enhance the rate of technological progress because there are more scientists and engineers.

KEY CONCEPTS

productivity, p. 138
physical capital, p. 139
human capital, p. 140

natural resources, p. 140
technological knowledge, p. 140

diminishing returns, p. 143
catch-up effect, p. 144

QUESTIONS FOR REVIEW

1. What does the level of a nation's GDP measure? What does the growth rate of GDP measure? Would you rather live in a nation with a high level of GDP and a low growth rate or in a nation with a low level of GDP and a high growth rate?

2. List and describe four determinants of productivity.

3. In what way is a college degree a form of capital?

4. Explain how higher saving leads to a higher standard of living. What might deter a policymaker from trying to raise the rate of saving?

5. Does a higher rate of saving lead to higher growth temporarily or indefinitely?

6. Why would removing a trade restriction, such as a tariff, lead to more rapid economic growth?

7. How does the rate of population growth influence the level of GDP per person?

8. Describe two ways the U.S. government tries to encourage advances in technological knowledge.

PROBLEMS AND APPLICATIONS

1. Most countries, including the United States, import substantial amounts of goods and services from other countries. Yet the chapter says that a nation can enjoy a high standard of living only if it can produce a large quantity of goods and services itself. Can you reconcile these two facts?

2. Suppose that society decided to reduce consumption and increase investment.
   a. How would this change affect economic growth?
   b. What groups in society would benefit from this change? What groups might be hurt?

3. Societies choose what share of their resources to devote to consumption and what share to devote to investment. Some of these decisions involve private spending; others involve government spending.
   a. Describe some forms of private spending that represent consumption and some forms that represent investment. The national income accounts include tuition as a part of consumer spending. In your opinion, are the resources you devote to your education a form of consumption or a form of investment?
   b. Describe some forms of government spending that represent consumption and some forms that represent investment. In your opinion, should we view government spend-

ing on health programs as a form of consumption or investment? Would you distinguish between health programs for the young and health programs for the elderly?

4. What is the opportunity cost of investing in capital? Do you think a country can "overinvest" in capital? What is the opportunity cost of investing in human capital? Do you think a country can "overinvest" in human capital? Explain.

5. Suppose that an auto company owned entirely by German citizens opens a new factory in South Carolina.
   a. What sort of foreign investment would this represent?
   b. What would be the effect of this investment on U.S. GDP? Would the effect on U.S. GNP be larger or smaller?

6. In the 1980s, Japanese investors made significant direct and portfolio investments in the United States. At the time, many Americans were unhappy that this investment was occurring.
   a. In what way was it better for the United States to receive this Japanese investment than not to receive it?
   b. In what way would it have been better still for Americans to have made this investment?

7. In the countries of South Asia in 1992, only 56 young women were enrolled in secondary school for every 100 young men. Describe several ways in which greater educational opportu-

nities for young women could lead to faster economic growth in these countries.

8. International data show a positive correlation between income per person and the health of the population.
   a. Explain how higher income might cause better health outcomes.
   b. Explain how better health outcomes might cause higher income.
   c. How might the relative importance of your two hypotheses be relevant for public policy?

9. International data show a positive correlation between political stability and economic growth.
   a. Through what mechanism could political stability lead to strong economic growth?
   b. Through what mechanism could strong economic growth lead to political stability?

10. From 1950 to 2000, manufacturing employment as a percentage of total employment in the U.S. economy fell from 28 percent to 13 percent. At the same time, manufacturing output experienced slightly more rapid growth than the overall economy.
   a. What do these facts say about growth in labor productivity (defined as output per worker) in manufacturing?
   b. In your opinion, should policymakers be concerned about the decline in the share of manufacturing employment? Explain.

 For further information on topics in this chapter, additional problems, examples, applications, online quizzes, and more, please visit our website at http://mankiw.swlearning.com.

Saving, Investment, and the Financial System

Imagine that you have just graduated from college (with a degree in economics, of course) and you decide to start your own business—an economic forecasting firm. Before you make any money selling your forecasts, you have to incur substantial costs to set up your business. You have to buy computers with which to make your forecasts, as well as desks, chairs, and filing cabinets to furnish your new office. Each of these items is a type of capital that your firm will use to produce and sell its services.

How do you obtain the funds to invest in these capital goods? Perhaps you are able to pay for them out of your past savings. More likely, however, like most entrepreneurs, you do not have enough money of your own to finance the start of your business. As a result, you have to get the money you need from other sources.

There are various ways to finance these capital investments. You could borrow the money, perhaps from a bank or from a friend or relative. In this case, you would promise not only to return the money at a later date but also to pay interest for the use of the money. Alternatively, you could convince someone to provide the money you need for your business in exchange for a share of your future profits, whatever they might happen to be. In either case, your investment in computers and office equipment is being financed by someone else's saving.

financial system
the group of institutions in the economy that help to match one person's saving with another person's investment

The **financial system** consists of those institutions in the economy that help to match one person's saving with another person's investment. As we discussed in the previous chapter, saving and investment are key ingredients to long-run economic growth: When a country saves a large portion of its GDP, more resources are available for investment in capital, and higher capital raises a country's productivity and living standard. The previous chapter, however, did not explain how the economy coordinates saving and investment. At any time, some people want to save some of their income for the future, and others want to borrow to finance investments in new and growing businesses. What brings these two groups of people together? What ensures that the supply of funds from those who want to save balances the demand for funds from those who want to invest?

This chapter examines how the financial system works. First, we discuss the large variety of institutions that make up the financial system in our economy. Second, we discuss the relationship between the financial system and some key macroeconomic variables—notably saving and investment. Third, we develop a model of the supply and demand for funds in financial markets. In the model, the interest rate is the price that adjusts to balance supply and demand. The model shows how various government policies affect the interest rate and, thereby, society's allocation of scarce resources.

FINANCIAL INSTITUTIONS IN THE U.S. ECONOMY

At the broadest level, the financial system moves the economy's scarce resources from savers (people who spend less than they earn) to borrowers (people who spend more than they earn). Savers save for various reasons—to put a child through college in several years or to retire comfortably in several decades. Similarly, borrowers borrow for various reasons—to buy a house in which to live or to start a business with which to make a living. Savers supply their money to the financial system with the expectation that they will get it back with interest at a later date. Borrowers demand money from the financial system with the knowledge that they will be required to pay it back with interest at a later date.

The financial system is made up of various financial institutions that help coordinate savers and borrowers. As a prelude to analyzing the economic forces that drive the financial system, let's discuss the most important of these institutions. Financial institutions can be grouped into two categories: financial markets and financial intermediaries. We consider each category in turn.

Financial Markets

financial markets
financial institutions through which savers can directly provide funds to borrowers

Financial markets are the institutions through which a person who wants to save can directly supply funds to a person who wants to borrow. The two most important financial markets in our economy are the bond market and the stock market.

bond
a certificate of indebtedness

The Bond Market   When Intel, the giant maker of computer chips, wants to borrow to finance construction of a new factory, it can borrow directly from the public. It does this by selling bonds. A **bond** is a certificate of indebtedness that specifies the obligations of the borrower to the holder of the bond. Put simply, a bond is an IOU. It identifies the time at which the loan will be repaid, called the *date of maturity,* and the rate of interest that will be paid periodically until the loan matures. The buyer of a bond gives his or her money to Intel in exchange for this promise of interest and eventual repayment of the amount borrowed (called the *principal*). The buyer can hold the bond until maturity or can sell the bond at an earlier date to someone else.

There are literally millions of different bonds in the U.S. economy. When large corporations, the federal government, or state and local governments need to borrow to finance the purchase of a new factory, a new jet fighter, or a new school, they usually do so by issuing bonds. If you look at *The Wall Street Journal* or the business section of your local newspaper, you will find a listing of the prices and interest rates on some of the most important bond issues. Although these bonds differ in many ways, three characteristics of bonds are most important.

The first characteristic is a bond's *term*—the length of time until the bond matures. Some bonds have short terms, such as a few months, while others have terms as long as 30 years. (The British government has even issued a bond that never matures, called a *perpetuity.* This bond pays interest forever, but the principal is never repaid.) The interest rate on a bond depends, in part, on its term. Long-term bonds are riskier than short-term bonds because holders of long-term bonds have to wait longer for repayment of principal. If a holder of a long-term bond needs his money earlier than the distant date of maturity, he has no choice but to sell the bond to someone else, perhaps at a reduced price. To compensate for this risk, long-term bonds usually pay higher interest rates than short-term bonds.

The second important characteristic of a bond is its *credit risk*—the probability that the borrower will fail to pay some of the interest or principal. Such a failure to pay is called a *default.* Borrowers can (and sometimes do) default on their loans by declaring bankruptcy. When bond buyers perceive that the probability of default is high, they demand a higher interest rate to compensate them for this risk. Because the U.S. government is considered a safe credit risk, government bonds tend to pay low interest rates. By contrast, financially shaky corporations raise money by issuing *junk bonds,* which pay very high interest rates. Buyers of bonds can judge credit risk by checking with various private agencies, such as Standard & Poor's, which rate the credit risk of different bonds.

The third important characteristic of a bond is its *tax treatment*—the way the tax laws treat the interest earned on the bond. The interest on most bonds is taxable income so that the bond owner has to pay a portion of the interest in income taxes. By contrast, when state and local governments issue bonds, called *municipal bonds,* the bond owners are not required to pay federal income tax on the interest income. Because of this tax advantage, bonds issued by state and local governments pay a lower interest rate than bonds issued by corporations or the federal government.

The Stock Market Another way for Intel to raise funds to build a new semi-conductor factory is to sell stock in the company. **Stock** represents ownership in a firm and is, therefore, a claim to the profits that the firm makes. For example, if Intel sells a total of 1,000,000 shares of stock, then each share represents ownership of 1/1,000,000 of the business.

stock
a claim to partial ownership in a firm

The sale of stock to raise money is called *equity finance,* whereas the sale of bonds is called *debt finance.* Although corporations use both equity and debt finance to raise money for new investments, stocks and bonds are very different.

The owner of shares of Intel stock is a part owner of Intel; the owner of an Intel bond is a creditor of the corporation. If Intel is very profitable, the stockholders enjoy the benefits of these profits, whereas the bondholders get only the interest on their bonds. And if Intel runs into financial difficulty, the bondholders are paid what they are due before stockholders receive anything at all. Compared to bonds, stocks offer the holder both higher risk and potentially higher return.

After a corporation issues stock by selling shares to the public, these shares trade among stockholders on organized stock exchanges. In these transactions, the corporation itself receives no money when its stock changes hands. The most important stock exchanges in the U.S. economy are the New York Stock Exchange, the American Stock Exchange, and NASDAQ (National Association of Securities Dealers Automated Quotation system). Most of the world's countries have their own stock exchanges on which the shares of local companies trade.

The prices at which shares trade on stock exchanges are determined by the supply of and demand for the stock in these companies. Because stock represents ownership in a corporation, the demand for a stock (and thus its price) reflects people's perception of the corporation's future profitability. When people become optimistic about a company's future, they raise their demand for its stock and thereby bid up the price of a share of stock. Conversely, when people come to expect a company to have little profit or even losses, the price of a share falls.

Various stock indexes are available to monitor the overall level of stock prices. A *stock index* is computed as an average of a group of stock prices. The most famous stock index is the Dow Jones Industrial Average, which has been computed regularly since 1896. It is now based on the prices of the stocks of 30 major U.S. companies, such as General Motors, General Electric, Microsoft, Coca-Cola, AT&T, and IBM. Another well-known stock index is the Standard & Poor's 500 Index, which is based on the prices of 500 major companies. Because stock prices reflect expected profitability, these stock indexes are watched closely as possible indicators of future economic conditions.

Financial Intermediaries

financial intermediaries
financial institutions through which savers can indirectly provide funds to borrowers

Financial intermediaries are financial institutions through which savers can indirectly provide funds to borrowers. The term *intermediary* reflects the role of these institutions in standing between savers and borrowers. Here we consider two of the most important financial intermediaries: banks and mutual funds.

Banks   If the owner of a small grocery store wants to finance an expansion of his business, he probably takes a strategy quite different from Intel. Unlike Intel, a small grocer would find it difficult to raise funds in the bond and stock markets. Most buyers of stocks and bonds prefer to buy those issued by larger, more familiar companies. The small grocer, therefore, most likely finances his business expansion with a loan from a local bank.

Banks are the financial intermediaries with which people are most familiar. A primary job of banks is to take in deposits from people who want to save and use these deposits to make loans to people who want to borrow. Banks pay depositors interest on their deposits and charge borrowers slightly higher interest on their loans. The difference between these rates of interest covers the banks' costs and returns some profit to the owners of the banks.

FYI

How to Read the Newspaper's Stock Tables

Most daily newspapers include stock tables, which contain information about recent trading in the stocks of several thousand companies. Here is the kind of information these tables usually provide:

- *Price.* The single most important piece of information about a stock is the price of a share. The newspaper usually presents several prices. The "last" or "closing" price is the price of the last transaction that occurred before the stock exchange closed the previous day. Many newspapers also give the "high" and "low" prices over the past day of trading and, sometimes, over the past year as well. They may also report the change from the previous day's closing price.
- *Volume.* Most newspapers present the number of shares sold during the past day of trading. This figure is called the *daily volume.*
- *Dividend.* Corporations pay out some of their profits to their stockholders; this amount is called the *dividend.* (Profits not paid out are called *retained earnings* and are used by the corporation for additional investment.) Newspapers often report the dividend paid over the previous year for each share of stock. They sometimes report the *dividend yield,* which is the dividend expressed as a percentage of the stock's price.

- *Price-earnings ratio.* A corporation's earnings, or profit, is the amount of revenue it receives for the sale of its products minus its costs of production as measured by its accountants. Earnings per share is the company's total earnings divided by the number of shares of stock outstanding. Companies use some of their earnings to pay dividends to stockholders; the rest is kept in the firm to make new investments. The price-earnings ratio, often called the P/E, is the price of a corporation's stock divided by the amount the corporation earned per share over the past year. Historically, the typical price-earnings ratio is about 15. A higher P/E indicates that a corporation's stock is expensive relative to its recent earnings; this might indicate either that people expect earnings to rise in the future or that the stock is overvalued. Conversely, a lower P/E indicates that a corporation's stock is cheap relative to its recent earnings; this might indicate either that people expect earnings to fall or that the stock is undervalued.

Why does the newspaper report all these data every day? Many people who invest their savings in stock follow these numbers closely when deciding which stocks to buy and sell. By contrast, other stockholders follow a buy-and-hold strategy: They buy the stock of well-run companies, hold it for long periods of time, and do not respond to the daily fluctuations reported in the paper.

Highest and lowest price over the past year		Name of company	Dividend amount	Dividend yield	Price-earnings ratio	Trading volume over the previous day	Last price at which the stock traded	Change in closing price from the day before
52 Weeks								
Hi	**Lo**	**Stock**	**Div**	**Yld %**	**PE**	**Vol 100s**	**Close**	**Net Chg**
66.04	48.90	Clorox	1.12	2.0	10	15099	56.83	0.95
36.42	17.99	Coach s		...	35	32236	34.97	– 0.47
17.99	11.22	Coachmen	.24	1.9	30	352	12.72	– 0.29
45.88	38.30	CocaCola	1.12	2.5	22	49150	44.36	– 0.31

Besides being financial intermediaries, banks play a second important role in the economy: They facilitate purchases of goods and services by allowing people to write checks against their deposits. In other words, banks help create a special asset that people can use as a *medium of exchange*. A medium of exchange is an item that people can easily use to engage in transactions. A bank's role in providing a medium of exchange distinguishes it from many other financial institutions. Stocks and bonds, like bank deposits, are a possible *store of value* for the wealth that people have accumulated in past saving, but access to this wealth is not as easy, cheap, and immediate as just writing a check. For now, we ignore this second role of banks, but we will return to it when we discuss the monetary system later in the book.

Mutual Funds   A financial intermediary of increasing importance in the U.S. economy is the mutual fund. A **mutual fund** is an institution that sells shares to the public and uses the proceeds to buy a selection, or *portfolio*, of various types of stocks, bonds, or both stocks and bonds. The shareholder of the mutual fund accepts all the risk and return associated with the portfolio. If the value of the portfolio rises, the shareholder benefits; if the value of the portfolio falls, the shareholder suffers the loss.

The primary advantage of mutual funds is that they allow people with small amounts of money to diversify. Buyers of stocks and bonds are well advised to heed the adage: Don't put all your eggs in one basket. Because the value of any single stock or bond is tied to the fortunes of one company, holding a single kind of stock or bond is very risky. By contrast, people who hold a diverse portfolio of stocks and bonds face less risk because they have only a small stake in each company. Mutual funds make this diversification easy. With only a few hundred dollars, a person can buy shares in a mutual fund and, indirectly, become the part owner or creditor of hundreds of major companies. For this service, the company operating the mutual fund charges shareholders a fee, usually between 0.5 and 2.0 percent of assets each year.

A second advantage claimed by mutual fund companies is that mutual funds give ordinary people access to the skills of professional money managers. The managers of most mutual funds pay close attention to the developments and prospects of the companies in which they buy stock. These managers buy the stock of those companies that they view as having a profitable future and sell the stock of companies with less promising prospects. This professional management, it is argued, should increase the return that mutual fund depositors earn on their savings.

mutual fund
an institution that sells shares to the public and uses the proceeds to buy a portfolio of stocks and bonds

ARLO AND JANIS by Jimmy Johnson

Financial economists, however, are often skeptical of this second argument. With thousands of money managers paying close attention to each company's prospects, the price of a company's stock is usually a good reflection of the company's true value. As a result, it is hard to "beat the market" by buying good stocks and selling bad ones. In fact, mutual funds called *index funds,* which buy all the stocks in a given stock index, perform somewhat better on average than mutual funds that take advantage of active management by professional money managers. The explanation for the superior performance of index funds is that they keep costs low by buying and selling very rarely and by not having to pay the salaries of the professional money managers.

Summing Up

The U.S. economy contains a large variety of financial institutions. In addition to the bond market, the stock market, banks, and mutual funds, there are also pension funds, credit unions, insurance companies, and even the local loan shark. These institutions differ in many ways. When analyzing the macroeconomic role of the financial system, however, it is more important to keep in mind the similarity of these institutions than the differences. These financial institutions all serve the same goal: directing the resources of savers into the hands of borrowers.

Quick Quiz   What is stock? What is a bond? How are they different? How are they similar?

SAVING AND INVESTMENT IN THE NATIONAL INCOME ACCOUNTS

Events that occur within the financial system are central to understanding developments in the overall economy. As we have just seen, the institutions that make up this system—the bond market, the stock market, banks, and mutual funds— have the role of coordinating the economy's saving and investment. And as we saw in the previous chapter, saving and investment are important determinants of long-run growth in GDP and living standards. As a result, macroeconomists need to understand how financial markets work and how various events and policies affect them.

As a starting point for an analysis of financial markets, we discuss in this section the key macroeconomic variables that measure activity in these markets. Our emphasis here is not on behavior but on accounting. *Accounting* refers to how various numbers are defined and added up. A personal accountant might help an individual add up his income and expenses. A national income accountant does the same thing for the economy as a whole. The national income accounts include, in particular, GDP and the many related statistics.

The rules of national income accounting include several important identities. Recall that an *identity* is an equation that must be true because of the way the variables in the equation are defined. Identities are useful to keep in mind, for they clarify how different variables are related to one another. Here we consider some accounting identities that shed light on the macroeconomic role of financial markets.

Some Important Identities

Recall that gross domestic product (GDP) is both total income in an economy and the total expenditure on the economy's output of goods and services. GDP (denoted as Y) is divided into four components of expenditure: consumption (C), investment (I), government purchases (G), and net exports (NX). We write

$$Y = C + I + G + NX.$$

This equation is an identity because every dollar of expenditure that shows up on the left side also shows up in one of the four components on the right side. Because of the way each of the variables is defined and measured, this equation must always hold.

In this chapter, we simplify our analysis by assuming that the economy we are examining is closed. A *closed economy* is one that does not interact with other economies. In particular, a closed economy does not engage in international trade in goods and services, nor does it engage in international borrowing and lending. Actual economies are *open economies*—that is, they interact with other economies around the world. Nonetheless, assuming a closed economy is a useful simplification with which we can learn some lessons that apply to all economies. Moreover, this assumption applies perfectly to the world economy (for interplanetary trade is not yet common).

Because a closed economy does not engage in international trade, imports and exports are exactly zero. Therefore, net exports (NX) are also zero. In this case, we can write

$$Y = C + I + G.$$

This equation states that GDP is the sum of consumption, investment, and government purchases. Each unit of output sold in a closed economy is consumed, invested, or bought by the government.

To see what this identity can tell us about financial markets, subtract C and G from both sides of this equation. We obtain

$$Y - C - G = I.$$

The left side of this equation ($Y - C - G$) is the total income in the economy that remains after paying for consumption and government purchases: This amount is called **national saving,** or just **saving,** and is denoted S. Substituting S for $Y - C - G$, we can write the last equation as

national saving (saving) the total income in the economy that remains after paying for consumption and government purchases

$$S = I.$$

This equation states that saving equals investment.

To understand the meaning of national saving, it is helpful to manipulate the definition a bit more. Let T denote the amount that the government collects from households in taxes minus the amount it pays back to households in the form of transfer payments (such as Social Security and welfare). We can then write national saving in either of two ways:

$$S = Y - C - G$$

or

$$S = (Y - T - C) + (T - G).$$

These equations are the same because the two Ts in the second equation cancel each other, but each reveals a different way of thinking about national saving. In particular, the second equation separates national saving into two pieces: private saving $(Y - T - C)$ and public saving $(T - G)$.

Consider each of these two pieces. **Private saving** is the amount of income that households have left after paying their taxes and paying for their consumption. In particular, because households receive income of Y, pay taxes of T, and spend C on consumption, private saving is $Y - T - C$. **Public saving** is the amount of tax revenue that the government has left after paying for its spending. The government receives T in tax revenue and spends G on goods and services. If T exceeds G, the government runs a **budget surplus** because it receives more money than it spends. This surplus of $T - G$ represents public saving. If the government spends more than it receives in tax revenue, then G is larger than T. In this case, the government runs a **budget deficit,** and public saving $T - G$ is a negative number.

Now consider how these accounting identities are related to financial markets. The equation $S = I$ reveals an important fact: *For the economy as a whole, saving must be equal to investment.* Yet this fact raises some important questions: What mechanisms lie behind this identity? What coordinates those people who are deciding how much to save and those people who are deciding how much to invest? The answer is the financial system. The bond market, the stock market, banks, mutual funds, and other financial markets and intermediaries stand between the two sides of the $S = I$ equation. They take in the nation's saving and direct it to the nation's investment.

private saving
the income that households have left after paying for taxes and consumption

public saving
the tax revenue that the government has left after paying for its spending

budget surplus
an excess of tax revenue over government spending

budget deficit
a shortfall of tax revenue from government spending

The Meaning of Saving and Investment

The terms *saving* and *investment* can sometimes be confusing. Most people use these terms casually and sometimes interchangeably. By contrast, the macroeconomists who put together the national income accounts use these terms carefully and distinctly.

Consider an example. Suppose that Larry earns more than he spends and deposits his unspent income in a bank or uses it to buy a bond or some stock from a corporation. Because Larry's income exceeds his consumption, he adds to the nation's saving. Larry might think of himself as "investing" his money, but a macroeconomist would call Larry's act saving rather than investment.

In the language of macroeconomics, investment refers to the purchase of new capital, such as equipment or buildings. When Moe borrows from the bank to build himself a new house, he adds to the nation's investment. Similarly, when the Curly Corporation sells some stock and uses the proceeds to build a new factory, it also adds to the nation's investment.

Although the accounting identity $S = I$ shows that saving and investment are equal for the economy as a whole, this does not have to be true for every individual household or firm. Larry's saving can be greater than his investment, and he can deposit the excess in a bank. Moe's saving can be less than his investment, and he can borrow the shortfall from a bank. Banks and other financial institutions make these individual differences between saving and investment possible by allowing one person's saving to finance another person's investment.

Quick Quiz   Define *private saving, public saving, national saving,* and *investment.* How are they related?

THE MARKET FOR LOANABLE FUNDS

Having discussed some of the important financial institutions in our economy and the macroeconomic role of these institutions, we are ready to build a model of financial markets. Our purpose in building this model is to explain how financial markets coordinate the economy's saving and investment. The model also gives us a tool with which we can analyze various government policies that influence saving and investment.

market for loanable funds

the market in which those who want to save supply funds and those who want to borrow to invest demand funds

To keep things simple, we assume that the economy has only one financial market, called the **market for loanable funds.** All savers go to this market to deposit their saving, and all borrowers go to this market to get their loans. Thus, the term *loanable funds* refers to all income that people have chosen to save and lend out, rather than use for their own consumption. In the market for loanable funds, there is one interest rate, which is both the return to saving and the cost of borrowing.

The assumption of a single financial market, of course, is not literally true. As we have seen, the economy has many types of financial institutions. But as we discussed in Chapter 2, the art in building an economic model is simplifying the world in order to explain it. For our purposes here, we can ignore the diversity of financial institutions and assume that the economy has a single financial market.

Supply and Demand for Loanable Funds

The economy's market for loanable funds, like other markets in the economy, is governed by supply and demand. To understand how the market for loanable funds operates, therefore, we first look at the sources of supply and demand in that market.

The supply of loanable funds comes from people who have some extra income they want to save and lend out. This lending can occur directly, such as when a household buys a bond from a firm, or it can occur indirectly, such as when a household makes a deposit in a bank, which in turn uses the funds to make loans. In both cases, *saving is the source of the supply of loanable funds.*

The demand for loanable funds comes from households and firms who wish to borrow to make investments. This demand includes families taking out mortgages to buy new homes. It also includes firms borrowing to buy new equipment or build factories. In both cases, *investment is the source of the demand for loanable funds.*

The interest rate is the price of a loan. It represents the amount that borrowers pay for loans and the amount that lenders receive on their saving. Because a high interest rate makes borrowing more expensive, the quantity of loanable funds demanded falls as the interest rate rises. Similarly, because a high interest rate makes saving more attractive, the quantity of loanable funds supplied rises as the interest rate rises. In other words, the demand curve for loanable funds slopes downward, and the supply curve for loanable funds slopes upward.

Figure 1 shows the interest rate that balances the supply and demand for loanable funds. In the equilibrium shown, the interest rate is 5 percent, and the quantity of loanable funds demanded and the quantity of loanable funds supplied both equal $1,200 billion.

The adjustment of the interest rate to the equilibrium level occurs for the usual reasons. If the interest rate were lower than the equilibrium level, the

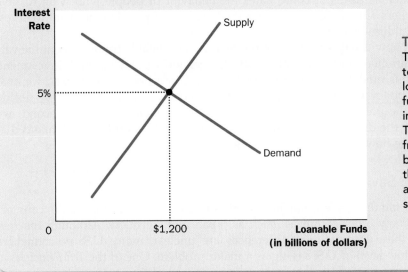

F I G U R E   1

The Market for Loanable Funds
The interest rate in the economy adjusts to balance the supply and demand for loanable funds. The supply of loanable funds comes from national saving, including both private saving and public saving. The demand for loanable funds comes from firms and households that want to borrow for purposes of investment. Here the equilibrium interest rate is 5 percent, and $1,200 billion of loanable funds are supplied and demanded.

quantity of loanable funds supplied would be less than the quantity of loanable funds demanded. The resulting shortage of loanable funds would encourage lenders to raise the interest rate they charge. A higher interest rate would encourage saving (thereby increasing the quantity of loanable funds supplied) and discourage borrowing for investment (thereby decreasing the quantity of loanable funds demanded). Conversely, if the interest rate were higher than the equilibrium level, the quantity of loanable funds supplied would exceed the quantity of loanable funds demanded. As lenders competed for the scarce borrowers, interest rates would be driven down. In this way, the interest rate approaches the equilibrium level at which the supply and demand for loanable funds exactly balance.

Recall that economists distinguish between the real interest rate and the nominal interest rate. The nominal interest rate is the interest rate as usually reported—-the monetary return to saving and the monetary cost of borrowing. The real interest rate is the nominal interest rate corrected for inflation; it equals the nominal interest rate minus the inflation rate. Because inflation erodes the value of money over time, the real interest rate more accurately reflects the real return to saving and the real cost of borrowing. Therefore, the supply and demand for loanable funds depend on the real (rather than nominal) interest rate, and the equilibrium in Figure 1 should be interpreted as determining the real interest rate in the economy. For the rest of this chapter, when you see the term *interest rate,* you should remember that we are talking about the real interest rate.

This model of the supply and demand for loanable funds shows that financial markets work much like other markets in the economy. In the market for milk, for instance, the price of milk adjusts so that the quantity of milk supplied balances the quantity of milk demanded. In this way, the invisible hand coordinates the behavior of dairy farmers and the behavior of milk drinkers. Once we realize that saving represents the supply of loanable funds and investment represents the demand, we can see how the invisible hand coordinates saving and investment. When the interest rate adjusts to balance supply and demand in the market for loanable funds, it coordinates the behavior of people who want to save (the suppliers of loanable funds) and the behavior of people who want to invest (the demanders of loanable funds).

We can now use this analysis of the market for loanable funds to examine various government policies that affect the economy's saving and investment. Because this model is just supply and demand in a particular market, we analyze any policy using the three steps discussed in Chapter 4. First, we decide whether the policy shifts the supply curve or the demand curve. Second, we determine the direction of the shift. Third, we use the supply-and-demand diagram to see how the equilibrium changes.

Policy 1: Saving Incentives

American families save a smaller fraction of their incomes than their counterparts in many other countries, such as Japan and Germany. Although the reasons for these international differences are unclear, many U.S. policymakers view the low level of U.S. saving as a major problem. One of the *Ten Principles of Economics* in Chapter 1 is that a country's standard of living depends on its ability to produce goods and services. And as we discussed in the preceding chapter, saving is an important long-run determinant of a nation's productivity. If the United States could somehow raise its saving rate to the level that prevails in other countries, the growth rate of GDP would increase, and over time, U.S. citizens would enjoy a higher standard of living.

Another of the *Ten Principles of Economics* is that people respond to incentives. Many economists have used this principle to suggest that the low saving rate in the United States is at least partly attributable to tax laws that discourage saving. The U.S. federal government, as well as many state governments, collects revenue by taxing income, including interest and dividend income. To see the effects of this policy, consider a 25-year-old who saves $1,000 and buys a 30-year bond that pays an interest rate of 9 percent. In the absence of taxes, the $1,000 grows to $13,268 when the individual reaches age 55. Yet if that interest is taxed at a rate of, say, 33 percent, then the after-tax interest rate is only 6 percent. In this case, the $1,000 grows to only $5,743 after 30 years. The tax on interest income substantially reduces the future payoff from current saving and, as a result, reduces the incentive for people to save.

In response to this problem, many economists and lawmakers have proposed reforming the tax code to encourage greater saving. For example, one proposal is to expand eligibility for special accounts, such as Individual Retirement Accounts, that allow people to shelter some of their saving from taxation. Let's consider the effect of such a saving incentive on the market for loanable funds, as illustrated in Figure 2. We analyze this policy following our three steps.

First, which curve would this policy affect? Because the tax change would alter the incentive for households to save *at any given interest rate,* it would affect the quantity of loanable funds supplied at each interest rate. Thus, the supply of loanable funds would shift. The demand for loanable funds would remain the same because the tax change would not directly affect the amount that borrowers want to borrow at any given interest rate.

Second, which way would the supply curve shift? Because saving would be taxed less heavily than under current law, households would increase their sav-

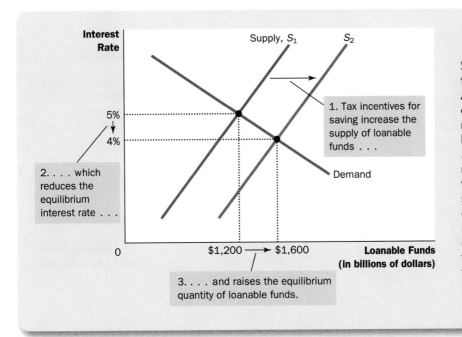

FIGURE **2**

Saving Incentives Increase the Supply of Loanable Funds
A change in the tax laws to encourage Americans to save more would shift the supply of loanable funds to the right from S_1 to S_2. As a result, the equilibrium interest rate would fall, and the lower interest rate would stimulate investment. Here the equilibrium interest rate falls from 5 percent to 4 percent, and the equilibrium quantity of loanable funds saved and invested rises from $1,200 billion to $1,600 billion.

Figure labels:
- Interest Rate
- Supply, S_1
- S_2
- 5%
- 4%
- 1. Tax incentives for saving increase the supply of loanable funds . . .
- 2. . . . which reduces the equilibrium interest rate . . .
- Demand
- 0
- $1,200 → $1,600
- Loanable Funds (in billions of dollars)
- 3. . . . and raises the equilibrium quantity of loanable funds.

ing by consuming a smaller fraction of their income. Households would use this additional saving to increase their deposits in banks or to buy more bonds. The supply of loanable funds would increase, and the supply curve would shift to the right from S_1 to S_2, as shown in Figure 2.

Finally, we can compare the old and new equilibria. In the figure, the increased supply of loanable funds reduces the interest rate from 5 percent to 4 percent. The lower interest rate raises the quantity of loanable funds demanded from $1,200 billion to $1,600 billion. That is, the shift in the supply curve moves the market equilibrium along the demand curve. With a lower cost of borrowing, households and firms are motivated to borrow more to finance greater investment. Thus, *if a reform of the tax laws encouraged greater saving, the result would be lower interest rates and greater investment.*

Although this analysis of the effects of increased saving is widely accepted among economists, there is less consensus about what kinds of tax changes should be enacted. Many economists endorse tax reform aimed at increasing saving to stimulate investment and growth. Yet others are skeptical that these tax changes would have much effect on national saving. These skeptics also doubt the equity of the proposed reforms. They argue that, in many cases, the benefits of the tax changes would accrue primarily to the wealthy, who are least in need of tax relief.

Policy 2: Investment Incentives

Suppose that Congress passed a tax reform aimed at making investment more attractive. In essence, this is what Congress does when it institutes an *investment tax credit*, which it does from time to time. An investment tax credit gives a tax advantage to any firm building a new factory or buying a new piece of

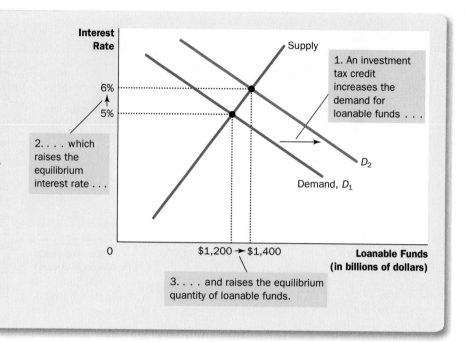

3 FIGURE

Investment Incentives Increase the Demand for Loanable Funds

If the passage of an investment tax credit encouraged firms to invest more, the demand for loanable funds would increase. As a result, the equilibrium interest rate would rise, and the higher interest rate would stimulate saving. Here, when the demand curve shifts from D_1 to D_2, the equilibrium interest rate rises from 5 percent to 6 percent, and the equilibrium quantity of loanable funds saved and invested rises from $1,200 billion to $1,400 billion.

equipment. Let's consider the effect of such a tax reform on the market for loanable funds, as illustrated in Figure 3.

First, would the law affect supply or demand? Because the tax credit would reward firms that borrow and invest in new capital, it would alter investment at any given interest rate and, thereby, change the demand for loanable funds. By contrast, because the tax credit would not affect the amount that households save at any given interest rate, it would not affect the supply of loanable funds.

Second, which way would the demand curve shift? Because firms would have an incentive to increase investment at any interest rate, the quantity of loanable funds demanded would be higher at any given interest rate. Thus, the demand curve for loanable funds would move to the right, as shown by the shift from D_1 to D_2 in the figure.

Third, consider how the equilibrium would change. In Figure 3, the increased demand for loanable funds raises the interest rate from 5 percent to 6 percent, and the higher interest rate in turn increases the quantity of loanable funds supplied from $1,200 billion to $1,400 billion, as households respond by increasing the amount they save. This change in household behavior is represented here as a movement along the supply curve. Thus, *if a reform of the tax laws encouraged greater investment, the result would be higher interest rates and greater saving.*

Policy 3: Government Budget Deficits and Surpluses

A perpetual topic of political debate is the status of the government budget. Recall that a *budget deficit* is an excess of government spending over tax revenue. Governments finance budget deficits by borrowing in the bond market, and the accumulation of past government borrowing is called the *government debt*. A *budget surplus*, an excess of tax revenue over government spending, can be used

When the government spends more than it receives in tax revenue, the resulting budget deficit lowers national saving. The supply of loanable funds decreases, and the equilibrium interest rate rises. Thus, when the government borrows to finance its budget deficit, it crowds out households and firms that otherwise would borrow to finance investment. Here, when the supply shifts from S_1 to S_2, the equilibrium interest rate rises from 5 percent to 6 percent, and the equilibrium quantity of loanable funds saved and invested falls from $1,200 billion to $800 billion.

FIGURE 4

The Effect of a Government Budget Deficit

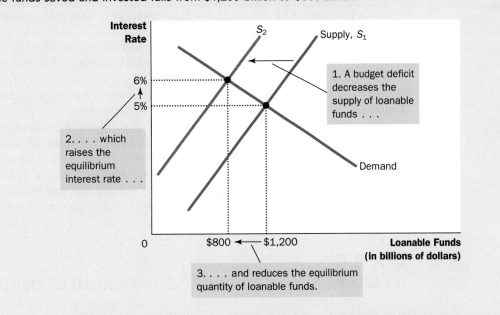

to repay some of the government debt. If government spending exactly equals tax revenue, the government is said to have a *balanced budget*.

Imagine that the government starts with a balanced budget and then, because of a tax cut or a spending increase, starts running a budget deficit. We can analyze the effects of the budget deficit by following our three steps in the market for loanable funds, as illustrated in Figure 4.

First, which curve shifts when the government starts running a budget deficit? Recall that national saving—the source of the supply of loanable funds—is composed of private saving and public saving. A change in the government budget balance represents a change in public saving and, thereby, in the supply of loanable funds. Because the budget deficit does not influence the amount that households and firms want to borrow to finance investment at any given interest rate, it does not alter the demand for loanable funds.

Second, which way does the supply curve shift? When the government runs a budget deficit, public saving is negative, and this reduces national saving. In other words, when the government borrows to finance its budget deficit, it reduces the supply of loanable funds available to finance investment by households and firms. Thus, a budget deficit shifts the supply curve for loanable funds to the left from S_1 to S_2, as shown in Figure 4.

Third, we can compare the old and new equilibria. In the figure, when the budget deficit reduces the supply of loanable funds, the interest rate rises from 5 percent to 6 percent. This higher interest rate then alters the behavior of the households and firms that participate in the loan market. In particular, many demanders of loanable funds are discouraged by the higher interest rate. Fewer families buy new homes, and fewer firms choose to build new factories. The fall in investment because of government borrowing is called **crowding out** and is represented in the figure by the movement along the demand curve from a quantity of $1,200 billion in loanable funds to a quantity of $800 billion. That is, when the government borrows to finance its budget deficit, it crowds out private borrowers who are trying to finance investment.

Thus, the most basic lesson about budget deficits follows directly from their effects on the supply and demand for loanable funds: *When the government reduces national saving by running a budget deficit, the interest rate rises, and investment falls.* Because investment is important for long-run economic growth, government budget deficits reduce the economy's growth rate.

Government budget surpluses work just the opposite as budget deficits. When government collects more in tax revenue than it spends, its saves the difference by retiring some of the outstanding government debt. This budget surplus, or public saving, contributes to national saving. Thus, *a budget surplus increases the supply of loanable funds, reduces the interest rate, and stimulates investment.* Higher investment, in turn, means greater capital accumulation and more rapid economic growth.

crowding out
a decrease in investment that results from government borrowing

CASE STUDY | THE HISTORY OF U.S. GOVERNMENT DEBT

How indebted is the U.S. government? The answer to this question varies substantially over time. Figure 5 shows the debt of the U.S. federal government expressed as a percentage of U.S. GDP. It shows that the government debt has fluctuated from zero in 1836 to 107 percent of GDP in 1945. In recent years, government debt has been between 30 and 40 percent of GDP.

The behavior of the debt-GDP ratio is one gauge of what's happening with the government's finances. Because GDP is a rough measure of the government's tax base, a declining debt-GDP ratio indicates that the government indebtedness is shrinking relative to its ability to raise tax revenue. This suggests that the government is, in some sense, living within its means. By contrast, a rising debt-GDP ratio means that the government indebtedness is increasing relative to its ability to raise tax revenue. It is often interpreted as meaning that fiscal policy—government spending and taxes—cannot be sustained forever at current levels.

Throughout history, the primary cause of fluctuations in government debt is war. When wars occur, government spending on national defense rises substantially to pay for soldiers and military equipment. Taxes typically rise as well but by much less than the increase in spending. The result is a budget deficit and increasing government debt. When the war is over, government spending declines, and the debt-GDP ratio starts declining as well.

There are two reasons to believe that debt financing of war is an appropriate policy. First, it allows the government to keep tax rates smooth over time. Without debt financing, tax rates would have to rise sharply during wars, and this

The debt of the U.S. federal government, expressed here as a percentage of GDP, has varied substantially throughout history. It reached its highest level after the large expenditures of World War II but then declined throughout the 1950s and 1960s. It began rising again in the early 1980s when Ronald Reagan's tax cuts were not accompanied by similar cuts in government spending. It then stabilized and even declined slightly in the late 1990s.

Source: U.S. Department of Treasury, U.S. Department of Commerce; and T. S. Berry, "Production and Population since 1789," Bostwick Paper No. 6, Richmond, 1988.

F I G U R E 5

The U.S. Government Debt

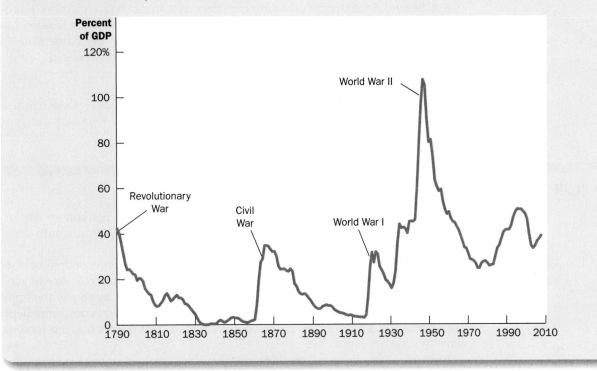

would cause a substantial decline in economic efficiency. Second, debt financing of wars shifts part of the cost of wars to future generations, who will have to pay off the government debt. This is arguably a fair distribution of the burden, for future generations get some of the benefit when one generation fights a war to defend the nation against foreign aggressors.

One large increase in government debt that cannot be explained by war is the increase that occurred beginning around 1980. When President Ronald Reagan took office in 1981, he was committed to smaller government and lower taxes. Yet he found cutting government spending to be more difficult politically than cutting taxes. The result was the beginning of a period of large budget deficits that continued not only through Reagan's time in office but also for many years thereafter. As a result, government debt rose from 26 percent of GDP in 1980 to 50 percent of GDP in 1993.

As we discussed earlier, government budget deficits reduce national saving, investment, and long-run economic growth, and this is precisely why the rise in government debt during the 1980s troubled many economists and policymakers.

When Bill Clinton moved into the Oval Office in 1993, deficit reduction was his first major goal. Similarly, when the Republicans took control of Congress in 1995, deficit reduction was high on their legislative agenda. Both of these efforts substantially reduced the size of the government budget deficit, and it eventually turned into a surplus. As a result, by the late 1990s, the debt-GDP ratio was declining.

The debt-GDP ratio started rising again during the first few years of the George W. Bush presidency, as the budget surplus turned into a budget deficit. There were three reasons for this change. First, President Bush signed into law several major tax cuts, which he had promised during the 2000 presidential campaign. Second, in 2001, the economy experienced a *recession* (a reduction in economic activity), which automatically decreases tax revenue and increases government spending. Third, the war on terrorism following the September 11 attacks and then the war in Iraq led to increases in government spending.   •

Quick Quiz If more Americans adopted a "live for today" approach to life, how would this affect saving, investment, and the interest rate?

CONCLUSION

"Neither a borrower nor a lender be," Polonius advises his son in Shakespeare's *Hamlet*. If everyone followed this advice, this chapter would have been unnecessary.

Few economists would agree with Polonius. In our economy, people borrow and lend often, and usually for good reason. You may borrow one day to start your own business or to buy a home. And people may lend to you in the hope that the interest you pay will allow them to enjoy a more prosperous retirement. The financial system has the job of coordinating all this borrowing and lending activity.

In many ways, financial markets are like other markets in the economy. The price of loanable funds—the interest rate—is governed by the forces of supply and demand, just as other prices in the economy are. And we can analyze shifts in supply or demand in financial markets as we do in other markets. One of the *Ten Principles of Economics* introduced in Chapter 1 is that markets are usually a good way to organize economic activity. This principle applies to financial markets as well. When financial markets bring the supply and demand for loanable funds into balance, they help allocate the economy's scarce resources to their most efficient use.

In one way, however, financial markets are special. Financial markets, unlike most other markets, serve the important role of linking the present and the future. Those who supply loanable funds—savers—do so because they want to convert some of their current income into future purchasing power. Those who demand loanable funds—borrowers—do so because they want to invest today in order to have additional capital in the future to produce goods and services. Thus, well-functioning financial markets are important not only for current generations but also for future generations who will inherit many of the resulting benefits.

SUMMARY

- The U.S. financial system is made up of many types of financial institutions, such as the bond market, the stock market, banks, and mutual funds. All these institutions act to direct the resources of households who want to save some of their income into the hands of households and firms who want to borrow.

- National income accounting identities reveal some important relationships among macroeconomic variables. In particular, for a closed economy, national saving must equal investment. Financial institutions are the mechanism through which the economy matches one person's saving with another person's investment.

- The interest rate is determined by the supply and demand for loanable funds. The supply of loan-

able funds comes from households who want to save some of their income and lend it out. The demand for loanable funds comes from households and firms who want to borrow for investment. To analyze how any policy or event affects the interest rate, one must consider how it affects the supply and demand for loanable funds.

- National saving equals private saving plus public saving. A government budget deficit represents negative public saving and, therefore, reduces national saving and the supply of loanable funds available to finance investment. When a government budget deficit crowds out investment, it reduces the growth of productivity and GDP.

KEY CONCEPTS

financial system, p. 160
financial markets, p. 160
bond, p. 160
stock, p. 161
financial intermediaries, p. 162

mutual fund, p. 164
national saving (saving), p. 166
private saving, p. 167
public saving, p. 167
budget surplus, p. 167

budget deficit, p. 167
market for loanable funds, p. 168
crowding out, p. 174

QUESTIONS FOR REVIEW

1. What is the role of the financial system? Name and describe two markets that are part of the financial system in the U.S. economy. Name and describe two financial intermediaries.

2. Why is it important for people who own stocks and bonds to diversify their holdings? What type of financial institution makes diversification easier?

3. What is national saving? What is private saving? What is public saving? How are these three variables related?

4. What is investment? How is it related to national saving?

5. Describe a change in the tax code that might increase private saving. If this policy were implemented, how would it affect the market for loanable funds?

6. What is a government budget deficit? How does it affect interest rates, investment, and economic growth?

PROBLEMS AND APPLICATIONS

1. For each of the following pairs, which bond would you expect to pay a higher interest rate? Explain.
   a. a bond of the U.S. government or a bond of an East European government
   b. a bond that repays the principal in year 2005 or a bond that repays the principal in year 2025
   c. a bond from Coca-Cola or a bond from a software company you run in your garage
   d. a bond issued by the federal government or a bond issued by New York State

2. Theodore Roosevelt once said, "There is no moral difference between gambling at cards or in lotteries or on the race track and gambling in the stock market." What social purpose do you think is served by the existence of the stock market?

3. When the Russian government defaulted on its debt to foreigners in 1998, interest rates rose on bonds issued by many other developing countries. Why do you suppose this happened?

4. Many workers hold large amounts of stock issued by the firms at which they work. Why do you suppose companies encourage this behavior? Why might a person *not* want to hold stock in the company where he works?

5. Explain the difference between saving and investment as defined by a macroeconomist. Which of the following situations represent investment? Saving? Explain.
   a. Your family takes out a mortgage and buys a new house.
   b. You use your $200 paycheck to buy stock in AT&T.
   c. Your roommate earns $100 and deposits it in her account at a bank.
   d. You borrow $1,000 from a bank to buy a car to use in your pizza delivery business.

6. Suppose GDP is $8 trillion, taxes are $1.5 trillion, private saving is $0.5 trillion, and public saving is $0.2 trillion. Assuming this economy is closed, calculate consumption, government purchases, national saving, and investment.

7. Suppose that Intel is considering building a new chip-making factory.
   a. Assuming that Intel needs to borrow money in the bond market, why would an increase in interest rates affect Intel's decision about whether to build the factory?
   b. If Intel has enough of its own funds to finance the new factory without borrowing, would an increase in interest rates still affect Intel's decision about whether to build the factory? Explain.

8. Suppose the government borrows $20 billion more next year than this year.
   a. Use a supply-and-demand diagram to analyze this policy. Does the interest rate rise or fall?
   b. What happens to investment? To private saving? To public saving? To national saving? Compare the size of the changes to the $20 billion of extra government borrowing.
   c. How does the elasticity of supply of loanable funds affect the size of these changes?
   d. How does the elasticity of demand for loanable funds affect the size of these changes?
   e. Suppose households believe that greater government borrowing today implies higher taxes to pay off the government debt in the future. What does this belief do to private saving and the supply of loanable funds today? Does it increase or decrease the effects you discussed in parts (a) and (b)?

9. Over the past decade, new computer technology has enabled firms to reduce substantially the amount of inventories they hold for each dollar of sales. Illustrate the effect of this change on the market for loanable funds. (Hint: Expenditure on inventories is a type of investment.) What do you think has been the effect on investment in factories and equipment?

10. "Some economists worry that the aging populations of industrial countries are going to start running down their savings just when the investment appetite of emerging economies is growing" (*Economist,* May 6, 1995). Illustrate the effect of these phenomena on the world market for loanable funds.

11. This chapter explains that investment can be increased both by reducing taxes on private saving and by reducing the government budget deficit.
    a. Why is it difficult to implement both of these policies at the same time?
    b. What would you need to know about private saving to judge which of these two policies would be a more effective way to raise investment?

 For further information on topics in this chapter, additional problems, examples, applications, online quizzes, and more, please visit our website at http://mankiw.swlearning.com.

The Basic Tools of Finance

Sometime in your life, you will have to deal with the economy's financial system. You will deposit your savings in a bank account, or you will take out a mortgage to buy a house. After you take a job, you will decide whether to invest your retirement account in stocks, bonds, or other financial instruments. You may try to put together your own stock portfolio, and then you will have to decide between betting on established companies such as General Electric or newer ones such as Google. And whenever you watch the evening news, you will hear reports about whether the stock market is up or down, together with the often feeble attempts to explain why the market behaves as it does.

If you reflect for a moment on the many financial decisions you will make during your life, you will see two related elements in almost all of them: time and risk. As we saw in the preceding chapter, the financial system coordinates the economy's saving and investment. Thus, it concerns decisions we make today that will affect our lives in the future. But the future is unknown. When a person decides to allocate some saving, or a firm decides to undertake an investment, the decision is based on a guess about the likely future result, but the actual result could end up being very different.

This chapter introduces some tools that help us understand the decisions that people make as they participate in financial markets. The field of **finance** develops these tools in great detail, and you may choose to take courses that focus on

finance
the field that studies how people make decisions regarding the allocation of resources over time and the handling of risk

this topic. But because the financial system is so important to the functioning of the economy, many of the basic insights of finance are central to understanding how the economy works. The tools of finance may also help you think through some of the decisions that you will make in your own life.

This chapter takes up three topics. First, we discuss how to compare sums of money at different points in time. Second, we discuss how to manage risk. Third, we build on our analysis of time and risk to examine what determines the value of an asset, such as a share of stock.

PRESENT VALUE: MEASURING THE TIME VALUE OF MONEY

Imagine that someone offered to give you $100 today or $100 in 10 years. Which would you choose? This is an easy question. Getting $100 today is better because you can always deposit the money in a bank, still have it in 10 years, and earn interest on the $100 along the way. The lesson: Money today is more valuable than the same amount of money in the future.

Now consider a harder question: Imagine that someone offered you $100 today or $200 in 10 years. Which would you choose? To answer this question, you need some way to compare sums of money from different points in time. Economists do this with a concept called present value. The **present value** of any future sum of money is the amount today that would be needed, at current interest rates, to produce that future sum.

present value
the amount of money today that would be needed, using prevailing interest rates, to produce a given future amount of money

To learn how to use the concept of present value, let's work through a couple of simple examples:

Question: If you put $100 in a bank account today, how much will it be worth in N years? That is, what will be the **future value** of this $100?

future value
the amount of money in the future that an amount of money today will yield, given prevailing interest rates

Answer: Let's use r to denote the interest rate expressed in decimal form (so an interest rate of 5 percent means $r = 0.05$). Suppose that interest is paid annually and that the interest paid remains in the bank account to earn more interest—a process called **compounding.** Then the $100 will become

compounding
the accumulation of a sum of money in, say, a bank account, where the interest earned remains in the account to earn additional interest in the future

$(1 + r) \times \$100$	after 1 year,
$(1 + r) \times (1 + r) \times \$100 = (1 + r)^2 \times \$100$	after 2 years,
$(1 + r) \times (1 + r) \times (1 + r) \times \$100 = (1 + r)^3 \times \$100$	after 3 years, . . .
$(1 + r)^N \times \$100$	after N years.

For example, if we are investing at an interest rate of 5 percent for 10 years, then the future value of the $100 will be $(1.05)^{10} \times \$100$, which is $163.

Question: Now suppose you are going to be paid $200 in N years. What is the *present value* of this future payment? That is, how much would you have to deposit in a bank right now to yield $200 in N years?

Answer: To answer this question, just turn the previous answer on its head. In the last question, we computed a future value from a present value by *multiplying* by the factor $(1 + r)^N$. To compute a present value from a future value, we *divide* by the factor $(1 + r)^N$. Thus, the present value of $200 in N years is $200/(1 + r)^N$. If that amount is deposited in a bank today, after N years it would become $(1 + r)^N \times [\$200/(1 + r)^N]$, which is $200. For instance, if the interest rate is 5 percent, the present value of $200 in 10 years is $200/(1.05)^{10}$, which is

$123. This means that $123 deposited today in a bank account that earned 5 percent would produce $200 after 10 years.

This illustrates the general formula:

- If r is the interest rate, then an amount X to be received in N years has a present value of $X/(1 + r)^N$.

Because the possibility of earning interest reduces the present value below the amount X, the process of finding a present value of a future sum of money is called *discounting*. This formula shows precisely how much future sums should be discounted.

Let's now return to our earlier question: Should you choose $100 today or $200 in 10 years? We can infer from our calculation of present value that if the interest rate is 5 percent, you should prefer the $200 in 10 years. The future $200 has a present value of $123, which is greater than $100. You are better off waiting for the future sum.

Notice that the answer to our question depends on the interest rate. If the interest rate were 8 percent, then the $200 in 10 years would have a present value of $200/(1.08)^{10}$, which is only $93. In this case, you should take the $100 today. Why should the interest rate matter for your choice? The answer is that the higher the interest rate, the more you can earn by depositing your money at the bank, so the more attractive getting $100 today becomes.

The concept of present value is useful in many applications, including the decisions that companies face when evaluating investment projects. For instance, imagine that General Motors is thinking about building a new factory. Suppose that the factory will cost $100 million today and will yield the company $200 million in 10 years. Should General Motors undertake the project? You can see that this decision is exactly like the one we have been studying. To make its decision, the company will compare the present value of the $200 million return to the $100 million cost.

The company's decision, therefore, will depend on the interest rate. If the interest rate is 5 percent, then the present value of the $200 million return from the factory is $123 million, and the company will choose to pay the $100 million cost. By contrast, if the interest rate is 8 percent, then the present value of the return is only $93 million, and the company will decide to forgo the project. Thus, the concept of present value helps explain why investment—and thus the quantity of loanable funds demanded—declines when the interest rate rises.

Here is another application of present value: Suppose you win a million-dollar lottery and are given a choice between $20,000 a year for 50 years (totaling $1,000,000) or an immediate payment of $400,000. Which would you choose? To make the right choice, you need to calculate the present value of the stream of payments. Suppose the interest rate is 7 percent. After performing 50 calculations similar to those above (one calculation for each payment) and adding up the results, you would learn that the present value of this million-dollar prize at a 7 percent interest rate is only $276,000. You are better off picking the immediate payment of $400,000. The million dollars may seem like more money, but the future cash flows, once discounted to the present, are worth far less.

Quick Quiz   The interest rate is 7 percent. What is the present value of $150 to be received in 10 years?

FYI

The Magic of Compounding and the Rule of 70

Suppose you observe that one country has an average growth rate of 1 percent per year, while another has an average growth rate of 3 percent per year. At first, this might not seem like a big deal. What difference can 2 percent make?

The answer is: a big difference. Even growth rates that seem small when written in percentage terms seem large after they are compounded for many years.

Consider an example. Suppose that two college graduates—Jerry and Elaine—both take their first jobs at the age of 22 earning $30,000 a year. Jerry lives in an economy where all incomes grow at 1 percent per year, while Elaine lives in one where incomes grow at 3 percent per year. Straightforward calculations show what happens. Forty years later, when both are 62 years old, Jerry earns $45,000 a year, while Elaine earns $98,000. Because of that difference of 2 percentage points in the growth rate, Elaine's salary is more than twice Jerry's.

An old rule of thumb, called the *rule of 70,* is helpful in understanding growth rates and the effects of compounding. According to the rule of 70, if some variable grows at a rate of *x* percent per year, then that variable doubles in approximately 70/*x* years. In Jerry's economy, incomes grow at 1 percent per year, so it takes about 70 years for incomes to double. In Elaine's economy, incomes grow at 3 percent per year, so it takes about 70/3, or 23, years for incomes to double.

The rule of 70 applies not only to a growing economy but also to a growing savings account. Here is an example: In 1791, Ben Franklin died and left $5,000 to be invested for a period of 200 years to benefit medical students and scientific research. If this money had earned 7 percent per year (which would, in fact, have been possible to do), the investment would have doubled in value every 10 years. Over 200 years, it would have doubled 20 times. At the end of 200 years of compounding, the investment would have been worth $2^{20} \times \$5,000$, which is about $5 billion. (In fact, Franklin's $5,000 grew to only $2 million over 200 years because some of the money was spent along the way.)

As these examples show, growth rates and interest rates compounded over many years can lead to some spectacular results. That is probably why Albert Einstein once called compounding "the greatest mathematical discovery of all time."

MANAGING RISK

Life is full of gambles. When you go skiing, you risk breaking your leg in a fall. When you drive to work, you risk a car accident. When you put some of your savings in the stock market, you risk a fall in prices. The rational response to this risk is not necessarily to avoid it at any cost but to take it into account in your decision making. Let's consider how a person might do that.

Risk Aversion

risk aversion
a dislike of uncertainty

Most people are **risk averse.** This means more than that people dislike bad things happening to them. It means that they dislike bad things more than they like comparable good things.

For example, suppose a friend offers you the following opportunity. He will toss a coin. If it comes up heads, he will pay you $1,000. But if it comes up tails, you will have to pay him $1,000. Would you accept the bargain? You wouldn't if

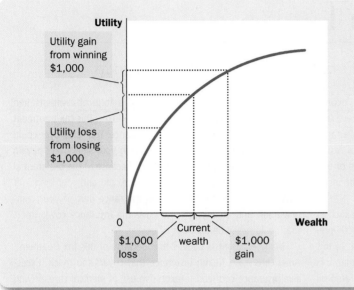

FIGURE 1

The Utility Function
This utility function shows how utility, a subjective measure of satisfaction, depends on wealth. As wealth rises, the utility function becomes flatter, reflecting the property of diminishing marginal utility. Because of diminishing marginal utility, a $1,000 loss decreases utility by more than a $1,000 gain increases it.

you were risk averse. For a risk-averse person, the pain of losing the $1,000 would exceed the pleasure from winning $1,000.

Economists have developed models of risk aversion using the concept of *utility*, which is a person's subjective measure of well-being or satisfaction. Every level of wealth provides a certain amount of utility, as shown by the utility function in Figure 1. But the function exhibits the property of diminishing marginal utility: The more wealth a person has, the less utility he gets from an additional dollar. Thus, in the figure, the utility function gets flatter as wealth increases. Because of diminishing marginal utility, the utility lost from losing the $1,000 bet is more than the utility gained from winning it. As a result, people are risk averse.

Risk aversion provides the starting point for explaining various things we observe in the economy. Let's consider three of them: insurance, diversification, and the risk-return trade-off.

The Markets for Insurance

One way to deal with risk is to buy insurance. The general feature of insurance contracts is that a person facing a risk pays a fee to an insurance company, which in return agrees to accept all or part of the risk. There are many types of insurance. Car insurance covers the risk of your being in an auto accident, fire insurance covers the risk that your house will burn down, health insurance covers the risk that you might need expensive medical treatment, and life insurance covers the risk that you will die and leave your family without your income. There is also insurance against the risk of living too long: For a fee paid today, an insurance company will pay you an *annuity*—a regular income every year until you die.

In a sense, every insurance contract is a gamble. It is possible that you will not be in an auto accident, that your house will not burn down, and that you will not need expensive medical treatment. In most years, you will pay the

FYI

The Peculiarities of Health Insurance

Many economists believe that health insurance in the United States is often poorly designed and, as a result, Americans spend too much on healthcare. Three features of typical health insurance distinguish it from other kinds of insurance, such as car insurance.

First, health insurance often covers routine expenses, such as annual checkups and vaccinations. If an expense is perfectly predictable, there is no reason to buy insurance to cover it. In this sense, health insurance is more like a prepayment plan than it is protection against risk. It is as if your car insurance covered oil changes and tire replacement.

Second, health insurance often covers small, random expenses, such as a doctor's visit for a child with an earache. For most people, such expenses would not have a major financial impact, so there is no need to buy insurance to protect against them. It is as if your car insurance covered the contingency that your taillight might burn out.

Third, many people obtain their health insurance through their employers rather than directly from an insurance company. As a result, when a person loses a job, he or she often loses health insurance as well. By contrast, a person's car insurance continues as long as the premiums are paid.

Why does health insurance have these three unusual features? One reason is the tax system. According to U.S. tax law, employer-provided health insurance is a form of compensation that is exempt from income and payroll taxes. This tax treatment does not apply to other types of insurance: Your employer could not reduce your tax burden by reducing your salary and paying your car insurance premiums for you. Because of the preferential tax treatment given to health insurance, you and your employer have an incentive to make health insurance part of your compensation and an incentive to have the insurance cover items that could easily be paid out of pocket.

Many economists believe that because of this tax treatment, Americans have health insurance that covers too much. Excessive insurance can lead to excessive use of medical care, driving up the amount Americans pay to stay healthy. It would be better, these economists argue, if people bought less expensive insurance that covered only catastrophic losses and paid for small, routine, and discretionary medical expenses out of pocket.

There are various ways policymakers might induce people to change the kind of health insurance they have. Some economists have advocated eliminating the preferential tax treatment now given to health insurance. Others have proposed giving similar tax treatment to medical expenses paid out of pocket. Either reform would level the playing field between different ways of paying for healthcare, thereby reducing the current incentive for employer-provided health insurance.

insurance company the premium and get nothing in return except peace of mind. Indeed, the insurance company is counting on the fact that most people will not make claims on their policies; otherwise, it couldn't pay out the large claims to those few who are unlucky and still stay in business.

From the standpoint of the economy as a whole, the role of insurance is not to eliminate the risks inherent in life but to spread them around more efficiently. Consider fire insurance, for instance. Owning fire insurance does not reduce the risk of losing your home in a fire. But if that unlucky event occurs, the insurance company compensates you. The risk, rather than being borne by you alone, is shared among the thousands of insurance-company shareholders. Because people are risk averse, it is easier for 10,000 people to bear 1/10,000 of the risk than for one person to bear the entire risk himself.

The markets for insurance suffer from two types of problems that impede their ability to spread risk. One problem is *adverse selection:* A high-risk person is more likely to apply for insurance than a low-risk person because a high-risk person would benefit more from insurance protection. A second problem is *moral hazard:* After people buy insurance, they have less incentive to be careful about their risky behavior because the insurance company will cover much of the resulting losses. Insurance companies are aware of these problems, but they cannot fully guard against them. An insurance company cannot perfectly distinguish between high-risk and low-risk customers, and it cannot monitor all of its customers' risky behavior. The price of insurance reflects the actual risks that the insurance company will face after the insurance is bought. The high price of insurance is why some people, especially those who know themselves to be low-risk, decide against buying it and, instead, endure some of life's uncertainty on their own.

Diversification of Firm-Specific Risk

In 2002, Enron, a large and once widely respected company, went bankrupt amid accusations of fraud and accounting irregularities. Several of the company's top executives were prosecuted and ended up going to prison. The saddest part of the story, however, involved thousands of lower-level employees. Not only did they lose their jobs, but many lost their life savings as well. The employees had about two-thirds of their retirement funds in Enron stock, which became worthless.

If there is one piece of practical advice that finance offers to risk-averse people, it is this: "Don't put all your eggs in one basket." You may have heard this before, but finance has turned this folk wisdom into a science. It goes by the name **diversification.**

The market for insurance is one example of diversification. Imagine a town with 10,000 homeowners, each facing the risk of a house fire. If someone starts an insurance company and each person in town becomes both a shareholder and a policyholder of the company, they all reduce their risk through diversification. Each person now faces 1/10,000 of the risk of 10,000 possible fires, rather than the entire risk of a single fire in his own home. Unless the entire town catches fire at the same time, the downside that each person faces is much smaller.

When people use their savings to buy financial assets, they can also reduce risk through diversification. A person who buys stock in a company is placing a bet on the future profitability of that company. That bet is often quite risky because companies' fortunes are hard to predict. Microsoft evolved from a start-up by some geeky teenagers to one of the world's most valuable companies in only a few years; Enron went from one of the world's most respected companies to an almost worthless one in only a few months. Fortunately, a shareholder need not tie his own fortune to that of any single company. Risk can be reduced by placing a large number of small bets, rather than a small number of large ones.

Figure 2 shows how the risk of a portfolio of stocks depends on the number of stocks in the portfolio. Risk is measured here with a statistic called the *standard deviation,* which you may have learned about in a math or statistics class. The standard deviation measures the volatility of a variable—that is, how much the variable is likely to fluctuate. The higher the standard deviation of a portfolio's return, the riskier it is.

The figure shows that the risk of a stock portfolio falls substantially as the number of stocks increases. For a portfolio with single stock, the standard deviation is

diversification
the reduction of risk achieved by replacing a single risk with a large number of smaller unrelated risks

2 FIGURE

Diversification Reduces Risk
This figure shows how the risk of a portfolio, measured here with a statistic called the *standard deviation*, depends on the number of stocks in the portfolio. The investor is assumed to put an equal percentage of his portfolio in each of the stocks. Increasing the number of stocks reduces the amount of risk in a stock portfolio, but it does not eliminate it.

Source: Adapted from Meir Statman, "How Many Stocks Make a Diversified Portfolio?" *Journal of Financial and Quantitative Analysis* 22 (September 1987): 353–364.

Risk (standard deviation of portfolio return)

(More risk)

49

1. Increasing the number of stocks in a portfolio reduces firm-specific risk through diversification . . .

20

2. . . . but market risk remains.

(Less risk)

0   1   4 6 8 10   20   30   40   **Number of Stocks in Portfolio**

---

49 percent. Going from 1 stock to 10 stocks eliminates about half the risk. Going from 10 to 20 stocks reduces the risk by another 13 percent. As the number of stocks continues to increase, risk continues to fall, although the reductions in risk after 20 or 30 stocks are small.

Notice that it is impossible to eliminate all risk by increasing the number of stocks in the portfolio. Diversification can eliminate **firm-specific risk**—the uncertainty associated with the specific companies. But diversification cannot eliminate **market risk**—the uncertainty associated with the entire economy, which affects all companies traded on the stock market. For example, when the economy goes into a recession, most companies experience falling sales, reduced profit, and low stock returns. Diversification reduces the risk of holding stocks, but it does not eliminate it.

firm-specific risk
risk that affects only a single company

market risk
risk that affects all companies in the stock market

The Trade-off between Risk and Return

One of the *Ten Principles of Economics* in Chapter 1 is that people face trade-offs. The trade-off that is most relevant for understanding financial decisions is the trade-off between risk and return.

As we have seen, there are risks inherent in holding stocks, even in a diversified portfolio. But risk-averse people are willing to accept this uncertainty because they are compensated for doing so. Historically, stocks have offered much higher rates of return than alternative financial assets, such as bonds and bank savings accounts. Over the past two centuries, stocks offered an average real return of about 8 percent per year, while short-term government bonds paid a real return of only 3 percent per year.

When deciding how to allocate their savings, people have to decide how much risk they are willing to undertake to earn the higher return. Figure 3 illustrates the risk-return trade-off for a person choosing how to allocate his portfolio between two asset classes:

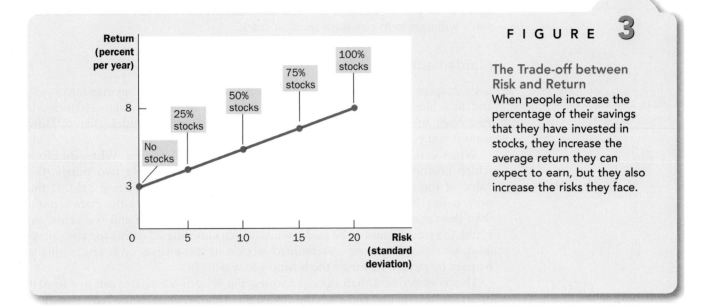

FIGURE 3

The Trade-off between Risk and Return
When people increase the percentage of their savings that they have invested in stocks, they increase the average return they can expect to earn, but they also increase the risks they face.

- The first asset class is a diversified group of risky stocks, with an average return of 8 percent and a standard deviation of 20 percent. (You may recall from a math or statistics class that a normal random variable stays within two standard deviations of its average about 95 percent of the time. Thus, while actual returns are centered around 8 percent, they typically vary from a gain of 48 percent to a loss of 32 percent.)
- The second asset class is a safe alternative, with a return of 3 percent and a standard deviation of zero. The safe alternative can be either a bank savings account or a government bond.

Each point in this figure represents a particular allocation of a portfolio between risky stocks and the safe asset. The figure shows that the more a person puts into stocks, the greater is both the risk and the return.

Acknowledging the risk-return trade-off does not, by itself, tell us what a person should do. The choice of a particular combination of risk and return depends on a person's risk aversion, which reflects a person's own preferences. But it is important for stockholders to realize that the higher average return that they enjoy comes at the price of higher risk.

Quick Quiz Describe three ways that a risk-averse person might reduce the risk he faces.

ASSET VALUATION

Now that we have developed a basic understanding of the two building blocks of finance—time and risk—let's apply this knowledge. This section considers a simple question: What determines the price of a share of stock? Like most prices, the answer is supply and demand. But that is not the end of the story. To understand stock prices, we need to think more deeply about what determines a person's willingness to pay for a share of stock.

Fundamental Analysis

Let's imagine that you have decided to put 60 percent of your savings into stock, and to achieve diversification, you have decided to buy 20 different stocks. If you open up the newspaper, you will find thousands of stocks listed. How should you pick the 20 for your portfolio?

When you buy stock, you are buying shares in a business. When deciding which businesses you want to own, it is natural to consider two things: the value of the business and the price at which the shares are being sold. If the price is less than the value, the stock is said to be *undervalued.* If the price is more than the value, the stock is said to be *overvalued.* If the price and the value are equal, the stock is said to be *fairly valued.* When choosing 20 stocks for your portfolio, you should prefer undervalued stocks. In these cases, you are getting a bargain by paying less than the business is worth.

This is easier said than done. Learning the price is easy: You can just look it up in the newspaper. Determining the value of the business is the hard part. The term **fundamental analysis** refers to the detailed analysis of a company to determine its value. Many Wall Street firms hire stock analysts to conduct such fundamental analysis and offer advice about which stocks to buy.

The value of a stock to a stockholder is what he gets out of owning it, which includes the present value of the stream of dividend payments and the final sale price. Recall that *dividends* are the cash payments that a company makes to its shareholders. A company's ability to pay dividends, as well as the value of the stock when the stockholder sells his shares, depends on the company's ability to earn profits. Its profitability, in turn, depends on a large number of factors: the demand for its product, how much competition it faces, how much capital it has in place, whether its workers are unionized, how loyal its customers are, what kinds of government regulations and taxes it faces, and so on. The job of fundamental analysts is to take all these factors into account to determine how much a share of stock in the company is worth.

If you want to rely on fundamental analysis to pick a stock portfolio, there are three ways to do it. One way is to do all the necessary research yourself, such as by reading through companies' annual reports. A second way is to rely on the advice of Wall Street analysts. A third way is to buy a mutual fund, which has a manager who conducts fundamental analysis and makes the decision for you.

The Efficient Markets Hypothesis

There is another way to choose 20 stocks for your portfolio: Pick them randomly by, for instance, putting the stock pages on your bulletin board and throwing darts at the page. This may sound crazy, but there is reason to believe that it won't lead you too far astray. That reason is called the **efficient markets hypothesis.**

To understand this theory, the starting point is to acknowledge that each company listed on a major stock exchange is followed closely by many money managers, such as the individuals who run mutual funds. Every day, these managers monitor news stories and conduct fundamental analysis to try to determine the stock's value. Their job is to buy a stock when its price falls below its value and to sell it when its price rises above its value.

fundamental analysis
the study of a company's accounting statements and future prospects to determine its value

efficient markets hypothesis
the theory that asset prices reflect all publicly available information about the value of an asset

The second piece to the efficient markets hypothesis is that the equilibrium of supply and demand sets the market price. This means that, at the market price, the number of shares being offered for sale exactly equals the number of shares that people want to buy. In other words, at the market price, the number of people who think the stock is overvalued exactly balances the number of people who think it's undervalued. As judged by the typical person in the market, all stocks are fairly valued all the time.

According to this theory, the stock market is **informationally efficient:** It reflects all available information about the value of the asset. Stock prices change when information changes. When good news about the company's prospects becomes public, the value and the stock price both rise. When the company's prospects deteriorate, the value and price both fall. But at any moment in time, the market price is the best guess of the company's value based on available information.

One implication of the efficient markets hypothesis is that stock prices should follow a **random walk.** This means that the changes in stock prices are impossible to predict from available information. If, based on publicly available information, a person could predict that a stock price would rise by 10 percent tomorrow, then the stock market must be failing to incorporate that information today. According to this theory, the only thing that can move stock prices is news that changes the market's perception of the company's value. But news must be unpredictable—otherwise, it wouldn't really be news. For the same reason, changes in stock prices should be unpredictable.

If the efficient markets hypothesis is correct, then there is little point in spending many hours studying the business page to decide which 20 stocks to add to your portfolio. If prices reflect all available information, no stock is a better buy than any other. The best you can do is buy a diversified portfolio.

informational efficiency the description of asset prices that rationally reflect all available information

random walk the path of a variable whose changes are impossible to predict

CASE STUDY | RANDOM WALKS AND INDEX FUNDS

The efficient markets hypothesis is a theory about how financial markets work. The theory is probably not completely true: As we discuss in the next section, there is reason to doubt that stockholders are always rational and that stock prices are informationally efficient at every moment. Nonetheless, the efficient markets hypothesis does much better as a description of the world than you might think.

There is much evidence that stock prices, even if not exactly a random walk, are very close to it. For example, you might be tempted to buy stocks that have recently risen and avoid stocks that have recently fallen (or perhaps just the opposite). But statistical studies have shown that following such trends (or bucking them) fails to outperform the market. The correlation between how well a stock does one year and how well it does the following year is almost exactly zero.

Some of the best evidence in favor of the efficient markets hypothesis comes from the performance of index funds. An index fund is a mutual fund that buys all the stocks in a given stock index. The performance of these funds can be compared with that of actively managed mutual funds, where a professional portfolio manager picks stocks based on extensive research and alleged expertise. In essence, an index fund buys all stocks, whereas active funds are supposed to buy only the best stocks.

In The News

Nobel Caliber Investment Advice

The field of behavioral economics combines the insights of psychology and economics. One of the pioneers in this field is Daniel Kahneman.

For a Nobel Prize Winner, Less Is More
By John Wasik

If you've won the Nobel Prize in economics, society assumes you're probably brilliant at managing your own money.

Daniel Kahneman, who shared the Nobel Prize in 2002, didn't win the prize for his investing acumen. He made some key insights into how human psychology consistently flummoxes investing decisions.

Prof Kahneman's research has shown that since we use overconfident, highly emotional logic in making investment decisions, the best approach is often the simplest. For portfolio advice, Prof Kahneman defers to his financial planner.

No matter where you are on the investment learning curve, you can apply Prof Kahneman's research to build a better portfolio. The first step is to ignore your gut feelings about investing.

Instincts, Prof Kahneman has found, are the enemy of sound investing. Working with his research partner Amos Tversky, who died in 1996, Prof Kahneman discovered that our biggest nemesis was our own ego. We think we know more than we know and act upon it.

Excessive optimism leads us to "underestimate uncertainty." The researchers developed prospect theory, which states that we are loath to accept our losses because they trigger emotional pain. As a result, we hold on to losing investments far too long and sell winners. When we do make decisions, it's based on loss aversion since "losses loom larger than gains." . . .

Prof Kahneman and his colleagues also discovered that we have "an illusion of control" over events such as the stock market that no one can predict with certainty. For example, during the stock market bubble of the last three years, Prof Kahneman observed "a high percentage of investors knew it was a bubble and still invested because they thought they could get out in time."

Prof Kahneman said he believed our brains were hard-wired for small decisions imbued with optimism. "Optimism is a force in capitalism, it may be the engine of capitalism."

Prof Kahneman suggests making fewer financial decisions and focusing on wealth from a big-picture perspective of several decades instead of following the market day to day. . . .

By investing in index mutual funds and US Treasury Inflation-Protected Securities, Prof Kahneman said his primary retirement planning focus was beating inflation and maintaining steady income—a strategy at odds with Wall Street's mantra of maximizing return.

Keep it simple and aim to beat inflation. Don't try to beat the market. Prof Kahneman's approach is an efficient path that won't get derailed by psychology. When it comes to investing, less is more. And if you try to do more, you'll often end up with less.

Source: *The Financial Times,* May 14, 2003.

In practice, active managers usually fail to beat index funds, and in fact, most of them do worse. For example, in the 10 years ending July 2005, 80 percent of stock mutual funds failed to beat an index fund holding all 500 stocks in the Standard & Poor's 500 Index. Most active portfolio managers give a lower return than index funds because they trade more frequently, incurring more trading costs, and because they charge greater fees as compensation for their alleged expertise.

What about those 20 percent of managers who did beat the market? Perhaps they are smarter than average, or perhaps they were luckier. If you have 5,000 people flipping coins ten times, on average about five will flip ten heads; these five might claim an exceptional coin-flipping skill, but they would have trouble replicating the feat. Similarly, studies have shown that mutual fund managers with a history of superior performance usually fail to maintain it in subsequent periods.

The efficient markets hypothesis says that it is impossible to beat the market. The accumulation of many studies in financial markets confirms that beating the market is, at best, extremely difficult. Even if the efficient markets hypothesis is not an exact description of the world, it contains a large element of truth.   •

Market Irrationality

The efficient markets hypothesis assumes that people buying and selling stock rationally process the information they have about the stock's underlying value. But is the stock market really that rational? Or do stock prices sometimes deviate from reasonable expectations of their true value?

There is a long tradition suggesting that fluctuations in stock prices are partly psychological. In the 1930s, economist John Maynard Keynes suggested that asset markets are driven by the "animal spirits" of investors—irrational waves of optimism and pessimism. In the 1990s, as the stock market soared to new heights, Fed Chairman Alan Greenspan questioned whether the boom reflected "irrational exuberance." Stock prices did subsequently fall, but whether the exuberance of the 1990s was irrational given the information available at the time remains debatable.

The possibility of such speculative bubbles arises in part because the value of the stock to a stockholder depends not only on the stream of dividend payments but also on the final sale price. Thus, a person might be willing to pay more than a stock is worth today if he expects another person to pay even more for it tomorrow. When you evaluate a stock, you have to estimate not only the value of the business but also what other people will think the business is worth in the future.

There is much debate among economists about whether departures from rational pricing are important or rare. Believers in market irrationality point out (correctly) that the stock market often moves in ways that are hard to explain on the basis of news that might alter a rational valuation. Believers in the efficient markets hypothesis point out (correctly) that it is impossible to know the correct, rational valuation of a company, so one should not quickly jump to the conclusion that any particular valuation is irrational. Moreover, if the market were irrational, a rational person should be able to take advantage of this fact; yet as the previous case study discussed, beating the market is nearly impossible.

Quick Quiz *Fortune* magazine regularly publishes a list of the "most respected" companies. According to the efficient markets hypothesis, if you restrict your stock portfolio to these companies, will you earn a better than average return? Explain.

CONCLUSION

This chapter has developed some of the basic tools that people should (and often do) use as they make financial decisions. The concept of present value reminds us that a dollar in the future is less valuable than a dollar today, and it gives us a way to compare sums of money at different points in time. The theory of risk management reminds us that the future is uncertain and that risk-averse people can take precautions to guard against this uncertainty. The study of asset valuation tells us that the stock price of any company should reflect its expected future profitability.

Although most of the tools of finance are well established, there is more controversy about the validity of the efficient markets hypothesis and whether stock prices are, in practice, rational estimates of a company's true worth. Rational or not, the large movements in stock prices that we observe have important macroeconomic implications. Stock market fluctuations often go hand in hand with fluctuations in the economy more broadly. We will revisit the stock market when we study economic fluctuations later in the book.

SUMMARY

- Because savings can earn interest, a sum of money today is more valuable than the same sum of money in the future. A person can compare sums from different times using the concept of present value. The present value of any future sum is the amount that would be needed today, given prevailing interest rates, to produce that future sum.

- Because of diminishing marginal utility, most people are risk averse. Risk-averse people can reduce risk using insurance, through diversification, and by choosing a portfolio with lower risk and lower return.

- The value of an asset, such as a share of stock, equals the present value of the cash flows the owner of the share will receive, including the stream of dividends and the final sale price. According to the efficient markets hypothesis, financial markets process available information rationally, so a stock price always equals the best estimate of the value of the underlying business. Some economists question the efficient markets hypothesis, however, and believe that irrational psychological factors also influence asset prices.

KEY CONCEPTS

finance, p. 181
present value, p. 182
future value, p. 182
compounding, p. 182
risk aversion, p. 184

diversification, p. 187
firm-specific risk, p. 188
market risk, p. 188
fundamental analysis, p. 190

efficient markets hypothesis,
   p. 190
informational efficiency, p. 191
random walk, p. 191

QUESTIONS FOR REVIEW

1. The interest rate is 7 percent. Use the concept of present value to compare $200 to be received in 10 years and $300 to be received in 20 years.

2. What benefit do people get from the market for insurance? What two problems impede the insurance company from working perfectly?

3. What is diversification? Does a stockholder get more diversification going from 1 to 10 stocks or going from 100 to 120 stocks?

4. Comparing stocks and government bonds, which has more risk? Which pays a higher average return?

5. What factors should a stock analyst think about in determining the value of a share of stock?

6. Describe the efficient markets hypothesis and give a piece of evidence consistent with this hypothesis.

7. Explain the view of those economists who are skeptical of the efficient markets hypothesis.

PROBLEMS AND APPLICATIONS

1. According to an old myth, Native Americans sold the island of Manhattan about 400 years ago for $24. If they had invested this amount at an interest rate of 7 percent per year, how much would they have today?

2. A company has an investment project that would cost $10 million today and yield a payoff of $15 million in 4 years.
   a. Should the firm undertake the project if the interest rate is 11 percent? 10 percent? 9 percent? 8 percent?
   b. Can you figure out the exact cutoff for the interest rate between profitability and non-profitability?

3. For each of the following kinds of insurance, give an example of behavior that can be called *moral hazard* and another example of behavior that can be called *adverse selection.*
   a. health insurance
   b. car insurance

4. Imagine that the U.S. Congress, recognizing the importance of being well dressed, started giving preferential tax treatment to "clothing insurance." Under this new type of insurance, you would pay the insurance company an annual premium, the insurance company would then pay for 80 percent of your clothing expenses (you pay the remaining 20 percent), and the tax laws would partly subsidize your insurance premiums.
   a. How would the existence of such insurance affect the amount of clothing that people buy? How would you evaluate this change in behavior from the standpoint of economic efficiency?
   b. Who would choose to buy clothing insurance?

   c. Suppose that the average person now spends $2,000 a year on clothes. Would clothing insurance cost more or less than $2,000? Explain.
   d. In your view, is this congressional action a good idea? How would you compare this idea with the current tax treatment of health insurance?

5. Imagine that you intend to buy a portfolio of ten stocks with some of your savings. Should the stocks be of companies in the same industry? Should the stocks be of companies located in the same country? Explain.

6. Which kind of stock would you expect to pay the higher average return: stock in an industry that is very sensitive to economic conditions (such as an automaker) or stock in an industry that is relatively insensitive to economic conditions (such as a water company)? Why?

7. A company faces two kinds of risk. A firm-specific risk is that a competitor might enter its market and take some of its customers. A market risk is that the economy might enter a recession, reducing sales. Which of these two risks would more likely cause the company's shareholders to demand a higher return? Why?

8. You have two roommates who invest in the stock market.
   a. One roommate says that he buys stock only in companies that everyone believes will experience big increases in profits in the future. How do you suppose the price-earnings ratio of these companies compares to the price-earnings ratio of other companies? What might be the disadvantage of buying stock in these companies?

b. Another roommate says he only buys stock in companies that are cheap, which he measures by a low price-earnings ratio. How do you suppose the earnings prospects of these companies compare to those of other companies? What might be the disadvantage of buying stock in these companies?

9. When company executives buy and sell stock based on private information they obtain as part of their jobs, they are engaged in *insider trading*.

a. Give an example of inside information that might be useful for buying or selling stock.

b. Those who trade stocks based on inside information usually earn very high rates of return. Does this fact violate the efficient markets hypothesis?

c. Insider trading is illegal. Why do you suppose that is?

10. Find some information on an index fund (such as the Vanguard 500 Index, ticker symbol VFINX). How has this fund performed compared with other stock mutual funds over the past 5 or 10 years? (Hint: One place to look for data on mutual funds is http://www.morningstar.com.) What do you learn from this comparison?

 For further information on topics in this chapter, additional problems, examples, applications, online quizzes, and more, please visit our website at http://mankiw.swlearning.com.

Unemployment

Losing a job can be the most distressing economic event in a person's life. Most people rely on their labor earnings to maintain their standard of living, and many people get from their work not only income but also a sense of personal accomplishment. A job loss means a lower living standard in the present, anxiety about the future, and reduced self-esteem. It is not surprising, therefore, that politicians campaigning for office often speak about how their proposed policies will help create jobs.

In previous chapters, we have seen some of the forces that determine the level and growth of a country's standard of living. A country that saves and invests a high fraction of its income, for instance, enjoys more rapid growth in its capital stock and its GDP than a similar country that saves and invests less. An even more obvious determinant of a country's standard of living is the amount of unemployment it typically experiences. People who would like to work but cannot find a job are not contributing to the economy's production of goods and services. Although some degree of unemployment is inevitable in a complex economy with thousands of firms and millions of workers, the amount of unemployment varies substantially over time and across countries. When a country keeps its workers as fully employed as possible, it achieves a higher level of GDP than it would if it left many of its workers standing idle.

This chapter begins our study of unemployment. The problem of unemployment is usefully divided into two categories: the long-run problem and the short-run problem. The economy's *natural rate of unemployment* refers to the amount of unemployment that the economy normally experiences. *Cyclical unemployment* refers to the year-to-year fluctuations in unemployment around its natural rate, and it is closely associated with the short-run ups and downs of economic activity. Cyclical unemployment has its own explanation, which we defer until we study short-run economic fluctuations later in this book. In this chapter, we discuss the determinants of an economy's natural rate of unemployment. As we will see, the designation *natural* does not imply that this rate of unemployment is desirable. Nor does it imply that it is constant over time or impervious to economic policy. It merely means that this unemployment does not go away on its own even in the long run.

We begin the chapter by looking at some of the relevant facts that describe unemployment. In particular, we examine three questions: How does the government measure the economy's rate of unemployment? What problems arise in interpreting the unemployment data? How long are the unemployed typically without work?

We then turn to the reasons economies always experience some unemployment and the ways in which policymakers can help the unemployed. We discuss four explanations for the economy's natural rate of unemployment: job search, minimum-wage laws, unions, and efficiency wages. As we will see, long-run unemployment does not arise from a single problem that has a single solution. Instead, it reflects a variety of related problems. As a result, there is no easy way for policymakers to reduce the economy's natural rate of unemployment and, at the same time, to alleviate the hardships experienced by the unemployed.

IDENTIFYING UNEMPLOYMENT

Let's start by examining more precisely what the term *unemployment* means.

How Is Unemployment Measured?

Measuring unemployment is the job of the Bureau of Labor Statistics (BLS), which is part of the Department of Labor. Every month, the BLS produces data on unemployment and on other aspects of the labor market, such as types of employment, length of the average workweek, and the duration of unemployment. These data come from a regular survey of about 60,000 households, called the Current Population Survey.

Based on the answers to survey questions, the BLS places each adult (aged 16 and older) in each surveyed household into one of three categories:

- *Employed:* This category includes those who worked as paid employees, worked in their own business, or worked as unpaid workers in a family member's business. It also includes those who were not working but who had jobs from which they were temporarily absent because of, for example, vacation, illness, or bad weather.
- *Unemployed:* This category includes those who were not employed, were available for work, and had tried to find employment during the previous 4 weeks. It also includes those waiting to be recalled to a job from which they had been laid off.

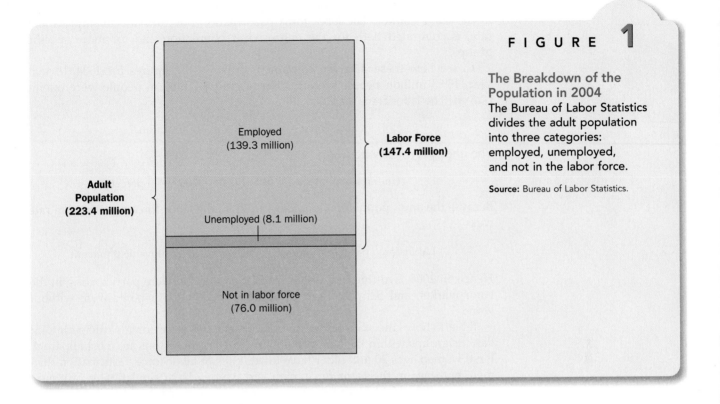

FIGURE 1

The Breakdown of the Population in 2004
The Bureau of Labor Statistics divides the adult population into three categories: employed, unemployed, and not in the labor force.

Source: Bureau of Labor Statistics.

- *Not in the labor force:* This category includes those who fit neither of the first two categories, such as a full-time student, homemaker, or retiree.

Figure 1 shows the breakdown into these categories for 2004.

Once the BLS has placed all the individuals covered by the survey in a category, it computes various statistics to summarize the state of the labor market. The BLS defines the **labor force** as the sum of the employed and the unemployed:

$$\text{Labor force} = \text{Number of employed} + \text{Number of unemployed}.$$

labor force
the total number of workers, including both the employed and the unemployed

The BLS defines the **unemployment rate** as the percentage of the labor force that is unemployed:

$$\text{Unemployment rate} = \frac{\text{Number of unemployed}}{\text{Labor force}} \times 100.$$

unemployment rate
the percentage of the labor force that is unemployed

The BLS computes unemployment rates for the entire adult population and for more narrowly defined groups such as blacks, whites, men, women, and so on.

The BLS uses the same survey to produce data on labor-force participation. The **labor-force participation rate** measures the percentage of the total adult population of the United States that is in the labor force:

$$\text{Labor-force participation rate} = \frac{\text{Labor force}}{\text{Adult population}} \times 100.$$

labor-force participation rate
the percentage of the adult population that is in the labor force

This statistic tells us the fraction of the population that has chosen to participate in the labor market. The labor-force participation rate, like the unemployment rate, is computed both for the entire adult population and for more specific groups.

To see how these data are computed, consider the figures for 2004. In that year, 139.3 million people were employed, and 8.1 million people were unemployed. The labor force was

$$\text{Labor force} = 139.3 + 8.1 = 147.4 \text{ million.}$$

The unemployment rate was

$$\text{Unemployment rate} = (8.1/147.4) \times 100 = 5.5 \text{ percent.}$$

Because the adult population was 223.4 million, the labor-force participation rate was

$$\text{Labor-force participation rate} = (147.4/223.4) \times 100 = 66.0 \text{ percent.}$$

Hence, in 2004, two-thirds of the U.S. adult population were participating in the labor market, and 5.5 percent of those labor-market participants were without work.

Table 1 shows the statistics on unemployment and labor-force participation for various groups within the U.S. population. Three comparisons are most apparent. First, women ages 20 and older have lower rates of labor-force participation than men, but once in the labor force, men and women have similar rates of unemployment. Second, blacks ages 20 and older have similar rates of labor-force participation as whites, but they have much higher rates of unemployment. Third, teenagers have lower rates of labor-force participation and much higher rates of unemployment than older workers. More generally, these data show that labor-market experiences vary widely among groups within the economy.

The BLS data on the labor market also allow economists and policymakers to monitor changes in the economy over time. Figure 2 shows the unemployment rate in the United States since 1960. The figure shows that the economy always has some unemployment and that the amount changes from year to year. The normal rate of unemployment around which the unemployment rate fluctuates is called the **natural rate of unemployment,** and the deviation of unemployment

natural rate of unemployment
the normal rate of unemployment around which the unemployment rate fluctuates

1 TABLE

The Labor-Market Experiences of Various Demographic Groups
This table shows the unemployment rate and the labor-force participation rate of various groups in the U.S. population for 2004.

Source: Bureau of Labor Statistics.

Demographic Group	Unemployment Rate	Labor-Force Participation Rate
Adults (ages 20 and older)		
White, male	4.4%	76.2%
White, female	4.2	59.7
Black, male	9.9	70.9
Black, female	8.9	64.2
Teenagers (ages 16–19)		
White, male	16.3	47.4
White, female	13.6	46.7
Black, male	35.6	30.0
Black, female	28.2	32.8

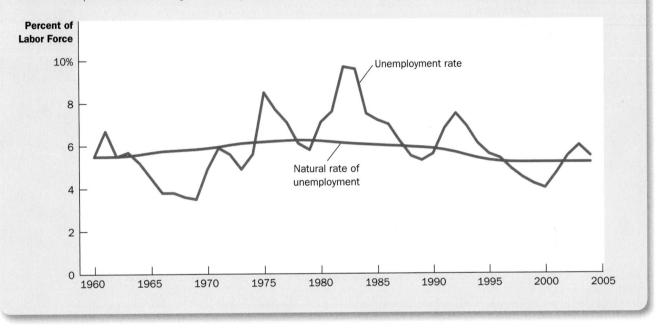

FIGURE **2**

Unemployment Rate since 1960

This graph uses annual data on the U.S. unemployment rate to show the percentage of the labor force without a job. The natural rate of unemployment is the normal level of unemployment around which the unemployment rate fluctuates.

Source: U.S. Department of Labor, Congressional Budget Office.

from its natural rate is called **cyclical unemployment.** The natural rate of unemployment shown in the figure is a series estimated by economists at the Congressional Budget Office. For 2004, they estimated a natural rate of 5.2, only slightly lower than the actual unemployment rate of 5.5 percent. Later in this book, we discuss short-run economic fluctuations, including the year-to-year fluctuations in unemployment around its natural rate. In the rest of this chapter, however, we ignore the short-run fluctuations and examine why there is always some unemployment in market economies.

cyclical unemployment
the deviation of unemployment from its natural rate

CASE STUDY   LABOR-FORCE PARTICIPATION OF MEN AND WOMEN IN THE U.S. ECONOMY

Women's role in American society has changed dramatically over the past century. Social commentators have pointed to many causes for this change. In part, it is attributable to new technologies, such as the washing machine, clothes dryer, refrigerator, freezer, and dishwasher, which have reduced the amount of time required to complete routine household tasks. In part, it is attributable to improved birth control, which has reduced the number of children born to the typical family. This change in women's role is also partly attributable to changing political and social attitudes, which in turn may have been facilitated by the

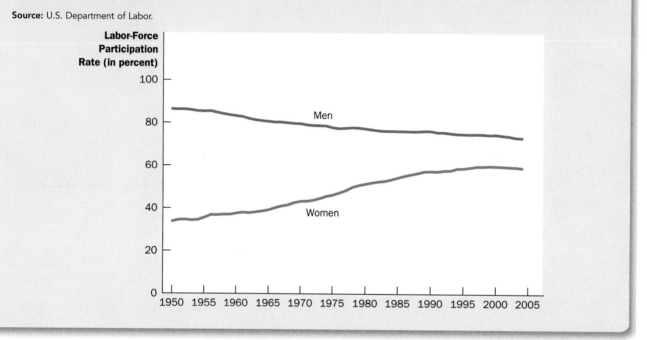

3 FIGURE

Labor-Force Participation Rates for
Men and Women since 1950

Source: U.S. Department of Labor.

This figure shows the percentage of adult men and women who are
members of the labor force. It shows that over the past several
decades, women have entered the labor force, and men have left it.

advances in technology and birth control. Together these developments have
had a profound impact on society in general and on the economy in particular.

Nowhere is that impact more obvious than in data on labor-force participation. Figure 3 shows the labor-force participation rates of men and women in the
United States since 1950. Just after World War II, men and women had very different roles in society. Only 33 percent of women were working or looking for
work, in contrast to 87 percent of men. Over the past several decades, the difference between the participation rates of men and women has gradually diminished, as growing numbers of women have entered the labor force and some
men have left it. Data for 2004 show that 59 percent of women were in the labor
force, in contrast to 73 percent of men. As measured by labor-force participation,
men and women are now playing a more equal role in the economy.

The increase in women's labor-force participation is easy to understand, but
the fall in men's may seem puzzling. There are several reasons for this decline.
First, young men now stay in school longer than their fathers and grandfathers
did. Second, older men now retire earlier and live longer. Third, with more
women employed, more fathers now stay at home to raise their children. Full-
time students, retirees, and stay-at-home fathers are all counted as out of the
labor force. •

Does the Unemployment Rate Measure What We Want It To?

Measuring the amount of unemployment in the economy might seem a straightforward task, but it is not. While it is easy to distinguish between a person with

a full-time job and a person who is not working at all, it is much harder to distinguish between a person who is unemployed and a person who is not in the labor force.

Movements into and out of the labor force are, in fact, common. More than one-third of the unemployed are recent entrants into the labor force. These entrants include young workers looking for their first jobs, such as recent college graduates. They also include, in greater numbers, older workers who had previously left the labor force but have now returned to look for work. Moreover, not all unemployment ends with the job seeker finding a job. Almost half of all spells of unemployment end when the unemployed person leaves the labor force.

Because people move into and out of the labor force so often, statistics on unemployment are difficult to interpret. On the one hand, some of those who report being unemployed may not, in fact, be trying hard to find a job. They may be calling themselves unemployed because they want to qualify for a government program that financially assists the unemployed or because they are actually working and paid "under the table." It may be more realistic to view these individuals as out of the labor force or, in some cases, employed. On the other hand, some of those who report being out of the labor force may want to work. These individuals may have tried to find a job and may have given up after an unsuccessful search. Such individuals, called **discouraged workers,** do not show up in unemployment statistics, even though they are truly workers without jobs.

discouraged workers individuals who would like to work but have given up looking for a job

Because of these and other problems, the BLS calculates several other measures of labor underutilization, in addition to the official unemployment rate. These alternative measures are presented in Table 2. In the end, it is best to view the official unemployment rate as a useful but imperfect measure of joblessness.

Measure and Description	Rate
U-1 Persons unemployed 15 weeks or longer, as a percent of the civilian labor force (includes only very long-term unemployed)	1.6%
U-2 Job losers and persons who have completed temporary jobs, as a percent of the civilian labor force (excludes job leavers)	2.4
U-3 Total unemployed, as a percent of the civilian labor force (official unemployment rate)	5.0
U-4 Total unemployed, plus discouraged workers, as a percent of the civilian labor force plus discouraged workers	5.3
U-5 Total unemployed plus all marginally attached workers, as a percent of the civilian labor force plus all marginally attached workers	6.0
U-6 Total unemployed, plus all marginally attached workers, plus total employed part-time for economic reasons, as a percent of the civilian labor force plus all marginally attached workers	8.9

TABLE 2

Alternative Measures of Labor Underutilization
The table shows various measures of joblessness for the U.S. economy. The data are for July 2005.

Source: U.S. Department of Labor.

Note: The Bureau of Labor Statistics defines terms as follows.
- *Marginally attached workers* are persons who currently are neither working nor looking for work but indicate that they want and are available for a job and have looked for work sometime in the recent past.
- *Discouraged workers* are marginally attached workers who have given a job-market related reason for not currently looking for a job.
- *Persons employed part-time for economic reasons* are those who want and are available for full-time work but have had to settle for a part-time schedule.

In The News

The Rise of Adult Male Joblessness

An increasing number of men are neither working nor looking for work.

A Growing Number of Men Are Not Working, So What Are They Doing?

By Alan B. Krueger

A growing number of men in their prime working years are pursuing what might be called the Kramer lifestyle, after the enigmatic "Seinfeld" character: neither working nor attending school. In 1967, 2.2 percent of noninstitutionalized men age 25 to 54 spent the entire year without working for pay or attending school. That figure climbed to 8 percent in 2002, the latest year available from the Bureau of Labor Statistics.

This trend is partly related to the rising disability rolls. More than half of male nonworkers reported themselves as sick or disabled. But the number of long-term jobless men who were able-bodied—a diverse group including young retirees, men who cannot find work, and family care providers—grew at a faster rate than the number who were disabled over the last 35 years.

The problem is much more severe for some groups than others. Nearly one in five men age 25 to 54 with less than a high school degree did not work even one week in 2002. The nonworking rate for college graduates was only 3.3 percent. In central cities, 10.8 percent of men spent the year without work, compared with 7.1 percent elsewhere.

Joblessness is persistent over time, so it ends up being highly concentrated among a small cadre of men who frequently spend long stretches without work. Just 3 percent of men accounted for more than two-thirds of the total number of years that men spent not

"YOU WOULDN'T CATCH ME IN THE LABOR FORCE."

working in the period from 1987 to 1997, according to an analysis by Jay Stewart, an economist at the Bureau of Labor Statistics.

How Long Are the Unemployed without Work?

In judging how serious the problem of unemployment is, one question to consider is whether unemployment is typically a short-term or long-term condition. If unemployment is short-term, one might conclude that it is not a big problem. Workers may require a few weeks between jobs to find the openings that best suit their tastes and skills. Yet if unemployment is long-term, one might conclude that it is a serious problem. Workers unemployed for many months are more likely to suffer economic and psychological hardship.

Because the duration of unemployment can affect our view about how big a problem unemployment is, economists have devoted much energy to studying data on the duration of unemployment spells. In this work, they have uncovered a

Long-term joblessness among mature men has become a much more important phenomenon than unemployment. Many jobless men do not actively search for work, so they are not counted as unemployed. Yet they still represent a significant loss of productive human resources for the economy.

The conventional wisdom is that joblessness has grown since the early 1980's because the demand for less-skilled workers has dropped, causing their pay to fall. The decline in unions and erosion of the real value of the minimum wage have also caused their pay to fall. Rather than toil at low pay, more and more men have withdrawn from the job market.

How are these men spending their time and getting by?

A new working paper by Mr. Stewart of the Labor Bureau provides the most comprehensive answers to date. The study, "What Do Male Nonworkers Do?", draws on information from several national data sets on the time allocation, living arrangements and income sources of male nonworkers in their prime earning years. . . .

In short, the average day of a male nonworker looks very much like the average day of a worker—on his day off. Nonworkers devoted 8.4 hours a day to leisure and recreation and 3.3 hours to housework. On their days off, workers devoted almost the same amount of time—8 and 3.4 hours, respectively—to these activities.

On workdays, the average full-time worker devoted only 3.5 hours to leisure and recreation and one hour to housework. Men worked an average of 8.6 hours on days when they performed some work for pay.

Comparing workers and nonworkers over a full week, nonworkers spent about a quarter of their extra time in "home production," which includes household chores, cleaning and repairs. The bulk of their extra time went into leisure and recreation, particularly watching television, socializing and playing sports and games. Nonworkers also slept 10 percent more (44 minutes) a night than workers. Both groups devoted relatively little time to child care, at least as a primary activity.

By contrast, nonworking women spend half their extra time engaged in household work and child care.

Supporting a Kramer lifestyle is not easy, especially if your neighbors are less magnanimous than Jerry Seinfeld. Nearly two-thirds of nonworking men age 25 to 54 received income from some source in 2002. Among those with unearned income, the average amount was $11,551, with the largest sums coming from Social Security and disability payments. . . .

Not surprisingly, wives are also an important source of financial support for nonworking men, but only 42 percent of male nonworkers between age 25 and 54 are married, compared with 68 percent of their employed counterparts. Twenty-nine percent of nonworkers live with their parents or other relatives, substantially higher than the 9 percent of workers in such a living arrangement. . . .

The experiences of nonworking adult men are quite varied, and many have severe disabilities. Although these statistics paint a picture of nonworking men struggling to get by financially, many manage to live as if every day were Sunday. As one man from Brooklyn who has not worked since 1998 told me this week, he thinks of the Off-Track Betting parlor in Midtown Manhattan as his "club," and he sees many of the same men there day after day.

Source: *The New York Times*, April 29, 2004.

result that is important, subtle, and seemingly contradictory: *Most spells of unemployment are short, and most unemployment observed at any given time is long-term.*

To see how this statement can be true, consider an example. Suppose that you visited the government's unemployment office every week for a year to survey the unemployed. Each week you find that there are four unemployed workers. Three of these workers are the same individuals for the whole year, while the fourth person changes every week. Based on this experience, would you say that unemployment is typically short-term or long-term?

Some simple calculations help answer this question. In this example, you meet a total of 55 unemployed people; 52 of them are unemployed for 1 week, and 3 are unemployed for the full year. This means that 52/55, or 95 percent, of unemployment spells end in 1 week. Yet whenever you walk into the unemployment office, three of the four people you meet will be unemployed for the entire year. So, even though 95 percent of unemployment spells end in 1 week, 75 percent of unemployment is attributable to those individuals who are unemployed for a full year. In this example, as in the world, most spells of unemployment are short, and most unemployment observed at any given time is long-term.

This subtle conclusion implies that economists and policymakers must be careful when interpreting data on unemployment and when designing policies to help the unemployed. Most people who become unemployed will soon find jobs. Yet most of the economy's unemployment problem is attributable to the relatively few workers who are jobless for long periods of time.

Why Are There Always Some People Unemployed?

We have discussed how the government measures the amount of unemployment, the problems that arise in interpreting unemployment statistics, and the findings of labor economists on the duration of unemployment. You should now have a good idea about what unemployment is.

This discussion, however, has not explained why economies experience unemployment. In most markets in the economy, prices adjust to bring quantity supplied and quantity demanded into balance. In an ideal labor market, wages would adjust to balance the quantity of labor supplied and the quantity of labor demanded. This adjustment of wages would ensure that all workers are always fully employed.

Of course, reality does not resemble this ideal. There are always some workers without jobs, even when the overall economy is doing well. In other words, the unemployment rate never falls to zero; instead, it fluctuates around the natural rate of unemployment. To understand this natural rate, the remaining sections of this chapter examine the reasons actual labor markets depart from the ideal of full employment.

To preview our conclusions, we will find that there are four ways to explain unemployment in the long run. The first explanation is that it takes time for workers to search for the jobs that are best suited for them. The unemployment that results from the process of matching workers and jobs is sometimes called **frictional unemployment,** and it is often thought to explain relatively short spells of unemployment.

The next three explanations for unemployment suggest that the number of jobs available in some labor markets may be insufficient to give a job to everyone who wants one. This occurs when the quantity of labor supplied exceeds the quantity demanded. Unemployment of this sort is sometimes called **structural unemployment,** and it is often thought to explain longer spells of unemployment. As we will see, this kind of unemployment results when wages are, for some reason, set above the level that brings supply and demand into equilibrium. We will examine three possible reasons for an above-equilibrium wage: minimum-wage laws, unions, and efficiency wages.

frictional unemployment unemployment that results because it takes time for workers to search for the jobs that best suit their tastes and skills

structural unemployment unemployment that results because the number of jobs available in some labor markets is insufficient to provide a job for everyone who wants one

Quick Quiz   How is the unemployment rate measured?   •   How might the unemployment rate overstate the amount of joblessness? How might it understate the amount of joblessness?

JOB SEARCH

One reason economies always experience some unemployment is job search. **Job search** is the process of matching workers with appropriate jobs. If all workers and all jobs were the same, so that all workers were equally well suited for all jobs, job search would not be a problem. Laid-off workers would quickly find new jobs that were well suited for them. But in fact, workers differ in their tastes and skills, jobs differ in their attributes, and information about job candidates and job vacancies is disseminated slowly among the many firms and households in the economy.

job search
the process by which workers find appropriate jobs given their tastes and skills

Why Some Frictional Unemployment Is Inevitable

Frictional unemployment is often the result of changes in the demand for labor among different firms. When consumers decide that they prefer Dell to Gateway computers, Dell increases employment, and Gateway lays off workers. The former Gateway workers must now search for new jobs, and Dell must decide which new workers to hire for the various jobs that have opened up. The result of this transition is a period of unemployment.

Similarly, because different regions of the country produce different goods, employment can rise in one region while it falls in another. Consider, for instance, what happens when the world price of oil falls. Oil-producing firms in Texas respond to the lower price by cutting back on production and employment. At the same time, cheaper gasoline stimulates car sales, so auto-producing firms in Michigan raise production and employment. Changes in the composition of demand among industries or regions are called *sectoral shifts*. Because it takes time for workers to search for jobs in the new sectors, sectoral shifts temporarily cause unemployment.

Frictional unemployment is inevitable simply because the economy is always changing. A century ago, the four industries with the largest employment in the United States were cotton goods, woolen goods, men's clothing, and lumber. Today, the four largest industries are autos, aircraft, communications, and electrical components. As this transition took place, jobs were created in some firms and destroyed in others. The end result of this process has been higher productivity and higher living standards. But along the way, workers in declining industries found themselves out of work and searching for new jobs.

Data show that at least 10 percent of U.S. manufacturing jobs are destroyed every year. In addition, more than 3 percent of workers leave their jobs in a typical month, sometimes because they realize that the jobs are not a good match for their tastes and skills. Many of these workers, especially younger ones, find new jobs at higher wages. This churning of the labor force is normal in a well-functioning and dynamic market economy, but the result is some amount of frictional unemployment.

Public Policy and Job Search

Even if some frictional unemployment is inevitable, the precise amount is not. The faster information spreads about job openings and worker availability, the more rapidly the economy can match workers and firms. The Internet, for instance, may help facilitate job search and reduce frictional unemployment. In

In The News

German Unemployment

Traditionally, many European countries have had unemployment insurance that is far more generous than that offered to U.S. workers. But some are starting to rethink that policy.

In a Deep Crisis, Germany Begins to Revamp Its Vast Welfare State

By Christopher Rhoads

Essen, Germany—Four years ago, the German social-welfare system rescued Renate Franke.

Soon after her mother died of cancer that year, her son was diagnosed with the same disease. Emotionally drained, Ms. Franke, then 48 years old, quit her job at an electronics company. The state stepped in, sending her to a spa for three weeks and paying her jobless benefits that were close to 60% of her former wage.

But last year, the state got tough with Ms. Franke. It cut her unemployment aid after she refused to take full-time jobs. It told her to sell her car, as a condition for receiving any further social assistance. Sitting one recent morning in her one-bedroom apartment on the outskirts of this industrial city, she said: "I began to fear for my future."

So, too, does Germany. Faced with its worst economic slump since World War II, Germany is beginning to broach some long-held taboos as it comes to terms with a cold reality: The country's economic system doesn't work anymore. The world's third-largest economy after the U.S. and Japan has slid into its second recession within the past three years—making it the weakest of the world's major economies. Unemployment is hovering at nearly 11%.

The dire conditions are prompting an unprecedented rethinking of the paternalistic role of the state in the country's economic life. In the decades since the war, West Germany and then united Germany had to deal with a catastrophic legacy of military and moral defeat. One source of pride, however, remained constant: the country's economic power tethered to a strong social-welfare system.

Now, the country's downward spiral has made this model no longer affordable. Social spending has reached close to 30% of gross domestic product, the most of any country in the world except for Sweden and more than twice that of the U.S. . . .

Within the past few months, Berlin's center-left government has proposed reducing unemployment benefits, opening the public health-care system to private insurers, cutting hundreds of millions of dollars of subsidies and easing laws that protect workers from being fired. Late last month, the government brought forward by a year a planned tax cut. Some ministers even want to cut back on the country's famously large amount of free time—30 vacation days on average, compared with 12 in the U.S. . . .

addition, public policy may play a role. If policy can reduce the time it takes unemployed workers to find new jobs, it can reduce the economy's natural rate of unemployment.

Government programs try to facilitate job search in various ways. One way is through government-run employment agencies, which give out information about job vacancies. Another way is through public training programs, which aim to ease the transition of workers from declining to growing industries and to help disadvantaged groups escape poverty. Advocates of these programs believe that they make the economy operate more efficiently by keeping the labor force more fully employed and that they reduce the inequities inherent in a constantly changing market economy.

Declining birth rates, longer life-spans, earlier retirement ages, less working time and steadily higher unemployment mean that those paying into the system can no longer support those living off of it. Since 1970, the total number of pensioners and jobless increased by 80% to 16.3 million in western Germany. The number of workers, who together with employers finance the system through payroll taxes, grew by just 4% in that time, to 30.7 million.

In the early part of the 20th century most social needs, such as care for children and the elderly, were handled by the family across Europe. After World War II, much of the responsibility shifted to the state, and the social-welfare system began to grow exponentially. Driving the expansion were European growth rates of 5% or more, spurred by the rebuilding after the destruction of the war. Jobs were so plentiful that countries had to import workers from Turkey and elsewhere. Birth rates soared, which meant that there were plenty of young workers to finance the retirement needs of the relatively few elderly.

Europe could afford to be generous. In the 1960s and '70s, the social role of governments grew well beyond caring for the needy to providing health care, higher-level education, child and old-age care—for all citizens. "The instruments of redistribution got hijacked by the middle class," says Dennis Snower, a professor of international economics at Birkbeck College, at the University of London. That meant that reversing direction became increasingly difficult, since an ever-larger number of citizens—and voters—benefited from the system.

While at the beginning of the 1960s social spending in Europe was only slightly higher than in the U.S., by the end of the 1990s, it was twice as much. "Americans are not as obsessed with social insurance because they think if they work hard they will get rich," says Robert MacCulloch, a professor of economics at Princeton University. And they think that once they get rich, they won't want to be burdened with high taxes to cover welfare costs. In Europe, many feel their chances of improving their lot are lower, increasing their appetite for assistance from the state, he says. Europeans also favor income equality more than Americans, surveys show.

But in some ways, the massive growth of the welfare state has led to just the opposite of what was intended: a less-integrated society through the creation of a growing underclass of long-term unemployed. More than 50% of Germany's 4.5 million unemployed have been without a job for a year or more, making them less employable and more wedded to welfare. The equivalent figure in the U.S. is 6%. . . .

In an effort to prevent the newly jobless from becoming permanently unemployed, the government is becoming less forgiving. As of this year, singles must move anywhere in the country to fill open positions or lose benefits. Other measures include cutting benefits when a jobless person refuses to accept an opening and enforcing participation in state-sponsored temp agencies.

For Ms. Franke, the former worker in the electronics firm, the tightening of the screws made a difference. She had worked several off-the-books part-time secretarial jobs to augment her welfare payments—a common practice. But with her state assistance dwindling, in recent months she began looking more actively for full-time work. In May, she landed a job in charge of bookkeeping for another electronics company nearby.

Critics of these programs question whether the government should get involved with the process of job search. They argue that it is better to let the private market match workers and jobs. In fact, most job search in our economy takes place without intervention by the government. Newspaper ads, Internet job sites, college placement offices, headhunters, and word of mouth all help spread information about job openings and job candidates. Similarly, much worker education is done privately, either through schools or through on-the-job training. These critics contend that the government is no better—and most likely worse—at disseminating the right information to the right workers and deciding what kinds of worker training would be most valuable. They claim that these decisions are best made privately by workers and employers.

Unemployment Insurance

unemployment insurance
a government program that partially protects workers' incomes when they become unemployed

One government program that increases the amount of frictional unemployment, without intending to do so, is **unemployment insurance.** This program is designed to offer workers partial protection against job loss. The unemployed who quit their jobs, were fired for cause, or just entered the labor force are not eligible. Benefits are paid only to the unemployed who were laid off because their previous employers no longer needed their skills. Although the terms of the program vary over time and across states, a typical American worker covered by unemployment insurance receives 50 percent of his or her former wages for 26 weeks.

While unemployment insurance reduces the hardship of unemployment, it also increases the amount of unemployment. The explanation is based on one of the *Ten Principles of Economics* in Chapter 1: People respond to incentives. Because unemployment benefits stop when a worker takes a new job, the unemployed devote less effort to job search and are more likely to turn down unattractive job offers. In addition, because unemployment insurance makes unemployment less onerous, workers are less likely to seek guarantees of job security when they negotiate with employers over the terms of employment.

Many studies by labor economists have examined the incentive effects of unemployment insurance. One study examined an experiment run by the state of Illinois in 1985. When unemployed workers applied to collect unemployment insurance benefits, the state randomly selected some of them and offered each a $500 bonus if they found new jobs within 11 weeks. This group was then compared to a control group not offered the incentive. The average spell of unemployment for the group offered the bonus was 7 percent shorter than the average spell for the control group. This experiment shows that the design of the unemployment insurance system influences the effort that the unemployed devote to job search.

Several other studies examined the search effort by following a group of workers over time. Unemployment insurance benefits, rather than lasting forever, usually run out after 6 months or 1 year. These studies found that when the unemployed become ineligible for benefits, the probability of their finding a new job rises markedly. Thus, receiving unemployment insurance benefits does reduce the search effort of the unemployed.

Even though unemployment insurance reduces search effort and raises unemployment, we should not necessarily conclude that the policy is a bad one. The program does achieve its primary goal of reducing the income uncertainty that workers face. In addition, when workers turn down unattractive job offers, they have the opportunity to look for jobs that better suit their tastes and skills. Some economists have argued that unemployment insurance improves the ability of the economy to match each worker with the most appropriate job.

The study of unemployment insurance shows that the unemployment rate is an imperfect measure of a nation's overall level of economic well-being. Most economists agree that eliminating unemployment insurance would reduce the amount of unemployment in the economy. Yet economists disagree on whether economic well-being would be enhanced or diminished by this change in policy.

Quick Quiz How would an increase in the world price of oil affect the amount of frictional unemployment? Is this unemployment undesirable? What public policies might affect the amount of unemployment caused by this price change?

MINIMUM-WAGE LAWS

Having seen how frictional unemployment results from the process of matching workers and jobs, let's now examine how structural unemployment results when the number of jobs is insufficient for the number of workers.

To understand structural unemployment, we begin by reviewing how unemployment arises from minimum-wage laws. Although minimum wages are not the predominant reason for unemployment in our economy, they have an important effect on certain groups with particularly high unemployment rates. Moreover, the analysis of minimum wages is a natural place to start because, as we will see, it can be used to understand some of the other reasons for structural unemployment.

Figure 4 reviews the basic economics of a minimum wage. When a minimum-wage law forces the wage to remain above the level that balances supply and demand, it raises the quantity of labor supplied and reduces the quantity of labor demanded compared to the equilibrium level. There is a surplus of labor. Because there are more workers willing to work than there are jobs, some workers are unemployed.

While minimum-wage laws are one reason there is always some unemployment in the U.S. economy, they do not affect everyone. Most workers have wages well above the legal minimum, so the law does not prevent the wage from adjusting to balance supply and demand. Minimum-wage laws matter most for the least skilled and least experienced members of the labor force, such as teenagers. Their equilibrium wages tend to be low and, therefore, are more likely to fall below the legal minimum. It is only among these workers that minimum-wage laws explain the existence of unemployment.

Although Figure 4 is drawn to show the effects of a minimum-wage law, it also illustrates a more general lesson: *If the wage is kept above the equilibrium level*

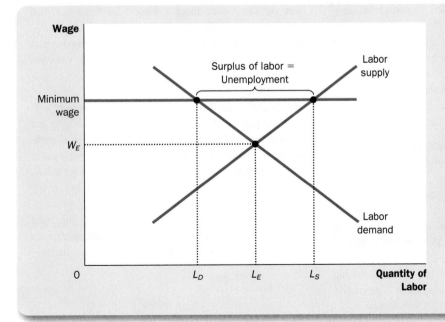

FIGURE 4

Unemployment from a Wage above the Equilibrium Level
In this labor market, the wage at which supply and demand balance is W_E. At this equilibrium wage, the quantity of labor supplied and the quantity of labor demanded both equal L_E. By contrast, if the wage is forced to remain above the equilibrium level, perhaps because of a minimum-wage law, the quantity of labor supplied rises to L_S, and the quantity of labor demanded falls to L_D. The resulting surplus of labor, $L_S - L_D$, represents unemployment.

for any reason, the result is unemployment. Minimum-wage laws are just one reason wages may be "too high." In the remaining two sections of this chapter, we consider two other reasons wages may be kept above the equilibrium level: unions and efficiency wages. The basic economics of unemployment in these cases is the same as that shown in Figure 4, but these explanations of unemployment can apply to many more of the economy's workers.

At this point, however, we should stop and notice that the structural unemployment that arises from an above-equilibrium wage is, in an important sense, different from the frictional unemployment that arises from the process of job search. The need for job search is not due to the failure of wages to balance labor supply and labor demand. When job search is the explanation for unemployment, workers are *searching* for the jobs that best suit their tastes and skills. By contrast, when the wage is above the equilibrium level, the quantity of labor supplied exceeds the quantity of labor demanded, and workers are unemployed because they are *waiting* for jobs to open up.

Quick Quiz   Draw the supply curve and the demand curve for a labor market in which the wage is fixed above the equilibrium level. Show the quantity of labor supplied, the quantity demanded, and the amount of unemployment.

FYI

Who Earns the Minimum Wage?

In 2005, the Department of Labor released a study of what workers reported earnings at or below the minimum wage, which at the time was $5.15 per hour. (A reported wage below the minimum is possible because some workers are exempt from the statute, because enforcement is imperfect, and because some workers round down to $5.00 when reporting their wages on surveys.) Here is a summary of the findings:

- Of those workers paid an hourly rate, about 2 percent of men and 4 percent of women reported wages at or below the prevailing federal minimum.
- Minimum-wage workers tend to be young. About half of all hourly paid workers earning $5.15 or less were under age 25, and about one-fourth were age 16–19. Among teenagers, about 9 percent earned $5.15 or less, compared with about 2 percent of workers age 25 and older.
- Minimum-wage workers tend to be less educated. Among hourly paid workers age 16 and older, about 2 percent of

those who had only a high school diploma earned $5.15 or less, compared with about 1 percent for those who had obtained a college degree.

- Minimum-wage workers are more likely to be working part time. Among part-time workers (those who usually work less than 35 hours per week), 7 percent were paid $5.15 or less, compared to 1 percent of full-time workers.
- The industry with the highest proportion of workers with reported hourly wages at or below $5.15 was leisure and hospitality (about 15 percent). About three-fifths of all workers paid at or below the minimum wage were employed in this industry, primarily in food services and drinking places. For many of these workers, tips supplement the hourly wages received.
- The proportion of hourly paid workers earning the prevailing federal minimum wage or less has trended downward since 1979, when data collection first began on a regular basis.

UNIONS AND COLLECTIVE BARGAINING

A **union** is a worker association that bargains with employers over wages, benefits, and working conditions. Whereas only 13 percent of U.S. workers now belong to unions, unions played a much larger role in the U.S. labor market in the past. In the 1940s and 1950s, when unions were at their peak, about a third of the U.S. labor force was unionized. Moreover, unions continue to play a large role in many European countries. In Sweden and Denmark, for instance, more than three-fourths of workers belong to unions.

union
a worker association that bargains with employers over wages, benefits, and working conditions

The Economics of Unions

A union is a type of cartel. Like any cartel, a union is a group of sellers acting together in the hope of exerting their joint market power. Most workers in the U.S. economy discuss their wages, benefits, and working conditions with their employers as individuals. By contrast, workers in a union do so as a group. The process by which unions and firms agree on the terms of employment is called **collective bargaining.**

When a union bargains with a firm, it asks for higher wages, better benefits, and better working conditions than the firm would offer in the absence of a union. If the union and the firm do not reach agreement, the union can organize a withdrawal of labor from the firm, called a **strike.** Because a strike reduces production, sales, and profit, a firm facing a strike threat is likely to agree to pay higher wages than it otherwise would. Economists who study the effects of unions typically find that union workers earn about 10 to 20 percent more than similar workers who do not belong to unions.

collective bargaining
the process by which unions and firms agree on the terms of employment

strike
the organized withdrawal of labor from a firm by a union

When a union raises the wage above the equilibrium level, it raises the quantity of labor supplied and reduces the quantity of labor demanded, resulting in unemployment. Workers who remain employed are better off, but those who were previously employed and are now unemployed at the higher wage are worse off. Indeed, unions are often thought to cause conflict between different groups of workers—between the *insiders* who benefit from high union wages and the *outsiders* who do not get the union jobs.

The outsiders can respond to their status in one of two ways. Some of them remain unemployed and wait for the chance to become insiders and earn the high union wage. Others take jobs in firms that are not unionized. Thus, when unions raise wages in one part of the economy, the supply of labor increases in other parts of the economy. This increase in labor supply, in turn, reduces wages in industries that are not unionized. In other words, workers in unions reap the benefit of collective bargaining, while workers not in unions bear some of the cost.

The role of unions in the economy depends in part on the laws that govern union organization and collective bargaining. Normally, explicit agreements among members of a cartel are illegal. If firms that sell a common product were to agree to set a high price for that product, the agreement would be a "conspiracy in restraint of trade." The government would prosecute these firms in civil and criminal court for violating the antitrust laws. By contrast, unions are exempt from these laws. The policymakers who wrote the antitrust laws believed that workers needed greater market power as they bargained with employers. Indeed, various laws are designed to encourage the formation of unions. In particular, the Wagner Act of 1935 prevents employers from interfering when workers try

"GENTLEMEN, NOTHING STANDS IN THE WAY OF A FINAL ACCORD EXCEPT THAT MANAGEMENT WANTS PROFIT MAXIMIZATION AND THE UNION WANTS MORE MOOLA."

to organize unions and requires employers to bargain with unions in good faith. The National Labor Relations Board (NLRB) is the government agency that enforces workers' right to unionize.

Legislation affecting the market power of unions is a perennial topic of political debate. State lawmakers sometimes debate *right-to-work laws,* which give workers in a unionized firm the right to choose whether to join the union. In the absence of such laws, unions can insist during collective bargaining that firms make union membership a requirement for employment. Lawmakers in Washington have also at times debated a proposed law that would prevent firms from hiring permanent replacements for workers who are on strike. This law would make strikes more costly for firms and, thereby, would increase the market power of unions. These and similar policy decisions will help determine the future of the union movement.

Are Unions Good or Bad for the Economy?

Economists disagree about whether unions are good or bad for the economy as a whole. Let's consider both sides of the debate.

Critics argue that unions are merely a type of cartel. When unions raise wages above the level that would prevail in competitive markets, they reduce the quantity of labor demanded, cause some workers to be unemployed, and reduce the wages in the rest of the economy. The resulting allocation of labor is, critics argue, both inefficient and inequitable. It is inefficient because high union wages reduce employment in unionized firms below the efficient, competitive level. It is inequitable because some workers benefit at the expense of other workers.

Advocates contend that unions are a necessary antidote to the market power of the firms that hire workers. The extreme case of this market power is the "company town," where a single firm does most of the hiring in a geographical region. In a company town, if workers do not accept the wages and working conditions that the firm offers, they have little choice but to move or stop working. In the absence of a union, therefore, the firm could use its market power to pay lower wages and offer worse working conditions than would prevail if it had to compete with other firms for the same workers. In this case, a union may balance the firm's market power and protect the workers from being at the mercy of the firm owners.

Advocates of unions also claim that unions are important for helping firms respond efficiently to workers' concerns. Whenever a worker takes a job, the worker and the firm must agree on many attributes of the job in addition to the wage: hours of work, overtime, vacations, sick leave, health benefits, promotion schedules, job security, and so on. By representing workers' views on these issues, unions allow firms to provide the right mix of job attributes. Even if unions have the adverse effect of pushing wages above the equilibrium level and causing unemployment, they have the benefit of helping firms keep a happy and productive work force.

In the end, there is no consensus among economists about whether unions are good or bad for the economy. Like many institutions, their influence is probably beneficial in some circumstances and adverse in others.

Quick Quiz   How does a union in the auto industry affect wages and employment at General Motors and Ford? How does it affect wages and employment in other industries?

In The News

Should You Join a Union?

Someday you may face the decision about whether to vote for or against a union in your workplace. The following article discusses some issues you might consider.

On Payday, Union Jobs Stack Up Very Well

By David Cay Johnston

With the teamsters' success in their two-week strike against United Parcel Service, and with the A.F.L.-C.I.O. training thousands of union organizers in a drive to reverse a quarter-century of declining membership, millions of workers will be asked over the next few years whether they want a union to represent them.

It is a complicated question, the answer to which rests on a jumble of determinations: Do you favor collective action or individual initiative? Do you trust the union's leaders? Do you want somebody else speaking for you in dealings with your employer? Do you think you will be dismissed if you sign a union card—or that the company will send your job overseas if a union is organized?

But in one regard, the choice is simple—and it is not the choice that most workers have made during the labor movement's recent decades in the economic wilderness.

From a pocketbook perspective, workers are absolutely better off joining a union. Economists across the political spectrum agree. Turning a nonunion job into a union job very likely will have a bigger effect on lifetime finances than all the advice employees will ever read about investing their 401(k) plans, buy-

ing a home or otherwise making more of what they earn.

Here is how the equation works, said Prof. Richard B. Freeman of Harvard University: "For an existing worker in a firm, if you can carry out an organizing drive, it is all to your benefit. If there are going to be losers, they are people who might have gotten a job in the future, the shareholders whose profits will go down, the managers because there will be less profit to distribute to them in pay and, maybe, consumers will pay a little more for the product. But as a worker, it is awfully hard to see why you wouldn't want a union."

Over all, union workers are paid about 20 percent more than nonunion workers, and their fringe benefits are typically worth two to four times as much, economists with a wide array of views have found. The financial advantage is even greater for workers with little formal education and training and for women, blacks, and Hispanic workers.

Moreover, 85 percent of union members have health insurance, compared with 57 percent of nonunion workers, said Barry Bluestone, a labor-friendly economics professor at the University of Massachusetts.

The conclusion draws no argument even from Prof. Leo Troy of Rutgers University, who is widely known in academic circles and among union leaders for his hostility to organized labor.

"From a standpoint of wages and fringe benefits," Professor Troy said, "the answer is yes, you are better off in a union."

His objections to unions concern how they reduce profits for owners and distort investment decisions in ways that slow the overall growth of the economy—not how they affect workers who bargain collectively. Professor Troy points out that he belongs to a union himself—the American Association of University Professors.

Donald R. Deere, an economist at the Bush School of Government and Public Service at Texas A & M University, studied the wage differential for comparable union and nonunion workers between 1974 and 1996, a period when union membership fell to 15 percent of American workers from 22 percent.

In every educational and age category that he studied, Professor Deere found that union members increased their wage advantage over nonunion workers during those years. Last year, he estimates, unionized workers with less than a high school education earned 22 percent more than their nonunion counterparts. The differential declined as education levels rose, reaching 10 percent for college graduates.

"It makes sense to belong to a union," Professor Deere said, "so long as you don't lose your job in the long term."

Source: *The New York Times* Money & Business section, August 31, 1997, p. 1. Copyright © 1997 by the New York Times Co. Reprinted by permission.

THE THEORY OF EFFICIENCY WAGES

efficiency wages
above-equilibrium wages
paid by firms to increase
worker productivity

A fourth reason economies always experience some unemployment—in addition to job search, minimum-wage laws, and unions—is suggested by the theory of **efficiency wages.** According to this theory, firms operate more efficiently if wages are above the equilibrium level. Therefore, it may be profitable for firms to keep wages high even in the presence of a surplus of labor.

In some ways, the unemployment that arises from efficiency wages is similar to the unemployment that arises from minimum-wage laws and unions. In all three cases, unemployment is the result of wages above the level that balances the quantity of labor supplied and the quantity of labor demanded. Yet there is also an important difference. Minimum-wage laws and unions prevent firms from lowering wages in the presence of a surplus of workers. Efficiency-wage theory states that such a constraint on firms is unnecessary in many cases because firms may be better off keeping wages above the equilibrium level.

Why should firms want to keep wages high? This decision may seem odd at first, for wages are a large part of firms' costs. Normally, we expect profit-maximizing firms to want to keep costs—and therefore wages—as low as possible. The novel insight of efficiency-wage theory is that paying high wages might be profitable because they might raise the efficiency of a firm's workers.

There are several types of efficiency-wage theory. Each type suggests a different explanation for why firms may want to pay high wages. Let's now consider four of these types.

Worker Health

The first and simplest type of efficiency-wage theory emphasizes the link between wages and worker health. Better paid workers eat a more nutritious diet, and workers who eat a better diet are healthier and more productive. A firm may find it more profitable to pay high wages and have healthy, productive workers than to pay lower wages and have less healthy, less productive workers.

This type of efficiency-wage theory is not relevant for firms in rich countries such as the United States. In these countries, the equilibrium wages for most workers are well above the level needed for an adequate diet. Firms are not concerned that paying equilibrium wages would place their workers' health in jeopardy.

This type of efficiency-wage theory is more relevant for firms in less developed countries where inadequate nutrition is a more common problem. Unemployment is high in the cities of many poor African countries, for example. In these countries, firms may fear that cutting wages would, in fact, adversely influence their workers' health and productivity. In other words, concern over nutrition may explain why firms do not cut wages despite a surplus of labor.

Worker Turnover

A second type of efficiency-wage theory emphasizes the link between wages and worker turnover. Workers quit jobs for many reasons: to take jobs in other firms, to move to other parts of the country, to leave the labor force, and so on. The frequency with which they quit depends on the entire set of incentives they face, including the benefits of leaving and the benefits of staying. The more a firm pays its workers, the less often its workers will choose to leave. Thus, a firm can reduce turnover among its workers by paying them a high wage.

Why do firms care about turnover? The reason is that it is costly for firms to hire and train new workers. Moreover, even after they are trained, newly hired workers are not as productive as experienced workers. Firms with higher turnover, therefore, will tend to have higher production costs. Firms may find it profitable to pay wages above the equilibrium level to reduce worker turnover.

Worker Quality

A third type of efficiency-wage theory emphasizes the link between wages and worker quality. All firms want workers who are talented, and they try to pick the best applicants to fill job openings. But because firms cannot perfectly gauge the quality of applicants, hiring has a degree of randomness to it. When a firm pays a high wage, it attracts a better pool of workers to apply for its jobs and thereby increases the quality of its work force. If the firm responded to a surplus of labor by reducing the wage, the most competent applicants—who are more likely to have better alternative opportunities than less competent applicants—may choose not to apply. If this influence of the wage on worker quality is strong enough, it may be profitable for the firm to pay a wage above the level that balances supply and demand.

Worker Effort

A fourth and final type of efficiency-wage theory emphasizes the link between wages and worker effort. In many jobs, workers have some discretion over how hard to work. As a result, firms monitor the efforts of their workers, and workers caught shirking their responsibilities are fired. But not all shirkers are caught immediately because monitoring workers is costly and imperfect. A firm can respond to this problem by paying wages above the equilibrium level. High wages make workers more eager to keep their jobs and, thereby, give workers an incentive to put forward their best effort.

This particular type of efficiency-wage theory is similar to the old Marxist idea of the "reserve army of the unemployed." Marx thought that employers benefited from unemployment because the threat of unemployment helped to discipline those workers who had jobs. In the worker-effort variant of efficiency-wage theory, unemployment fills a similar role. If the wage were at the level that balanced supply and demand, workers would have less reason to work hard because if they were fired, they could quickly find new jobs at the same wage. Therefore, firms raise wages above the equilibrium level, causing unemployment and providing an incentive for workers not to shirk their responsibilities.

CASE STUDY | HENRY FORD AND THE VERY GENEROUS $5-A-DAY WAGE

Henry Ford was an industrial visionary. As founder of the Ford Motor Company, he was responsible for introducing modern techniques of production. Rather than building cars with small teams of skilled craftsmen, Ford built cars on assembly lines in which unskilled workers were taught to perform the same simple tasks over and over again. The output of this assembly process was the Model T Ford, one of the most famous early automobiles.

In 1914, Ford introduced another innovation: the $5 workday. This might not seem like much today, but back then $5 was about twice the going wage. It was also far above the wage that balanced supply and demand. When the new $5-a-day wage was announced, long lines of job seekers formed outside the Ford factories. The number of workers willing to work at this wage far exceeded the number of workers Ford needed.

Ford's high-wage policy had many of the effects predicted by efficiency-wage theory. Turnover fell, absenteeism fell, and productivity rose. Workers were so much more efficient that Ford's production costs were lower even though wages were higher. Thus, paying a wage above the equilibrium level was profitable for the firm. Henry Ford himself called the $5-a-day wage "one of the finest cost-cutting moves we ever made."

Historical accounts of this episode are also consistent with efficiency-wage theory. An historian of the early Ford Motor Company wrote, "Ford and his associates freely declared on many occasions that the high-wage policy turned out to be good business. By this they meant that it had improved the discipline of the workers, given them a more loyal interest in the institution, and raised their personal efficiency."

Why did it take Henry Ford to introduce this efficiency wage? Why were other firms not already taking advantage of this seemingly profitable business strategy? According to some analysts, Ford's decision was closely linked to his use of the assembly line. Workers organized in an assembly line are highly interdependent. If one worker is absent or works slowly, other workers are less able to complete their own tasks. Thus, while assembly lines made production more efficient, they also raised the importance of low worker turnover, high worker effort, and high worker quality. As a result, paying efficiency wages may have been a better strategy for the Ford Motor Company than for other businesses at the time. •

Quick Quiz Give four explanations for why firms might find it profitable to pay wages above the level that balances quantity of labor supplied and quantity of labor demanded.

CONCLUSION

In this chapter, we discussed the measurement of unemployment and the reasons economies always experience some degree of unemployment. We have seen how job search, minimum-wage laws, unions, and efficiency wages can all help explain why some workers do not have jobs. Which of these four explanations for the natural rate of unemployment are the most important for the U.S. economy and other economies around the world? Unfortunately, there is no easy way to tell. Economists differ in which of these explanations of unemployment they consider most important.

The analysis of this chapter yields an important lesson: Although the economy will always have some unemployment, its natural rate does change over time. Many events and policies can alter the amount of unemployment the economy typically experiences. As the information revolution changes the process of job search, as Congress adjusts the minimum wage, as workers form or quit unions, and as firms change their reliance on efficiency wages, the natural rate of unemployment evolves. Unemployment is not a simple problem with a simple solution. But how we choose to organize our society can profoundly influence how prevalent a problem it is.

SUMMARY

- The unemployment rate is the percentage of those who would like to work who do not have jobs. The Bureau of Labor Statistics calculates this statistic monthly based on a survey of thousands of households.

- The unemployment rate is an imperfect measure of joblessness. Some people who call themselves unemployed may actually not want to work, and some people who would like to work have left the labor force after an unsuccessful search.

- In the U.S. economy, most people who become unemployed find work within a short period of time. Nonetheless, most unemployment observed at any given time is attributable to the few people who are unemployed for long periods of time.

- One reason for unemployment is the time it takes workers to search for jobs that best suit their tastes and skills. Unemployment insurance is a government policy that, while protecting workers' incomes, increases the amount of frictional unemployment.

- A second reason our economy always has some unemployment is minimum-wage laws. By raising the wage of unskilled and inexperienced workers above the equilibrium level, minimum-wage laws raise the quantity of labor supplied and reduce the quantity demanded. The resulting surplus of labor represents unemployment.

- A third reason for unemployment is the market power of unions. When unions push the wages in unionized industries above the equilibrium level, they create a surplus of labor.

- A fourth reason for unemployment is suggested by the theory of efficiency wages. According to this theory, firms find it profitable to pay wages above the equilibrium level. High wages can improve worker health, lower worker turnover, raise worker quality, and increase worker effort.

KEY CONCEPTS

labor force, p. 199
unemployment rate, p. 199
labor-force participation rate, p. 199
natural rate of unemployment, p. 200

cyclical unemployment, p. 201
discouraged workers, p. 203
frictional unemployment, p. 206
structural unemployment, p. 206
job search, p. 207

unemployment insurance, p. 210
union, p. 213
collective bargaining, p. 213
strike, p. 213
efficiency wages, p. 216

QUESTIONS FOR REVIEW

1. What are the three categories into which the Bureau of Labor Statistics divides everyone? How does the BLS compute the labor force, the unemployment rate, and the labor-force participation rate?

2. Is unemployment typically short-term or long-term? Explain.

3. Why is frictional unemployment inevitable? How might the government reduce the amount of frictional unemployment?

4. Are minimum-wage laws a better explanation for structural unemployment among teenagers or among college graduates? Why?

5. How do unions affect the natural rate of unemployment?

6. What claims do advocates of unions make to argue that unions are good for the economy?

7. Explain four ways in which a firm might increase its profits by raising the wages it pays.

PROBLEMS AND APPLICATIONS

1. The Bureau of Labor Statistics announced that in July 2005, of all adult Americans, 142,076,000 were employed, 7,497,000 were unemployed, and 76,580,000 were not in the labor force. Use this information to calculate:
   a. the adult population
   b. the labor force
   c. the labor-force participation rate
   d. the unemployment rate

2. Go to the website of the Bureau of Labor Statistics (http://www.bls.gov). What is the national unemployment rate right now? Find the unemployment rate for the demographic group that best fits a description of you (for example, based on age, sex, and race). Is it higher or lower than the national average? Why do you think this is so?

3. As shown in Figure 3, the overall labor-force participation rate of men declined between 1970 and 1990. This overall decline reflects different patterns for different age groups, however, as shown in the following table.

	All Men	Men 16–24	Men 25–54	Men 55 and older
1970	80%	69%	96%	56%
1990	76	72	93	40

Which group experienced the largest decline? Given this information, what factor may have played an important role in the decline in overall male labor-force participation over this period?

4. The labor-force participation rate of women increased sharply between 1970 and 1990, as shown in Figure 3. As with men, however, there were different patterns for different age groups, as shown in this table.

	All Women	Women 25–54	Women 25–34	Women 35–44	Women 45–54
1970	43%	50%	45%	51%	54%
1990	58	74	74	77	71

Why do you think younger women experienced a bigger increase in labor-force participation than older women?

5. Between 2003 and 2004, total U.S. employment increased by 1.5 million workers, but the number of unemployed workers declined by only 0.6 million. How are these numbers consistent with each other? Why might one expect a reduction in the number of people counted as unemployed to be smaller than the increase in the number of people employed?

6. Are the following workers more likely to experience short-term or long-term unemployment? Explain.
   a. A construction worker laid off because of bad weather
   b. A manufacturing worker who loses her job at a plant in an isolated area
   c. A stagecoach-industry worker laid off because of competition from railroads

d. A short-order cook who loses his job when a new restaurant opens across the street

e. An expert welder with little formal education who loses her job when the company installs automatic welding machinery

7. Using a diagram of the labor market, show the effect of an increase in the minimum wage on the wage paid to workers, the number of workers supplied, the number of workers demanded, and the amount of unemployment.

8. Consider an economy with two labor markets—one for manufacturing workers and one for service workers. Suppose initially that neither is unionized.

   a. If manufacturing workers formed a union, what impact on the wages and employment in manufacturing would you predict?

   b. How would these changes in the manufacturing labor market affect the supply of labor in the market for service workers? What would happen to the equilibrium wage and employment in this labor market?

9. It can be shown that an industry's demand for labor will become more elastic when the demand for the industry's product becomes more elastic. Let's consider the implications of this fact for the U.S. automobile industry and the United Autoworkers Union (UAW).

   a. What happened to the elasticity of demand for American cars when the Japanese developed a strong auto industry? What happened to the elasticity of demand for American auto workers? Explain.

   b. As the chapter explains, a union generally faces a trade-off in deciding how much to raise wages because a bigger increase is bet-

ter for workers who remain employed but also results in a greater reduction in employment. How did the rise in auto imports from Japan affect the wage-employment trade-off faced by the UAW?

   c. Do you think the growth of the Japanese auto industry increased or decreased the gap between the competitive wage and the wage chosen by the UAW? Explain.

10. Suppose that Congress passes a law requiring employers to provide employees some benefit (such as healthcare) that raises the cost of an employee by $4 per hour.

   a. What effect does this employer mandate have on the demand for labor? (In answering this and the following questions, be quantitative when you can.)

   b. If employees place a value on this benefit exactly equal to its cost, what effect does this employer mandate have on the supply of labor?

   c. If the wage is free to balance supply and demand, how does this law affect the wage and the level of employment? Are employers better or worse off? Are employees better or worse off?

   d. Suppose that, before the mandate, the wage in this market was $3 above the minimum wage. In this case, how does the employer mandate affect the wage, the level of employment, and the level of unemployment?

   e. Now suppose that workers do not value the mandated benefit at all. How does this alternative assumption change your answers to parts (b) and (c)?

For further information on topics in this chapter, additional problems, examples, applications, online quizzes, and more, please visit our website at http://mankiw.swlearning.com.

5

Money and Prices in the Long Run

The Monetary System

When you walk into a restaurant to buy a meal, you get something of value—a full stomach. To pay for this service, you might hand the restaurateur several worn-out pieces of greenish paper decorated with strange symbols, government buildings, and the portraits of famous dead Americans. Or you might hand him a single piece of paper with the name of a bank and your signature. Whether you pay by cash or check, the restaurateur is happy to work hard to satisfy your gastronomical desires in exchange for these pieces of paper which, in and of themselves, are worthless.

To anyone who has lived in a modern economy, this social custom is not at all odd. Even though paper money has no intrinsic value, the restaurateur is confident that, in the future, some third person will accept it in exchange for something that the restaurateur does value. And that third person is confident that some fourth person will accept the money, with the knowledge that yet a fifth person will accept the money . . . and so on. To the restaurateur and to other people in our society, your cash or check represents a claim to goods and services in the future.

The social custom of using money for transactions is extraordinarily useful in a large, complex society. Imagine, for a moment, that there was no item in the economy widely accepted in exchange for goods and services. People would have to rely on *barter*—the exchange of one good or service for another—to obtain the things they need. To get your restaurant meal, for instance, you would have to offer the restaurateur something of immediate value. You could offer to wash some dishes, clean his car, or give him your family's secret recipe for meat loaf. An economy that relies on barter will have trouble allocating its scarce resources efficiently. In such an economy, trade is said to require the *double coincidence of wants*—the unlikely occurrence that two people each have a good or service that the other wants.

The existence of money makes trade easier. The restaurateur does not care whether you can produce a valuable good or service for him. He is happy to accept your money, knowing that other people will do the same for him. Such a convention allows trade to be roundabout. The restaurateur accepts your money and uses it to pay his chef; the chef uses her paycheck to send her child to day care; the day care center uses this tuition to pay a teacher; and the teacher hires you to mow his lawn. As money flows from person to person in the economy, it facilitates production and trade, thereby allowing each person to specialize in what he or she does best and raising everyone's standard of living.

In this chapter, we begin to examine the role of money in the economy. We discuss what money is, the various forms that money takes, how the banking system helps create money, and how the government controls the quantity of money in circulation. Because money is so important in the economy, we devote much effort in the rest of this book to learning how changes in the quantity of money affect various economic variables, including inflation, interest rates, production, and employment. Consistent with our long-run focus in the previous three chapters, in the next chapter we will examine the long-run effects of changes in the quantity of money. The short-run effects of monetary changes are a more complex topic, which we will take up later in the book. This chapter provides the background for all of this further analysis.

THE MEANING OF MONEY

money
the set of assets in an economy that people regularly use to buy goods and services from other people

What is money? This might seem like an odd question. When you read that billionaire Bill Gates has a lot of money, you know what that means: He is so rich that he can buy almost anything he wants. In this sense, the term *money* is used to mean *wealth*.

Economists, however, use the word in a more specific sense: **Money** is the set of assets in the economy that people regularly use to buy goods and services from other people. The cash in your wallet is money because you can use it to buy a meal at a restaurant or a shirt at a clothing store. By contrast, if you happened to own most of Microsoft Corporation, as Bill Gates does, you would be wealthy, but this asset is not considered a form of money. You could not buy a meal or a shirt with this wealth without first obtaining some cash. According to the economist's definition, money includes only those few types of wealth that are regularly accepted by sellers in exchange for goods and services.

The Functions of Money

Money has three functions in the economy: It is a *medium of exchange*, a *unit of account*, and a *store of value*. These three functions together distinguish money from other assets in the economy, such as stocks, bonds, real estate, art, and even baseball cards. Let's examine each of these functions of money in turn.

A **medium of exchange** is an item that buyers give to sellers when they purchase goods and services. When you buy a shirt at a clothing store, the store gives you the shirt, and you give the store your money. This transfer of money from buyer to seller allows the transaction to take place. When you walk into a store, you are confident that the store will accept your money for the items it is selling because money is the commonly accepted medium of exchange.

A **unit of account** is the yardstick people use to post prices and record debts. When you go shopping, you might observe that a shirt costs $20 and a hamburger costs $2. Even though it would be accurate to say that the price of a shirt is 10 hamburgers and the price of a hamburger is $1/10$ of a shirt, prices are never quoted in this way. Similarly, if you take out a loan from a bank, the size of your future loan repayments will be measured in dollars, not in a quantity of goods and services. When we want to measure and record economic value, we use money as the unit of account.

A **store of value** is an item that people can use to transfer purchasing power from the present to the future. When a seller accepts money today in exchange for a good or service, that seller can hold the money and become a buyer of another good or service at another time. Of course, money is not the only store of value in the economy, for a person can also transfer purchasing power from the present to the future by holding other assets. The term *wealth* is used to refer to the total of all stores of value, including both money and nonmonetary assets.

Economists use the term **liquidity** to describe the ease with which an asset can be converted into the economy's medium of exchange. Because money is the economy's medium of exchange, it is the most liquid asset available. Other assets vary widely in their liquidity. Most stocks and bonds can be sold easily with small cost, so they are relatively liquid assets. By contrast, selling a house, a Rembrandt painting, or a 1948 Joe DiMaggio baseball card requires more time and effort, so these assets are less liquid.

When people decide in what form to hold their wealth, they have to balance the liquidity of each possible asset against the asset's usefulness as a store of value. Money is the most liquid asset, but it is far from perfect as a store of value. When prices rise, the value of money falls. In other words, when goods and services become more expensive, each dollar in your wallet can buy less. This link between the price level and the value of money will turn out to be important for understanding how money affects the economy.

The Kinds of Money

When money takes the form of a commodity with intrinsic value, it is called **commodity money.** The term *intrinsic value* means that the item would have value even if it were not used as money. One example of commodity money is gold. Gold has intrinsic value because it is used in industry and in the making of jewelry. Although today we no longer use gold as money, historically gold has been a common form of money because it is relatively easy to carry, measure, and verify for impurities. When an economy uses gold as money (or uses paper money that is convertible into gold on demand), it is said to be operating under a *gold standard.*

Another example of commodity money is cigarettes. In prisoner-of-war camps during World War II, prisoners traded goods and services with one another using cigarettes as the store of value, unit of account, and medium of

---

medium of exchange
an item that buyers give to sellers when they want to purchase goods and services

unit of account
the yardstick people use to post prices and record debts

store of value
an item that people can use to transfer purchasing power from the present to the future

liquidity
the ease with which an asset can be converted into the economy's medium of exchange

commodity money
money that takes the form of a commodity with intrinsic value

In The News

The History of Money

The social custom of money evolved along with human society.

At This Museum, Money Talks

By Cleo Paskal

Let us think about money as an abstract concept. One place that encourages this concept is the Bank of Canada's Currency Museum in Ottawa. . . . The Currency Museum is the only place you can see a 2-ton chunk of rock that was used as money on the island of Yap. This alone should help us understand money as an abstract, because you know they didn't drag the boulder from store to store.

We used to think there were many things that made humans human. That is, we use tools, we laugh, we have language. But so, it seems, do various other animals. Pretty much the only fundamental we have that these other species do not have is money.

Money is one of those convenient theories, like standardized time, that provides a skeleton for modern society. It is so much a part of our daily lives that we take it for granted (presuming we have money). But, if you think about it, why should I give you a perfectly good cheeseburger in exchange for a small piece of paper?

The museum begins with a bit of history. At first, we humans lived in small family units, and we just shared.

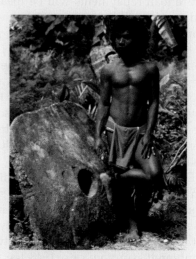

MONEY ON THE ISLAND OF YAP: NOT EXACTLY POCKET CHANGE.

exchange. Similarly, as the Soviet Union was breaking up in the late 1980s, cigarettes started replacing the ruble as the preferred currency in Moscow. In both cases, even nonsmokers were happy to accept cigarettes in an exchange, knowing that they could use the cigarettes to buy other goods and services.

fiat money
money without intrinsic value that is used as money because of government decree

Money without intrinsic value is called **fiat money.** A *fiat* is simply an order or decree, and fiat money is established as money by government decree. For example, compare the paper dollars in your wallet (printed by the U.S. government) and the paper dollars from a game of Monopoly (printed by the Parker Brothers game company). Why can you use the first to pay your bill at a restaurant but not the second? The answer is that the U.S. government has decreed its dollars to be valid money. Each paper dollar in your wallet reads: "This note is legal tender for all debts, public and private."

Although the government is central to establishing and regulating a system of fiat money (by prosecuting counterfeiters, for example), other factors are also required for the success of such a monetary system. To a large extent, the acceptance of fiat money depends as much on expectations and social convention as on government decree. The Soviet government in the 1980s never abandoned the

As societies grew bigger, we bartered. Then we used basic goods (tea bricks in Mongolia, salt blocks in the Madura Islands, cocoa beans in South America).

Livestock was often the "gold" standard. In both Latin and Anglo-Saxon, the word for cattle and money is the same. But it became too unwieldy to lug around cows every time you wanted to buy a canoe, so representative objects were introduced.

Eventually, the objects became purely abstract: elephant hair bracelets (central Africa), glass trade beads (Africa), stone disks (Togo). But, usually, the objects were made out of metal. This gave them intrinsic value, durability, portability and perhaps also divisibility.

This separation between value and specific goods made all sorts of societal changes possible, including specialized craftsmen. It was such a good idea that, by the seventh century B.C., the government (in this case Lydia, which is in western Asia Minor) got involved by creating coins.

Lydia mined huge quantities of gold, and you may have heard of one of the kings of Lydia, referred to in the phrase "as rich as Croesus."

By the third century B.C., the Romans had perfected a coin-based monetary system and used it to expand their empire. Their silver denarii dominated Europe for about 500 years.

The coins were also used for propaganda. Usually the emperor had an image of his head put on one side, and a pro-empire message on the other. Julius Caesar minted coins to finance his conquest of Gaul that featured a fine depiction of Caesar's elephant trampling Gaul's dragon. . . .

It was the Chinese that made that quantum financial leap forward, the acceptance of paper money. About a thousand years ago, carrying around all those coins was impractical if you wanted to run a complex empire over a large territory.

But how do you get a no-nonsense farmer to accept an inedible piece of mulberry tree bark in exchange for several sacks of grain?

It helps if you print on the mulberry bark that not only is it redeemable for "hard" currency but also that forgers will be decapitated. The Chinese were particularly clear when it came to money. For instance, mint-operators who diluted their coins with metals of lesser value had their faces tattooed.

It took longer for paper money to catch on in Europe. In the 16th century, an oversized coin was minted using silver from the mine in Joachimsthal, Bohemia. The coin became known as thalers. The Dutch changed that to daalder, and by the time the coins were used in England, they were being called dollars.

Source: *St. Petersburg Times* (Florida), March 14, 2004. Copyright St. Petersburg Times 2004.

ruble as the official currency. Yet the people of Moscow preferred to accept cigarettes (or even American dollars) in exchange for goods and services because they were more confident that these alternative monies would be accepted by others in the future.

Money in the U.S. Economy

As we will see, the quantity of money circulating in the economy, called the *money stock,* has a powerful influence on many economic variables. But before we consider why that is true, we need to ask a preliminary question: What is the quantity of money? In particular, suppose you were given the task of measuring how much money there is in the U.S. economy. What would you include in your measure?

The most obvious asset to include is **currency**—the paper bills and coins in the hands of the public. Currency is clearly the most widely accepted medium of exchange in our economy. There is no doubt that it is part of the money stock.

currency
the paper bills and coins in the hands of the public

demand deposits
balances in bank
accounts that depositors
can access on demand
by writing a check

Yet currency is not the only asset that you can use to buy goods and services. Many stores also accept personal checks. Wealth held in your checking account is almost as convenient for buying things as wealth held in your wallet. To measure the money stock, therefore, you might want to include **demand deposits**—balances in bank accounts that depositors can access on demand simply by writing a check.

Once you start to consider balances in checking accounts as part of the money stock, you are led to consider the large variety of other accounts that people hold at banks and other financial institutions. Bank depositors usually cannot write checks against the balances in their savings accounts, but they can easily transfer funds from savings into checking accounts. In addition, depositors in money market mutual funds can often write checks against their balances. Thus, these other accounts should plausibly be part of the U.S. money stock.

In a complex economy such as ours, it is not easy to draw a line between assets that can be called "money" and assets that cannot. The coins in your pocket are clearly part of the money stock, and the Empire State Building clearly is not, but there are many assets in between these extremes for which the choice is less clear. Because different analysts can reasonably disagree about where to draw the dividing line between monetary and nonmonetary assets, various measures of the money stock are available for the U.S. economy. Figure 1 shows the two most commonly used, designated M1 and M2. M2 includes more assets in its measure of money than does M1.

For our purposes in this book, we need not dwell on the differences between the various measures of money. None of our discussion will hinge on the distinction between M1 and M2. The important point is that the money stock for the U.S.

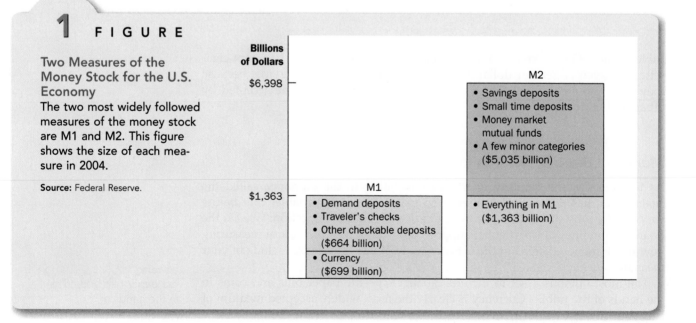

1 FIGURE

Two Measures of the
Money Stock for the U.S.
Economy
The two most widely followed
measures of the money stock
are M1 and M2. This figure
shows the size of each measure in 2004.

Source: Federal Reserve.

FYI

Credit Cards, Debit Cards, and Money

It might seem natural to include credit cards as part of the economy's stock of money. After all, people use credit cards to make many of their purchases. Aren't credit cards, therefore, a medium of exchange?

Although at first this argument may seem persuasive, credit cards are excluded from all measures of the quantity of money. The reason is that credit cards are not really a method of payment but a method of *deferring* payment. When you buy a meal with a credit card, the bank that issued the card pays the restaurant what it is due. At a later date, you will have to repay the bank (perhaps with interest). When the time comes to pay your credit card bill, you will probably do so by writing a check against your checking account. The balance in this checking account is part of the economy's stock of money.

Notice that credit cards are very different from debit cards, which automatically withdraw funds from a bank account to pay for items bought. Rather than allowing the user to postpone payment for a purchase, a debit card allows the user immediate access to deposits in a bank account. In this sense, a debit card is more similar to a check than to a credit card. The account balances that lie behind debit cards are included in measures of the quantity of money.

Even though credit cards are not considered a form of money, they are nonetheless important for analyzing the monetary system. People who have credit cards can pay many of their bills all at once at the end of the month, rather than sporadically as they make purchases. As a result, people who have credit cards probably hold less money on average than people who do not have credit cards. Thus, the introduction and increased popularity of credit cards may reduce the amount of money that people choose to hold.

economy includes not just currency but also deposits in banks and other financial institutions that can be readily accessed and used to buy goods and services.

CASE STUDY | WHERE IS ALL THE CURRENCY?

One puzzle about the money stock of the U.S. economy concerns the amount of currency. In 2004, there was $699 billion of currency outstanding. To put this number in perspective, we can divide it by 223 million, the number of adults (age 16 and older) in the United States. This calculation implies that the average adult holds about $3,134 of currency. Most people are surprised to learn that our economy has so much currency because they carry far less than this in their wallets.

Who is holding all this currency? No one knows for sure, but there are two plausible explanations.

The first explanation is that much of the currency is held abroad. In foreign countries without a stable monetary system, people often prefer U.S. dollars to domestic assets. It is, in fact, not unusual to see U.S. dollars used overseas as the medium of exchange, unit of account, and store of value.

The second explanation is that much of the currency is held by drug dealers, tax evaders, and other criminals. For most people in the U.S. economy, currency is not a particularly good way to hold wealth. Not only can currency be lost or stolen, but it also does not earn interest, whereas a bank deposit does. Thus, most people hold only small amounts of currency. By contrast, criminals may avoid putting their wealth in banks because a bank deposit gives police a paper trail with which to trace their illegal activities. For criminals, currency may be the best store of value available.   •

Quick Quiz   List and describe the three functions of money.

THE FEDERAL RESERVE SYSTEM

Federal Reserve (Fed)
the central bank of the United States

central bank
an institution designed to oversee the banking system and regulate the quantity of money in the economy

Whenever an economy relies on a system of fiat money, as the U.S. economy does, some agency must be responsible for regulating the system. In the United States, that agency is the **Federal Reserve,** often simply called the **Fed.** If you look at the top of a dollar bill, you will see that it is called a "Federal Reserve Note." The Fed is an example of a **central bank**—an institution designed to oversee the banking system and regulate the quantity of money in the economy. Other major central banks around the world include the Bank of England, the Bank of Japan, and the European Central Bank.

The Fed's Organization

The Federal Reserve was created in 1913 after a series of bank failures in 1907 convinced Congress that the United States needed a central bank to ensure the health of the nation's banking system. Today, the Fed is run by its board of governors, which has seven members appointed by the president and confirmed by the Senate. The governors have 14-year terms. Just as federal judges are given lifetime appointments to insulate them from politics, Fed governors are given long terms to give them independence from short-term political pressures when they formulate monetary policy.

Among the seven members of the board of governors, the most important is the chairman. The chairman directs the Fed staff, presides over board meetings, and testifies regularly about Fed policy in front of congressional committees. The president appoints the chairman to a four-year term. As this book was going to press, the chairman of the Fed was Alan Greenspan, who was originally appointed in 1987 by President Reagan and was later reappointed by Presidents Bush, Clinton, and Bush.

The Federal Reserve System is made up of the Federal Reserve Board in Washington, D.C., and twelve regional Federal Reserve Banks located in major cities around the country. The presidents of the regional banks are chosen by each bank's board of directors, whose members are typically drawn from the region's banking and business community.

The Fed has two related jobs. The first is to regulate banks and ensure the health of the banking system. This task is largely the responsibility of the regional Federal Reserve Banks. In particular, the Fed monitors each bank's financial condition and facilitates bank transactions by clearing checks. It also acts as a bank's bank. That is, the Fed makes loans to banks when banks themselves want to borrow. When financially troubled banks find themselves short of cash, the Fed acts as a *lender of last resort*—a lender to those who cannot borrow anywhere else—to maintain stability in the overall banking system.

The Fed's second and more important job is to control the quantity of money that is made available in the economy, called the **money supply**. Decisions by policymakers concerning the money supply constitute **monetary policy**. At the Federal Reserve, monetary policy is made by the Federal Open Market Committee (FOMC). The FOMC meets about every six weeks in Washington, D.C., to discuss the condition of the economy and consider changes in monetary policy.

money supply
the quantity of money available in the economy

monetary policy
the setting of the money supply by policymakers in the central bank

The Federal Open Market Committee

The Federal Open Market Committee is made up of the seven members of the board of governors and five of the twelve regional bank presidents. All twelve regional presidents attend each FOMC meeting, but only five get to vote. The five with voting rights rotate among the twelve regional presidents over time. The president of the New York Fed always gets a vote, however, because New York is the traditional financial center of the U.S. economy and because all Fed purchases and sales of government bonds are conducted at the New York Fed's trading desk.

Through the decisions of the FOMC, the Fed has the power to increase or decrease the number of dollars in the economy. In simple metaphorical terms, you can imagine the Fed printing dollar bills and dropping them around the country by helicopter. Similarly, you can imagine the Fed using a giant vacuum cleaner to suck dollar bills out of people's wallets. Although in practice the Fed's methods for changing the money supply are more complex and subtle than this, the helicopter-vacuum metaphor is a good first step to understanding the meaning of monetary policy.

Later in this chapter, we discuss how the Fed actually changes the money supply, but it is worth noting here that the Fed's primary tool is the *open-market operation*—the purchase and sale of U.S. government bonds. (Recall that a U.S. government bond is a certificate of indebtedness of the federal government.) If the FOMC decides to increase the money supply, the Fed creates dollars and uses them to buy government bonds from the public in the nation's bond markets. After the purchase, these dollars are in the hands of the public. Thus, an open-market purchase of bonds by the Fed increases the money supply. Conversely, if the FOMC decides to decrease the money supply, the Fed sells government bonds from its portfolio to the public in the nation's bond markets. After the sale, the dollars it receives for the bonds are out of the hands of the public. Thus, an open-market sale of bonds by the Fed decreases the money supply.

Central banks are important institutions because changes in the money supply can profoundly affect the economy. One of the *Ten Principles of Economics* in Chapter 1 is that prices rise when the government prints too much money. Another of the *Ten Principles of Economics* is that society faces a short-run trade-off between inflation and unemployment. The power of the Fed rests on these principles. For reasons we discuss more fully in the coming chapters, the Fed's policy decisions have an important influence on the economy's rate of inflation in the long run and the economy's employment and production in the short run. Indeed, the chairman of the Federal Reserve has been called the second most powerful person in the United States.

Quick Quiz   What are the primary responsibilities of the Federal Reserve? If the Fed wants to increase the supply of money, how does it usually do so?

BANKS AND THE MONEY SUPPLY

So far, we have introduced the concept of "money" and discussed how the Federal Reserve controls the supply of money by buying and selling government bonds in open-market operations. Although this explanation of the money supply is correct, it is not complete. In particular, it omits the central role that banks play in the monetary system.

Recall that the amount of money you hold includes both currency (the bills in your wallet and coins in your pocket) and demand deposits (the balance in your checking account). Because demand deposits are held in banks, the behavior of banks can influence the quantity of demand deposits in the economy and, therefore, the money supply. This section examines how banks affect the money supply and how they complicate the Fed's job of controlling the money supply.

The Simple Case of 100-Percent-Reserve Banking

To see how banks influence the money supply, it is useful to imagine first a world without any banks at all. In this simple world, currency is the only form of money. To be concrete, let's suppose that the total quantity of currency is $100. The supply of money is, therefore, $100.

Now suppose that someone opens a bank, appropriately called First National Bank. First National Bank is only a depository institution—that is, it accepts deposits but does not make loans. The purpose of the bank is to give depositors a safe place to keep their money. Whenever a person deposits some money, the bank keeps the money in its vault until the depositor comes to withdraw it or writes a check against his or her balance. Deposits that banks have received but have not loaned out are called **reserves.** In this imaginary economy, all deposits are held as reserves, so this system is called *100-percent-reserve banking*.

reserves
deposits that banks have received but have not loaned out

We can express the financial position of First National Bank with a *T-account*, which is a simplified accounting statement that shows changes in a bank's assets and liabilities. Here is the T-account for First National Bank if the economy's entire $100 of money is deposited in the bank:

FIRST NATIONAL BANK

Assets		Liabilities	
Reserves	$100.00	Deposits	$100.00

On the left side of the T-account are the bank's assets of $100 (the reserves it holds in its vaults). On the right side are the bank's liabilities of $100 (the amount it owes to its depositors). Notice that the assets and liabilities of First National Bank exactly balance.

Now consider the money supply in this imaginary economy. Before First National Bank opens, the money supply is the $100 of currency that people are holding. After the bank opens and people deposit their currency, the money sup-

"I'VE HEARD A LOT ABOUT MONEY, AND NOW I'D LIKE TO TRY SOME."

ply is the $100 of demand deposits. (There is no longer any currency outstanding, for it is all in the bank vault.) Each deposit in the bank reduces currency and raises demand deposits by exactly the same amount, leaving the money supply unchanged. Thus, *if banks hold all deposits in reserve, banks do not influence the supply of money.*

Money Creation with Fractional-Reserve Banking

Eventually, the bankers at First National Bank may start to reconsider their policy of 100-percent-reserve banking. Leaving all that money idle in their vaults seems unnecessary. Why not lend some of it out and earn a profit by charging interest on the loans? Families buying houses, firms building new factories, and students paying for college would all be happy to pay interest to borrow some of that money for a while. First National Bank has to keep some reserves so that currency is available if depositors want to make withdrawals. But if the flow of new deposits is roughly the same as the flow of withdrawals, First National needs to keep only a fraction of its deposits in reserve. Thus, First National adopts a system called **fractional-reserve banking.**

The fraction of total deposits that a bank holds as reserves is called the **reserve ratio.** This ratio is determined by a combination of government regulation and bank policy. As we discuss more fully later in the chapter, the Fed sets a minimum amount of reserves that banks must hold, called a *reserve requirement.* In addition, banks may hold reserves above the legal minimum, called *excess reserves,* so they can be more confident that they will not run short of cash. For our purpose here, we take the reserve ratio as given to examine what fractional-reserve banking means for the money supply.

Let's suppose that First National has a reserve ratio of 10 percent. This means that it keeps 10 percent of its deposits in reserve and loans out the rest. Now let's look again at the bank's T-account:

fractional-reserve banking
a banking system in which banks hold only a fraction of deposits as reserves

reserve ratio
the fraction of deposits that banks hold as reserves

FIRST NATIONAL BANK

Assets		Liabilities	
Reserves	$10.00	Deposits	$100.00
Loans	90.00		

First National still has $100 in liabilities because making the loans did not alter the bank's obligation to its depositors. But now the bank has two kinds of assets: It has $10 of reserves in its vault, and it has loans of $90. (These loans are liabilities of the people taking out the loans, but they are assets of the bank making the loans because the borrowers will later repay the bank.) In total, First National's assets still equal its liabilities.

Once again consider the supply of money in the economy. Before First National makes any loans, the money supply is the $100 of deposits in the bank. Yet when First National makes these loans, the money supply increases. The depositors still have demand deposits totaling $100, but now the borrowers hold $90 in currency. The money supply (which equals currency plus demand deposits) equals $190. Thus, *when banks hold only a fraction of deposits in reserve, banks create money.*

At first, this creation of money by fractional-reserve banking may seem too good to be true because it appears that the bank has created money out of thin air. To make this creation of money seem less miraculous, note that when First

National Bank loans out some of its reserves and creates money, it does not create any wealth. Loans from First National give the borrowers some currency and thus the ability to buy goods and services. Yet the borrowers are also taking on debts, so the loans do not make them any richer. In other words, as a bank creates the asset of money, it also creates a corresponding liability for its borrowers. At the end of this process of money creation, the economy is more liquid in the sense that there is more of the medium of exchange, but the economy is no wealthier than before.

The Money Multiplier

The creation of money does not stop with First National Bank. Suppose the borrower from First National uses the $90 to buy something from someone who then deposits the currency in Second National Bank. Here is the T-account for Second National Bank:

SECOND NATIONAL BANK

Assets		Liabilities	
Reserves	$9.00	Deposits	$90.00
Loans	81.00		

After the deposit, this bank has liabilities of $90. If Second National also has a reserve ratio of 10 percent, it keeps assets of $9 in reserve and makes $81 in loans. In this way, Second National Bank creates an additional $81 of money. If this $81 is eventually deposited in Third National Bank, which also has a reserve ratio of 10 percent, this bank keeps $8.10 in reserve and makes $72.90 in loans. Here is the T-account for Third National Bank:

THIRD NATIONAL BANK

Assets		Liabilities	
Reserves	$8.10	Deposits	$81.00
Loans	72.90		

The process goes on and on. Each time that money is deposited and a bank loan is made, more money is created.

How much money is eventually created in this economy? Let's add it up:

Original deposit	= $	100.00
First National lending	= $	90.00 [= .9 × $100.00]
Second National lending	= $	81.00 [= .9 × $90.00]
Third National lending	= $	72.90 [= .9 × $81.00]
•		•
•		•
•		•
Total money supply	= $1,000.00	

It turns out that even though this process of money creation can continue forever, it does not create an infinite amount of money. If you laboriously add the infinite sequence of numbers in the foregoing example, you find the $100 of reserves generates $1,000 of money. The amount of money the banking system generates with each dollar of reserves is called the **money multiplier.** In this imaginary economy, where the $100 of reserves generates $1,000 of money, the money multiplier is 10.

What determines the size of the money multiplier? It turns out that the answer is simple: *The money multiplier is the reciprocal of the reserve ratio.* If R is the reserve ratio for all banks in the economy, then each dollar of reserves generates $1/R$ dollars of money. In our example, $R = 1/10$, so the money multiplier is 10.

This reciprocal formula for the money multiplier makes sense. If a bank holds $1,000 in deposits, then a reserve ratio of 1/10 (10 percent) means that the bank must hold $100 in reserves. The money multiplier just turns this idea around: If the banking system as a whole holds a total of $100 in reserves, it can have only $1,000 in deposits. In other words, if R is the ratio of reserves to deposits at each bank (that is, the reserve ratio), then the ratio of deposits to reserves in the banking system (that is, the money multiplier) must be $1/R$.

This formula shows how the amount of money banks create depends on the reserve ratio. If the reserve ratio were only 1/20 (5 percent), then the banking system would have 20 times as much in deposits as in reserves, implying a money multiplier of 20. Each dollar of reserves would generate $20 of money. Similarly, if the reserve ratio were 1/5 (20 percent), deposits would be 5 times reserves, the money multiplier would be 5, and each dollar of reserves would generate $5 of money. *Thus, the higher the reserve ratio, the less of each deposit banks loan out, and the smaller the money multiplier.* In the special case of 100-percent-reserve banking, the reserve ratio is 1, the money multiplier is 1, and banks do not make loans or create money.

The Fed's Tools of Monetary Control

As we have already discussed, the Federal Reserve is responsible for controlling the supply of money in the economy. Now that we understand how fractional-reserve banking works, we are in a better position to understand how the Fed carries out this job. Because banks create money in a system of fractional-reserve banking, the Fed's control of the money supply is indirect. When the Fed decides to change the money supply, it must consider how its actions will work through the banking system.

The Fed has three tools in its monetary toolbox: open-market operations, reserve requirements, and the discount rate. Let's discuss how the Fed uses each of these tools.

Open-Market Operations   As we noted earlier, the Fed conducts **open-market operations** when it buys or sells government bonds. To increase the money supply, the Fed instructs its bond traders at the New York Fed to buy bonds from the public in the nation's bond markets. The dollars the Fed pays for the bonds increase the number of dollars in the economy. Some of these new dollars are held as currency, and some are deposited in banks. Each new dollar held as currency increases the money supply by exactly $1. Each new dollar deposited in a bank increases the money supply to an even greater extent because it increases reserves and, thereby, the amount of money that the banking system can create.

To reduce the money supply, the Fed does just the opposite: It sells government bonds to the public in the nation's bond markets. The public pays for these

money multiplier
the amount of money the banking system generates with each dollar of reserves

open-market operations
the purchase and sale of U.S. government bonds by the Fed

bonds with its holdings of currency and bank deposits, directly reducing the amount of money in circulation. In addition, as people make withdrawals from banks, banks find themselves with a smaller quantity of reserves. In response, banks reduce the amount of lending, and the process of money creation reverses itself.

Open-market operations are easy to conduct. In fact, the Fed's purchases and sales of government bonds in the nation's bond markets are similar to the transactions that any individual might undertake for his own portfolio. (Of course, when an individual buys or sells a bond, money changes hands, but the amount of money in circulation remains the same.) In addition, the Fed can use open-market operations to change the money supply by a small or large amount on any day without major changes in laws or bank regulations. Therefore, open-market operations are the tool of monetary policy that the Fed uses most often.

reserve requirements
regulations on the minimum amount of reserves that banks must hold against deposits

Reserve Requirements   The Fed also influences the money supply with **reserve requirements,** which are regulations on the minimum amount of reserves that banks must hold against deposits. Reserve requirements influence how much money the banking system can create with each dollar of reserves. An increase in reserve requirements means that banks must hold more reserves and, therefore, can loan out less of each dollar that is deposited; as a result, it raises the reserve ratio, lowers the money multiplier, and decreases the money supply. Conversely, a decrease in reserve requirements lowers the reserve ratio, raises the money multiplier, and increases the money supply.

The Fed uses changes in reserve requirements only rarely because frequent changes would disrupt the business of banking. When the Fed increases reserve requirements, for instance, some banks find themselves short of reserves, even though they have seen no change in deposits. As a result, they have to curtail lending until they build their level of reserves to the new required level.

discount rate
the interest rate on the loans that the Fed makes to banks

The Discount Rate   The third tool in the Fed's toolbox is the **discount rate,** the interest rate on the loans that the Fed makes to banks. A bank borrows from the Fed when it has too few reserves to meet its reserve requirements. This might occur because the bank made too many loans or because it has experienced unexpectedly high withdrawals. When the Fed makes such a loan to a bank, the banking system has more reserves than it otherwise would, and these additional reserves allow the banking system to create more money.

The Fed can alter the money supply by changing the discount rate. A higher discount rate discourages banks from borrowing reserves from the Fed. Thus, an increase in the discount rate reduces the quantity of reserves in the banking system, which in turn reduces the money supply. Conversely, a lower discount rate encourages banks to borrow from the Fed, increases the quantity of reserves, and increases the money supply.

The Fed uses discount lending not only to control the money supply but also to help financial institutions when they are in trouble. For example, in 1984, rumors circulated that Continental Illinois National Bank had made a large number of bad loans, and these rumors induced many depositors to withdraw their deposits. As part of an effort to save the bank, the Fed acted as a lender of last resort and loaned Continental Illinois more than $5 billion. Similarly, when the stock market crashed on October 19, 1987, many Wall Street brokerage firms found themselves temporarily in need of funds to finance the high volume of stock trading. The next morning, before the stock market opened, Fed Chairman

Alan Greenspan announced the Fed's "readiness to serve as a source of liquidity to support the economic and financial system." Many economists believe that Greenspan's reaction to the stock crash was an important reason it had so few repercussions.

Problems in Controlling the Money Supply

The Fed's three tools—open-market operations, reserve requirements, and the discount rate—have powerful effects on the money supply. Yet the Fed's control of the money supply is not precise. The Fed must wrestle with two problems, each of which arises because much of the money supply is created by our system of fractional-reserve banking.

The first problem is that the Fed does not control the amount of money that households choose to hold as deposits in banks. The more money households deposit, the more reserves banks have, and the more money the banking system can create. And the less money households deposit, the less reserves banks have, and the less money the banking system can create. To see why this is a problem, suppose that one day people begin to lose confidence in the banking system and, therefore, decide to withdraw deposits and hold more currency. When this happens, the banking system loses reserves and creates less money. The money supply falls, even without any Fed action.

The second problem of monetary control is that the Fed does not control the amount that bankers choose to lend. When money is deposited in a bank, it creates more money only when the bank loans it out. Because banks can choose to hold excess reserves instead, the Fed cannot be sure how much money the banking system will create. For instance, suppose that one day bankers become more cautious about economic conditions and decide to make fewer loans and hold greater reserves. In this case, the banking system creates less money than it otherwise would. Because of the bankers' decision, the money supply falls.

Hence, in a system of fractional-reserve banking, the amount of money in the economy depends in part on the behavior of depositors and bankers. Because the Fed cannot control or perfectly predict this behavior, it cannot perfectly control the money supply. Yet if the Fed is vigilant, these problems need not be large. The Fed collects data on deposits and reserves from banks every week, so it is quickly aware of any changes in depositor or banker behavior. It can, therefore, respond to these changes and keep the money supply close to whatever level it chooses.

CASE STUDY | BANK RUNS AND THE MONEY SUPPLY

A NOT-SO-WONDERFUL BANK RUN

Although you have probably never witnessed a bank run in real life, you may have seen one depicted in movies such as *Mary Poppins* or *It's a Wonderful Life*. A bank run occurs when depositors suspect that a bank may go bankrupt and, therefore, "run" to the bank to withdraw their deposits.

Bank runs are a problem for banks under fractional-reserve banking. Because a bank holds only a fraction of its deposits in reserve, it cannot satisfy withdrawal requests from all depositors. Even if the bank is in fact *solvent* (meaning that its assets exceed its liabilities), it will not have enough cash on hand to allow all depositors immediate access to all of their money. When a run occurs,

FYI

The Federal Funds Rate

If you read about U.S. monetary policy in the newspaper, you will find much discussion of the *federal funds rate*. This raises several questions:

Q: What is the federal funds rate?

A: The federal funds rate is the short-term interest rate that banks charge one another for loans. If one bank finds itself short of reserves while another bank has excess reserves, the second bank can lend some reserves to the first. The loans are temporary—typically overnight. The price of the loan is the federal funds rate.

Q: Does the federal funds rate matter only for banks?

A: Not at all. While only banks borrow directly in the federal funds market, the economic impact of this market is much broader. Because different parts of the financial system are highly interconnected, interest rates on different kinds of loans are strongly correlated with one another. So when the federal funds rate rises or falls, other interest rates often move in the same direction.

Q: What does the Federal Reserve have to do with the federal funds rate?

A: In recent years, the Federal Reserve has set a target goal for the federal funds rate. When the Federal Open Market Committee meets approximately every six weeks, it decides whether to raise or lower that target.

Q: How can the Fed make the federal funds rate hit the target it sets?

A: Although the actual federal funds rate is set by supply and demand in the market for loans among banks, the Fed can use open-market operations to influence that market. For example, when the Fed buys bonds in open-market operations, it injects reserves into the banking system. With more reserves in the system, fewer banks find themselves in need of borrowing reserves to meet reserve requirements. The fall in demand for borrowing reserves decreases the price of such borrowing, which is the federal funds rate. Conversely, when the Fed sells bonds and withdraws reserves from the banking system, more banks find themselves short of reserves, and they bid up the price of borrowing reserves. Thus, open-market purchases lower the federal funds rate, and open-market sales raise the federal funds rate.

Q: But don't these open-market operations affect the money supply?

A: Yes, absolutely. When the Fed announces a change in the federal funds rate, it is committing itself to the open-market operations necessary to make change happen, and these open-market operations will change the supply of money. Decisions by the FOMC to change the target for the federal funds rate are also decisions to change the money supply. They are two sides of the same coin. Other things equal, a decrease in the target for the federal funds rate means an expansion in the money supply, and an increase in the target for the federal funds rate means a contraction in the money supply.

the bank is forced to close its doors until some bank loans are repaid or until some lender of last resort (such as the Fed) provides it with the currency it needs to satisfy depositors.

Bank runs complicate the control of the money supply. An important example of this problem occurred during the Great Depression in the early 1930s. After a wave of bank runs and bank closings, households and bankers became more cautious. Households withdrew their deposits from banks, preferring to hold their money in the form of currency. This decision reversed the process of money creation, as bankers responded to falling reserves by reducing bank loans. At the same time, bankers increased their reserve ratios so that they would have enough cash on hand to meet their depositors' demands in any future bank runs. The higher reserve ratio reduced the money multiplier, which also reduced the money supply. From 1929 to 1933, the money supply fell by 28 percent, even without the Federal Reserve taking any deliberate contractionary action. Many economists point to this massive fall in the money supply to explain the high unemployment and falling prices that prevailed during this period. (In future chapters, we examine the mechanisms by which changes in the money supply affect unemployment and prices.)

Today, bank runs are not a major problem for the U.S. banking system or the Fed. The federal government now guarantees the safety of deposits at most banks, primarily through the Federal Deposit Insurance Corporation (FDIC). Depositors do not run on their banks because they are confident that, even if their bank goes bankrupt, the FDIC will make good on the deposits. The policy of government deposit insurance has costs: Bankers whose deposits are guaranteed may have too little incentive to avoid bad risks when making loans. But one benefit of deposit insurance is a more stable banking system. As a result, most people see bank runs only in the movies. •

Quick Quiz Describe how banks create money. • If the Fed wanted to use all three of its policy tools to decrease the money supply, what would it do?

CONCLUSION

Some years ago, a book made the best-seller list with the title *Secrets of the Temple: How the Federal Reserve Runs the Country.* Although no doubt an exaggeration, this title did highlight the important role of the monetary system in our daily lives. Whenever we buy or sell anything, we are relying on the extraordinarily useful social convention called "money." Now that we know what money is and what determines its supply, we can discuss how changes in the quantity of money affect the economy. We begin to address that topic in the next chapter.

SUMMARY

- The term *money* refers to assets that people regularly use to buy goods and services.

- Money serves three functions. As a medium of exchange, it provides the item used to make transactions. As a unit of account, it provides the way in which prices and other economic values are recorded. As a store of value, it provides a way of transferring purchasing power from the present to the future.

- Commodity money, such as gold, is money that has intrinsic value: It would be valued even if it were not used as money. Fiat money, such as paper dollars, is money without intrinsic value: It would be worthless if it were not used as money.

- In the U.S. economy, money takes the form of currency and various types of bank deposits, such as checking accounts.

- The Federal Reserve, the central bank of the United States, is responsible for regulating the U.S. monetary system. The Fed chairman is appointed by the president and confirmed by Congress every 4 years. The chairman is the lead member of the Federal Open Market Committee, which meets about every 6 weeks to consider changes in monetary policy.

- The Fed controls the money supply primarily through open-market operations: The purchase of government bonds increases the money supply, and the sale of government bonds decreases the money supply. The Fed can also expand the money supply by lowering reserve requirements or decreasing the discount rate, and it can contract the money supply by raising reserve requirements or increasing the discount rate.

- When banks loan out some of their deposits, they increase the quantity of money in the economy. Because of this role of banks in determining the money supply, the Fed's control of the money supply is imperfect.

KEY CONCEPTS

money, p. 226
medium of exchange, p. 227
unit of account, p. 227
store of value, p. 227
liquidity, p. 227
commodity money, p. 227
fiat money, p. 228

currency, p. 229
demand deposits, p. 230
Federal Reserve (Fed), p. 232
central bank, p. 232
money supply, p. 233
monetary policy, p. 233
reserves, p. 234

fractional-reserve banking, p. 235
reserve ratio, p. 235
money multiplier, p. 237
open-market operations, p. 237
reserve requirements, p. 238
discount rate, p. 238

QUESTIONS FOR REVIEW

1. What distinguishes money from other assets in the economy?

2. What is commodity money? What is fiat money? Which kind do we use?

3. What are demand deposits and why should they be included in the stock of money?

4. Who is responsible for setting monetary policy in the United States? How is this group chosen?

5. If the Fed wants to increase the money supply with open-market operations, what does it do?

6. Why don't banks hold 100 percent reserves? How is the amount of reserves banks hold related to the amount of money the banking system creates?

7. What is the discount rate? What happens to the money supply when the Fed raises the discount rate?

8. What are reserve requirements? What happens to the money supply when the Fed raises reserve requirements?

9. Why can't the Fed control the money supply perfectly?

PROBLEMS AND APPLICATIONS

1. Which of the following are money in the U.S. economy? Which are not? Explain your answers by discussing each of the three functions of money.
   a. a U.S. penny
   b. a Mexican peso
   c. a Picasso painting
   d. a plastic credit card

2. What characteristics of an asset make it useful as a medium of exchange? As a store of value?

3. Go to the website of the Federal Reserve Bank of St. Louis (http://www.stlouisfed.org) to find some information about the Fed.   Find a map of the Federal Reserve districts. If you live in the United States, find what district you live in. Where is the Federal Reserve Bank for your dis-

trict located? (Extra credit: What state has two Federal Reserve Banks?)

4. Your uncle repays a $100 loan from Tenth National Bank (TNB) by writing a $100 check from his TNB checking account. Use T-accounts to show the effect of this transaction on your uncle and on TNB. Has your uncle's wealth changed? Explain.

5. Beleaguered State Bank (BSB) holds $250 million in deposits and maintains a reserve ratio of 10 percent.
   a. Show a T-account for BSB.
   b. Now suppose that BSB's largest depositor withdraws $10 million in cash from her account. If BSB decides to restore its reserve ratio by reducing the amount of loans outstanding, show its new T-account.
   c. Explain what effect BSB's action will have on other banks.
   d. Why might it be difficult for BSB to take the action described in part (b)? Discuss another way for BSB to return to its original reserve ratio.

6. You take $100 you had kept under your pillow and deposit it in your bank account. If this $100 stays in the banking system as reserves and if banks hold reserves equal to 10 percent of deposits, by how much does the total amount of deposits in the banking system increase? By how much does the money supply increase?

7. The Federal Reserve conducts a $10 million open-market purchase of government bonds. If the required reserve ratio is 10 percent, what is the largest possible increase in the money supply that could result? Explain. What is the smallest possible increase? Explain.

8. Suppose that the T-account for First National Bank is as follows:

Assets		Liabilities	
Reserves	$100,000	Deposits	$500,000
Loans	400,000		

   a. If the Fed requires banks to hold 5 percent of deposits as reserves, how much in excess reserves does First National now hold?

   b. Assume that all other banks hold only the required amount of reserves. If First National decides to reduce its reserves to only the required amount, by how much would the economy's money supply increase?

9. Suppose that the reserve requirement for checking deposits is 10 percent and that banks do not hold any excess reserves.
   a. If the Fed sells $1 million of government bonds, what is the effect on the economy's reserves and money supply?
   b. Now suppose the Fed lowers the reserve requirement to 5 percent, but banks choose to hold another 5 percent of deposits as excess reserves. Why might banks do so? What is the overall change in the money multiplier and the money supply as a result of these actions?

10. Assume that the banking system has total reserves of $100 billion. Assume also that required reserves are 10 percent of checking deposits and that banks hold no excess reserves and households hold no currency.
   a. What is the money multiplier? What is the money supply?
   b. If the Fed now raises required reserves to 20 percent of deposits, what is the change in reserves and the change in the money supply?

11. The economy of Elmendyn contains 2,000 $1 bills.
   a. If people hold all money as currency, what is the quantity of money?
   b. If people hold all money as demand deposits and banks maintain 100 percent reserves, what is the quantity of money?
   c. If people hold equal amounts of currency and demand deposits and banks maintain 100 percent reserves, what is the quantity of money?
   d. If people hold all money as demand deposits and banks maintain a reserve ratio of 10 percent, what is the quantity of money?
   e. If people hold equal amounts of currency and demand deposits and banks maintain a reserve ratio of 10 percent, what is the quantity of money?

For further information on topics in this chapter, additional problems, examples, applications, online quizzes, and more, please visit our website at http://mankiw.swlearning.com.

Money Growth and Inflation

Although today you need a couple of dollars to buy yourself an ice-cream cone, life was very different 70 years ago. In one Trenton, New Jersey, candy store (run, incidentally, by my grandmother in the 1930s), ice-cream cones came in two sizes. A cone with a small scoop of ice cream cost three cents. Hungry customers could buy a large scoop for a nickel.

You are probably not surprised at the increase in the price of ice cream. In our economy, most prices tend to rise over time. This increase in the overall level of prices is called *inflation*. Earlier in the book, we examined how economists measure the inflation rate as the percentage change in the consumer price index (CPI), the GDP deflator, or some other index of the overall price level. These price indexes show that, over the past 70 years, prices have risen on average about 4 percent per year. Accumulated over so many years, a 4 percent annual inflation rate leads to a 16-fold increase in the price level.

Inflation may seem natural and inevitable to a person who grew up in the United States during the second half of the 20th century, but in fact, it is not inevitable at all. There were long periods in the 19th century during which most prices fell—a phenomenon called *deflation*. The average level of prices in the U.S. economy was 23 percent lower in 1896 than in 1880, and this deflation was a major issue in the presidential election of 1896. Farmers, who had accumulated large debts, were suffering when the fall in crop prices reduced their incomes and thus their ability to pay off their debts. They advocated government policies to reverse the deflation.

Although inflation has been the norm in more recent history, there has been substantial variation in the rate at which prices rise. During the 1990s, prices rose at an average rate of about 2 percent per year. By contrast, in the 1970s, prices rose by 7 percent per year, which meant a doubling of the price level over the decade. The public often views such high rates of inflation as a major economic problem. In fact, when President Jimmy Carter ran for reelection in 1980, challenger Ronald Reagan pointed to high inflation as one of the failures of Carter's economic policy.

International data show an even broader range of inflation experiences. In 2005, while the U.S. inflation rate was about 3 percent, inflation was 12 percent in Russia and 15 percent in Venezuela. And even these higher inflation rates are moderate by historical standards. In Germany after World War I, the price of a newspaper rose from 0.3 marks in January 1921 to 70,000,000 marks less than two years later, with other prices rising by similar amounts. An extraordinarily high rate of inflation such as this is called *hyperinflation*.

What determines whether an economy experiences inflation and, if so, how much? This chapter answers this question by developing the *quantity theory of money.* Chapter 1 summarized this theory as one of the *Ten Principles of Economics:* Prices rise when the government prints too much money. This insight has a long and venerable tradition among economists. The quantity theory was discussed by the famous 18th-century philosopher and economist David Hume and has been advocated more recently by the prominent economist Milton Friedman. This theory of inflation can explain both moderate inflations, such as those we have experienced in the United States, and hyperinflations, such as those experienced in interwar Germany and, more recently, in some Latin American countries.

After developing a theory of inflation, we turn to a related question: Why is inflation a problem? At first glance, the answer to this question may seem obvious: Inflation is a problem because people don't like it. In the 1970s, when the United States experienced a relatively high rate of inflation, opinion polls placed inflation as the most important issue facing the nation. President Ford echoed this sentiment in 1974 when he called inflation "public enemy number one." Ford wore a "WIN" button on his lapel—for Whip Inflation Now.

But what, exactly, are the costs that inflation imposes on a society? The answer may surprise you. Identifying the various costs of inflation is not as straightforward as it first appears. As a result, although all economists decry hyperinflation, some economists argue that the costs of moderate inflation are not nearly as large as the general public believes.

THE CLASSICAL THEORY OF INFLATION

We begin our study of inflation by developing the quantity theory of money. This theory is often called "classical" because it was developed by some of the earliest thinkers about economic issues. Most economists today rely on this theory to explain the long-run determinants of the price level and the inflation rate.

The Level of Prices and the Value of Money

Suppose we observe over some period of time the price of an ice-cream cone rising from a nickel to a dollar. What conclusion should we draw from the fact that people are willing to give up so much more money in exchange for a cone? It is possible that people have come to enjoy ice cream more (perhaps because some chemist has developed a miraculous new flavor). Yet that is probably not the case. It is more likely that people's enjoyment of ice cream has stayed roughly the same and that, over time, the money used to buy ice cream has become less valuable. Indeed, the first insight about inflation is that it is more about the value of money than about the value of goods.

This insight helps point the way toward a theory of inflation. When the consumer price index and other measures of the price level rise, commentators are often tempted to look at the many individual prices that make up these price indexes: "The CPI rose by 3 percent last month, led by a 20 percent rise in the price of coffee and a 30 percent rise in the price of heating oil." Although this approach does contain some interesting information about what's happening in the economy, it also misses a key point: Inflation is an economy-wide phenomenon that concerns, first and foremost, the value of the economy's medium of exchange.

The economy's overall price level can be viewed in two ways. So far, we have viewed the price level as the price of a basket of goods and services. When the price level rises, people have to pay more for the goods and services they buy. Alternatively, we can view the price level as a measure of the value of money. A rise in the price level means a lower value of money because each dollar in your wallet now buys a smaller quantity of goods and services.

It may help to express these ideas mathematically. Suppose P is the price level as measured, for instance, by the consumer price index or the GDP deflator. Then P measures the number of dollars needed to buy a basket of goods and services. Now turn this idea around: The quantity of goods and services that can be bought with $1 equals $1/P$. In other words, if P is the price of goods and services measured in terms of money, $1/P$ is the value of money measured in terms of goods and services. Thus, when the overall price level rises, the value of money falls.

"SO WHAT'S IT GOING TO BE? THE SAME SIZE AS LAST YEAR OR THE SAME PRICE AS LAST YEAR?"

Money Supply, Money Demand, and Monetary Equilibrium

What determines the value of money? The answer to this question, like many in economics, is supply and demand. Just as the supply and demand for bananas determines the price of bananas, the supply and demand for money determines the value of money. Thus, our next step in developing the quantity theory of money is to consider the determinants of money supply and money demand.

First consider money supply. In the preceding chapter, we discussed how the Federal Reserve, together with the banking system, determines the supply of money. When the Fed sells bonds in open-market operations, it receives dollars in exchange and contracts the money supply. When the Fed buys government bonds, it pays out dollars and expands the money supply. In addition, if any of these dollars are deposited in banks which then hold them as reserves, the money multiplier swings into action, and these open-market operations can have an even greater effect on the money supply. For our purposes in this chapter, we ignore the complications introduced by the banking system and simply take the quantity of money supplied as a policy variable that the Fed controls.

Now consider money demand. Most fundamentally, the demand for money reflects how much wealth people want to hold in liquid form. Many factors influence the quantity of money demanded. The amount of currency that people hold in their wallets, for instance, depends on how much they rely on credit cards and on whether an automatic teller machine is easy to find. And as we will emphasize in Chapter 16, the quantity of money demanded depends on the interest rate that a person could earn by using the money to buy an interest-bearing bond rather than leaving it in a wallet or low-interest checking account.

Although many variables affect the demand for money, one variable stands out in importance: the average level of prices in the economy. People hold money because it is the medium of exchange. Unlike other assets, such as bonds or stocks, people can use money to buy the goods and services on their shopping lists. How much money they choose to hold for this purpose depends on the prices of those goods and services. The higher prices are, the more money the typical transaction requires, and the more money people will choose to hold in their wallets and checking accounts. That is, a higher price level (a lower value of money) increases the quantity of money demanded.

What ensures that the quantity of money the Fed supplies balances the quantity of money people demand? The answer, it turns out, depends on the time horizon being considered. Later in this book, we will examine the short-run answer, and we will see that interest rates play a key role. In the long run, however, the answer is different and much simpler. *In the long run, the overall level of prices adjusts to the level at which the demand for money equals the supply.* If the price level is above the equilibrium level, people will want to hold more money than the Fed has created, so the price level must fall to balance supply and demand. If the price level is below the equilibrium level, people will want to hold less money than the Fed has created, and the price level must rise to balance supply and demand. At the equilibrium price level, the quantity of money that people want to hold exactly balances the quantity of money supplied by the Fed.

Figure 1 illustrates these ideas. The horizontal axis of this graph shows the quantity of money. The left vertical axis shows the value of money $1/P$, and the right vertical axis shows the price level P. Notice that the price-level axis on the right is inverted: A low price level is shown near the top of this axis, and a high price level is shown near the bottom. This inverted axis illustrates that when the value of money is high (as shown near the top of the left axis), the price level is low (as shown near the top of the right axis).

The two curves in this figure are the supply and demand curves for money. The supply curve is vertical because the Fed has fixed the quantity of money available. The demand curve for money is downward sloping, indicating that when the value of money is low (and the price level is high), people demand a larger quantity of it to buy goods and services. At the equilibrium, shown in the figure as point A, the quantity of money demanded balances the quantity of money supplied. This equilibrium of money supply and money demand determines the value of money and the price level.

The Effects of a Monetary Injection

Let's now consider the effects of a change in monetary policy. To do so, imagine that the economy is in equilibrium and then, suddenly, the Fed doubles the supply of money by printing some dollar bills and dropping them around the country from helicopters. (Or less dramatically and more realistically, the Fed could inject money into the economy by buying some government bonds from the public in open-market operations.) What happens after such a monetary injection? How does the new equilibrium compare to the old one?

Thus, the greater demand for goods and services causes the prices of goods and services to increase. The increase in the price level, in turn, increases the quantity of money demanded because people are using more dollars for every transaction. Eventually, the economy reaches a new equilibrium (point B in Figure 2) at which the quantity of money demanded again equals the quantity of money supplied. In this way, the overall price level for goods and services adjusts to bring money supply and money demand into balance.

The Classical Dichotomy and Monetary Neutrality

We have seen how changes in the money supply lead to changes in the average level of prices of goods and services. How do monetary changes affect other economic variables, such as production, employment, real wages, and real interest rates? This question has long intrigued economists, including David Hume in the 18th century.

Hume and his contemporaries suggested that economic variables should be divided into two groups. The first group consists of **nominal variables**—variables measured in monetary units. The second group consists of **real variables**—variables measured in physical units. For example, the income of corn farmers is a nominal variable because it is measured in dollars, whereas the quantity of corn they produce is a real variable because it is measured in bushels. Nominal GDP is a nominal variable because it measures the dollar value of the economy's output of goods and services; real GDP is a real variable because it measures the total quantity of goods and services produced and is not influenced by the current prices of those goods and services. The separation of real and nominal variables is now called the **classical dichotomy.** (A *dichotomy* is a division into two groups, and *classical* refers to the earlier economic thinkers.)

Application of the classical dichotomy is tricky when we turn to prices. Most prices are quoted in units of money and, therefore, are nominal variables. When we say that the price of corn is $2 a bushel or that the price of wheat is $1 a bushel, both prices are nominal variables. But what about a *relative* price—the price of one thing compared to another? In our example, we could say that the price of a bushel of corn is 2 bushels of wheat. This relative price is not measured in terms of money. When comparing the prices of any two goods, the dollar signs cancel, and the resulting number is measured in physical units. Thus, while dollar prices are nominal variables, relative prices are real variables.

This lesson has many applications. For instance, the real wage (the dollar wage adjusted for inflation) is a real variable because it measures the rate at which people exchange goods and services for a unit of labor. Similarly, the real interest rate (the nominal interest rate adjusted for inflation) is a real variable because it measures the rate at which people exchange goods and services today for goods and services in the future.

Why separate variables into these groups? The classical dichotomy is useful because different forces influence real and nominal variables. According to classical analysis, nominal variables are influenced by developments in the economy's monetary system, whereas money is largely irrelevant for explaining real variables.

This idea was implicit in our discussion of the real economy in the long run. In previous chapters, we examined how real GDP, saving, investment, real interest rates, and unemployment are determined without mentioning the existence

nominal variables
variables measured in monetary units

real variables
variables measured in physical units

classical dichotomy
the theoretical separation of nominal and real variables

of money. In that analysis, the economy's production of goods and services depends on productivity and factor supplies, the real interest rate balances the supply and demand for loanable funds, the real wage balances the supply and demand for labor, and unemployment results when the real wage is for some reason kept above its equilibrium level. These conclusions have nothing to do with the quantity of money supplied.

Changes in the supply of money, according to classical analysis, affect nominal variables but not real variables. When the central bank doubles the money supply, the price level doubles, the dollar wage doubles, and all other dollar values double. Real variables, such as production, employment, real wages, and real interest rates, are unchanged. The irrelevance of monetary changes for real variables is called **monetary neutrality.**

An analogy helps explain monetary neutrality. As the unit of account, money is the yardstick we use to measure economic transactions. When a central bank doubles the money supply, all prices double, and the value of the unit of account falls by half. A similar change would occur if the government were to reduce the length of the yard from 36 to 18 inches: With the new unit of measurement, all *measured* distances (nominal variables) would double, but the *actual* distances (real variables) would remain the same. The dollar, like the yard, is merely a unit of measurement, so a change in its value should not have real effects.

Is monetary neutrality realistic? Not completely. A change in the length of the yard from 36 to 18 inches would not matter in the long run, but in the short run, it would lead to confusion and mistakes. Similarly, most economists today believe that over short periods of time—within the span of a year or two—monetary changes affect real variables. Hume himself also doubted that monetary neutrality would apply in the short run. (We will study short-run nonneutrality later in the book, and this topic will help explain why the Fed changes the money supply over time.)

Yet classical analysis is right about the economy in the long run. Over the course of a decade, monetary changes have significant effects on nominal variables (such as the price level) but only negligible effects on real variables (such as real GDP). When studying long-run changes in the economy, the neutrality of money offers a good description of how the world works.

Velocity and the Quantity Equation

We can obtain another perspective on the quantity theory of money by considering the following question: How many times per year is the typical dollar bill used to pay for a newly produced good or service? The answer to this question is given by a variable called the **velocity of money.** In physics, the term *velocity* refers to the speed at which an object travels. In economics, the velocity of money refers to the speed at which the typical dollar bill travels around the economy from wallet to wallet.

To calculate the velocity of money, we divide the nominal value of output (nominal GDP) by the quantity of money. If P is the price level (the GDP deflator), Y the quantity of output (real GDP), and M the quantity of money, then velocity is

$$V = (P \times Y)/M.$$

To see why this makes sense, imagine a simple economy that produces only pizza. Suppose that the economy produces 100 pizzas in a year, that a pizza sells

monetary neutrality the proposition that changes in the money supply do not affect real variables

velocity of money the rate at which money changes hands

for $10, and that the quantity of money in the economy is $50. Then the velocity of money is

$$V = (\$10 \times 100)/\$50$$
$$= 20.$$

In this economy, people spend a total of $1,000 per year on pizza. For this $1,000 of spending to take place with only $50 of money, each dollar bill must change hands on average 20 times per year.

With slight algebraic rearrangement, this equation can be rewritten as

$$M \times V = P \times Y.$$

This equation states that the quantity of money (M) times the velocity of money (V) equals the price of output (P) times the amount of output (Y). It is called the **quantity equation** because it relates the quantity of money (M) to the nominal value of output ($P \times Y$). The quantity equation shows that an increase in the quantity of money in an economy must be reflected in one of the other three variables: The price level must rise, the quantity of output must rise, or the velocity of money must fall.

In many cases, it turns out that the velocity of money is relatively stable. For example, Figure 3 shows nominal GDP, the quantity of money (as measured by M2), and the velocity of money for the U.S. economy since 1960. During the

quantity equation
the equation $M \times V = P \times Y$, which relates the quantity of money, the velocity of money, and the dollar value of the economy's output of goods and services

This figure shows the nominal value of output as measured by nominal GDP, the quantity of money as measured by M2, and the velocity of money as measured by their ratio. For comparability, all three series have been scaled to equal 100 in 1960. Notice that nominal GDP and the quantity of money have grown dramatically over this period, while velocity has been relatively stable.

FIGURE 3

Nominal GDP, the Quantity of Money, and the Velocity of Money

Source: U.S. Department of Commerce; Federal Reserve Board.

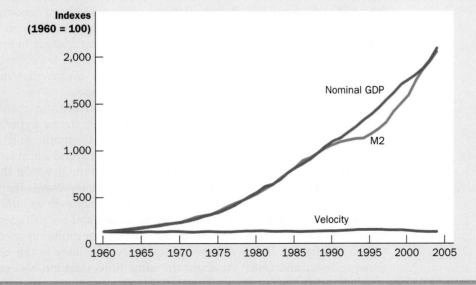

period, the money supply and nominal GDP both increased about 20-fold. By contrast, the velocity of money, although not exactly constant, has not changed dramatically. Thus, for some purposes, the assumption of constant velocity may be a good approximation.

We now have all the elements necessary to explain the equilibrium price level and inflation rate. Here they are:

1. The velocity of money is relatively stable over time.
2. Because velocity is stable, when the central bank changes the quantity of money (M), it causes proportionate changes in the nominal value of output ($P \times Y$).
3. The economy's output of goods and services (Y) is primarily determined by factor supplies (labor, physical capital, human capital, and natural resources) and the available production technology. In particular, because money is neutral, money does not affect output.
4. With output (Y) determined by factor supplies and technology, when the central bank alters the money supply (M) and induces proportional changes in the nominal value of output ($P \times Y$), these changes are reflected in changes in the price level (P).
5. Therefore, when the central bank increases the money supply rapidly, the result is a high rate of inflation.

These five steps are the essence of the quantity theory of money.

CASE STUDY | MONEY AND PRICES DURING FOUR HYPERINFLATIONS

Although earthquakes can wreak havoc on a society, they have the beneficial by-product of providing much useful data for seismologists. These data can shed light on alternative theories and, thereby, help society predict and deal with future threats. Similarly, hyperinflations offer monetary economists a natural experiment they can use to study the effects of money on the economy.

Hyperinflations are interesting in part because the changes in the money supply and price level are so large. Indeed, hyperinflation is generally defined as inflation that exceeds 50 percent *per month*. This means that the price level increases more than 100-fold over the course of a year.

The data on hyperinflation show a clear link between the quantity of money and the price level. Figure 4 graphs data from four classic hyperinflations that occurred during the 1920s in Austria, Hungary, Germany, and Poland. Each graph shows the quantity of money in the economy and an index of the price level. The slope of the money line represents the rate at which the quantity of money was growing, and the slope of the price line represents the inflation rate. The steeper the lines, the higher the rates of money growth or inflation.

Notice that in each graph the quantity of money and the price level are almost parallel. In each instance, growth in the quantity of money is moderate at first and so is inflation. But over time, the quantity of money in the economy starts growing faster and faster. At about the same time, inflation also takes off. Then

This figure shows the quantity of money and the price level during four hyperinflations. (Note that these variables are graphed on *logarithmic* scales. This means that equal vertical distances on the graph represent equal *percentage* changes in the variable.) In each case, the quantity of money and the price level move closely together. The strong association between these two variables is consistent with the quantity theory of money, which states that growth in the money supply is the primary cause of inflation.

FIGURE **4**

Money and Prices during Four Hyperinflations

Source: Adapted from Thomas J. Sargent, "The End of Four Big Inflations," in Robert Hall, ed., *Inflation* (Chicago: University of Chicago Press, 1983), pp. 41–93.

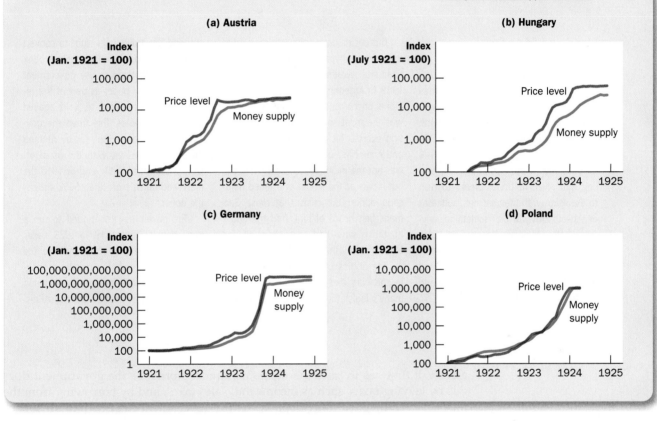

when the quantity of money stabilizes, the price level stabilizes as well. These episodes illustrate well one of the *Ten Principles of Economics:* Prices rise when the government prints too much money. •

The Inflation Tax

If inflation is so easy to explain, why do countries experience hyperinflation? That is, why do the central banks of these countries choose to print so much money that its value is certain to fall rapidly over time?

The answer is that the governments of these countries are using money creation as a way to pay for their spending. When the government wants to build roads, pay salaries to police officers, or give transfer payments to the poor or

In The News

The German Hyperinflation

The German experience between the two world wars remains one of history's most vivid examples of hyperinflation and its horrific consequences.

Loads of Money

"For these ten marks I sold my virtue," were the words a Berliner noticed written on a banknote in 1923. He was buying a box of matches, all the note was worth by then. That was in the early days. By November 5th, a loaf of bread cost 140 billion marks. Workers were paid twice a day, and given half-hour breaks to rush to the shops with their satchels, suitcases or wheelbarrow, to buy something, anything, before their paper money halved in value yet again. By mid-November, when a new currency was issued, prices had added twelve zeros since the first world war began in 1914.

Currencies have collapsed, and inflation turned hyper-, in other places: in Shanghai awaiting Maoist takeover in 1949, in Argentina in 1989, when, in July alone, prices rose 197%. But Germany's was the most spectacular bout of inflation ever to hit an advanced economy; and none has had more awful results. It was not the main reason for Hitler's rise, but it was as the leader of a failed mini-coup during the crisis that most Germans first heard of him. And the anger of those who had lost their all fed Nazism's growth.

The origins of the hyperinflation lay in the war, and the readiness of Germany's legislature to let the authorities suspend the individual's right to convert banknotes into gold. The central bank was also authorized to use government and commercial paper as part of the reserves it was required to hold against newly issued notes. This freed the government to finance the war by running the printing presses, with the usual effect: prices rose. By the end of 1918 the mark had fallen more than 50% against the dollar.

The government continued to run a huge deficit. From 1919 to 1923, taxes never exceeded 35% of expenditure. The gap was covered by heroic money-printing. The public finances, bad enough anyway, were worsened by the Allies'

---

elderly, it first has to raise the necessary funds. Normally, the government does this by levying taxes, such as income and sales taxes, and by borrowing from the public by selling government bonds. Yet the government can also pay for spending simply by printing the money it needs.

When the government raises revenue by printing money, it is said to levy an **inflation tax.** The inflation tax is not exactly like other taxes, however, because no one receives a bill from the government for this tax. Instead, the inflation tax is subtler. When the government prints money, the price level rises, and the dollars in your wallet are less valuable. Thus, *the inflation tax is like a tax on everyone who holds money.*

The importance of the inflation tax varies from country to country and over time. In the United States in recent years, the inflation tax has been a trivial source of revenue: It has accounted for less than 3 percent of government revenue. During the 1770s, however, the Continental Congress of the fledgling United States relied heavily on the inflation tax to pay for military spending. Because the new government had a limited ability to raise funds through regular taxes or borrowing, printing dollars was the easiest way to pay the American

inflation tax
the revenue the government raises by creating money

demands for reparations, enough not just to compensate for damage done but to pay the pensions of Allied combatants. Even ignoring the part due to be paid in some bonds of dubious worth, the total was $12.5 billion—a huge amount for the time, about half Britain's GDP. How could it be found? The Allies did not want to see German exports boom, nor were they united in encouraging payment in labor to rebuild Europe. So—roll the presses. Notes in circulation increased from 29.2 billion marks in November 1918 to 497 quintillion (497 plus 18 zeros) five years later.

As early as 1919, when the peace treaty was signed, Keynes had warned that the settlement imposed on Germany would ruin it. By early 1922, even the *Times,* much given to berating Germany for allegedly failing to meet its promises to disarm, was warning that the Allied demands would lead to "further production of paper marks on a massive scale. In the present state of German finances, that would mean a big step on the way to Moscow." To Auschwitz, in the event, but the analysis of money-printing was sound enough. In vain: the victorious powers shut their ears.

Later that year, the German government defaulted on its reparations payments. In response, in January 1923 French and Belgian troops occupied the Ruhr, Germany's industrial heartland. The direct economic cost was huge; the Ruhr provided 85% of Germany's coal. But, besides that, the government backed a campaign of passive resistance—in effect, a general strike. To pay the 2 million workers involved, it printed more money. This was enough to tip the economy over the edge.

Prices roared up. So did unemployment, modest as 1923 began. As October ended, 19% of metal-workers were officially out of work, and half of those left were on short time. Feeble attempts had been made to stabilize prices. Some German states had issued their own would-be stable currency: Baden's was secured on the revenue of state forests, Hanover's convertible into a given quantity of rye. The central authorities issued what became known as "gold loan" notes, payable in 1935. Then, on November 15th, came the Rentenmark, worth 1,000 billion paper marks, or just under 24 American cents, like the gold mark of 1914.

Prices quite soon stabilized, but the damage was done. Millions had seen their life savings evaporate, and were ready later to believe that Germany had been stabbed in the back by a conspiracy of Jews, international financiers and local appeasers. Elias Canetti, a German writer, likened the Nazis' treatment of Jews to the great inflation: depreciation to the point where they could be "destroyed with impunity by the million." He strained the analogy. But he was right that a debauched currency was one reason why a whole country could lose its virtue.

soldiers. As the quantity theory predicts, the result was a high rate of inflation: Prices measured in terms of the continental dollar rose more than 100-fold over a few years.

Almost all hyperinflations follow the same pattern as the hyperinflation during the American Revolution. The government has high spending, inadequate tax revenue, and limited ability to borrow. As a result, it turns to the printing press to pay for its spending. The massive increases in the quantity of money lead to massive inflation. The inflation ends when the government institutes fiscal reforms—such as cuts in government spending—that eliminate the need for the inflation tax.

The Fisher Effect

According to the principle of monetary neutrality, an increase in the rate of money growth raises the rate of inflation but does not affect any real variable. An important application of this principle concerns the effect of money on interest rates. Interest rates are important variables for macroeconomists to understand because they link the economy of the present and the economy of the future through their effects on saving and investment.

To understand the relationship between money, inflation, and interest rates, recall the distinction between the nominal interest rate and the real interest rate. The *nominal interest rate* is the interest rate you hear about at your bank. If you have a savings account, for instance, the nominal interest rate tells you how fast the number of dollars in your account will rise over time. The *real interest rate* corrects the nominal interest rate for the effect of inflation to tell you how fast the purchasing power of your savings account will rise over time. The real interest rate is the nominal interest rate minus the inflation rate:

$$\text{Real interest rate} = \text{Nominal interest rate} - \text{Inflation rate.}$$

For example, if the bank posts a nominal interest rate of 7 percent per year and the inflation rate is 3 percent per year, then the real value of the deposits grows by 4 percent per year.

We can rewrite this equation to show that the nominal interest rate is the sum of the real interest rate and the inflation rate:

$$\text{Nominal interest rate} = \text{Real interest rate} + \text{Inflation rate.}$$

This way of looking at the nominal interest rate is useful because different economic forces determine each of the two terms on the right side of this equation. As we discussed earlier in the book, the supply and demand for loanable funds determine the real interest rate. And according to the quantity theory of money, growth in the money supply determines the inflation rate.

Let's now consider how the growth in the money supply affects interest rates. In the long run over which money is neutral, a change in money growth should not affect the real interest rate. The real interest rate is, after all, a real variable. For the real interest rate not to be affected, the nominal interest rate must adjust one-for-one to changes in the inflation rate. Thus, *when the Fed increases the rate of money growth, the long-run result is both a higher inflation rate and a higher nominal interest rate.* This adjustment of the nominal interest rate to the inflation rate is called the **Fisher effect,** after economist Irving Fisher (1867–1947), who first studied it.

Fisher effect
the one-for-one adjustment of the nominal interest rate to the inflation rate

Keep in mind that our analysis of the Fisher effect has maintained a long-run perspective. The Fisher effect does not hold in the short run to the extent that inflation is unanticipated. A nominal interest rate is a payment on a loan, and it is typically set when the loan is first made. If inflation catches the borrower and lender by surprise, the nominal interest rate they set will fail to reflect the rise in prices. To be precise, the Fisher effect states that the nominal interest rate adjusts to expected inflation. Expected inflation moves with actual inflation in the long run but not necessarily in the short run.

The Fisher effect is crucial for understanding changes over time in the nominal interest rate. Figure 5 shows the nominal interest rate and the inflation rate in the U.S. economy since 1960. The close association between these two variables is clear. The nominal interest rate rose from the early 1960s through the 1970s because inflation was also rising during this time. Similarly, the nominal interest rate fell from the early 1980s through the 1990s because the Fed got inflation under control.

This figure uses annual data since 1960 to show the nominal interest rate on 3-month Treasury bills and the inflation rate as measured by the consumer price index. The close association between these two variables is evidence for the Fisher effect: When the inflation rate rises, so does the nominal interest rate.

FIGURE 5

The Nominal Interest Rate and the Inflation Rate

Source: U.S. Department of Treasury; U.S. Department of Labor.

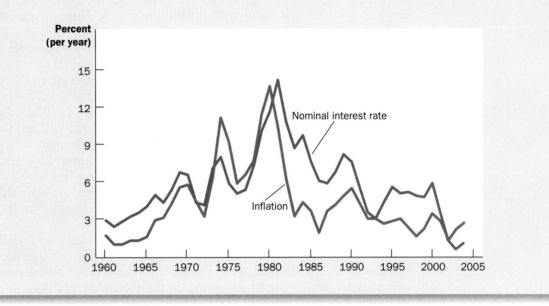

Quick Quiz The government of a country increases the growth rate of the money supply from 5 percent per year to 50 percent per year. What happens to prices? What happens to nominal interest rates? Why might the government be doing this?

THE COSTS OF INFLATION

In the late 1970s, when the U.S. inflation rate reached about 10 percent per year, inflation dominated debates over economic policy. And even though inflation has been low over the past decade, it remains a closely watched macroeconomic variable. One study found that *inflation* is the economic term mentioned most often in U.S. newspapers (far ahead of second-place finisher *unemployment* and third-place finisher *productivity*).

Inflation is closely watched and widely discussed because it is thought to be a serious economic problem. But is that true? And if so, why?

A Fall in Purchasing Power? The Inflation Fallacy

If you ask the typical person why inflation is bad, he will tell you that the answer is obvious: Inflation robs him of the purchasing power of his hard-earned dollars. When prices rise, each dollar of income buys fewer goods and services. Thus, it might seem that inflation directly lowers living standards.

Yet further thought reveals a fallacy in this answer. When prices rise, buyers of goods and services pay more for what they buy. At the same time, however, sellers of goods and services get more for what they sell. Because most people earn their incomes by selling their services, such as their labor, inflation in incomes goes hand in hand with inflation in prices. Thus, *inflation does not in itself reduce people's real purchasing power.*

People believe the inflation fallacy because they do not appreciate the principle of monetary neutrality. A worker who receives an annual raise of 10 percent tends to view that raise as a reward for her own talent and effort. When an inflation rate of 6 percent reduces the real value of that raise to only 4 percent, the worker might feel that she has been cheated of what is rightfully her due. In fact, as we discussed in the chapter on production and growth, real incomes are determined by real variables, such as physical capital, human capital, natural resources, and the available production technology. Nominal incomes are determined by those factors and the overall price level. If the Fed were to lower the inflation rate from 6 percent to zero, our worker's annual raise would fall from 10 percent to 4 percent. She might feel less robbed by inflation, but her real income would not rise more quickly.

If nominal incomes tend to keep pace with rising prices, why then is inflation a problem? It turns out that there is no single answer to this question. Instead, economists have identified several costs of inflation. Each of these costs shows some way in which persistent growth in the money supply does, in fact, have some effect on real variables.

Shoeleather Costs

As we have discussed, inflation is like a tax on the holders of money. The tax itself is not a cost to society: It is only a transfer of resources from households to the government. Yet most taxes give people an incentive to alter their behavior to avoid paying the tax, and this distortion of incentives causes deadweight losses for society as a whole. Like other taxes, the inflation tax also causes deadweight losses because people waste scarce resources trying to avoid it.

How can a person avoid paying the inflation tax? Because inflation erodes the real value of the money in your wallet, you can avoid the inflation tax by holding less money. One way to do this is to go to the bank more often. For example, rather than withdrawing $200 every four weeks, you might withdraw $50 once a week. By making more frequent trips to the bank, you can keep more of your wealth in your interest-bearing savings account and less in your wallet, where inflation erodes its value.

shoeleather costs
the resources wasted when inflation encourages people to reduce their money holdings

The cost of reducing your money holdings is called the **shoeleather cost** of inflation because making more frequent trips to the bank causes your shoes to wear out more quickly. Of course, this term is not to be taken literally: The actual cost of reducing your money holdings is not the wear and tear on your shoes but the time and convenience you must sacrifice to keep less money on hand than you would if there were no inflation.

The shoeleather costs of inflation may seem trivial. And in fact, they are in the U.S. economy, which has had only moderate inflation in recent years. But this cost is magnified in countries experiencing hyperinflation. Here is a description of one person's experience in Bolivia during its hyperinflation (as reported in the August 13, 1985, issue of *The Wall Street Journal*):

> When Edgar Miranda gets his monthly teacher's pay of 25 million pesos, he hasn't a moment to lose. Every hour, pesos drop in value. So, while his wife rushes to market to lay in a month's supply of rice and noodles, he is off with the rest of the pesos to change them into black-market dollars.
>
> Mr. Miranda is practicing the First Rule of Survival amid the most out-of-control inflation in the world today. Bolivia is a case study of how runaway inflation undermines a society. Price increases are so huge that the figures build up almost beyond comprehension. In one six-month period, for example, prices soared at an annual rate of 38,000 percent. By official count, however, last year's inflation reached 2,000 percent, and this year's is expected to hit 8,000 percent—though other estimates range many times higher. In any event, Bolivia's rate dwarfs Israel's 370 percent and Argentina's 1,100 percent—two other cases of severe inflation.
>
> It is easier to comprehend what happens to the thirty-eight-year-old Mr. Miranda's pay if he doesn't quickly change it into dollars. The day he was paid 25 million pesos, a dollar cost 500,000 pesos. So he received $50. Just days later, with the rate at 900,000 pesos, he would have received $27.

As this story shows, the shoeleather costs of inflation can be substantial. With the high inflation rate, Mr. Miranda does not have the luxury of holding the local money as a store of value. Instead, he is forced to convert his pesos quickly into goods or into U.S. dollars, which offer a more stable store of value. The time and effort that Mr. Miranda expends to reduce his money holdings are a waste of resources. If the monetary authority pursued a low-inflation policy, Mr. Miranda would be happy to hold pesos, and he could put his time and effort to more productive use. In fact, shortly after this article was written, the Bolivian inflation rate was reduced substantially with more restrictive monetary policy.

Menu Costs

Most firms do not change the prices of their products every day. Instead, firms often announce prices and leave them unchanged for weeks, months, or even years. One survey found that the typical U.S. firm changes its prices about once a year.

Firms change prices infrequently because there are costs of changing prices. Costs of price adjustment are called **menu costs,** a term derived from a restaurant's cost of printing a new menu. Menu costs include the cost of deciding on new prices, the cost of printing new price lists and catalogs, the cost of sending these new price lists and catalogs to dealers and customers, the cost of advertising the new prices, and even the cost of dealing with customer annoyance over price changes.

menu costs
the costs of changing prices

Inflation increases the menu costs that firms must bear. In the current U.S. economy, with its low inflation rate, annual price adjustment is an appropriate business strategy for many firms. But when high inflation makes firms' costs rise rapidly, annual price adjustment is impractical. During hyperinflations, for example, firms must change their prices daily or even more often just to keep up with all the other prices in the economy.

Relative-Price Variability and the Misallocation of Resources

Suppose that the Eatabit Eatery prints a new menu with new prices every January and then leaves its prices unchanged for the rest of the year. If there is no inflation, Eatabit's relative prices—the prices of its meals compared to other prices in the economy—would be constant over the course of the year. By contrast, if the inflation rate is 12 percent per year, Eatabit's relative prices will automatically fall by 1 percent each month. The restaurant's relative prices will be high in the early months of the year, just after it has printed a new menu, and low in the later months. And the higher the inflation rate, the greater is this automatic variability. Thus, because prices change only once in a while, inflation causes relative prices to vary more than they otherwise would.

Why does this matter? The reason is that market economies rely on relative prices to allocate scarce resources. Consumers decide what to buy by comparing the quality and prices of various goods and services. Through these decisions, they determine how the scarce factors of production are allocated among industries and firms. When inflation distorts relative prices, consumer decisions are distorted, and markets are less able to allocate resources to their best use.

Inflation-Induced Tax Distortions

Almost all taxes distort incentives, cause people to alter their behavior, and lead to a less efficient allocation of the economy's resources. Many taxes, however, become even more problematic in the presence of inflation. The reason is that lawmakers often fail to take inflation into account when writing the tax laws. Economists who have studied the tax code conclude that inflation tends to raise the tax burden on income earned from savings.

One example of how inflation discourages saving is the tax treatment of *capital gains*—the profits made by selling an asset for more than its purchase price. Suppose that in 1980 you used some of your savings to buy stock in Microsoft Corporation for $10 and that in 2005 you sold the stock for $50. According to the tax law, you have earned a capital gain of $40, which you must include in your income when computing how much income tax you owe. But suppose the overall price level doubled from 1980 to 2005. In this case, the $10 you invested in 1980 is equivalent (in terms of purchasing power) to $20 in 2005. When you sell your stock for $50, you have a real gain (an increase in purchasing power) of only $30. The tax code, however, does not take account of inflation and assesses you a tax on a gain of $40. Thus, inflation exaggerates the size of capital gains and inadvertently increases the tax burden on this type of income.

Another example is the tax treatment of interest income. The income tax treats the *nominal* interest earned on savings as income, even though part of the nominal interest rate merely compensates for inflation. To see the effects of this policy,

In the presence of zero inflation, a 25 percent tax on interest income reduces the real interest rate from 4 percent to 3 percent. In the presence of 8 percent inflation, the same tax reduces the real interest rate from 4 percent to 1 percent.

	Economy A (price stability)	Economy B (inflation)
Real interest rate	4%	4%
Inflation rate	0	8
Nominal interest rate	4	12
(real interest rate + inflation rate)		
Reduced interest due to 25 percent tax	1	3
(.25 × nominal interest rate)		
After-tax nominal interest rate	3	9
(.75 × nominal interest rate)		
After-tax real interest rate	3	1
(after-tax nominal interest rate − inflation rate)		

consider the numerical example in Table 1. The table compares two economies, both of which tax interest income at a rate of 25 percent. In Economy A, inflation is zero, and the nominal and real interest rates are both 4 percent. In this case, the 25 percent tax on interest income reduces the real interest rate from 4 percent to 3 percent. In Economy B, the real interest rate is again 4 percent, but the inflation rate is 8 percent. As a result of the Fisher effect, the nominal interest rate is 12 percent. Because the income tax treats this entire 12 percent interest as income, the government takes 25 percent of it, leaving an after-tax nominal interest rate of only 9 percent and an after-tax real interest rate of only 1 percent. In this case, the 25 percent tax on interest income reduces the real interest rate from 4 percent to 1 percent. Because the after-tax real interest rate provides the incentive to save, saving is much less attractive in the economy with inflation (Economy B) than in the economy with stable prices (Economy A).

The taxes on nominal capital gains and on nominal interest income are two examples of how the tax code interacts with inflation. There are many others. Because of these inflation-induced tax changes, higher inflation tends to discourage people from saving. Recall that the economy's saving provides the resources for investment, which in turn is a key ingredient to long-run economic growth. Thus, when inflation raises the tax burden on saving, it tends to depress the economy's long-run growth rate. There is, however, no consensus among economists about the size of this effect.

One solution to this problem, other than eliminating inflation, is to index the tax system. That is, the tax laws could be rewritten to take account of the effects of inflation. In the case of capital gains, for example, the tax code could adjust the purchase price using a price index and assess the tax only on the real gain. In the case of interest income, the government could tax only real interest income by excluding that portion of the interest income that merely compensates for inflation. To some extent, the tax laws have moved in the direction of indexation. For example, the income levels at which income tax rates change are adjusted automatically each year based on changes in the consumer price index. Yet many other aspects of the tax laws—such as the tax treatment of capital gains and interest income—are not indexed.

In an ideal world, the tax laws would be written so that inflation would not alter anyone's real tax liability. In the world in which we live, however, tax laws are far from perfect. More complete indexation would probably be desirable, but it would further complicate a tax code that many people already consider too complex.

Confusion and Inconvenience

Imagine that we took a poll and asked people the following question: "This year the yard is 36 inches. How long do you think it should be next year?" Assuming we could get people to take us seriously, they would tell us that the yard should stay the same length—36 inches. Anything else would just complicate life needlessly.

What does this finding have to do with inflation? Recall that money, as the economy's unit of account, is what we use to quote prices and record debts. In other words, money is the yardstick with which we measure economic transactions. The job of the Federal Reserve is a bit like the job of the Bureau of Standards—to ensure the reliability of a commonly used unit of measurement. When the Fed increases the money supply and creates inflation, it erodes the real value of the unit of account.

It is difficult to judge the costs of the confusion and inconvenience that arise from inflation. Earlier, we discussed how the tax code incorrectly measures real incomes in the presence of inflation. Similarly, accountants incorrectly measure firms' earnings when prices are rising over time. Because inflation causes dollars at different times to have different real values, computing a firm's profit—the difference between its revenue and costs—is more complicated in an economy with inflation. Therefore, to some extent, inflation makes investors less able to sort out successful from unsuccessful firms, which in turn impedes financial markets in their role of allocating the economy's saving to alternative types of investment.

A Special Cost of Unexpected Inflation: Arbitrary Redistributions of Wealth

So far, the costs of inflation we have discussed occur even if inflation is steady and predictable. Inflation has an additional cost, however, when it comes as a surprise. Unexpected inflation redistributes wealth among the population in a way that has nothing to do with either merit or need. These redistributions occur because many loans in the economy are specified in terms of the unit of account—money.

Consider an example. Suppose that Sam Student takes out a $20,000 loan at a 7 percent interest rate from Bigbank to attend college. In 10 years, the loan will come due. After his debt has compounded for 10 years at 7 percent, Sam will owe Bigbank $40,000. The real value of this debt will depend on inflation over the decade. If Sam is lucky, the economy will have a hyperinflation. In this case, wages and prices will rise so high that Sam will be able to pay the $40,000 debt out of pocket change. By contrast, if the economy goes through a major deflation, then wages and prices will fall, and Sam will find the $40,000 debt a greater burden than he anticipated.

This example shows that unexpected changes in prices redistribute wealth among debtors and creditors. A hyperinflation enriches Sam at the expense of Bigbank because it diminishes the real value of the debt; Sam can repay the loan in less valuable dollars than he anticipated. Deflation enriches Bigbank at Sam's expense because it increases the real value of the debt; in this case, Sam has to repay the loan in more valuable dollars than he anticipated. If inflation were predictable, then Bigbank and Sam could take inflation into account when setting the nominal interest rate. (Recall the Fisher effect.) But if inflation is hard to predict, it imposes risk on Sam and Bigbank that both would prefer to avoid.

This cost of unexpected inflation is important to consider together with another fact: Inflation is especially volatile and uncertain when the average rate of inflation is high. This is seen most simply by examining the experience of different countries. Countries with low average inflation, such as Germany in the late 20th century, tend to have stable inflation. Countries with high average inflation, such as many countries in Latin America, tend to have unstable inflation. There are no known examples of economies with high, stable inflation. This relationship between the level and volatility of inflation points to another cost of inflation. If a country pursues a high-inflation monetary policy, it will have to bear not only the costs of high expected inflation but also the arbitrary redistributions of wealth associated with unexpected inflation.

CASE STUDY   *THE WIZARD OF OZ* AND THE FREE-SILVER DEBATE

As a child, you probably saw the movie *The Wizard of Oz,* based on a children's book written in 1900. The movie and book tell the story of a young girl, Dorothy, who finds herself lost in a strange land far from home. You probably did not know, however, that the story is actually an allegory about U.S. monetary policy in the late 19th century.

From 1880 to 1896, the price level in the U.S. economy fell by 23 percent. Because this event was unanticipated, it led to a major redistribution of wealth. Most farmers in the western part of the country were debtors. Their creditors were the bankers in the east. When the price level fell, it caused the real value of these debts to rise, which enriched the banks at the expense of the farmers.

According to Populist politicians of the time, the solution to the farmers' problem was the free coinage of silver. During this period, the United States was operating with a gold standard. The quantity of gold determined the money supply and, thereby, the price level. The free-silver advocates wanted silver, as well as gold, to be used as money. If adopted, this proposal would have

In The News

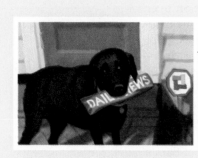

How to Protect Your Savings from Inflation

As we have seen, unexpected changes in the price level redistribute wealth among debtors and creditors. This would no longer be true if debt contracts were written in real, rather than nominal, terms. In 1997, the U.S. Treasury started issuing bonds with a return indexed to the price level. In the following article, written a few months before the policy was implemented, two prominent economists discuss the merits of this policy.

Inflation Fighters for the Long Term

By John Y. Campbell and Robert J. Shiller

Treasury Secretary Robert Rubin announced on Thursday that the government plans to issue inflation-indexed bonds—that is, bonds whose interest and principal payments are adjusted upward for inflation, guaranteeing their real purchasing power in the future.

This is a historic moment. Economists have been advocating such bonds for many long and frustrating years.

Index bonds were first called for in 1822 by the economist Joseph Lowe. In the 1870s, they were championed by the British economist William Stanley Jevons. In the early part of this century, the legendary Irving Fisher made a career of advocating them.

In recent decades, economists of every political stripe—from Milton Friedman to James Tobin, Alan Blinder to Alan Greenspan—have supported them. Yet, because there was little public clamor for such an investment, the government never issued indexed bonds.

Let's hope this lack of interest does not continue now that they will become available. The success of the indexed bonds depends on whether the public understands them—and buys them. Until now, inflation has made government bonds a risky investment. In 1966, when the inflation rate was only 3 percent, if someone had bought a 30-year government bond yielding 5 percent, he would have expected that by now his investment would be worth 180 percent of its original value. However, after years of higher-than-expected inflation, the in-

AN EARLY DEBATE OVER MONETARY POLICY

increased the money supply, pushed up the price level, and reduced the real burden of the farmers' debts.

The debate over silver was heated, and it was central to the politics of the 1890s. A common election slogan of the Populists was "We Are Mortgaged. All but Our Votes." One prominent advocate of free silver was William Jennings Bryan, the Democratic nominee for president in 1896. He is remembered in part for a speech at the Democratic party's nominating convention in which he said, "You shall not press down upon the brow of labor this crown of thorns. You shall not crucify mankind upon a cross of gold." Rarely since then have politicians waxed so poetic about alternative approaches to monetary policy. Nonetheless, Bryan lost the election to Republican William McKinley, and the United States remained on the gold standard.

L. Frank Baum, author of the book *The Wonderful Wizard of Oz,* was a midwestern journalist. When he sat down to write a story for children, he made the characters represent protagonists in the major political battle of his time.

vestment is worth only 85 percent of its original value.

Because inflation has been modest in recent years, many people today are not worried about how it will affect their savings. This complacency is dangerous: Even a low rate of inflation can seriously erode savings over long periods of time.

Imagine that you retire today with a pension invested in Treasury bonds that pay a fixed $10,000 each year, regardless of inflation. If there is no inflation, in 20 years the pension will have the same purchasing power that it does today. But if there is an inflation rate of only 3 percent per year, in 20 years your pension will be worth only $5,540 in today's dollars. Five percent inflation over 20 years will cut your purchasing power to $3,770, and 10 percent will reduce it to a pitiful $1,390. Which of these scenarios is likely? No one knows. Inflation ultimately depends on the people who are elected and appointed as guardians of our money supply.

At a time when Americans are living longer and planning for several decades of retirement, the insidious effects of inflation should be of serious concern. For this reason alone, the creation of inflation-indexed bonds, with their guarantee of a safe return over long periods of time, is a welcome development.

No other investment offers this kind of safety. Conventional government bonds make payments that are fixed in dollar terms; but investors should be concerned about purchasing power, not about the number of dollars they receive. Money market funds make dollar payments that increase with inflation to some degree, since short-term interest rates tend to rise with inflation. But many other factors also influence interest rates, so the real income from a money market fund is not secure.

The stock market offers a high rate of return on average, but it can fall as well as rise. Investors should remember the bear market of the 1970s as well as the bull market of the 1980s and 1990s.

Inflation-indexed government bonds have been issued in Britain for 15 years, in Canada for 5 years, and in many other countries, including Australia, New Zealand, and Sweden. In Britain, which has the world's largest indexed-bond market, the bonds have offered a yield 3 to 4 percent higher than the rate of inflation. In the United States, a safe long-term return of this sort should make indexed bonds an important part of retirement savings.

We expect that financial institutions will take advantage of the new inflation-indexed bonds and offer innovative new products. Indexed-bond funds will probably appear first, but indexed annuities and even indexed mortgages—monthly payments would be adjusted for inflation—should also become available. [*Author's note:* Since this article was written, some of these indexed products have been introduced, but their use is not yet widespread.]

Although the Clinton administration may not get much credit for it today, the decision to issue inflation-indexed bonds is an accomplishment that historians decades hence will single out for special recognition.

Source: *The New York Times*, May 18, 1996. Copyright © 1996 by the New York Times Co. Reprinted by permission.

Although modern commentators on the story differ somewhat in the interpretation they assign to each character, there is no doubt that the story highlights the debate over monetary policy. Here is how economic historian Hugh Rockoff, writing in the *Journal of Political Economy* in 1990, interprets the story:

DOROTHY:	Traditional American values
TOTO:	Prohibitionist party, also called the Teetotalers
SCARECROW:	Farmers
TIN WOODSMAN:	Industrial workers
COWARDLY LION:	William Jennings Bryan
MUNCHKINS:	Citizens of the East
WICKED WITCH OF THE EAST:	Grover Cleveland
WICKED WITCH OF THE WEST:	William McKinley

WIZARD: Marcus Alonzo Hanna, chairman of the Republican party

OZ: Abbreviation for ounce of gold

YELLOW BRICK ROAD: Gold standard

In the end of Baum's story, Dorothy does find her way home, but it is not by just following the yellow brick road. After a long and perilous journey, she learns that the wizard is incapable of helping her or her friends. Instead, Dorothy finally discovers the magical power of her *silver* slippers. (When the book was made into a movie in 1939, Dorothy's slippers were changed from silver to ruby. The Hollywood filmmakers were more interested in showing off the new technology of Technicolor than telling a story about 19th-century monetary policy.)

Although the Populists lost the debate over the free coinage of silver, they did eventually get the monetary expansion and inflation that they wanted. In 1898, prospectors discovered gold near the Klondike River in the Canadian Yukon. Increased supplies of gold also arrived from the mines of South Africa. As a result, the money supply and the price level started to rise in the United States and other countries operating on the gold standard. Within 15 years, prices in the United States were back to the levels that had prevailed in the 1880s, and farmers were better able to handle their debts.   •

Quick Quiz   List and describe six costs of inflation.

CONCLUSION

This chapter discussed the causes and costs of inflation. The primary cause of inflation is simply growth in the quantity of money. When the central bank creates money in large quantities, the value of money falls quickly. To maintain stable prices, the central bank must maintain strict control over the money supply.

The costs of inflation are subtler. They include shoeleather costs, menu costs, increased variability of relative prices, unintended changes in tax liabilities, confusion and inconvenience, and arbitrary redistributions of wealth. Are these costs, in total, large or small? All economists agree that they become huge during hyperinflation. But their size for moderate inflation—when prices rise by less than 10 percent per year—is more open to debate.

Although this chapter presented many of the most important lessons about inflation, the discussion is incomplete. When the central bank reduces the rate of money growth, prices rise less rapidly, as the quantity theory suggests. Yet as the economy makes the transition to this lower inflation rate, the change in monetary policy will have disruptive effects on production and employment. That is, even though monetary policy is neutral in the long run, it has profound effects on real variables in the short run. Later in this book we will examine the reasons for short-run monetary nonneutrality to enhance our understanding of the causes and costs of inflation.

SUMMARY

- The overall level of prices in an economy adjusts to bring money supply and money demand into balance. When the central bank increases the supply of money, it causes the price level to rise. Persistent growth in the quantity of money supplied leads to continuing inflation.

- The principle of monetary neutrality asserts that changes in the quantity of money influence nominal variables but not real variables. Most economists believe that monetary neutrality approximately describes the behavior of the economy in the long run.

- A government can pay for some of its spending simply by printing money. When countries rely heavily on this "inflation tax," the result is hyperinflation.

- One application of the principle of monetary neutrality is the Fisher effect. According to the Fisher effect, when the inflation rate rises, the nominal interest rate rises by the same amount so that the real interest rate remains the same.

- Many people think that inflation makes them poorer because it raises the cost of what they buy. This view is a fallacy, however, because inflation also raises nominal incomes.

- Economists have identified six costs of inflation: shoeleather costs associated with reduced money holdings, menu costs associated with more frequent adjustment of prices, increased variability of relative prices, unintended changes in tax liabilities due to nonindexation of the tax code, confusion and inconvenience resulting from a changing unit of account, and arbitrary redistributions of wealth between debtors and creditors. Many of these costs are large during hyperinflation, but the size of these costs for moderate inflation is less clear.

KEY CONCEPTS

quantity theory of money, p. 249
nominal variables, p. 251
real variables, p. 251
classical dichotomy, p. 251

monetary neutrality, p. 252
velocity of money, p. 252
quantity equation, p. 253
inflation tax, p. 256

Fisher effect, p. 258
shoeleather costs, p. 260
menu costs, p. 261

QUESTIONS FOR REVIEW

1. Explain how an increase in the price level affects the real value of money.

2. According to the quantity theory of money, what is the effect of an increase in the quantity of money?

3. Explain the difference between nominal and real variables and give two examples of each. According to the principle of monetary neutrality, which variables are affected by changes in the quantity of money?

4. In what sense is inflation like a tax? How does thinking about inflation as a tax help explain hyperinflation?

5. According to the Fisher effect, how does an increase in the inflation rate affect the real interest rate and the nominal interest rate?

6. What are the costs of inflation? Which of these costs do you think are most important for the U.S. economy?

7. If inflation is less than expected, who benefits—debtors or creditors? Explain.

PROBLEMS AND APPLICATIONS

1. Suppose that this year's money supply is $500 billion, nominal GDP is $10 trillion, and real GDP is $5 trillion.
   a. What is the price level? What is the velocity of money?
   b. Suppose that velocity is constant and the economy's output of goods and services rises by 5 percent each year. What will happen to nominal GDP and the price level next year if the Fed keeps the money supply constant?
   c. What money supply should the Fed set next year if it wants to keep the price level stable?
   d. What money supply should the Fed set next year if it wants inflation of 10 percent?

2. Suppose that changes in bank regulations expand the availability of credit cards so that people need to hold less cash.
   a. How does this event affect the demand for money?
   b. If the Fed does not respond to this event, what will happen to the price level?
   c. If the Fed wants to keep the price level stable, what should it do?

3. It is often suggested that the Federal Reserve try to achieve zero inflation. If we assume that velocity is constant, does this zero-inflation goal require that the rate of money growth equal zero? If yes, explain why. If no, explain what the rate of money growth should equal.

4. Suppose that a country's inflation rate increases sharply. What happens to the inflation tax on the holders of money? Why is wealth that is held in savings accounts *not* subject to a change in the inflation tax? Can you think of any way holders of savings accounts are hurt by the increase in the inflation rate?

5. Hyperinflations are extremely rare in countries whose central banks are independent of the rest of the government. Why might this be so?

6. Let's consider the effects of inflation in an economy composed only of two people: Bob, a bean farmer, and Rita, a rice farmer. Bob and Rita both always consume equal amounts of rice and beans. In 2005, the price of beans was $1, and the price of rice was $3.
   a. Suppose that in 2006 the price of beans was $2 and the price of rice was $6. What was inflation? Was Bob better off, worse off, or unaffected by the changes in prices? What about Rita?
   b. Now suppose that in 2006 the price of beans was $2 and the price of rice was $4. What was inflation? Was Bob better off, worse off, or unaffected by the changes in prices? What about Rita?
   c. Finally, suppose that in 2006 the price of beans was $2 and the price of rice was $1.50. What was inflation? Was Bob better off, worse off, or unaffected by the changes in prices? What about Rita?
   d. What matters more to Bob and Rita—the overall inflation rate or the relative price of rice and beans?

7. If the tax rate is 40 percent, compute the before-tax real interest rate and the after-tax real interest rate in each of the following cases.

a. The nominal interest rate is 10 percent and the inflation rate is 5 percent.

b. The nominal interest rate is 6 percent and the inflation rate is 2 percent.

c. The nominal interest rate is 4 percent and the inflation rate is 1 percent.

8. What are your shoeleather costs of going to the bank? How might you measure these costs in dollars? How do you think the shoeleather costs of your college president differ from your own?

9. Recall that money serves three functions in the economy. What are those functions? How does inflation affect the ability of money to serve each of these functions?

10. Suppose that people expect inflation to equal 3 percent, but in fact, prices rise by 5 percent. Describe how this unexpectedly high inflation rate would help or hurt the following:

a. the government

b. a homeowner with a fixed-rate mortgage

c. a union worker in the second year of a labor contract

d. a college that has invested some of its endowment in government bonds

11. Explain one harm associated with unexpected inflation that is *not* associated with expected inflation. Then explain one harm associated with both expected and unexpected inflation.

12. Explain whether the following statements are true, false, or uncertain.

a. "Inflation hurts borrowers and helps lenders, because borrowers must pay a higher rate of interest."

b. "If prices change in a way that leaves the overall price level unchanged, then no one is made better or worse off."

c. "Inflation does not reduce the purchasing power of most workers."

 For further information on topics in this chapter, additional problems, examples, applications, online quizzes, and more, please visit our website at http://mankiw.swlearning.com.

6

The Macroeconomics of Open Economies

Open-Economy Macroeconomics: Basic Concepts

$\mathbf{W}$hen you decide to buy a car, you may compare the latest models offered by Ford and Toyota. When you take your next vacation, you may consider spending it on a beach in Florida or in Mexico. When you start saving for your retirement, you may choose between a mutual fund that buys stock in U.S. companies and one that buys stock in foreign companies. In all of these cases, you are participating not just in the U.S. economy but in economies around the world.

There are clear benefits to being open to international trade: Trade allows people to produce what they produce best and to consume the great variety of goods and services produced around the world. Indeed, one of the *Ten Principles of Economics* highlighted in Chapter 1 is that trade can make everyone better off. International trade can raise living standards in all countries by allowing each country to specialize in producing those goods and services in which it has a comparative advantage.

So far, our development of macroeconomics has largely ignored the economy's interaction with other economies around the world. For most questions in macroeconomics, international issues are peripheral. For instance, when we discussed the natural rate of unemployment and the causes of inflation, the effects of international trade could safely be ignored. Indeed, to keep their models simple, macroeconomists often assume a **closed economy**—an economy that does not interact with other economies.

closed economy
an economy that does not interact with other economies in the world

275

open economy
an economy that inter-
acts freely with other
economies around the
world

Yet new macroeconomic issues arise in an **open economy**—an economy that interacts freely with other economies around the world. This chapter and the next, therefore, provide an introduction to open-economy macroeconomics. We begin in this chapter by discussing the key macroeconomic variables that describe an open economy's interactions in world markets. You may have noticed mention of these variables—exports, imports, the trade balance, and exchange rates—when reading the newspaper or watching the nightly news. Our first job is to understand what these data mean. In the next chapter, we develop a model to explain how these variables are determined and how they are affected by various government policies.

THE INTERNATIONAL FLOWS OF GOODS AND CAPITAL

An open economy interacts with other economies in two ways: It buys and sells goods and services in world product markets, and it buys and sells capital assets such as stocks and bonds in world financial markets. Here we discuss these two activities and the close relationship between them.

The Flow of Goods: Exports, Imports, and Net Exports

exports
goods and services that
are produced domesti-
cally and sold abroad

imports
goods and services that
are produced abroad
and sold domestically

net exports
the value of a nation's
exports minus the value
of its imports; also called
the trade balance

trade balance
the value of a nation's
exports minus the value
of its imports; also called
net exports

trade surplus
an excess of exports
over imports

trade deficit
an excess of imports
over exports

balanced trade
a situation in which
exports equal imports

Exports are domestically produced goods and services that are sold abroad, and **imports** are foreign-produced goods and services that are sold domestically. When Boeing, the U.S. aircraft manufacturer, builds a plane and sells it to Air France, the sale is an export for the United States and an import for France. When Volvo, the Swedish car manufacturer, makes a car and sells it to a U.S. resident, the sale is an import for the United States and an export for Sweden.

The **net exports** of any country are the difference between the value of its exports and the value of its imports:

$$\text{Net exports} = \text{Value of country's exports} - \text{Value of country's imports.}$$

The Boeing sale raises U.S. net exports, and the Volvo sale reduces U.S. net exports. Because net exports tell us whether a country is, in total, a seller or a buyer in world markets for goods and services, net exports are also called the **trade balance.** If net exports are positive, exports are greater than imports, indicating that the country sells more goods and services abroad than it buys from other countries. In this case, the country is said to run a **trade surplus.** If net exports are negative, exports are less than imports, indicating that the country sells fewer goods and services abroad than it buys from other countries. In this case, the country is said to run a **trade deficit.** If net exports are zero, its exports and imports are exactly equal, and the country is said to have **balanced trade.**

In the next chapter, we develop a theory that explains an economy's trade balance, but even at this early stage, it is easy to think of many factors that might influence a country's exports, imports, and net exports. Those factors include the following:

- The tastes of consumers for domestic and foreign goods
- The prices of goods at home and abroad
- The exchange rates at which people can use domestic currency to buy foreign currencies

- The incomes of consumers at home and abroad
- The cost of transporting goods from country to country
- Government policies toward international trade

As these variables change, so does the amount of international trade.

CASE STUDY | THE INCREASING OPENNESS OF THE U.S. ECONOMY

"BUT WE'RE NOT JUST TALKING ABOUT BUYING A CAR—WE'RE TALKING ABOUT CONFRONTING THIS COUNTRY'S TRADE DEFICIT WITH JAPAN."

Perhaps the most dramatic change in the U.S. economy over the past five decades has been the increasing importance of international trade and finance. This change is illustrated in Figure 1, which shows the total value of goods and services exported to other countries and imported from other countries expressed as a percentage of gross domestic product. In the 1950s, imports and exports of goods and services were typically between 4 and 5 percent of GDP. In recent years, exports have been about twice that level, with imports about three times as high.

This increase in international trade is partly due to improvements in transportation. In 1950, the average merchant ship carried less than 10,000 tons of cargo; today, many ships carry more than 100,000 tons. The long-distance jet was introduced in 1958, and the wide-body jet in 1967, making air transport far cheaper than it had been. Because of these developments, goods that once had to be produced locally can now be traded around the world. Cut flowers, for instance, are now grown in Israel and flown to the United States to be sold. Fresh fruits and vegetables that can grow only in summer can now be consumed in winter as well because they can be shipped to the United States from countries in the Southern Hemisphere.

The increase in international trade has also been influenced by advances in telecommunications, which have allowed businesses to reach overseas customers

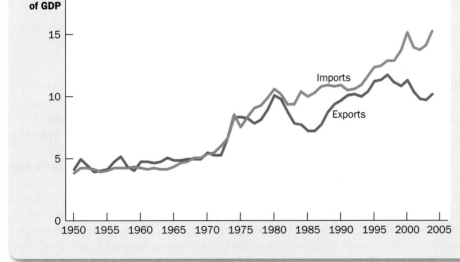

FIGURE 1

The Internationalization of the U.S. Economy
This figure shows exports and imports of the U.S. economy as a percentage of U.S. gross domestic product since 1950. The substantial increases over time show the increasing importance of international trade and finance.

Source: U.S. Department of Commerce.

more easily. For example, the first transatlantic telephone cable was not laid until 1956. As recently as 1966, the technology allowed only 138 simultaneous conversations between North America and Europe. Today, communications satellites permit more than 1 million conversations to occur at the same time.

Technological progress has also fostered international trade by changing the kinds of goods that economies produce. When bulky raw materials (such as steel) and perishable goods (such as foodstuffs) were a large part of the world's output, transporting goods was often costly and sometimes impossible. By contrast, goods produced with modern technology are often light and easy to transport. Consumer electronics, for instance, have low weight for every dollar of value, which makes them easy to produce in one country and sell in another. An even more extreme example is the film industry. Once a studio in Hollywood makes a movie, it can send copies of the film around the world at almost zero cost. And indeed, movies are a major export of the United States.

The government's trade policies have also been a factor in increasing international trade. As we discussed earlier in this book, economists have long believed that free trade between countries is mutually beneficial. Over time, most policymakers around the world have come to accept these conclusions. International agreements, such as the North American Free Trade Agreement (NAFTA) and the General Agreement on Tariffs and Trade (GATT), have gradually lowered tariffs, import quotas, and other trade barriers. The pattern of increasing trade illustrated in Figure 1 is a phenomenon that most economists and policymakers endorse and encourage.   •

The Flow of Financial Resources: Net Capital Outflow

So far, we have been discussing how residents of an open economy participate in world markets for goods and services. In addition, residents of an open economy participate in world financial markets. A U.S. resident with $20,000 could use that money to buy a car from Toyota, or he could instead use that money to buy stock in the Toyota corporation. The first transaction would represent a flow of goods, whereas the second would represent a flow of capital.

net capital outflow
the purchase of foreign assets by domestic residents minus the purchase of domestic assets by foreigners

The term **net capital outflow** refers to the difference between the purchase of foreign assets by domestic residents and the purchase of domestic assets by foreigners:

$$\text{Net capital outflow} = \text{Purchase of foreign assets by domestic residents} \\ - \text{Purchase of domestic assets by foreigners.}$$

When a U.S. resident buys stock in Telmex, the Mexican phone company, the purchase increases the first term on the right side of this equation and, therefore, increases U.S. net capital outflow. When a Japanese resident buys a bond issued by the U.S. government, the purchase increases the second term on the right side of this equation and, therefore, decreases U.S. net capital outflow.

The flow of capital abroad takes two forms. If McDonald's opens up a fast-food outlet in Russia, that is an example of *foreign direct investment*. Alternatively, if an American buys stock in a Russian corporation, that is an example of *foreign portfolio investment*. In the first case, the American owner is actively managing the investment, whereas in the second case, the American owner has a more passive role. In both cases, U.S. residents are buying assets located in another country, so both purchases increase U.S. net capital outflow.

The net capital outflow (sometimes called *net foreign investment*) can be either positive or negative. When it is positive, domestic residents are buying more foreign assets than foreigners are buying domestic assets. Capital is said to be flowing out of the country. When the net capital outflow is negative, domestic residents are buying less foreign assets than foreigners are buying domestic assets. Capital is said to be flowing into the country. That is, when net capital outflow is negative, a country is experiencing a capital inflow.

We develop a theory to explain net capital outflow in the next chapter. Here let's consider briefly some of the more important variables that influence net capital outflow:

- The real interest rates paid on foreign assets
- The real interest rates paid on domestic assets
- The perceived economic and political risks of holding assets abroad
- The government policies that affect foreign ownership of domestic assets

For example, consider U.S. investors deciding whether to buy Mexican government bonds or U.S. government bonds. (Recall that a bond is, in effect, an IOU of the issuer.) To make this decision, U.S. investors compare the real interest rates offered on the two bonds. The higher a bond's real interest rate, the more attractive it is. While making this comparison, however, U.S. investors must also take into account the risk that one of these governments might default on its debt (that is, not pay interest or principal when it is due), as well as any restrictions that the Mexican government has imposed, or might impose in the future, on foreign investors in Mexico.

The Equality of Net Exports and Net Capital Outflow

We have seen that an open economy interacts with the rest of the world in two ways—in world markets for goods and services and in world financial markets. Net exports and net capital outflow each measure a type of imbalance in these markets. Net exports measure an imbalance between a country's exports and its imports. Net capital outflow measures an imbalance between the amount of foreign assets bought by domestic residents and the amount of domestic assets bought by foreigners.

An important but subtle fact of accounting states that, for an economy as a whole, these variables must always be the same. That is, net capital outflow (*NCO*) equals net exports (*NX*):

$$NCO = NX.$$

This equation holds because every transaction that affects one side of this equation affects the other side by exactly the same amount. This equation is an *identity*—an equation that must hold because of the way the variables in the equation are defined and measured.

To see why this accounting identity is true, let's consider an example. Imagine that you are a computer programmer residing in the United States. One day, you write some software and sell it to a Japanese consumer for 10,000 yen. The sale of software is an export of the United States, so it increases U.S. net exports. What else happens to make the identity hold? The answer depends on what you do with the 10,000 yen.

First, let's suppose that you simply stuff the yen in your mattress. (We might say you have a yen for yen.) In this case, you are using some of your income to invest in the Japanese economy. That is, a domestic resident (you) has acquired a foreign asset (the Japanese currency). The increase in U.S. net exports is matched by an increase in the U.S. net capital outflow.

More realistically, however, if you want to invest in the Japanese economy, you won't hold currency. More likely, you would use the 10,000 yen to buy stock in a Japanese corporation, or you might buy a Japanese government bond. Yet the situation is much the same: A domestic resident ends up acquiring a foreign asset. The increase in U.S. net capital outflow (the purchase of the Japanese stock or bond) exactly equals the increase in U.S. net exports (the sale of software).

Let's now change the example. Suppose that instead of using the 10,000 yen to buy a Japanese asset, you use it to buy a good made in Japan, such as a Nintendo Gameboy. As a result of the Gameboy purchase, U.S. imports increase. The software export and the Gameboy import represent balanced trade. Because exports and imports increase by the same amount, net exports are unchanged. In this case, no American ends up acquiring foreign assets and no foreigner ends up acquiring U.S. assets, so there is also no impact on U.S. net capital outflow.

A final possibility is that you go to a local bank to exchange your 10,000 yen for U.S. dollars. But this doesn't change the situation because the bank now has to do something with the 10,000 yen. It can buy Japanese assets (a U.S. net capital outflow); it can buy a Japanese good (a U.S. import); or it can sell the yen to another American who wants to make such a transaction. In the end, U.S. net exports must equal U.S. net capital outflow.

From this example, we can generalize to the economy as a whole.

- When a nation is running a trade surplus ($NX > 0$), it is selling more goods and services to foreigners than it is buying from them. What is it doing with the foreign currency it receives from the net sale of goods and services abroad? It must be using it to buy foreign assets. Capital is flowing out of the country ($NCO > 0$).
- When a nation is running a trade deficit ($NX < 0$), it is buying more goods and services from foreigners than it is selling to them. How is it financing the net purchase of these goods and services in world markets? It must be selling assets abroad. Capital is flowing into the country ($NCO < 0$).

The international flow of goods and services and the international flow of capital are two sides of the same coin.

Saving, Investment, and Their Relationship to the International Flows

A nation's saving and investment are crucial to its long-run economic growth. As we have seen earlier in this book, saving and investment are equal in a closed economy. But matters are not as simple in an open economy. Let's now consider how saving and investment are related to the international flows of goods and capital as measured by net exports and net capital outflow.

As you may recall, the term *net exports* appeared earlier in the book when we discussed the components of gross domestic product. The economy's gross domestic product (Y) is divided among four components: consumption (C), investment (I), government purchases (G), and net exports (NX). We write this as

$$Y = C + I + G + NX.$$

In The News

Americans Rely on Capital Flows from Abroad

In 2004, the U.S. economy ran large trade deficits, financed by substantial net capital inflows.

U.S. Account Deficit Set Record in '04

By Sue Kirchhoff

The U.S. current account deficit—the broadest measure of the nation's trade balance—hit an all-time high in 2004, the government said Wednesday, raising fresh worries about the dollar even as other data showed the nation's economy on track. . . .

The Commerce Department said the current account . . . showed a $187.9 billion deficit in the fourth quarter of 2004, and $665.9 billion for the year. That's 25.5% above the 2003 gap of $530.7 billion. The deficit amounts to a record 5.7% of the economy.

The higher-than-expected numbers renewed concerns that the nation is too dependent on foreign investors, particularly Asian central banks, to finance the economy.

While foreign investment surged 51% in January to the second-highest level on record, funding needs are growing.

Ethan Harris, chief U.S. economist at Lehman Bros. in New York, called the current account numbers "abysmal."

"The counterpart to this is that we're asking foreigners, 'Don't just lend us $600 billion this year. We're asking for $700 billion.' So it creates this funding problem," Harris said. "Maybe they love to give us $300 billion or $400 billion, but you're really stretching the boundaries."

The White House says the trade deficit reflects that the U.S. economy is growing faster than other nations'. Federal Reserve Chairman Alan Greenspan expects the trade imbalance to gradually correct.

Other economists and business leaders are concerned that if foreign investors were to suddenly move away from U.S. dollar-denominated investments, the dollar and stock prices could plummet and interest rates and inflation could move higher. . . .

Influential investor Warren Buffett, in this year's letter to shareholders of Berkshire Hathaway, warned that the USA could become a "sharecropper's society" if it continued to transfer assets to foreigners.

Source: *USA Today*, March 17, 2005.

Total expenditure on the economy's output of goods and services is the sum of expenditure on consumption, investment, government purchases, and net exports. Because each dollar of expenditure is placed into one of these four components, this equation is an accounting identity: It must be true because of the way the variables are defined and measured.

Recall that national saving is the income of the nation that is left after paying for current consumption and government purchases. National saving (S) equals $Y - C - G$. If we rearrange the equation to reflect this fact, we obtain

$$Y - C - G = I + NX$$

$$S = I + NX.$$

Because net exports (*NX*) also equal net capital outflow (*NCO*), we can write this equation as

$$S \quad = \quad I \quad + \quad NCO$$

| Saving | = | Domestic investment | + | Net capital outflow. |

This equation shows that a nation's saving must equal its domestic investment plus its net capital outflow. In other words, when U.S. citizens save a dollar of their income for the future, that dollar can be used to finance accumulation of domestic capital or it can be used to finance the purchase of capital abroad.

This equation should look somewhat familiar. Earlier in the book, when we analyzed the role of the financial system, we considered this identity for the special case of a closed economy. In a closed economy, net capital outflow is zero ($NCO = 0$), so saving equals investment ($S = I$). By contrast, an open economy has two uses for its saving: domestic investment and net capital outflow.

As before, we can view the financial system as standing between the two sides of this identity. For example, suppose the Smith family decides to save some of its income for retirement. This decision contributes to national saving, the left side of our equation. If the Smiths deposit their saving in a mutual fund, the mutual fund may use some of the deposit to buy stock issued by General Motors, which uses the proceeds to build a factory in Ohio. In addition, the mutual fund may use some of the Smiths' deposit to buy stock issued by Toyota, which uses the proceeds to build a factory in Osaka. These transactions show up on the right side of the equation. From the standpoint of U.S. accounting, the General Motors' expenditure on a new factory is domestic investment, and the purchase of Toyota stock by a U.S. resident is net capital outflow. Thus, all saving in the U.S. economy shows up as investment in the U.S. economy or as U.S. net capital outflow.

The bottom line is that saving, investment, and international capital flows are inextricably linked. When a nation's saving exceeds its domestic investment, its net capital outflow is positive, indicating that the nation is using some of its saving to buy assets abroad. When a nation's domestic investment exceeds its saving, its net capital outflow is negative, indicating that foreigners are financing some of this investment by purchasing domestic assets.

Summing Up

Table 1 summarizes many of the ideas presented so far in this chapter. It describes the three possibilities for an open economy: a country with a trade deficit, a country with balanced trade, and a country with a trade surplus.

Consider first a country with a trade surplus. By definition, a trade surplus means that the value of exports exceeds the value of imports. Because net exports are exports minus imports, net exports *NX* are greater than zero. As a result, income $Y = C + I + G + NX$ must be greater than domestic spending $C + I + G$. But if income Y is more than spending $C + I + G$, then saving $S = Y - C - G$ must be more than investment I. Because the country is saving more than it is investing, it must be sending some of its saving abroad. That is, the net capital outflow must be greater than zero.

The converse logic applies to a country with a trade deficit (such as the U.S. economy in recent years). By definition, a trade deficit means that the value of exports is less than the value of imports. Because net exports are exports minus

	TABLE 1
This table shows the three possible outcomes for an open economy.	International Flows of Goods and Capital: Summary

Trade Deficit	Balanced Trade	Trade Surplus
Exports < Imports	Exports = Imports	Exports > Imports
Net Exports < 0	Net Exports = 0	Net Exports > 0
$Y < C + I + G$	$Y = C + I + G$	$Y > C + I + G$
Saving < Investment	Saving = Investment	Saving > Investment
Net Capital Outflow < 0	Net Capital Outflow = 0	Net Capital Outflow > 0

imports, net exports NX are negative. Thus, income $Y = C + I + G + NX$ must be less than domestic spending $C + I + G$. But if income Y is less than spending $C + I + G$, then saving $S = Y - C - G$ must be less than investment I. Because the country is investing more than it is saving, it must be financing some domestic investment by selling assets abroad. That is, the net capital outflow must be negative.

A country with balanced trade is between these cases. Exports equal imports, so net exports are zero. Income equals domestic spending, and saving equals investment. The net capital outflow equals zero.

CASE STUDY   IS THE U.S. TRADE DEFICIT A NATIONAL PROBLEM?

You may have heard the press call the United States "the world's largest debtor." The nation earned that description by borrowing heavily in world financial markets during the past two decades to finance large trade deficits. Why did the United States do this, and should this event give Americans reason to worry?

To answer these questions, let's see what the macroeconomic accounting identities tell us about the U.S. economy. Panel (a) of Figure 2 shows national saving and domestic investment as a percentage of GDP since 1960. Panel (b) shows net capital outflow (that is, the trade balance) as a percentage of GDP. Notice that, as the identities require, net capital outflow always equals national saving minus domestic investment.

The figure shows a dramatic change beginning in the early 1980s. Before 1980, national saving and domestic investment were close, and so net capital outflow was small. Yet after 1980, national saving fell below investment, and net capital outflow became a large negative number. That is, there was a capital inflow: Foreigners were buying more capital assets in the United States than Americans were buying abroad. The United States was going into debt.

History shows that changes in capital flows arise sometimes from changes in saving and sometimes from changes in investment. From 1980 to 1987, the flow of capital into the United States went from 0.5 to 3.1 percent of GDP. This 2.6 percentage point change is largely attributable to a fall in saving of 3.2 percentage points. This decline in national saving, in turn, is often explained by the decline in public saving—that is, the increase in the government budget deficit.

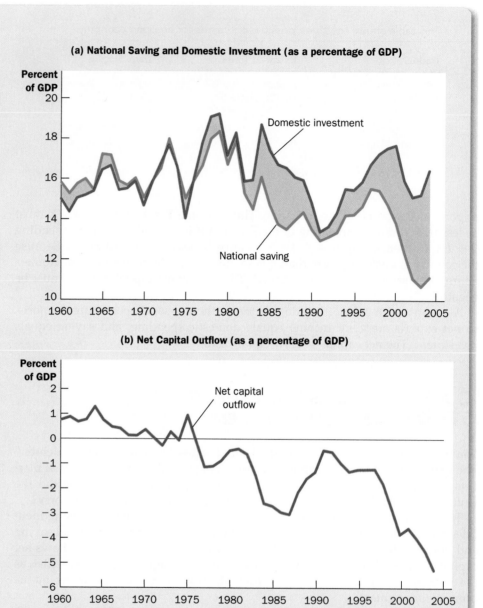

2 FIGURE

National Saving, Domestic Investment, and Net Capital Outflow
Panel (a) shows national saving and domestic investment as a percentage of GDP. Panel (b) shows net capital outflow as a percentage of GDP. You can see from the figure that national saving has been lower since 1980 than it was before 1980. This fall in national saving has been reflected primarily in reduced net capital outflow rather than in reduced domestic investment.

Source: U.S. Department of Commerce.

(a) National Saving and Domestic Investment (as a percentage of GDP)

(b) Net Capital Outflow (as a percentage of GDP)

A different story explains the events of the following decade. From 1991 to 2000, the capital flow into the United States went from 0.5 to 3.9 percent of GDP. None of this 3.4 percentage point change is attributable to a decline in saving; in fact, saving increased over this time, as the government's budget switched from deficit to surplus. But investment went from 13.4 to 17.7 percent of GDP, as the economy enjoyed a boom in information technology and many firms were eager to make these high-tech investments.

From 2000 to 2004, the capital flow into the United States increased further, reaching a record 5.3 percent of GDP. The investment boom abated after 2000, but once again, the federal government started running budget deficits, and national saving fell to extraordinarily low levels by historical standards.

Are these trade deficits a problem for the U.S. economy? To answer this question, it is important to keep an eye on the nation's saving and investment.

Consider first a trade deficit induced by a fall in saving, as occurred during the 1980s and the early 2000s. Lower saving means that the nation is putting away less of its income to provide for its future. Once national saving has fallen, however, there is no reason to deplore the resulting trade deficits. If national saving fell without inducing a trade deficit, investment in the United States would have to fall. This fall in investment, in turn, would adversely affect the growth in the capital stock, labor productivity, and real wages. In other words, given that U.S. saving has declined, it is better to have foreigners invest in the U.S. economy than no one at all.

Now consider a trade deficit induced by an investment boom, such as the trade deficits of the 1990s. In this case, the economy is borrowing from abroad to finance the purchase of new capital goods. If this additional capital provides a good return in the form of higher production of goods and services, then the economy should be able to handle the debts that are being accumulated. On the other hand, if the investment projects fail to yield the expected returns, the debts will look less desirable, at least with the benefit of hindsight.

There is no simple and correct answer to the question posed in the title to this case study. Just as an individual can go into debt in either a prudent or profligate manner, so can a nation. The trade deficit is not a problem in itself, but sometimes it can be a symptom of a problem. •

Quick Quiz Define *net exports* and *net capital outflow*. Explain how they are related.

THE PRICES FOR INTERNATIONAL TRANSACTIONS: REAL AND NOMINAL EXCHANGE RATES

So far, we have discussed measures of the flow of goods and services and the flow of capital across a nation's border. In addition to these quantity variables, macroeconomists also study variables that measure the prices at which these international transactions take place. Just as the price in any market serves the important role of coordinating buyers and sellers in that market, international prices help coordinate the decisions of consumers and producers as they interact in world markets. Here we discuss the two most important international prices: the nominal and real exchange rates.

Nominal Exchange Rates

The **nominal exchange rate** is the rate at which a person can trade the currency of one country for the currency of another. For example, if you go to a bank, you might see a posted exchange rate of 80 yen per dollar. If you give the bank one U.S. dollar, it will give you 80 Japanese yen; and if you give the bank 80 Japanese yen, it will give you one U.S. dollar. (In actuality, the bank will post slightly different prices for buying and selling yen. The difference gives the bank some profit for offering this service. For our purposes here, we can ignore these differences.)

nominal exchange rate
the rate at which a person can trade the currency of one country for the currency of another

An exchange rate can always be expressed in two ways. If the exchange rate is 80 yen per dollar, it is also 1/80 (= 0.0125) dollar per yen. Throughout this book, we always express the nominal exchange rate as units of foreign currency per U.S. dollar, such as 80 yen per dollar.

If the exchange rate changes so that a dollar buys more foreign currency, that change is called an **appreciation** of the dollar. If the exchange rate changes so that a dollar buys less foreign currency, that change is called a **depreciation** of the dollar. For example, when the exchange rate rises from 80 to 90 yen per dollar, the dollar is said to appreciate. At the same time, because a Japanese yen now buys less of the U.S. currency, the yen is said to depreciate. When the exchange rate falls from 80 to 70 yen per dollar, the dollar is said to depreciate, and the yen is said to appreciate.

At times, you may have heard the media report that the dollar is either "strong" or "weak." These descriptions usually refer to recent changes in the nominal exchange rate. When a currency appreciates, it is said to *strengthen* because it can then buy more foreign currency. Similarly, when a currency depreciates, it is said to *weaken*.

For any country, there are many nominal exchange rates. The U.S. dollar can be used to buy Japanese yen, British pounds, Mexican pesos, and so on. When economists study changes in the exchange rate, they often use indexes that average these many exchange rates. Just as the consumer price index turns the many prices in the economy into a single measure of the price level, an exchange rate index turns these many exchange rates into a single measure of the international value of a currency. So when economists talk about the dollar appreciating or depreciating, they often are referring to an exchange rate index that takes into account many individual exchange rates.

appreciation
an increase in the value of a currency as measured by the amount of foreign currency it can buy

depreciation
a decrease in the value of a currency as measured by the amount of foreign currency it can buy

Real Exchange Rates

real exchange rate
the rate at which a person can trade the goods and services of one country for the goods and services of another

The **real exchange rate** is the rate at which a person can trade the goods and services of one country for the goods and services of another. For example, suppose that you go shopping and find that a pound of Swiss cheese is twice as expensive as a pound of American cheese. We would then say that the real exchange rate is 1/2 pound of Swiss cheese per pound of American cheese. Notice that, like the nominal exchange rate, we express the real exchange rate as units of the foreign item per unit of the domestic item. But in this instance, the item is a good rather than a currency.

Real and nominal exchange rates are closely related. To see how, consider an example. Suppose that a bushel of American rice sells for $100, and a bushel of Japanese rice sells for 16,000 yen. What is the real exchange rate between American and Japanese rice? To answer this question, we must first use the nominal exchange rate to convert the prices into a common currency. If the nominal exchange rate is 80 yen per dollar, then a price for American rice of $100 per bushel is equivalent to 8,000 yen per bushel. American rice is half as expensive as Japanese rice. The real exchange rate is 1/2 bushel of Japanese rice per bushel of American rice.

We can summarize this calculation for the real exchange rate with the following formula:

$$\text{Real exchange rate} = \frac{\text{Nominal exchange rate} \times \text{Domestic price}}{\text{Foreign price}}.$$

FYI

The Euro

You may have once heard of, or perhaps even seen, currencies such as the French franc, the German mark, or the Italian lira. These types of money no longer exist. During the 1990s, many European nations decided to give up their national currencies and use a common currency called the *euro*. The euro started circulating on January 1, 2002. Monetary policy for the euro area is now set by the European Central Bank (ECB), with representatives from all of the participating countries. The ECB issues the euro and controls the supply of this money, much as the Federal Reserve controls the supply of dollars in the U.S. economy.

Why did these countries adopt a common currency? One benefit of a common currency is that it makes trade easier. Imagine that each of the fifty U.S. states had a different currency. Every time you crossed a state border, you would need to change your money and perform the kind of exchange-rate calculations discussed in the text. This would be inconvenient, and it might deter you from buying goods and ser-

vices outside your own state. The countries of Europe decided that as their economies became more integrated, it would be better to avoid this inconvenience.

To some extent, the adoption of a common currency in Europe was a political decision based on concerns beyond the scope of standard economics. Some advocates of the euro wanted to reduce nationalistic feelings and to make Europeans appreciate more fully their shared history and destiny. A single money for most of the continent, they argued, would help achieve this goal.

There are, however, costs of choosing a common currency. If the nations of Europe have only one money, they can have only one monetary policy. If they disagree about what monetary policy is best, they will have to reach some kind of agreement, rather than each going its own way. Because adopting a single money has both benefits and costs, there is debate among economists about whether Europe's recent adoption of the euro was a good decision.

Using the numbers in our example, the formula applies as follows

$$\text{Real exchange rate} = \frac{(80 \text{ yen per dollar}) \times (\$100 \text{ per bushel of American rice})}{16{,}000 \text{ yen per bushel of Japanese rice}}$$

$$= \frac{8{,}000 \text{ yen per bushel of American rice}}{16{,}000 \text{ yen per bushel of Japanese rice}}$$

$$= \text{}^1\!/_2 \text{ bushel of Japanese rice per bushel of American rice.}$$

Thus, the real exchange rate depends on the nominal exchange rate and on the prices of goods in the two countries measured in the local currencies.

Why does the real exchange rate matter? As you might guess, the real exchange rate is a key determinant of how much a country exports and imports. When Uncle Ben's, Inc., is deciding whether to buy U.S. rice or Japanese rice to put into its boxes, for example, it will ask which rice is cheaper. The real exchange rate gives the answer. As another example, imagine that you are deciding whether to take a seaside vacation in Miami, Florida, or in Cancún, Mexico. You might ask your travel agent the price of a hotel room in Miami (measured in dollars), the price of a hotel room in Cancún (measured in pesos), and the exchange rate between pesos and dollars. If you decide where to vacation by comparing costs, you are basing your decision on the real exchange rate.

When studying an economy as a whole, macroeconomists focus on overall prices rather than the prices of individual items. That is, to measure the real exchange rate, they use price indexes, such as the consumer price index, which measure the price of a basket of goods and services. By using a price index for a U.S. basket (P), a price index for a foreign basket (P^*), and the nominal exchange rate between the U.S. dollar and foreign currencies (e), we can compute the overall real exchange rate between the United States and other countries as follows:

$$\text{Real exchange rate} = (e \times P)/P^*.$$

This real exchange rate measures the price of a basket of goods and services available domestically relative to a basket of goods and services available abroad.

As we examine more fully in the next chapter, a country's real exchange rate is a key determinant of its net exports of goods and services. A depreciation (fall) in the U.S. real exchange rate means that U.S. goods have become cheaper relative to foreign goods. This change encourages consumers both at home and abroad to buy more U.S. goods and fewer goods from other countries. As a result, U.S. exports rise, and U.S. imports fall, and both of these changes raise U.S. net exports. Conversely, an appreciation (rise) in the U.S. real exchange rate means that U.S. goods have become more expensive compared to foreign goods, so U.S. net exports fall.

Quick Quiz Define *nominal exchange rate* and *real exchange rate*, and explain how they are related. • If the nominal exchange rate goes from 100 to 120 yen per dollar, has the dollar appreciated or depreciated?

A FIRST THEORY OF EXCHANGE-RATE DETERMINATION: PURCHASING-POWER PARITY

purchasing-power parity
a theory of exchange rates whereby a unit of any given currency should be able to buy the same quantity of goods in all countries

Exchange rates vary substantially over time. In 1970, a U.S. dollar could be used to buy 3.65 German marks or 627 Italian lira. In 1998, as both Germany and Italy were getting ready to adopt the euro as their common currency, a U.S. dollar bought 1.76 German marks or 1,737 Italian lira. In other words, over this period, the value of the dollar fell by more than half compared to the mark, while it more than doubled compared to the lira.

What explains these large and opposite changes? Economists have developed many models to explain how exchange rates are determined, each emphasizing just some of the many forces at work. Here we develop the simplest theory of exchange rates, called **purchasing-power parity.** This theory states that a unit of any given currency should be able to buy the same quantity of goods in all countries. Many economists believe that purchasing-power parity describes the forces that determine exchange rates in the long run. We now consider the logic on which this long-run theory of exchange rates is based, as well as the theory's implications and limitations.

The Basic Logic of Purchasing-Power Parity

The theory of purchasing-power parity is based on a principle called the *law of one price.* This law asserts that a good must sell for the same price in all locations. Otherwise, there would be opportunities for profit left unexploited. For example, suppose that coffee beans sold for less in Seattle than in Boston. A person could buy coffee in Seattle for, say, $4 a pound and then sell it in Boston for $5 a pound, making a profit of $1 per pound from the difference in price. The process of taking advantage of differences in prices for the same item in different markets is called *arbitrage.* In our example, as people took advantage of this arbitrage opportunity, they would increase the demand for coffee in Seattle and increase the supply in Boston. The price of coffee would rise in Seattle (in response to greater demand) and fall in Boston (in response to greater supply). This process would continue until, eventually, the prices were the same in the two markets.

Now consider how the law of one price applies to the international marketplace. If a dollar (or any other currency) could buy more coffee in the United States than in Japan, international traders could profit by buying coffee in the United States and selling it in Japan. This export of coffee from the United States to Japan would drive up the U.S. price of coffee and drive down the Japanese price. Conversely, if a dollar could buy more coffee in Japan than in the United States, traders could buy coffee in Japan and sell it in the United States. This import of coffee into the United States from Japan would drive down the U.S. price of coffee and drive up the Japanese price. In the end, the law of one price tells us that a dollar must buy the same amount of coffee in all countries.

This logic leads us to the theory of purchasing-power parity. According to this theory, a currency must have the same purchasing power in all countries. That is, a U.S. dollar must buy the same quantity of goods in the United States and Japan, and a Japanese yen must buy the same quantity of goods in Japan and the United States. Indeed, the name of this theory describes it well. *Parity* means equality, and *purchasing power* refers to the value of money in terms of the quantity of goods it can buy. *Purchasing-power parity* states that a unit of a currency must have the same real value in every country.

Implications of Purchasing-Power Parity

What does the theory of purchasing-power parity say about exchange rates? It tells us that the nominal exchange rate between the currencies of two countries depends on the price levels in those countries. If a dollar buys the same quantity of goods in the United States (where prices are measured in dollars) as in Japan (where prices are measured in yen), then the number of yen per dollar must reflect the prices of goods in the United States and Japan. For example, if a pound of coffee costs 500 yen in Japan and $5 in the United States, then the nominal exchange rate must be 100 yen per dollar (500 yen/$5 = 100 yen per dollar). Otherwise, the purchasing power of the dollar would not be the same in the two countries.

To see more fully how this works, it is helpful to use just a bit of mathematics. Suppose that P is the price of a basket of goods in the United States (measured in dollars), P^* is the price of a basket of goods in Japan (measured in yen), and e

is the nominal exchange rate (the number of yen a dollar can buy). Now consider the quantity of goods a dollar can buy at home and abroad. At home, the price level is P, so the purchasing power of \$1 at home is $1/P$. That is, a dollar can buy $1/P$ quantity of goods. Abroad, a dollar can be exchanged into e units of foreign currency, which in turn have purchasing power e/P^*. For the purchasing power of a dollar to be the same in the two countries, it must be the case that

$$1/P = e/P^*.$$

With rearrangement, this equation becomes

$$1 = eP/P^*.$$

Notice that the left side of this equation is a constant, and the right side is the real exchange rate. Thus, *if the purchasing power of the dollar is always the same at home and abroad, then the real exchange rate—the relative price of domestic and foreign goods—cannot change.*

To see the implication of this analysis for the nominal exchange rate, we can rearrange the last equation to solve for the nominal exchange rate:

$$e = P^*/P.$$

That is, the nominal exchange rate equals the ratio of the foreign price level (measured in units of the foreign currency) to the domestic price level (measured in units of the domestic currency). *According to the theory of purchasing-power parity, the nominal exchange rate between the currencies of two countries must reflect the price levels in those countries.*

A key implication of this theory is that nominal exchange rates change when price levels change. As we saw in the preceding chapter, the price level in any country adjusts to bring the quantity of money supplied and the quantity of money demanded into balance. Because the nominal exchange rate depends on the price levels, it also depends on the money supply and money demand in each country. When a central bank in any country increases the money supply and causes the price level to rise, it also causes that country's currency to depreciate relative to other currencies in the world. In other words, *when the central bank prints large quantities of money, that money loses value both in terms of the goods and services it can buy and in terms of the amount of other currencies it can buy.*

We can now answer the question that began this section: Why did the U.S. dollar lose value compared to the German mark and gain value compared to the Italian lira? The answer is that Germany pursued a less inflationary monetary policy than the United States, and Italy pursued a more inflationary monetary policy. From 1970 to 1998, inflation in the United States was 5.3 percent per year. By contrast, inflation was 3.5 percent in Germany and 9.6 percent in Italy. As U.S. prices rose relative to German prices, the value of the dollar fell relative to the mark. Similarly, as U.S. prices fell relative to Italian prices, the value of the dollar rose relative to the lira.

Germany and Italy now have a common currency—the euro. This means that the two countries share a single monetary policy and that the inflation rates in the two countries will be closely linked. But the historical lessons of the lira and the mark will apply to the euro as well. Whether the U.S. dollar buys more or fewer euros 20 years from now than it does today depends on whether the European Central Bank produces more or less inflation in Europe than the Federal Reserve does in the United States.

CASE STUDY | THE NOMINAL EXCHANGE RATE DURING A HYPERINFLATION

Macroeconomists can only rarely conduct controlled experiments. Most often, they must glean what they can from the natural experiments that history gives them. One natural experiment is hyperinflation—the high inflation that arises when a government turns to the printing press to pay for large amounts of government spending. Because hyperinflations are so extreme, they illustrate some basic economic principles with clarity.

Consider the German hyperinflation of the early 1920s. Figure 3 shows the German money supply, the German price level, and the nominal exchange rate (measured as U.S. cents per German mark) for that period. Notice that these series move closely together. When the supply of money starts growing quickly, the price level also takes off, and the German mark depreciates. When the money supply stabilizes, so do the price level and the exchange rate.

The pattern shown in this figure appears during every hyperinflation. It leaves no doubt that there is a fundamental link among money, prices, and the nominal exchange rate. The quantity theory of money discussed in the previous chapter explains how the money supply affects the price level. The theory of purchasing-power parity discussed here explains how the price level affects the nominal exchange rate.   •

This figure shows the money supply, the price level, and the exchange rate (measured as U.S. cents per mark) for the German hyperinflation from January 1921 to December 1924. Notice how similarly these three variables move. When the quantity of money started growing quickly, the price level followed, and the mark depreciated relative to the dollar. When the German central bank stabilized the money supply, the price level and exchange rate stabilized as well.

FIGURE 3

Money, Prices, and the Nominal Exchange Rate during the German Hyperinflation

Source: Adapted from Thomas J. Sargent, "The End of Four Big Inflations," in Robert Hall, ed., *Inflation* (Chicago: University of Chicago Press, 1983), pp. 41–93.

In The News

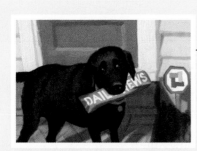

The Starbucks Index

A new application of purchasing-power parity is percolating through foreign-exchange markets.

Burgers or Beans?

Starbucks was due to open its first coffee shop in France on January 16th—a brave step, given that Paris invented café culture. Some of the French press are frothing at the mouth at the notion that Americans think they can make coffee. Jean-Paul Sartre, they scoff, would hardly have found the same inspiration slurping from a paper cup as sipping black coffee in Les Deux Magots. *The Economist,* however, has been pondering a more existential idea: what can the price of Starbucks coffee—now served in as many as 32 countries—tell us about exchange rates?

Readers may be familiar with *The Economist*'s long-running *Big Mac index:* by comparing burger prices around the world, it offers a light-hearted guide to whether currencies are at their "correct" level against the dollar. Given the dollar's recent plunge against the euro and growing complaints that China is unfairly holding down its currency, we cannot resist testing whether a Starbucks "tall latte index" reaches the same conclusions as our Big Mac index. Both are based on the theory of purchasing-power parity (PPP). This says that, in the long run, exchange rates should move towards levels that equalize the prices of a basket of goods and services in different countries—i.e., a dollar should buy the same everywhere.

By coincidence, the average price of a Starbucks tall latte in America is the same as the average price of a Big Mac, $2.80. By dividing the local currency price in each country by the dollar price we can calculate dollar PPPs. Comparing these with actual exchange rates is one test of whether a currency is undervalued or overvalued.

Our tall-latte index tells broadly the same story as the Big Mac index for most main currencies (see table). Economic trouble is surely brewing in Europe: the euro (based on the average price of €2.93—$3.70—in member countries where Starbucks operates) is about 30% overvalued against the dollar. Sterling is 17% too strong. By both

Limitations of Purchasing-Power Parity

Purchasing-power parity provides a simple model of how exchange rates are determined. For understanding many economic phenomena, the theory works well. In particular, it can explain many long-term trends, such as the depreciation of the U.S. dollar against the German mark and the appreciation of the U.S. dollar against the Italian lira. It can also explain the major changes in exchange rates that occur during hyperinflations.

Yet the theory of purchasing-power parity is not completely accurate. That is, exchange rates do not always move to ensure that a dollar has the same real value in all countries all the time. There are two reasons the theory of purchasing-power parity does not always hold in practice.

The first reason is that many goods are not easily traded. Imagine, for instance, that haircuts are more expensive in Paris than in New York. International travelers might avoid getting their haircuts in Paris, and some haircutters measures, the Swiss franc is the world's most overvalued currency. The Canadian, Australian and New Zealand dollars are still undervalued against the dollar despite their recent climb.

Where the two measures differ is in Asia. The burger index says the yen is 12% undervalued against the dollar; on the coffee standard, however, it is 13% overvalued. More startling is the Chi-nese yuan: it is 56% undervalued according to the Big Mac, but spot on its dollar PPP according to our Starbucks index. If so, American manufacturers have no grounds to complain about the yuan. The pricing differences probably reflect different competition in the markets for the two products.

Many readers will find burgernomics and lattenomics hard to swallow. Both are flawed as measures of PPP, because they are distorted by differences in the cost of non-tradables such as rents. Yet they are surely a more fun way to understand exchange rates than textbooks. [Author's Note: Except, of course, this one.] Many readers ask why don't we use the price of *The Economist* around the globe. Unlike the Big Mac or a tall latte, *The Economist* is not produced locally in lots of countries, so distribution accounts for a large chunk of its cost. Burgers and coffee are therefore likelier to give some clues about currencies.

Our Hot Tips

Local currency under (−)/over (+) valuation against the dollar, %, using:

	Starbucks tall latte index	McDonald's Big Mac index
Australia	−4	−17
Britain	+17	+23
Canada	−16	−16
China	−1	−56
Euro area	+33	+24
Hong Kong	+15	−45
Japan	+13	−12
Malaysia	−25	−53
Mexico	−15	−21
New Zealand	−12	−4
Singapore	+2	−31
South Korea	+6	0
Switzerland	+62	+82
Taiwan	−5	−21
Thailand	−31	−46
Turkey	+6	+5

Source: *The Economist*

---

might move from New York to Paris. Yet such arbitrage would be too limited to eliminate the differences in prices. Thus, the deviation from purchasing-power parity might persist, and a dollar (or euro) would continue to buy less of a haircut in Paris than in New York.

The second reason that purchasing-power parity does not always hold is that even tradable goods are not always perfect substitutes when they are produced in different countries. For example, some consumers prefer German cars, and others prefer American cars. Moreover, consumer tastes can change over time. If German cars suddenly become more popular, the increase in demand will drive up the price of German cars compared to American cars. But despite this difference in prices in the two markets, there might be no opportunity for profitable arbitrage because consumers do not view the two cars as equivalent.

Thus, both because some goods are not tradable and because some tradable goods are not perfect substitutes with their foreign counterparts, purchasing-power parity is not a perfect theory of exchange-rate determination. For these reasons, real exchange rates fluctuate over time. Nonetheless, the theory of purchasing-power parity does provide a useful first step in understanding exchange rates. The basic logic is persuasive: As the real exchange rate drifts from the level predicted by purchasing-power parity, people have greater incentive to move goods across national borders. Even if the forces of purchasing-power parity do not completely fix the real exchange rate, they provide a reason to expect that changes in the real exchange rate are most often small or temporary. As a result, large and persistent movements in nominal exchange rates typically reflect changes in price levels at home and abroad.

CASE STUDY | THE HAMBURGER STANDARD

When economists apply the theory of purchasing-power parity to explain exchange rates, they need data on the prices of a basket of goods available in different countries. One analysis of this sort is conducted by *The Economist,* an international newsmagazine. The magazine occasionally collects data on a basket of goods consisting of "two all-beef patties, special sauce, lettuce, cheese, pickles, onions, on a sesame seed bun." It's called the "Big Mac" and is sold by McDonald's around the world.

Once we have the prices of Big Macs in two countries denominated in the local currencies, we can compute the exchange rate predicted by the theory of purchasing-power parity. The predicted exchange rate is the one that makes the cost of the Big Mac the same in the two countries. For instance, if the price of a Big Mac is $3 in the United States and 300 yen in Japan, purchasing-power parity would predict an exchange rate of 100 yen per dollar.

How well does purchasing-power parity work when applied using Big Mac prices? Here are some examples from June 2005, when the price of a Big Mac was $3.06 in the United States:

IN THE UNITED STATES THE PRICE OF A BIG MAC IS $3.06; IN JAPAN IT IS 250 YEN.

Country	Price of a Big Mac	Predicted Exchange Rate	Actual Exchange Rate
South Korea	2,500 won	817 won/$	1,004 won/$
Japan	250 yen	82 yen/$	107 yen/$
Sweden	31 kronor	10.1 kronor/$	7.4 kronor/$
Mexico	28 pesos	9.2 pesos/$	10.8 pesos/$
Euro area	3.21 euros	1.05 euros/$	0.90 euros/$
Britain	1.88 pounds	0.61 pound/$	0.55 pound/$

You can see that the predicted and actual exchange rates are not exactly the same. After all, international arbitrage in Big Macs is not easy. Yet the two exchange rates are usually in the same ballpark. Purchasing-power parity is not a precise theory of exchange rates, but it often provides a reasonable first approximation. •

Quick Quiz Over the past 20 years, Spain has had high inflation, and Japan has had low inflation. What do you predict has happened to the number of Spanish pesetas a person can buy with a Japanese yen?

CONCLUSION

The purpose of this chapter has been to develop some basic concepts that macro-economists use to study open economies. You should now understand how a nation's trade balance is related to the international flow of capital and how national saving can differ from domestic investment in an open economy. You should understand that when a nation is running a trade surplus, it must be sending capital abroad, and that when it is running a trade deficit, it must be experiencing a capital inflow. You should also understand the meaning of the nominal and real exchange rates, as well as the implications and limitations of purchasing-power parity as a theory of how exchange rates are determined.

The macroeconomic variables defined here offer a starting point for analyzing an open economy's interactions with the rest of the world. In the next chapter, we develop a model that can explain what determines these variables. We can then discuss how various events and policies affect a country's trade balance and the rate at which nations make exchanges in world markets.

SUMMARY

- Net exports are the value of domestic goods and services sold abroad minus the value of foreign goods and services sold domestically. Net capital outflow is the acquisition of foreign assets by domestic residents minus the acquisition of domestic assets by foreigners. Because every international transaction involves an exchange of an asset for a good or service, an economy's net capital outflow always equals its net exports.

- An economy's saving can be used either to finance investment at home or to buy assets abroad. Thus, national saving equals domestic investment plus net capital outflow.

- The nominal exchange rate is the relative price of the currency of two countries, and the real exchange rate is the relative price of the goods and services of two countries. When the nominal exchange rate changes so that each dollar buys more foreign currency, the dollar is said to *appreciate* or *strengthen*. When the nominal exchange rate changes so that each dollar buys less foreign currency, the dollar is said to *depreciate* or *weaken*.

- According to the theory of purchasing-power parity, a dollar (or a unit of any other currency) should be able to buy the same quantity of goods in all countries. This theory implies that the nominal exchange rate between the currencies of two countries should reflect the price levels in those countries. As a result, countries with relatively high inflation should have depreciating currencies, and countries with relatively low inflation should have appreciating currencies.

KEY CONCEPTS

closed economy, p. 275
open economy, p. 276
exports, p. 276
imports, p. 276
net exports, p. 276

trade balance, p. 276
trade surplus, p. 276
trade deficit, p. 276
balanced trade, p. 276
net capital outflow, p. 278

nominal exchange rate, p. 285
appreciation, p. 286
depreciation, p. 286
real exchange rate, p. 286
purchasing-power parity, p. 288

QUESTIONS FOR REVIEW

1. Define *net exports* and *net capital outflow*. Explain how and why they are related.

2. Explain the relationship among saving, investment, and net capital outflow.

3. If a Japanese car costs 500,000 yen, a similar American car costs $10,000, and a dollar can buy 100 yen, what are the nominal and real exchange rates?

4. Describe the economic logic behind the theory of purchasing-power parity.

5. If the Fed started printing large quantities of U.S. dollars, what would happen to the number of Japanese yen a dollar could buy?

PROBLEMS AND APPLICATIONS

1. How would the following transactions affect U.S. exports, imports, and net exports?
   a. An American art professor spends the summer touring museums in Europe.
   b. Students in Paris flock to see the latest movie from Hollywood.
   c. Your uncle buys a new Volvo.
   d. The student bookstore at Oxford University sells a pair of Levi's 501 jeans.
   e. A Canadian citizen shops at a store in northern Vermont to avoid Canadian sales taxes.

2. Would each of the following transactions be included in net exports or net capital outflow? Be sure to say whether it would represent an increase or a decrease in that variable.
   a. An American buys a Sony TV.
   b. An American buys a share of Sony stock.
   c. The Sony pension fund buys a bond from the U.S. Treasury.
   d. A worker at Sony buys some Georgia peaches from an American farmer.

3. International trade in each of the following products has increased over time. Suggest some reasons this might be so.
   a. wheat
   b. banking services
   c. computer software
   d. automobiles

4. Describe the difference between foreign direct investment and foreign portfolio investment. Who is more likely to engage in foreign direct investment—a corporation or an individual investor? Who is more likely to engage in foreign portfolio investment?

5. How would the following transactions affect U.S. net capital outflow? Also, state whether each involves direct investment or portfolio investment.
   a. An American cellular phone company establishes an office in the Czech Republic.
   b. Harrod's of London sells stock to the General Electric pension fund.
   c. Honda expands its factory in Marysville, Ohio.
   d. A Fidelity mutual fund sells its Volkswagen stock to a French investor.

6. Holding national saving constant, does an increase in net capital outflow increase, decrease, or have no effect on a country's accumulation of domestic capital?

7. The business section of most major newspapers contains a table showing U.S. exchange rates. Find such a table and use it to answer the following questions.
   a. Does this table show nominal or real exchange rates? Explain.
   b. What are the exchange rates between the United States and Canada and between the United States and Japan? Calculate the exchange rate between Canada and Japan.
   c. If U.S. inflation exceeds Japanese inflation over the next year, would you expect the U.S. dollar to appreciate or depreciate relative to the Japanese yen?

8. Would each of the following groups be happy or unhappy if the U.S. dollar appreciated? Explain.
   a. Dutch pension funds holding U.S. government bonds
   b. U.S. manufacturing industries
   c. Australian tourists planning a trip to the United States
   d. An American firm trying to purchase property overseas

9. What is happening to the U.S. real exchange rate in each of the following situations? Explain.
   a. The U.S. nominal exchange rate is unchanged, but prices rise faster in the United States than abroad.
   b. The U.S. nominal exchange rate is unchanged, but prices rise faster abroad than in the United States.
   c. The U.S. nominal exchange rate declines, and prices are unchanged in the United States and abroad.
   d. The U.S. nominal exchange rate declines, and prices rise faster abroad than in the United States.

10. A can of soda costs $0.75 in the United States and 12 pesos in Mexico. What would the peso-dollar exchange rate be if purchasing-power parity holds? If a monetary expansion caused all prices in Mexico to double, so that soda rose to 24 pesos, what would happen to the peso-dollar exchange rate?

11. Assume that American rice sells for $100 per bushel, Japanese rice sells for 16,000 yen per bushel, and the nominal exchange rate is 80 yen per dollar.

    a. Explain how you could make a profit from this situation. What would be your profit per bushel of rice? If other people exploit the same opportunity, what would happen to the price of rice in Japan and the price of rice in the United States?
    b. Suppose that rice is the only commodity in the world. What would happen to the real exchange rate between the United States and Japan?

12. A case study in the chapter analyzed purchasing-power parity for several countries using the price of Big Macs. Here are data for a few more countries:

Country	Price of a Big Mac	Predicted Exchange Rate	Actual Exchange Rate
Indonesia	14,600 rupiah	_____ rupiah/$	9,541 rupiah/$
Hungary	529 forints	_____ forints/$	204 forints/$
Czech Republic	56.30 korunas	_____ korunas/$	24.5 korunas/$
Canada	3.27 C$	_____ C$/$	1.24 C$/$

    a. For each country, compute the predicted exchange rate of the local currency per U.S. dollar. (Recall that the U.S. price of a Big Mac was $3.06.)
    b. According to purchasing-power parity, what is the predicted exchange rate between the Hungarian forint and the Canadian dollar? What is the actual exchange rate?
    c. How well does the theory of purchasing-power parity explain exchange rates?

 For further information on topics in this chapter, additional problems, examples, applications, online quizzes, and more, please visit our website at http://mankiw.swlearning.com.

A Macroeconomic Theory of the Open Economy

Over the past two decades, the United States has persistently imported more goods and services than it has exported. That is, U.S. net exports have been negative. Although economists debate whether these trade deficits are a problem for the U.S. economy, the nation's business community has a strong opinion. Many business leaders claim that the trade deficits reflect unfair competition: Foreign firms are allowed to sell their products in U.S. markets, they contend, while foreign governments impede U.S. firms from selling U.S. products abroad.

Imagine that you are the president and you want to end these trade deficits. What should you do? Should you try to limit imports, perhaps by imposing a quota on the import of cars from Japan? Or should you try to influence the nation's trade deficit in some other way?

To understand the factors that determine a country's trade balance and how government policies can affect it, we need a macroeconomic theory that explains how an open economy works. The preceding chapter introduced some of the key macroeconomic variables that describe an economy's relationship with other economies, including net exports, net capital outflow, and the real and nominal exchange rates. This chapter develops a model that identifies the forces that determine these variables and shows how these variables are related to one another.

To develop this macroeconomic model of an open economy, we build on our previous analysis in two ways. First, the model takes the economy's GDP as given. We assume that the economy's output of goods and services, as measured by real GDP, is determined by the supplies of the factors of production and by the available production technology that turns these inputs into output. Second, the model takes the economy's price level as given. We assume that the price level adjusts to bring the supply and demand for money into balance. In other words, this chapter takes as a starting point the lessons learned in previous chapters about the determination of the economy's output and price level.

The goal of the model in this chapter is to highlight the forces that determine the economy's trade balance and exchange rate. In one sense, the model is simple: It applies the tools of supply and demand to an open economy. Yet the model is also more complicated than others we have seen because it involves looking simultaneously at two related markets: the market for loanable funds and the market for foreign-currency exchange. After we develop this model of the open economy, we use it to examine how various events and policies affect the economy's trade balance and exchange rate. We will then be able to determine the government policies that are most likely to reverse the trade deficits that the U.S. economy has experienced over the past two decades.

SUPPLY AND DEMAND FOR LOANABLE FUNDS AND FOR FOREIGN-CURRENCY EXCHANGE

To understand the forces at work in an open economy, we focus on supply and demand in two markets. The first is the market for loanable funds, which coordinates the economy's saving, investment, and the flow of loanable funds abroad (called the net capital outflow). The second is the market for foreign-currency exchange, which coordinates people who want to exchange the domestic currency for the currency of other countries. In this section, we discuss supply and demand in each of these markets. In the next section, we put these markets together to explain the overall equilibrium for an open economy.

The Market for Loanable Funds

When we first analyzed the role of the financial system in Chapter 8, we made the simplifying assumption that the financial system consists of only one market, called the *market for loanable funds*. All savers go to this market to deposit their saving, and all borrowers go to this market to get their loans. In this market, there is one interest rate, which is both the return to saving and the cost of borrowing.

To understand the market for loanable funds in an open economy, the place to start is the identity discussed in the preceding chapter:

$$S = I + NCO$$
$$\text{Saving} = \frac{\text{Domestic}}{\text{investment}} + \frac{\text{Net capital}}{\text{outflow.}}$$

Whenever a nation saves a dollar of its income, it can use that dollar to finance the purchase of domestic capital or to finance the purchase of an asset abroad. The two sides of this identity represent the two sides of the market for loanable funds. The supply of loanable funds comes from national saving (*S*), and the demand for loanable funds comes from domestic investment (*I*) and net capital outflow (*NCO*).

Loanable funds should be interpreted as the domestically generated flow of resources available for capital accumulation. The purchase of a capital asset adds to the demand for loanable funds, regardless of whether that asset is located at home (*I*) or abroad (*NCO*). Because net capital outflow can be either positive or negative, it can either add to or subtract from the demand for loanable funds that arises from domestic investment. When $NCO > 0$, the country is experiencing a net outflow of capital; the net purchase of capital overseas adds to the demand for domestically generated loanable funds. When $NCO < 0$, the country is experiencing a net inflow of capital; the capital resources coming from abroad reduce the demand for domestically generated loanable funds.

As we learned in our earlier discussion of the market for loanable funds, the quantity of loanable funds supplied and the quantity of loanable funds demanded depend on the real interest rate. A higher real interest rate encourages people to save and, therefore, raises the quantity of loanable funds supplied. A higher interest rate also makes borrowing to finance capital projects more costly; thus, it discourages investment and reduces the quantity of loanable funds demanded.

In addition to influencing national saving and domestic investment, the real interest rate in a country affects that country's net capital outflow. To see why, consider two mutual funds—one in the United States and one in Germany—deciding whether to buy a U.S. government bond or a German government bond. The mutual fund manager would make this decision in part by comparing the real interest rates in the United States and Germany. When the U.S. real interest rate rises, the U.S. bond becomes more attractive to both mutual funds. Thus, an increase in the U.S. real interest rate discourages Americans from buying foreign assets and encourages foreigners to buy U.S. assets. For both reasons, a high U.S. real interest rate reduces U.S. net capital outflow.

We represent the market for loanable funds on the familiar supply-and-demand diagram in Figure 1. As in our earlier analysis of the financial system, the supply curve slopes upward because a higher interest rate increases the quantity of loanable funds supplied, and the demand curve slopes downward because a higher interest rate decreases the quantity of loanable funds demanded. Unlike the situation in our previous discussion, however, the demand side of the market

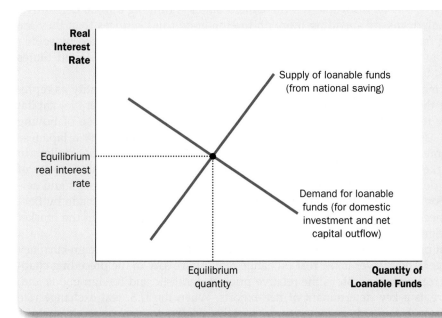

Real Interest Rate

Supply of loanable funds (from national saving)

Equilibrium real interest rate

Demand for loanable funds (for domestic investment and net capital outflow)

Equilibrium quantity

Quantity of Loanable Funds

FIGURE 1

The Market for Loanable Funds
The interest rate in an open economy, as in a closed economy, is determined by the supply and demand for loanable funds. National saving is the source of the supply of loanable funds. Domestic investment and net capital outflow are the sources of the demand for loanable funds. At the equilibrium interest rate, the amount that people want to save exactly balances the amount that people want to borrow for the purpose of buying domestic capital and foreign assets.

now represents the behavior of both domestic investment and net capital outflow. That is, in an open economy, the demand for loanable funds comes not only from those who want loanable funds to buy domestic capital goods but also from those who want loanable funds to buy foreign assets.

The interest rate adjusts to bring the supply and demand for loanable funds into balance. If the interest rate were below the equilibrium level, the quantity of loanable funds supplied would be less than the quantity demanded. The resulting shortage of loanable funds would push the interest rate upward. Conversely, if the interest rate were above the equilibrium level, the quantity of loanable funds supplied would exceed the quantity demanded. The surplus of loanable funds would drive the interest rate downward. At the equilibrium interest rate, the supply of loanable funds exactly balances the demand. That is, *at the equilibrium interest rate, the amount that people want to save exactly balances the desired quantities of domestic investment and net capital outflow.*

The Market for Foreign-Currency Exchange

The second market in our model of the open economy is the market for foreign-currency exchange. Participants in this market trade U.S. dollars in exchange for foreign currencies. To understand the market for foreign-currency exchange, we begin with another identity from the last chapter:

$$NCO = NX$$
$$\text{Net capital outflow} = \text{Net exports.}$$

This identity states that the imbalance between the purchase and sale of capital assets abroad (NCO) equals the imbalance between exports and imports of goods and services (NX). For example, when the U.S. economy is running a trade surplus ($NX > 0$), foreigners are buying more U.S. goods and services than Americans are buying foreign goods and services. What are Americans doing with the foreign currency they are getting from this net sale of goods and services abroad? They must be buying foreign assets, so U.S. capital is flowing abroad ($NCO > 0$). Conversely, if the United States is running a trade deficit ($NX < 0$), Americans are spending more on foreign goods and services than they are earning from selling abroad. Some of this spending must be financed by selling American assets abroad, so foreign capital is flowing into the United States ($NCO < 0$).

Our model of the open economy treats the two sides of this identity as representing the two sides of the market for foreign-currency exchange. Net capital outflow represents the quantity of dollars supplied for the purpose of buying foreign assets. For example, when a U.S. mutual fund wants to buy a Japanese government bond, it needs to change dollars into yen, so it supplies dollars in the market for foreign-currency exchange. Net exports represent the quantity of dollars demanded for the purpose of buying U.S. net exports of goods and services. For example, when a Japanese airline wants to buy a plane made by Boeing, it needs to change its yen into dollars, so it demands dollars in the market for foreign-currency exchange.

What price balances the supply and demand in the market for foreign-currency exchange? The answer is the real exchange rate. As we saw in the preceding chapter, the real exchange rate is the relative price of domestic and foreign goods and, therefore, is a key determinant of net exports. When the U.S. real exchange rate appreciates, U.S. goods become more expensive relative to foreign goods, making

U.S. goods less attractive to consumers both at home and abroad. As a result, exports from the United States fall, and imports into the United States rise. For both reasons, net exports fall. Hence, an appreciation of the real exchange rate reduces the quantity of dollars demanded in the market for foreign-currency exchange.

Figure 2 shows supply and demand in the market for foreign-currency exchange. The demand curve slopes downward for the reason we just discussed: A higher real exchange rate makes U.S. goods more expensive and reduces the quantity of dollars demanded to buy those goods. The supply curve is vertical because the quantity of dollars supplied for net capital outflow does not depend on the real exchange rate. (As discussed earlier, net capital outflow depends on the real interest rate. When discussing the market for foreign-currency exchange, we take the real interest rate and net capital outflow as given.)

The real exchange rate adjusts to balance the supply and demand for dollars just as the price of any good adjusts to balance supply and demand for that good. If the real exchange rate were below the equilibrium level, the quantity of dollars supplied would be less than the quantity demanded. The resulting shortage of dollars would push the value of the dollar upward. Conversely, if the real exchange rate were above the equilibrium level, the quantity of dollars supplied would exceed the quantity demanded. The surplus of dollars would drive the value of the dollar downward. *At the equilibrium real exchange rate, the demand for*

The real exchange rate is determined by the supply and demand for foreign-currency exchange. The supply of dollars to be exchanged into foreign currency comes from net capital outflow. Because net capital outflow does not depend on the real exchange rate, the supply curve is vertical. The demand for dollars comes from net exports. Because a lower real exchange rate stimulates net exports (and thus increases the quantity of dollars demanded to pay for these net exports), the demand curve is downward sloping. At the equilibrium real exchange rate, the number of dollars people supply to buy foreign assets exactly balances the number of dollars people demand to buy net exports.

FIGURE 2

The Market for Foreign-Currency Exchange

FYI

Purchasing-Power Parity as a Special Case

An alert reader of this book might ask: Why are we developing a theory of the exchange rate here? Didn't we already do that in the preceding chapter?

As you may recall, the preceding chapter developed a theory of the exchange rate called *purchasing-power parity*. This theory asserts that a dollar (or any other currency) must buy the same quantity of goods and services in every country. As a result, the real exchange rate is fixed, and all changes in the nominal exchange rate between two currencies reflect changes in the price levels in the two countries.

The model of the exchange rate developed here is related to the theory of purchasing-power parity. According to the theory of purchasing-power parity, international trade responds quickly to international price differences. If goods were cheaper in one country than in another, they would be exported from the first country and imported into the second until the price difference

disappeared. In other words, the theory of purchasing-power parity assumes that net exports are highly responsive to small changes in the real exchange rate. If net exports were in fact so responsive, the demand curve in Figure 2 would be horizontal.

Thus, the theory of purchasing-power parity can be viewed as a special case of the model considered here. In that special case, the demand curve for foreign-currency exchange, rather than being downward sloping, is horizontal at the level of the real exchange rate that ensures parity of purchasing power at home and abroad. That special case is a good place to start when studying exchange rates, but it is far from the end of the story.

This chapter, therefore, concentrates on the more realistic case in which the demand curve for foreign-currency exchange is downward sloping. This allows for the possibility that the real exchange rate changes over time, as in fact it sometimes does in the real world.

dollars by foreigners arising from the U.S. net exports of goods and services exactly balances the supply of dollars from Americans arising from U.S. net capital outflow.

Quick Quiz Describe the sources of supply and demand in the market for loanable funds and the market for foreign-currency exchange.

EQUILIBRIUM IN THE OPEN ECONOMY

So far, we have discussed supply and demand in two markets: the market for loanable funds and the market for foreign-currency exchange. Let's now consider how these markets are related to each other.

Net Capital Outflow: The Link between the Two Markets

We begin by recapping what we've learned so far in this chapter. We have been discussing how the economy coordinates four important macroeconomic variables: national saving (S), domestic investment (I), net capital outflow (NCO), and net exports (NX). Keep in mind the following identities:

$$S = I + NCO$$

and

$$NCO = NX.$$

In the market for loanable funds, supply comes from national saving, demand comes from domestic investment and net capital outflow, and the real interest rate balances supply and demand. In the market for foreign-currency exchange, supply comes from net capital outflow, demand comes from net exports, and the real exchange rate balances supply and demand.

Net capital outflow is the variable that links these two markets. In the market for loanable funds, net capital outflow is a piece of demand. A person who wants to buy an asset abroad must finance this purchase by obtaining resources in the market for loanable funds. In the market for foreign-currency exchange, net capital outflow is the source of supply. A person who wants to buy an asset in another country must supply dollars to exchange them for the currency of that country.

The key determinant of net capital outflow, as we have discussed, is the real interest rate. When the U.S. interest rate is high, owning U.S. assets is more attractive, and U.S. net capital outflow is low. Figure 3 shows this negative relationship between the interest rate and net capital outflow. This net-capital-outflow curve is the link between the market for loanable funds and the market for foreign-currency exchange.

Simultaneous Equilibrium in Two Markets

We can now put all the pieces of our model together in Figure 4. This figure shows how the market for loanable funds and the market for foreign-currency exchange jointly determine the important macroeconomic variables of an open economy.

Panel (a) of the figure shows the market for loanable funds (taken from Figure 1). As before, national saving is the source of the supply of loanable funds. Domestic investment and net capital outflow are the source of the demand for

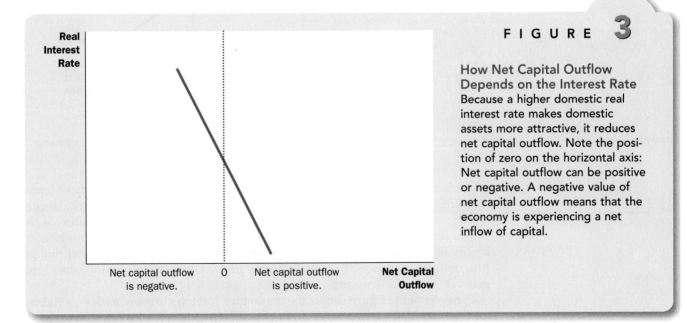

F I G U R E 3

How Net Capital Outflow Depends on the Interest Rate Because a higher domestic real interest rate makes domestic assets more attractive, it reduces net capital outflow. Note the position of zero on the horizontal axis: Net capital outflow can be positive or negative. A negative value of net capital outflow means that the economy is experiencing a net inflow of capital.

Real Interest Rate

Net capital outflow is negative.   0   Net capital outflow is positive.   **Net Capital Outflow**

4 FIGURE

The Real Equilibrium in an Open Economy

In panel (a), the supply and demand for loanable funds determine the real interest rate. In panel (b), the interest rate determines net capital outflow, which provides the supply of dollars in the market for foreign-currency exchange. In panel (c), the supply and demand for dollars in the market for foreign-currency exchange determine the real exchange rate.

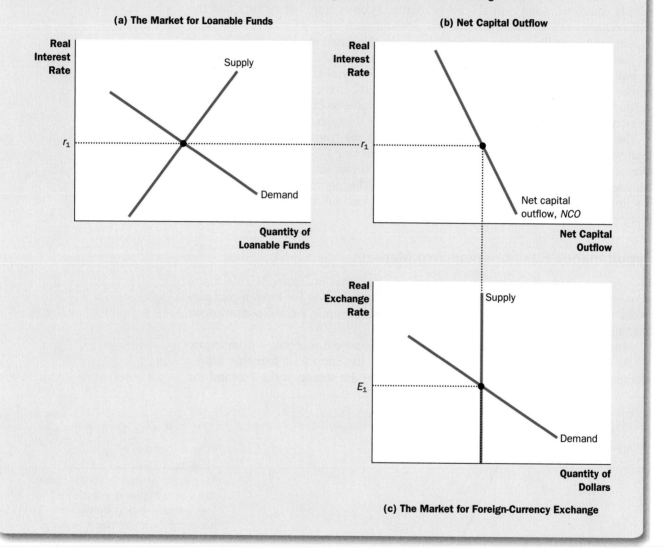

(a) The Market for Loanable Funds

(b) Net Capital Outflow

(c) The Market for Foreign-Currency Exchange

loanable funds. The equilibrium real interest rate (r_1) brings the quantity of loanable funds supplied and the quantity of loanable funds demanded into balance.

Panel (b) of the figure shows net capital outflow (taken from Figure 3). It shows how the interest rate from panel (a) determines net capital outflow. A higher interest rate at home makes domestic assets more attractive, and this in turn reduces net capital outflow. Therefore, the net-capital-outflow curve in panel (b) slopes downward.

Panel (c) of the figure shows the market for foreign-currency exchange (taken from Figure 2). Because foreign assets must be purchased with foreign currency,

FYI

Disentangling Supply and Demand

Suppose the owner of an apple orchard decides to consume some of his own apples. Does this decision represent an increase in the demand for apples or a decrease in the supply? Either answer is defensible, and as long as we are careful in our subsequent analysis, nothing important will hinge on which answer we choose. Sometimes it's a bit arbitrary how we divide things between supply and demand.

In the macroeconomic model of the open economy developed in this chapter, the division of transactions between "supply" and "demand" is also a bit arbitrary. This is true both in the market for loanable funds and in the market for foreign-currency exchange.

Consider first the market for loanable funds. The model treats the net capital outflow as part of the demand for loanable funds. Yet instead of writing $S = I + NCO$, we could just as easily have written $S - NCO = I$. When the equation is rewritten in this way, a capital outflow looks like a reduction in the supply of loanable funds. Either way would have worked. The first interpretation ($S = I + NCO$) emphasizes loanable funds generated domestically whether used at home or abroad. The second interpretation ($S - NCO = I$) emphasizes loanable funds available for domestic investment whether generated at home or abroad. The difference is more semantic than substantive.

Similarly, consider the market for foreign-currency exchange. In our model, net exports are the source of the demand for dollars, and net capital outflow is the source of the supply. Thus, when a U.S. resident imports a car made in Japan, our model treats that transaction as a decrease in the quantity of dollars demanded (because net exports fall) rather than an increase in the quantity of dollars supplied. Similarly, when a Japanese citizen buys a U.S. government bond, our model treats that transaction as a decrease in the quantity of dollars supplied (because net capital outflow falls) rather than an increase in the quantity of dollars demanded. This definition of terms may seem somewhat unnatural at first, but it will prove useful when analyzing the effects of various policies.

the quantity of net capital outflow from panel (b) determines the supply of dollars to be exchanged into foreign currencies. The real exchange rate does not affect net capital outflow, so the supply curve is vertical. The demand for dollars comes from net exports. Because a depreciation of the real exchange rate increases net exports, the demand curve for foreign-currency exchange slopes downward. The equilibrium real exchange rate (E_1) brings into balance the quantity of dollars supplied and the quantity of dollars demanded in the market for foreign-currency exchange.

The two markets shown in Figure 4 determine two relative prices: the real interest rate and the real exchange rate. The real interest rate determined in panel (a) is the price of goods and services in the present relative to goods and services in the future. The real exchange rate determined in panel (c) is the price of domestic goods and services relative to foreign goods and services. These two relative prices adjust simultaneously to balance supply and demand in these two markets. As they do so, they determine national saving, domestic investment, net capital outflow, and net exports. In a moment, we will use this model to see how all these variables change when some policy or event causes one of these curves to shift.

Quick Quiz   In the model of the open economy just developed, two markets determine two relative prices. What are the markets? What are the two relative prices?

HOW POLICIES AND EVENTS AFFECT AN OPEN ECONOMY

Having developed a model to explain how key macroeconomic variables are determined in an open economy, we can now use the model to analyze how changes in policy and other events alter the economy's equilibrium. As we proceed, keep in mind that our model is just supply and demand in two markets: the market for loanable funds and the market for foreign-currency exchange. When using the model to analyze any event, we can apply the three steps outlined in Chapter 4. First, we determine which of the supply and demand curves the event affects. Second, we determine which way the curves shift. Third, we use the supply-and-demand diagrams to examine how these shifts alter the economy's equilibrium.

Government Budget Deficits

When we first discussed the supply and demand for loanable funds earlier in the book, we examined the effects of government budget deficits, which occur when government spending exceeds government revenue. Because a government budget deficit represents *negative* public saving, it reduces national saving (the sum of public and private saving). Thus, a government budget deficit reduces the supply of loanable funds, drives up the interest rate, and crowds out investment.

Now let's consider the effects of a budget deficit in an open economy. First, which curve in our model shifts? As in a closed economy, the initial impact of the budget deficit is on national saving and, therefore, on the supply curve for loanable funds. Second, which way does this supply curve shift? Again as in a closed economy, a budget deficit represents *negative* public saving, so it reduces national saving and shifts the supply curve for loanable funds to the left. This is shown as the shift from S_1 to S_2 in panel (a) of Figure 5.

Our third and final step is to compare the old and new equilibria. Panel (a) shows the impact of a U.S. budget deficit on the U.S. market for loanable funds. With fewer funds available for borrowers in U.S. financial markets, the interest rate rises from r_1 to r_2 to balance supply and demand. Faced with a higher interest rate, borrowers in the market for loanable funds choose to borrow less. This change is represented in the figure as the movement from point A to point B along the demand curve for loanable funds. In particular, households and firms reduce their purchases of capital goods. As in a closed economy, budget deficits crowd out domestic investment.

In an open economy, however, the reduced supply of loanable funds has additional effects. Panel (b) shows that the increase in the interest rate from r_1 to r_2 reduces net capital outflow. (This fall in net capital outflow is also part of the decrease in the quantity of loanable funds demanded in the movement from point A to point B in panel (a).) Because saving kept at home now earns higher rates of return, investing abroad is less attractive, and domestic residents buy fewer foreign assets. Higher interest rates also attract foreign investors, who want to earn the higher returns on U.S. assets. Thus, when budget deficits raise interest rates, both domestic and foreign behavior cause U.S. net capital outflow to fall.

Panel (c) shows how budget deficits affect the market for foreign-currency exchange. Because net capital outflow is reduced, people need less foreign currency to buy foreign assets and, therefore, supply fewer dollars in the market for foreign-currency exchange. The supply curve for dollars shifts leftward from S_1 to S_2. The reduced supply of dollars causes the real exchange rate to appreciate

When the government runs a budget deficit, it reduces the supply of loanable funds from S_1 to S_2 in panel (a). The interest rate rises from r_1 to r_2 to balance the supply and demand for loanable funds. In panel (b), the higher interest rate reduces net capital outflow. Reduced net capital outflow, in turn, reduces the supply of dollars in the market for foreign-currency exchange from S_1 to S_2 in panel (c). This fall in the supply of dollars causes the real exchange rate to appreciate from E_1 to E_2. The appreciation of the exchange rate pushes the trade balance toward deficit.

FIGURE **5**

The Effects of a Government Budget Deficit

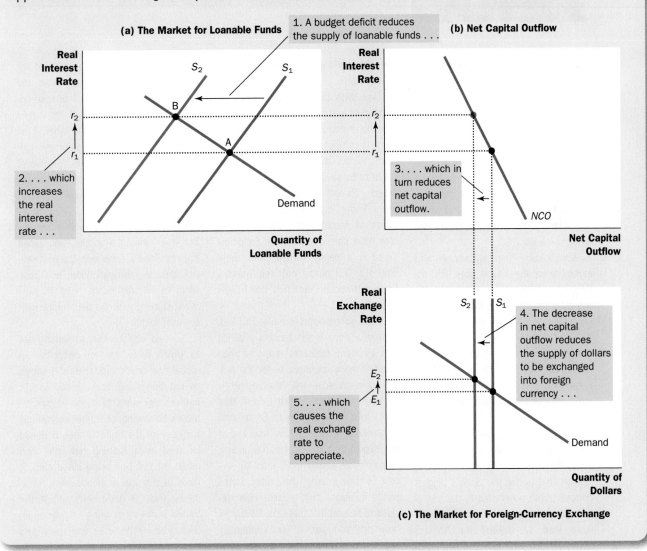

(a) The Market for Loanable Funds

1. A budget deficit reduces the supply of loanable funds . . .

2. . . . which increases the real interest rate . . .

(b) Net Capital Outflow

3. . . . which in turn reduces net capital outflow.

4. The decrease in net capital outflow reduces the supply of dollars to be exchanged into foreign currency . . .

5. . . . which causes the real exchange rate to appreciate.

(c) The Market for Foreign-Currency Exchange

from E_1 to E_2. That is, the dollar becomes more valuable compared to foreign currencies. This appreciation, in turn, makes U.S. goods more expensive compared to foreign goods. Because people both at home and abroad switch their purchases away from the more expensive U.S. goods, exports from the United States fall, and imports into the United States rise. For both reasons, U.S. net exports fall. Hence, *in an open economy, government budget deficits raise real interest*

In The News

The U.S. Trade Deficit

Economist Kenneth Rogoff discusses the U.S. trade deficit, which reached record levels in 2003 and 2004.

The Debtor's Empire

By Kenneth Rogoff

Isn't it just a little twisted that the United States, the world's richest country, is on track to borrow more than $500 billion from abroad this year? Isn't it even stranger that this borrowing includes sizable chunks from countries such as India and China, many of whose 2.3 billion people live on less than a dollar or two a day?

Sure, I know there are reasons why money flows the way it does. For one thing, the United States has a long history of treating foreign investors pretty decently, going back to the 1780s, when the first Treasury secretary, Alexander Hamilton, decided to honor pre-Revolutionary War debt. And the United States is growing decently (roughly 4 percent next year), albeit less than India (6 percent) or China (8 percent).

But whatever the reasons, and they are admittedly complex, isn't it still a bit nutty that the world's richest country has become by far the world's biggest borrower, with a net debt to the rest of the world (assets minus liabilities) of more than $2 trillion? The Romans would be jealous: They went to a lot of trouble to extract taxes from their em- pire; the world just gives money to the United States.

Even with the morality of it all set aside, pure self-interest ought to dictate that the United States be a net lender to the rest of the world rather than a bor- rower. We are an aging population that ought to be saving for retirement in real assets abroad. Unfortunately, you'd never know it from the consumption frenzy of recent years. We Americans may have coined the phrase "a penny saved is a penny earned," but these days it's "I'll gladly pay you Tuesday for a genetically modified hamburger today."

State governments are bleeding red. California alone is still running a deficit that by many measures is bigger than those of many countries. As for the fed- eral government—well, Washington is on track to achieve deficit records that could take a generation to break. And the American consumer? We save less of our income than any other rich economy. China's citizens save more than 40 per- cent of their income; the United States would be lucky if its citizens ever de- cided to save at half that rate. No matter how rich you are, if you continually spend more than you earn, you are even- tually going to run into problems. . . .

So what to do? Do we just hold our collective breath and pray that the biggest borrowing binge of all time un- winds smoothly, no sweat? Or should we be a little worried that when it all ends, we will be yearning for the hal- cyon days of the "jobless" recovery? Well, it would help if Europe and Japan grew a bit faster. But growth abroad can't be the whole story; China is al- ready growing much faster than we are, but it is running a surplus, and Japan has remained a saver over the past sev- eral decades, through boom and bust. Most of all, Americans need to save more, starting with the debt-happy gov- ernment sector.

Is it so obvious that something has to give? There are no certainties in global economics, but when a country's overall borrowing from abroad (public and private) starts to mirror its govern- ment's borrowing, as is now increasingly the case for the United States, it should be read as a flashing red light. And when the U.S. borrowing binge ends, it could be a global economic mess. Fortu- nately, there is good news too. If the United States starts being a lender again then, just maybe, after any mess gets cleaned up, the world will make a little bit more sense.

Source: *The Washington Post*, October 20, 2003. Copyright © 2003 by Kenneth Rogoff.

rates, crowd out domestic investment, cause the currency to appreciate, and push the trade balance toward deficit.

An important example of this lesson occurred in the United States in the 1980s. Shortly after Ronald Reagan was elected president in 1980, the fiscal policy of the U.S. federal government changed dramatically. The president and Congress enacted large cuts in taxes, but they did not cut government spending by nearly as much, so the result was a large budget deficit. Our model of the open economy predicts that such a policy should lead to a trade deficit, and in fact it did, as we saw in a case study in the preceding chapter. The budget deficit and trade deficit during this period were so closely related in both theory and practice that they earned the nickname the *twin deficits*. We should not, however, view these twins as identical, for many factors beyond fiscal policy can influence the trade deficit.

Trade Policy

A **trade policy** is a government policy that directly influences the quantity of goods and services that a country imports or exports. Trade policy takes various forms. One common trade policy is a *tariff*, a tax on imported goods. Another is an *import quota*, a limit on the quantity of a good produced abroad that can be sold domestically. Trade policies are common throughout the world, although sometimes they are disguised. For example, the U.S. government has sometimes pressured Japanese automakers to reduce the number of cars they sell in the United States. These so-called "voluntary export restrictions" are not really voluntary and, in essence, are a form of import quota.

Let's consider the macroeconomic impact of trade policy. Suppose that the U.S. auto industry, concerned about competition from Japanese automakers, convinces the U.S. government to impose a quota on the number of cars that can be imported from Japan. In making their case, lobbyists for the auto industry assert that the trade restriction would shrink the size of the U.S. trade deficit. Are they right? Our model, as illustrated in Figure 6, offers an answer.

The first step in analyzing the trade policy is to determine which curve shifts. The initial impact of the import restriction is, not surprisingly, on imports. Because net exports equal exports minus imports, the policy also affects net exports. And because net exports are the source of demand for dollars in the market for foreign-currency exchange, the policy affects the demand curve in this market.

The second step is to determine which way this demand curve shifts. Because the quota restricts the number of Japanese cars sold in the United States, it reduces imports at any given real exchange rate. Net exports, which equal exports minus imports, will therefore *rise* for any given real exchange rate. Because foreigners need dollars to buy U.S. net exports, there is an increased demand for dollars in the market for foreign-currency exchange. This increase in the demand for dollars is shown in panel (c) of Figure 6 as the shift from D_1 to D_2.

The third step is to compare the old and new equilibria. As we can see in panel (c), the increase in the demand for dollars causes the real exchange rate to appreciate from E_1 to E_2. Because nothing has happened in the market for loanable funds in panel (a), there is no change in the real interest rate. Because there is no change in the real interest rate, there is also no change in net capital outflow, shown in panel (b). And because there is no change in net capital outflow, there can be no change in net exports, even though the import quota has reduced imports.

The reason net exports can stay the same while imports fall is explained by the change in the real exchange rate: When the dollar appreciates in value in the market for foreign-currency exchange, domestic goods become more expensive

trade policy
a government policy that directly influences the quantity of goods and services that a country imports or exports

FIGURE

The Effects of an
Import Quota

When the U.S. government imposes a quota on the import of Japanese cars, nothing happens in the market for loanable funds in panel (a) or to net capital outflow in panel (b). The only effect is a rise in net exports (exports minus imports) for any given real exchange rate. As a result, the demand for dollars in the market for foreign-currency exchange rises, as shown by the shift from D_1 to D_2 in panel (c). This increase in the demand for dollars causes the value of the dollar to appreciate from E_1 to E_2. This appreciation of the dollar tends to reduce net exports, offsetting the direct effect of the import quota on the trade balance.

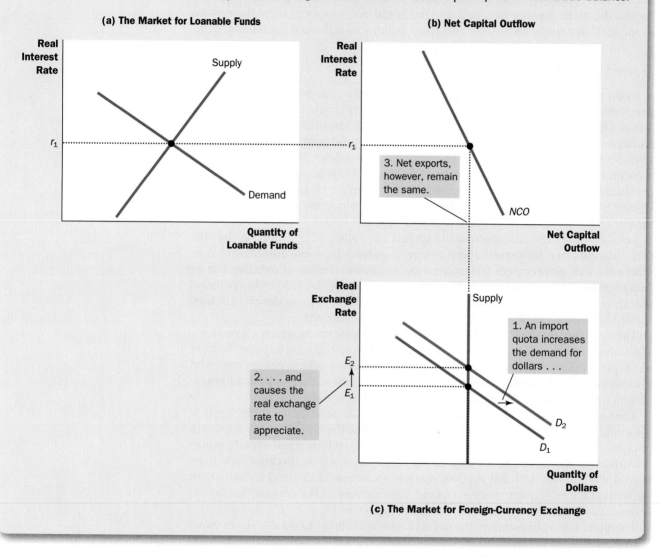

relative to foreign goods. This appreciation encourages imports and discourages exports, and both of these changes work to offset the direct increase in net exports due to the import quota. In the end, an import quota reduces both imports and exports, but net exports (exports minus imports) are unchanged.

We have thus come to a surprising implication: *Trade policies do not affect the trade balance.* That is, policies that directly influence exports or imports do not alter net exports. This conclusion seems less surprising if one recalls the accounting identity:

$$NX = NCO = S - I.$$

Net exports equal net capital outflow, which equals national saving minus domestic investment. Trade policies do not alter the trade balance because they do not alter national saving or domestic investment. For given levels of national saving and domestic investment, the real exchange rate adjusts to keep the trade balance the same, regardless of the trade policies the government puts in place.

Although trade policies do not affect a country's overall trade balance, these policies do affect specific firms, industries, and countries. When the U.S. government imposes an import quota on Japanese cars, General Motors has less competition from abroad and will sell more cars. At the same time, because the dollar has appreciated in value, Boeing, the U.S. aircraft maker, will find it harder to compete with Airbus, the European aircraft maker. U.S. exports of aircraft will fall, and U.S. imports of aircraft will rise. In this case, the import quota on Japanese cars will increase net exports of cars and decrease net exports of planes. In addition, it will increase net exports from the United States to Japan and decrease net exports from the United States to Europe. The overall trade balance of the U.S. economy, however, stays the same.

The effects of trade policies are, therefore, more microeconomic than macroeconomic. Although advocates of trade policies sometimes claim (incorrectly) that these policies can alter a country's trade balance, they are usually more motivated by concerns about particular firms or industries. One should not be surprised, for instance, to hear an executive from General Motors advocating import quotas for Japanese cars. Economists almost always oppose such trade policies. Free trade allows economies to specialize in doing what they do best, making residents of all countries better off. Trade restrictions interfere with these gains from trade and, thus, reduce overall economic well-being.

Political Instability and Capital Flight

In 1994, political instability in Mexico, including the assassination of a prominent political leader, made world financial markets nervous. People began to view Mexico as a much less stable country than they had previously thought. They decided to pull some of their assets out of Mexico to move these funds to the United States and other "safe havens." Such a large and sudden movement of funds out of a country is called **capital flight.** To see the implications of capital flight for the Mexican economy, we again follow our three steps for analyzing a change in equilibrium, but this time, we apply our model of the open economy from the perspective of Mexico rather than the United States.

Consider first which curves in our model capital flight affects. When investors around the world observe political problems in Mexico, they decide to sell some of their Mexican assets and use the proceeds to buy U.S. assets. This act increases Mexican net capital outflow and, therefore, affects both markets in our model. Most obviously, it affects the net-capital-outflow curve, and this in turn influences the supply of pesos in the market for foreign-currency exchange. In addition, because the demand for loanable funds comes from both domestic investment and net capital outflow, capital flight affects the demand curve in the market for loanable funds.

Now consider which way these curves shift. When net capital outflow increases, there is greater demand for loanable funds to finance these purchases

capital flight
a large and sudden reduction in the demand for assets located in a country

of capital assets abroad. Thus, as panel (a) of Figure 7 shows, the demand curve for loanable funds shifts to the right from D_1 to D_2. In addition, because net capital outflow is higher for any interest rate, the net-capital-outflow curve also shifts to the right from NCO_1 to NCO_2, as in panel (b).

7 FIGURE

The Effects of Capital Flight

If people decide that Mexico is a risky place to keep their savings, they will move their capital to safer havens such as the United States, resulting in an increase in Mexican net capital outflow. Consequently, the demand for loanable funds in Mexico rises from D_1 to D_2, as shown in panel (a), and this drives up the Mexican real interest rate from r_1 to r_2. Because net capital outflow is higher for any interest rate, that curve also shifts to the right from NCO_1 to NCO_2 in panel (b). At the same time, in the market for foreign-currency exchange, the supply of pesos rises from S_1 to S_2, as shown in panel (c). This increase in the supply of pesos causes the peso to depreciate from E_1 to E_2, so the peso becomes less valuable compared to other currencies.

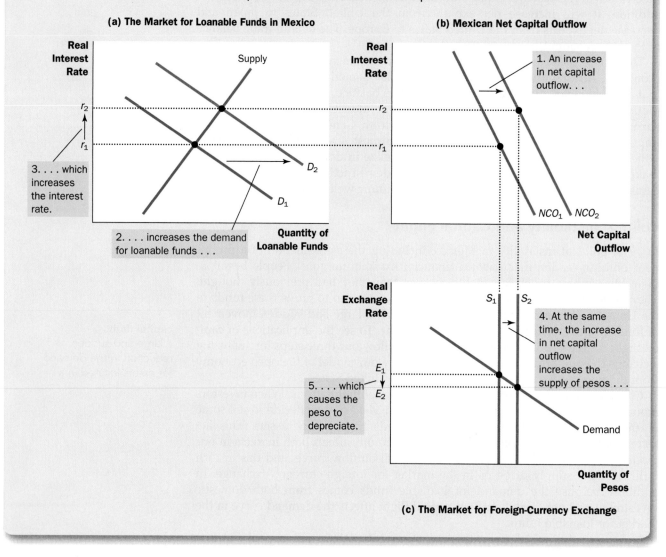

(a) The Market for Loanable Funds in Mexico

Real Interest Rate

Supply

r_2

r_1

3. . . . which increases the interest rate.

2. . . . increases the demand for loanable funds . . .

D_2

D_1

Quantity of Loanable Funds

(b) Mexican Net Capital Outflow

Real Interest Rate

1. An increase in net capital outflow. . .

r_2

r_1

NCO_1 NCO_2

Net Capital Outflow

Real Exchange Rate

S_1 S_2

4. At the same time, the increase in net capital outflow increases the supply of pesos . . .

E_1

5. . . . which causes the peso to depreciate.

E_2

Demand

Quantity of Pesos

(c) The Market for Foreign-Currency Exchange

To see the effects of capital flight on the Mexican economy, we compare the old and new equilibria. Panel (a) of Figure 7 shows that the increased demand for loanable funds causes the interest rate in Mexico to rise from r_1 to r_2. Panel (b) shows that Mexican net capital outflow increases. (Although the rise in the interest rate does make Mexican assets more attractive, this only partly offsets the impact of capital flight on net capital outflow.) Panel (c) shows that the increase in net capital outflow raises the supply of pesos in the market for foreign-currency exchange from S_1 to S_2. That is, as people try to get out of Mexican assets, there is a large supply of pesos to be converted into dollars. This increase in supply causes the peso to depreciate from E_1 to E_2. Thus, *capital flight from Mexico increases Mexican interest rates and decreases the value of the Mexican peso in the market for foreign-currency exchange.* This is exactly what was observed in 1994. From November 1994 to March 1995, the interest rate on short-term Mexican government bonds rose from 14 percent to 70 percent, and the peso depreciated in value from 29 to 15 U.S. cents per peso.

These price changes that result from capital flight influence some key macroeconomic quantities. The depreciation of the currency makes exports cheaper and imports more expensive, pushing the trade balance toward surplus. At the same time, the increase in the interest rate reduces domestic investment, which slows capital accumulation and economic growth.

Although capital flight has its largest impact on the country from which capital is fleeing, it also affects other countries. When capital flows out of Mexico into the United States, for instance, it has the opposite effect on the U.S. economy as it has on the Mexican economy. In particular, the rise in Mexican net capital outflow coincides with a fall in U.S. net capital outflow. As the peso depreciates in value and Mexican interest rates rise, the dollar appreciates in value and U.S. interest rates fall. The size of this impact on the U.S. economy is small, however, because the economy of the United States is so large compared to that of Mexico.

The events that we have been describing in Mexico could happen to any economy in the world, and in fact, they do from time to time. In 1997, the world learned that the banking systems of several Asian economies, including Thailand, South Korea, and Indonesia, were at or near the point of bankruptcy, and this news induced capital to flee from these nations. In 1998, the Russian government defaulted on its debt, inducing international investors to take whatever money they could and run. A similar (but more complicated) set of events unfolded in Argentina in 2002. In each of these cases of capital flight, the results were much as our model predicts: rising interest rates and a falling currency.

CASE STUDY | COULD CAPITAL FLEE FROM THE UNITED STATES?

The U.S. economy has long been viewed as a safe economy in which to invest. Historical examples of capital flight usually occur in less developed nations, which are more likely to follow policies that induce sudden fear among international investors. Yet lessons learned abroad can sometimes become relevant at home.

Political developments in the United States have at times induced small amounts of capital flight. For example, the September 22, 1995, issue of *The New York Times* reported that on the previous day, "House Speaker Newt Gingrich threatened to send the United States into default on its debt for the first time in the nation's history, to force the Clinton administration to balance the budget on

Republican terms" (p. A1). Even though most people believed such a default was unlikely, the effect of the announcement was, in a small way, similar to that experienced by Mexico in 1994. The interest rate on a 30-year U.S. government bond rose from 6.46 percent to 6.55 percent, and the exchange rate fell from 102.7 to 99.0 yen per dollar—unusually large moves over the course of a single day. Thus, even the stable U.S. economy is potentially susceptible to the effects of capital flight.

New York Times columnist Paul Krugman has in recent years suggested that the U.S. economy may be headed for a more dramatic episode. His concerns are based on the recurrence of the twin deficits under President George W. Bush. He has written (on January 6, 2004):

> The traditional immunity of advanced countries like America to third-world-style financial crises isn't a birthright. Financial markets give us the benefit of the doubt only because they believe in our political maturity—in the willingness of our leaders to do what is necessary to rein in deficits, paying a political cost if necessary. And in the past that belief has been justified. Even Ronald Reagan raised taxes when the budget deficit soared.
>
> But do we still have that kind of maturity? Here's the opening sentence of a recent *New York Times* article on the administration's budget plans: "Facing a record budget deficit, Bush administration officials say they have drafted an election-year budget that will rein in the growth of domestic spending without alienating politically influential constituencies." Needless to say, the proposed spending cuts—focused only on the powerless—are both cruel and trivial.
>
> If this kind of fecklessness goes on, investors will eventually conclude that America has turned into a third world country, and start to treat it like one. And the results for the U.S. economy won't be pretty.

Krugman is suggesting that the United States could experience a major bout of capital flight.

Most economists are less alarmist than Krugman. But all agree that the United States is not immune to the laws of economics.   •

Quick Quiz   Suppose that Americans decided to spend a smaller fraction of their incomes. What would be the effect on saving, investment, interest rates, the real exchange rate, and the trade balance?

CONCLUSION

International economics is a topic of increasing importance. More and more, American citizens are buying goods produced abroad and producing goods to be sold overseas. Through mutual funds and other financial institutions, they borrow and lend in world financial markets. As a result, a full analysis of the U.S. economy requires an understanding of how the U.S. economy interacts with other economies in the world. This chapter has provided a basic model for thinking about the macroeconomics of open economies.

Although the study of international economics is valuable, we should be careful not to exaggerate its importance. Policymakers and commentators are often quick to blame foreigners for problems facing the U.S. economy. By contrast, economists more often view these problems as homegrown. For example, politicians often discuss foreign competition as a threat to American living standards. Economists are more likely to lament the low level of national saving. Low saving impedes growth in capital, productivity, and living standards, regardless of whether the economy is open or closed. Foreigners are a convenient target for politicians because blaming foreigners provides a way to avoid responsibility without insulting any domestic constituency. Whenever you hear popular discussions of international trade and finance, therefore, it is especially important to try to separate myth from reality. The tools you have learned in the past two chapters should help in that endeavor.

SUMMARY

- To analyze the macroeconomics of open economies, two markets are central: the market for loanable funds and the market for foreign-currency exchange. In the market for loanable funds, the real interest rate adjusts to balance the supply of loanable funds (from national saving) and the demand for loanable funds (from domestic investment and net capital outflow). In the market for foreign-currency exchange, the real exchange rate adjusts to balance the supply of dollars (from net capital outflow) and the demand for dollars (for net exports). Because net capital outflow is part of the demand for loanable funds and because it provides the supply of dollars for foreign-currency exchange, it is the variable that connects these two markets.

- A policy that reduces national saving, such as a government budget deficit, reduces the supply of loanable funds and drives up the interest rate. The higher interest rate reduces net capital outflow, which reduces the supply of dollars in the

market for foreign-currency exchange. The dollar appreciates, and net exports fall.

- Although restrictive trade policies, such as tariffs or quotas on imports, are sometimes advocated as a way to alter the trade balance, they do not necessarily have that effect. A trade restriction increases net exports for a given exchange rate and, therefore, increases the demand for dollars in the market for foreign-currency exchange. As a result, the dollar appreciates in value, making domestic goods more expensive relative to foreign goods. This appreciation offsets the initial impact of the trade restriction on net exports.

- When investors change their attitudes about holding assets of a country, the ramifications for the country's economy can be profound. In particular, political instability can lead to capital flight, which tends to increase interest rates and cause the currency to depreciate.

KEY CONCEPTS

trade policy, p. 311
capital flight, p. 313

QUESTIONS FOR REVIEW

1. Describe supply and demand in the market for loanable funds and the market for foreign-currency exchange. How are these markets linked?

2. Why are budget deficits and trade deficits sometimes called the twin deficits?

3. Suppose that a textile workers' union encourages people to buy only American-made clothes. What would this policy do to the trade balance and the real exchange rate? What is the impact on the textile industry? What is the impact on the auto industry?

4. What is capital flight? When a country experiences capital flight, what is the effect on its interest rate and exchange rate?

PROBLEMS AND APPLICATIONS

1. Japan generally runs a significant trade surplus. Do you think this is most related to high foreign demand for Japanese goods, low Japanese demand for foreign goods, a high Japanese saving rate relative to Japanese investment, or structural barriers against imports into Japan? Explain your answer.

2. An article in *USA Today* (December 16, 2004) began "President Bush said Wednesday that the White House will shore up the sliding dollar by working to cut record budget and trade deficits."
   a. According to the model in this chapter, would a reduction in the budget deficit reduce the trade deficit? Would it raise the value of the dollar? Explain.
   b. Suppose that a reduction in the budget deficit made international investors more confident in the U.S. economy. How would this increase in confidence affect the value of the dollar? How would it affect the trade deficit?

3. Suppose that Congress passes an investment tax credit, which subsidizes domestic investment. How does this policy affect national saving, domestic investment, net capital outflow, the interest rate, the exchange rate, and the trade balance?

4. The chapter notes that the rise in the U.S. trade deficit during the 1980s was due largely to the rise in the U.S. budget deficit. On the other hand, the popular press sometimes claims that the increased trade deficit resulted from a decline in the quality of U.S. products relative to foreign products.
   a. Assume that U.S. products did decline in relative quality during the 1980s. How did this affect net exports *at any given exchange rate*?
   b. Draw a three-panel diagram to show the effect of this shift in net exports on the U.S. real exchange rate and trade balance.
   c. Is the claim in the popular press consistent with the model in this chapter? Does a decline in the quality of U.S. products have any effect on our standard of living? (Hint: When we sell our goods to foreigners, what do we receive in return?)

5. An economist discussing trade policy in *The New Republic* wrote: "One of the benefits of the United States removing its trade restrictions [is] the gain to U.S. industries that produce goods for export. Export industries would find it easier to sell their goods abroad—even if other countries didn't follow our example and reduce their trade barriers." Explain in words why U.S. *export* industries would benefit from a reduction in restrictions on *imports* to the United States.

6. Suppose the French suddenly develop a strong taste for California wines. Answer the following questions in words and with a diagram.
   a. What happens to the demand for dollars in the market for foreign-currency exchange?
   b. What happens to the value of dollars in the market for foreign-currency exchange?
   c. What happens to the quantity of net exports?

7. A senator renounces her past support for protectionism: "The U.S. trade deficit must be reduced, but import quotas only annoy our trading partners. If we subsidize U.S. exports instead, we

can reduce the deficit by increasing our competitiveness." Using a three-panel diagram, show the effect of an export subsidy on net exports and the real exchange rate. Do you agree with the senator?

8. Suppose that real interest rates increase across Europe. Explain how this development will affect U.S. net capital outflow. Then explain how it will affect U.S. net exports by using a formula from the chapter and by drawing a diagram. What will happen to the U.S. real interest rate and real exchange rate?

9. Suppose that Americans decide to increase their saving.
   a. If the elasticity of U.S. net capital outflow with respect to the real interest rate is very high, will this increase in private saving have a large or small effect on U.S. domestic investment?
   b. If the elasticity of U.S. exports with respect to the real exchange rate is very low, will this increase in private saving have a large or small effect on the U.S. real exchange rate?

10. Over the past decade, some of Japanese saving has been used to finance American investment. That is, the Japanese have been buying American capital assets.
    a. If the Japanese decided they no longer wanted to buy U.S. assets, what would happen in the U.S. market for loanable funds? In particular, what would happen to U.S. interest rates, U.S. saving, and U.S. investment?

    b. What would happen in the market for foreign-currency exchange? In particular, what would happen to the value of the dollar and the U.S. trade balance?

11. In 1998, the Russian government defaulted on its debt payments, leading investors worldwide to raise their preference for U.S. government bonds, which are considered very safe. What effect do you think this "flight to safety" had on the U.S. economy? Be sure to note the impact on national saving, domestic investment, net capital outflow, the interest rate, the exchange rate, and the trade balance.

12. Suppose that U.S. mutual funds suddenly decide to invest more in Canada.
    a. What happens to Canadian net capital outflow, Canadian saving, and Canadian domestic investment?
    b. What is the long-run effect on the Canadian capital stock?
    c. How will this change in the capital stock affect the Canadian labor market? Does this U.S. investment in Canada make Canadian workers better off or worse off?
    d. Do you think this will make U.S. workers better off or worse off? Can you think of any reason the impact on U.S. citizens generally may be different from the impact on U.S. workers?

 For further information on topics in this chapter, additional problems, examples, applications, online quizzes, and more, please visit our website at http://mankiw.swlearning.com.

Short-Run Economic Fluctuations

15

Aggregate Demand and Aggregate Supply

Economic activity fluctuates from year to year. In most years, the production of goods and services rises. Because of increases in the labor force, increases in the capital stock, and advances in technological knowledge, the economy can produce more and more over time. This growth allows everyone to enjoy a higher standard of living. On average over the past 50 years, the production of the U.S. economy as measured by real GDP has grown by about 3 percent per year.

In some years, however, this normal growth does not occur. Firms find themselves unable to sell all of the goods and services they have to offer, so they cut back on production. Workers are laid off, unemployment rises, and factories are left idle. With the economy producing fewer goods and services, real GDP and other measures of income fall. Such a period of falling incomes and rising unemployment is called a **recession** if it is relatively mild and a **depression** if it is more severe.

What causes short-run fluctuations in economic activity? What, if anything, can public policy do to prevent periods of falling incomes and rising unemployment? When recessions and depressions occur, how can policymakers reduce their length and severity? These are the questions that we take up now.

The variables that we study are largely those we have already seen in previous chapters. They include GDP, unemployment, interest rates, and the price

recession
a period of declining real incomes and rising unemployment

depression
a severe recession

level. Also familiar are the policy instruments of government spending, taxes, and the money supply. What differs from our earlier analysis is the time horizon. So far, our focus has been on the behavior of the economy in the long run. Our focus now is on the economy's short-run fluctuations around its long-run trend.

Although there remains some debate among economists about how to analyze short-run fluctuations, most economists use the *model of aggregate demand and aggregate supply.* Learning how to use this model for analyzing the short-run effects of various events and policies is the primary task ahead. This chapter introduces the model's two pieces: the aggregate-demand curve and the aggregate-supply curve. But before turning to the model, let's look at some of the key facts that describe the ups and downs in the economy.

THREE KEY FACTS ABOUT ECONOMIC FLUCTUATIONS

Short-run fluctuations in economic activity occur in all countries and have occurred throughout history. As a starting point for understanding these year-to-year fluctuations, let's discuss some of their most important properties.

Fact 1: Economic Fluctuations Are Irregular and Unpredictable

Fluctuations in the economy are often called *the business cycle.* As this term suggests, economic fluctuations correspond to changes in business conditions. When real GDP grows rapidly, business is good. During such periods of economic expansion, most firms find that customers are plentiful and that profits are growing. When real GDP falls during recessions, businesses have trouble. During such periods of economic contraction, most firms experience declining sales and dwindling profits.

The term *business cycle* is somewhat misleading because it suggests that economic fluctuations follow a regular, predictable pattern. In fact, economic fluctuations are not at all regular, and they are almost impossible to predict with much accuracy. Panel (a) of Figure 1 shows the real GDP of the U.S. economy since 1965. The shaded areas represent times of recession. As the figure shows, recessions do not come at regular intervals. Sometimes recessions are close together, such as the recessions of 1980 and 1982. Sometimes the economy goes many years without a recession. The longest period in U.S. history without a recession was the economic expansion from 1991 to 2001.

Fact 2: Most Macroeconomic Quantities Fluctuate Together

Real GDP is the variable that is most commonly used to monitor short-run changes in the economy because it is the most comprehensive measure of economic activity. Real GDP measures the value of all final goods and services produced within a given period of time. It also measures the total income (adjusted for inflation) of everyone in the economy.

It turns out, however, that for monitoring short-run fluctuations, it does not really matter which measure of economic activity one looks at. Most macroeconomic variables that measure some type of income, spending, or production fluctuate closely together. When real GDP falls in a recession, so do personal income, corporate profits, consumer spending, investment spending, industrial

HOW TO DELEGATE
DURING A RECESSION

MANKOFF

"YOU'RE FIRED. PASS IT ON."

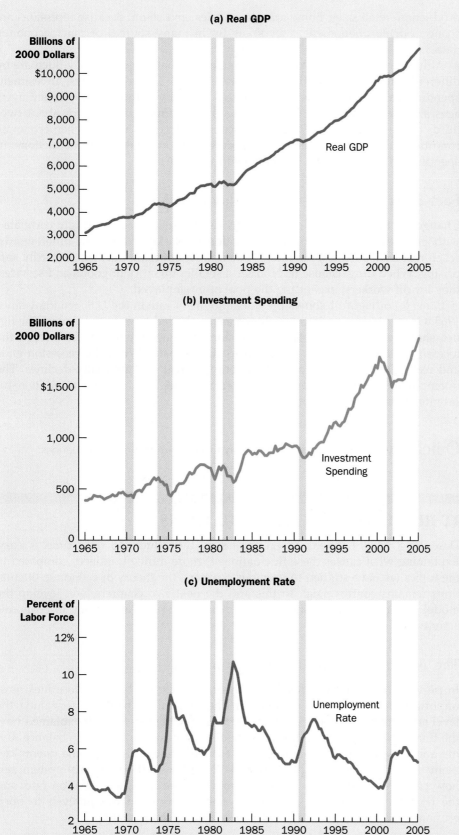

(a) Real GDP

(b) Investment Spending

(c) Unemployment Rate

FIGURE 1

A Look at Short-Run Economic Fluctuations
This figure shows real GDP in panel (a), investment spending in panel (b), and unemployment in panel (c) for the U.S. economy using quarterly data since 1965. Recessions are shown as the shaded areas. Notice that real GDP and investment spending decline during recessions, while unemployment rises.

Source: U.S. Department of Commerce; U.S. Department of Labor.

production, retail sales, home sales, auto sales, and so on. Because recessions are economy-wide phenomena, they show up in many sources of macroeconomic data.

Although many macroeconomic variables fluctuate together, they fluctuate by different amounts. In particular, as panel (b) of Figure 1 shows, investment spending varies greatly over the business cycle. Even though investment averages about one-seventh of GDP, declines in investment account for about two-thirds of the declines in GDP during recessions. In other words, when economic conditions deteriorate, much of the decline is attributable to reductions in spending on new factories, housing, and inventories.

Fact 3: As Output Falls, Unemployment Rises

Changes in the economy's output of goods and services are strongly correlated with changes in the economy's utilization of its labor force. In other words, when real GDP declines, the rate of unemployment rises. This fact is hardly surprising: When firms choose to produce a smaller quantity of goods and services, they lay off workers, expanding the pool of unemployed.

Panel (c) of Figure 1 shows the unemployment rate in the U.S. economy since 1965. Once again, recessions are shown as the shaded areas in the figure. The figure shows clearly the impact of recessions on unemployment. In each of the recessions, the unemployment rate rises substantially. When the recession ends and real GDP starts to expand, the unemployment rate gradually declines. The unemployment rate never approaches zero; instead, it fluctuates around its natural rate of about 5 or 6 percent.

Quick Quiz   List and discuss three key facts about economic fluctuations.

EXPLAINING SHORT-RUN ECONOMIC FLUCTUATIONS

Describing what happens to economies as they fluctuate over time is easy. Explaining what causes these fluctuations is more difficult. Indeed, compared to the topics we have studied in previous chapters, the theory of economic fluctuations remains controversial. In this and the next two chapters, we develop the model that most economists use to explain short-run fluctuations in economic activity.

The Assumptions of Classical Economics

In previous chapters, we developed theories to explain what determines most important macroeconomic variables in the long run. Chapter 7 explained the level and growth of productivity and real GDP. Chapters 8 and 9 explained how the financial system works and how the real interest rate adjusts to balance saving and investment. Chapter 10 explained why there is always some unemployment in the economy. Chapters 11 and 12 explained the monetary system and how changes in the money supply affect the price level, the inflation rate, and the nominal interest rate. Chapters 13 and 14 extended this analysis to open economies to explain the trade balance and the exchange rate.

In The News

Offbeat Indicators

When the economy goes into a recession, many economic variables are affected. This article, written during the recession of 2001, gives some examples.

Economic Numbers Befuddle Even the Best

By George Hager

Economists pore over scores of numbers every week, trying to sense when the recession is over. But quirky indicators and gut instinct might be almost as helpful—maybe even more so.

Is your dentist busy? Dentists say people put off appointments when times turn tough, then reschedule when the economy improves.

How far away do you have to park when you go to the mall? Fewer shoppers equal more parking spaces.

If you drive to work, has your commute time gotten shorter or longer?

Economist Michael Evans says a colleague with a pipeline into the garbage business swears by his own homegrown Chicago Trash index. Collections plunged after the Sept. 11 terror attacks, rebounded in October but then fell off again in mid-November. "Trash is a pretty good indicator of what people are buying," says Evans, an economist with Evans Carrol & Associates. "They've got to throw out the wrappings." . . .

What's actually happening is often clear only in hindsight. That's one reason the National Bureau of Economic Research waited until November to declare that a recession began last March—and why it took them until December 1992 to declare that the last recession had ended more than a year earlier, in March 1991.

"The data can fail you," says Allen Sinai, chief economist for Decision Economics. Sinai cautions that if numbers appear to be going up (or down), it's best to wait to see what happens over two or three months before drawing a conclusion—something hair-trigger financial markets routinely don't do.

"We have lots of false predictions of recoveries by (stock) markets that don't happen," he says.

Like a lot of economists, Sinai leavens the numbers with informal observations. These days, he's paying particular attention to what business executives say at meetings and cocktail parties because their mood—and their plans for investing and hiring—are key to a comeback.

Even the Federal Reserve, whose more than 200 economists monitor about every piece of the economy that can be measured, make room for anecdotes. Two weeks before every policy meeting, the Fed publishes its "beige book," a survey based on off-the-record conversations between officials at the Fed's 12 regional banks and local businesses.

The reports are peppered with quotes from unnamed business people ("Everybody's decided to go shopping again," someone told the Richmond Fed Bank last month) and the occasional odd detail that reveals just how far down the Fed inquisitors sometimes drill. Last March, the Dallas Fed Bank reported "healthy sales of singing gorillas" for Valentine's Day.

Source: *USA Today*, December 26, 2001. Reprinted with permission.

All of this previous analysis was based on two related ideas: the classical dichotomy and monetary neutrality. Recall that the classical dichotomy is the separation of variables into real variables (those that measure quantities or relative prices) and nominal variables (those measured in terms of money). According to classical macroeconomic theory, changes in the money supply affect nominal variables but not real variables. As a result of this monetary neutrality, Chapters 7 through 10 were able to examine the determinants of real variables (real GDP, the real interest rate, and unemployment) without introducing nominal variables (the money supply and the price level).

In a sense, money does not matter in a classical world. If the quantity of money in the economy were to double, everything would cost twice as much, and everyone's income would be twice as high. But so what? The change would be *nominal* (by the standard meaning of "nearly insignificant"). The things that people *really* care about—whether they have a job, how many goods and services they can afford, and so on—would be exactly the same.

This classical view is sometimes described by the saying, "Money is a veil." That is, nominal variables may be the first things we see when we observe an economy because economic variables are often expressed in units of money. But what's important are the real variables and the economic forces that determine them. According to classical theory, to understand these real variables, we need to look beneath the veil.

The Reality of Short-Run Fluctuations

Do these assumptions of classical macroeconomic theory apply to the world in which we live? The answer to this question is of central importance to understanding how the economy works. *Most economists believe that classical theory describes the world in the long run but not in the short run.*

Consider again the impact of money on the economy. Most economists believe that, beyond a period of several years, changes in the money supply affect prices and other nominal variables but do not affect real GDP, unemployment, or other real variables—just as classical theory says. When studying year-to-year changes in the economy, however, the assumption of monetary neutrality is no longer appropriate. In the short run, real and nominal variables are highly intertwined, and changes in the money supply can temporarily push real GDP away from its long-run trend.

Even the classical economists themselves, such as David Hume, realized that classical economic theory did not hold in the short run. From his vantage point in 18th-century England, Hume observed that when the money supply expanded after gold discoveries, it took some time for prices to rise, and in the meantime, the economy enjoyed higher employment and production.

To understand how the economy works in the short run, we need a new model. This new model can be built using many of the tools we developed in previous chapters, but it must abandon the classical dichotomy and the neutrality of money. We can no longer separate our analysis of real variables such as output and employment from our analysis of nominal variable such as money and the price level. Our new model focuses on how real and nominal variables interact.

The Model of Aggregate Demand and Aggregate Supply

Our model of short-run economic fluctuations focuses on the behavior of two variables. The first variable is the economy's output of goods and services, as measured by real GDP. The second is the average level of prices, as measured by the CPI or the GDP deflator. Notice that output is a real variable, whereas the price level is a nominal variable. By focusing on the relationship between these two variables, we are departing from the classical assumption that real and nominal variables can be studied separately.

We analyze fluctuations in the economy as a whole with the **model of aggregate demand and aggregate supply,** which is illustrated in Figure 2. On the vertical axis is the overall price level in the economy. On the horizontal axis is the overall quantity of goods and services produced in the economy. The **aggregate-demand curve** shows the quantity of goods and services that households, firms, the government, and customers abroad want to buy at each price level. The **aggregate-supply curve** shows the quantity of goods and services that firms produce and sell at each price level. According to this model, the price level and the quantity of output adjust to bring aggregate demand and aggregate supply into balance.

It is tempting to view the model of aggregate demand and aggregate supply as nothing more than a large version of the model of market demand and market supply introduced in Chapter 4. In fact, this model is quite different. When we consider demand and supply in a particular market—ice cream, for instance—the behavior of buyers and sellers depends on the ability of resources to move from one market to another. When the price of ice cream rises, the quantity demanded falls because buyers will use their incomes to buy products other than ice cream. Similarly, a higher price of ice cream raises the quantity supplied because firms that produce ice cream can increase production by hiring workers away from other parts of the economy. This *microeconomic* substitution from one market to another is impossible for the economy as a whole. After all, the quantity that our model is trying to explain—real GDP—measures the *total* quantity of goods and services produced in *all* markets. To understand why the aggregate-demand curve is downward sloping and why the aggregate-supply curve is upward sloping, we need a *macroeconomic* theory that explains the total quantity of goods and services demanded and the total quantity of goods and services supplied. Developing such a theory is our next task.

model of aggregate demand and aggregate supply
the model that most economists use to explain short-run fluctuations in economic activity around its long-run trend

aggregate-demand curve
a curve that shows the quantity of goods and services that households, firms, the government, and customers abroad want to buy at each price level

aggregate-supply curve
a curve that shows the quantity of goods and services that firms choose to produce and sell at each price level

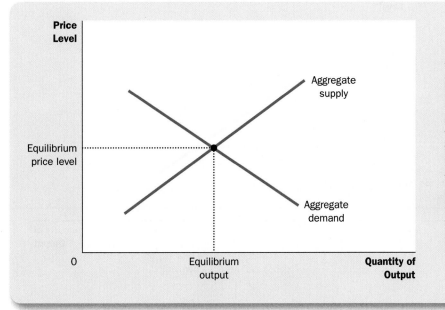

FIGURE 2

Aggregate Demand and Aggregate Supply
Economists use the model of aggregate demand and aggregate supply to analyze economic fluctuations. On the vertical axis is the overall level of prices. On the horizontal axis is the economy's total output of goods and services. Output and the price level adjust to the point at which the aggregate-supply and aggregate-demand curves intersect.

Quick Quiz How does the economy's behavior in the short run differ from its behavior in the long run?   •   Draw the model of aggregate demand and aggregate supply. What variables are on the two axes?

THE AGGREGATE-DEMAND CURVE

The aggregate-demand curve tells us the quantity of all goods and services demanded in the economy at any given price level. As Figure 3 illustrates, the aggregate-demand curve is downward sloping. This means that, other things equal, a decrease in the economy's overall level of prices (from, say, P_1 to P_2) raises the quantity of goods and services demanded (from Y_1 to Y_2). Conversely, an increase in the price level reduces the quantity of goods and services demanded.

Why the Aggregate-Demand Curve Slopes Downward

Why does a change in the price level move the quantity of goods and services demanded in the opposite direction? To answer this question, it is useful to recall that an economy's GDP (which we denote as Y) is the sum of its consumption (C), investment (I), government purchases (G), and net exports (NX):

$$Y = C + I + G + NX.$$

Each of these four components contributes to the aggregate demand for goods and services. For now, we assume that government spending is fixed by policy.

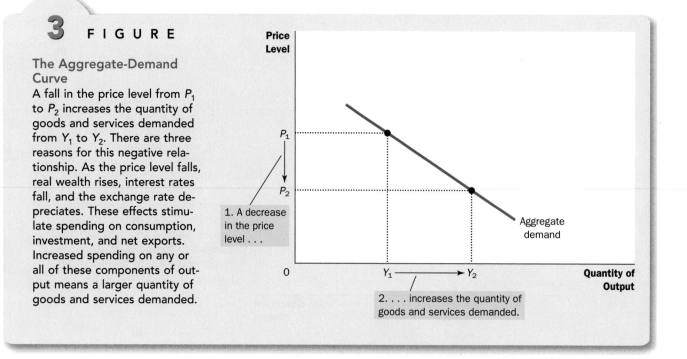

3 FIGURE

The Aggregate-Demand Curve
A fall in the price level from P_1 to P_2 increases the quantity of goods and services demanded from Y_1 to Y_2. There are three reasons for this negative relationship. As the price level falls, real wealth rises, interest rates fall, and the exchange rate depreciates. These effects stimulate spending on consumption, investment, and net exports. Increased spending on any or all of these components of output means a larger quantity of goods and services demanded.

Price Level

P_1

P_2

1. A decrease in the price level . . .

Aggregate demand

0   Y_1 ⟶ Y_2 Quantity of Output

2. . . . increases the quantity of goods and services demanded.

The other three components of spending—consumption, investment, and net exports—depend on economic conditions and, in particular, on the price level. To understand the downward slope of the aggregate-demand curve, therefore, we must examine how the price level affects the quantity of goods and services demanded for consumption, investment, and net exports.

The Price Level and Consumption: The Wealth Effect

Consider the money that you hold in your wallet and your bank account. The nominal value of this money is fixed: One dollar is always worth one dollar. Yet the *real* value of a dollar is not fixed. If a candy bar costs 1 dollar, then a dollar is worth one candy bar. If the price of a candy bar falls to 50 cents, then 1 dollar is worth two candy bars. Thus, when the price level falls, the dollars you are holding rise in value, which increases your real wealth and your ability to buy goods and services.

This logic gives us the first reason the aggregate demand curve is downward sloping. *A decrease in the price level raises the real value of money and makes consumers wealthier, which in turn encourages them to spend more. The increase in consumer spending means a larger quantity of goods and services demanded. Conversely, an increase in the price level reduces the real value of money, in turn reducing wealth, consumer spending, and the quantity of goods and services demanded.*

The Price Level and Investment: The Interest-Rate Effect

The price level is one determinant of the quantity of money demanded. The lower the price level, the less money households need to hold to buy the goods and services they want. Therefore, when the price level falls, households try to reduce their holdings of money by lending some of it out. For instance, a household might use its excess money to buy interest-bearing bonds. Or it might deposit its excess money in an interest-bearing savings account, and the bank would use these funds to make more loans. In either case, as households try to convert some of their money into interest-bearing assets, they drive down interest rates. (The next chapter analyzes this in more detail.)

Interest rates, in turn, affect spending on goods and services. Because a lower interest rate makes borrowing less expensive, it encourages firms to borrow more to invest in new plants and equipment, and it encourages households to borrow more to invest in new housing. (A lower interest rate might also stimulate consumer spending, especially large durable purchases such as cars, which are often bought on credit.) Thus, a lower interest rate increases the quantity of goods and services demanded.

This gives us a second reason the aggregate demand curve is downward sloping. *A lower price level reduces the interest rate, encourages greater spending on investment goods, and thereby increases the quantity of goods and services demanded. Conversely, a higher price level raises the interest rate, reducing investment spending and the quantity of goods and services demanded.*

The Price Level and Net Exports: The Exchange-Rate Effect

As we have just discussed, a lower price level in the United States lowers the U.S. interest rate. In response to the lower interest rate, some U.S. investors will seek higher returns by investing abroad. For instance, as the interest rate on U.S. government bonds falls, a mutual fund might sell U.S. government bonds to buy German government bonds. As the mutual fund tries to convert its dollars into euros to buy the German bonds, it increases the supply of dollars in the market for foreign-currency exchange.

The increased supply of dollars to be turned into euros causes the dollar to depreciate relative to the euro. This leads to a change in the real exchange rate—the relative price of domestic and foreign goods. Because each dollar buys fewer units of foreign currencies, foreign goods become more expensive relative to domestic goods.

The change in relative prices affects spending, both at home and abroad. Because foreign goods are now more expensive, Americans buy less from other countries, causing U.S. imports of goods and services to decrease. At the same time, because U.S. goods are now cheaper, foreigners buy more from the United States, so U.S. exports increase. Net exports equal exports minus imports, so both of these changes cause U.S. net exports to increase. Thus, the fall in the real exchange value of the dollar leads to an increase in the quantity of goods and services demanded.

This gives us a third reason the aggregate demand curve is downward sloping. *When a fall in the U.S. price level causes U.S. interest rates to fall, the real value of the dollar declines in foreign exchange markets, and this depreciation stimulates U.S. net exports and thereby increases the quantity of goods and services demanded. Conversely, when the U.S. price level rises and causes U.S interest rates to rise, the real value of the dollar increases, and this appreciation reduces U.S. net exports and the quantity of goods and services demanded.*

Summary There are three distinct but related reasons a fall in the price level increases the quantity of goods and services demanded:

1. Consumers are wealthier, which stimulates the demand for consumption goods.
2. Interest rates fall, which stimulates the demand for investment goods.
3. The currency depreciates, which stimulates the demand for net exports.

The same three effects work in reverse: When the price level rises, decreased wealth depresses consumer spending, higher interest rates depress investment spending, and a currency appreciation depresses net exports.

Here is a thought experiment to hone your intuition about these effects. Imagine that one day you wake up and notice that, for some mysterious reason, the prices of all goods and services have fallen by half, so the dollars you are holding are worth twice as much. In real terms, you now have twice as much money as you had when you went to bed the night before. What would you do with the extra money? You could spend it at your favorite restaurant, increasing consumer spending. You could lend it out (by buying a bond or depositing it in your bank), reducing interest rates and increasing investment spending. Or you could invest it overseas (by buying shares in an international mutual fund), reducing the real exchange value of the dollar and increasing net exports. Whichever of these three responses you choose, the fall in the price level leads to an increase in the quantity of goods and services demanded. This is what the downward slope of the aggregate-demand curve represents.

It is important to keep in mind that the aggregate-demand curve (like all demand curves) is drawn holding "other things equal." In particular, our three explanations of the downward-sloping aggregate-demand curve assume that the money supply is fixed. That is, we have been considering how a change in the price level affects the demand for goods and services, holding the amount of money in the economy constant. As we will see, a change in the quantity of money shifts the aggregate-demand curve. At this point, just keep in mind that the aggregate-demand curve is drawn for a given quantity of money.

Why the Aggregate-Demand Curve Might Shift

The downward slope of the aggregate-demand curve shows that a fall in the price level raises the overall quantity of goods and services demanded. Many other factors, however, affect the quantity of goods and services demanded at a given price level. When one of these other factors changes, the aggregate-demand curve shifts.

Let's consider some examples of events that shift aggregate demand. We can categorize them according to which component of spending is most directly affected.

Shifts Arising from Changes in Consumption

Suppose Americans suddenly become more concerned about saving for retirement and, as a result, reduce their current consumption. Because the quantity of goods and services demanded at any price level is lower, the aggregate-demand curve shifts to the left. Conversely, imagine that a stock-market boom makes people wealthier and less concerned about saving. The resulting increase in consumer spending means a greater quantity of goods and services demanded at any given price level, so the aggregate-demand curve shifts to the right.

Thus, any event that changes how much people want to consume at a given price level shifts the aggregate-demand curve. One policy variable that has this effect is the level of taxation. When the government cuts taxes, it encourages people to spend more, so the aggregate-demand curve shifts to the right. When the government raises taxes, people cut back on their spending, and the aggregate-demand curve shifts to the left.

Shifts Arising from Changes in Investment

Any event that changes how much firms want to invest at a given price level also shifts the aggregate-demand curve. For instance, imagine that the computer industry introduces a faster line of computers, and many firms decide to invest in new computer systems. Because the quantity of goods and services demanded at any price level is higher, the aggregate-demand curve shifts to the right. Conversely, if firms become pessimistic about future business conditions, they may cut back on investment spending, shifting the aggregate-demand curve to the left.

Tax policy can also influence aggregate demand through investment. As we saw in Chapter 8, an investment tax credit (a tax rebate tied to a firm's investment spending) increases the quantity of investment goods that firms demand at any given interest rate. It therefore shifts the aggregate-demand curve to the right. The repeal of an investment tax credit reduces investment and shifts the aggregate-demand curve to the left.

Another policy variable that can influence investment and aggregate demand is the money supply. As we discuss more fully in the next chapter, an increase in the money supply lowers the interest rate in the short run. This makes borrowing less costly, which stimulates investment spending and thereby shifts the aggregate-demand curve to the right. Conversely, a decrease in the money supply raises the interest rate, discourages investment spending, and thereby shifts the aggregate-demand curve to the left. Many economists believe that throughout U.S. history, changes in monetary policy have been an important source of shifts in aggregate demand.

Shifts Arising from Changes in Government Purchases   The most direct way that policymakers shift the aggregate-demand curve is through government purchases. For example, suppose Congress decides to reduce purchases of new weapons systems. Because the quantity of goods and services demanded at any price level is lower, the aggregate-demand curve shifts to the left. Conversely, if state governments start building more highways, the result is a greater quantity of goods and services demanded at any price level, so the aggregate-demand curve shifts to the right.

Shifts Arising from Changes in Net Exports   Any event that changes net exports for a given price level also shifts aggregate demand. For instance, when Europe experiences a recession, it buys fewer goods from the United States. This reduces U.S. net exports at every price level and shifts the aggregate-demand curve for the U.S. economy to the left. When Europe recovers from its recession, it starts buying U.S. goods again, and the aggregate-demand curve shifts to the right.

Net exports sometimes change because international speculators cause movements in the exchange rate. Suppose, for instance, that these speculators lose confidence in foreign economies and want to move some of their wealth into the U.S. economy. In doing so, they bid up the value of the U.S. dollar in the foreign exchange market. This appreciation of the dollar makes U.S. goods more expensive compared to foreign goods, which depresses net exports and shifts the aggregate-demand curve to the left. Conversely, speculation that causes a depreciation of the dollar stimulates net exports and shifts the aggregate-demand curve to the right.

Summary   In the next chapter, we analyze the aggregate-demand curve in more detail. There we examine more precisely how the tools of monetary and fiscal policy can shift aggregate demand and whether policymakers should use these tools for that purpose. At this point, however, you should have some idea about why the aggregate-demand curve slopes downward and what kinds of events and policies can shift this curve. Table 1 summarizes what we have learned so far.

Quick Quiz   Explain the three reasons the aggregate-demand curve slopes downward.   •   Give an example of an event that would shift the aggregate-demand curve. Which way would this event shift the curve?

THE AGGREGATE-SUPPLY CURVE

The aggregate-supply curve tells us the total quantity of goods and services that firms produce and sell at any given price level. Unlike the aggregate-demand curve, which is always downward sloping, the aggregate-supply curve shows a relationship that depends crucially on the time horizon examined. *In the long run, the aggregate-supply curve is vertical, whereas in the short run, the aggregate-supply*

	TABLE **1**
Why Does the Aggregate-Demand Curve Slope Downward? 1. *The Wealth Effect:* A lower price level increases real wealth, which encourages spending on consumption. 2. *The Interest-Rate Effect:* A lower price level reduces the interest rate, which encourages spending on investment. 3. *The Exchange-Rate Effect:* A lower price level causes the real exchange rate to depreciate, which encourages spending on net exports. **Why Might the Aggregate-Demand Curve Shift?** 1. *Shifts Arising from Consumption:* An event that makes consumers spend more at a given price level (a tax cut, a stock-market boom) shifts the aggregate-demand curve to the right. An event that makes consumers spend less at a given price level (a tax hike, a stock-market decline) shifts the aggregate-demand curve to the left. 2. *Shifts Arising from Investment:* An event that makes firms invest more at a given price level (optimism about the future, a fall in interest rates due to an increase in the money supply) shifts the aggregate-demand curve to the right. An event that makes firms invest less at a given price level (pessimism about the future, a rise in interest rates due to a decrease in the money supply) shifts the aggregate-demand curve to the left. 3. *Shifts Arising from Government Purchases:* An increase in government purchases of goods and services (greater spending on defense or highway construction) shifts the aggregate-demand curve to the right. A decrease in government purchases on goods and services (a cutback in defense or highway spending) shifts the aggregate-demand curve to the left. 4. *Shifts Arising from Net Exports:* An event that raises spending on net exports at a given price level (a boom overseas, speculation that causes an exchange-rate depreciation) shifts the aggregate-demand curve to the right. An event that reduces spending on net exports at a given price level (a recession overseas, speculation that causes an exchange-rate appreciation) shifts the aggregate-demand curve to the left.	The Aggregate-Demand Curve: Summary

curve is upward sloping. To understand short-run economic fluctuations, and how the short-run behavior of the economy deviates from its long-run behavior, we need to examine both the long-run aggregate-supply curve and the short-run aggregate-supply curve.

Why the Aggregate-Supply Curve Is Vertical in the Long Run

What determines the quantity of goods and services supplied in the long run? We implicitly answered this question earlier in the book when we analyzed the process of economic growth. *In the long run, an economy's production of goods and services (its real GDP) depends on its supplies of labor, capital, and natural resources and on the available technology used to turn these factors of production into goods and services.*

When we analyzed these forces that govern long-run growth, we did not need to make any reference to the overall level of prices. We examined the price level in a separate chapter, where we saw that it was determined by the quantity of money. We learned that if two economies were identical except that one had twice as much money in circulation as the other, the price level would be twice as high in the economy with more money, but the output of goods and services would be the same.

Because the price level does not affect the long-run determinants of real GDP, the long-run aggregate-supply curve is vertical, as in Figure 4. In other words, in the long run, the economy's labor, capital, natural resources, and technology determine the total quantity of goods and services supplied, and this quantity supplied is the same regardless of what the price level happens to be.

The vertical long-run aggregate-supply curve is a graphical representation of the classical dichotomy and monetary neutrality. As we have already discussed, classical macroeconomic theory is based on the assumption that real variables do not depend on nominal variables. The long-run aggregate-supply curve is consistent with this idea because it implies that the quantity of output (a real variable) does not depend on the level of prices (a nominal variable). As noted earlier, most economists believe that this principle works well when studying the economy over a period of many years but not when studying year-to-year changes. Thus, the aggregate-supply curve is vertical only in the long run.

Why the Long-Run Aggregate-Supply Curve Might Shift

Because classical macroeconomic theory predicts the quantity of goods and services produced by an economy in the long run, it also explains the position of the long-run aggregate-supply curve. The long-run level of production is sometimes called *potential output* or *full-employment output*. To be more precise, we call it the **natural rate of output** because it shows what the economy produces when unemployment is at its natural, or normal, rate. The natural rate of output is the level of production toward which the economy gravitates in the long run.

Any change in the economy that alters the natural rate of output shifts the long-run aggregate-supply curve. Because output in the classical model depends on labor, capital, natural resources, and technological knowledge, we can categorize shifts in the long-run aggregate-supply curve as arising from these four sources.

Shifts Arising from Changes in Labor   Imagine that an economy experiences an increase in immigration. Because there would be a greater number of

natural rate of output
the production of goods and services that an economy achieves in the long run when unemployment is at its normal rate

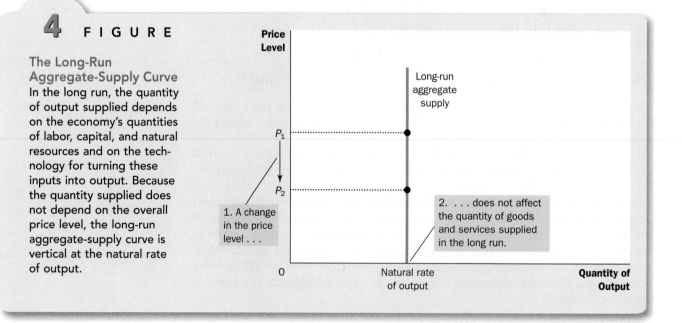

4   FIGURE

The Long-Run Aggregate-Supply Curve
In the long run, the quantity of output supplied depends on the economy's quantities of labor, capital, and natural resources and on the technology for turning these inputs into output. Because the quantity supplied does not depend on the overall price level, the long-run aggregate-supply curve is vertical at the natural rate of output.

workers, the quantity of goods and services supplied would increase. As a result, the long-run aggregate-supply curve would shift to the right. Conversely, if many workers left the economy to go abroad, the long-run aggregate-supply curve would shift to the left.

The position of the long-run aggregate-supply curve also depends on the natural rate of unemployment, so any change in the natural rate of unemployment shifts the long-run aggregate-supply curve. For example, if Congress were to raise the minimum wage substantially, the natural rate of unemployment would rise, and the economy would produce a smaller quantity of goods and services. As a result, the long-run aggregate-supply curve would shift to the left. Conversely, if a reform of the unemployment insurance system were to encourage unemployed workers to search harder for new jobs, the natural rate of unemployment would fall, and the long-run aggregate-supply curve would shift to the right.

Shifts Arising from Changes in Capital An increase in the economy's capital stock increases productivity and, thereby, the quantity of goods and services supplied. As a result, the long-run aggregate-supply curve shifts to the right. Conversely, a decrease in the economy's capital stock decreases productivity and the quantity of goods and services supplied, shifting the long-run aggregate-supply curve to the left.

Notice that the same logic applies regardless of whether we are discussing physical capital such as machines and factories or human capital such as college degrees. An increase in either type of capital will raise the economy's ability to produce goods and services and, thus, shift the long-run aggregate-supply curve to the right.

Shifts Arising from Changes in Natural Resources An economy's production depends on its natural resources, including its land, minerals, and weather. A discovery of a new mineral deposit shifts the long-run aggregate-supply curve to the right. A change in weather patterns that makes farming more difficult shifts the long-run aggregate-supply curve to the left.

In many countries, important natural resources are imported. A change in the availability of these resources can also shift the aggregate-supply curve. As we discuss later in this chapter, events occurring in the world oil market have historically been an important source of shifts in aggregate supply for the United States and other oil-importing nations.

Shifts Arising from Changes in Technological Knowledge Perhaps the most important reason that the economy today produces more than it did a generation ago is that our technological knowledge has advanced. The invention of the computer, for instance, has allowed us to produce more goods and services from any given amounts of labor, capital, and natural resources. As computer use has spread throughout the economy, it has shifted the long-run aggregate-supply curve to the right.

Although not literally technological, there are many other events that act like changes in technology. For instance, opening up international trade has effects similar to inventing new production processes because it allows a country to specialize in higher-productivity industries, so it also shifts the long-run aggregate-supply curve to the right. Conversely, if the government passed new regulations preventing firms from using some production methods, perhaps to address worker safety or environmental concerns, the result would be a leftward shift in the long-run aggregate-supply curve.

Summary   Because the long-run aggregate-supply curve reflects the classical model of the economy we developed in previous chapters, it provides a new way to describe our earlier analysis. Any policy or event that raised real GDP in previous chapters can now be described as increasing the quantity of goods and services supplied and shifting the long-run aggregate-supply curve to the right. Any policy or event that lowered real GDP in previous chapters can now be described as decreasing the quantity of goods and services supplied and shifting the long-run aggregate-supply curve to the left.

Using Aggregate Demand and Aggregate Supply to Depict Long-Run Growth and Inflation

Having introduced the economy's aggregate-demand curve and the long-run aggregate-supply curve, we now have a new way to describe the economy's long-run trends. Figure 5 illustrates the changes that occur in an economy from

5   FIGURE

Long-Run Growth and Inflation in the Model of Aggregate Demand and Aggregate Supply

As the economy becomes better able to produce goods and services over time, primarily because of technological progress, the long-run aggregate-supply curve shifts to the right. At the same time, as the Fed increases the money supply, the aggregate-demand curve also shifts to the right. In this figure, output grows from Y_{1980} to Y_{1990} and then to Y_{2000}, and the price level rises from P_{1980} to P_{1990} and then to P_{2000}. Thus, the model of aggregate demand and aggregate supply offers a new way to describe the classical analysis of growth and inflation.

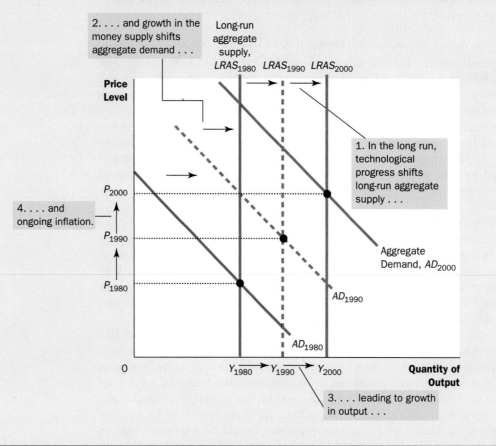

decade to decade. Notice that both curves are shifting. Although there are many forces that govern the economy in the long run and can in theory cause such shifts, the two most important in the real world are technology and monetary policy. Technological progress enhances an economy's ability to produce goods and services, and this increase in output is reflected in the continual shifts of the long-run aggregate-supply curve to the right. At the same time, because the Fed increases the money supply over time, the aggregate-demand curve also shifts to the right. As the figure illustrates, the result is trend growth in output (as shown by increasing Y) and continuing inflation (as shown by increasing P). This is just another way of representing the classical analysis of growth and inflation we conducted in earlier chapters.

The purpose of developing the model of aggregate demand and aggregate supply, however, is not to dress our previous long-run conclusions in new clothing. Instead, it is to provide a framework for short-run analysis, as we will see in a moment. As we develop the short-run model, we keep the analysis simple by not showing the continuing growth and inflation depicted by the shifts in Figure 5. But always remember that long-run trends provide the background for short-run fluctuations. *Short-run fluctuations in output and the price level should be viewed as deviations from the continuing long-run trends of output growth and inflation.*

Why the Aggregate-Supply Curve Slopes Upward in the Short Run

The key difference between the economy in the short run and in the long run is the behavior of aggregate supply. The long-run aggregate-supply curve is vertical because, in the long run, the overall level of prices does not affect the economy's ability to produce goods and services. By contrast, in the short run, the price level *does* affect the economy's output. That is, over a period of a year or two, an increase in the overall level of prices in the economy tends to raise the quantity of goods and services supplied, and a decrease in the level of prices tends to reduce the quantity of goods and services supplied. As a result, the short-run aggregate-supply curve is upward sloping, as shown in Figure 6.

Why do changes in the price level affect output in the short run? Macroeconomists have proposed three theories for the upward slope of the short-run aggregate-supply curve. In each theory, a specific market imperfection causes the supply side of the economy to behave differently in the short run than it does in the long run. Although the following theories differ in their details, they share a common theme: *The quantity of output supplied deviates from its long-run, or "natural," level when the actual price level in the economy deviates from the price level that people expected to prevail.* When the price level rises above the level that people expected, output rises above its natural rate, and when the price level falls below the expected level, output falls below its natural rate.

The Sticky-Wage Theory The first explanation of the upward slope of the short-run aggregate-supply curve is the sticky-wage theory. Because this theory is the simplest of the three approaches to aggregate supply, it is the one we emphasize in this book.

According to this theory, the short-run aggregate-supply curve slopes upward because nominal wages are slow to adjust to changing economic conditions. In other words, wages are "sticky" in the short run. To some extent, the slow adjustment of nominal wages is attributable to long-term contracts between workers and firms that fix nominal wages, sometimes for as long as three years.

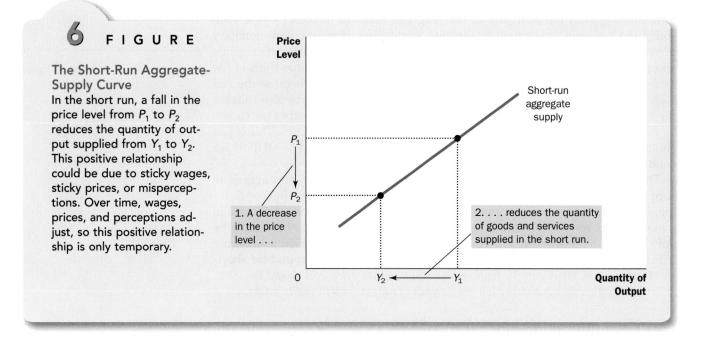

6   FIGURE

The Short-Run Aggregate-Supply Curve
In the short run, a fall in the price level from P_1 to P_2 reduces the quantity of output supplied from Y_1 to Y_2. This positive relationship could be due to sticky wages, sticky prices, or misperceptions. Over time, wages, prices, and perceptions adjust, so this positive relationship is only temporary.

Price Level

P_1

P_2

Short-run aggregate supply

1. A decrease in the price level . . .

2. . . . reduces the quantity of goods and services supplied in the short run.

0   Y_2 ← Y_1 Quantity of Output

In addition, this slow adjustment may be attributable to social norms and notions of fairness that influence wage setting and that change only slowly over time.

An example helps explain how sticky nominal wages can result in a short-run aggregate-supply curve that slopes upward. Imagine that a year ago a firm expected the price level to be 100, and based on this expectation, it signed a contract with its workers agreeing to pay them, say, $20 an hour. In fact, the price level, P, turns out to be only 95. Because prices have fallen below expectations, the firm gets 5 percent less than expected for each unit of its product that it sells. The cost of labor used to make the output, however, is stuck at $20 per hour. Production is now less profitable, so the firm hires fewer workers and reduces the quantity of output supplied. Over time, the labor contract will expire, and the firm can renegotiate with its workers for a lower wage (which they may accept because prices are lower), but in the meantime, employment and production will remain below their long-run levels.

The same logic works in reverse. Suppose the price level turns out to be 105, and the wage remains stuck at $20. The firm sees that the amount it is paid for each unit sold is up by 5 percent, while its labor costs are not. In response, it hires more workers and increases the quantity supplied. Eventually, the workers will demand higher nominal wages to compensate for the higher price level, but for a while, the firm can take advantage of the profit opportunity by increasing employment and the quantity of output supplied above their long-run levels.

In short, according to the sticky-wage theory, the short-run aggregate-supply curve is upward sloping because nominal wages are based on the expected prices and do not respond immediately when the actual price level turns out to be different from what was expected. This stickiness of wages gives firms an incentive to produce less than the natural rate of output when the price level turns out lower than expected and to produce more when the price level turns out higher than expected.

The Sticky-Price Theory   Some economists have advocated another approach to explaining the upward slope of the short-run aggregate-supply curve, called the sticky-price theory. As we just discussed, the sticky-wage theory emphasizes that nominal wages adjust slowly over time. The sticky-price theory emphasizes that the prices of some goods and services also adjust sluggishly in response to changing economic conditions. This slow adjustment of prices occurs in part because there are costs to adjusting prices, called *menu costs*. These menu costs include the cost of printing and distributing catalogs and the time required to change price tags. As a result of these costs, prices as well as wages may be sticky in the short run.

To see how sticky prices explain the aggregate-supply curve's upward slope, suppose that each firm in the economy announces its prices in advance based on the economic conditions it expects to prevail over the coming year. Suppose further that after prices are announced, the economy experiences an unexpected contraction in the money supply, which (as we have learned) will reduce the overall price level in the long run. Although some firms can reduce their prices immediately in response to an unexpected change in economic conditions, other firms may not want to incur additional menu costs. As a result, they may temporarily lag behind in reducing their prices. Because these lagging firms have prices that are too high, their sales decline. Declining sales, in turn, cause these firms to cut back on production and employment. In other words, because not all prices adjust instantly to changing economic conditions, an unexpected fall in the price level leaves some firms with higher-than-desired prices, and these higher-than-desired prices depress sales and induce firms to reduce the quantity of goods and services they produce.

The same reasoning applies when the money supply and price level turn out to be above what firms expected when they originally set their prices. While some firms raise their prices immediately in response to the new economic environment, other firms lag behind, keeping their prices at the lower-than-desired levels. These low prices attract customers, which induces these firms to increase employment and production. Thus, during the time these lagging firms are operating with outdated prices, there is a positive association between the overall price level and the quantity of output. This positive association is represented by the upward slope of the short-run aggregate-supply curve.

The Misperceptions Theory   A third approach to explaining the upward slope of the short-run aggregate-supply curve is the misperceptions theory. According to this theory, changes in the overall price level can temporarily mislead suppliers about what is happening in the individual markets in which they sell their output. As a result of these short-run misperceptions, suppliers respond to changes in the level of prices, and this response leads to an upward-sloping aggregate-supply curve.

To see how this might work, suppose the overall price level falls below the level that suppliers expected. When suppliers see the prices of their products fall, they may mistakenly believe that their *relative* prices have fallen; that is, they may believe that their prices have fallen compared to other prices in the economy. For example, wheat farmers may notice a fall in the price of wheat before they notice a fall in the prices of the many items they buy as consumers. They may infer from this observation that the reward to producing wheat is temporarily low, and they may respond by reducing the quantity of wheat they supply. Similarly, workers may notice a fall in their nominal wages before they notice that the prices of the goods they buy are also falling. They may infer that the reward for working is temporarily low and respond by reducing the quantity of labor they supply. In both cases, a lower price level causes misperceptions about relative prices, and these misperceptions induce suppliers to respond to the lower price level by decreasing the quantity of goods and services supplied.

Similar misperceptions arise when the price level is above what was expected. Suppliers of goods and services may notice the price of their output rising and infer, mistakenly, that their relative prices are rising. They would conclude that it is a good time to produce. Until their misperceptions are corrected, they respond to the higher price level by increasing the quantity of goods and services supplied. This behavior results in a short-run aggregate-supply curve that slopes upward.

Summary   There are three alternative explanations for the upward slope of the short-run aggregate-supply curve: (1) sticky wages, (2) sticky prices, and (3) misperceptions about relative prices. Economists debate which of these theories is correct, and it is very possible each contains an element of truth. For our purposes in this book, the similarities of the theories are more important than the differences. All three theories suggest that output deviates in the short run from its long-run level (the natural rate) when the actual price level deviates from the price level that people had expected to prevail. We can express this mathematically as follows:

$$
\begin{pmatrix} \text{Quantity} \\ \text{of output} \\ \text{supplied} \end{pmatrix} = \begin{pmatrix} \text{Natural} \\ \text{rate of} \\ \text{output} \end{pmatrix} + a \begin{pmatrix} \text{Actual} \\ \text{price} \\ \text{level} \end{pmatrix} - \begin{pmatrix} \text{Expected} \\ \text{price} \\ \text{level} \end{pmatrix}
$$

where a is a number that determines how much output responds to unexpected changes in the price level.

Notice that each of the three theories of short-run aggregate supply emphasizes a problem that is likely to be temporary. Whether the upward slope of the aggregate-supply curve is attributable to sticky wages, sticky prices, or misperceptions, these conditions will not persist forever. Over time, nominal wages will become unstuck, prices will become unstuck, and misperceptions about relative prices will be corrected. In the long run, it is reasonable to assume that wages and prices are flexible rather than sticky and that people are not confused about relative prices. Thus, while we have several good theories to explain why the short-run aggregate-supply curve is upward sloping, they are all consistent with a long-run aggregate-supply curve that is vertical.

Why the Short-Run Aggregate-Supply Curve Might Shift

The short-run aggregate-supply curve tells us the quantity of goods and services supplied in the short run for any given level of prices. This curve is similar to the long-run aggregate-supply curve, but it is upward sloping rather than vertical because of sticky wages, sticky prices, and misperceptions. Thus, when thinking about what shifts the short-run aggregate-supply curve, we have to consider all those variables that shift the long-run aggregate-supply curve plus a new variable—the expected price level—that influences the wages that are stuck, the prices that are stuck, and the perceptions about relative prices.

Let's start with what we know about the long-run aggregate-supply curve. As we discussed earlier, shifts in the long-run aggregate-supply curve normally arise from changes in labor, capital, natural resources, or technological knowledge. These same variables shift the short-run aggregate-supply curve. For example, when an increase in the economy's capital stock increases productivity, the economy is able to produce more output, so both the long-run and short-run aggregate-supply curves shift to the right. When an increase in the minimum wage raises the natural rate of unemployment, the economy has fewer employed workers and thus produces less output, so both the long-run and short-run aggregate-supply curves shift to the left.

The important new variable that affects the position of the short-run aggregate-supply curve is the price level that people expected to prevail. As we have discussed, the quantity of goods and services supplied depends, in the short run, on sticky wages, sticky prices, and misperceptions. Yet wages, prices, and perceptions are set on the basis of the expected price level. So when people change their expectations of the price level, the short-run aggregate-supply curve shifts.

To make this idea more concrete, let's consider a specific theory of aggregate supply—the sticky-wage theory. According to this theory, when workers and firms expect the price level to be high, they are more likely to reach a bargain with a high level of nominal wages. High wages raise firms' costs, and for any given actual price level, higher costs reduce the quantity of goods and services that firms supply. Thus, when the expected price level rises, wages are higher, costs increase, and firms supply a smaller quantity of goods and services at any given actual price level. Thus, the short-run aggregate-supply curve shifts to the left. Conversely, when the expected price level falls, wages are lower, costs decline, firms increase output at any given price level, and the short-run aggregate-supply curve shifts to the right.

A similar logic applies in each theory of aggregate supply. The general lesson is the following: *An increase in the expected price level reduces the quantity of goods and services supplied and shifts the short-run aggregate-supply curve to the left. A decrease in the expected price level raises the quantity of goods and services supplied and shifts the short-run aggregate-supply curve to the right.* As we will see in the next section, this influence of expectations on the position of the short-run aggregate-supply curve plays a key role in explaining how the economy makes the transition from the short run to the long run. In the short run, expectations are fixed, and the economy finds itself at the intersection of the aggregate-demand curve and the short-run aggregate-supply curve. In the long run, if people observe that the price level is different from what they expected, their expectations adjust, and the short-run aggregate-supply curve shifts. This shift ensures that the economy eventually finds itself at the intersection of the aggregate-demand curve and the long-run aggregate-supply curve.

You should now have some understanding about why the short-run aggregate-supply curve slopes upward and what events and policies can cause this curve to shift. Table 2 summarizes our discussion.

Quick Quiz   Explain why the long-run aggregate-supply curve is vertical.   • Explain three theories for why the short-run aggregate-supply curve is upward sloping.   •   What variables shift both the long-run and short-run aggregate-supply curves?   •   What variable shifts the short-run aggregate-supply curve but not the long-run aggregate-supply curve?

2 TABLE

The Short-Run
Aggregate-Supply
Curve: Summary

Why Does the Short-Run Aggregate-Supply Curve Slope Upward?

1. *The Sticky-Wage Theory:* An unexpectedly low price level raises the real wage, which causes firms to hire fewer workers and produce a smaller quantity of goods and services.
2. *The Sticky-Price Theory:* An unexpectedly low price level leaves some firms with higher-than-desired prices, which depresses their sales and leads them to cut back production.
3. *The Misperceptions Theory:* An unexpectedly low price level leads some suppliers to think their relative prices have fallen, which induces a fall in production.

Why Might the Short-Run Aggregate-Supply Curve Shift?

1. *Shifts Arising from Labor:* An increase in the quantity of labor available (perhaps due to a fall in the natural rate of unemployment) shifts the aggregate-supply curve to the right. A decrease in the quantity of labor available (perhaps due to a rise in the natural rate of unemployment) shifts the aggregate-supply curve to the left.
2. *Shifts Arising from Capital:* An increase in physical or human capital shifts the aggregate-supply curve to the right. A decrease in physical or human capital shifts the aggregate-supply curve to the left.
3. *Shifts Arising from Natural Resources:* An increase in the availability of natural resources shifts the aggregate-supply curve to the right. A decrease in the availability of natural resources shifts the aggregate-supply curve to the left.
4. *Shifts Arising from Technology:* An advance in technological knowledge shifts the aggregate-supply curve to the right. A decrease in the available technology (perhaps due to government regulation) shifts the aggregate-supply curve to the left.
5. *Shifts Arising from the Expected Price Level:* A decrease in the expected price level shifts the short-run aggregate-supply curve to the right. An increase in the expected price level shifts the short-run aggregate-supply curve to the left.

TWO CAUSES OF ECONOMIC FLUCTUATIONS

Now that we have introduced the model of aggregate demand and aggregate supply, we have the basic tools we need to analyze fluctuations in economic activity. In particular, we can use what we have learned about aggregate demand and aggregate supply to examine the two basic causes of short-run fluctuations: shifts in aggregate demand and shifts in aggregate supply.

To keep things simple, we assume the economy begins in long-run equilibrium, as shown in Figure 7. Output and the price level are determined in the long run by the intersection of the aggregate-demand curve and the long-run aggregate-supply curve, shown as point A in the figure. At this point, output is at its natural rate. Because the economy is always in a short-run equilibrium, the short-run aggregate-supply curve passes through this point as well, indicating that the expected price level has adjusted to this long-run equilibrium. That is, when an economy is in its long-run equilibrium, the expected price level must equal the actual price level so that the intersection of aggregate demand with short-run aggregate supply is the same as the intersection of aggregate demand with long-run aggregate supply.

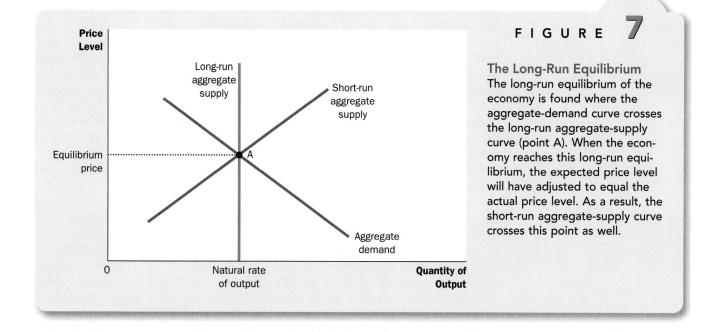

The Long-Run Equilibrium
The long-run equilibrium of the economy is found where the aggregate-demand curve crosses the long-run aggregate-supply curve (point A). When the economy reaches this long-run equilibrium, the expected price level will have adjusted to equal the actual price level. As a result, the short-run aggregate-supply curve crosses this point as well.

The Effects of a Shift in Aggregate Demand

Suppose that a wave of pessimism suddenly overtakes the economy. The cause might be a scandal in the White House, a crash in the stock market, or the outbreak of war overseas. Because of this event, many people lose confidence in the future and alter their plans. Households cut back on their spending and delay major purchases, and firms put off buying new equipment.

What is the macroeconomic impact of such a wave of pessimism? In answering this question, we can follow the three steps we used in Chapter 4 when analyzing supply and demand in specific markets. First, we determine whether the event affects aggregate demand or aggregate supply. Second, we decide which direction the curve shifts. Third, we use the diagram of aggregate demand and aggregate supply to compare the initial and the new equilibrium. The new wrinkle is that we need to add a fourth step: We have to keep track of a new short-run equilibrium, a new long-run equilibrium, and the transition between them. Table 3 summarizes the four steps to analyzing economic fluctuations.

The first two steps are easy. First, because the wave of pessimism affects spending plans, it affects the aggregate-demand curve. Second, because households and

1. Decide whether the event shifts the aggregate demand curve or the aggregate supply curve (or perhaps both).
2. Decide in which direction the curve shifts.
3. Use the diagram of aggregate demand and aggregate supply to see how the shift changes output and the price level in the short run.
4. Use the diagram of aggregate demand and aggregate supply to analyze how the economy moves from its new short-run equilibrium to its long-run equilibrium.

Four Steps for Analyzing Macroeconomic Fluctuations

firms now want to buy a smaller quantity of goods and services for any given price level, the event reduces aggregate demand. As Figure 8 shows, the aggregate-demand curve shifts to the left from AD_1 to AD_2.

With this figure, we can perform step three: By comparing the initial and new equilibrium, we can see the effects of the fall in aggregate demand. In the short run, the economy moves along the initial short-run aggregate-supply curve, AS_1, going from point A to point B. As the economy moves between these two points, output falls from Y_1 to Y_2, and the price level falls from P_1 to P_2. The falling level of output indicates that the economy is in a recession. Although not shown in the figure, firms respond to lower sales and production by reducing employment. Thus, the pessimism that caused the shift in aggregate demand is, to some extent, self-fulfilling: Pessimism about the future leads to falling incomes and rising unemployment.

Now comes step four—the transition from the short-run equilibrium to the long-run equilibrium. Because of the reduction in aggregate demand, the price level initially falls from P_1 to P_2. The price level is thus below the level that people had come to expect (P_1) before the sudden fall in aggregate demand. Although people are surprised in the short run, they will not remain surprised. Over time, expectations catch up with this new reality, and the expected price level falls as well. The fall in the expected price level alters wages, prices, and perceptions, which in turn influences the position of the short-run aggregate-supply curve. For example, according to the sticky-wage theory, once workers and firms come to expect a lower level of prices, they start to strike bargains for lower nominal wages; the reduction in labor costs encourages firms to hire more workers and expands production at any given level of prices. Thus, the fall in the expected price level shifts the short-run aggregate-supply curve to the right

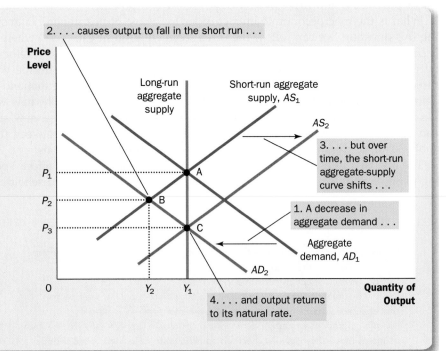

8 FIGURE

A Contraction in Aggregate Demand

A fall in aggregate demand is represented with a leftward shift in the aggregate-demand curve from AD_1 to AD_2. In the short run, the economy moves from point A to point B. Output falls from Y_1 to Y_2, and the price level falls from P_1 to P_2. Over time, as the expected price level adjusts, the short-run aggregate-supply curve shifts to the right from AS_1 to AS_2, and the economy reaches point C, where the new aggregate-demand curve crosses the long-run aggregate-supply curve. In the long run, the price level falls to P_3, and output returns to its natural rate, Y_1.

2. . . . causes output to fall in the short run . . .

Long-run aggregate supply

Short-run aggregate supply, AS_1

AS_2

3. . . . but over time, the short-run aggregate-supply curve shifts . . .

1. A decrease in aggregate demand . . .

Aggregate demand, AD_1

AD_2

4. . . . and output returns to its natural rate.

FYI

Monetary Neutrality Revisited

According to classical economic theory, money is neutral. That is, changes in the quantity of money affect nominal variables such as the price level but not real variables such as output. Earlier in this chapter, we noted that most economists accept this conclusion as a description of how the economy works in the long run but not in the short run. With the model of aggregate demand and aggregate supply, we can illustrate this conclusion and explain it more fully.

Suppose that the Federal Reserve reduces the quantity of money in the economy. What effect does this change have? As we discussed, the money supply is one determinant of aggregate demand. The reduction in the money supply shifts the aggregate-demand curve to the left.

The analysis looks just like Figure 8. Even though the cause of the shift in aggregate demand is different, we would observe the same effects on output and the price level. In the short run, both output and the price level fall. The economy experiences a recession. But over time, the expected price level falls as well. Firms and workers respond to their new expectations by, for instance, agreeing to lower nominal wages. As they do so, the short-run aggregate-supply curve shifts to the right. Eventually, the economy finds itself back on the long-run aggregate-supply curve.

Figure 8 shows when money matters for real variables and when it does not. In the long run, money is neutral, as represented by the movement of the economy from point A to point C. But in the short run, a change in the money supply has real effects, as represented by the movement of the economy from point A to point B. An old saying summarizes the analysis: "Money is a veil, but when the veil flutters, real output sputters."

from AS_1 to AS_2 in Figure 8. This shift allows the economy to approach point C, where the new aggregate-demand curve (AD_2) crosses the long-run aggregate-supply curve.

In the new long-run equilibrium, point C, output is back to its natural rate. The economy has corrected itself: The decline in output is reversed in the long run, even without action by policymakers. Although the wave of pessimism has reduced aggregate demand, the price level has fallen sufficiently (to P_3) to offset the shift in the aggregate-demand curve, and people have come to expect this new lower price level as well. Thus, in the long run, the shift in aggregate demand is reflected fully in the price level and not at all in the level of output. In other words, the long-run effect of a shift in aggregate demand is a nominal change (the price level is lower) but not a real change (output is the same).

What should policymakers do when faced with a sudden fall in aggregate demand? In this analysis, we assumed they did nothing. Another possibility is that, as soon as the economy heads into recession (moving from point A to point B), policymakers could take action to increase aggregate demand. As we noted earlier, an increase in government spending or an increase in the money supply would increase the quantity of goods and services demanded at any price and, therefore, would shift the aggregate-demand curve to the right. If policymakers act with sufficient speed and precision, they can offset the initial shift in aggregate demand, return the aggregate-demand curve back to AD_1, and bring the economy back to point A. If the policy is successful, the painful period of depressed output and employment can be reduced in length and severity. The next chapter discusses in more detail the ways in which monetary and fiscal policy influence aggregate demand, as well as some of the practical difficulties in using these policy instruments.

To sum up, this story about shifts in aggregate demand has three important lessons:

- In the short run, shifts in aggregate demand cause fluctuations in the economy's output of goods and services.
- In the long run, shifts in aggregate demand affect the overall price level but do not affect output.
- Policymakers who influence aggregate demand can potentially mitigate the severity of economic fluctuations.

CASE STUDY | TWO BIG SHIFTS IN AGGREGATE DEMAND: THE GREAT DEPRESSION AND WORLD WAR II

At the beginning of this chapter, we established three key facts about economic fluctuations by looking at data since 1965. Let's now take a longer look at U.S. economic history. Figure 9 shows data since 1900 on the percentage change in real GDP over the previous 3 years. In an average 3-year period, real GDP grows about 10 percent—a bit more than 3 percent per year. The business cycle, however, causes fluctuations around this average. Two episodes jump out as being particularly significant: the large drop in real GDP in the early 1930s and the large increase in real GDP in the early 1940s. Both of these events are attributable to shifts in aggregate demand.

9 FIGURE

U.S. Real GDP Growth since 1900

Source: U.S. Department of Commerce.

Over the course of U.S. economic history, two fluctuations stand out as especially large. During the early 1930s, the economy went through the Great Depression, when the production of goods and services plummeted. During the early 1940s, the United States entered World War II, and the economy experienced rapidly rising production. Both of these events are usually explained by large shifts in aggregate demand.

The economic calamity of the early 1930s is called the *Great Depression*, and it is by far the largest economic downturn in U.S. history. Real GDP fell by 27 percent from 1929 to 1933, and unemployment rose from 3 percent to 25 percent. At the same time, the price level fell by 22 percent over these 4 years. Many other countries experienced similar declines in output and prices during this period.

Economic historians continue to debate the causes of the Great Depression, but most explanations center on a large decline in aggregate demand. What caused aggregate demand to contract? Here is where the disagreement arises.

Many economists place primary blame on the decline in the money supply: From 1929 to 1933, the money supply fell by 28 percent. As you may recall from our discussion of the monetary system, this decline in the money supply was due to problems in the banking system. As households withdrew their money from financially shaky banks and bankers became more cautious and started holding greater reserves, the process of money creation under fractional-reserve banking went into reverse. The Fed, meanwhile, failed to offset this fall in the money multiplier with expansionary open-market operations. As a result, the money supply declined. Many economists blame the Fed's failure to act for the Great Depression's severity.

Other economists have suggested alternative reasons for the collapse in aggregate demand. For example, stock prices fell about 90 percent during this period, depressing household wealth and thereby consumer spending. In addition, the banking problems may have prevented some firms from obtaining the financing they wanted for investment projects, and this would have depressed investment spending. Of course, all of these forces may have acted together to contract aggregate demand during the Great Depression.

The second significant episode in Figure 9—the economic boom of the early 1940s—is easier to explain. The obvious cause of this event was World War II. As the United States entered the war overseas, the federal government had to devote more resources to the military. Government purchases of goods and services increased almost fivefold from 1939 to 1944. This huge expansion in aggregate demand almost doubled the economy's production of goods and services and led to a 20 percent increase in the price level (although widespread government price controls limited the rise in prices). Unemployment fell from 17 percent in 1939 to about 1 percent in 1944—the lowest level in U.S. history. •

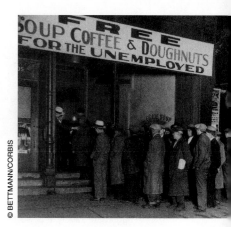

THE OUTCOME OF A MASSIVE DECREASE IN AGGREGATE DEMAND

CASE STUDY | THE RECESSION OF 2001

After the longest economic expansion in history, the U.S. economy experienced a recession in 2001. The unemployment rate rose from 3.9 percent in December 2000 to 4.9 percent in August 2001 and to 6.3 percent in June 2003. The unemployment rate then began to decline. By January 2005, unemployment had fallen back to 5.2 percent.

What caused the recession, and what ended it? The answer to both questions is shifts in aggregate demand.

The recession began with the end of the dot-com bubble in the stock market. During the 1990s, many stock-market investors became optimistic about information technology, and they bid up stock prices, particularly of high-tech companies. With hindsight, it is fair to say that this optimism was excessive. Eventually, the optimism faded, and stock prices fell by about 25 percent from August 2000 to August 2001. The fall in the stock market reduced household wealth,

FYI

The Origins of Aggregate Demand and Aggregate Supply

Now that we have a preliminary understanding of the model of aggregate demand and aggregate supply, it is worthwhile to step back from it and consider its history. How did this model of short-run fluctuations develop? The answer is that this model, to a large extent, is a by-product of the Great Depression of the 1930s. Economists and policymakers at the time were puzzled about what had caused this calamity and were uncertain about how to deal with it.

In 1936, economist John Maynard Keynes published a book titled *The General Theory of Employment, Interest, and Money,* which attempted to explain short-run economic fluctuations in general and the Great Depression in particular. Keynes's primary message was that recessions and depressions can occur because of inadequate aggregate demand for goods and services.

Keynes had long been a critic of classical economic theory—the theory we examined earlier in the book—because it could

John Maynard Keynes

explain only the long-run effects of policies. A few years before offering *The General Theory,* Keynes had written the following about classical economics:

> The long run is a misleading guide to current affairs. In the long run we are all dead. Economists set themselves too easy, too useless a task if in tempestuous seasons they can only tell us when the storm is long past, the ocean will be flat.

Keynes's message was aimed at policymakers as well as economists. As the world's economies suffered with high unemployment, Keynes advocated policies to increase aggregate demand, including government spending on public works.

In the next chapter, we examine in detail how policymakers can use the tools of monetary and fiscal policy to influence aggregate demand. The analysis in the next chapter, as well as in this one, owes much to the legacy of John Maynard Keynes.

---

which in turn reduced consumer spending. In addition, when the new technologies started to appear less profitable than they had originally seemed, investment spending fell. The aggregate-demand curve shifted to the left.

The second shock to the economy was the terrorist attacks on New York and Washington on September 11, 2001. In the week after the attacks, the stock market fell another 12 percent, its biggest weekly loss since the Great Depression of the 1930s. Moreover, the attacks increased uncertainty about what the future would hold. Uncertainty can reduce spending, as households and firms postpone plans, waiting for the uncertainty to be resolved. Thus, the terrorist attacks also shifted the aggregate-demand curve further to the left.

The third event that put downward pressure on aggregate demand was a series of corporate accounting scandals. During 2001 and 2002, several major corporations, including Enron and WorldCom, were found to have misled the public about their profitability. When the truth became known, the value of their stock plummeted. Even honest companies experienced stock declines, as stock-market investors became less trustful of all accounting data. This fall in the stock market further depressed aggregate demand.

Policymakers were quick to respond to these events. As soon as the economic slowdown became apparent, the Federal Reserve pursued expansionary monetary policy. Money growth accelerated, and interest rates fell. The federal funds rate (the interest rate on loans between banks that the Fed uses as its short-term policy target) fell from 6.5 percent in December 2000 to 1.0 percent in June 2003. Lower interest rates stimulated spending by reducing the cost of borrowing. At the same time, with the president's urging, Congress passed a tax cut in 2001, including an immediate tax rebate, and another tax cut in 2003. One goal of these tax cuts was to stimulate consumer and investment spending. Interest-rate cuts and tax cuts both shifted the aggregate-demand curve to the right, offsetting the three contractionary shocks the economy had experienced.

The recession of 2001 is a reminder of the many kinds of events that can influence aggregate demand and, thus, the direction of the economy.   •

The Effects of a Shift in Aggregate Supply

Imagine once again an economy in its long-run equilibrium. Now suppose that suddenly some firms experience an increase in their costs of production. For example, bad weather in farm states might destroy some crops, driving up the cost of producing food products. Or a war in the Middle East might interrupt the shipping of crude oil, driving up the cost of producing oil products.

To analyze the macroeconomic impact of such an increase in production costs, we follow the same four steps. First, which curve is affected? Because production costs affect the firms that supply goods and services, changes in production costs alter the position of the aggregate-supply curve. Second, which direction does the curve shift? Because higher production costs make selling goods and services less profitable, firms now supply a smaller quantity of output for any given price level. Thus, as Figure 10 shows, the short-run aggregate-supply curve shifts to the left from AS_1 to AS_2. (Depending on the event, the long-run aggregate-supply curve might also shift. To keep things simple, however, we will assume that it does not.)

The figure allows us to perform step three of comparing the initial and new equilibrium. In the short run, the economy goes from point A to point B, moving along the existing aggregate-demand curve. The output of the economy falls from Y_1 to Y_2, and the price level rises from P_1 to P_2. Because the economy is experiencing both *stagnation* (falling output) and *inflation* (rising prices), such an event is sometimes called **stagflation.**

Now consider step four—the transition from the short-run equilibrium to the long-run equilibrium. According to the sticky-wage theory, the key issue is how stagflation affects nominal wages. Firms and workers may at first respond to the higher level of prices by raising their expectations of the price level and setting higher nominal wages. In this case, firms' costs will rise yet again, and the short-run aggregate-supply curve will shift further to the left, making the problem of stagflation even worse. This phenomenon of higher prices leading to higher wages, in turn leading to even higher prices, is sometimes called a *wage-price spiral.*

At some point, this spiral of ever-rising wages and prices will slow. The low level of output and employment will put downward pressure on workers' wages because workers have less bargaining power when unemployment is high. As nominal wages fall, producing goods and services becomes more profitable, and

stagflation
a period of falling output and rising prices

10 F I G U R E

An Adverse Shift in Aggregate Supply
When some event increases firms' costs, the short-run aggregate-supply curve shifts to the left from AS_1 to AS_2. The economy moves from point A to point B. The result is stagflation: Output falls from Y_1 to Y_2, and the price level rises from P_1 to P_2.

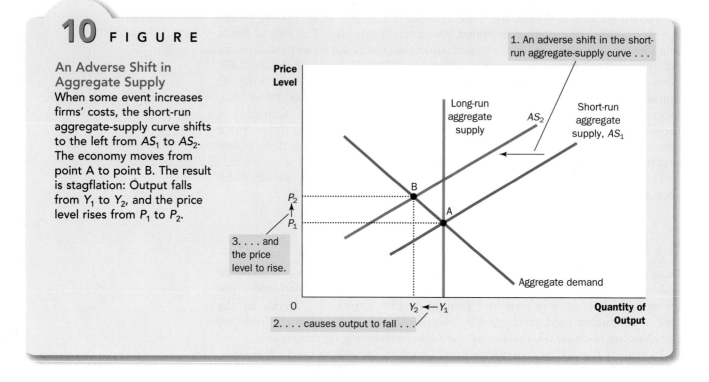

the short-run aggregate-supply curve shifts to the right. As it shifts back toward AS_1, the price level falls, and the quantity of output approaches its natural rate. In the long run, the economy returns to point A, where the aggregate-demand curve crosses the long-run aggregate-supply curve.

This transition back to the initial equilibrium assumes, however, that aggregate demand is held constant throughout the process. In the real world, that may not be the case. Policymakers who control monetary and fiscal policy might attempt to offset some of the effects of the shift in the short-run aggregate-supply curve by shifting the aggregate-demand curve. This possibility is shown in Figure 11. In this case, changes in policy shift the aggregate-demand curve to the right from AD_1 to AD_2—exactly enough to prevent the shift in aggregate supply from affecting output. The economy moves directly from point A to point C. Output remains at its natural rate, and the price level rises from P_1 to P_3. In this case, policymakers are said to *accommodate* the shift in aggregate supply. An accommodative policy accepts a permanently higher level of prices to maintain a higher level of output and employment.

To sum up, this story about shifts in aggregate supply has two important lessons:

- Shifts in aggregate supply can cause stagflation—a combination of recession (falling output) and inflation (rising prices).
- Policymakers who can influence aggregate demand can potentially mitigate the adverse impact on output but only at the cost of exacerbating the problem of inflation.

1. When short-run aggregate supply falls . . .

FIGURE **11**

Accommodating an Adverse Shift in Aggregate Supply
Faced with an adverse shift in aggregate supply from AS_1 to AS_2, policymakers who can influence aggregate demand might try to shift the aggregate-demand curve to the right from AD_1 to AD_2. The economy would move from point A to point C. This policy would prevent the supply shift from reducing output in the short run, but the price level would permanently rise from P_1 to P_3.

2. . . . policymakers can accommodate the shift by expanding aggregate demand . . .

3. . . . which causes the price level to rise further . . .

4. . . . but keeps output at its natural rate.

CASE STUDY | OIL AND THE ECONOMY

Some of the largest economic fluctuations in the U.S. economy since 1970 have originated in the oil fields of the Middle East. Crude oil is a key input into the production of many goods and services, and much of the world's oil comes from Saudi Arabia, Kuwait, and other Middle Eastern countries. When some event (usually political in origin) reduces the supply of crude oil flowing from this region, the price of oil rises around the world. U.S. firms that make gasoline, tires, and many other products experience rising costs, and they find it less profitable to supply their output of goods and services at any given price level. The result is a leftward shift in the aggregate-supply curve, which in turn leads to stagflation.

The first episode of this sort occurred in the mid-1970s. The countries with large oil reserves got together as members of OPEC, the Organization of Petroleum Exporting Countries. OPEC is a *cartel*—a group of sellers that attempts to thwart competition and reduce production to raise prices. And indeed, oil prices rose substantially. From 1973 to 1975, oil approximately doubled in price. Oil-importing countries around the world experienced simultaneous inflation and recession. The U.S. inflation rate as measured by the CPI exceeded 10 percent for the first time in decades. Unemployment rose from 4.9 percent in 1973 to 8.5 percent in 1975.

Almost the same thing happened a few years later. In the late 1970s, the OPEC countries again restricted the supply of oil to raise the price. From 1978 to 1981, the price of oil more than doubled. Once again, the result was stagflation.

FYI

The Macroeconomic Impact of Hurricane Katrina

In August 2005, as this book was going to press, the Gulf Coast of the United States was hit by Hurricane Katrina, devastating New Orleans and the surrounding area. While the human toll was the primary focus of policymakers' attentions, economists in and out of government immediately started analyzing the economic impact. Here are some excerpts from the analysis of the Congressional Budget Office (CBO), prepared just a few days after the disaster:

Katrina could dampen real gross domestic product (GDP) growth in the second half of the year by 1/2 to 1 percentage point and reduce employment through the end of this year by about 400,000. Most economic forecasters had expected 3 percent to 4 percent growth during the second half, and employment growth of 150,000 to 200,000 per month. Economic growth and employment are likely to rebound during the first half of 2006 as rebuilding accelerates. . . .

Katrina's macroeconomic effects will be greater than those of previous major hurricanes such as Andrew and Hugo, which caused a great deal of devastation but which had a small effect on the macroeconomy. Katrina's effects will be greater because of the greater devastation, the long-term flooding of New Orleans (which will preclude immediate rebuilding), and the destruction of energy and port infrastructure. . . .

The gross state product of Louisiana is about 1.2 percent of U.S. GDP, and that for Mississippi is about 0.7 percent. If half of that product were lost for three months (September to November), the level of real GDP would be lowered by about 1 percent from what it otherwise would be. . . . It is unlikely that production would be hurt that much for that long, however. Presumably some people in New Orleans and other parts of the coast will be able to return to work in one or two months, and construction employment will be picking up during the fourth quarter. . . .

Economic activity in the rest of the United States will be adversely affected through higher energy prices, which will temporarily reduce other consumption. . . . [This fall in consumption occurs because] the increase in gasoline prices is basically a temporary redistribution of income from consumers of gasoline to the stockholders of refiners. . . . If sustained, that would reduce annualized GDP growth for the third quarter by 0.4 percent and for the fourth quarter by 0.9 percent. That effect is temporary: as gasoline prices return to pre-Katrina levels, consumption would bounce back, meaning higher GDP growth.

In other words, the hurricane was expected to reduce aggregate supply by making unavailable some of the productive capacity of the Gulf area. In addition, it was expected to reduce aggregate demand because consumers might respond to higher gasoline prices by cutting back their overall level of spending. The predicted decline in GDP growth from these two shifts was significant, but according to CBO, it was not large enough to push the economy into recession.

As you read this book, you should know if this analysis proved correct.

Inflation, which had subsided somewhat after the first OPEC event, again rose above 10 percent per year. But because the Fed was not willing to accommodate such a large rise in inflation, a recession was soon to follow. Unemployment rose from about 6 percent in 1978 and 1979 to about 10 percent a few years later.

The world market for oil can also be a source of favorable shifts in aggregate supply. In 1986, squabbling broke out among members of OPEC. Member countries reneged on their agreements to restrict oil production. In the world market for crude oil, prices fell by about half. This fall in oil prices reduced costs to U.S. firms, which now found it more profitable to supply goods and services at any given price level. As a result, the aggregate-supply curve shifted to the right. The U.S. economy experienced the opposite of stagflation: Output grew rapidly, unemployment fell, and the inflation rate reached its lowest level in many years.

In recent years, the world market for oil has not been as important a source of economic fluctuations. Part of the reason is that OPEC has been less effective as a cartel: Adjusted for inflation, the price of oil has never again reached the record levels set in the early 1980s. In addition, conservation efforts and changes in technology have reduced the economy's dependence on oil. The amount of oil used to produce a unit of real GDP has declined about 40 percent since the OPEC shocks of the 1970s. As a result, the economic impact of any change in oil prices is smaller today than it was in the past.

Nonetheless, it would be premature to conclude that the United States no longer needs to worry about oil prices. Political troubles in the Middle East or greater cooperation among the members of OPEC could always send oil prices higher. And indeed, during the Iraq war, the price of crude oil did rise significantly. If the rise in oil prices were ever large enough, the macroeconomic result would most likely resemble the stagflation of the 1970s. •

CHANGES IN MIDDLE EAST OIL PRODUCTION ARE ONE SOURCE OF U.S. ECONOMIC FLUCTUATIONS.

Quick Quiz Suppose that the election of a popular presidential candidate suddenly increases people's confidence in the future. Use the model of aggregate demand and aggregate supply to analyze the effect on the economy.

CONCLUSION

This chapter has achieved two goals. First, we have discussed some of the important facts about short-run fluctuations in economic activity. Second, we have introduced a basic model to explain those fluctuations, called the model of aggregate demand and aggregate supply. We continue our study of this model in the next chapter to understand more fully what causes fluctuations in the economy and how policymakers might respond to these fluctuations.

SUMMARY

- All societies experience short-run economic fluctuations around long-run trends. These fluctuations are irregular and largely unpredictable. When recessions do occur, real GDP and other measures of income, spending, and production fall, and unemployment rises.

- Classical economic theory is based on the assumption that nominal variables such as the money supply and the price level do not influence real variables such as output and employment. Most economists believe that this assump-

tion is accurate in the long run but not in the short run. Economists analyze short-run economic fluctuations using the model of aggregate demand and aggregate supply. According to this model, the output of goods and services and the overall level of prices adjust to balance aggregate demand and aggregate supply.

- The aggregate-demand curve slopes downward for three reasons. The first is the wealth effect: A lower price level raises the real value of households' money holdings, which stimulates consumer spending. The second is the interest-rate effect: A lower price level reduces the quantity of money households demand; as households try to convert money into interest-bearing assets, interest rates fall, which stimulates investment spending. The third is the exchange-rate effect: As a lower price level reduces interest rates, the dollar depreciates in the market for foreign-currency exchange, which stimulates net exports.

- Any event or policy that raises consumption, investment, government purchases, or net exports at a given price level increases aggregate demand. Any event or policy that reduces consumption, investment, government purchases, or net exports at a given price level decreases aggregate demand.

- The long-run aggregate-supply curve is vertical. In the long run, the quantity of goods and services supplied depends on the economy's labor, capital, natural resources, and technology but not on the overall level of prices.

- Three theories have been proposed to explain the upward slope of the short-run aggregate-supply curve. According to the sticky-wage theory, an unexpected fall in the price level temporarily raises real wages, which induces firms to reduce employment and production. According to the sticky-price theory, an unexpected fall in the price level leaves some firms with prices that are temporarily too high, which reduces their sales and causes them to cut back production. According to

the misperceptions theory, an unexpected fall in the price level leads suppliers to mistakenly believe that their relative prices have fallen, which induces them to reduce production. All three theories imply that output deviates from its natural rate when the actual price level deviates from the price level that people expected.

- Events that alter the economy's ability to produce output, such as changes in labor, capital, natural resources, or technology, shift the short-run aggregate-supply curve (and may shift the long-run aggregate-supply curve as well). In addition, the position of the short-run aggregate-supply curve depends on the expected price level.

- One possible cause of economic fluctuations is a shift in aggregate demand. When the aggregate-demand curve shifts to the left, for instance, output and prices fall in the short run. Over time, as a change in the expected price level causes wages, prices, and perceptions to adjust, the short-run aggregate-supply curve shifts to the right, and the economy returns to its natural rate of output at a new, lower price level.

- A second possible cause of economic fluctuations is a shift in aggregate supply. When the aggregate-supply curve shifts to the left, the short-run effect is falling output and rising prices—a combination called stagflation. Over time, as wages, prices, and perceptions adjust, the price level falls back to its original level, and output recovers.

KEY CONCEPTS

recession, p. 323
depression, p. 323
model of aggregate demand and
  aggregate supply, p. 329

aggregate-demand curve, p. 329
aggregate-supply curve, p. 329

natural rate of output, p. 336
stagflation, p. 351

QUESTIONS FOR REVIEW

1. Name two macroeconomic variables that decline when the economy goes into a recession. Name one macroeconomic variable that rises during a recession.

2. Draw a diagram with aggregate demand, short-run aggregate supply, and long-run aggregate supply. Be careful to label the axes correctly.

3. List and explain the three reasons the aggregate-demand curve is downward sloping.

4. Explain why the long-run aggregate-supply curve is vertical.

5. List and explain the three theories for why the short-run aggregate-supply curve is upward sloping.

6. What might shift the aggregate-demand curve to the left? Use the model of aggregate demand and aggregate supply to trace through the short-run and long-run effects of such a shift on output and the price level.

7. What might shift the aggregate-supply curve to the left? Use the model of aggregate demand and aggregate supply to trace through the short-run and long-run effects of such a shift on output and the price level.

PROBLEMS AND APPLICATIONS

1. Suppose that the economy is in a long-run equilibrium.
   a. Draw a diagram to illustrate the state of the economy. Be sure to show aggregate demand, short-run aggregate supply, and long-run aggregate supply.
   b. Now suppose that a stock-market crash causes aggregate demand to fall. Use your diagram to show what happens to output and the price level in the short run. What happens to the unemployment rate?
   c. Use the sticky-wage theory of aggregate supply to explain what will happen to output and the price level in the long run (assuming there is no change in policy). What role does the expected price level play in this adjustment? Be sure to illustrate your analysis in a graph.

2. Explain whether each of the following events will increase, decrease, or have no effect on long-run aggregate supply.
   a. The United States experiences a wave of immigration.
   b. Congress raises the minimum wage to $10 per hour.
   c. Intel invents a new and more powerful computer chip.
   d. A severe hurricane damages factories along the East Coast.

3. Suppose an economy is in long-run equilibrium.
   a. Use the model of aggregate demand and aggregate supply to illustrate the initial equilibrium (call it point A). Be sure to include both short-run and long-run aggregate supply.
   b. The central bank raises the money supply by 5 percent. Use your diagram to show what happens to output and the price level as the economy moves from the initial to the new short-run equilibrium (call it point B).
   c. Now show the new long-run equilibrium (call it point C). What causes the economy to move from point B to point C?
   d. According to the sticky-wage theory of aggregate supply, how do nominal wages at point A compare to nominal wages at point B? How do nominal wages at point A compare to nominal wages at point C?
   e. According to the sticky-wage theory of aggregate supply, how do real wages at point A compare to real wages at point B? How do real wages at point A compare to real wages at point C?
   f. Judging by the impact of the money supply on nominal and real wages, is this analysis consistent with the proposition that money has real effects in the short run but is neutral in the long run?

4. In 1939, with the U.S. economy not yet fully recovered from the Great Depression, President Roosevelt proclaimed that Thanksgiving would fall a week earlier than usual so that the shopping period before Christmas would be longer. Explain what President Roosevelt might have been trying to achieve, using the model of aggregate demand and aggregate supply.

5. Explain why the following statements are false.
   a. "The aggregate-demand curve slopes downward because it is the horizontal sum of the demand curves for individual goods."

b. "The long-run aggregate-supply curve is vertical because economic forces do not affect long-run aggregate supply."

c. "If firms adjusted their prices every day, then the short-run aggregate-supply curve would be horizontal."

d. "Whenever the economy enters a recession, its long-run aggregate-supply curve shifts to the left."

6. For each of the three theories for the upward slope of the short-run aggregate-supply curve, carefully explain the following:

a. How the economy recovers from a recession and returns to its long-run equilibrium without any policy intervention.

b. What determines the speed of that recovery.

7. Suppose the Fed expands the money supply, but because the public expects this Fed action, it simultaneously raises its expectation of the price level. What will happen to output and the price level in the short run? Compare this result to the outcome if the Fed expanded the money supply but the public didn't change its expectation of the price level.

8. Suppose that the economy is currently in a recession. If policymakers take no action, how will the economy change over time? Explain in words and using an aggregate-demand/aggregate-supply diagram.

9. The economy begins in long-run equilibrium. Then one day, the president appoints a new chairman of the Federal Reserve. This new chairman is well-known for his view that inflation is not a major problem for an economy.

a. How would this news affect the price level that people would expect to prevail?

b. How would this change in the expected price level affect the nominal wage that workers and firms agree to in their new labor contracts?

c. How would this change in the nominal wage affect the profitability of producing goods and services at any given price level?

d. How does this change in profitability affect the short-run aggregate-supply curve?

e. If aggregate demand is held constant, how does this shift in the aggregate-supply curve affect the price level and the quantity of output produced?

f. Do you think this Fed chairman was a good appointment?

10. Explain whether each of the following events shifts the short-run aggregate-supply curve, the aggregate-demand curve, both, or neither. For each event that does shift a curve, draw a diagram to illustrate the effect on the economy.

a. Households decide to save a larger share of their income.

b. Florida orange groves suffer a prolonged period of below-freezing temperatures.

c. Increased job opportunities overseas cause many people to leave the country.

11. For each of the following events, explain the short-run and long-run effects on output and the price level, assuming policymakers take no action.

a. The stock market declines sharply, reducing consumers' wealth.

b. The federal government increases spending on national defense.

c. A technological improvement raises productivity.

d. A recession overseas causes foreigners to buy fewer U.S. goods.

12. Suppose that firms become very optimistic about future business conditions and invest heavily in new capital equipment.

a. Draw an aggregate-demand/aggregate-supply diagram to show the short-run effect of this optimism on the economy. Label the new levels of prices and real output. Explain in words why the aggregate quantity of output *supplied* changes.

b. Now use the diagram from part (a) to show the new long-run equilibrium of the economy. (For now, assume there is no change in the long-run aggregate-supply curve.) Explain in words why the aggregate quantity of output *demanded* changes between the short run and the long run.

c. How might the investment boom affect the long-run aggregate-supply curve? Explain.

13. In economy A, all workers agree in advance on the nominal wages that their employers will pay them. In economy B, half of all workers have these nominal wage contracts, while the other half have indexed employment contracts, so their wages rise and fall automatically with the

price level. According to the sticky-wage theory of aggregate supply, which economy has a more steeply sloped short-run aggregate-supply curve? In which economy would a 5 percent increase in the money supply have a larger impact on output? In which economy would it have a larger impact on the price level? Explain.

14. The National Bureau of Economic Research is a nonprofit economic research group that sets the official dates for the beginning and end of recessions in the United States. Go to its website, http://www.nber.org, and find information about business cycle dating. Notice that the NBER often uses the term *contraction* for a recession and the term *expansion* for the period of growth between recessions.

a. What was the U.S. economy's most recent turning point? Is the U.S economy now in an expansion or a contraction?

b. When was the most recent completed contraction? How long was it? By historical standards, was this contraction short or long?

c. When was the most recent completed expansion? How long was it? By historical standards, was this expansion short or long?

 For further information on topics in this chapter, additional problems, examples, applications, online quizzes, and more, please visit our website at http://mankiw.swlearning.com.

The Influence of Monetary and Fiscal Policy on Aggregate Demand

Imagine that you are a member of the Federal Open Market Committee, the group at the Federal Reserve that sets monetary policy. You observe that the president and Congress have agreed to cut government spending. How should the Fed respond to this change in fiscal policy? Should it expand the money supply, contract the money supply, or leave the money supply the same?

To answer this question, you need to consider the impact of monetary and fiscal policy on the economy. In the preceding chapter, we used the model of aggregate demand and aggregate supply to explain short-run economic fluctuations. We saw that shifts in the aggregate-demand curve or the aggregate-supply curve cause fluctuations in the economy's overall output of goods and services and its overall level of prices. As we noted in the previous chapter, monetary and fiscal policy can each influence aggregate demand. Thus, a change in one of these policies can lead to short-run fluctuations in output and prices. Policymakers will want to anticipate this effect and, perhaps, adjust the other policy in response.

In this chapter, we examine in more detail how the government's policy tools influence the position of the aggregate-demand curve. These tools include monetary policy (the supply of money set by the central bank) and fiscal policy (the levels of government spending and taxation set by the president and Congress).

We have previously discussed the long-run effects of these policies. In Chapters 7 and 8, we saw how fiscal policy affects saving, investment, and long-run economic growth. In Chapters 11 and 12, we saw how the Fed controls the money supply and how the money supply affects the price level in the long run. We now see how these policy tools can shift the aggregate-demand curve and, in doing so, affect macroeconomic variables in the short run.

As we have already learned, many factors influence aggregate demand besides monetary and fiscal policy. In particular, desired spending by households and firms determines the overall demand for goods and services. When desired spending changes, aggregate demand shifts. If policymakers do not respond, such shifts in aggregate demand cause short-run fluctuations in output and employment. As a result, monetary and fiscal policymakers sometimes use the policy levers at their disposal to try to offset these shifts in aggregate demand and thereby stabilize the economy. Here we discuss the theory behind these policy actions and some of the difficulties that arise in using this theory in practice.

HOW MONETARY POLICY INFLUENCES AGGREGATE DEMAND

The aggregate-demand curve shows the total quantity of goods and services demanded in the economy for any price level. The preceding chapter discussed three reasons the aggregate-demand curve slopes downward:

- *The wealth effect:* A lower price level raises the real value of households' money holdings, which are part of their wealth. Higher real wealth stimulates consumer spending and thus increases the quantity of goods and services demanded.
- *The interest-rate effect:* A lower price level reduces the amount of money people want to hold. As people try to lend out their excess money holdings, the interest rate falls. The lower interest rate stimulates investment spending and thus increases the quantity of goods and services demanded.
- *The exchange-rate effect:* When a lower price level reduces the interest rate, investors move some of their funds overseas in search of higher returns. This movement of funds causes the real value of the domestic currency to fall in the market for foreign-currency exchange. Domestic goods become less expensive relative to foreign goods. This change in the real exchange rate stimulates spending on net exports and thus increases the quantity of goods and services demanded.

These three effects occur simultaneously to increase the quantity of goods and services demanded when the price level falls and to decrease it when the price level rises.

Although all three effects work together to explain the downward slope of the aggregate-demand curve, they are not of equal importance. Because money holdings are a small part of household wealth, the wealth effect is the least important of the three. In addition, because exports and imports represent only a small fraction of U.S. GDP, the exchange-rate effect is not large for the U.S. economy. (This effect is more important for smaller countries, which typically export and import a higher fraction of their GDP.) *For the U.S. economy, the most important reason for the downward slope of the aggregate-demand curve is the interest-rate effect.*

To better understand aggregate demand, we now examine the short-run determination of interest rates in more detail. Here we develop the **theory of liquidity preference.** This theory of interest-rate determination will help explain the downward slope of the aggregate-demand curve, as well as how monetary and fiscal policy can shift this curve. By shedding new light on aggregate demand, the theory of liquidity preference expands our understanding of what causes short-run economic fluctuations and what policymakers can potentially do about them.

theory of liquidity preference
Keynes's theory that the interest rate adjusts to bring money supply and money demand into balance

The Theory of Liquidity Preference

In his classic book *The General Theory of Employment, Interest, and Money*, John Maynard Keynes proposed the theory of liquidity preference to explain what factors determine an economy's interest rate. The theory is, in essence, just an application of supply and demand. According to Keynes, the interest rate adjusts to balance the supply and demand for money.

You may recall that economists distinguish between two interest rates: The *nominal interest rate* is the interest rate as usually reported, and the *real interest rate* is the interest rate corrected for the effects of inflation. When there is no inflation, the two rates are the same. But when borrowers and lenders expect prices to rise over the course of the loan, they agree to a nominal interest rate that exceeds the real interest rate by the expected rate of inflation. The higher nominal interest rate compensates for the fact that they expect the loan to be repaid in less valuable dollars.

Which interest rate are we now trying to explain with the theory of liquidity preference? The answer is both. In the analysis that follows, we hold constant the expected rate of inflation. This assumption is reasonable for studying the economy in the short run, as we are now doing. Thus, when the nominal interest rate rises or falls, the real interest rate that people expect to earn rises or falls as well. For the rest of this chapter, when we refer to changes in the interest rate, you should envision the real and nominal interest rates moving in the same direction.

Let's now develop the theory of liquidity preference by considering the supply and demand for money and how each depends on the interest rate.

Money Supply   The first piece of the theory of liquidity preference is the supply of money. As we first discussed in Chapter 11, the money supply in the U.S. economy is controlled by the Federal Reserve. The Fed alters the money supply primarily by changing the quantity of reserves in the banking system through the purchase and sale of government bonds in open-market operations. When the Fed buys government bonds, the dollars it pays for the bonds are typically deposited in banks, and these dollars are added to bank reserves. When the Fed sells government bonds, the dollars it receives for the bonds are withdrawn from the banking system, and bank reserves fall. These changes in bank reserves, in turn, lead to changes in banks' ability to make loans and create money. In addition to these open-market operations, the Fed can alter the money supply by changing reserve requirements (the amount of reserves banks must hold against deposits) or the discount rate (the interest rate at which banks can borrow reserves from the Fed).

These details of monetary control are important for the implementation of Fed policy, but they are not crucial in this chapter. Our goal here is to examine how changes in the money supply affect the aggregate demand for goods and services. For this purpose, we can ignore the details of how Fed policy is implemented and simply assume that the Fed controls the money supply directly. In other words, the quantity of money supplied in the economy is fixed at whatever level the Fed decides to set it.

Because the quantity of money supplied is fixed by Fed policy, it does not depend on other economic variables. In particular, it does not depend on the interest rate. Once the Fed has made its policy decision, the quantity of money supplied is the same, regardless of the prevailing interest rate. We represent a fixed money supply with a vertical supply curve, as in Figure 1.

Money Demand   The second piece of the theory of liquidity preference is the demand for money. As a starting point for understanding money demand, recall that any asset's *liquidity* refers to the ease with which that asset is converted into the economy's medium of exchange. Money is the economy's medium of exchange, so it is by definition the most liquid asset available. The liquidity of money explains the demand for it: People choose to hold money instead of other assets that offer higher rates of return because money can be used to buy goods and services.

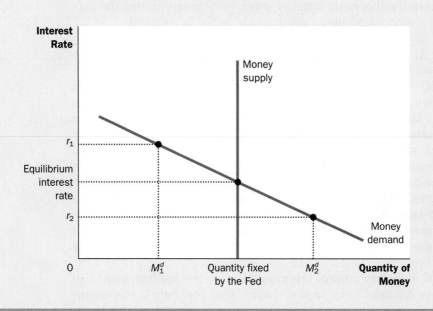

1 **FIGURE**

Equilibrium in the Money Market

According to the theory of liquidity preference, the interest rate adjusts to bring the quantity of money supplied and the quantity of money demanded into balance. If the interest rate is above the equilibrium level (such as at r_1), the quantity of money people want to hold (M_1^d) is less than the quantity the Fed has created, and this surplus of money puts downward pressure on the interest rate. Conversely, if the interest rate is below the equilibrium level (such as at r_2), the quantity of money people want to hold (M_2^d) is greater than the quantity the Fed has created, and this shortage of money puts upward pressure on the interest rate. Thus, the forces of supply and demand in the market for money push the interest rate toward the equilibrium interest rate, at which people are content holding the quantity of money the Fed has created.

Although many factors determine the quantity of money demanded, the one emphasized by the theory of liquidity preference is the interest rate. The reason is that the interest rate is the opportunity cost of holding money. That is, when you hold wealth as cash in your wallet, instead of as an interest-bearing bond, you lose the interest you could have earned. An increase in the interest rate raises the cost of holding money and, as a result, reduces the quantity of money demanded. A decrease in the interest rate reduces the cost of holding money and raises the quantity demanded. Thus, as shown in Figure 1, the money-demand curve slopes downward.

Equilibrium in the Money Market   According to the theory of liquidity preference, the interest rate adjusts to balance the supply and demand for money. There is one interest rate, called the *equilibrium interest rate*, at which the quantity of money demanded exactly balances the quantity of money supplied. If the interest rate is at any other level, people will try to adjust their portfolios of assets and, as a result, drive the interest rate toward the equilibrium.

For example, suppose that the interest rate is above the equilibrium level, such as r_1 in Figure 1. In this case, the quantity of money that people want to hold, M_1^d, is less than the quantity of money that the Fed has supplied. Those people who are holding the surplus of money will try to get rid of it by buying interest-bearing bonds or by depositing it in an interest-bearing bank account. Because bond issuers and banks prefer to pay lower interest rates, they respond to this surplus of money by lowering the interest rates they offer. As the interest rate falls, people become more willing to hold money until, at the equilibrium interest rate, people are happy to hold exactly the amount of money the Fed has supplied.

Conversely, at interest rates below the equilibrium level, such as r_2 in Figure 1, the quantity of money that people want to hold, M_2^d, is greater than the quantity of money that the Fed has supplied. As a result, people try to increase their holdings of money by reducing their holdings of bonds and other interest-bearing assets. As people cut back on their holdings of bonds, bond issuers find that they have to offer higher interest rates to attract buyers. Thus, the interest rate rises and approaches the equilibrium level.

The Downward Slope of the Aggregate-Demand Curve

Having seen how the theory of liquidity preference explains the economy's equilibrium interest rate, we now consider its implications for the aggregate demand for goods and services. As a warm-up exercise, let's begin by using the theory to reexamine a topic we already understand—the interest-rate effect and the downward slope of the aggregate-demand curve. In particular, suppose that the overall level of prices in the economy rises. What happens to the interest rate that balances the supply and demand for money, and how does that change affect the quantity of goods and services demanded?

As we discussed in Chapter 12, the price level is one determinant of the quantity of money demanded. At higher prices, more money is exchanged every time a good or service is sold. As a result, people will choose to hold a larger quantity of money. That is, a higher price level increases the quantity of money demanded for any given interest rate. Thus, an increase in the price level from P_1 to P_2 shifts the money-demand curve to the right from MD_1 to MD_2, as shown in panel (a) of Figure 2.

FYI

Interest Rates in the Long Run and the Short Run

At this point, we should pause and reflect on a seemingly awkward embarrassment of riches. It might appear as if we now have two theories for how interest rates are determined. In an earlier chapter, we said that the interest rate adjusts to balance the supply and demand for loanable funds (that is, national saving and desired investment). By contrast, we just established here that the interest rate adjusts to balance the supply and demand for money. How can we reconcile these two theories?

To answer this question, we must again consider the differences between the long-run and short-run behavior of the economy. Three macroeconomic variables are of central importance: the economy's output of goods and services, the interest rate, and the price level. According to the classical macroeconomic theory we developed earlier in the book, these variables are determined as follows:

1. *Output* is determined by the supplies of capital and labor and the available production technology for turning capital and labor into output. (We call this the natural rate of output.)
2. For any given level of output, the *interest rate* adjusts to balance the supply and demand for loanable funds.
3. Given output and the interest rate, the *price level* adjusts to balance the supply and demand for money. Changes in the supply of money lead to proportionate changes in the price level.

These are three of the essential propositions of classical economic theory. Most economists believe that these propositions do a good job of describing how the economy works *in the long run.*

Yet these propositions do not hold in the short run. As we discussed in the preceding chapter, many prices are slow to adjust to changes in the money supply; this is reflected in a short-run aggregate-supply curve that is upward sloping rather than vertical. As a result, the overall price level cannot, by itself, move to balance the supply and demand for money in the short run. This stickiness of the price level forces the interest rate to move to bring the money market into equilibrium. These changes in the interest rate, in turn, affect the aggregate demand for goods and services. As aggregate demand fluctuates, the economy's output of goods and services moves away from the level determined by factor supplies and technology.

For issues concerning the short run, then, it is best to think about the economy as follows:

1. The *price level* is stuck at some level (based on previously formed expectations) and, in the short run, is relatively unresponsive to changing economic conditions.
2. For any given price level, the *interest rate* adjusts to balance the supply and demand for money.
3. The interest rate that balances the money market influences the quantity of goods and services demanded and thus the level of *output.*

Notice that this precisely reverses the order of analysis used to study the economy in the long run.

The different theories of the interest rate are useful for different purposes. When thinking about the long-run determinants of interest rates, it is best to keep in mind the loanable-funds theory. This approach highlights the importance of an economy's saving propensities and investment opportunities. By contrast, when thinking about the short-run determinants of interest rates, it is best to keep in mind the liquidity-preference theory. This theory highlights the importance of monetary policy.

Notice how this shift in money demand affects the equilibrium in the money market. For a fixed money supply, the interest rate must rise to balance money supply and money demand. The higher price level has increased the amount of money people want to hold and has shifted the money demand curve to the

An increase in the price level from P_1 to P_2 shifts the money-demand curve to the right, as in panel (a). This increase in money demand causes the interest rate to rise from r_1 to r_2. Because the interest rate is the cost of borrowing, the increase in the interest rate reduces the quantity of goods and services demanded from Y_1 to Y_2. This negative relationship between the price level and quantity demanded is represented with a downward-sloping aggregate-demand curve, as in panel (b).

FIGURE 2

The Money Market and the Slope of the Aggregate-Demand Curve

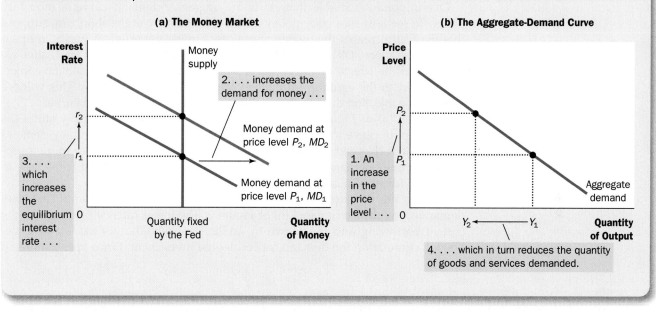

right. Yet the quantity of money supplied is unchanged, so the interest rate must rise from r_1 to r_2 to discourage the additional demand.

This increase in the interest rate has ramifications not only for the money market but also for the quantity of goods and services demanded, as shown in panel (b). At a higher interest rate, the cost of borrowing and the return to saving are greater. Fewer households choose to borrow to buy a new house, and those who do buy smaller houses, so the demand for residential investment falls. Fewer firms choose to borrow to build new factories and buy new equipment, so business investment falls. Thus, when the price level rises from P_1 to P_2, increasing money demand from MD_1 to MD_2 and raising the interest rate from r_1 to r_2, the quantity of goods and services demanded falls from Y_1 to Y_2.

This analysis of the interest-rate effect can be summarized in three steps: (1) A higher price level raises money demand. (2) Higher money demand leads to a higher interest rate. (3) A higher interest rate reduces the quantity of goods and services demanded. Of course, the same logic works in reverse as well: A lower price level reduces money demand, which leads to a lower interest rate, and this in turn increases the quantity of goods and services demanded. The end result of this analysis is a negative relationship between the price level and the quantity of goods and services demanded, as illustrated by a downward-sloping aggregate-demand curve.

Changes in the Money Supply

So far, we have used the theory of liquidity preference to explain more fully how the total quantity demanded of goods and services in the economy changes as the price level changes. That is, we have examined movements along the downward-sloping aggregate-demand curve. The theory also sheds light, however, on some of the other events that alter the quantity of goods and services demanded. Whenever the quantity of goods and services demanded changes *for a given price level*, the aggregate-demand curve shifts.

One important variable that shifts the aggregate-demand curve is monetary policy. To see how monetary policy affects the economy in the short run, suppose that the Fed increases the money supply by buying government bonds in open-market operations. (Why the Fed might do this will become clear later, after we understand the effects of such a move.) Let's consider how this monetary injection influences the equilibrium interest rate for a given price level. This will tell us what the injection does to the position of the aggregate-demand curve.

As panel (a) of Figure 3 shows, an increase in the money supply shifts the money-supply curve to the right from MS_1 to MS_2. Because the money-demand curve has not changed, the interest rate falls from r_1 to r_2 to balance money supply and money demand. That is, the interest rate must fall to induce people to hold the additional money the Fed has created.

Once again, the interest rate influences the quantity of goods and services demanded, as shown in panel (b) of Figure 3. The lower interest rate reduces the cost of borrowing and the return to saving. Households buy more and larger houses, stimulating the demand for residential investment. Firms spend more on

3 FIGURE

A Monetary Injection

In panel (a), an increase in the money supply from MS_1 to MS_2 reduces the equilibrium interest rate from r_1 to r_2. Because the interest rate is the cost of borrowing, the fall in the interest rate raises the quantity of goods and services demanded at a given price level from Y_1 to Y_2. Thus, in panel (b), the aggregate-demand curve shifts to the right from AD_1 to AD_2.

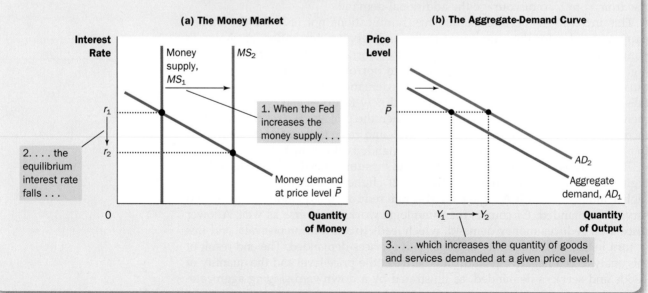

(a) The Money Market

(b) The Aggregate-Demand Curve

new factories and new equipment, stimulating business investment. As a result, the quantity of goods and services demanded at a given price level, $\bar{P}$, rises from Y_1 to Y_2. Of course, there is nothing special about $\bar{P}$: The monetary injection raises the quantity of goods and services demanded at every price level. Thus, the entire aggregate-demand curve shifts to the right.

To sum up: *When the Fed increases the money supply, it lowers the interest rate and increases the quantity of goods and services demanded for any given price level, shifting the aggregate-demand curve to the right. Conversely, when the Fed contracts the money supply, it raises the interest rate and reduces the quantity of goods and services demanded for any given price level, shifting the aggregate-demand curve to the left.*

The Role of Interest-Rate Targets in Fed Policy

How does the Federal Reserve affect the economy? Our discussion here and earlier in the book has treated the money supply as the Fed's policy instrument. When the Fed buys government bonds in open-market operations, it increases the money supply and expands aggregate demand. When the Fed sells government bonds in open-market operations, it decreases the money supply and contracts aggregate demand.

Discussions of Fed policy often treat the interest rate, rather than the money supply, as the Fed's policy instrument. Indeed, in recent years, the Federal Reserve has conducted policy by setting a target for the *federal funds rate*—the interest rate that banks charge one another for short-term loans. This target is reevaluated every six weeks at meetings of the Federal Open Market Committee (FOMC). The FOMC has chosen to set a target for the federal funds rate (rather than for the money supply, as it has done at times in the past) in part because the money supply is hard to measure with sufficient precision.

The Fed's decision to target an interest rate does not fundamentally alter our analysis of monetary policy. The theory of liquidity preference illustrates an important principle: *Monetary policy can be described either in terms of the money supply or in terms of the interest rate.* When the FOMC sets a target for the federal funds rate of, say, 6 percent, the Fed's bond traders are told: "Conduct whatever open-market operations are necessary to ensure that the equilibrium interest rate equals 6 percent." In other words, when the Fed sets a target for the interest rate, it commits itself to adjusting the money supply to make the equilibrium in the money market hit that target.

As a result, changes in monetary policy can be viewed either in terms of changing the interest rate target or in terms of changing the money supply. When you read in the newspaper that "the Fed has lowered the federal funds rate from 6 to 5 percent," you should understand that this occurs only because the Fed's bond traders are doing what it takes to make it happen. To lower the federal funds rate, the Fed's bond traders buy government bonds, and this purchase increases the money supply and lowers the equilibrium interest rate (just as in Figure 3). Similarly, when the FOMC raises the target for the federal funds rate, the bond traders sell government bonds, and this sale decreases the money supply and raises the equilibrium interest rate.

The lessons from this analysis are simple: Changes in monetary policy aimed at expanding aggregate demand can be described either as increasing the money supply or as lowering the interest rate. Changes in monetary policy aimed at contracting aggregate demand can be described either as decreasing the money supply or as raising the interest rate.

CASE STUDY | WHY THE FED WATCHES THE STOCK MARKET (AND VICE VERSA)

"Irrational exuberance." That was how Federal Reserve Chairman Alan Greenspan once described the booming stock market of the late 1990s. He was right that the market was exuberant: Average stock prices increased about four-fold during this decade. And perhaps it was even irrational: In the first few years of the following decade, the stock market took back some of these large gains, as stock prices experienced a pronounced decline, falling by about 40 percent from 2000 to 2003.

Regardless of how we view the booming market, it does raise an important question: How should the Fed respond to stock-market fluctuations? The Fed has no reason to care about stock prices in themselves, but it does have the job of monitoring and responding to developments in the overall economy, and the stock market is a piece of that puzzle. When the stock market booms, households become wealthier, and this increased wealth stimulates consumer spending. In addition, a rise in stock prices makes it more attractive for firms to sell new shares of stock, and this stimulates investment spending. For both reasons, a booming stock market expands the aggregate demand for goods and services.

As we discuss more fully later in the chapter, one of the Fed's goals is to stabilize aggregate demand, for greater stability in aggregate demand means greater stability in output and the price level. To do this, the Fed might respond to a stock-market boom by keeping the money supply lower and interest rates higher than it otherwise would. The contractionary effects of higher interest rates would offset the expansionary effects of higher stock prices. In fact, this analysis does describe Fed behavior: Real interest rates were kept high by historical standards during the "irrationally exuberant" stock-market boom of the late 1990s.

The opposite occurs when the stock market falls. Spending on consumption and investment declines, depressing aggregate demand and pushing the economy toward recession. To stabilize aggregate demand, the Fed needs to increase the money supply and lower interest rates. And indeed, that is what it typically does. For example, on October 19, 1987, the stock market fell by 22.6 percent—its biggest one-day drop in history. The Fed responded to the market crash by increasing the money supply and lowering interest rates. The federal funds rate fell from 7.7 percent at the beginning of October to 6.6 percent at the end of the month. In part because of the Fed's quick action, the economy avoided a recession. Similarly, as we discussed in a case study in the preceding chapter, the Fed also reduced interest rates during the stock market declines of 2001 and 2002, although this time monetary policy was not quick enough to avert a recession.

While the Fed keeps an eye on the stock market, stock-market participants also keep an eye on the Fed. Because the Fed can influence interest rates and economic activity, it can alter the value of stocks. For example, when the Fed raises interest rates by reducing the money supply, it makes owning stocks less attractive for two reasons. First, a higher interest rate means that bonds, the alternative to stocks, are earning a higher return. Second, the Fed's tightening of monetary policy reduces the demand for goods and services, which reduces profits. As a result, stock prices often fall when the Fed raises interest rates.   •

Quick Quiz Use the theory of liquidity preference to explain how a decrease in the money supply affects the equilibrium interest rate. How does this change in monetary policy affect the aggregate-demand curve?

HOW FISCAL POLICY INFLUENCES AGGREGATE DEMAND

The government can influence the behavior of the economy not only with monetary policy but also with fiscal policy. **Fiscal policy** refers to the government's choices regarding the overall level of government purchases or taxes. Earlier in the book, we examined how fiscal policy influences saving, investment, and growth in the long run. In the short run, however, the primary effect of fiscal policy is on the aggregate demand for goods and services.

fiscal policy
the setting of the level of government spending and taxation by government policymakers.

Changes in Government Purchases

When policymakers change the money supply or the level of taxes, they shift the aggregate-demand curve indirectly by influencing the spending decisions of firms or households. By contrast, when the government alters its own purchases of goods and services, it shifts the aggregate-demand curve directly.

Suppose, for instance, that the U.S. Department of Defense places a $20 billion order for new fighter planes with Boeing, the large aircraft manufacturer. This order raises the demand for the output produced by Boeing, which induces the company to hire more workers and increase production. Because Boeing is part of the economy, the increase in the demand for Boeing planes means an increase in the total quantity of goods and services demanded at each price level. As a result, the aggregate-demand curve shifts to the right.

By how much does this $20 billion order from the government shift the aggregate-demand curve? At first, one might guess that the aggregate-demand curve shifts to the right by exactly $20 billion. It turns out, however, that this is not the case. There are two macroeconomic effects that make the size of the shift in aggregate demand differ from the change in government purchases. The first—the multiplier effect—suggests that the shift in aggregate demand could be *larger* than $20 billion. The second—the crowding-out effect—suggests that the shift in aggregate demand could be *smaller* than $20 billion. We now discuss each of these effects in turn.

The Multiplier Effect

When the government buys $20 billion of goods from Boeing, that purchase has repercussions. The immediate impact of the higher demand from the government is to raise employment and profits at Boeing. Then, as the workers see higher earnings and the firm owners see higher profits, they respond to this increase in income by raising their own spending on consumer goods. As a result, the government purchase from Boeing raises the demand for the products of many other firms in the economy. Because each dollar spent by the government can raise the aggregate demand for goods and services by more than a dollar, government purchases are said to have a **multiplier effect** on aggregate demand.

multiplier effect
the additional shifts in aggregate demand that result when expansionary fiscal policy increases income and thereby increases consumer spending

This multiplier effect continues even after this first round. When consumer spending rises, the firms that produce these consumer goods hire more people and experience higher profits. Higher earnings and profits stimulate consumer spending once again and so on. Thus, there is positive feedback as higher demand leads to higher income, which in turn leads to even higher demand. Once all these effects are added together, the total impact on the quantity of goods and services demanded can be much larger than the initial impulse from higher government spending.

Figure 4 illustrates the multiplier effect. The increase in government purchases of $20 billion initially shifts the aggregate-demand curve to the right from AD_1 to AD_2 by exactly $20 billion. But when consumers respond by increasing their spending, the aggregate-demand curve shifts still further to AD_3.

This multiplier effect arising from the response of consumer spending can be strengthened by the response of investment to higher levels of demand. For instance, Boeing might respond to the higher demand for planes by deciding to buy more equipment or build another plant. In this case, higher government demand spurs higher demand for investment goods. This positive feedback from demand to investment is sometimes called the *investment accelerator*.

A Formula for the Spending Multiplier

A little high school algebra permits us to derive a formula for the size of the multiplier effect that arises when an increase in government purchases induces increases in consumer spending. An important number in this formula is the *marginal propensity to consume* (*MPC*)—the fraction of extra income that a household consumes rather than saves. For example, suppose that the marginal propensity to consume is $3/4$. This means that for every extra dollar that a household earns, the household spends $0.75 ($3/4$ of the dollar) and saves $0.25. With an *MPC* of $3/4$, when the workers and owners of Boeing earn $20 billion from the government contract, they increase their consumer spending by $3/4 \times$ $20 billion, or $15 billion.

To gauge the impact on aggregate demand of a change in government purchases, we follow the effects step by step. The process begins when the government spends $20 billion, which implies that national income (earnings and profits) also rises by this amount. This increase in income in turn raises consumer

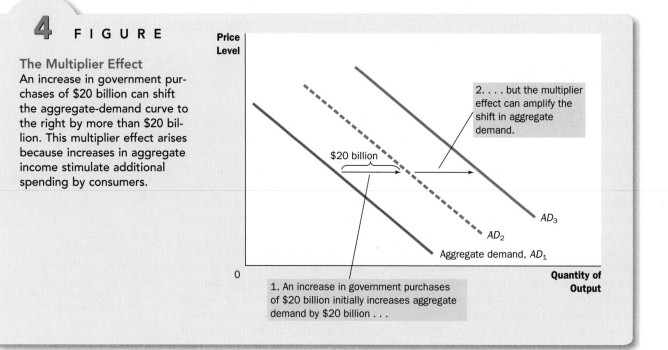

4   FIGURE

The Multiplier Effect
An increase in government purchases of $20 billion can shift the aggregate-demand curve to the right by more than $20 billion. This multiplier effect arises because increases in aggregate income stimulate additional spending by consumers.

Price Level

2. . . . but the multiplier effect can amplify the shift in aggregate demand.

$20 billion

AD_3

AD_2

Aggregate demand, AD_1

0

Quantity of Output

1. An increase in government purchases of $20 billion initially increases aggregate demand by $20 billion . . .

spending by $MPC \times \$20$ billion, which in turn raises the income for the workers and owners of the firms that produce the consumption goods. This second increase in income again raises consumer spending, this time by $MPC \times (MPC \times \$20$ billion). These feedback effects go on and on.

To find the total impact on the demand for goods and services, we add up all these effects:

Change in government purchases	=	$\$20$ billion
First change in consumption	=	$MPC \times \$20$ billion
Second change in consumption	=	$MPC^2 \times \$20$ billion
Third change in consumption	=	$MPC^3 \times \$20$ billion

$$\text{Total change in demand} = (1 + MPC + MPC^2 + MPC^3 + \ldots) \times \$20 \text{ billion.}$$

Here "..." represents an infinite number of similar terms. Thus, we can write the multiplier as follows:

$$\text{Multiplier} = 1 + MPC + MPC^2 + MPC^3 + \ldots.$$

This multiplier tells us the demand for goods and services that each dollar of government purchases generates.

To simplify this equation for the multiplier, recall from math class that this expression is an infinite geometric series. For x between -1 and $+1$,

$$1 + x + x^2 + x^3 + \ldots = 1 / (1 - x).$$

In our case, $x = MPC$. Thus,

$$\text{Multiplier} = 1 / (1 - MPC).$$

For example, if MPC is $^3/_4$, the multiplier is $1 / (1 - ^3/_4)$, which is 4. In this case, the $\$20$ billion of government spending generates $\$80$ billion of demand for goods and services.

This formula for the multiplier shows an important conclusion: The size of the multiplier depends on the marginal propensity to consume. While an MPC of $^3/_4$ leads to a multiplier of 4, an MPC of $^1/_2$ leads to a multiplier of only 2. Thus, a larger MPC means a larger multiplier. To see why this is true, remember that the multiplier arises because higher income induces greater spending on consumption. The larger the MPC is, the greater is this induced effect on consumption, and the larger is the multiplier.

Other Applications of the Multiplier Effect

Because of the multiplier effect, a dollar of government purchases can generate more than a dollar of aggregate demand. The logic of the multiplier effect, however, is not restricted to changes in government purchases. Instead, it applies to any event that alters spending on any component of GDP—consumption, investment, government purchases, or net exports.

For example, suppose that a recession overseas reduces the demand for U.S. net exports by $10 billion. This reduced spending on U.S. goods and services depresses U.S. national income, which reduces spending by U.S. consumers. If the marginal propensity to consume is $3/4$ and the multiplier is 4, then the $10 billion fall in net exports means a $40 billion contraction in aggregate demand.

As another example, suppose that a stock-market boom increases households' wealth and stimulates their spending on goods and services by $20 billion. This extra consumer spending increases national income, which in turn generates even more consumer spending. If the marginal propensity to consume is $3/4$ and the multiplier is 4, then the initial impulse of $20 billion in consumer spending translates into an $80 billion increase in aggregate demand.

The multiplier is an important concept in macroeconomics because it shows how the economy can amplify the impact of changes in spending. A small initial change in consumption, investment, government purchases, or net exports can end up having a large effect on aggregate demand and, therefore, the economy's production of goods and services.

The Crowding-Out Effect

The multiplier effect seems to suggest that when the government buys $20 billion of planes from Boeing, the resulting expansion in aggregate demand is necessarily larger than $20 billion. Yet another effect is working in the opposite direction. While an increase in government purchases stimulates the aggregate demand for goods and services, it also causes the interest rate to rise, and a higher interest rate reduces investment spending and puts downward pressure on aggregate demand. The reduction in aggregate demand that results when a fiscal expansion raises the interest rate is called the **crowding-out effect.**

crowding-out effect
the offset in aggregate demand that results when expansionary fiscal policy raises the interest rate and thereby reduces investment spending

To see why crowding out occurs, let's consider what happens in the money market when the government buys planes from Boeing. As we have discussed, this increase in demand raises the incomes of the workers and owners of this firm (and because of the multiplier effect, of other firms as well). As incomes rise, households plan to buy more goods and services and, as a result, choose to hold more of their wealth in liquid form. That is, the increase in income caused by the fiscal expansion raises the demand for money.

The effect of the increase in money demand is shown in panel (a) of Figure 5. Because the Fed has not changed the money supply, the vertical supply curve remains the same. When the higher level of income shifts the money-demand curve to the right from MD_1 to MD_2, the interest rate must rise from r_1 to r_2 to keep supply and demand in balance.

The increase in the interest rate, in turn, reduces the quantity of goods and services demanded. In particular, because borrowing is more expensive, the demand for residential and business investment goods declines. That is, as the increase in government purchases increases the demand for goods and services, it may also crowd out investment. This crowding-out effect partially offsets the impact of government purchases on aggregate demand, as illustrated in panel (b) of Figure 5. The increase in government purchases initially shifts the aggregate-demand curve from AD_1 to AD_2, but once crowding out takes place, the aggregate-demand curve drops back to AD_3.

To sum up: *When the government increases its purchases by $20 billion, the aggregate demand for goods and services could rise by more or less than $20 billion depending on whether the multiplier effect or the crowding-out effect is larger.*

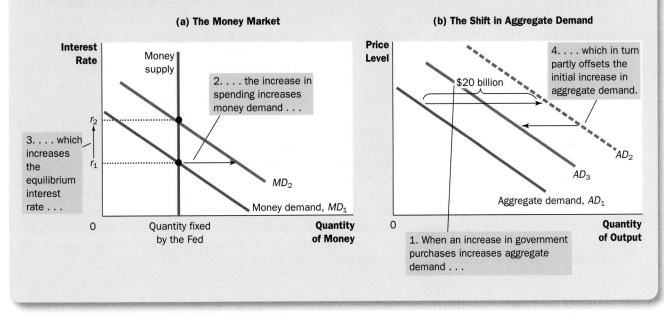

Panel (a) shows the money market. When the government increases its purchases of goods and services, the resulting increase in income raises the demand for money from MD_1 to MD_2, and this causes the equilibrium interest rate to rise from r_1 to r_2. Panel (b) shows the effects on aggregate demand. The initial impact of the increase in government purchases shifts the aggregate-demand curve from AD_1 to AD_2. Yet because the interest rate is the cost of borrowing, the increase in the interest rate tends to reduce the quantity of goods and services demanded, partic-ularly for investment goods. This crowding out of investment partially offsets the impact of the fiscal expansion on aggregate demand. In the end, the aggregate-demand curve shifts only to AD_3.

FIGURE 5

The Crowding-Out Effect

(a) The Money Market

Interest Rate

Money supply

2. . . . the increase in spending increases money demand . . .

r_2

3. . . . which increases the equilibrium interest rate . . .

r_1

MD_2

Money demand, MD_1

0

Quantity fixed by the Fed

Quantity of Money

(b) The Shift in Aggregate Demand

Price Level

$20 billion

4. . . . which in turn partly offsets the initial increase in aggregate demand.

AD_2

AD_3

Aggregate demand, AD_1

0

1. When an increase in government purchases increases aggregate demand . . .

Quantity of Output

Changes in Taxes

The other important instrument of fiscal policy, besides the level of government purchases, is the level of taxation. When the government cuts personal income taxes, for instance, it increases households' take-home pay. Households will save some of this additional income, but they will also spend some of it on consumer goods. Because it increases consumer spending, the tax cut shifts the aggregate-demand curve to the right. Similarly, a tax increase depresses consumer spend-ing and shifts the aggregate-demand curve to the left.

The size of the shift in aggregate demand resulting from a tax change is also affected by the multiplier and crowding-out effects. When the government cuts taxes and stimulates consumer spending, earnings and profits rise, which fur-ther stimulates consumer spending. This is the multiplier effect. At the same time, higher income leads to higher money demand, which tends to raise inter-est rates. Higher interest rates make borrowing more costly, which reduces investment spending. This is the crowding-out effect. Depending on the size of the multiplier and crowding-out effects, the shift in aggregate demand could be larger or smaller than the tax change that causes it.

FYI

How Fiscal Policy Might Affect Aggregate Supply

So far, our discussion of fiscal policy has stressed how changes in government purchases and changes in taxes influence the quantity of goods and services demanded. Most economists believe that the short-run macroeconomic effects of fiscal policy work primarily through aggregate demand. Yet fiscal policy can potentially also influence the quantity of goods and services supplied.

For instance, consider the effects of tax changes on aggregate supply. One of the *Ten Principles of Economics* in Chapter 1 is that people respond to incentives. When government policymakers cut tax rates, workers get to keep more of each dollar they earn, so they have a greater incentive to work and produce goods and services. If they respond to this incentive, the quantity of goods and services supplied will be greater at each price level, and the aggregate-supply curve will shift to the right.

Some economists, called *supply-siders*, have argued that the influence of tax cuts on aggregate supply is large. According to some supply-siders, the influence is so large that a cut in tax rates will stimulate enough additional production and income that tax revenue will actually increase. This is certainly a theoretical possibility, but most economists do not consider it the normal case. While the supply-side effects of taxes are important to consider, they are usually not large enough to cause tax revenue to rise when tax rates fall.

Like changes in taxes, changes in government purchases can also potentially affect aggregate supply. Suppose, for instance, that the government increases expenditure on a form of government-provided capital, such as roads. Roads are used by private businesses to make deliveries to their customers; an increase in the quantity of roads increases these businesses' productivity. Hence, when the government spends more on roads, it increases the quantity of goods and services supplied at any given price level and, thus, shifts the aggregate-supply curve to the right. This effect on aggregate supply is probably more important in the long run than in the short run, however, because it would take some time for the government to build the new roads and put them into use.

In addition to the multiplier and crowding-out effects, there is another important determinant of the size of the shift in aggregate demand that results from a tax change: households' perceptions about whether the tax change is permanent or temporary. For example, suppose that the government announces a tax cut of $1,000 per household. In deciding how much of this $1,000 to spend, households must ask themselves how long this extra income will last. If households expect the tax cut to be permanent, they will view it as adding substantially to their financial resources and, therefore, increase their spending by a large amount. In this case, the tax cut will have a large impact on aggregate demand. By contrast, if households expect the tax change to be temporary, they will view it as adding only slightly to their financial resources and, therefore, will increase their spending by only a small amount. In this case, the tax cut will have a small impact on aggregate demand.

An extreme example of a temporary tax cut was the one announced in 1992. In that year, President George H. W. Bush faced a lingering recession and an upcoming reelection campaign. He responded to these circumstances by announcing a reduction in the amount of income tax that the federal government was withholding from workers' paychecks. Because legislated income tax rates did not change, however, every dollar of reduced withholding in 1992 meant an extra dollar of taxes due on April 15, 1993, when income tax returns for 1992 were to be filed. Thus, this "tax cut" actually represented only a short-term loan from the government. Not surprisingly, the impact of the policy on consumer spending and aggregate demand was relatively small.

Quick Quiz   Suppose that the government reduces spending on highway construction by $10 billion. Which way does the aggregate-demand curve shift? Explain why the shift might be larger than $10 billion. Explain why the shift might be smaller than $10 billion.

USING POLICY TO STABILIZE THE ECONOMY

We have seen how monetary and fiscal policy can affect the economy's aggregate demand for goods and services. These theoretical insights raise some important policy questions: Should policymakers use these instruments to control aggregate demand and stabilize the economy? If so, when? If not, why not?

The Case for Active Stabilization Policy

Let's return to the question that began this chapter: When the president and Congress cut government spending, how should the Federal Reserve respond? As we have seen, government spending is one determinant of the position of the aggregate-demand curve. When the government cuts spending, aggregate demand will fall, which will depress production and employment in the short run. If the Federal Reserve wants to prevent this adverse effect of the fiscal policy, it can act to expand aggregate demand by increasing the money supply. A monetary expansion would reduce interest rates, stimulate investment spending, and expand aggregate demand. If monetary policy responds appropriately, the combined changes in monetary and fiscal policy could leave the aggregate demand for goods and services unaffected.

This analysis is exactly the sort followed by members of the Federal Open Market Committee. They know that monetary policy is an important determinant of aggregate demand. They also know that there are other important determinants as well, including fiscal policy set by the president and Congress. As a result, the Fed's Open Market Committee watches the debates over fiscal policy with a keen eye.

This response of monetary policy to the change in fiscal policy is an example of a more general phenomenon: the use of policy instruments to stabilize aggregate demand and, as a result, production and employment. Economic stabilization has been an explicit goal of U.S. policy since the Employment Act of 1946. This act states that "it is the continuing policy and responsibility of the federal government to . . . promote full employment and production." In essence, the government has chosen to hold itself accountable for short-run macroeconomic performance.

The Employment Act has two implications. The first, more modest, implication is that the government should avoid being a cause of economic fluctuations. Thus, most economists advise against large and sudden changes in monetary and fiscal policy, for such changes are likely to cause fluctuations in aggregate demand. Moreover, when large changes do occur, it is important that monetary and fiscal policymakers be aware of and respond to the other's actions.

The second, more ambitious, implication of the Employment Act is that the government should respond to changes in the private economy to stabilize aggregate demand. The act was passed not long after the publication of Keynes's *The General Theory of Employment, Interest, and Money*, which has been one of the most influential books ever written about economics. In it, Keynes emphasized the key role of aggregate demand in explaining short-run economic fluctuations. Keynes claimed that the government should actively stimulate aggregate demand when aggregate demand appeared insufficient to maintain production at its full-employment level.

Keynes (and his many followers) argued that aggregate demand fluctuates because of largely irrational waves of pessimism and optimism. He used the term "animal spirits" to refer to these arbitrary changes in attitude. When pessimism reigns, households reduce consumption spending, and firms reduce investment spending. The result is reduced aggregate demand, lower production, and higher unemployment. Conversely, when optimism reigns, households and firms increase spending. The result is higher aggregate demand, higher production, and inflationary pressure. Notice that these changes in attitude are, to some extent, self-fulfilling.

In principle, the government can adjust its monetary and fiscal policy in response to these waves of optimism and pessimism and, thereby, stabilize the economy. For example, when people are excessively pessimistic, the Fed can expand the money supply to lower interest rates and expand aggregate demand. When they are excessively optimistic, it can contract the money supply to raise interest rates and dampen aggregate demand. Former Fed chairman William McChesney Martin described this view of monetary policy very simply: "The Federal Reserve's job is to take away the punch bowl just as the party gets going."

|CASE STUDY| KEYNESIANS IN THE WHITE HOUSE

When a reporter in 1961 asked President John F. Kennedy why he advocated a tax cut, Kennedy replied, "To stimulate the economy. Don't you remember your Economics 101?" Kennedy's policy was, in fact, based on the analysis of fiscal policy we have developed in this chapter. His goal was to enact a tax cut, which would raise consumer spending, expand aggregate demand, and increase the economy's production and employment.

In choosing this policy, Kennedy was relying on his team of economic advisers. This team included such prominent economists as James Tobin and Robert Solow, who later would win Nobel prizes for their contributions to economics. As students in the 1940s, these economists had closely studied John Maynard Keynes's *General Theory*, which then was only a few years old. When the Kennedy advisers proposed cutting taxes, they were putting Keynes's ideas into action.

Although tax changes can have a potent influence on aggregate demand, they have other effects as well. In particular, by changing the incentives that people face, taxes can alter the aggregate supply of goods and services. Part of the Kennedy proposal was an investment tax credit, which gives a tax break to firms that invest in new capital. Higher investment would not only stimulate aggregate demand immediately but would also increase the economy's productive capacity over time. Thus, the short-run goal of increasing production through higher aggregate demand was coupled with a long-run goal of increasing production through higher aggregate supply. And indeed, when the tax cut Kennedy proposed was finally enacted in 1964, it helped usher in a period of robust economic growth.

Since the 1964 tax cut, policymakers have from time to time used fiscal policy as a tool for controlling aggregate demand. For example, when President George W. Bush moved into the Oval Office in 2001, he faced an economy that was heading into recession. One of his first policy initiatives was a substantial and permanent tax cut. Bush explained, "The best way to increase demand for goods and services is to let people keep more of their own money. And when somebody meets that demand by additional production, somebody is more likely to find a job."   •

The Case against Active Stabilization Policy

Some economists argue that the government should avoid active use of monetary and fiscal policy to try to stabilize the economy. They claim that these policy instruments should be set to achieve long-run goals, such as rapid economic growth and low inflation, and that the economy should be left to deal with short-run fluctuations on its own. Although these economists may admit that monetary and fiscal policy can stabilize the economy in theory, they doubt whether it can do so in practice.

The primary argument against active monetary and fiscal policy is that these policies affect the economy with a long lag. As we have seen, monetary policy works by changing interest rates, which in turn influence investment spending. But many firms make investment plans far in advance. Thus, most economists believe that it takes at least six months for changes in monetary policy to have much effect on output and employment. Moreover, once these effects occur, they can last for several years. Critics of stabilization policy argue that because of this lag, the Fed should not try to fine-tune the economy. They claim that the Fed often reacts too late to changing economic conditions and, as a result, ends up being a cause of rather than a cure for economic fluctuations. These critics advocate a passive monetary policy, such as slow and steady growth in the money supply.

Fiscal policy also works with a lag, but unlike the lag in monetary policy, the lag in fiscal policy is largely attributable to the political process. In the United States, most changes in government spending and taxes must go through congressional committees in both the House and the Senate, be passed by both legislative bodies, and then be signed by the president. Completing this process can take months and, in some cases, years. By the time the change in fiscal policy is passed and ready to implement, the condition of the economy may well have changed.

These lags in monetary and fiscal policy are a problem in part because economic forecasting is so imprecise. If forecasters could accurately predict the condition of the economy a year in advance, then monetary and fiscal policymakers could look ahead when making policy decisions. In this case, policymakers could stabilize the economy despite the lags they face. In practice, however, major recessions and depressions arrive without much advance warning. The best policymakers can do at any time is to respond to economic changes as they occur.

Automatic Stabilizers

automatic stabilizers
changes in fiscal policy
that stimulate aggregate
demand when the econ-
omy goes into a reces-
sion without policymak-
ers having to take any
deliberate action

All economists—both advocates and critics of stabilization policy—agree that the lags in implementation render policy less useful as a tool for short-run stabilization. The economy would be more stable, therefore, if policymakers could find a way to avoid some of these lags. In fact, they have. **Automatic stabilizers** are changes in fiscal policy that stimulate aggregate demand when the economy goes into a recession without policymakers having to take any deliberate action.

The most important automatic stabilizer is the tax system. When the economy goes into a recession, the amount of taxes collected by the government falls automatically because almost all taxes are closely tied to economic activity. The personal income tax depends on households' incomes, the payroll tax depends on workers' earnings, and the corporate income tax depends on firms' profits. Because incomes, earnings, and profits all fall in a recession, the government's tax revenue falls as well. This automatic tax cut stimulates aggregate demand and, thereby, reduces the magnitude of economic fluctuations.

Government spending also acts as an automatic stabilizer. In particular, when the economy goes into a recession and workers are laid off, more people apply for unemployment insurance benefits, welfare benefits, and other forms of income support. This automatic increase in government spending stimulates aggregate demand at exactly the time when aggregate demand is insufficient to maintain full employment. Indeed, when the unemployment insurance system was first enacted in the 1930s, economists who advocated this policy did so in part because of its power as an automatic stabilizer.

The automatic stabilizers in the U.S. economy are not sufficiently strong to prevent recessions completely. Nonetheless, without these automatic stabilizers, output and employment would probably be more volatile than they are. For this reason, many economists oppose a constitutional amendment that would require the federal government always to run a balanced budget, as some politicians have proposed. When the economy goes into a recession, taxes fall, government spending rises, and the government's budget moves toward deficit. If the government faced a strict balanced-budget rule, it would be forced to look for ways to raise taxes or cut spending in a recession. In other words, a strict balanced-budget rule would eliminate the automatic stabilizers inherent in our current system of taxes and government spending.

Quick Quiz   Suppose a wave of negative "animal spirits" overruns the economy, and people become pessimistic about the future. What happens to aggregate demand? If the Fed wants to stabilize aggregate demand, how should it alter the money supply? If it does this, what happens to the interest rate? Why might the Fed choose not to respond in this way?

CONCLUSION

Before policymakers make any change in policy, they need to consider all the effects of their decisions. Earlier in the book, we examined classical models of the economy, which describe the long-run effects of monetary and fiscal policy. There we saw how fiscal policy influences saving, investment, and long-run growth and how monetary policy influences the price level and the inflation rate.

In this chapter, we examined the short-run effects of monetary and fiscal policy. We saw how these policy instruments can change the aggregate demand for goods and services and, thereby, alter the economy's production and employment in the short run. When Congress reduces government spending to balance the budget, it needs to consider both the long-run effects on saving and growth and the short-run effects on aggregate demand and employment. When the Fed reduces the growth rate of the money supply, it must take into account the long-run effect on inflation as well as the short-run effect on production. In all parts of government, policymakers must keep in mind both long-run and short-run goals.

SUMMARY

- In developing a theory of short-run economic fluctuations, Keynes proposed the theory of liquidity preference to explain the determinants of the interest rate. According to this theory, the interest rate adjusts to balance the supply and demand for money.

- An increase in the price level raises money demand and increases the interest rate that brings the money market into equilibrium. Because the interest rate represents the cost of borrowing, a higher interest rate reduces investment and, thereby, the quantity of goods and services demanded. The downward-sloping aggregate-demand curve expresses this negative relationship between the price level and the quantity demanded.

- Policymakers can influence aggregate demand with monetary policy. An increase in the money supply reduces the equilibrium interest rate for any given price level. Because a lower interest rate stimulates investment spending, the aggregate-demand curve shifts to the right. Conversely, a decrease in the money supply raises the equilibrium interest rate for any given price level and shifts the aggregate-demand curve to the left.

- Policymakers can also influence aggregate demand with fiscal policy. An increase in government purchases or a cut in taxes shifts the aggregate-demand curve to the right. A decrease in government purchases or an increase in taxes shifts the aggregate-demand curve to the left.

- When the government alters spending or taxes, the resulting shift in aggregate demand can be larger or smaller than the fiscal change. The multiplier effect tends to amplify the effects of fiscal policy on aggregate demand. The crowding-out effect tends to dampen the effects of fiscal policy on aggregate demand.

- Because monetary and fiscal policy can influence aggregate demand, the government sometimes uses these policy instruments in an attempt to stabilize the economy. Economists disagree about how active the government should be in this effort. According to advocates of active stabilization policy, changes in attitudes by households and firms shift aggregate demand; if the government does not respond, the result is undesirable and unnecessary fluctuations in output and employment. According to critics of active stabilization policy, monetary and fiscal policy work with such long lags that attempts at stabilizing the economy often end up being destabilizing.

KEY CONCEPTS

theory of liquidity preference, p. 363

fiscal policy, p. 371

multiplier effect, p. 371

crowding-out effect, p. 374

automatic stabilizers, p. 380

QUESTIONS FOR REVIEW

1. What is the theory of liquidity preference? How does it help explain the downward slope of the aggregate-demand curve?

2. Use the theory of liquidity preference to explain how a decrease in the money supply affects the aggregate-demand curve.

3. The government spends $3 billion to buy police cars. Explain why aggregate demand might increase by more than $3 billion. Explain why aggregate demand might increase by less than $3 billion.

4. Suppose that survey measures of consumer confidence indicate a wave of pessimism is sweeping the country. If policymakers do nothing, what will happen to aggregate demand? What should the Fed do if it wants to stabilize aggregate demand? If the Fed does nothing, what might Congress do to stabilize aggregate demand?

5. Give an example of a government policy that acts as an automatic stabilizer. Explain why the policy has this effect.

PROBLEMS AND APPLICATIONS

1. Explain how each of the following developments would affect the supply of money, the demand for money, and the interest rate. Illustrate your answers with diagrams.
   a. The Fed's bond traders buy bonds in open-market operations.
   b. An increase in credit-card availability reduces the cash people hold.
   c. The Federal Reserve reduces banks' reserve requirements.
   d. Households decide to hold more money to use for holiday shopping.
   e. A wave of optimism boosts business investment and expands aggregate demand.

2. The Federal Reserve expands the money supply by 5 percent.
   a. Use the theory of liquidity preference to illustrate the impact of this policy on the interest rate.
   b. Use the model of aggregate demand and aggregate supply to illustrate the impact of this change in the interest rate on output and the price level in the short run.
   c. When the economy makes the transition from its short-run equilibrium to its long-run equilibrium, what will happen to the price level?
   d. How will this change in the price level affect the demand for money and the equilibrium interest rate?
   e. Is this analysis consistent with the proposition that money has real effects in the short run but is neutral in the long run?

3. Suppose banks install automatic teller machines on every block and, by making cash readily available, reduce the amount of money people want to hold.
   a. Assume the Fed does not change the money supply. According to the theory of liquidity preference, what happens to the interest rate? What happens to aggregate demand?
   b. If the Fed wants to stabilize aggregate demand, how should it respond?

4. Consider two policies—a tax cut that will last for only 1 year and a tax cut that is expected to be permanent. Which policy will stimulate greater spending by consumers? Which policy will have the greater impact on aggregate demand? Explain.

5. The economy is in a recession with high unemployment and low output.
   a. Draw a graph of aggregate demand and aggregate supply to illustrate the current situation. Be sure to include the aggregate-demand curve, the short-run aggregate-supply curve, and the long-run aggregate-supply curve.
   b. Identify an open-market operation that would restore the economy to its natural rate.
   c. Draw a graph of the money market to illustrate the effect of this open-market operation. Show the resulting change in the interest rate.
   d. Draw a graph similar to the one in part (a) to show the effect of the open-market operation

on output and the price level. Explain in words why the policy has the effect that you have shown in the graph.

6. In the early 1980s, new legislation allowed banks to pay interest on checking deposits, which they could not do previously.

   a. If we define money to include checking deposits, what effect did this legislation have on money demand? Explain.

   b. If the Federal Reserve had maintained a constant money supply in the face of this change, what would have happened to the interest rate? What would have happened to aggregate demand and aggregate output?

   c. If the Federal Reserve had maintained a constant market interest rate (the interest rate on nonmonetary assets) in the face of this change, what change in the money supply would have been necessary? What would have happened to aggregate demand and aggregate output?

7. Suppose economists observe that an increase in government spending of $10 billion raises the total demand for goods and services by $30 billion.

   a. If these economists ignore the possibility of crowding out, what would they estimate the marginal propensity to consume (*MPC*) to be?

   b. Now suppose the economists allow for crowding out. Would their new estimate of the *MPC* be larger or smaller than their initial one?

8. Suppose the government reduces taxes by $20 billion, that there is no crowding out, and that the marginal propensity to consume is $3/4$.

   a. What is the initial effect of the tax reduction on aggregate demand?

   b. What additional effects follow this initial effect? What is the total effect of the tax cut on aggregate demand?

   c. How does the total effect of this $20 billion tax cut compare to the total effect of a $20 billion increase in government purchases? Why?

9. Suppose government spending increases. Would the effect on aggregate demand be larger if the Federal Reserve took no action in response or if the Fed were committed to maintaining a fixed interest rate? Explain.

10. In which of the following circumstances is expansionary fiscal policy more likely to lead to a short-run increase in investment? Explain.

    a. When the investment accelerator is large or when it is small?

    b. When the interest sensitivity of investment is large or when it is small?

11. For various reasons, fiscal policy changes automatically when output and employment fluctuate.

    a. Explain why tax revenue changes when the economy goes into a recession.

    b. Explain why government spending changes when the economy goes into a recession.

    c. If the government were to operate under a strict balanced-budget rule, what would it have to do in a recession? Would that make the recession more or less severe?

12. Some members of Congress have proposed a law that would make price stability the sole goal of monetary policy. Suppose such a law were passed.

    a. How would the Fed respond to an event that contracted aggregate demand?

    b. How would the Fed respond to an event that caused an adverse shift in short-run aggregate supply?

    In each case, is there another monetary policy that would lead to greater stability in output?

13. Go to the website of the Federal Reserve, http://www.federalreserve.gov, to learn more about monetary policy. Find a recent report, speech, or testimony by the Fed chairman or another Fed governor. What does it say about the state of the economy and recent decisions about monetary policy?

 For further information on topics in this chapter, additional problems, examples, applications, online quizzes, and more, please visit our website at http://mankiw.swlearning.com.

The Short-Run Trade-off between Inflation and Unemployment

Two closely watched indicators of economic performance are inflation and unemployment. When the Bureau of Labor Statistics releases data on these variables each month, policymakers are eager to hear the news. Some commentators have added together the inflation rate and the unemployment rate to produce a *misery index*, which purports to measure the health of the economy.

How are these two measures of economic performance related to each other? Earlier in the book, we discussed the long-run determinants of unemployment and the long-run determinants of inflation. We saw that the natural rate of unemployment depends on various features of the labor market, such as minimum-wage laws, the market power of unions, the role of efficiency wages, and the effectiveness of job search. By contrast, the inflation rate depends primarily on growth in the money supply, which a nation's central bank controls. In the long run, therefore, inflation and unemployment are largely unrelated problems.

In the short run, just the opposite is true. One of the *Ten Principles of Economics* discussed in Chapter 1 is that society faces a short-run trade-off between inflation and unemployment. If monetary and fiscal policymakers expand aggregate demand and move the economy up along the short-run aggregate-supply curve, they can expand output and lower unemployment for a while, but only at the cost of a more rapidly rising price level. If policymakers contract aggregate demand and move the economy down the short-run aggregate-supply curve, they can lower inflation, but only at the cost of temporarily lower output and higher unemployment.

In this chapter, we examine the inflation-unemployment trade-off more closely. The relationship between inflation and unemployment is a topic that has attracted the attention of some of the most important economists of the last half-century. The best way to understand this relationship is to see how thinking about it has evolved. As we will see, the history of thought regarding inflation and unemployment since the 1950s is inextricably connected to the history of the U.S. economy. These two histories will show why the trade-off between inflation and unemployment holds in the short run, why it does not hold in the long run, and what issues the trade-off raises for economic policymakers.

THE PHILLIPS CURVE

Phillips curve
a curve that shows the short-run trade-off between inflation and unemployment

"Probably the single most important macroeconomic relationship is the Phillips curve." These are the words of economist George Akerlof from the lecture he gave when he received the Nobel prize in 2001. The **Phillips curve** is the short-run relationship between inflation and unemployment. We begin our story with the discovery of the Phillips curve and its migration to America.

Origins of the Phillips Curve

In 1958, economist A. W. Phillips published an article in the British journal *Economica* that would make him famous. The article was titled "The Relationship between Unemployment and the Rate of Change of Money Wages in the United Kingdom, 1861–1957." In it, Phillips showed a negative correlation between the rate of unemployment and the rate of inflation. That is, Phillips showed that years with low unemployment tend to have high inflation, and years with high unemployment tend to have low inflation. (Phillips examined inflation in nominal wages rather than inflation in prices, but for our purposes, that distinction is not important. These two measures of inflation usually move together.) Phillips concluded that two important macroeconomic variables—inflation and unemployment—were linked in a way that economists had not previously appreciated.

Although Phillips's discovery was based on data for the United Kingdom, researchers quickly extended his finding to other countries. Two years after Phillips published his article, economists Paul Samuelson and Robert Solow published an article in the *American Economic* Review called "Analytics of Anti-Inflation Policy" in which they showed a similar negative correlation between inflation and unemployment in data for the United States. They reasoned that this correlation arose because low unemployment was associated with high aggregate demand, which in turn puts upward pressure on wages and prices throughout the economy. Samuelson and Solow dubbed the negative association between inflation and unemployment the *Phillips curve.* Figure 1 shows an example of a Phillips curve like the one found by Samuelson and Solow.

As the title of their paper suggests, Samuelson and Solow were interested in the Phillips curve because they believed it held important lessons for policymakers. In particular, they suggested that the Phillips curve offers policymakers a

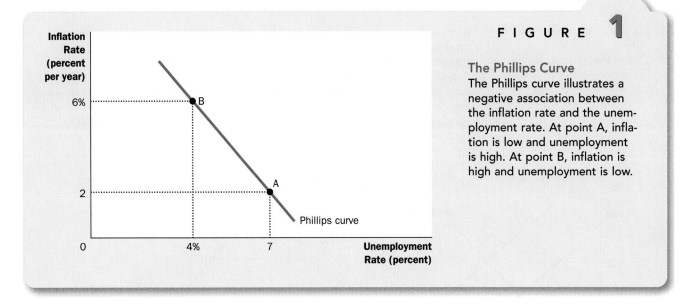

FIGURE **1**

The Phillips Curve
The Phillips curve illustrates a negative association between the inflation rate and the unemployment rate. At point A, inflation is low and unemployment is high. At point B, inflation is high and unemployment is low.

menu of possible economic outcomes. By altering monetary and fiscal policy to influence aggregate demand, policymakers could choose any point on this curve. Point A offers high unemployment and low inflation. Point B offers low unemployment and high inflation. Policymakers might prefer both low inflation and low unemployment, but the historical data as summarized by the Phillips curve indicate that this combination is impossible. According to Samuelson and Solow, policymakers face a trade-off between inflation and unemployment, and the Phillips curve illustrates that trade-off.

Aggregate Demand, Aggregate Supply, and the Phillips Curve

The model of aggregate demand and aggregate supply provides an easy explanation for the menu of possible outcomes described by the Phillips curve. *The Phillips curve simply shows the combinations of inflation and unemployment that arise in the short run as shifts in the aggregate-demand curve move the economy along the short-run aggregate-supply curve.* As we saw in the preceding two chapters, an increase in the aggregate demand for goods and services leads, in the short run, to a larger output of goods and services and a higher price level. Larger output means greater employment and, thus, a lower rate of unemployment. In addition, whatever the previous year's price level happened to be, the higher the price level in the current year, the higher the rate of inflation. Thus, shifts in aggregate demand push inflation and unemployment in opposite directions in the short run—a relationship illustrated by the Phillips curve.

To see more fully how this works, let's consider an example. To keep the numbers simple, imagine that the price level (as measured, for instance, by the consumer price index) equals 100 in the year 2010. Figure 2 shows two possible

2 FIGURE

How the Phillips Curve
Is Related to the Model
of Aggregate Demand
and Aggregate Supply

This figure assumes a price level of 100 for the year 2010 and charts possible outcomes for the year 2011. Panel (a) shows the model of aggregate demand and aggregate supply. If aggregate demand is low, the economy is at point A; output is low (7,500), and the price level is low (102). If aggregate demand is high, the economy is at point B; output is high (8,000), and the price level is high (106). Panel (b) shows the implications for the Phillips curve. Point A, which arises when aggregate demand is low, has high unemployment (7 percent) and low inflation (2 percent). Point B, which arises when aggregate demand is high, has low unemployment (4 percent) and high inflation (6 percent).

(a) The Model of Aggregate Demand and Aggregate Supply

(b) The Phillips Curve

outcomes that might occur in the year 2011 depending of the strength of aggregate demand. One outcome occurs if aggregate demand is high, and the other occurs if aggregate demand is low. Panel (a) shows these two outcomes using the model of aggregate demand and aggregate supply. Panel (b) illustrates the same two outcomes using the Phillips curve.

Panel (a) of the figure shows what happens to output and the price level in the year 2011. If the aggregate demand for goods and services is low, the economy experiences outcome A. The economy produces output of 7,500, and the price level is 102. By contrast, if aggregate demand is high, the economy experiences outcome B. Output is 8,000, and the price level is 106. This is just an example of a familiar conclusion: Higher aggregate demand moves the economy to an equilibrium with higher output and a higher price level.

Panel (b) shows what these two possible outcomes mean for unemployment and inflation. Because firms need more workers when they produce a greater output of goods and services, unemployment is lower in outcome B than in outcome A. In this example, when output rises from 7,500 to 8,000, unemployment falls from 7 percent to 4 percent. Moreover, because the price level is higher at outcome B than at outcome A, the inflation rate (the percentage change in the price level from the previous year) is also higher. In particular, since the price level was 100 in the year 2010, outcome A has an inflation rate of 2 percent, and outcome B has an inflation rate of 6 percent. The two possible outcomes for the economy can be compared either in terms of output and the price level (using the model of aggregate demand and aggregate supply) or in terms of unemployment and inflation (using the Phillips curve).

Because monetary and fiscal policy can shift the aggregate-demand curve, they can move an economy along the Phillips curve. Increases in the money supply, increases in government spending, or cuts in taxes expand aggregate demand and move the economy to a point on the Phillips curve with lower unemployment and higher inflation. Decreases in the money supply, cuts in government spending, or increases in taxes contract aggregate demand and move the economy to a point on the Phillips curve with lower inflation and higher unemployment. In this sense, the Phillips curve offers policymakers a menu of combinations of inflation and unemployment.

Quick Quiz   Draw the Phillips curve. Use the model of aggregate demand and aggregate supply to show how policy can move the economy from a point on this curve with high inflation to a point with low inflation.

SHIFTS IN THE PHILLIPS CURVE: THE ROLE OF EXPECTATIONS

The Phillips curve seems to offer policymakers a menu of possible inflation-unemployment outcomes. But does this menu of choices remain the same over time? Is the downward-sloping Phillips curve a stable relationship on which policymakers can rely? Economists took up these questions in the late 1960s, shortly after Samuelson and Solow had introduced the Phillips curve into the macroeconomic policy debate.

The Long-Run Phillips Curve

In 1968, economist Milton Friedman published a paper in the *American Economic Review*, based on an address he had recently given as president of the American Economic Association. The paper, titled "The Role of Monetary Policy," contained sections on "What Monetary Policy Can Do" and "What Monetary Policy Cannot Do." Friedman argued that one thing monetary policy cannot do, other than for only a short time, is lower unemployment by raising inflation. At about the same time, another economist, Edmund Phelps, also published a paper denying the existence of a long-run trade-off between inflation and unemployment.

Friedman and Phelps based their conclusions on classical principles of macroeconomics. Classical theory points to growth in the money supply as the primary determinant of inflation. But classical theory also states that monetary growth does not affect real variables such as output and employment; it merely alters all prices and nominal incomes proportionately. In particular, monetary growth does not influence those factors that determine the economy's unemployment rate, such as the market power of unions, the role of efficiency wages, or the process of job search. Friedman and Phelps concluded that there is no reason to think that the rate of inflation would, in the long run, be related to the rate of unemployment.

Here, in his own words, is Friedman's view about what the Federal Reserve can hope to accomplish for the economy in the long run:

> The monetary authority controls nominal quantities—directly, the quantity of its own liabilities [currency plus bank reserves]. In principle, it can use this control to peg a nominal quantity—an exchange rate, the price level, the nominal level of national income, the quantity of money by one definition or another—or to peg the change in a nominal quantity—the rate of inflation or deflation, the rate of growth or decline in nominal national income, the rate of growth of the quantity of money. It cannot use its control over nominal quantities to peg a real quantity—the real rate of interest, the rate of unemployment, the level of real national income, the real quantity of money, the rate of growth of real national income, or the rate of growth of the real quantity of money.

These views have important implications for the Phillips curve. In particular, they imply that monetary policymakers face a long-run Phillips curve that is vertical, as in Figure 3. If the Fed increases the money supply slowly, the inflation rate is low, and the economy finds itself at point A. If the Fed increases the money supply quickly, the inflation rate is high, and the economy finds itself at point B. In either case, the unemployment rate tends toward its normal level, called the *natural rate of unemployment*. The vertical long-run Phillips curve illustrates the conclusion that unemployment does not depend on money growth and inflation in the long run.

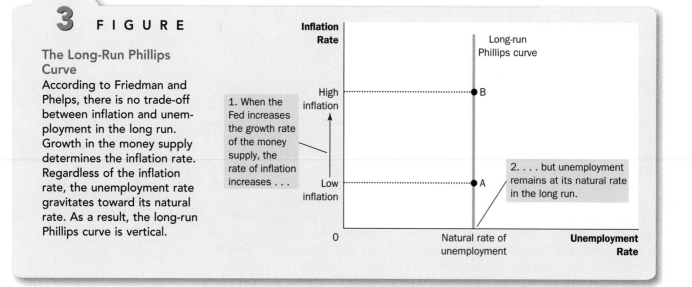

3 **FIGURE**

The Long-Run Phillips Curve

According to Friedman and Phelps, there is no trade-off between inflation and unemployment in the long run. Growth in the money supply determines the inflation rate. Regardless of the inflation rate, the unemployment rate gravitates toward its natural rate. As a result, the long-run Phillips curve is vertical.

1. When the Fed increases the growth rate of the money supply, the rate of inflation increases . . .

2. . . . but unemployment remains at its natural rate in the long run.

Long-run Phillips curve

Inflation Rate

High inflation

Low inflation

0

Natural rate of unemployment

Unemployment Rate

The vertical long-run Phillips curve is, in essence, one expression of the classical idea of monetary neutrality. Previously, we expressed monetary neutrality with a vertical long-run aggregate-supply curve. Figure 4 shows that the vertical long-run Phillips curve and the vertical long-run aggregate-supply curve are two sides of the same coin. In panel (a) of this figure, an increase in the money supply shifts the aggregate-demand curve to the right from AD_1 to AD_2. As a result of this shift, the long-run equilibrium moves from point A to point B. The price level rises from P_1 to P_2, but because the aggregate-supply curve is vertical, output remains the same. In panel (b), more rapid growth in the money supply raises the inflation rate by moving the economy from point A to point B. But because the Phillips curve is vertical, the rate of unemployment is the same at these two points. Thus, the vertical long-run aggregate-supply curve and the vertical long-run Phillips curve both imply that monetary policy influences nominal variables (the price level and the inflation rate) but not real variables (output and unemployment). Regardless of the monetary policy pursued by the Fed, output and unemployment are, in the long run, at their natural rates.

Panel (a) shows the model of aggregate demand and aggregate supply with a vertical aggregate-supply curve. When expansionary monetary policy shifts the aggregate-demand curve to the right from AD_1 to AD_2, the equilibrium moves from point A to point B. The price level rises from P_1 to P_2, while output remains the same. Panel (b) shows the long-run Phillips curve, which is vertical at the natural rate of unemployment. Expansionary monetary policy moves the economy from lower inflation (point A) to higher inflation (point B) without changing the rate of unemployment.

FIGURE 4

How the Long-Run Phillips Curve Is Related to the Model of Aggregate Demand and Aggregate Supply

The Meaning of "Natural"

What is so "natural" about the natural rate of unemployment? Friedman and Phelps used this adjective to describe the unemployment rate toward which the economy gravitates in the long run. Yet the natural rate of unemployment is not necessarily the socially desirable rate of unemployment. Nor is the natural rate of unemployment constant over time.

For example, suppose that a newly formed union uses its market power to raise the real wages of some workers above the equilibrium level. The result is an excess supply of workers and, therefore, a higher natural rate of unemployment. This unemployment is natural not because it is good but because it is beyond the influence of monetary policy. More rapid money growth would not reduce the market power of the union or the level of unemployment; it would lead only to more inflation.

Although monetary policy cannot influence the natural rate of unemployment, other types of policy can. To reduce the natural rate of unemployment, policymakers should look to policies that improve the functioning of the labor market. Earlier in the book, we discussed how various labor-market policies, such as minimum-wage laws, collective-bargaining laws, unemployment insurance, and job-training programs, affect the natural rate of unemployment. A policy change that reduced the natural rate of unemployment would shift the long-run Phillips curve to the left. In addition, because lower unemployment means more workers are producing goods and services, the quantity of goods and services supplied would be larger at any given price level, and the long-run aggregate-supply curve would shift to the right. The economy could then enjoy lower unemployment and higher output for any given rate of money growth and inflation.

Reconciling Theory and Evidence

At first, the conclusion of Friedman and Phelps that there is no long-run trade-off between inflation and unemployment might not seem persuasive. Their argument was based on an appeal to *theory*, specifically classical theory's prediction of monetary neutrality. By contrast, the negative correlation between inflation and unemployment documented by Phillips, Samuelson, and Solow was based on actual *evidence* from the real world. Why should anyone believe that policymakers faced a vertical Phillips curve when the world seemed to offer a downward-sloping one? Shouldn't the findings of Phillips, Samuelson, and Solow lead us to reject monetary neutrality?

Friedman and Phelps were well aware of these questions, and they offered a way to reconcile classical macroeconomic theory with the finding of a downward-sloping Phillips curve in data from the United Kingdom and the United States. They claimed that a negative relationship between inflation and unemployment exists in the short run but that it cannot be used by policymakers as a menu of outcomes in the long run. Policymakers can pursue expansionary monetary policy to achieve lower unemployment for a while, but eventually, unemployment returns to its natural rate, and more expansionary monetary policy leads only to higher inflation.

Friedman's and Phelps's work was the basis of our discussion of the difference between the short-run and long-run aggregate-supply curves in Chapter 15. As you may recall, the long-run aggregate-supply curve is vertical, indicating that the price level does not influence quantity supplied in the long run. But the short-run aggregate-supply curve is upward sloping, indicating that an increase in the price level raises the quantity of goods and services that firms supply. According to the sticky-wage theory of aggregate supply, for instance, nominal wages are set in advance based on the price level that workers and firms expected to prevail. When prices come in higher than expected, firms have an incentive to increase production and employment; when prices are less than expected, firms reduce production and employment. Yet because the expected price level and nominal wages will eventually adjust, the positive relationship between the actual price level and quantity supplied applies only in the short run.

Friedman and Phelps applied this same logic to the Phillips curve. Just as the aggregate-supply curve slopes upward only in the short run, the trade-off between inflation and unemployment holds only in the short run. And just as the long-run aggregate-supply curve is vertical, the long-run Phillips curve is also vertical. Once again, expectations are the key for understanding how the short run and the long run are related.

Friedman and Phelps introduced a new variable into the analysis of the inflation-unemployment trade-off: *expected inflation*. Expected inflation measures how much people expect the overall price level to change. Because the expected price level affects nominal wages, expected inflation is one factor that determines the position of the short-run aggregate-supply curve. In the short run, the Fed can take expected inflation (and thus, the short-run aggregate-supply curve) as already determined. When the money supply changes, the aggregate-demand curve shifts, and the economy moves along a given short-run aggregate-supply curve. In the short run, therefore, monetary changes lead to unexpected fluctuations in output, prices, unemployment, and inflation. In this way, Friedman and Phelps explained the downward-sloping Phillips curve that Phillips, Samuelson, and Solow had documented.

The Fed's ability to create unexpected inflation by increasing the money supply exists only in the short run. In the long run, people come to expect whatever inflation rate the Fed chooses to produce, and nominal wages will adjust to keep pace with inflation. As a result, the long-run aggregate-supply curve is vertical. Changes in aggregate demand, such as those due to changes in the money supply, affect neither the economy's output of goods and services nor the number of workers that firms need to hire to produce those goods and services. Friedman and Phelps concluded that unemployment returns to its natural rate in the long run.

The Short-Run Phillips Curve

The analysis of Friedman and Phelps can be summarized in the following equation:

$$\text{Unemployment rate} = \text{Natural rate of unemployment} - a\left(\text{Actual inflation} - \text{Expected inflation}\right).$$

This equation (which is, in essence, another expression of the aggregate-supply equation we have seen previously) relates the unemployment rate to the natural rate of unemployment, actual inflation, and expected inflation. In the short run, expected inflation is given, so higher actual inflation is associated with lower unemployment. (The variable *a* is a parameter that measures how much unemployment responds to unexpected inflation.) In the long run, people come to expect whatever inflation the Fed produces, so actual inflation equals expected inflation, and unemployment is at its natural rate.

This equation implies there can be no stable short-run Phillips curve. Each short-run Phillips curve reflects a particular expected rate of inflation. (To be precise, if you graph the equation, you'll find that the downward-sloping short-run Phillips curve intersects the vertical long-run Phillips curve at the expected rate of inflation.) When expected inflation changes, the short-run Phillips curve shifts.

According to Friedman and Phelps, it is dangerous to view the Phillips curve as a menu of options available to policymakers. To see why, imagine an economy at its natural rate of unemployment with low inflation and low expected inflation, shown in Figure 5 as point A. Now suppose that policymakers try to take advantage of the trade-off between inflation and unemployment by using monetary or fiscal policy to expand aggregate demand. In the short run, when expected inflation is given, the economy goes from point A to point B. Unemployment falls below its natural rate, and the actual inflation rate rises above expected inflation. As the economy moves from point A to point B, policymakers might think they have achieved permanently lower unemployment at the cost of higher inflation—a bargain that, if possible, might be worth making.

5 FIGURE

How Expected Inflation Shifts the Short-Run Phillips Curve
The higher the expected rate of inflation, the higher the short-run trade-off between inflation and unemployment. At point A, expected inflation and actual inflation are both low, and unemployment is at its natural rate. If the Fed pursues an expansionary monetary policy, the economy moves from point A to point B in the short run. At point B, expected inflation is still low, but actual inflation is high. Unemployment is below its natural rate. In the long run, expected inflation rises, and the economy moves to point C. At point C, expected inflation and actual inflation are both high, and unemployment is back to its natural rate.

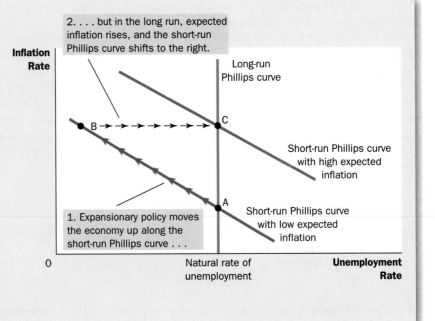

This situation, however, will not persist. Over time, people get used to this higher inflation rate, and they raise their expectations of inflation. When expected inflation rises, firms and workers start taking higher inflation into account when setting wages. The short-run Phillips curve then shifts to the right, as shown in the figure. The economy ends up at point C, with higher inflation than at point A but with the same level of unemployment. Thus, Friedman and Phelps concluded that policymakers face only a temporary trade-off between inflation and unemployment. In the long run, expanding aggregate demand more rapidly will yield higher inflation without any reduction in unemployment.

The Natural Experiment for the Natural-Rate Hypothesis

Friedman and Phelps had made a bold prediction in 1968: If policymakers try to take advantage of the Phillips curve by choosing higher inflation to reduce unemployment, they will succeed at reducing unemployment only temporarily. This view—that unemployment eventually returns to its natural rate, regardless of the rate of inflation—is called the **natural-rate hypothesis.** A few years after Friedman and Phelps proposed this hypothesis, monetary and fiscal policymakers inadvertently created a natural experiment to test it. Their laboratory was the U.S. economy.

Before we see the outcome of this test, however, let's look at the data that Friedman and Phelps had when they made their prediction in 1968. Figure 6 shows the unemployment and inflation rates for the period from 1961 to 1968.

natural-rate hypothesis
the claim that unemployment eventually returns to its normal, or natural, rate, regardless of the rate of inflation

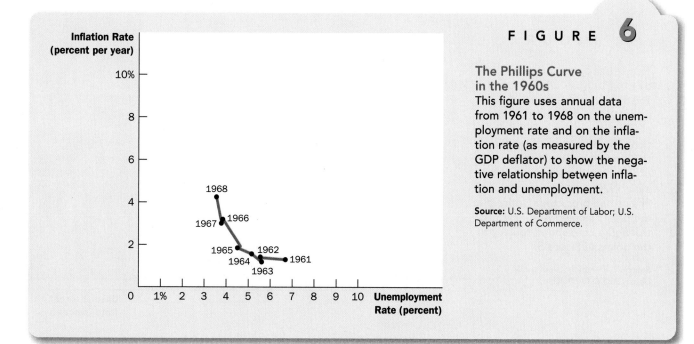

FIGURE **6**

The Phillips Curve in the 1960s
This figure uses annual data from 1961 to 1968 on the unemployment rate and on the inflation rate (as measured by the GDP deflator) to show the negative relationship between inflation and unemployment.

Source: U.S. Department of Labor; U.S. Department of Commerce.

These data trace out an almost perfect Phillips curve. As inflation rose over these eight years, unemployment fell. The economic data from this era seemed to confirm that policymakers faced a trade-off between inflation and unemployment.

The apparent success of the Phillips curve in the 1960s made the prediction of Friedman and Phelps all the bolder. In 1958, Phillips had suggested a negative association between inflation and unemployment. In 1960, Samuelson and Solow had shown it existed in U.S. data. Another decade of data had confirmed the relationship. To some economists at the time, it seemed ridiculous to claim that the historically reliable Phillips curve would start shifting once policymakers tried to take advantage of it.

In fact, that is exactly what happened. Beginning in the late 1960s, the government followed policies that expanded the aggregate demand for goods and services. In part, this expansion was due to fiscal policy: Government spending rose as the Vietnam War heated up. In part, it was due to monetary policy: Because the Fed was trying to hold down interest rates in the face of expansionary fiscal policy, the money supply (as measured by M2) rose about 13 percent per year during the period from 1970 to 1972, compared to 7 percent per year in the early 1960s. As a result, inflation stayed high (about 5 to 6 percent per year in the late 1960s and early 1970s, compared to about 1 to 2 percent per year in the early 1960s). But as Friedman and Phelps had predicted, unemployment did not stay low.

Figure 7 displays the history of inflation and unemployment from 1961 to 1973. It shows that the simple negative relationship between these two variables started to break down around 1970. In particular, as inflation remained high in the early 1970s, people's expectations of inflation caught up with reality, and the

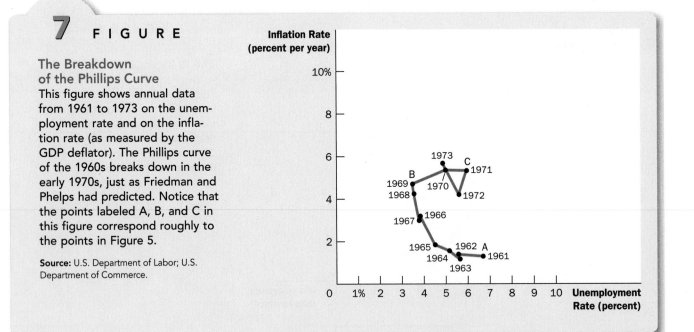

7 **FIGURE**

The Breakdown of the Phillips Curve
This figure shows annual data from 1961 to 1973 on the unemployment rate and on the inflation rate (as measured by the GDP deflator). The Phillips curve of the 1960s breaks down in the early 1970s, just as Friedman and Phelps had predicted. Notice that the points labeled A, B, and C in this figure correspond roughly to the points in Figure 5.

Source: U.S. Department of Labor; U.S. Department of Commerce.

unemployment rate reverted to the 5 percent to 6 percent range that had prevailed in the early 1960s. Notice that the history illustrated in Figure 7 resembles the theory of a shifting short-run Phillips curve shown in Figure 5. By 1973, policymakers had learned that Friedman and Phelps were right: There is no trade-off between inflation and unemployment in the long run.

In The News

How to Keep Expected Inflation Low

In 2004, Finn Kydland and Edward Prescott won the Nobel prize in economics, in part for their work on the role of expectations in policymaking.

Resist the Siren Song: The Nobel Laureates' Classical Refrain Has Modern Resonance

Odysseus legendarily had himself tied to his ship's mast before it passed the island of the Sirens, so that he could hear their entrancing song without steering his vessel to its destruction on the surrounding rocks. The deserving winners of this year's Nobel economics prize, the Norwegian Finn Kydland and the American Edward Prescott, would instantly recognize this as a fine example of overcoming a time consistency problem by using credible commitment to follow an ex ante optimal policy.

The independence of Europe's central banks, along with most others across the world, shows that, in the area of monetary policy, its politicians have largely absorbed the lesson exemplified by their mythical ancestor and codified by Kydland and Prescott. . . .

The work of the Kydland-Prescott duo has become synonymous with the idea that policy needs to be "time-consistent." If the public knows it is in the interest of policymakers to change direction in the future, decisions they make now will lack credibility.

That insight underlies what is now an almost universal acceptance that monetary policy, the chief means of steering the economy, should be in the hands of independent central bankers focused firmly on long-term stability, not finance ministers keeping one eye on the next election. The public will always rightly be suspicious that even if interest rates are set to ensure low inflation today, it will be in ministers' interests tomorrow to exploit the fact that wages have been set with that low inflation in mind and hence loosen monetary policy to steal a little more short-term growth. The inability of politicians credibly to commit to an outcome of low inflation will thus in fact raise expectations of in-

flation and mean interest rates have to be higher than otherwise.

In other words, policymakers need to find ways of tying themselves to the mast now to prevent the damaging belief that siren calls will make them stray later. Establishing independent central banks that focus on inflation is one such means. The events of recent months have shown the benefits in the US, the eurozone and the UK: Inflation expectations have remained subdued despite the rise in oil prices, enabling interest rates to stay low. . . .

Through careful policy design, Odysseus was able both to hear the Sirens' song and to avoid wrecking his vessel. Those steering the ships of state should learn from his example and the newly rewarded work of professors Kydland and Prescott.

Source: *The Financial Times*, October 12, 2004.

Quick Quiz Draw the short-run Phillips curve and the long-run Phillips curve. Explain why they are different.

SHIFTS IN THE PHILLIPS CURVE: THE ROLE OF SUPPLY SHOCKS

Friedman and Phelps had suggested in 1968 that changes in expected inflation shift the short-run Phillips curve, and the experience of the early 1970s convinced most economists that Friedman and Phelps were right. Within a few years, however, the economics profession would turn its attention to a different source of shifts in the short-run Phillips curve: shocks to aggregate supply.

This time, the change in focus came not from two American economics professors but from a group of Arab sheiks. In 1974, the Organization of Petroleum Exporting Countries (OPEC) began to exert its market power as a cartel in the world oil market to increase its members' profits. The countries of OPEC, such as Saudi Arabia, Kuwait, and Iraq, restricted the amount of crude oil they pumped and sold on world markets. Within a few years, this reduction in supply caused the world price of oil to almost double.

supply shock
an event that directly alters firms' costs and prices, shifting the economy's aggregate-supply curve and thus the Phillips curve

A large increase in the world price of oil is an example of a supply shock. A **supply shock** is an event that directly affects firms' costs of production and thus the prices they charge; it shifts the economy's aggregate-supply curve and, as a result, the Phillips curve. For example, when an oil price increase raises the cost of producing gasoline, heating oil, tires, and many other products, it reduces the quantity of goods and services supplied at any given price level. As panel (a) of Figure 8 shows, this reduction in supply is represented by the leftward shift in the aggregate-supply curve from AS_1 to AS_2. The price level rises from P_1 to P_2, and output falls from Y_1 to Y_2. The combination of rising prices and falling output is sometimes called *stagflation*.

This shift in aggregate supply is associated with a similar shift in the short-run Phillips curve, shown in panel (b). Because firms need fewer workers to produce the smaller output, employment falls and unemployment rises. Because the price level is higher, the inflation rate—the percentage change in the price level from the previous year—is also higher. Thus, the shift in aggregate supply leads to higher unemployment and higher inflation. The short-run trade-off between inflation and unemployment shifts to the right from PC_1 to PC_2.

Confronted with an adverse shift in aggregate supply, policymakers face a difficult choice between fighting inflation and fighting unemployment. If they contract aggregate demand to fight inflation, they will raise unemployment further. If they expand aggregate demand to fight unemployment, they will raise inflation further. In other words, policymakers face a less favorable trade-off between inflation and unemployment than they did before the shift in aggregate supply: They have to live with a higher rate of inflation for a given rate of unemployment, a higher rate of unemployment for a given rate of inflation, or some combination of higher unemployment and higher inflation.

Faced with such an adverse shift in the Phillips curve, policymakers will ask whether the shift is temporary or permanent. The answer depends on how peo-

Panel (a) shows the model of aggregate demand and aggregate supply. When the aggregate-supply curve shifts to the left from AS_1 to AS_2, the equilibrium moves from point A to point B. Output falls from Y_1 to Y_2, and the price level rises from P_1 to P_2. Panel (b) shows the short-run trade-off between inflation and unemployment. The adverse shift in aggregate supply moves the economy from a point with lower unemployment and lower inflation (point A) to a point with higher unemployment and higher inflation (point B). The short-run Phillips curve shifts to the right from PC_1 to PC_2. Policymakers now face a worse trade-off between inflation and unemployment.

FIGURE **8**

An Adverse Shock to Aggregate Supply

(a) The Model of Aggregate Demand and Aggregate Supply

(b) The Phillips Curve

ple adjust their expectations of inflation. If people view the rise in inflation due to the supply shock as a temporary aberration, expected inflation will not change, and the Phillips curve will soon revert to its former position. But if people believe the shock will lead to a new era of higher inflation, then expected inflation will rise, and the Phillips curve will remain at its new, less desirable position.

In the United States during the 1970s, expected inflation did rise substantially. This rise in expected inflation was partly attributable to the Fed's decision to accommodate the supply shock with higher money growth. (Recall that policymakers are said to *accommodate* an adverse supply shock when they respond to it by increasing aggregate demand in an effort to keep output from falling.) Because of this policy decision, the recession that resulted from the supply shock was smaller than it otherwise might have been, but the U.S. economy faced an unfavorable trade-off between inflation and unemployment for many years. The problem was compounded in 1979, when OPEC once again started to exert its market power, more than doubling the price of oil. Figure 9 shows inflation and unemployment in the U.S. economy during this period.

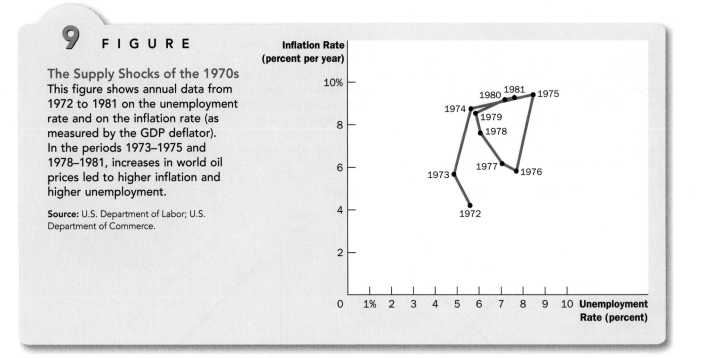

9 FIGURE

The Supply Shocks of the 1970s
This figure shows annual data from 1972 to 1981 on the unemployment rate and on the inflation rate (as measured by the GDP deflator). In the periods 1973–1975 and 1978–1981, increases in world oil prices led to higher inflation and higher unemployment.

Source: U.S. Department of Labor; U.S. Department of Commerce.

In 1980, after two OPEC supply shocks, the U.S. economy had an inflation rate of more than 9 percent and an unemployment rate of about 7 percent. This combination of inflation and unemployment was not at all near the trade-off that seemed possible in the 1960s. (In the 1960s, the Phillips curve suggested that an unemployment rate of 7 percent would be associated with an inflation rate of only 1 percent. Inflation of more than 9 percent was unthinkable.) With the misery index in 1980 near a historic high, the public was widely dissatisfied with the performance of the economy. Largely because of this dissatisfaction, President Jimmy Carter lost his bid for reelection in November 1980 and was replaced by Ronald Reagan. Something had to be done, and soon it would be.

Quick Quiz Give an example of a favorable shock to aggregate supply. Use the model of aggregate demand and aggregate supply to explain the effects of such a shock. How does it affect the Phillips curve?

THE COST OF REDUCING INFLATION

In October 1979, as OPEC was imposing adverse supply shocks on the world's economies for the second time in a decade, Fed Chairman Paul Volcker decided that the time for action had come. Volcker had been appointed chairman by

President Carter only two months earlier, and he had taken the job knowing that inflation had reached unacceptable levels. As guardian of the nation's monetary system, he felt he had little choice but to pursue a policy of *disinflation*—a reduction in the rate of inflation. Volcker had no doubt that the Fed could reduce inflation through its ability to control the quantity of money. But what would be the short-run cost of disinflation? The answer to this question was much less certain.

The Sacrifice Ratio

To reduce the inflation rate, the Fed has to pursue contractionary monetary policy. Figure 10 shows some of the effects of such a decision. When the Fed slows the rate at which the money supply is growing, it contracts aggregate demand. The fall in aggregate demand, in turn, reduces the quantity of goods and services that firms produce, and this fall in production leads to a rise in unemployment. The economy begins at point A in the figure and moves along the short-run Phillips curve to point B, which has lower inflation and higher unemployment. Over time, as people come to understand that prices are rising more slowly, expected inflation falls, and the short-run Phillips curve shifts downward. The economy moves from point B to point C. Inflation is lower than it was initially at point A, and unemployment is back at its natural rate.

Thus, if a nation wants to reduce inflation, it must endure a period of high unemployment and low output. In Figure 10, this cost is represented by the movement of the economy through point B as it travels from point A to point C.

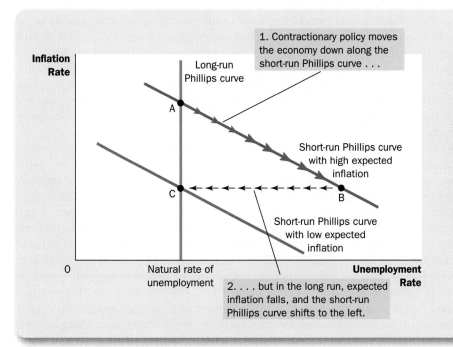

FIGURE 10

Disinflationary Monetary Policy in the Short Run and Long Run
When the Fed pursues contractionary monetary policy to reduce inflation, the economy moves along a short-run Phillips curve from point A to point B. Over time, expected inflation falls, and the short-run Phillips curve shifts downward. When the economy reaches point C, unemployment is back at its natural rate.

1. Contractionary policy moves the economy down along the short-run Phillips curve . . .

2. . . . but in the long run, expected inflation falls, and the short-run Phillips curve shifts to the left.

Inflation Rate

Long-run Phillips curve

Short-run Phillips curve with high expected inflation

Short-run Phillips curve with low expected inflation

Natural rate of unemployment

Unemployment Rate

sacrifice ratio
the number of percentage points of annual output lost in the process of reducing inflation by 1 percentage point

The size of this cost depends on the slope of the Phillips curve and how quickly expectations of inflation adjust to the new monetary policy.

Many studies have examined the data on inflation and unemployment to estimate the cost of reducing inflation. The findings of these studies are often summarized in a statistic called the **sacrifice ratio.** The sacrifice ratio is the number of percentage points of annual output lost in the process of reducing inflation by 1 percentage point. A typical estimate of the sacrifice ratio is 5. That is, for each percentage point that inflation is reduced, 5 percent of annual output must be sacrificed in the transition.

Such estimates surely must have made Paul Volcker apprehensive as he confronted the task of reducing inflation. Inflation was running at almost 10 percent per year. To reach moderate inflation of, say, 4 percent per year would mean reducing inflation by 6 percentage points. If each percentage point cost 5 percent of the economy's annual output, then reducing inflation by 6 percentage points would require sacrificing 30 percent of annual output.

According to studies of the Phillips curve and the cost of disinflation, this sacrifice could be paid in various ways. An immediate reduction in inflation would depress output by 30 percent for a single year, but that outcome was surely too harsh even for an inflation hawk like Paul Volcker. It would be better, many argued, to spread out the cost over several years. If the reduction in inflation took place over 5 years, for instance, then output would have to average only 6 percent below trend during that period to add up to a sacrifice of 30 percent. An even more gradual approach would be to reduce inflation slowly over a decade so that output would have to be only 3 percent below trend. Whatever path was chosen, however, it seemed that reducing inflation would not be easy.

Rational Expectations and the Possibility of Costless Disinflation

rational expectations
the theory according to which people optimally use all the information they have, including information about government policies, when forecasting the future

Just as Paul Volcker was pondering how costly reducing inflation might be, a group of economics professors was leading an intellectual revolution that would challenge the conventional wisdom on the sacrifice ratio. This group included such prominent economists as Robert Lucas, Thomas Sargent, and Robert Barro. Their revolution was based on a new approach to economic theory and policy called **rational expectations.** According to the theory of rational expectations, people optimally use all the information they have, including information about government policies, when forecasting the future.

This new approach has had profound implications for many areas of macroeconomics, but none is more important than its application to the trade-off between inflation and unemployment. As Friedman and Phelps had first emphasized, expected inflation is an important variable that explains why there is a trade-off between inflation and unemployment in the short run but not in the long run. How quickly the short-run trade-off disappears depends on how quickly people adjust their expectations of inflation. Proponents of rational expectations built on the Friedman-Phelps analysis to argue that when economic policies change, people adjust their expectations of inflation accordingly. The studies of inflation and unemployment that had tried to estimate the sacrifice ratio had failed to take account of the direct effect of the policy regime on expectations. As a result, estimates of the sacrifice ratio were, according to the rational-expectations theorists, unreliable guides for policy.

In a 1981 paper titled "The End of Four Big Inflations," Thomas Sargent described this new view as follows:

An alternative "rational expectations" view denies that there is any inherent momentum to the present process of inflation. This view maintains that firms and workers have now come to expect high rates of inflation in the future and that they strike inflationary bargains in light of these expectations. However, it is held that people expect high rates of inflation in the future precisely because the government's current and prospective monetary and fiscal policies warrant those expectations. . . . An implication of this view is that inflation can be stopped much more quickly than advocates of the "momentum" view have indicated and that their estimates of the length of time and the costs of stopping inflation in terms of forgone output are erroneous. . . . This is not to say that it would be easy to eradicate inflation. On the contrary, it would require more than a few temporary restrictive fiscal and monetary actions. It would require a change in the policy regime. . . . How costly such a move would be in terms of forgone output and how long it would be in taking effect would depend partly on how resolute and evident the government's commitment was.

According to Sargent, the sacrifice ratio could be much smaller than suggested by previous estimates. Indeed, in the most extreme case, it could be zero: If the government made a credible commitment to a policy of low inflation, people would be rational enough to lower their expectations of inflation immediately. The short-run Phillips curve would shift downward, and the economy would reach low inflation quickly without the cost of temporarily high unemployment and low output.

The Volcker Disinflation

As we have seen, when Paul Volcker faced the prospect of reducing inflation from its peak of about 10 percent, the economics profession offered two conflicting predictions. One group of economists offered estimates of the sacrifice ratio and concluded that reducing inflation would have great cost in terms of lost output and high unemployment. Another group offered the theory of rational expectations and concluded that reducing inflation could be much less costly and, perhaps, could even have no cost at all. Who was right?

Figure 11 shows inflation and unemployment from 1979 to 1987. As you can see, Volcker did succeed at reducing inflation. Inflation came down from almost 10 percent in 1981 and 1982 to about 4 percent in 1983 and 1984. Credit for this reduction in inflation goes completely to monetary policy. Fiscal policy at this time was acting in the opposite direction: The increases in the budget deficit during the Reagan administration were expanding aggregate demand, which tends to raise inflation. The fall in inflation from 1981 to 1984 is attributable to the tough anti-inflation policies of Fed Chairman Paul Volcker.

The figure shows that the Volcker disinflation did come at the cost of high unemployment. In 1982 and 1983, the unemployment rate was about 10 percent—about 4 percentage points above its level when Paul Volcker was appointed Fed chairman. At the same time, the production of goods and services as measured by real GDP was well below its trend level. The Volcker disinflation

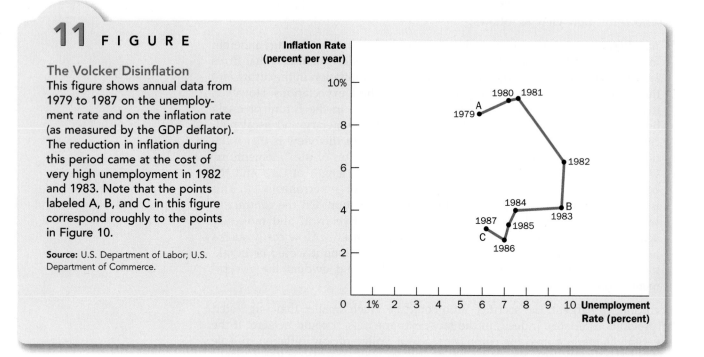

11 FIGURE

The Volcker Disinflation
This figure shows annual data from 1979 to 1987 on the unemployment rate and on the inflation rate (as measured by the GDP deflator). The reduction in inflation during this period came at the cost of very high unemployment in 1982 and 1983. Note that the points labeled A, B, and C in this figure correspond roughly to the points in Figure 10.

Source: U.S. Department of Labor; U.S. Department of Commerce.

produced the deepest recession in the United States since the Great Depression of the 1930s.

Does this experience refute the possibility of costless disinflation as suggested by the rational-expectations theorists? Some economists have argued that the answer to this question is a resounding yes. Indeed, the pattern of disinflation shown in Figure 11 is similar to the pattern predicted in Figure 10. To make the transition from high inflation (point A in both figures) to low inflation (point C), the economy had to experience a painful period of high unemployment (point B).

Yet there are two reasons not to reject the conclusions of the rational-expectations theorists so quickly. First, even though the Volcker disinflation did impose a cost of temporarily high unemployment, the cost was not as large as many economists had predicted. Most estimates of the sacrifice ratio based on the Volcker disinflation are smaller than estimates that had been obtained from previous data. Perhaps Volcker's tough stand on inflation did have some direct effect on expectations, as the rational-expectations theorists claimed.

Second, and more important, even though Volcker announced that he would aim monetary policy to lower inflation, much of the public did not believe him. Because few people thought Volcker would reduce inflation as quickly as he did, expected inflation did not fall, and the short-run Phillips curve did not shift down as quickly as it might have. Some evidence for this hypothesis comes from the forecasts made by commercial forecasting firms: Their forecasts of inflation fell more slowly in the 1980s than did actual inflation. Thus, the Volcker disinflation does not necessarily refute the rational-expectations view that credible disinflation can be costless. It does show, however, that policymakers cannot count on people immediately believing them when they announce a policy of disinflation.

The Greenspan Era

Since the OPEC inflation of the 1970s and the Volcker disinflation of the 1980s, the U.S. economy has experienced relatively mild fluctuations in inflation and unemployment. Figure 12 shows inflation and unemployment from 1984 to 2004. This period is called the Greenspan era, after Alan Greenspan who in 1987 followed Paul Volcker as chairman of the Federal Reserve.

This period began with a favorable supply shock. In 1986, OPEC members started arguing over production levels, and their longstanding agreement to restrict supply broke down. Oil prices fell by about half. As the figure shows, this favorable supply shock led to falling inflation and falling unemployment from 1984 to 1986.

Since then, the Fed has been careful to avoid repeating the policy mistakes of the 1960s, when excessive aggregate demand pushed unemployment below the natural rate and raised inflation. When unemployment fell and inflation rose in 1989 and 1990, the Fed raised interest rates and contracted aggregate demand, leading to a small recession in 1991 and 1992. Unemployment then rose above most estimates of the natural rate, and inflation fell once again.

The rest of the 1990s witnessed a period of economic prosperity. Inflation gradually drifted downward, approaching zero by the end of the decade. Unemployment also drifted downward, leading many observers to believe that the natural rate of unemployment had fallen. Part of the credit for this good economic performance goes to Alan Greenspan and his colleagues at the Federal Reserve, for low inflation can be achieved only with prudent monetary policy.

FED CHAIRMAN ALAN GREENSPAN: A HARD ACT TO FOLLOW?

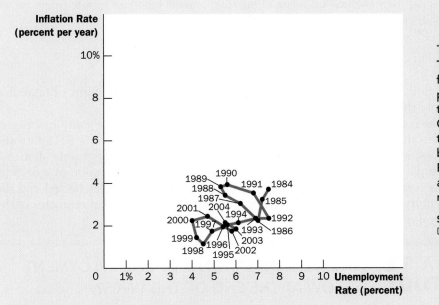

FIGURE 12

The Greenspan Era
This figure shows annual data from 1984 to 2004 on the unemployment rate and on the inflation rate (as measured by the GDP deflator). During most of this period, Alan Greenspan has been chairman of the Federal Reserve. Fluctuations in inflation and unemployment have been relatively small.

Source: U.S. Department of Labor; U.S. Department of Commerce.

In The News

The Case for Inflation Targeting

As this book was going to press, Alan Greenspan's tenure as Fed chairman was coming to a close. In this article, three economists offer his successor some advice. In October 2005, President Bush nominated Greenspan's successor: Ben Bernanke, the first author of this article.

What Happens When Greenspan Is Gone?

By Ben S. Bernanke, Frederic S. Mishkin and Adam S. Posen

U.S. monetary policy has been remarkably successful during Alan Greenspan's $12\frac{1}{2}$ years as Federal Reserve chairman. But although President Clinton yesterday reappointed the 73-year-old Mr. Greenspan to a new term ending in 2004, the chairman will not be around forever. To ensure that monetary policy stays on track after Mr. Greenspan, the Fed should be thinking through its approach to monetary policy now. The Fed needs an approach that consolidates the gains of the Greenspan years and ensures that those successful policies will continue—even if future Fed chairmen are less skillful or less committed to price stability than Mr. Greenspan has been.

We think the best bet lies in a framework known as inflation targeting, which has been employed with great success in recent years by most of the world's biggest economies, except for Japan. Inflation targeting is a monetary-policy framework that commits the central bank to a forward-looking pursuit of low inflation—the source of the Fed's current great performance—but also promotes a more open and accountable policy-making process. More transparency and accountability would help keep the Fed on track, and a more open Fed would be good for financial markets and more consistent with our democratic political system. . . .

Successful inflation targeting requires that the central bank and elected officials make a public commitment to an explicit numerical target level for inflation (usually around 2%), to be achieved over a specified horizon (usually two years). Equally important, the central bank must agree to provide the

---

But as the following case study discusses, good luck in the form of favorable supply shocks is also part of the story.

The economy, however, ran into problems in 2001, as a case study in Chapter 15 described. The end of the dot-com stock-market bubble, the 9/11 terrorist attacks, and corporate accounting scandals all depressed aggregate demand. Unemployment rose as the economy experienced its first recession in a decade. But a combination of expansionary monetary and fiscal policies helped end the downturn, and by early 2005, unemployment was close to most estimates of the natural rate.

CASE STUDY | WHY WERE INFLATION AND UNEMPLOYMENT SO LOW AT THE END OF THE 1990S?

As the 20th century drew to a close, the U.S. economy was experiencing some of the lowest rates of inflation and unemployment in many years. In 1999, for markets and the public with enough information to evaluate its performance, and to understand its reasoning when policy and inflation deviate from the long-run goal—as they inevitably will at times. . . .

Adoption of inflation targeting by the Federal Reserve would bring several major advantages over the current, less structured approach. First, it would transform the commitment to price stability—which has served us so well under Mr. Greenspan and his predecessor, Paul Volcker—from a personal preference of the chairman into an official policy. By depersonalizing and institutionalizing the Greenspan policy approach, the Fed would increase the likelihood that future U.S. monetary policy will look like the 1980s and 1990s rather than the 1930s or the 1970s.

Second, the transparency of the inflation-targeting approach would encourage politicians and the public to focus on what monetary policy can do (namely, maintain long-run price stability), rather than on what it can't do (create permanent increases in growth through expansionary policies). In place of politically expedient demands and scapegoating by politicians—a particular danger in election years—public oversight of the Fed would be directed toward discussion of the appropriate level for the inflation target and evaluation of the Fed's effectiveness in meeting that target. The Fed would retain the sole authority for specific policy actions—such as setting the federal-funds rate—in pursuit of its target. This allocation of responsibility for monetary policy between elected officials and technocrats would serve both democratic principles and good policy. . . .

Third, increased transparency would diminish financial and economic uncertainty. More information from the Fed about its plans and expectations would reduce the perpetual, and wasteful, attempts by financial market participants to guess what the Fed will do next. An inflation target would also make it easier for businesses and consumers to plan.

Fourth, inflation targeting is particularly good insurance against the threat of falling prices. Deflation has been associated with deep recessions or even depressions, as in the 1930s and recently in Japan. Targeting an annual inflation rate a couple of percentage points above zero, as all inflation targeters have done, commits the central bank to maintaining a floor under price level movements (as well as a ceiling over them). . . .

Mr. Greenspan's reappointment should not make us complacent about the future of Fed policy. On the principle that it is better to fix the roof when skies are sunny, the Fed should announce its intentions to establish a more open policy framework now, rather than waiting to be confronted by difficult policy decisions. An explicit commitment to inflation targeting would increase the odds that those decisions would be the right ones, and that they would receive public support—whether or not Alan Greenspan is chairman of the Fed.

instance, unemployment had fallen to 4.2 percent, while inflation was running at a mere 1.3 percent per year. As measured by these two important macroeconomic variables, the United States was enjoying a period of unusual prosperity.

Some observers argued that this experience cast doubt on the theory of the Phillips curve. Indeed, the combination of low inflation and low unemployment might seem to suggest that there was no longer a trade-off between these two variables. Yet most economists took a less radical view of events. As we have discussed throughout this chapter, the short-run trade-off between inflation and unemployment shifts over time. In the 1990s, this trade-off shifted leftward, allowing the economy to enjoy low unemployment and low inflation simultaneously.

What caused this favorable shift in the short-run Phillips curve? Part of the answer lies in a fall in expected inflation. Under Paul Volcker and Alan Greenspan, the Fed pursued a policy aimed at reducing inflation and keeping it low. Over time, as this policy succeeded, the Fed gained credibility with the public that it would continue to fight inflation as necessary. The increased credibility lowered inflation expectations, which shifted the short-run Phillips curve to the left.

In addition to this shift from reduced expected inflation, many economists believe that the U.S. economy experienced some favorable supply shocks during this period. (Recall that a favorable supply shock shifts the short-run aggregate-supply curve to the right, raising output and reducing prices. It therefore reduces both unemployment and inflation and shifts the short-run Phillips curve to the left.) Here are three events that get credit for the favorable shift to aggregate supply:

- *Declining Commodity Prices.* In the late 1990s, the prices of many basic commodities, including oil, fell on world markets. This fall in commodity prices, in turn, was partly due to a deep recession in Japan and other Asian economies, which reduced the demand for these products. Because commodities are an important input into production, the fall in their prices reduced producers' costs and acted as a favorable supply shock for the U.S. economy.
- *Labor-Market Changes.* Some economists believe that the aging of the large baby-boom generation born after World War II has caused fundamental changes in the labor market. Because older workers are typically in more stable jobs than younger workers, an increase in the average age of the labor force reduces the economy's natural rate of unemployment.
- *Technological Advance.* In the second half of the 1990s, the U.S. economy entered a period of rapid technological progress. Advances in information technology, such as the Internet, have been profound and have influenced many parts of the economy. Such technological advance increases productivity and, therefore, is a type of favorable supply shock.

Economists debate which of these explanations of the shifting Phillips curve is the most important. Most likely, the complete story contains elements of each.

Keep in mind that none of these hypotheses denies the fundamental lesson of the Phillips curve—that policymakers who control aggregate demand always face a short-run trade-off between inflation and unemployment. Yet the 1990s remind us that this short-run trade-off changes over time, sometimes in ways that are hard to predict.   •

Quick Quiz   What is the sacrifice ratio? How might the credibility of the Fed's commitment to reduce inflation affect the sacrifice ratio?

CONCLUSION

This chapter has examined how economists' thinking about inflation and unemployment has evolved. We have discussed the ideas of many of the best economists of the 20th century: from the Phillips curve of Phillips, Samuelson, and Solow, to the natural-rate hypothesis of Friedman and Phelps, to the rational-expectations theory of Lucas, Sargent, and Barro. Four of this group have already won Nobel prizes for their work in economics, and more are likely to be so honored in the years to come.

Although the trade-off between inflation and unemployment has generated much intellectual turmoil over the past half century, certain principles have developed that today command consensus. Here is how Milton Friedman expressed the relationship between inflation and unemployment in 1968:

> There is always a temporary tradeoff between inflation and unemployment; there is no permanent tradeoff. The temporary tradeoff comes not from inflation per se, but from unanticipated inflation, which generally means from a rising rate of inflation. The widespread belief that there is a permanent trade-off is a sophisticated version of the confusion between "high" and "rising" that we all recognize in simpler forms. A rising rate of inflation may reduce unemployment, a high rate will not.
>
> But how long, you will say, is "temporary"? . . . I can at most venture a personal judgment, based on some examination of the historical evidence, that the initial effects of a higher and unanticipated rate of inflation last for something like two to five years.

Today, about 40 years later, this statement still summarizes the view of most macroeconomists.

SUMMARY

- The Phillips curve describes a negative relationship between inflation and unemployment. By expanding aggregate demand, policymakers can choose a point on the Phillips curve with higher inflation and lower unemployment. By contracting aggregate demand, policymakers can choose a point on the Phillips curve with lower inflation and higher unemployment.

- The trade-off between inflation and unemployment described by the Phillips curve holds only in the short run. In the long run, expected inflation adjusts to changes in actual inflation, and the short-run Phillips curve shifts. As a result, the long-run Phillips curve is vertical at the natural rate of unemployment.

- The short-run Phillips curve also shifts because of shocks to aggregate supply. An adverse supply shock, such as an increase in world oil prices, gives policymakers a less favorable trade-off between inflation and unemployment. That is, after an adverse supply shock, policymakers have to accept a higher rate of inflation for any given rate of unemployment or a higher rate of unemployment for any given rate of inflation.

- When the Fed contracts growth in the money supply to reduce inflation, it moves the economy along the short-run Phillips curve, which results in temporarily high unemployment. The cost of disinflation depends on how quickly expectations of inflation fall. Some economists argue that a credible commitment to low inflation can reduce the cost of disinflation by inducing a quick adjustment of expectations.

KEY CONCEPTS

Phillips curve, p. 386
natural-rate hypothesis, p. 395

supply shock, p. 398
sacrifice ratio, p. 402

rational expectations, p. 402

QUESTIONS FOR REVIEW

1. Draw the short-run trade-off between inflation and unemployment. How might the Fed move the economy from one point on this curve to another?

2. Draw the long-run trade-off between inflation and unemployment. Explain how the short-run and long-run trade-offs are related.

3. What is "natural" about the natural rate of unemployment? Why might the natural rate of unemployment differ across countries?

4. Suppose a drought destroys farm crops and drives up the price of food. What is the effect on the short-run trade-off between inflation and unemployment?

5. The Fed decides to reduce inflation. Use the Phillips curve to show the short-run and long-run effects of this policy. How might the short-run costs be reduced?

PROBLEMS AND APPLICATIONS

1. Suppose the natural rate of unemployment is 6 percent. On one graph, draw two Phillips curves that describe the four situations listed here. Label the point that shows the position of the economy in each case.
   a. Actual inflation is 5 percent and expected inflation is 3 percent.
   b. Actual inflation is 3 percent and expected inflation is 5 percent.
   c. Actual inflation is 5 percent and expected inflation is 5 percent.
   d. Actual inflation is 3 percent and expected inflation is 3 percent.

2. Illustrate the effects of the following developments on both the short-run and long-run Phillips curves. Give the economic reasoning underlying your answers.
   a. A rise in the natural rate of unemployment
   b. A decline in the price of imported oil
   c. A rise in government spending
   d. A decline in expected inflation

3. Suppose that a fall in consumer spending causes a recession.
   a. Illustrate the immediate change in the economy using both an aggregate-supply/ aggregate-demand diagram and a Phillips-curve diagram. What happens to inflation and unemployment in the short run?
   b. Now suppose that over time expected inflation changes in the same direction that actual inflation changes. What happens to the position of the short-run Phillips curve? After the recession is over, does the economy face a better or worse set of inflation-unemployment combinations?

4. Suppose the economy is in a long-run equilibrium.
   a. Draw the economy's short-run and long-run Phillips curves.
   b. Suppose a wave of business pessimism reduces aggregate demand. Show the effect of this shock on your diagram from part (a).

If the Fed undertakes expansionary monetary policy, can it return the economy to its original inflation rate and original unemployment rate?

c. Now suppose the economy is back in long-run equilibrium, and then the price of imported oil rises. Show the effect of this shock with a new diagram like that in part (a). If the Fed undertakes expansionary monetary policy, can it return the economy to its original inflation rate and original unemployment rate? If the Fed undertakes contractionary monetary policy, can it return the economy to its original inflation rate and original unemployment rate? Explain why this situation differs from that in part (b).

5. The inflation rate is 10 percent, and the central bank is considering slowing the rate of money growth to reduce inflation to 5 percent. Economist Milton believes that expectations of inflation change quickly in response to new policies, whereas economist James believes that expectations are very sluggish. Which economist is more likely to favor the proposed change in monetary policy? Why?

6. Suppose the Federal Reserve's policy is to maintain low and stable inflation by keeping unemployment at its natural rate. However, the Fed believes that the natural rate of unemployment is 4 percent when the actual natural rate was 5 percent. If the Fed based its policy decisions on its belief, what would happen to the economy? How might the Fed come to realize that its belief about the natural rate was mistaken?

7. Suppose the price of oil falls sharply (as it did in 1986 and again in 1998).

a. Show the impact of such a change in both the aggregate-demand/aggregate-supply diagram and in the Phillips-curve diagram. What happens to inflation and unemployment in the short run?

b. Do the effects of this event mean there is no short-run trade-off between inflation and unemployment? Why or why not?

8. Suppose the Federal Reserve announced that it would pursue contractionary monetary policy to reduce the inflation rate. Would the following conditions make the ensuing recession more or less severe? Explain.
   a. Wage contracts have short durations.
   b. There is little confidence in the Fed's determination to reduce inflation.
   c. Expectations of inflation adjust quickly to actual inflation.

9. Given the unpopularity of inflation, why don't elected leaders always support efforts to reduce inflation? Many economists believe that countries can reduce the cost of disinflation by letting their central banks make decisions about monetary policy without interference from politicians. Why might this be so?

10. Suppose Federal Reserve policymakers accept the theory of the short-run Phillips curve and the natural-rate hypothesis and want to keep unemployment close to its natural rate. Unfortunately, because the natural rate of unemployment can change over time, they aren't certain about the value of the natural rate. What macroeconomic variables do you think they should look at when conducting monetary policy?

 For further information on topics in this chapter, additional problems, examples, applications, online quizzes, and more, please visit our website at http://mankiw.swlearning.com.

Final Thoughts

Five Debates over Macroeconomic Policy

It is hard to open up the newspaper without finding some politician or editorial writer advocating a change in economic policy. The president should raise taxes to reduce the budget deficit, or he should stop worrying about the budget deficit. The Federal Reserve should cut interest rates to stimulate a flagging economy, or it should avoid such moves in order not to risk higher inflation. Congress should reform the tax system to promote faster economic growth, or it should reform the tax system to achieve a more equal distribution of income. Such economic issues are central to the continuing political debate in the United States and other countries around the world.

Previous chapters have developed the tools that economists use when analyzing the behavior of the economy as a whole and the impact of policies on the economy. This final chapter presents both sides in five leading debates over macroeconomic policy. The knowledge you have accumulated in this course provides the background with which we can discuss these important, unsettled issues. It should help you choose a side in these debates or, at least, help you see why choosing a side is so difficult.

SHOULD MONETARY AND FISCAL POLICYMAKERS TRY TO STABILIZE THE ECONOMY?

In the preceding three chapters, we saw how changes in aggregate demand and aggregate supply can lead to short-run fluctuations in production and employment. We also saw how monetary and fiscal policy can shift aggregate demand and, thereby, influence these fluctuations. But even if policymakers *can* influence short-run economic fluctuations, does that mean they *should*? Our first debate concerns whether monetary and fiscal policymakers should use the tools at their disposal in an attempt to smooth the ups and downs of the business cycle.

Pro: Policymakers Should Try to Stabilize the Economy

Left on their own, economies tend to fluctuate. When households and firms become pessimistic, for instance, they cut back on spending, and this reduces the aggregate demand for goods and services. The fall in aggregate demand, in turn, reduces the production of goods and services. Firms lay off workers, and the unemployment rate rises. Real GDP and other measures of income fall. Rising unemployment and falling income help confirm the pessimism that initially generated the economic downturn.

Such a recession has no benefit for society—it represents a sheer waste of resources. Workers who become unemployed because of inadequate aggregate demand would rather be working. Business owners whose factories are left idle during a recession would rather be producing valuable goods and services and selling them at a profit.

There is no reason for society to suffer through the booms and busts of the business cycle. The development of macroeconomic theory has shown policymakers how to reduce the severity of economic fluctuations. By "leaning against the wind" of economic change, monetary and fiscal policy can stabilize aggregate demand and, thereby, production and employment. When aggregate demand is inadequate to ensure full employment, policymakers should boost government spending, cut taxes, and expand the money supply. When aggregate demand is excessive, risking higher inflation, policymakers should cut government spending, raise taxes, and reduce the money supply. Such policy actions put macroeconomic theory to its best use by leading to a more stable economy, which benefits everyone.

Con: Policymakers Should Not Try to Stabilize the Economy

Although monetary and fiscal policy can be used to stabilize the economy in theory, there are substantial obstacles to the use of such policies in practice.

One problem is that monetary and fiscal policy do not affect the economy immediately but instead work with a long lag. Monetary policy affects aggregate demand by changing interest rates, which in turn affect spending, especially residential and business investment. But many households and firms set their spending plans in advance. As a result, it takes time for changes in interest rates to alter the aggregate demand for goods and services. Many studies indicate that changes in monetary policy have little effect on aggregate demand until about six months after the change is made.

Fiscal policy works with a lag because of the long political process that governs changes in spending and taxes. To make any change in fiscal policy, a bill must go through congressional committees, pass both the House and the Senate, and be signed by the president. It can take years to propose, pass, and implement a major change in fiscal policy.

Because of these long lags, policymakers who want to stabilize the economy need to look ahead to economic conditions that are likely to prevail when their actions will take effect. Unfortunately, economic forecasting is highly imprecise, in part because macroeconomics is such a primitive science and in part because the shocks that cause economic fluctuations are intrinsically unpredictable. Thus, when policymakers change monetary or fiscal policy, they must rely on educated guesses about future economic conditions.

All too often, policymakers trying to stabilize the economy do just the opposite. Economic conditions can easily change between when a policy action begins and when it takes effect. Because of this, policymakers can inadvertently exacerbate rather than mitigate the magnitude of economic fluctuations. Some economists have claimed that many of the major economic fluctuations in history, including the Great Depression of the 1930s, can be traced to destabilizing policy actions.

One of the first rules taught to physicians is "do no harm." The human body has natural restorative powers. Confronted with a sick patient and an uncertain diagnosis, often a doctor should do nothing but leave the patient's body to its own devices. Intervening in the absence of reliable knowledge merely risks making matters worse.

The same can be said about treating an ailing economy. It might be desirable if policymakers could eliminate all economic fluctuations, but that is not a realistic goal given the limits of macroeconomic knowledge and the inherent unpredictability of world events. Economic policymakers should refrain from intervening often with monetary and fiscal policy and be content if they do no harm.

In The News

The Fine-Tuning of George W. Bush

In 2003, as the economy was struggling to recover from a recent recession, President Bush proposed a package of tax cuts in an attempt to strengthen the economy. Was it the right economic medicine?

Bush's Push

"I understand the politics of economic stimulus," said President George Bush on January 2nd. What worries some observers is whether he and his advisers have got their economics right. . . .

Mr Bush is certain that an extra push is needed to consolidate the sluggish and somewhat erratic recovery that has been under way since the beginning of 2002. He has his eye on two crucial American elections: that of 1992, which saw his father swept from office after a one-term presidency; and that of 2004, in which he is determined not to suffer the same fate. The conventional wisdom asserts that Mr Bush senior was turfed out because he had paid insufficient attention to the economy.

But is there a risk that Mr Bush junior is putting too much effort into kick-starting the economy? Has the case for further government intervention been convincingly made? After all, America grew at a pretty healthy pace in the year to last September, surpassed in the industrial world only by Australia and Canada. . . .

Overall, though, the picture remains confused. In December [2002], figures showed that unemployment is at its highest level for eight years. . . . Even Alan Greenspan, the influential chairman of the Federal Reserve, America's central bank, has admitted that the economy has been going through what he called a "soft patch." . . .

Mr Greenspan and his colleagues at the Fed have not been idle. In the past two years they have cut interest rates aggressively: 12 times in all, most recently in November. American interest rates are now at their lowest level for more than 40 years. The Fed has made clear that it does not expect to need to make further cuts—but stands ready to do so if necessary. Interest-rate reductions take time to work through the

Quick Quiz Explain why monetary and fiscal policy work with a lag. Why do these lags matter in the choice between active and passive policy?

SHOULD MONETARY POLICY BE MADE BY RULE RATHER THAN BY DISCRETION?

As we learned in the chapter on the monetary system, the Federal Open Market Committee sets monetary policy in the United States. The committee meets about every six weeks to evaluate the state of the economy. Based on this evaluation and forecasts of future economic conditions, it chooses whether to raise, lower, or leave unchanged the level of short-term interest rates. The Fed then adjusts the money supply to reach that interest-rate target until the next meeting, when the target is reevaluated.

The Federal Open Market Committee operates with almost complete discretion over how to conduct monetary policy. The laws that created the Fed give economy and most economists reckon the full impact of the recent cuts has yet to be felt.

Monetary policy is now regarded as the main short-term policy lever. The lags with which it operates may be uncertain, and their impact difficult to forecast, but the drawbacks of discretionary fiscal policy are far greater. Disastrous attempts at fiscal fine-tuning, in the 1970s in particular, largely discredited such government intervention across the rich world.

So why is Mr Bush so keen on stimulus packages? The one now eagerly awaited is, after all, his second. The first was finally enacted early in 2002, after a battle with Congress and, especially, Mr Bush's Democratic opponents in the Senate. . . .

But clearing the political hurdles is only part of the challenge facing Mr Bush. The package still has to be judged effective—a much more daunting task. . . .

Two main obstacles make fiscal stimulus difficult to get right. The first is timing. It is never easy to know when action is appropriate. That's a problem with monetary policy too, of course, but if the Fed concludes that a cut in interest rates is appropriate it can implement one immediately—and can reverse it with equal dispatch.

That is simply not possible with fiscal policy, even with political opposition silenced. Tax cuts or government spending take time to arrange: the inevitable gap between announcement and implementation can mean the measures have lost their relevance by the time they start to have any impact—let alone by the time they have fully worked through. The risk is, for example, that such fiscal measures coincide with an economic upturn, fuelling inflationary pressures. And fiscal measures are fiendishly difficult to unwind.

They are also much more unpredictable even than monetary policy. How

will individuals respond to tax cuts? By spending more readily, Mr Bush presumably hopes. But if they remain uncertain about the economic outlook because of the international security situation, for instance, or because unemployment remains high, they may instead decide to save more. While desirable in itself, more saving will not fuel economic demand—and nor will extra tax breaks for business stimulate investment if firms aren't convinced it will be profitable.

Author's note: President Bush's proposed tax reductions were passed in the summer of 2003, after which the economy started growing more quickly. Economists can debate, however, the extent to which the change in fiscal policy was responsible for the subsequent improvement in economic performance.

the institution only vague recommendations about what goals it should pursue. And they do not tell the Fed how to pursue whatever goals it might choose. Once members are appointed to the Federal Open Market Committee, they have little mandate but to "do the right thing."

Some economists are critical of this institutional design. Our second debate over macroeconomic policy, therefore, focuses on whether the Federal Reserve should have its discretionary powers reduced and, instead, be committed to following a rule for how it conducts monetary policy.

Pro: Monetary Policy Should Be Made by Rule

Discretion in the conduct of monetary policy has two problems. The first is that it does not limit incompetence and abuse of power. When the government sends police into a community to maintain civic order, it gives them strict guidelines about how to carry out their job. Because police have great power, allowing them to exercise that power in whatever way they want would be dangerous. Yet when the government gives central bankers the authority to maintain economic order, it gives them no guidelines. Monetary policymakers are allowed undisciplined discretion.

In The News

Inflation Targeting as a Rule for Monetary Policy

Many central banks around the world have adopted explicit targets for inflation. Should the Fed follow suit?

Slaves to the Mechanical Rules of Central Banking

By Stephen Cecchetti

In his speech to the central bank elite last week in Jackson Hole, Alan Greenspan argued that it is dangerous for central bankers to adhere slavishly to mechanical rules. Instead, the Federal Reserve chairman said, faced with inevitable uncertainties, they should constantly use their own judgment.

Mr Greenspan is absolutely right that real-world monetary policy is about managing risks that are difficult to quantify, and so discretion is required. In defending his own practices, he implicitly criticized the monetary policy framework now commonly known as "inflation targeting" and the manner in which it is implemented in a number of countries. He is correct about the pitfalls in the practice of inflation targeting. But it is difficult to justify the unstated extension of his argument from flexibility in the execution of policy to flexibility in formulating policy objectives. To see why, we need to look at a little history.

Some 25 years ago, economists realized that a central bank controlled by politicians yields high inflation. The problem is that a monetary policy easing produces higher growth and employment in the short term, driving inflation up only several years later. Politicians are notoriously myopic, caring primarily about the next election.

Everyone agrees that this "inflation bias" is a problem and that the solution is to take monetary policy out of the hands of the politicians and hand it over to an independent central bank. The answer is to create a system with two basic elements. First, the politicians would dictate a set of goals and, sec-

As an example of the abuse of power, central bankers are sometimes tempted to use monetary policy to affect the outcome of elections. Suppose that the vote for the incumbent president is based on economic conditions at the time he is up for reelection. A central banker sympathetic to the incumbent might be tempted to pursue expansionary policies just before the election to stimulate production and employment, knowing that the resulting inflation will not show up until after the election. Thus, to the extent that central bankers ally themselves with politicians, discretionary policy can lead to economic fluctuations that reflect the electoral calendar. Economists call such fluctuations the *political business cycle*.

The second, subtler problem with discretionary monetary policy is that it might lead to more inflation than is desirable. Central bankers, knowing that there is no long-run trade-off between inflation and unemployment, often announce that their goal is zero inflation. Yet they rarely achieve price stability. Why? Perhaps it is because, once the public forms expectations of inflation, policymakers face a short-run trade-off between inflation and unemployment. They are tempted to renege on their announcement of price stability to achieve lower unemployment. This discrepancy between announcements (what policymakers ond, the central bankers would publicly report their progress on meeting these goals. Explicit goals foster accountability, while disclosure requirements create transparency. . . .

The exact institutional arrangements establishing accountability and transparency differ from country to country. In some cases the government gives central bankers explicit numerical targets for inflation, while in others the central banks are left to define the exact goals. The British government sets a specific inflation target each year, while the treaty establishing the European Central Bank as well as the statutes governing the Fed simply refer to a goal of "price stability" and provide no technical definition. . . .

This brings us back to inflation targeting. In principle, it is no different from any other framework in which objectives are announced and policymakers' actions are explained to the public and the markets. The problem is in the practice. . . .

If you were to survey the academic literature that provides the conceptual underpinning for inflation targeting, you would find that most economists are discussing something called "inflation-forecast targeting." It is logical that policymakers should adjust interest rates in response to forecast deviations from the objective. That means having accurate forecasts as well as a quantitative estimate of the impact of interest rate changes on these forecasts. Getting these means building and using sophisticated models of a country's economy. . . .

My concern is that inflation-targeting central banks will employ economists to build models and then mechanically adjust policy in response to them. As one inflation-targeting central banker said to me once: "Forecasting is too important to be left to forecasters." Models are fine; but central bankers earn their pay on the days when the models fail. Here Mr Greenspan's warning about the dan-

gers of following policy rules is well placed. . . .

So we can agree with Mr Greenspan's warnings. Central banking is an art and it would be dangerous for any policy maker to adhere slavishly to mechanical rules. But no one has proposed that we replace informed decision makers with a bunch of econometric model-builders armed with ever-faster computers. Instead, critics have asked that Mr Greenspan and his colleagues give us a clearer sense of what their objectives really are. We are happy to leave them alone to do their jobs; we just want to understand some of the details of what that job is. Would it really do that much harm to the policymaking process if the Fed were to announce a medium-term numerical inflation objective?

Source: *The Financial Times*, September 3, 2003.

say they are going to do) and actions (what they subsequently in fact do) is called the *time inconsistency of policy.* Because policymakers are so often time inconsistent, people are skeptical when central bankers announce their intentions to reduce the rate of inflation. As a result, people always expect more inflation than monetary policymakers claim they are trying to achieve. Higher expectations of inflation, in turn, shift the short-run Phillips curve upward, making the short-run trade-off between inflation and unemployment less favorable than it otherwise might be.

One way to avoid these two problems with discretionary policy is to commit the central bank to a policy rule. For example, suppose that Congress passed a law requiring the Fed to increase the money supply by exactly 3 percent per year. (Why 3 percent? Because real GDP grows on average about 3 percent per year and because money demand grows with real GDP, 3 percent growth in the money supply is roughly the rate necessary to produce long-run price stability.) Such a law would eliminate incompetence and abuse of power on the part of the Fed, and it would make the political business cycle impossible. In addition, policy could no longer be time inconsistent. People would now believe the Fed's announcement of low inflation because the Fed would be legally required to pursue a low-inflation monetary policy. With low expected inflation, the economy would face a more favorable short-run trade-off between inflation and unemployment.

Other rules for monetary policy are also possible. A more active rule might allow some feedback from the state of the economy to changes in monetary policy. For example, a more active rule might require the Fed to increase monetary growth by 1 percentage point for every percentage point that unemployment rises above its natural rate. Regardless of the precise form of the rule, committing the Fed to some rule would yield advantages by limiting incompetence, abuse of power, and time inconsistency in the conduct of monetary policy.

Con: Monetary Policy Should Not Be Made by Rule

Although there may be pitfalls with discretionary monetary policy, there is also an important advantage to it: flexibility. The Fed has to confront various circumstances, not all of which can be foreseen. In the 1930s, banks failed in record numbers. In the 1970s, the price of oil skyrocketed around the world. In October 1987, the stock market fell by 22 percent in a single day. The Fed must decide how to respond to these shocks to the economy. A designer of a policy rule could not possibly consider all the contingencies and specify in advance the right policy response. It is better to appoint good people to conduct monetary policy and then give them the freedom to do the best they can.

Moreover, the alleged problems with discretion are largely hypothetical. The practical importance of the political business cycle, for instance, is far from clear. In some cases, just the opposite seems to occur. For example, President Jimmy Carter appointed Paul Volcker to head the Federal Reserve in 1979. Nonetheless, in October of that year, Volcker moved to contract monetary policy to combat the high rate of inflation that he had inherited from his predecessor. The predictable result of Volcker's decision was a recession, and the predictable result of the recession was a decline in Carter's popularity. Rather than using monetary policy to help the president who had appointed him, Volcker took actions he thought were in the national interest, even though they helped to ensure Carter's defeat by Ronald Reagan in the November 1980 election.

The practical importance of time inconsistency is also far from clear. Although most people are skeptical of central-bank announcements, central bankers can achieve credibility over time by backing up their words with actions. In the 1990s, the Fed has achieved and maintained a low rate of inflation, despite the ever-present temptation to take advantage of the short-run trade-off between inflation and unemployment. This experience shows that low inflation does not require that the Fed be committed to a policy rule.

Any attempt to replace discretion with a rule must confront the difficult task of specifying a precise rule. Despite much research examining the costs and benefits of alternative rules, economists have not reached a consensus about what a good rule would be. Until there is a consensus, society has little choice but to give central bankers discretion to conduct monetary policy as they see fit.

Quick Quiz   Give an example of a monetary policy rule. Why might your rule be better than discretionary policy? Why might it be worse?

SHOULD THE CENTRAL BANK AIM FOR ZERO INFLATION?

One of the *Ten Principles of Economics* discussed in Chapter 1, and developed more fully in the chapter on money growth and inflation, is that prices rise when the government prints too much money. Another of the *Ten Principles of Economics* discussed in Chapter 1, and developed more fully in the last chapter, is that society faces a short-run trade-off between inflation and unemployment. Put together, these two principles raise a question for policymakers: How much inflation should the central bank be willing to tolerate? Our third debate is whether zero is the right target for the inflation rate.

Pro: The Central Bank Should Aim for Zero Inflation

Inflation confers no benefit on society, but it imposes several real costs. As we have discussed, economists have identified six costs of inflation:

- Shoeleather costs associated with reduced money holdings
- Menu costs associated with more frequent adjustment of prices
- Increased variability of relative prices
- Unintended changes in tax liabilities due to nonindexation of the tax code
- Confusion and inconvenience resulting from a changing unit of account
- Arbitrary redistributions of wealth associated with dollar-denominated debts

Some economists argue that these costs are small, at least for moderate rates of inflation, such as the 3 percent inflation experienced in the United States during the 1990s. But other economists claim these costs can be substantial, even for moderate inflation. Moreover, there is no doubt that the public dislikes inflation. When inflation heats up, opinion polls identify inflation as one of the nation's leading problems.

The benefits of zero inflation have to be weighed against the costs of achieving it. Reducing inflation usually requires a period of high unemployment and low output, as illustrated by the short-run Phillips curve. But this disinflationary recession is only temporary. Once people come to understand that policymakers are aiming for zero inflation, expectations of inflation will fall, and the short-run trade-off will improve. Because expectations adjust, there is no trade-off between inflation and unemployment in the long run.

Reducing inflation is, therefore, a policy with temporary costs and permanent benefits. Once the disinflationary recession is over, the benefits of zero inflation would persist into the future. If policymakers are farsighted, they should be willing to incur the temporary costs for the permanent benefits. This is precisely the calculation made by Paul Volcker in the early 1980s, when he tightened monetary policy and reduced inflation from about 10 percent in 1980 to about 4 percent in 1983. Although in 1982 unemployment reached its highest level since the Great Depression, the economy eventually recovered from the recession, leaving a legacy of low inflation. Today, Volcker is considered a hero among central bankers.

Moreover, the costs of reducing inflation need not be as large as some economists claim. If the Fed announces a credible commitment to zero inflation, it can directly influence expectations of inflation. Such a change in expectations can improve the short-run trade-off between inflation and unemployment, allowing the economy to reach lower inflation at a reduced cost. The key to this strategy is credibility: People must believe that the Fed is actually going to carry through on its announced policy. Congress could help in this regard by passing legislation that made price stability the Fed's primary goal. Such a law would make it less costly to achieve zero inflation without reducing any of the resulting benefits.

One advantage of a zero-inflation target is that zero provides a more natural focal point for policymakers than any other number. Suppose, for instance, that the Fed were to announce that it would keep inflation at 3 percent—the rate experienced during the 1990s. Would the Fed really stick to that 3 percent target? If events inadvertently pushed inflation up to 4 or 5 percent, why wouldn't they just raise the target? There is, after all, nothing special about the number 3. By contrast, zero is the only number for the inflation rate at which the Fed can claim that it achieved price stability and fully eliminated the costs of inflation.

Con: The Central Bank Should Not Aim for Zero Inflation

Although price stability may be desirable, the benefits of zero inflation compared to moderate inflation are small, whereas the costs of reaching zero inflation are large. Estimates of the sacrifice ratio suggest that reducing inflation by 1 percentage point requires giving up about 5 percent of one year's output. Reducing inflation from, say, 4 percent to zero requires a loss of 20 percent of a year's output. Although people might dislike inflation of 4 percent, it is not at all clear that they would (or should) be willing to pay 20 percent of a year's income to get rid of it.

The social costs of disinflation are even larger than this 20 percent figure suggests, for the lost income is not spread equitably over the population. When the economy goes into recession, all incomes do not fall proportionately. Instead, the fall in aggregate income is concentrated on those workers who lose their jobs. The vulnerable workers are often those with the least skills and experience. Hence, much of the cost of reducing inflation is borne by those who can least afford to pay it.

Although economists can list several costs of inflation, there is no professional consensus that these costs are substantial. The shoeleather costs, menu costs, and others that economists have identified do not seem great, at least for moderate rates of inflation. It is true that the public dislikes inflation, but the public may be misled into believing the inflation fallacy—the view that inflation erodes living standards. Economists understand that living standards depend on productivity, not monetary policy. Because inflation in nominal incomes goes hand in hand with inflation in prices, reducing inflation would not cause real incomes to rise more rapidly.

Moreover, policymakers can reduce many of the costs of inflation without actually reducing inflation. They can eliminate the problems associated with the nonindexed tax system by rewriting the tax laws to take account of the effects of inflation. They can also reduce the arbitrary redistributions of wealth between creditors and debtors caused by unexpected inflation by issuing indexed government bonds, as in fact the Clinton administration did in 1997. Such an act insulates holders of government debt from inflation. In addition, by setting an example, the policy might encourage private borrowers and lenders to write debt contracts indexed for inflation.

Reducing inflation might be desirable if it could be done at no cost, as some economists argue is possible. Yet this trick seems hard to carry out in practice.

In The News

The Optimal Rate of Inflation

Over the past two decades, central banks around the world have beaten inflation. Yet in recent years, some commentators have worried that inflation might get too low.

The Joy of Inflation

Inflation in the developed world is at its lowest in almost half a century. This should be a moment of triumph for inflation-busting central banks. Yet instead, many economists are fretting that they have succeeded too well. Prices have been falling in Japan since 1995; in America and Germany the risk of deflation is greater than at any time since the 1930s. The longer growth remains below trend, the further inflation will fall. . . .

Recent statements by both America's Federal Reserve and the European Central Bank (ECB) signal that they recognize the danger of deflation, even if they still consider it a minor risk. So can they, unlike the Bank of Japan, prevent deflation? The biggest problem is that nominal interest rates cannot go below zero; if prices fall, this can make it impossible to deliver the negative real rates necessary to boost demand. . . .

A more fundamental question is whether central banks might themselves have aggravated the risk of deflation, by aiming for a needlessly low target for inflation. Everybody agrees that high inflation is bad for growth, because it distorts relative prices and hence the allocation of resources. But there is room for disagreement about how low inflation ought to be. There is little evidence that pushing inflation below, say, 3% will raise growth. Indeed, there is plenty of academic support for the view that a little bit of inflation is better for growth than none at all.

One reason is the danger of deflation. A study by the IMF concludes that, given the range of economic shocks over the past 40 years, the risk of interest rates hitting zero and deflation setting in rises markedly once an inflation target is set below 2%. This suggests that the mid-point of any target should be above 2%. The ECB regards 2% as its ceiling. . . .

Another argument for a little bit of inflation is that it can smooth the path of adjustment. If inflation is 3%, workers might accept a pay freeze, implying a real pay cut of 3%; but if inflation is zero, they may not accept a 3% nominal pay cut. Without some inflation, it is hard to trim real wages in a declining industry or region, meaning that unemployment will rise. The less flexible a country's labour market, the higher its optimal inflation is likely to be: and Europe's are notoriously inflexible. All in all, if the appropriate rate for America is 2–3%, say, then in the euro area it might be 3–4%. Instead, the ECB has the lowest inflation target of any central bank in the world.

A decade or so ago, when inflation still loomed large, some (including *The Economist*) argued that 0–2% was the right inflation goal for central banks. Seeking a little bit of inflation was, after all, like wanting to be a little bit pregnant: it could quickly get out of hand. At that time, when the priority was to reduce inflationary expectations and deflation was confined to dusty old textbooks, this made sense. Today, with Japan so clearly demonstrating the perils of deflation, central banks need to aim a little higher.

When economies reduce their rate of inflation, they almost always experience a period of high unemployment and low output. It is risky to believe that the central bank could achieve credibility so quickly as to make disinflation painless.

Indeed, a disinflationary recession can potentially leave permanent scars on the economy. Firms in all industries reduce their spending on new plants and equipment substantially during recessions, making investment the most volatile component of GDP. Even after the recession is over, the smaller stock of capital reduces productivity, incomes, and living standards below the levels they otherwise would have achieved. In addition, when workers become unemployed in recessions, they lose valuable job skills, permanently reducing their value as workers. Some economists have argued that the high unemployment in many European economies during the past decade is the aftermath of the disinflations of the 1980s.

Why should policymakers put the economy through a costly, inequitable disinflationary recession to achieve zero inflation, which may have only modest benefits? Economist Alan Blinder, who was once vice chairman of the Federal Reserve, argued in his book *Hard Heads, Soft Hearts* that policymakers should not make this choice:

> The costs that attend the low and moderate inflation rates experienced in the United States and in other industrial countries appear to be quite modest—more like a bad cold than a cancer on society. . . . As rational individuals, we do not volunteer for a lobotomy to cure a head cold. Yet, as a collectivity, we routinely prescribe the economic equivalent of lobotomy (high unemployment) as a cure for the inflationary cold.

Blinder concludes that it is better to learn to live with moderate inflation.

Quick Quiz Explain the costs and benefits of reducing inflation to zero. Which are temporary and which are permanent?

SHOULD THE GOVERNMENT BALANCE ITS BUDGET?

A persistent macroeconomic debate concerns the government's finances. Whenever the government spends more than it collects in tax revenue, it covers this budget deficit by issuing government debt. In 2005, for example, the U.S. federal government was expected to run a budget deficit of $365 billion.

When we studied financial markets, we saw how budget deficits affect saving, investment, and interest rates. But how big a problem are budget deficits? Our fourth debate concerns whether fiscal policymakers should make balancing the government's budget a high priority.

Pro: The Government Should Balance Its Budget

The U.S. federal government is far more indebted today than it was two decades ago. In 1980, the federal debt was $710 billion; in 2005, it was $4.7 trillion. If we divide today's debt by the size of the population, we learn that each person's share of the government debt is about $16,000.

The most direct effect of the government debt is to place a burden on future generations of taxpayers. When these debts and accumulated interest come due, future taxpayers will face a difficult choice. They can pay higher taxes, enjoy less government spending, or both to make resources available to pay off the debt and accumulated interest. Or they can delay the day of reckoning and put the government into even deeper debt by borrowing once again to pay off the old debt and interest. In essence, when the government runs a budget deficit and issues government debt, it allows current taxpayers to pass the bill for some of their government spending on to future taxpayers. Inheriting such a large debt cannot help but lower the living standard of future generations.

In addition to this direct effect, budget deficits also have various macroeconomic effects. Because budget deficits represent *negative* public saving, they lower national saving (the sum of private and public saving). Reduced national saving causes real interest rates to rise and investment to fall. Reduced investment leads over time to a smaller stock of capital. A lower capital stock reduces labor productivity, real wages, and the economy's production of goods and services. Thus, when the government increases its debt, future generations are born into an economy with lower incomes as well as higher taxes.

There are, nevertheless, situations in which running a budget deficit is justifiable. Throughout history, the most common cause of increased government debt has been war. When a military conflict raises government spending temporarily, it is reasonable to finance this extra spending by borrowing. Otherwise, taxes during wartime would have to rise precipitously. Such high tax rates would greatly distort the incentives faced by those who are taxed, leading to large deadweight losses. In addition, such high tax rates would be unfair to current generations of taxpayers, who already have to make the sacrifice of fighting the war.

Similarly, it is reasonable to allow a budget deficit during a temporary downturn in economic activity. When the economy goes into a recession, tax revenue falls automatically because the income tax and the payroll tax are levied on measures of income. If the government tried to balance its budget during a recession, it would have to raise taxes or cut spending at a time of high unemployment. Such a policy would tend to depress aggregate demand at precisely the time it needed to be stimulated and, therefore, would tend to increase the magnitude of economic fluctuations.

Yet not all budget deficits can be justified by appealing to war or recession. U.S. government debt as a percentage of GDP increased from 26 percent in 1980 to 50 percent in 1995. During this period, the United States avoided major military conflict and major economic downturn. Nonetheless, the government consistently ran a large budget deficit, largely because the president and Congress found it easier to increase government spending than to increase taxes.

The budget deficits of the early 2000s can, perhaps, be rationalized by the lingering effects of the recession of 2001 and by the war on terrorism. But it is imperative that this deficit not signal a return to the unsustainable fiscal policy of an earlier era. Compared to the alternative of ongoing budget deficits, a balanced budget means greater national saving, investment, and economic growth. It means that future college graduates will enter a more prosperous economy.

Con: The Government Should Not Balance Its Budget

The problem of government debt is often exaggerated. Although the government debt does represent a tax burden on younger generations, it is not large compared to the average person's lifetime income. The debt of the U.S. federal government is about $16,000 per person. A person who works 40 years for

"MY SHARE OF THE GOVERNMENT DEBT IS $16,000."

In The News

Dealing with Deficits

The nation's trade deficit and the federal government's budget deficit remain a focus of debate among U.S. policymakers.

Cutting Deficit Now May Spare Pain Later

By David Wessel

If the economy came in for credit counseling, the advice would sound like this: You're smart, ambitious, flexible—and in better shape than others. But you're living beyond your means. You spent every penny you made last year, and then borrowed a further 6% of your income at favorable rates. Don't count on this continuing.

There is widespread, though not universal, agreement that the U.S. economy is on an unsustainable trajectory. It isn't prudent to expect foreigners to lend the U.S. 6% or more of gross domestic product indefinitely. It isn't prudent for the U.S. to keep expecting to consume more than it produces (importing from abroad to make up the difference) and to invest more than it saves (borrowing from abroad to make up the difference).

The only question is whether all this ends with a bang or a whimper. "While the basic facts are undisputed . . . every actor in this tale is spinning a different interpretation, blaming someone else and providing a different solution,"

notes Nouriel Roubini, a New York University economist.

Europeans and Asians tell us that the global economy would be safer if we saved more and imported less. The U.S. replies that the economy would be safer if Europeans and Asians saved less and imported more. Some analysts say the key is for China to let its currency rise against the dollar so it imports more and exports less. Other analysts say the key is for the U.S. to save more so it relies less on borrowing from China. They're all right: No one of those solutions will suffice.

$30,000 a year will earn $1.2 million over his lifetime. His share of the government debt represents less than 2 percent of his lifetime resources.

Moreover, it is misleading to view the effects of budget deficits in isolation. The budget deficit is just one piece of a large picture of how the government chooses to raise and spend money. In making these decisions over fiscal policy, policymakers affect different generations of taxpayers in many ways. The government's budget deficit or surplus should be considered together with these other policies.

For example, suppose the government reduces the budget deficit by cutting spending on public investments, such as education. Does this policy make young generations better off? The government debt will be smaller when they enter the labor force, which means a smaller tax burden. Yet if they are less educated than they could be, their productivity and incomes will be lower. Many estimates of the return to schooling (the increase in a worker's wage that results from an additional year in school) find that it is quite large. Reducing the budget deficit rather than funding more education spending could, all things considered, make future generations worse off.

But the U.S. government, as is painfully evident, can't make China revalue its currency or prod European or Japanese consumers to buy more. It can't even make Americans save more. The one lever the government controls, sort of, is its own budget deficit, the amount that it subtracts from overall national saving.

There is no hard link between the budget deficit and the current-account deficit—the amount (now more than $1.8 billion a day, or $2,250 per man, woman and child per year) that the U.S. borrows from abroad. When the U.S. ran budget surpluses in the late 1990s, it still borrowed a lot; foreigners readily lent to and invested in the booming U.S. economy.

But at some point—and don't believe anyone who predicts precisely when—foreigners aren't going to be willing to put increasing amounts into U.S. dollars. They'll invest elsewhere or use the money at home. (It's bizarre that a country like China with so much thirst for improving the lot of its people is pouring money into the U.S. so that Americans can save a few bucks a month on their mortgages.)

When that day comes, the dollar will fall and interest rates will rise. Americans will be forced to borrow less, spend less (particularly on imports) and thus save more to replace foreigners' savings. The challenge to the U.S. is what to do now to reduce the risk that inevitable belt-tightening will cause a recession. "We shouldn't use all the rope that the rest of the world will give us to hang ourselves," advises William Kline, an international economist at the Center for Global Development, a Washington think tank.

That's where the budget deficit comes in. The bond market and the Federal Reserve will push up interest rates when the foreign appetite for lending to the U.S. wanes, but the increases will be less sharp if the government is borrowing less. And the only way to reduce future government borrowing is to act now to reduce deficits projected for the future. It's unpleasant, but it's the only plausible way to reduce the risk of a more painful outcome.

In contrast to his deficit-increasing first term, President Bush says he wants to reduce the deficit in his second term. But his goal is unambitious: His budget shows the deficit falling to 2.3% of GDP by fiscal year 2007 even though he projects the economy will have been operating at full speed for several years by then. And there's justified global skepticism about whether the U.S. will actually hit the target: Congress already has rejected or reduced Mr. Bush's proposals to restrain Medicaid health spending and farm subsidies. . . .

The U.S. budget deficit isn't the primary cause of the nation's risky overreliance on foreign savings. But reducing it is a big part of a prudent solution.

Source: *The Wall Street Journal*, May 12, 2005. Copyright 2005 by DOW JONES & CO INC. Reproduced with permission of DOW JONES & CO INC.

Single-minded concern about the budget deficit is also dangerous because it draws attention away from various other policies that redistribute income across generations. For example, in the 1960s and 1970s, the U.S. federal government raised Social Security benefits for the elderly. It financed this higher spending by increasing the payroll tax on the working-age population. This policy redistributed income away from younger generations toward older generations, even though it did not affect the government debt. Thus, the budget deficit is only a small part of the larger issue of how government policy affects the welfare of different generations.

To some extent, the adverse effects of government debt can be reversed by forward-looking parents. Suppose a parent is worried about the impact of the government debt on his children. The parent can offset the impact simply by saving and leaving a larger bequest. The bequest would enhance the children's ability to bear the burden of future taxes. Some economists claim that people do in fact behave this way. If this were true, higher private saving by parents would offset the public dissaving of budget deficits, and deficits would not affect the economy. Most economists doubt that parents are so farsighted, but some people probably do act this way, and anyone could. Deficits give people the opportunity to consume at the expense of their children, but deficits do not require them to do so. If the government debt were actually a great problem facing future generations, some parents would help to solve it.

Critics of budget deficits sometimes assert that the government debt cannot continue to rise forever, but in fact, it can. Just as a bank evaluating a loan application would compare a person's debts to his income, we should judge the burden of the government debt relative to the size of the nation's income. Population growth and technological progress cause the total income of the U.S. economy to grow over time. As a result, the nation's ability to pay the interest on the government debt grows over time as well. As long as the government debt grows more slowly than the nation's income, there is nothing to prevent the government debt from growing forever.

Some numbers can put this into perspective. The real output of the U.S. economy grows on average about 3 percent per year. If the inflation rate is 2 percent per year, then nominal income grows at a rate of 5 percent per year. The government debt, therefore, can rise by 5 percent per year without increasing the ratio of debt to income. In 2005, the federal government debt was $4.7 trillion; 5 percent of this figure is $235 billion. As long as the federal budget deficit is smaller than $235 billion, the policy is sustainable. There will never be any day of reckoning that forces the budget deficits to end or the economy to collapse.

Quick Quiz Explain how reducing a government budget deficit makes future generations better off. What fiscal policy might improve the lives of future generations more than reducing a government budget deficit?

SHOULD THE TAX LAWS BE REFORMED TO ENCOURAGE SAVING?

 A nation's standard of living depends on its ability to produce goods and services. This was one of the *Ten Principles of Economics* in Chapter 1. As we saw in the chapter on production and growth, a nation's productive capability, in turn, is determined largely by how much it saves and invests for the future. Our fifth debate is whether policymakers should reform the tax laws to encourage greater saving and investment.

Pro: The Tax Laws Should Be Reformed to Encourage Saving

A nation's saving rate is a key determinant of its long-run economic prosperity. When the saving rate is higher, more resources are available for investment in new plant and equipment. A larger stock of plant and equipment, in turn, raises labor productivity, wages, and incomes. It is, therefore, no surprise that international data show a strong correlation between national saving rates and measures of economic well-being.

Another of the *Ten Principles of Economics* presented in Chapter 1 is that people respond to incentives. This lesson should apply to people's decisions about how much to save. If a nation's laws make saving attractive, people will save a higher fraction of their incomes, and this higher saving will lead to a more prosperous future.

Unfortunately, the U.S. tax system discourages saving by taxing the return to saving quite heavily. For example, consider a 25-year-old worker who saves $1,000 of her income to have a more comfortable retirement at the age of 70. If she buys a bond that pays an interest rate of 10 percent, the $1,000 will accumulate at the end of 45 years to $72,900 in the absence of taxes on interest. But suppose she faces a marginal tax rate on interest income of 40 percent, which is typical of many workers once federal and state income taxes are added together. In this case, her after-tax interest rate is only 6 percent, and the $1,000 will accumulate at the end of 45 years to only $13,800. That is, accumulated over this long span of time, the tax rate on interest income reduces the benefit of saving $1,000 from $72,900 to $13,800—or by about 80 percent.

The tax code further discourages saving by taxing some forms of capital income twice. Suppose a person uses some of his saving to buy stock in a corporation. When the corporation earns a profit from its capital investments, it first pays tax on this profit in the form of the corporate income tax. If the corporation pays out the rest of the profit to the stockholder in the form of dividends, the stockholder pays tax on this income a second time in the form of the individual income tax. This double taxation substantially reduces the return to the stockholder, thereby reducing the incentive to save.

The tax laws again discourage saving if a person wants to leave his accumulated wealth to his children (or anyone else) rather than consuming it during his lifetime. Parents can bequeath some money to their children without tax, but if the bequest becomes large, the inheritance tax rate can be as high as 55 percent. To a large extent, concern about national saving is motivated by a desire to ensure economic prosperity for future generations. It is odd, therefore, that the tax laws discourage the most direct way in which one generation can help the next.

In addition to the tax code, many other policies and institutions in our society reduce the incentive for households to save. Some government benefits, such as welfare and Medicaid, are means-tested; that is, the benefits are reduced for those who in the past have been prudent enough to save some of their income. Colleges and universities grant financial aid as a function of the wealth of the students and their parents. Such a policy is like a tax on wealth and, as such, discourages students and parents from saving.

There are various ways in which the tax code could provide an incentive to save, or at least reduce the disincentive that households now face. Already the tax laws give preferential treatment to some types of retirement saving. When a taxpayer puts income into an Individual Retirement Account (IRA), for instance, that income and the interest it earns are not taxed until the funds are withdrawn at retirement. The tax code gives a similar tax advantage to retirement accounts that go by other names, such as 401(k), 403(b), Keogh plan, and profit-sharing plans. There are, however, limits to who is eligible to use these plans and, for those who are eligible, limits on the amount that can be put in them. Moreover, because there are penalties for withdrawal before retirement age, these retirement plans provide little incentive for other types of saving, such as saving to buy a house or pay for college. A small step to encourage greater saving would be to expand the ability of households to use such tax-advantaged savings accounts.

A more comprehensive approach would be to reconsider the entire basis by which the government collects revenue. The centerpiece of the U.S. tax system is

In The News

Tax Reform

In 2005, President Bush appointed a panel of experts to study options for reforming the tax system. Here is what economist Alan Greenspan advised the panel.

Greenspan Backs Consumption Tax in His Principles for Reform

By Andrew Balls

Alan Greenspan, the Federal Reserve chairman, laid out the principles he believed should guide US tax reform and voiced support yesterday for the introduction of a consumption tax alongside the present system.

Mr Greenspan, who appeared before President George W. Bush's advisory panel on tax reform, steered clear of direct prescriptions. But in response to questions he said that introducing a consumption tax, such as a value-added tax or national sales tax, in addition to income tax was a sensible approach.

"I would suspect that probably that may be the best route to go," he said.

The tax panel is considering a broad range of possible tax reforms, including introducing a consumption tax. Given the broad respect he is held in on both sides of the political debate, Mr Greenspan's comments will be welcomed by those who favor some form of consumption tax.

But he said it was impractical to move fully to that system because of a host of practical and political difficulties, and stressed a number of transition problems in introducing such a tax. On the income tax, Mr Greenspan said the emphasis should be on broadening the income tax base, by eliminating deductions and exemptions. He praised the 1986 tax reform, which focused on these matters, but said much good work had been undone by congressional meddling. "The tax code has drifted back to be overly complicated and burdened by higher marginal tax rates and by many special provisions that have undesirably narrowed the tax base," he said.

Source: *The Financial Times*, March 4, 2005.

the income tax. A dollar earned is taxed the same whether it is spent or saved. An alternative advocated by many economists is a consumption tax. Under a consumption tax, a household pays taxes only on the basis of what it spends. Income that is saved is exempt from taxation until the saving is later withdrawn and spent on consumption goods. In essence, a consumption tax puts all saving automatically into a tax-advantaged savings account, much like an IRA. A switch from income to consumption taxation would greatly increase the incentive to save.

Con: The Tax Laws Should Not Be Reformed to Encourage Saving

Increasing saving may be desirable, but it is not the only goal of tax policy. Policymakers also must be sure to distribute the tax burden fairly. The problem with proposals to increase the incentive to save is that they increase the tax burden on those who can least afford it.

It is an undeniable fact that high-income households save a greater fraction of their income than low-income households. As a result, any tax change that favors people who save will also tend to favor people with high income. Policies such as tax-advantaged retirement accounts may seem appealing, but they lead to a less egalitarian society. By reducing the tax burden on the wealthy who can take advantage of these accounts, they force the government to raise the tax burden on the poor.

Moreover, tax policies designed to encourage saving may not be effective at achieving that goal. Many studies have found that saving is relatively inelastic—that is, the amount of saving is not very sensitive to the rate of return on saving. If this is indeed the case, then tax provisions that raise the effective return by reducing the taxation of capital income will further enrich the wealthy without inducing them to save more than they otherwise would.

Economic theory does not give a clear prediction about whether a higher rate of return would increase saving. The outcome depends on the relative size of two conflicting effects, called the *substitution effect* and the *income effect.* On the one hand, a higher rate of return raises the benefit of saving: Each dollar saved today produces more consumption in the future. This substitution effect tends to increase saving. On the other hand, a higher rate of return lowers the need for saving: A household has to save less to achieve any target level of consumption in the future. This income effect tends to reduce saving. If the substitution and income effects approximately cancel each other, as some studies suggest, then saving will not change when lower taxation of capital income raises the rate of return.

There are other ways to raise national saving than by giving tax breaks to the rich. National saving is the sum of private and public saving. Instead of trying to alter the tax code to encourage greater private saving, policymakers can simply raise public saving by reducing the budget deficit, perhaps by raising taxes on the wealthy. This offers a direct way of raising national saving and increasing prosperity for future generations.

Indeed, once public saving is taken into account, tax provisions to encourage saving might backfire. Tax changes that reduce the taxation of capital income reduce government revenue and, thereby, lead to a budget deficit. To increase national saving, such a change in the tax code must stimulate private saving by more than the decline in public saving. If this is not the case, so-called saving incentives can potentially make matters worse.

Quick Quiz   Give three examples of how our society discourages saving. What are the drawbacks of eliminating these disincentives?

CONCLUSION

This chapter has considered five debates over macroeconomic policy. For each, it began with a controversial proposition and then offered the arguments pro and con. If you find it hard to choose a side in these debates, you may find some comfort in the fact that you are not alone. The study of economics does not always make it easy to choose among alternative policies. Indeed, by clarifying the inevitable trade-offs that policymakers face, it can make the choice more difficult.

Difficult choices, however, have no right to seem easy. When you hear politicians or commentators proposing something that sounds too good to be true, it probably is. If they sound like they are offering you a free lunch, you should look for the hidden price tag. Few if any policies come with benefits but no costs. By helping you see through the fog of rhetoric so common in political discourse, the study of economics should make you a better participant in our national debates.

SUMMARY

- Advocates of active monetary and fiscal policy view the economy as inherently unstable and believe that policy can manage aggregate demand to offset the inherent instability. Critics of active monetary and fiscal policy emphasize that policy affects the economy with a lag and that our ability to forecast future economic conditions is poor. As a result, attempts to stabilize the economy can end up being destabilizing.

- Advocates of rules for monetary policy argue that discretionary policy can suffer from incompetence, the abuse of power, and time inconsistency. Critics of rules for monetary policy argue that discretionary policy is more flexible in responding to changing economic circumstances.

- Advocates of a zero-inflation target emphasize that inflation has many costs and few if any benefits. Moreover, the cost of eliminating inflation—depressed output and employment—is only temporary. Even this cost can be reduced if the central bank announces a credible plan to reduce inflation, thereby directly lowering expectations of inflation. Critics of a zero-inflation target claim that moderate inflation imposes only small costs on society, whereas the recession necessary to reduce inflation is quite costly.

- Advocates of a balanced government budget argue that budget deficits impose an unjustifiable burden on future generations by raising their taxes and lowering their incomes. Critics of a balanced government budget argue that the deficit is only one small piece of fiscal policy. Single-minded concern about the budget deficit can obscure the many ways in which policy, including various spending programs, affects different generations.

- Advocates of tax incentives for saving point out that our society discourages saving in many ways, such as by heavily taxing the income from capital and by reducing benefits for those who have accumulated wealth. They endorse reforming the tax laws to encourage saving, perhaps by switching from an income tax to a consumption tax. Critics of tax incentives for saving argue that many proposed changes to stimulate saving would primarily benefit the wealthy, who do not need a tax break. They also argue that such changes might have only a small effect on private saving. Raising public saving by decreasing the government's budget deficit would provide a more direct and equitable way to increase national saving.

QUESTIONS FOR REVIEW

1. What causes the lags in the effect of monetary and fiscal policy on aggregate demand? What are the implications of these lags for the debate over active versus passive policy?

2. What might motivate a central banker to cause a political business cycle? What does the political business cycle imply for the debate over policy rules?

3. Explain how credibility might affect the cost of reducing inflation.

4. Why are some economists against a target of zero inflation?

5. Explain two ways in which a government budget deficit hurts a future worker.

6. What are two situations in which most economists view a budget deficit as justifiable?

7. Give an example of how the government might hurt young generations, even while reducing the government debt they inherit.

8. Some economists say that the government can continue running a budget deficit forever. How is that possible?

9. Some income from capital is taxed twice. Explain.

10. Give an example, other than tax policy, of how our society discourages saving.

11. What adverse effect might be caused by tax incentives to raise saving?

PROBLEMS AND APPLICATIONS

1. The chapter suggests that the economy, like the human body, has "natural restorative powers."
   a. Illustrate the short-run effect of a fall in aggregate demand using an aggregate-demand/aggregate-supply diagram. What happens to total output, income, and employment?
   b. If the government does not use stabilization policy, what happens to the economy over time? Illustrate on your diagram. Does this adjustment generally occur in a matter of months or a matter of years?
   c. Do you think the "natural restorative powers" of the economy mean that policymakers

   should be passive in response to the business cycle?

2. Policymakers who want to stabilize the economy must decide how much to change the money supply, government spending, or taxes. Why is it difficult for policymakers to choose the appropriate strength of their actions?

3. Suppose that people suddenly wanted to hold more money balances.
   a. What would be the effect of this change on the economy if the Federal Reserve followed

a rule of increasing the money supply by 3 percent per year? Illustrate your answer with a money-market diagram and an aggregate-demand/aggregate-supply diagram.

b. What would be the effect of this change on the economy if the Fed followed a rule of increasing the money supply by 3 percent per year *plus* 1 percentage point for every percentage point that unemployment rises above its normal level? Illustrate your answer.

c. Which of the foregoing rules better stabilizes the economy? Would it help to allow the Fed to respond to predicted unemployment instead of current unemployment? Explain.

4. Economist John Taylor has suggested that the Fed use the following rule for choosing its target for the federal funds interest rate (*r*):

$$r = 2\% + \pi + \tfrac{1}{2}\,(y - y^*)/y^* + \tfrac{1}{2}\,(\pi - \pi^*),$$

where π is the average of the inflation rate over the past year, y is real GDP as recently measured, y^* is an estimate of the natural rate of output, and π^* is the Fed's goal for inflation.

a. Explain the logic that might lie behind this rule for setting interest rates. Would you support the Fed's use of this rule?

b. Some economists advocate such a rule for monetary policy but believe π and y should be the *forecasts* of future values of inflation and output. What are the advantages of using forecasts instead of actual values? What are the disadvantages?

5. The problem of time inconsistency applies to fiscal policy as well as to monetary policy. Suppose the government announced a reduction in taxes on income from capital investments, like new factories.

a. If investors believed that capital taxes would remain low, how would the government's action affect the level of investment?

b. After investors have responded to the announced tax reduction, does the government have an incentive to renege on its policy? Explain.

c. Given your answer to part (b), would investors believe the government's announcement? What can the government do to increase the credibility of announced policy changes?

d. Explain why this situation is similar to the time inconsistency problem faced by monetary policymakers.

6. Chapter 2 explains the difference between positive analysis and normative analysis. In the debate about whether the central bank should aim for zero inflation, which areas of disagreement involve positive statements and which involve normative judgments?

7. Why are the benefits of reducing inflation permanent and the costs temporary? Why are the costs of increasing inflation permanent and the benefits temporary? Use Phillips-curve diagrams in your answer.

8. Suppose the federal government cuts taxes and increases spending, raising the budget deficit to 12 percent of GDP. If nominal GDP is rising 5 percent per year, are such budget deficits sustainable forever? Explain. If budget deficits of this size are maintained for 20 years, what is likely to happen to your taxes and your children's taxes in the future? Can you personally do something today to offset this future effect?

9. Explain how each of the following policies redistributes income across generations. Is the redistribution from young to old or from old to young?

a. an increase in the budget deficit
b. more generous subsidies for education loans
c. greater investments in highways and bridges
d. an increase in Social Security benefits

10. The chapter says that budget deficits reduce the income of future generations but can boost output and income during a recession. Explain how both of these statements can be true.

11. What is the fundamental trade-off that society faces if it chooses to save more? How might the government increase national saving?

12. Suppose the government reduced the tax rate on income from savings and raised taxes on labor income to avoid increasing the budget deficit.

   a. Who would benefit from this tax change most directly?

   b. What would happen to the capital stock over time? What would happen to the capital available to each worker? What would happen to productivity? What would happen to wages?

   c. In light of your answer to part (b), how might the long-run distributional effects differ from the answer you gave in part (a)?

 For further information on topics in this chapter, additional problems, examples, applications, online quizzes, and more, please visit our website at http://mankiw.swlearning.com.

Chapter 1

Page 8 The four principles of economic decision making are: (1) people face trade-offs; (2) the cost of something is what you give up to get it; (3) rational people think at the margin; and (4) people respond to incentives. People face trade-offs because to get one thing that they like, they usually have to give up another thing that they like. The cost of something is what you give up to get it, not just in terms of monetary costs but all opportunity costs. Rational people think at the margin by taking an action if and only if the marginal benefit exceeds the marginal cost. People respond to incentives because they choose activities by comparing benefits to costs; therefore, a change in these benefits or costs may cause their behavior to change.

Page 11 The three principles concerning people's economic interactions are: (1) trade can make everyone better off; (2) markets are usually a good way to organize economic activity; and (3) governments can sometimes improve market outcomes. Trade can make everyone better off because it allows countries to specialize in what they do best and to enjoy a wider variety of goods and services. Markets are usually a good way to organize economic activity because the invisible hand leads markets to desirable outcomes. Governments can sometimes improve market outcomes because markets may fail to allocate resources efficiently due to an externality or market power.

Page 14 The three principles that describe how the economy as a whole works are: (1) a country's standard of living depends on its ability to produce goods and services; (2) prices rise when the government prints too much money; and (3) society faces a short-run trade-off between inflation and unemployment. A country's standard of living depends largely on the productivity of its workers, which in turn depends on the education of its workers and the access its workers have to the necessary tools and technology. Prices rise when the government prints too much money because more money in circulation reduces the value of money, causing inflation. Society faces a short-run trade-off between inflation and unemployment that is only temporary. Policymakers have some short-term ability to exploit this relationship using various policy instruments.

Chapter 2

Page 28 Economics is like a science because economists devise theories, collect data, and analyze the data in an attempt to verify or refute their theories. In other words, economics is based on the scientific method.

Figure 2–1 shows the production possibilities frontier for a society that produces food and clothing. Point A is an efficient point (on the frontier), point B is an inefficient point (inside the frontier), and point C is an infeasible point (outside the frontier).

The effects of a drought are shown in Figure 2–2. The drought reduces the amount of food that can be produced, shifting the production possibilities frontier inward.

Figure 2–2

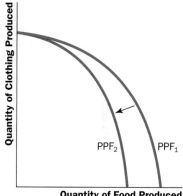

Quantity of Food Produced

Microeconomics is the study of how households and firms make decisions and how they interact in markets. Macroeconomics is the study of economy-wide phenomena, including inflation, unemployment, and economic growth.

Page 32 An example of a positive statement is "higher taxes discourage work effort." It is a positive statement because it is a claim that describes the world as it is. An example of a normative statement is "the government should reduce tax rates." It is a normative statement because it is a claim that prescribes how the world should be. Many other examples are possible.

Parts of the government that regularly rely on advice from economists are the Department of the Treasury in designing tax policy, the Department of Labor in analyzing data on the employment situation, the Department of Justice in

Figure 2–1

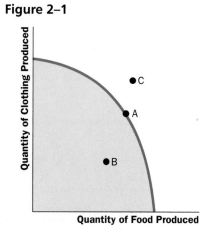

Quantity of Food Produced

enforcing the nation's antitrust laws, the Congressional Budget Office in evaluating policy proposals, and the Federal Reserve in analyzing economic developments. Many other answers are possible.

Page 34 Economic advisers to the president might disagree about a question of policy because of differences in scientific judgments or differences in values.

Chapter 3

Page 52 Figure 3–1 shows Robinson Crusoe's production possibilities frontier for gathering coconuts and catching fish. If Crusoe lives by himself, this frontier limits his consumption of coconuts and fish, but if he can trade with natives on the island, he will possibly be able to consume at a point outside his production possibilities frontier.

Figure 3–1

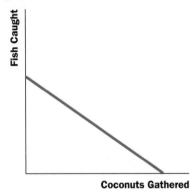

Page 54 Crusoe's opportunity cost of catching one fish is 10 coconuts, since he can gather 10 coconuts in the same amount of time it takes to catch one fish. Friday's opportunity cost of catching one fish is 15 coconuts, since he can gather 30 coconuts in the same amount of time it takes to catch two fish. Friday has an absolute advantage in catching fish, since he can catch two per hour, while Crusoe can catch only one per hour. But Crusoe has a comparative advantage in catching fish, since his opportunity cost of catching a fish is less than Friday's.

Page 58 If the world's fastest typist happens to be trained in brain surgery, he should hire a secretary because the secretary will give up less for each hour spent typing. Although the brain surgeon has an absolute advantage in typing, the secretary has a comparative advantage in typing because of the lower opportunity cost of typing.

Chapter 4

Page 65 A market is a group of buyers (who determine demand) and a group of sellers (who determine supply) of a particular good or service. A competitive market is one in which there are many buyers and many sellers of an identical product so that each has a negligible impact on the market price.

Page 71 Here is an example of a demand schedule for pizza:

Price of Pizza Slice	Number of Pizza Slices Demanded
$0.00	10
0.25	9
0.50	8
0.75	7
1.00	6
1.25	5
1.50	4
1.75	3
2.00	2
2.25	1
2.50	0

The demand curve is graphed in Figure 4–1.

Figure 4–1

Examples of things that would shift the demand curve include changes in income, prices of related goods like soda or hot dogs, tastes, expectations about future income or prices, and the number of buyers.

A change in the price of pizza would not shift this demand curve; it would only lead to a movement from one point to another along the same demand curve.

Page 75 Here is an example of a supply schedule for pizza:

Price of Pizza Slice	Number of Pizza Slices Supplied
$0.00	0
0.25	100
0.50	200
0.75	300
1.00	400
1.25	500
1.50	600
1.75	700
2.00	800
2.25	900
2.50	1000

The supply curve is graphed in Figure 4–2.

Figure 4–2

Examples of things that would shift the supply curve include changes in prices of inputs like tomato sauce and cheese, changes in technology like more efficient pizza ovens or automatic dough makers, changes in expectations about the future price of pizza, or a change in the number of sellers.

A change in the price of pizza would not shift this supply curve;

it would only lead to a movement from one point to another along the same supply curve.

Page 82 If the price of tomatoes rises, the supply curve for pizza shifts to the left because there has been an increase in the price of an input into pizza production, but there is no shift in demand. The shift to the left of the supply curve causes the equilibrium price to rise and the equilibrium quantity to decline, as Figure 4–3 shows.

Figure 4–3

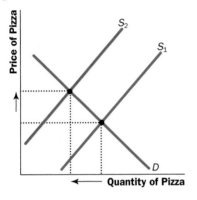

If the price of hamburgers falls, the demand curve for pizza shifts to the left because the lower price of hamburgers will lead consumers to buy more hamburgers and fewer pizzas, but there is no shift in supply. The shift to the left of the demand curve causes the equilibrium price to fall and the equilibrium quantity to decline, as Figure 4–4 shows.

Figure 4–4

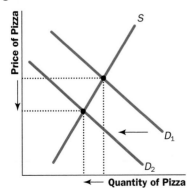

Chapter 5

Page 94 Gross domestic product measures two things at once: (1) the total income of everyone in the economy and (2) the total expenditure on the economy's output of final goods and services. It can measure both of these things at once because all expenditure in the economy ends up as someone's income.

Page 96 The production of a pound of caviar contributes more to GDP than the production of a pound of hamburger because the contribution to GDP is measured by market value and the price of a pound of caviar is much higher than the price of a pound of hamburger.

Page 99 The four components of expenditure are: (1) consumption; (2) investment; (3) government purchases; and (4) net exports. The largest component is consumption, which accounts for more than two-thirds of total expenditure.

Page 104 Real GDP is the production of goods and services valued at constant prices. Nominal GDP is the production of goods and services valued at current prices. Real GDP is a better measure of economic well-being because changes in real GDP reflect changes in the amount of output being produced. Thus, a rise in real GDP means people have produced more goods and services, but a rise in nominal GDP could occur either because of increased production or because of higher prices.

Page 108 Although GDP is not a perfect measure of well-being, policymakers should care about it because a larger GDP means that a nation can afford better healthcare, better educational systems, and more of the material necessities of life.

Chapter 6

Page 122 The consumer price index tries to measure the overall cost of the goods and services bought by a typical consumer. It is constructed

by surveying consumers to determine a basket of goods and services that the typical consumer buys. Prices of these goods and services are used to compute the cost of the basket at different times, and a base year is chosen. To compute the index, we divide the cost of the market basket in the current year by the cost of the market basket in the base year and multiply by 100.

Page 126 Since Henry Ford paid his workers $5 a day in 1914 and the consumer price index was 10 in 1914 and 195 in 2005, then the Ford paycheck was worth $5 × 195/10 = $97.50 a day in 2005 dollars.

Chapter 7

Page 135 The approximate growth rate of real GDP per person in the United States is 1.82 percent (based on Table 1) from 1870 to 2003. Countries that have had faster growth include Japan, Brazil, Mexico, China, Germany, and Canada; countries that have had slower growth include Argentina, India, United Kingdom, Indonesia, Pakistan, and Bangladesh.

Page 142 The four determinants of a country's productivity are: (1) physical capital, which is the stock of equipment and structures that are used to produce goods and services; (2) human capital, which is the knowledge and skills that workers acquire through education, training, and experience; (3) natural resources, which are inputs into production that are provided by nature, such as land, rivers, and mineral deposits; and (4) technological knowledge, which is society's understanding of the best ways to produce goods and services.

Page 155 Ways in which a government policymaker can try to raise the growth in living standards in a society include: (1) investing more current resources in the production of capital, which has the drawback of reducing the resources used for producing current consumption; (2) encouraging investment from abroad, which has the drawback that some of the benefits of investment flow to foreigners; (3) increasing education, which has an opportunity cost in that students are not engaged in current production; (4) protecting property rights and promoting political stability, for which no drawbacks are obvious; (5) pursuing outward-oriented policies to encourage free trade, which may have the drawback of making a country more dependent on its trading partners; (6) reducing the rate of population growth, which may have the drawbacks of reducing individual freedom and lowering the rate of technological progress; and (7) encouraging research and development, which (like investment) may have the drawback of reducing current consumption.

Chapter 8

Page 165 A stock is a claim to partial ownership in a firm. A bond is a certificate of indebtedness. They are different in numerous ways: (1) a bond pays interest (a fixed payment determined when the bond is issued), while a stock pays dividends (a share of the firm's profits that can increase if the firm is more profitable); (2) a bond has a fixed time to maturity, while a stock never matures; and (3) if a company that has issued both stock and bonds goes bankrupt, the bondholders get paid off before the stockholders, so stocks have greater risk and potentially greater return than bonds. Stocks and bonds are similar in that both are financial instruments that are used by companies to raise money for investment, both are traded on exchanges, both entail a degree of risk, and the returns to both are taxed (usually).

Page 167 Private saving is the amount of income that households have left after paying their taxes and paying for their consumption. Public saving is the amount of tax revenue that the government has left after paying for its spending. National saving is equal to the total income in the economy that remains after paying for consumption and government purchases. Investment is the purchase of new capital, such as equipment or buildings.

These terms are related in two ways: (1) National saving is the sum of public saving and private saving. (2) In a closed economy, national saving equals investment.

Page 176 If more Americans adopted a "live for today" approach to life, they would spend more and save less. This would shift the supply curve to the left in the market for loanable funds. At the new equilibrium, there would be less saving and investment and a higher interest rate.

Chapter 9

Page 183 The present value of $150 to be received in 10 years if the interest rate is 7 percent is $150/(1.07)^{10} = 76.25.

Page 189 There are three ways in which a risk-averse person may reduce the risk he faces: (1) purchase insurance, (2) diversify his portfolio, or (3) choose safer alternatives by accepting a lower rate of return.

Page 193 No. According to the efficient markets hypothesis, the price of a share of stock should reflect all available information about its value. Thus, the stocks on this list should perform no better on average than other stocks listed on the stock exchange.

Chapter 10

Page 206 The unemployment rate is measured through a survey of 60,000 households to determine the percentage of the labor force that is unemployed. The unemployment rate overstates the amount of job-lessness because some of those who report being unemployed may not, in fact, be trying hard to find a job. But the unemployment rate may understate the amount of joblessness because discouraged workers are considered not in the labor force even though they are workers without jobs.

Page 210 An increase in the world price of oil increases the amount of frictional unemployment as oil-producing firms increase output and employment, but other firms, such as those in the auto industry, reduce output and employment. The sectoral shift from the auto industry to oil firms causes higher frictional unemployment for a time until workers have shifted from the auto industry to the oil industry. Although no increase in unemployment is really desirable, this type of frictional unemployment is a natural outcome of the reallocation of resources between different sectors. Public policies that might affect the unemployment caused by this change in the price of oil include government-run employment agencies, which can help autoworkers move into the oil industry, job-training programs to help workers adapt to a new industry, and unemployment insurance, which keeps workers from suffering economic hardship while changing from one industry to another.

Page 212 Figure 10–1 shows the supply curve (S) and the demand curve (D)

Figure 10–1

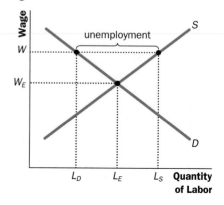

for labor. The wage (W) is above the equilibrium wage (W_E). The result is unemployment, equal to the amount by which the quantity of labor supplied (L_S) exceeds the quantity of labor demanded (L_D).

Page 214 A union in the auto industry raises the wages of workers employed by General Motors and Ford by threatening to strike. To prevent the costs of a strike, the firms generally pay higher wages than they would if there were no union. However, the higher wages reduce employment at General Motors and Ford. The unemployed autoworkers seek jobs elsewhere, reducing wages and increasing employment in the nonunion sector.

Page 218 There are four reasons that firms might find it profitable to pay wages above the level that balances the quantity of labor supplied and the quantity of labor demanded: (1) to ensure that workers are in good health so they will be more productive; (2) to reduce worker turnover because it is costly to hire new workers; (3) to make workers eager to keep their jobs, thus discouraging them from shirking; and (4) to attract a better pool of workers.

Chapter 11

Page 232 The three functions of money are: (1) medium of exchange; (2) unit of account; and (3) store of value. Money is a medium of exchange because money is the item people use to purchase goods and services. Money is a unit of account because it is the yardstick people use to post prices and record debts. Money is a store of value because people use it to transfer purchasing power from the present to the future.

Page 234 The primary responsibilities of the Federal Reserve are to regulate banks, to ensure the health of the banking system, and to control the quantity of money that is made

available in the economy. If the Fed wants to increase the supply of money, it usually does so by creating dollars and using them to purchase government bonds from the public in the nation's bond markets.

Page 241 Banks create money when they hold a fraction of their deposits in reserve and lend out the remainder. If the Fed wanted to use all three of its tools to decrease the money supply, it would: (1) sell government bonds from its portfolio in the open market to reduce the number of dollars in circulation; (2) increase reserve requirements to reduce the money created by banks; and (3) increase the discount rate to discourage banks from borrowing reserves from the Fed.

Chapter 12

Page 259 When the government of a country increases the growth rate of the money supply from 5 percent per year to 50 percent per year, the average level of prices will start rising very quickly, as predicted by the quantity theory of money. Nominal interest rates will increase dramatically as well, as predicted by the Fisher effect. The government may be increasing the money supply to finance its expenditures.

Page 268 Six costs of inflation are: (1) shoeleather costs; (2) menu costs; (3) relative-price variability and the misallocation of resources; (4) inflation-induced tax distortions; (5) confusion and inconvenience; and (6) arbitrary redistributions of wealth. Shoeleather costs arise because inflation causes people to spend resources going to the bank more often. Menu costs occur when people spend resources changing their posted prices. Relative-price variability occurs because as general prices rise, a fixed dollar price translates into a declining relative price, so the relative prices of goods are constantly changing, causing a misallocation of re-

sources. The combination of inflation and taxation causes distortions in incentives because people are taxed on their nominal capital gains and interest income instead of their real income from these sources. Inflation causes confusion and inconvenience because it reduces money's ability to function as a unit of account. Unexpected inflation redistributes wealth between borrowers and lenders.

Chapter 13

Page 285 Net exports are the value of a nation's exports minus the value of its imports, also called the trade balance. Net capital outflow is the purchase of foreign assets by domestic residents minus the purchase of domestic assets by foreigners. Net exports equal net capital outflow.

Page 288 The nominal exchange rate is the rate at which a person can trade the currency of one country for the currency of another. The real exchange rate is the rate at which a person can trade the goods and services of one country for the goods and services of another. They are related through the expression: Real exchange rate equals nominal exchange rate times domestic price divided by foreign price.

If the nominal exchange rate goes from 100 to 120 yen per dollar, the dollar has appreciated because a dollar now buys more yen.

Page 294 If Spain has had high inflation and Japan has had low inflation, then, according to the theory of purchasing-power parity, the number of Spanish pesetas a person can buy with Japanese yen should have increased.

Chapter 14

Page 304 The supply of loanable funds comes from national saving. The demand for loanable funds comes from domestic investment and net capital outflow. The supply in the market for foreign-currency exchange comes from net capital outflow. The demand in the market for foreign-currency exchange comes from net exports.

Page 307 The two markets in the model of the open economy are the market for loanable funds and the market for foreign-currency exchange. These markets determine two relative prices: (1) the market for loanable funds determines the real interest rate and (2) the market for foreign-currency exchange determines the real exchange rate.

Page 316 If Americans decided to spend a smaller fraction of their incomes, the increase in saving would shift the supply curve for loanable funds to the right, as shown in Figure 14–1. The decline in the real interest

Figure 14–1

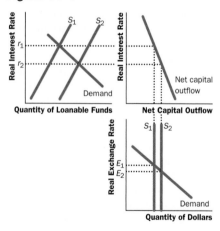

rate increases net capital outflow and shifts the supply of dollars to the right in the market for foreign-currency exchange. The result is a decline in the real exchange rate. Since the real interest rate is lower, domestic investment increases. Since the real exchange rate declines, net exports increase and the trade balance moves toward surplus. Overall, saving and domestic investment increase, the real interest rate and real exchange rate

decrease, and the trade balance moves toward surplus.

Chapter 15

Page 326 Three key facts about economic fluctuations are: (1) economic fluctuations are irregular and unpredictable; (2) most macroeconomic quantities fluctuate together; and (3) as output falls, unemployment rises.

Economic fluctuations are irregular and unpredictable, as you can see by looking at a graph of real GDP over time. Some recessions are close together and others are far apart. There appears to be no recurring pattern.

Most macroeconomic quantities fluctuate together. In recessions, real GDP, consumer spending, investment spending, corporate profits, and other macroeconomic variables decline or grow much more slowly than during economic expansions. However, the variables fluctuate by different amounts over the business cycle, with investment varying much more than other variables.

As output falls, unemployment rises, because when firms want to produce less, they lay off workers, thus causing a rise in unemployment.

Page 330 The economy's behavior in the short run differs from its behavior in the long run because the assumption of monetary neutrality applies only to the long run, not the short run. In the short run, real and nominal variables are highly intertwined.

Figure 15–1 shows the model of aggregate demand and aggregate supply. The horizontal axis shows the quantity of output, and the vertical axis shows the price level.

Page 334 The aggregate-demand curve slopes downward for three reasons. First, when prices fall, the value of dollars in people's wallets and

Figure 15–1

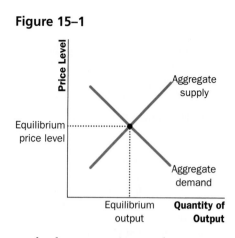

bank accounts rises, so they are wealthier. As a result, they spend more, thereby increasing the quantity of goods and services demanded. Second, when prices fall, people need less money to make their purchases, so they lend more out, which reduces the interest rate. The lower interest rate encourages businesses to invest more, increasing the quantity of goods and services demanded. Third, since lower prices lead to a lower interest rate, some U.S. investors will invest abroad, supplying dollars to the foreign-exchange market, thus causing the dollar to depreciate. The decline in the real exchange rate causes net exports to increase, which increases the quantity of goods and services demanded.

Any event that alters the level of consumption, investment, government purchases, or net exports at a given price level will lead to a shift in aggregate demand. An increase in expenditure will shift the aggregate-demand curve to the right, while a decline in expenditure will shift the aggregate-demand curve to the left.

Page 343 The long-run aggregate-supply curve is vertical because the price level does not affect the long-run determinants of real GDP, which include supplies of labor, capital, natural resources, and the level of available technology. This is just an application of the classical dichotomy and monetary neutrality.

There are three reasons the short-run aggregate-supply curve slopes upward. First, the sticky-wage theory suggests that because nominal wages are slow to adjust, a decline in the price level means real wages are higher, so firms hire fewer workers and produce less, causing the quantity of goods and services supplied to decline. Second, the sticky-price theory suggests that the prices of some goods and services are slow to change. If some economic event causes the overall price level to decline, the relative prices of goods whose prices are sticky will rise and the quantity of those goods sold will decline, leading firms to cut back on production. Thus, a lower price level reduces the quantity of goods and services supplied. Third, the misperceptions theory suggests that changes in the overall price level can temporarily mislead suppliers. When the price level falls below the level that was expected, suppliers think that the relative prices of their products have declined, so they produce less. Thus, a lower price level reduces the quantity of goods and services supplied.

The long-run and short-run aggregate-supply curves will both shift if the supplies of labor, capital, or natural resources change or if technology changes. A change in the expected price level will shift the short-run aggregate-supply curve but will have no effect on the long-run aggregate-supply curve.

Page 355 When a popular presidential candidate is elected, causing people to be more confident about the future, they will spend more, causing the aggregate-demand curve to shift to the right, as shown in Figure 15–2. The economy begins at point A with aggregate-demand curve AD_1 and short-run aggregate-supply curve AS_1. The equilibrium has price level P_1 and output level Y_1. In-

Figure 15–2

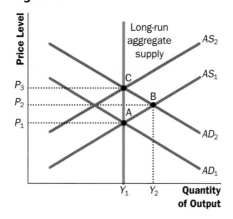

creased confidence about the future causes the aggregate-demand curve to shift to AD_2. The economy moves to point B, with price level P_2 and output level Y_2. Over time, price expectations adjust and the short-run aggregate-supply curve shifts up to AS_2 and the economy moves to equilibrium at point C, with price level P_3 and output level Y_1.

Chapter 16
Page 370 According to the theory of liquidity preference, the interest rate adjusts to balance the supply and demand for money. Therefore, a decrease in the money supply will increase the equilibrium interest rate. This decrease in the money supply reduces aggregate demand because the higher interest rate causes households to buy fewer houses, reducing the demand for residential investment, and causes firms to spend less on new factories and new equipment, reducing business investment.

Page 377 If the government reduces spending on highway construction by $10 billion, the aggregate-demand curve shifts to the left because government purchases are lower. The shift to the left of the aggregate-demand curve could be more than $10 billion if the multiplier effect outweighs the crowding-

out effect, or it could be less than $10 billion if the crowding-out effect outweighs the multiplier effect.

Page 380 If people become pessimistic about the future, they will spend less, causing the aggregate-demand curve to shift to the left. If the Fed wants to stabilize aggregate demand, it should increase the money supply. The increase in the money supply will cause the interest rate to decline, thus stimulating residential and business investment. The Fed might choose not to do this because by the time the policy action takes effect, the long lag time might mean the economy would have recovered on its own, and the increase in the money supply will cause inflation.

Chapter 17
Page 389 The Phillips curve is shown in Figure 17–1.

Figure 17–1

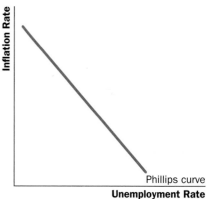

To see how policy can move the economy from a point with high inflation to a point with low inflation, suppose the economy begins at point A in Figure 17–2. If policy is used to reduce aggregate demand (such as a decrease in the money supply or a decrease in government purchases), the aggregate-demand curve shifts from AD_1 to AD_2, and the economy moves from

Figure 17–2

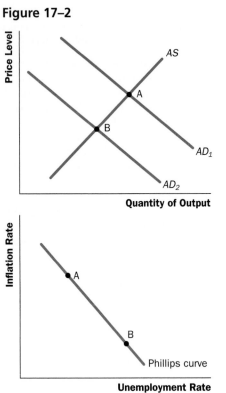

point A to point B with lower inflation, a reduction in real GDP, and an increase in the unemployment rate.

Page 398 Figure 17–3 shows the short-run Phillips curve and the long-run Phillips curve. The curves are dif-

Figure 17–3

ferent because in the long run, monetary policy has no effect on unemployment, which tends toward its natural rate. However, in the short run, monetary policy can affect the unemployment rate. An increase in the growth rate of money raises actual inflation above expected inflation, causing firms to produce more since the short-run aggregate supply curve is positively sloped, which reduces unemployment temporarily.

Page 400 Examples of favorable shocks to aggregate supply include improved productivity and a decline in oil prices. Either shock shifts the aggregate-supply curve to the right, increasing output and reducing the price level, moving the economy from point A to point B in Figure 17–4. As a result, the Phillips curve shifts to the left, as the figure shows.

Figure 17–4

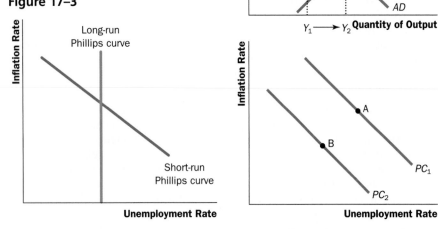

Page 408 The sacrifice ratio is the number of percentage points of annual output lost in the process of reducing inflation by 1 percentage point. The credibility of the Fed's commitment to reduce inflation might affect the sacrifice ratio because it affects the speed at which expectations of inflation adjust. If the Fed's commitment to reduce inflation is credible, people will reduce their expectations of inflation quickly, the short-run Phillips curve will shift downward, and the cost of reducing inflation will be low in terms of lost output. But if the Fed is not credible, people will not reduce their expectations of inflation quickly, and the cost of reducing inflation will be high in terms of lost output.

Chapter 18

Page 420 Monetary and fiscal policies work with a lag. Monetary policy works with a lag because it affects spending for residential and business investment, but spending plans for such investment are often set in advance. Thus, it takes time for changes in monetary policy, working through interest rates, to affect investment. Fiscal policy works with a lag because of the long political process that governs changes in spending and taxes.

These lags matter for the choice between active and passive policy because if the lags are long, policy must be set today for conditions far in the future, about which we can only guess. Since economic conditions may change between the time a policy is implemented and when it takes effect, policy changes may be destabilizing. Thus, long lags suggest a policy that is passive rather than active.

Page 424 There are many possible rules for monetary policy. One example is a rule that sets money growth at 3 percent per year. This rule might be better than discretionary policy because it prevents a political business cycle and the time inconsistency problem. It might be worse than discretionary policy because it would tie the Fed's hands when there are shocks to the economy. For example, in response to a stock-market crash, the rule would prevent the Fed from easing monetary policy, even if it saw the economy slipping into recession.

Page 428 The benefits of reducing inflation to zero include: (1) reducing shoeleather costs; (2) reducing menu costs; (3) reducing the variability of relative prices; (4) preventing unintended changes in tax liabilities due to nonindexation of the tax code; (5) eliminating the confusion and inconvenience resulting from a changing unit of account; and (6) preventing arbitrary redistribution of wealth associated with dollar-denominated debts. These benefits are all permanent. The costs of reducing inflation to zero are the high unemployment and low output needed to reduce inflation. According to the natural rate hypothesis, these costs are temporary.

Page 432 Reducing the budget deficit makes future generations better off because with lower debt, future taxes will be lower. In addition, lower debt will reduce real interest rates, causing investment to increase, leading to a larger stock of capital in the future, which means higher future labor productivity and higher real wages. A fiscal policy that might improve the lives of future generations even more than reducing the budget deficit is increased spending on education, which will also increase incomes in the future.

Page 435 Our society discourages saving in a number of ways: (1) taxing the return on interest income; (2) taxing some forms of capital twice; (3) taxing bequests; (4) having means tests for welfare and Medicaid; and (5) granting financial aid as a function of wealth. The drawback of eliminating these disincentives is that, in many cases, doing so would reduce the tax burden on wealthy taxpayers. The lost revenue to the government could require raising other taxes, which might increase the tax burden on the poor.

absolute advantage the ability to produce a good using fewer inputs than another producer

aggregate-demand curve a curve that shows the quantity of goods and services that households, firms, the government, and customers abroad want to buy at each price level

aggregate-supply curve a curve that shows the quantity of goods and services that firms choose to produce and sell at each price level

appreciation an increase in the value of a currency as measured by the amount of foreign currency it can buy

automatic stabilizers changes in fiscal policy that stimulate aggregate demand when the economy goes into a recession without policymakers having to take any deliberate action

balanced trade a situation in which exports equal imports

bond a certificate of indebtedness

budget deficit a shortfall of tax revenue from government spending

budget surplus an excess of tax revenue over government spending

business cycle fluctuations in economic activity, such as employment and production

capital flight a large and sudden reduction in the demand for assets located in a country

catch-up effect the property whereby countries that start off poor tend to grow more rapidly than countries that start off rich

central bank an institution designed to oversee the banking system and regulate the quantity of money in the economy

circular-flow diagram a visual model of the economy that shows how dollars flow through markets among households and firms

classical dichotomy the theoretical separation of nominal and real variables

closed economy an economy that does not interact with other economies in the world

collective bargaining the process by which unions and firms agree on the terms of employment

commodity money money that takes the form of a commodity with intrinsic value

comparative advantage the ability to produce a good at a lower opportunity cost than another producer

competitive market a market in which there are many buyers and many sellers so that each has a negligible impact on the market price

complements two goods for which an increase in the price of one leads to a decrease in the demand for the other

compounding the accumulation of a sum of money in, say, a bank account, where the interest earned remains in the account to earn additional interest in the future

consumer price index (CPI) a measure of the overall cost of the goods and services bought by a typical consumer

consumption spending by households on goods and services, with the exception of purchases of new housing

crowding out a decrease in investment that results from government borrowing

crowding-out effect the offset in aggregate demand that results when expansionary fiscal policy raises the interest rate and thereby reduces investment spending

currency the paper bills and coins in the hands of the public

cyclical unemployment the deviation of unemployment from its natural rate

demand curve a graph of the relationship between the price of a good and the quantity demanded

demand deposits balances in bank accounts that depositors can access on demand by writing a check

demand schedule a table that shows the relationship between the price of a good and the quantity demanded

depreciation a decrease in the value of a currency as measured by the amount of foreign currency it can buy

depression a severe recession

diminishing returns the property whereby the benefit from an extra unit of an input declines as the quantity of the input increases

discount rate the interest rate on the loans that the Fed makes to banks

discouraged workers individuals who would like to work but have given up looking for a job

diversification the reduction of risk achieved by replacing a single risk with a large number of smaller unrelated risks

economics the study of how society manages its scarce resources

efficiency the property of society getting the most it can from its scarce resources

efficiency wages above-equilibrium wages paid by firms to increase worker productivity

efficient markets hypothesis the theory that asset prices reflect all publicly available information about the value of an asset

equilibrium   a situation in which the market price has reached the level at which quantity supplied equals quantity demanded

equilibrium price   the price that balances quantity supplied and quantity demanded

equilibrium quantity   the quantity supplied and the quantity demanded at the equilibrium price

equity   the property of distributing economic prosperity fairly among the members of society

exports   goods and services that are produced domestically and sold abroad

externality   the impact of one person's actions on the well-being of a bystander

Federal Reserve (Fed)   the central bank of the United States

fiat money   money without intrinsic value that is used as money because of government decree

finance   the field that studies how people make decisions regarding the allocation of resources over time and the handling of risk

financial intermediaries   financial institutions through which savers can indirectly provide funds to borrowers

financial markets   financial institutions through which savers can directly provide funds to borrowers

financial system   the group of institutions in the economy that help to match one person's saving with another person's investment

firm-specific risk   risk that affects only a single company

fiscal policy   the setting of the level of government spending and taxation by government policymakers.

Fisher effect   the one-for-one adjustment of the nominal interest rate to the inflation rate

fractional-reserve banking   a banking system in which banks hold only a fraction of deposits as reserves

frictional unemployment   unemployment that results because it takes time for workers to search for the jobs that best suit their tastes and skills

fundamental analysis   the study of a company's accounting statements and future prospects to determine its value

future value   the amount of money in the future that an amount of money today will yield, given prevailing interest rates

GDP deflator   a measure of the price level calculated as the ratio of nominal GDP to real GDP times 100

government purchases   spending on goods and services by local, state, and federal governments

gross domestic product (GDP)   the market value of all final goods and services produced within a country in a given period of time

human capital   the knowledge and skills that workers acquire through education, training, and experience

imports   goods and services that are produced abroad and sold domestically

incentive   something that induces a person to act

indexation   the automatic correction of a dollar amount for the effects of inflation by law or contract

inferior good   a good for which, other things equal, an increase in income leads to a decrease in demand

inflation   an increase in the overall level of prices in the economy

inflation rate   the percentage change in the price index from the preceding period

inflation tax   the revenue the government raises by creating money

informational efficiency   the description of asset prices that rationally reflect all available information

investment   spending on capital equipment, inventories, and structures, including household purchases of new housing

job search   the process by which workers find appropriate jobs given their tastes and skills

labor force   the total number of workers, including both the employed and the unemployed

labor-force participation rate   the percentage of the adult population that is in the labor force

law of demand   the claim that, other things equal, the quantity demanded of a good falls when the price of the good rises

law of supply   the claim that, other things equal, the quantity supplied of a good rises when the price of the good rises

law of supply and demand   the claim that the price of any good adjusts to bring the quantity supplied and the quantity demanded for that good into balance

liquidity   the ease with which an asset can be converted into the economy's medium of exchange

macroeconomics   the study of economywide phenomena, including inflation, unemployment, and economic growth

marginal changes   small incremental adjustments to a plan of action

market   a group of buyers and sellers of a particular good or service

market economy   an economy that allocates resources through the decentralized decisions of many firms and households as they interact in markets for goods and services

market failure   a situation in which a market left on its own fails to allocate resources efficiently

market for loanable funds   the market in which those who want to save supply funds and those who want to borrow to invest demand funds

market power   the ability of a single economic actor (or small group of actors) to have a substantial influence on market prices

market risk   risk that affects all companies in the stock market

medium of exchange   an item that buyers give to sellers when they want to purchase goods and services

menu costs   the costs of changing prices

microeconomics   the study of how households and firms make decisions and how they interact in markets

model of aggregate demand and aggregate supply   the model that most economists use to explain short-run fluctuations in economic activity around its long-run trend

monetary neutrality   the proposition that changes in the money supply do not affect real variables

monetary policy   the setting of the money supply by policymakers in the central bank

money   the set of assets in an economy that people regularly use to buy goods and services from other people

money multiplier   the amount of money the banking system generates with each dollar of reserves

money supply   the quantity of money available in the economy

multiplier effect   the additional shifts in aggregate demand that result when expansionary fiscal policy increases income and thereby increases consumer spending

mutual fund   an institution that sells shares to the public and uses the proceeds to buy a portfolio of stocks and bonds

national saving (saving)   the total income in the economy that remains after paying for consumption and government purchases

natural-rate hypothesis   the claim that unemployment eventually returns to its normal, or natural, rate, regardless of the rate of inflation

natural rate of output   the production of goods and services that an economy achieves in the long run when unemployment is at its normal rate

natural rate of unemployment   the normal rate of unemployment around which the unemployment rate fluctuates

natural resources   the inputs into the production of goods and services that are provided by nature, such as land, rivers, and mineral deposits

net capital outflow   the purchase of foreign assets by domestic residents minus the purchase of domestic assets by foreigners

net exports   the value of a nation's exports minus the value of its imports; also called the trade balance

nominal exchange rate   the rate at which a person can trade the currency of one country for the currency of another

nominal GDP   the production of goods and services valued at current prices

nominal interest rate   the interest rate as usually reported without a correction for the effects of inflation

nominal variables   variables measured in monetary units

normal good   a good for which, other things equal, an increase in income leads to an increase in demand

normative statements   claims that attempt to prescribe how the world should be

open economy   an economy that interacts freely with other economies around the world

open-market operations   the purchase and sale of U.S. government bonds by the Fed

opportunity cost   whatever must be given up to obtain some item

Phillips curve   a curve that shows the short-run trade-off between inflation and unemployment

physical capital   the stock of equipment and structures that are used to produce goods and services

positive statements   claims that attempt to describe the world as it is

present value   the amount of money today that would be needed, using prevailing interest rates, to produce a given future amount of money

private saving   the income that households have left after paying for taxes and consumption

producer price index   a measure of the cost of a basket of goods and services bought by firms

production possibilities frontier   a graph that shows the combinations of output that the economy can possibly produce given the available factors of production and the available production technology

productivity   the quantity of goods and services produced from each hour of a worker's time

property rights   the ability of an individual to own and exercise control over scarce resources

public saving   the tax revenue that the government has left after paying for its spending

purchasing-power parity   a theory of exchange rates whereby a unit of any given currency should be able to buy the same quantity of goods in all countries

quantity demanded   the amount of a good that buyers are willing and able to purchase

quantity equation   the equation $M \times V = P \times Y$, which relates the quantity of money, the velocity of money, and the dollar value of the economy's output of goods and services

quantity supplied   the amount of a good that sellers are willing and able to sell

quantity theory of money   a theory asserting that the quantity of money available determines the price level and that the growth rate in the quantity of money available determines the inflation rate

random walk   the path of a variable whose changes are impossible to predict

rational expectations the theory according to which people optimally use all the information they have, including information about government policies, when forecasting the future

rational people people who systematically and purposefully do the best they can to achieve their objectives

real exchange rate the rate at which a person can trade the goods and services of one country for the goods and services of another

real GDP the production of goods and services valued at constant prices

real interest rate the interest rate corrected for the effects of inflation

real variables variables measured in physical units

recession a period of declining real incomes and rising unemployment

reserve ratio the fraction of deposits that banks hold as reserves

reserve requirements regulations on the minimum amount of reserves that banks must hold against deposits

reserves deposits that banks have received but have not loaned out

risk aversion a dislike of uncertainty

sacrifice ratio the number of percentage points of annual output lost in the process of reducing inflation by 1 percentage point

scarcity the limited nature of society's resources

shoeleather costs the resources wasted when inflation encourages people to reduce their money holdings

shortage a situation in which quantity demanded is greater than quantity supplied

stagflation a period of falling output and rising prices

stock a claim to partial ownership in a firm

store of value an item that people can use to transfer purchasing power from the present to the future

strike the organized withdrawal of labor from a firm by a union

structural unemployment unemployment that results because the number of jobs available in some labor markets is insufficient to provide a job for everyone who wants one

substitutes two goods for which an increase in the price of one leads to an increase in the demand for the other

supply curve a graph of the relationship between the price of a good and the quantity supplied

supply schedule a table that shows the relationship between the price of a good and the quantity supplied

supply shock an event that directly alters firms' costs and prices, shifting the economy's aggregate-supply curve and thus the Phillips curve

surplus a situation in which quantity supplied is greater than quantity demanded

technological knowledge society's understanding of the best ways to produce goods and services

theory of liquidity preference Keynes's theory that the interest rate adjusts to bring money supply and money demand into balance

trade balance the value of a nation's exports minus the value of its imports; also called net exports

trade deficit an excess of imports over exports

trade policy a government policy that directly influences the quantity of goods and services that a country imports or exports

trade surplus an excess of exports over imports

unemployment insurance a government program that partially protects workers' incomes when they become unemployed

unemployment rate the percentage of the labor force that is unemployed

union a worker association that bargains with employers over wages, benefits, and working conditions

unit of account the yardstick people use to post prices and record debts

velocity of money the rate at which money changes hands

INDEX

Note: Page numbers in **boldface** refer to pages where key terms are defined.

SUGGESTIONS FOR SUMMER READING

IF YOU ENJOYED THE ECONOMICS COURSE THAT YOU HAVE JUST FINISHED, YOU MIGHT LIKE TO READ MORE ABOUT ECONOMIC ISSUES IN THE FOLLOWING BOOKS.

PAUL BLUSTEIN

The Chastening: Inside the Crisis That Rocked the Global Financial System and Humbled the IMF

New York: Public Affairs, 2001

A journalist tells the story of how economic policymakers around the world muddled through the financial crises of the late 1990s.

WILLIAM BREIT AND BARRY T. HIRSCH

Lives of the Laureates

Cambridge, MA: MIT Press, 2004

Eighteen winners of the Nobel prize in economics offer autobiographical essays about their life and work.

COUNCIL OF ECONOMIC ADVISERS

Economic Report of the President

Washington, DC: U.S. Government Printing Office, released every year

The annual report of the CEA surveys the state of economy and presents the case for the president's economic program.

DIANE COYLE

Sex, Drugs, and Economics

New York: Texere, 2002

Basic economics applied to a wide range of sometimes unconventional topics.

AVINASH DIXIT AND BARRY NALEBUFF

Thinking Strategically: A Competitive Edge in Business, Politics, and Everyday Life

New York: Norton, 1991

This introduction to game theory discusses how all people—from corporate executives to criminals under arrest—should and do make strategic decisions.

WILLIAM EASTERLY

The Elusive Quest for Growth: Economists' Adventures and Misadventures in the Tropics

Cambridge, MA: MIT Press, 2001

A World Bank economist examines the many attempts to help the world's poorest nations and why they have so often failed.